MW01170663

Comprehensive

Microsoft® Access 2.0 for Windows®

Comprehensive

Microsoft® ACCESS 2.0 for Windows®

Joseph J. Adamski

Grand Valley State University

A Susan Solomon Book

CTI

A DIVISION OF COURSE TECHNOLOGY

ONE MAIN STREET, CAMBRIDGE, MA 02142

an International Thomson Publishing company I(T)P

Cambridge • Albany • Bonn • Boston • Cincinnati • London • Madrid • Melbourne • Mexico City
New York • Paris • San Francisco • Singapore • Tokyo • Toronto • Washington

Comprehensive Microsoft Access 2.0 for Windows is published by Course Technology, Inc.

Managing Editor: Mac Mendelsohn
Product Managers: David Crocco, Barbara Clemens
Production Editor: Donna Whiting
Text Designer: Sally Steele
Cover Designer: John Gamache

For more information contact:
Course Technology, Inc.
One Main Street
Cambridge, MA 02142

International Thomson Publishing Europe
Berkshire House 168-173
High Holborn
London WCIV 7AA
England

Thomas Nelson Australia
102 Dodds Street
South Melbourne, 3205
Victoria, Australia

Nelson Canada
1120 Birchmount Road
Scarborough, Ontario
Canada M1K 5G4

International Thomson Editores
Campos Eliseos 385, Piso 7
Col. Polanco
11560 Mexico D.F. Mexico

International Thomson Publishing GmbH
Königswinterer Strasse 418
53227 Bonn
Germany

International Thomson Publishing Asia
211 Henderson Road
#05-10 Henderson Building
Singapore 0315

International Thomson Publishing Japan
Hirakawacho Kyowa Building, 3F
2-2-1 Hirakawacho
Chiyoda-ku, Tokyo 102
Japan

ISBN 0-7600-4582-8

Printed in the United States of America

10 9 8 7 6 5 4 3

From the Publisher

At Course Technology, Inc., we believe that technology will transform the way that people teach and learn. We are excited about bringing you, college professors and students, the most practical and affordable technology-related products available.

The Course Technology Development Process

Our development process is unparalleled in the higher education publishing industry. Every product we create goes through an exacting process of design, development, review, and testing.

Reviewers give us direction and insight that shape our manuscripts and bring them up to the latest standards. Every manuscript is quality tested. Students whose backgrounds match the intended audience work through every keystroke, carefully checking for clarity and pointing out errors in logic and sequence. Together with our own technical reviewers, these testers help us ensure that everything that carries our name is error-free and easy to use.

Course Technology Products

We show both *how* and *why* technology is critical to solving problems in college and in whatever field you choose to teach or pursue. Our time-tested, step-by-step instructions provide unparalleled clarity. Examples and applications are chosen and crafted to motivate students.

The Course Technology Team

This book will suit your needs because it was delivered quickly, efficiently, and affordably. In every aspect of our business, we rely on a commitment to quality and the use of technology. Every employee contributes to this process. The names of all of our employees are listed below:
Diana Armington, Tim Ashe, Stephen M. Bayle, Ann Marie Buconjic, Jody Buttafoco, Kerry Cannell, Jim Chrysikos, Barbara Clemens, Susan Collins, John M. Connolly, Myrna D'Addario, Lisa D'Alessandro, Jodi Davis, Howard S. Diamond, Kathryn Dinovo, Joseph B. Dougherty, Laurie Duncan, Karen Dwyer, MaryJane Dwyer, Kristin Dyer, Chris Elkhill, Don Fabricant, Viktor Frengut, Jeff Goding, Laurie Gomes, Eileen Gorham, Catherine Griffin, Jamie Harper, Roslyn Hooley, Marjorie Hunt, Matt Kenslea, Marybeth LaFauci, Susannah Lean, Kim Mai, Margaret Makowski, Tammy Marciano, Elizabeth Martinez, Debbie Masi, Don Maynard, Kathleen McCann, Sarah McLean, Jay McNamara, Mac Mendelsohn, Karla Mitchell, Kim Munsell, Michael Ormsby, Debbie Parlee, Kristin Patrick, Charlie Patsios, Darren Perl, Kevin Phaneuf, George J. Pilla, Nicole Jones Pinard, Nancy Ray, Brian Romer, Laura Sacks, Carla Sharpe, Deborah Shute, Roger Skilling, Jennifer Slivinski, Christine Spillett, Audrey Tortolani, Michelle Tucker, David Upton, Mark Valentine, Karen Wadsworth, Renee Walkup, Tracy Wells, Donna Whiting, Rob Williams, Janet Wilson, Lisa Yameen.

Preface

Course Technology, Inc. is proud to present this new book in its Windows Series. *Comprehensive Microsoft Access 2.0 for Windows* is designed for a full-term course on Microsoft Access. This book capitalizes on the energy and enthusiasm students naturally have for Windows-based applications and clearly teaches students how to take full advantage of Access' power. It assumes no prerequisite knowledge of computers, the Windows environment, or Microsoft Access 2.0.

Organization and Coverage

Comprehensive Microsoft Access 2.0 for Windows contains ten tutorials that present hands-on instruction. In these tutorials students learn how to plan, create, and maintain Access databases. They learn to retrieve information by creating queries and developing professional-looking reports. Students also learn to create customized forms, and work with macros and Access Basic.

The text emphasizes the ease-of-use features included in the Access software: toolbar and toolbox buttons, Shortcut menus, graphical relationship tools, graphical query by example (QBE), Cue Cards, and Wizards. Using this book, students will be able to do more advanced tasks sooner than they would using other texts; a perusal of the table of contents affirms this. By the end of the book, students will have learned "advanced" tasks such as creating input masks, importing data, creating parameter queries, linking multiple tables, creating custom forms and reports, creating macros, switchboards, and custom menus. They will also know how to create functions and event procedures using Access Basic.

Approach

Comprehensive Microsoft Access 2.0 for Windows distinguishes itself from other Windows textbooks because of its unique two-pronged approach. First, it motivates students by demonstrating why they need to learn the concepts and skills. This book teaches Access using a task-driven rather than a feature-driven approach. By working through the tutorials—each motivated by a realistic case—students learn how to use Access in situations they are likely to encounter in the workplace, rather than learn a list of features one-by-one, out of context. Second, the content, organization, and pedagogy of this book make full use of the Windows environment. What content is presented, when it's presented, and how it's presented capitalizes on Access' power to perform complex database tasks earlier and more easily than was possible under DOS.

Features

Comprehensive Microsoft Access 2.0 for Windows is an exceptional textbook also because it includes the following features:

- **"Read This Before You Begin" Pages** These pages are consistent with Course Technology, Inc.'s unequaled commitment to helping instructors introduce technology into the classroom. Technical considerations and assumptions about hardware, software, and default settings are listed to help instructors save time and eliminate unnecessary aggravation. There is a "Read This Before You Begin" page before the Windows tutorials, and another before the Access tutorials.
- **Tutorial Case** Each tutorial begins with a database-related problem that students could reasonably encounter in business. Thus, the process of solving the problem will be meaningful to students.
- **Step-by-Step Methodology** The unique Course Technology, Inc. methodology keeps students on track. They click or press keys always within the context of solving the problem posed in the Tutorial Case. The text constantly guides students, letting them know where they are in the process of solving the problem. The numerous screen shots include labels that direct students' attention to what they should look at on the screen.
- **Page Design** Each *full-color* page is designed to help students easily differentiate between what they are to *do* and what they are to *read*. The steps are easily identified by their color background and numbered bullets. Windows' default colors are used in the screen shots so instructors can more easily assure that students' screens look like those in the book.
- **TROUBLE?** TROUBLE? paragraphs anticipate the mistakes that students are likely to make and help them recover from these mistakes. This feature facilitates independent learning and frees the instructor to focus on substantive conceptual issues rather than common procedural errors.
- **Reference Windows and Task Reference** Reference Windows provide short, generic summaries of frequently used procedures. The Task Reference appears at the end of the book and summarizes how to accomplish tasks using the mouse, the menus, and the keyboard. Both of these features are specially designed and written so students can use the book as a reference manual after completing the course.
- **Questions, Tutorial Assignments, and Case Problems** Each tutorial concludes with meaningful, conceptual Questions that test students' understanding of what they learned in the tutorial. The Questions are followed by Tutorial Assignments, which provide students with additional hands-on practice of the skills they learned in the Tutorial. Each Tutorial Assignment (except Tutorial 1) is followed by four complete Case Problems that have approximately the same scope as the Tutorial Case.
- **Exploration Exercises** Unlike DOS, the Windows environment allows students to learn by exploring and discovering what they can do. The Exploration Exercises are Questions, Tutorial Assignments, or Case Problems designated by an **E** that encourage students to explore the capabilities of the computing environment they are using and to extend their knowledge using the Windows on-line Help facility and other reference materials.
- **Reference Section** This section provides lists of Microsoft Access commands, toolbar buttons, and functions.
- **Additional Cases** Three interactive cases help students incorporate all their knowledge of Microsoft Access in new, real-life settings.
- **Relational Database Appendix** For those instructors who want their students to explore Relational Databases in more detail, the Appendix contains the basics of Relational Databases and Database Design.

The CTI WinApps Setup Disk

The CTI WinApps Setup Disk, bundled with the Instructor's copy of this book, contains an innovative Student Disk generating program that is designed to save instructors time. Once this software is installed on a network or a standalone workstation, students can double click the "Make Access2 Comprehensive Student Disks" icon in the CTI WinApps icon group. Double clicking this icon transfers all the data files students need to complete the tutorials, Tutorial Assignments, Case Problems, and Additional Cases to a high-density disk in drive A or B. These files free students from tedious keystroking and allow them to concentrate on mastering the concept or task at hand. Tutorial 1 provides complete step-by-step instructions for making the Student Disks.

Adopters of this text are granted the right to install the CTI WinApps group window on any standalone computer or network used by students who have purchased this text.

For more information of the CTI WinApps Setup Disk, see the page in this book called "Read This Before You Begin" before the Microsoft Access tutorials.

Supplements

- **Instructor's Manual** The Instructor's Manual is written by the author and is quality assurance tested. It includes:
  - Answers and solutions to all of the Questions, Tutorial Assignments, Case Problems, and Additional Cases. Suggested solutions are also included for the Exploration Exercises
  - A 3.5-inch disk containing solutions to all the Questions, Tutorial Assignments, Case Problems, and Additional Cases.
  - Tutorial Notes, which contain background information from the author about the Tutorial Case and the instructional progression of the tutorial
  - Technical Notes, which include troubleshooting tips as well as information on how to customize the students' screens to closely emulate the screen shots in the book
  - Transparency Masters of key concepts
- **Test Bank** The Test Bank contains 50 questions per tutorial in true/false, multiple choice, and fill-in-the-blank formats, plus two essay questions. Each question has been quality assurance tested by students to achieve clarity and accuracy.
- **Electronic Test Bank** The Electronic Test Bank allows instructors to edit individual test questions, select questions individually or at random, and print out scrambled versions of the same test to any supported printer.

Acknowledgments

I want to thank the many people who contributed to this book. I thank the many reviewers of this book, in particular: Dr. Michael Paul, Barry University; James M. Kraushaar, University of Vermont; Minnie Yen, University of Alaska Anchorage; Tim O'Keefe, Mayville State University, Joey George, Florida State University, and Jeffrey Frates, Los Medanos College.

I also thank the dedicated and enthusiastic Course Technology, Inc. staff, including the excellent production team: Donna Whiting, Production Editor; Nancy Ray, Production Assistant; the student testers: Brenda Domingo, Mark Vodnik, David Vislosky and Morten Eidal; and Reference Section writers Laura Bergs and Robert Gillett.

My special thanks to Susan Solomon for her friendship, advice, and support. Special thanks also to developmental editor Joan Carey for her expert advice, grace under pressure and positive support, and to David Crocco and Barbara Clemens, Product Managers, for their assistance, suggestions, and positive nature.

Many thanks also to Cary Prague at Book & Software for permission to use figures from Picture Builder Wizard.

Joseph J. Adamski

Brief Contents

Contents

Microsoft® Windows™ 3.1 Tutorials

1 **Essential Windows Skills**

2 **Effective File Management**

Read This Before You Begin

To the Student

To use this book, you must have a Student Disk. Your instructor will either provide you with a Student Disk or ask you to make your own by following the instructions in the section called "Preparing Your Student Disk" in Windows Tutorial 2. See your instructor or lab manager for further information.

Using Your Own Computer If you are going to work through this book using your own computer, you need:

- The Student Disk. ***You will not be able to complete the tutorials and exercises in this book using your own computer until you have the Student Disk.*** Ask your instructor or lab manager for details on how to get it.
- A computer system running Microsoft Windows 3.1 and DOS.

To the Instructor

Making the Student Disk To complete the tutorials in this book, your students must have a copy of the Student Disk. To relieve you of having to make multiple Student Disks from a single master copy, we provide you with the CTI WinApps Setup Disk, which contains an automatic Student Disk generating program. Once you install the Setup Disk on a network or standalone workstation, students can easily make their own Student Disks by double clicking on the "Make Win 3.1 Student Disk" icon in the CTI WinApps icon group. Double clicking this icon transfers all the data files students will need to complete the tutorials and Tutorial Assignments to a high-density disk in drive A or B. If some of your students will use their own computers to complete the tutorials and exercises in this book, they must first get the Student Disk. The section called "Preparing Your Student Disk" in Windows Tutorial 2 provides complete instructions on how to make the Student Disk.

If you have disk copying resources available, you might choose to use them for making quantities of the Student Disk. The "Make Win 3.1 Student Disk" provides an easy and fast way to make multiple Student Disks.

Installing the CTI WinApps Setup Disk: To install the CTI WinApps icon group from the Setup Disk, follow the instructions either on the disk label or inside the disk envelope that was bundled with your book. By adopting this book, you are granted a license to install this software on any computer or computer network used by you or your students.

Readme File: A Readme.txt file located on the Setup Disk provides additional technical notes, troubleshooting advice, and tips for using the CTI WinApps software in your school's computer lab. You can view the Readme file using any word processor you choose.

System Requirements for installing the CTI WinApps Disk The minimum software and hardware requirements your computer system needs to install the CTI WinApps icon group are as follows:

- Microsoft Windows version 3.1 on a local hard drive or on a network drive
- A 286 (or higher) processor with a minimum of 2 MB RAM (4 MB RAM or more is strongly recommended).
- A mouse supported by Windows
- A printer that is supported by Windows 3.1
- A VGA 640 x 480 16-color display is recommended; an 800 x 600 or 1024 x 768 SVGA, VGA monochrome, or EGA display is also acceptable
- 1.5 MB of free hard disk space
- Student workstations with at least 1 high-density 3.5 inch-disk drive.
- If you wish to install the CTI WinApps Setup Disk on a network drive, your network must support Microsoft Windows.

T U T O R I A L 1

Essential Windows Skills

Using the Program Manager, CTI WinApps, and Help

OBJECTIVES

In this tutorial you will:

- Start your computer
- Launch and exit Windows
- Use the mouse and the keyboard
- Identify the components of the Windows desktop
- Launch and exit applications
- Organize your screen-based desktop
- Switch tasks in a multi-tasking environment.
- Use Windows menus
- Explore Windows toolbars

CASE **A New Computer, Anywhere, Inc.** You're a busy employee without a minute of spare time. But now, to top it all off, a computer technician appears at your office door, introduces himself as Steve Laslow, and begins unpacking your new computer!

You wonder out loud, "How long is it going to take me to learn this?"

Steve explains that your new computer uses Microsoft Windows 3.1 software and that the **interface**—the way you interact with the computer and give it instructions—is very easy to use. He describes the Windows software as a "gooey," a **graphical user interface (GUI)**, which uses pictures of familiar objects such as file folders and documents to represent a desktop on your screen.

Steve unpacks your new computer and begins to connect the components. He talks as he works, commenting on three things he really likes about Microsoft Windows. First, Windows applications have a standard interface, which means that once you learn how to use one Windows application, you are well on your way to understanding how to use others. Second, Windows lets you use more than one application at a time, a capability called **multitasking**, so you can easily switch between applications such as your word processor and your calendar. Third, Windows lets you do more than one task at a time, such as printing a document while you create a pie chart. All in all, Windows makes your computer an effective and easy-to-use productivity tool.

Using the Windows Tutorials Effectively

This tutorial will help you learn about Windows 3.1. Begin by reading the text that explains the concepts. Then when you come to numbered steps on a colored background, follow those steps as you work at your computer. Read each step carefully and completely *before* you try it.

Don't worry if parts of your screen display are different from the figures in the tutorials. The important parts of the screen display are labeled in each figure. Just be sure these parts are on your screen.

Don't worry about making mistakes—that's part of the learning process. **TROUBLE?** paragraphs identify common problems and explain how to get back on track. Do the steps in the **TROUBLE?** paragraph *only* if you are having the problem described.

Starting Your Computer and Launching Windows

The process of starting Windows is sometimes referred to as **launching**. If your computer system requires procedures different from those in the steps below, your instructor or technical support person will provide you with step-by-step instructions for turning on your monitor, starting or resetting your computer, logging into a network if you have one, and launching Windows.

To start your computer and launch Windows:

❶ Make sure your disk drives are empty.

❷ Find the power switch for your monitor and turn it on.

❸ Locate the power switch for your computer and turn it on. After a few seconds you should see C:\> or C> on the screen.

TROUBLE? If your computer displays a "non-system disk" error message, a floppy disk was left in a disk drive at startup. To continue, remove the disk and press [Enter].

❹ Type **win** to launch Windows. See Figure 1-1.

Figure 1-1
Launching Windows

❺ Press the key labeled **[Enter]**. Soon the Windows 3.1 title screen appears. Next you might notice an hourglass on the screen. This symbol means your computer is busy with a task and you must wait until it has finished.

After a brief wait, the title screen is replaced by one similar to Figure 1-2. Don't worry if your screen is not exactly the same as Figure 1-2. You are ready to continue the Tutorial when you see the Program Manager title at the top of the screen. If you do not see this title, ask your technical support person for assistance.

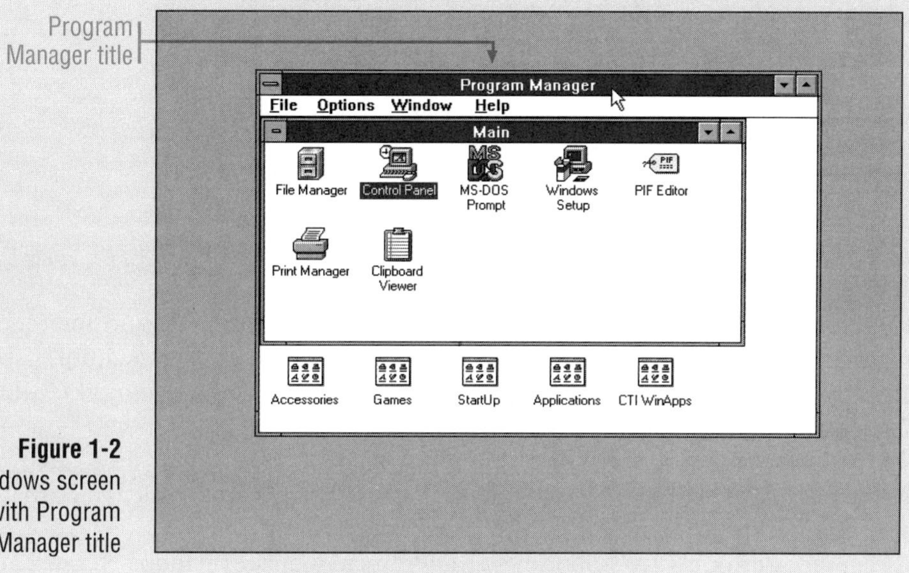

Figure 1-2
Windows screen display with Program Manager title

Basic Windows Controls and Concepts

Windows has a variety of **controls** that enable you to communicate with the computer. In this section you'll learn how to use the basic Windows controls.

The Windows Desktop

Look at your screen display and compare it to Figure 1-3 on the following page. Your screen may not be exactly the same as the illustration. You should, however, be able to locate components on your screen similar to those in Figure 1-3 on the following page.

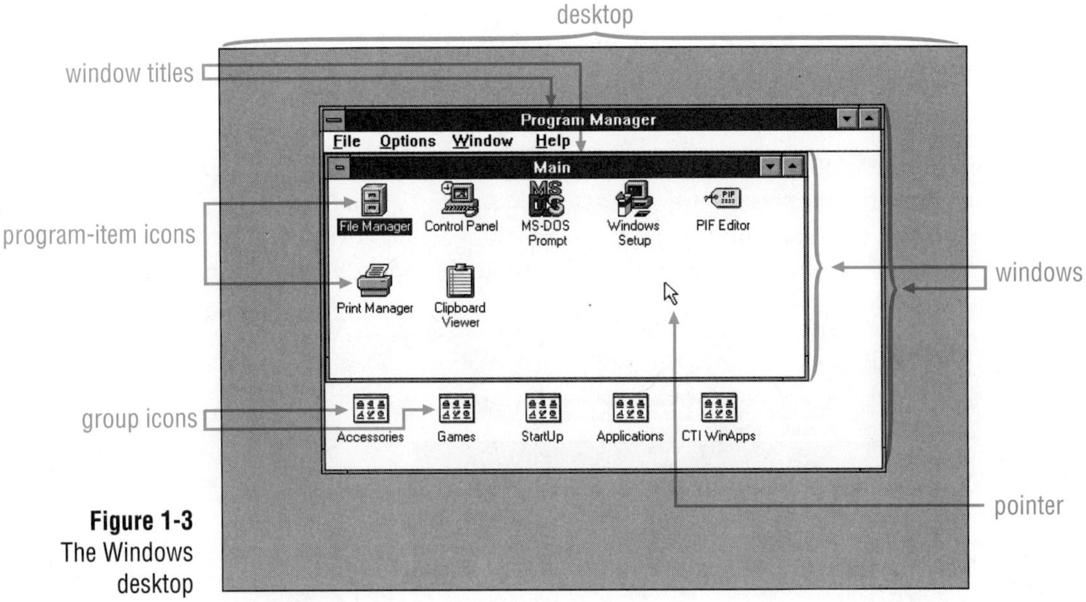

Figure 1-3 The Windows desktop

The screen represents a **desktop**, a workspace for projects and for the tools that are needed to manipulate those projects. Rectangular **windows** (with a lowercase *w*) define work areas on the desktop. The desktop in Figure 1-3 contains the Program Manager window and the Main window.

Icons are small pictures that represent real objects, such as disk drives, software, and documents. Each icon in the Main window represents an **application**, that is, a computer program. These icons are called **program-item icons**.

Each **group icon** at the bottom of the Program Manager window represents a collection of applications. For example, the CTI WinApps icon represents a collection of tutorial and practice applications, which you can use to learn more about Windows. A group icon expands into a group window that contains program-item icons.

The **pointer** helps you manipulate objects on the Windows desktop. The pointer can assume different shapes, depending on what is happening on the desktop. In Figure 1-3 the pointer is shaped like an arrow.

The Program Manager

When you launch Windows, the Program Manager application starts automatically and continues to run as long as you are working with Windows. Think of the Program Manager as a launching pad for other applications. The **Program Manager** displays icons for the applications on your system. To launch an application, you would select its icon.

Using the Mouse

The **mouse** is a pointing device that helps you interact with the screen-based objects in the Windows environment. As you move the mouse on a flat surface, the pointer on the screen moves in the direction corresponding to the movement of the mouse. You can also control the Windows environment from the keyboard; however, the mouse is much more efficient for most operations, so the tutorials in this book assume you are using one.

Find the arrow-shaped pointer on your screen. If you do not see the pointer, move your mouse until the pointer comes into view. You will begin most Windows-based operations by **pointing**.

To position the pointer:

➊ Position your right index finger over the left mouse button, as shown in Figure 1-4.

TROUBLE? If you want to use your mouse with your left hand, ask your technical support person to help you. Be sure you find out how to change back to the right-handed mouse setting, so you can reset the mouse each time you are finished in the lab.

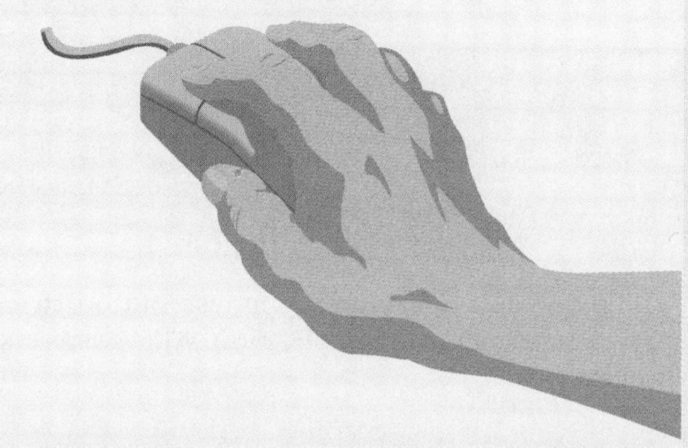

Figure 1-4
How to hold the mouse

➋ Locate the arrow-shaped pointer on the screen.

➌ Move the mouse and watch the movement of the pointer.

➍ Next, move the mouse to each of the four corners of the screen.

TROUBLE? If your mouse runs out of room, lift it, move it into the middle of a clear area on your desk, and then place it back on the table. The pointer does not move when the mouse is not in contact with the tabletop.

➎ Continue experimenting with mouse pointing until you feel comfortable with your "eye-mouse coordination."

Pointing is usually followed by clicking, double-clicking, or dragging. **Clicking** means pressing a mouse button (usually the left button) and then quickly releasing it. Clicking is used to select an object on the desktop. Windows shows you which object is selected by highlighting it.

To click an icon:

➊ Locate the Print Manager icon in the Main window. If you cannot see the Print Manager icon, use any other icon for this activity.

➋ Position the pointer on the icon.

➌ Once the pointer is on the icon, *do not move the mouse*.

➍ Press the left mouse button and then quickly release it. Your icon should have a highlighted title like the one in Figure 1-5 on the following page.

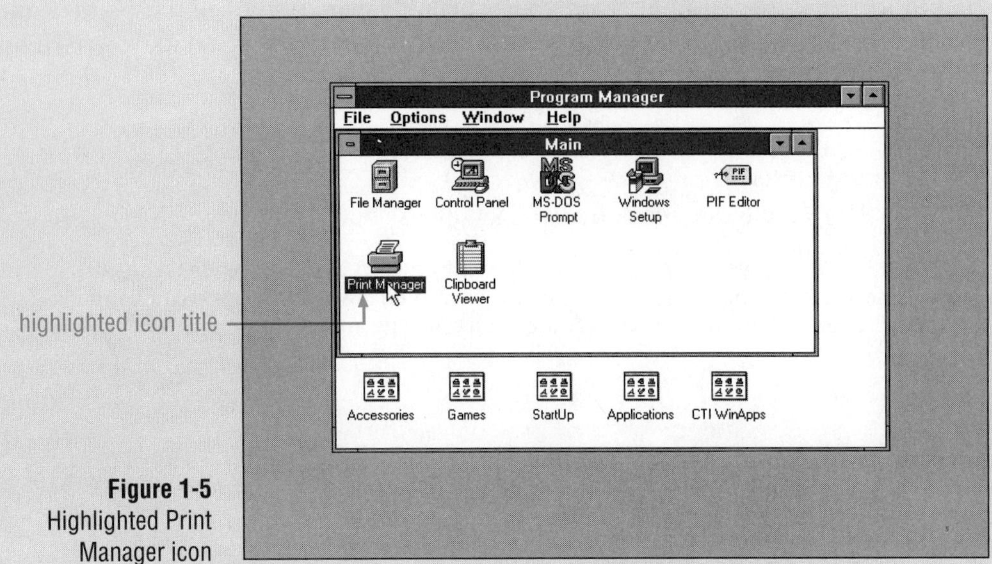

Figure 1-5
Highlighted Print Manager icon

Double-clicking means clicking the mouse button twice in rapid succession. Double-clicking is a shortcut. For example, most Windows users double-click to launch and exit applications.

To double click:

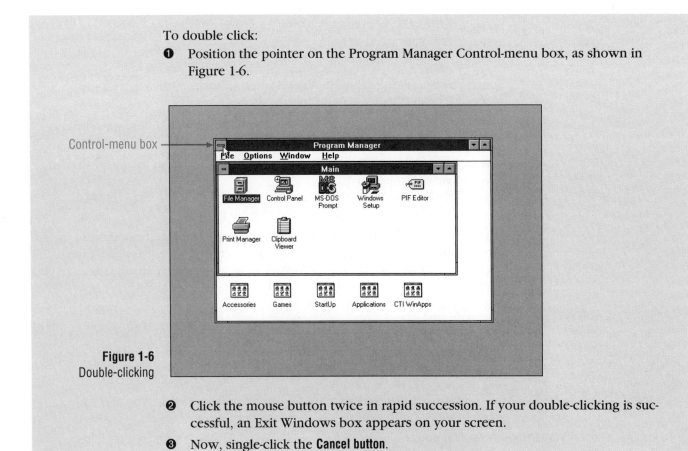

❶ Position the pointer on the Program Manager Control-menu box, as shown in Figure 1-6.

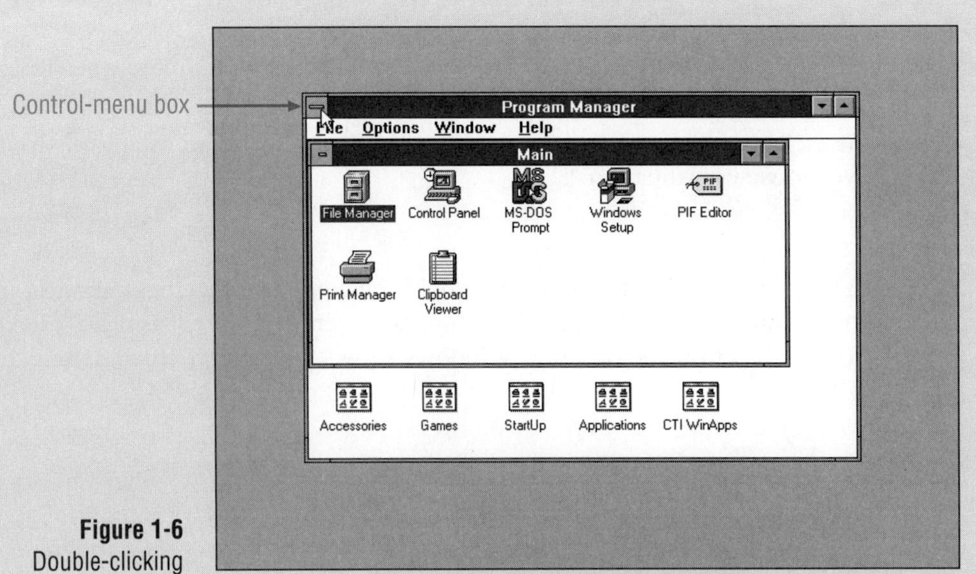

Figure 1-6
Double-clicking

❷ Click the mouse button twice in rapid succession. If your double-clicking is successful, an Exit Windows box appears on your screen.

❸ Now, single-click the **Cancel button**.

Dragging means moving an object to a new location on the desktop. To drag an object, you would position the pointer on the object, then hold the left mouse button down while you move the mouse. Let's drag one of the icons to a new location.

To drag an icon:

❶ Position the pointer on any icon on the screen, such as on the Clipboard Viewer icon. Figure 1-7 shows you where to put the pointer and what happens on your screen as you carry out the next step.

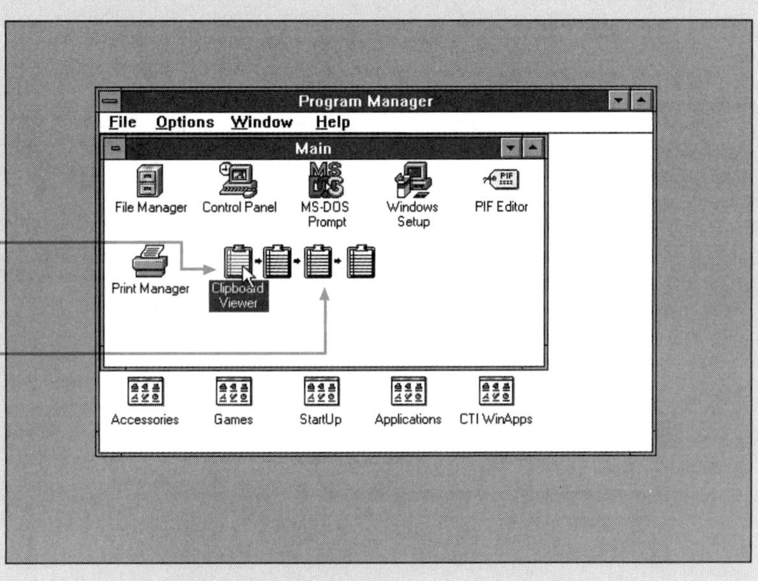

begin with pointer on Clipboard Viewer

outline of the icon moves as you drag

Figure 1-7
Dragging an icon

❷ Hold the left mouse button down while you move the mouse to the right. Notice that an outline of the icon moves as you move the mouse.

❸ Release the mouse button. Now the icon is in a new location.

TROUBLE? If the icon snaps back to its original position, don't worry. Your technical support person probably has instructed Windows to do this. If your icon automatically snapped back to its original position, skip Step 4.

❹ Drag the icon back to its original location.

Using the Keyboard

You use the keyboard to type documents, enter numbers, and activate some commands. You can use the on-screen CTI Keyboard Tutorial to learn the special features of your computer keyboard. To do this, you need to learn how to launch the Keyboard Tutorial and other applications.

Launching Applications

Earlier in this tutorial you launched Windows. Once you have launched Windows, you can launch other Windows applications such as Microsoft Works. When you launch an application, an application window opens. Later, when you have finished using the application, you close the window to exit.

Launching the CTI Keyboard Tutorial

To launch the CTI Keyboard Tutorial, you need to have the CTI WinApps software installed on your computer. If you are working in a computer lab, these applications should already be installed on your computer system. Look on your screen for a group icon or a window labeled "CTI WinApps."

If you don't have anything labeled "CTI WinApps" on your screen's desktop, ask your technical support person for help. If you are using your own computer, you will need to install the CTI WinApps applications yourself. See your technical support person or your instructor for a copy of the Setup Disk and the Installation Instructions that come with it.

To open the CTI Win Apps group window:

1. Double-click the **CTI WinApps group icon**. Your screen displays a CTI WinApps group window similar to the one in Figure 1-8.

Control-menu box

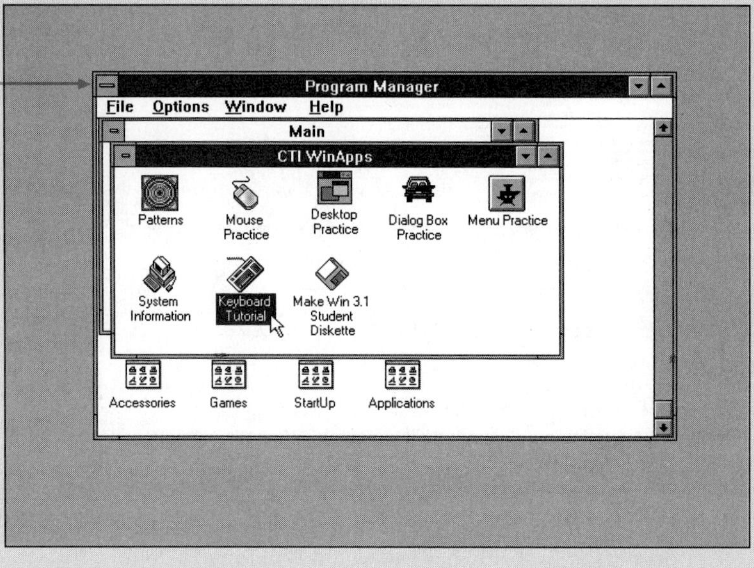

Figure 1-8
Double-clicking

The CTI WinApps group window contains an icon for each application provided with these tutorials. Right now we want to use the Keyboard Tutorial application.

To launch the Keyboard Tutorial:

1. Double-click the **Keyboard Tutorial icon**. Within a few seconds, the tutorial begins.
2. Read the opening screen, then click the **Continue button**. The CTI Keyboard Tutorial window appears. Follow the instructions on your screen to complete the tutorial. See Figure 1-9.

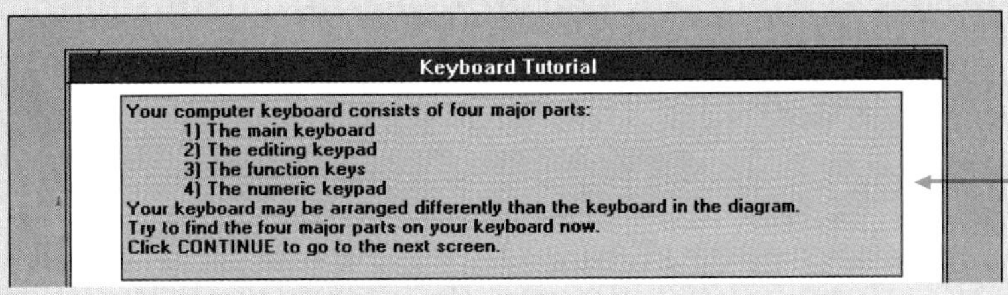

Figure 1-9 Instructions in the CTI Keyboard Tutorial window

TROUBLE? Click the Quit button at any time if you want to exit the Tutorial.

3. When you have completed the Keyboard Tutorial, click the **Quit button**. This takes you back to the Program Manager and CTI WinApps group window.

   TROUBLE? *If you did not have trouble in Step 3, skip this entire paragraph!* If the Program Manager window is not open, look for its icon at the bottom of your screen. Double-click this icon to open the Program Manager window. To prevent this problem from happening again, click the word Options on the Program Manager menu bar, then click Minimize on Use.

Launching the CTI Mouse Practice

To discover how to use the mouse to manipulate Windows controls, you should launch the Mouse Practice.

To launch the Mouse Practice:

1. Make sure the Program Manager and the CTI WinApps windows are open. It is not a problem if you have additional windows open.

   TROUBLE? If the Program Manager window is not open, look for its icon at the bottom of your screen. Double-click this icon to open the Program Manager window. To prevent this problem from happening again, click the word Options that appears near the top of the Program Manager window, then click Minimize.

2. Double-click the **Mouse Practice icon**. The Mouse Practice window opens.

   TROUBLE? If you don't see the Mouse Practice icon, try clicking the scroll bar arrow button or see your technical support person.

3. Click, drag, or double-click the objects on the screen to see what happens. Don't hesitate to experiment.

4. When you have finished using the Mouse Practice, click the **Exit button** to go back to the Program Manager and continue the tutorial steps.

Organizing Application Windows on the Desktop

The Windows desktop provides you with capabilities similar to your desk; it lets you stack many different items on your screen-based desktop and activate the one you want to use.

There is a problem, though. Like your real desk, your screen-based desktop can become cluttered. That's why you need to learn how to organize the applications on your Windows desktop.

Launching the CTI Desktop Practice

The Desktop Practice application will help you learn the controls for organizing your screen-based desktop.

To Launch the Desktop Practice:

1. Double-click the **Desktop Practice icon** to open the Desktop Practice window, shown in Figure 1-10. Your windows might be a different size or in a slightly different position. Don't worry. What's important is that you see a window with the title "Desktop Practice."

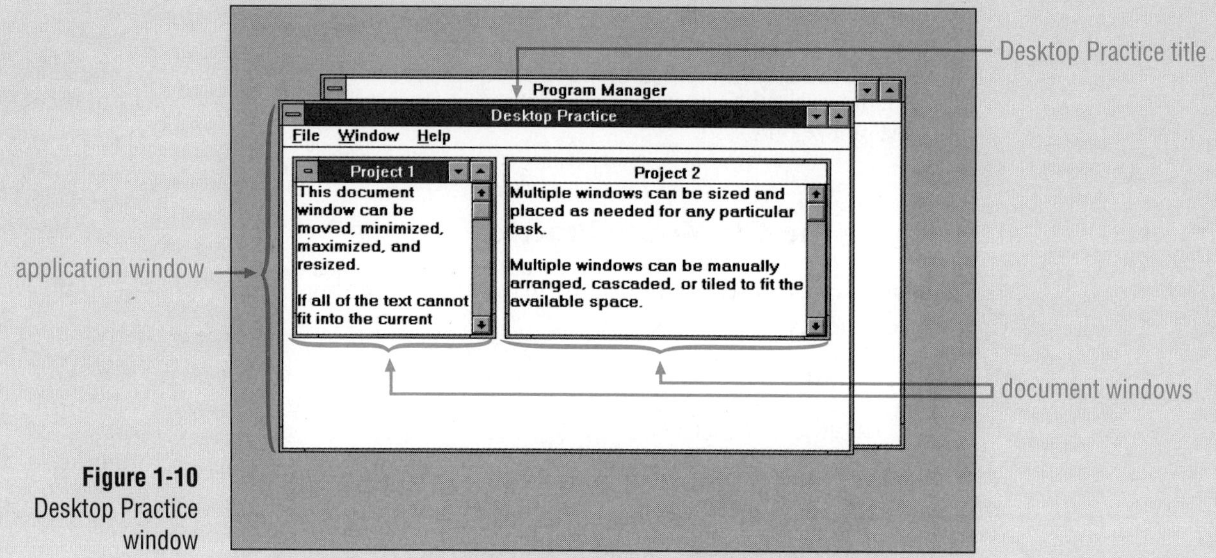

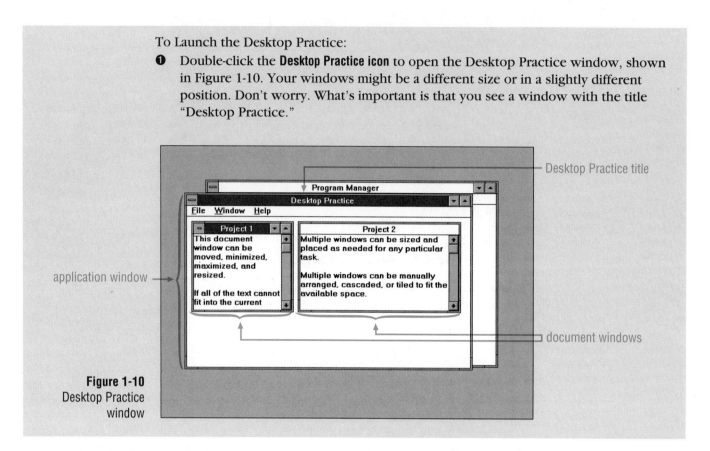

Figure 1-10
Desktop Practice window

Launching the Desktop Practice application opens three new windows on the desktop: Desktop Practice, Project 1, and Project 2. You might be able to see the edges of the Program Manager window "under" the Desktop Practice window. Essentially, you have stacked one project on top of another on your desktop.

The Desktop Practice window is an **application window**, a window that opens when you launch an application. The Project 1 and Project 2 windows are referred to as **document windows**, because they contain the documents, graphs, and lists you create using the application. Document windows are also referred to as **child windows**, because they belong to and are controlled by a "parent" application window.

The ability to have more than one document window open is one of many useful features of the Windows operating environment. Without this capability, you would have to print the documents that aren't being displayed so you could refer to them.

The Anatomy of a Window

Application windows and document windows are similar in many respects. Take a moment to study the Desktop Practice window on your screen and in Figure 1-11 on the following page to familiarize yourself with the terminology. Notice the location of each component but *don't* activate the controls.

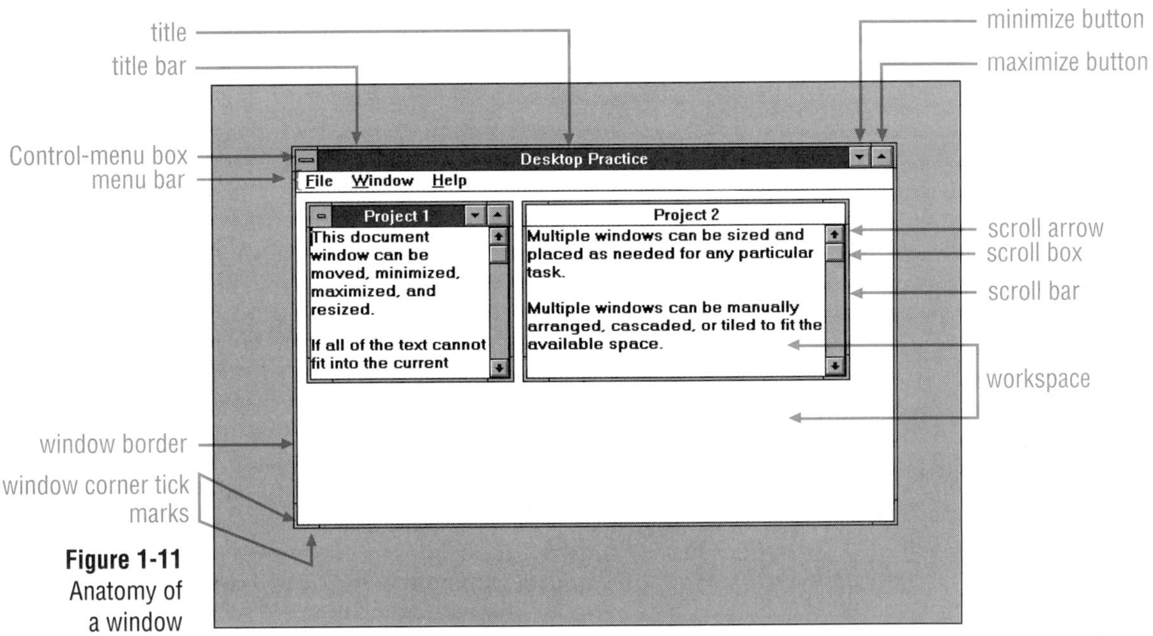

Figure 1-11
Anatomy of a window

At the top of each window is a **title bar**, which contains the window title. A darkened or highlighted title bar indicates that the application window is active. In Figure 1-11, the Desktop Practice application and the Project 1 document windows are active.

In the upper-right of the application window are two buttons used to change the size of a window. The **minimize button—**a square containing a triangle with the point down—is used to shrink the window. The **maximize button**, with the triangle pointing up, is used to enlarge the window so it fills the screen. When a window is maximized, a **restore button** with two triangles replaces the maximize button. Clicking the restore button reduces a maximized window to its previous size.

The **Control-menu box**, located in the upper-left of the Desktop Practice application window, is used to open the **Control menu**, which allows you to switch between application windows.

The **menu bar** is located just below the title bar on application windows. Notice that child windows do not contain menu bars.

The thin line running around the entire perimeter of the window is called the **window border**. The **window corners** are indicated by tick marks on the border.

The gray bar on the right side of each document window is a **scroll bar**, which you use to view window contents that don't initially fit in the window. Both application windows and document windows can contain scroll bars. Scroll bars can appear on the bottom of a window as well as on the side.

The space inside a window where you type text, design graphics, and so forth is called the **workspace**.

Maximizing and Minimizing Windows

The buttons on the right of the title bar are sometimes referred to as **resizing buttons**. You can use the resizing buttons to **minimize** the window so it shrinks down to an icon, **maximize** the window so it fills the screen, or **restore** the window to its previous size.

Because a minimized program is still running, you have quick access to the materials you're using for the project without taking up space on the desktop. You don't need to launch the program when you want to use it again because it continues to run.

A maximized window is useful when you want to focus your attention on the project in that window without being distracted by other windows and projects.

To maximize, restore, and minimize the Desktop Practice window:

1. Locate the maximize button (the one with the triangle pointing up) for the Desktop Practice window. You might see a portion of the Program Manager window behind the Desktop Practice window. Be sure you have found the Desktop Practice maximize button. See Figure 1-12.

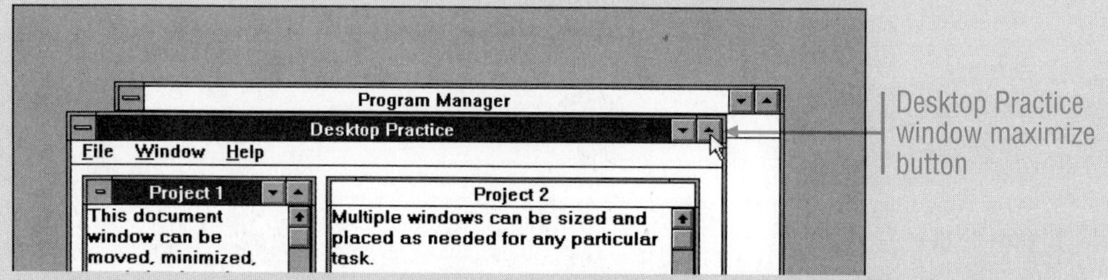

Figure 1-12
Maximizing a window

2. Click the **maximize button** to expand the window to fill the screen. Notice that in place of the maximize button there is now a restore button that contains double triangles.
3. Click the **restore button**. The Desktop Practice window returns to its original size.
4. Next, click the **minimize button** (the one with the triangle pointing down) to shrink the window to an icon.
5. Locate the minimized Desktop Practice icon at the bottom of your screen. See Figure 1-13.

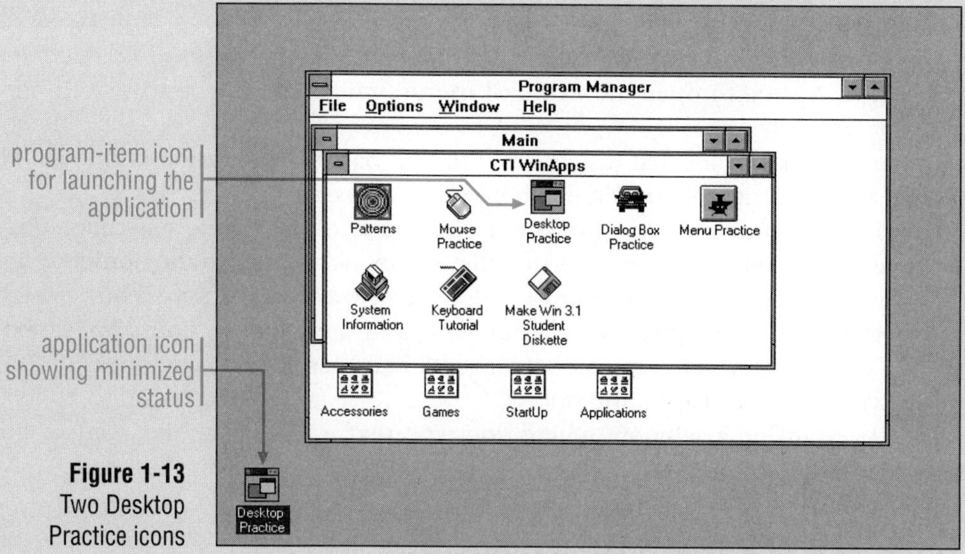

Figure 1-13
Two Desktop Practice icons

TROUBLE? If you cannot locate the Desktop Practice icon at the bottom of your screen, the Program Manager is probably maximized. To remedy this situtation, click the restore button on the Program Manager Window.

When you *close* an application window, you exit the application and it stops running. But when you *minimize* an application, it is still running even though it has been shrunk to an icon. It is important to remember that minimizing a window is not the same as closing it.

The icon for a minimized application is called an **application icon**. As Figure 1-13 illustrates, your screen shows two icons for the Desktop Practice application. The icon at the bottom of your screen is the application icon and represents a program that is currently running even though it is minimized. The other Desktop Practice icon is inside the CTI WinApps window. If you were to double-click this icon, you would launch a second version of the Desktop Practice application. *Don't launch two versions of the same application.* You should restore the Desktop Practice window by double-clicking the minimized icon at the bottom of your screen. Let's do that now.

To restore the Desktop Practice window:

❶ Double-click the minimized **Desktop Practice icon** at the bottom of your screen. The Desktop Practice window opens.

Changing the Dimensions of a Window

Changing the dimensions of a window is useful when you want to arrange more than one project on your desktop. Suppose you want to work with the Desktop Practice application and at the same time view the contents of the Program Manager window. To do this, you will need to change the dimensions of both windows so they don't overlap each other.

To change the dimensions of the Desktop Practice window:

❶ Move the pointer slowly over the top border of the Desktop Practice window until the pointer changes shape to a double-ended arrow. See Figure 1-14.

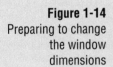

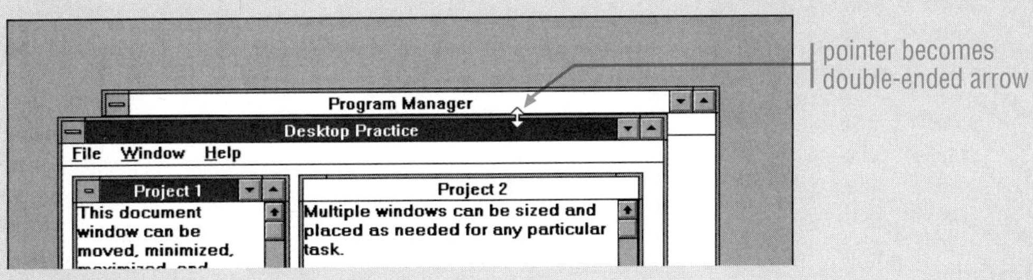

Figure 1-14
Preparing to change the window dimensions

❷ Press the left mouse button and hold it down while you drag the border to the top of the screen. Notice how an outline of the border follows your mouse movement.

❸ Release the mouse button. As a result the window adjusts to the new border.

❹ Drag the left border of the Desktop Practice window to the left edge of the screen.

❺ Move the pointer slowly over the lower-right corner of the Desktop Practice window until the pointer changes shape to a double-ended diagonal arrow. Figure 1-15 on the following page shows you how to do this step and the next one.

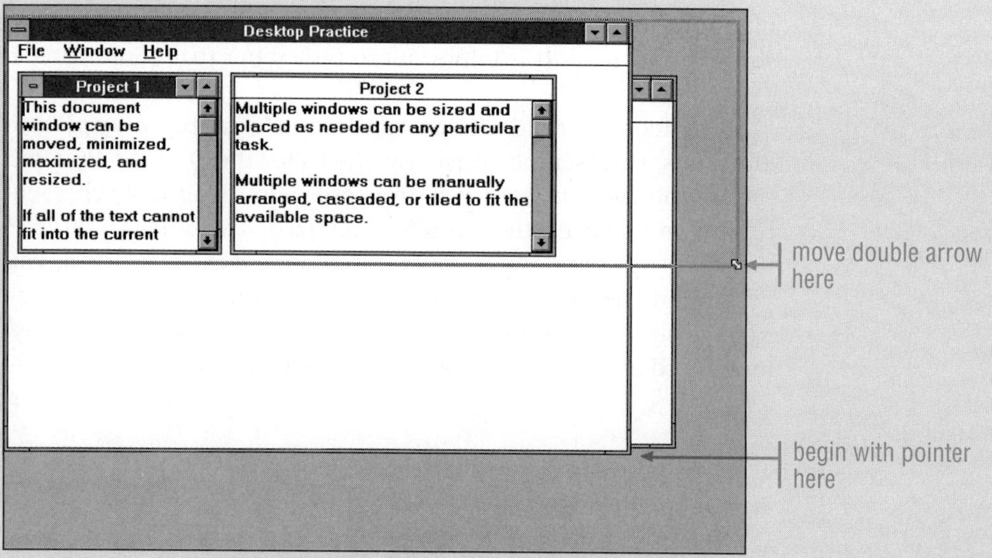

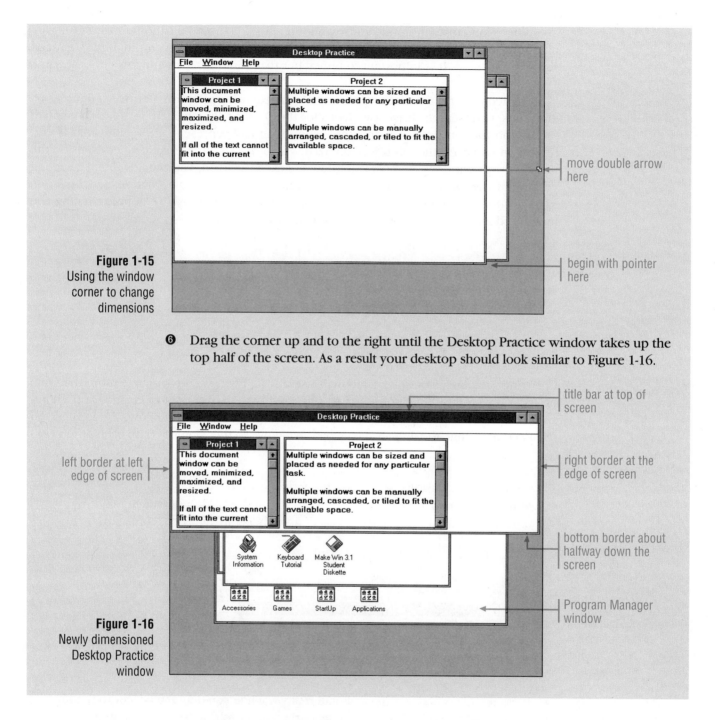

Figure 1-15 Using the window corner to change dimensions

❻ Drag the corner up and to the right until the Desktop Practice window takes up the top half of the screen. As a result your desktop should look similar to Figure 1-16.

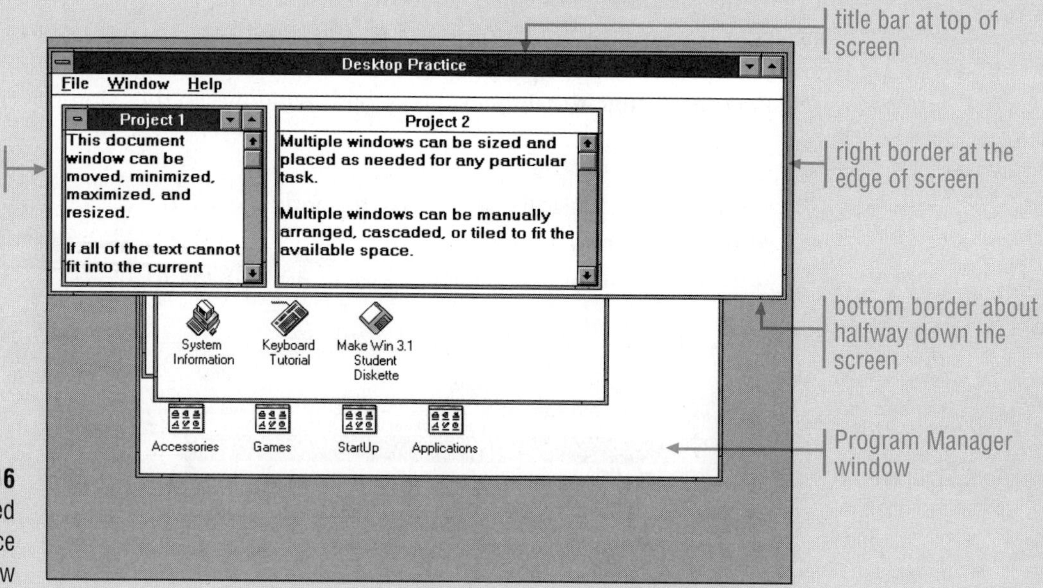

Figure 1-16 Newly dimensioned Desktop Practice window

Switching Applications

In the preceding steps you arranged the application windows so they were both visible at the same time. A different approach to organizing windows is to maximize the windows and then switch between them using the **Task List**, which contains a list of all open applications.

Let's maximize the Desktop Practice window. Then, using the Task List, let's switch to the Program Manager window, which will be hidden behind it.

To maximize the Desktop Practice window and then switch to the Program Manager:

❶ Click the **maximize button** on the Desktop Practice title bar. As a result the maximized Desktop Practice window hides the Program Manager window.

❷ Click the **Control-menu box** on the left side of the Desktop Practice title bar. Figure 1-17 shows you the location of the Control-menu box and also the Control menu, which appears after you click.

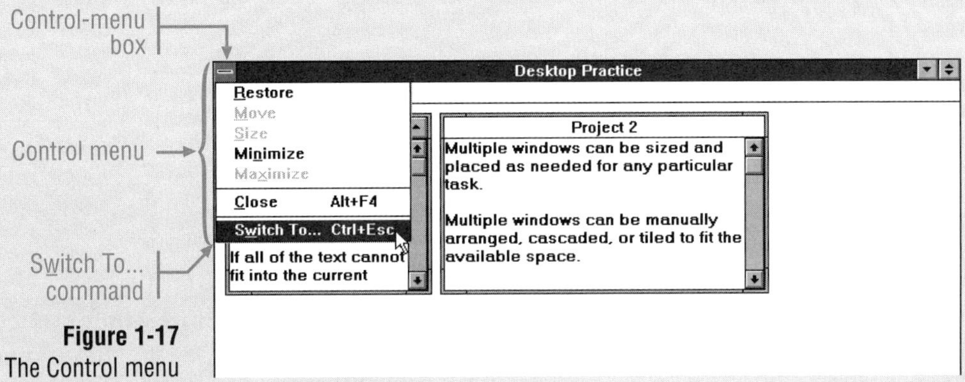

Figure 1-17
The Control menu

❸ Click **Switch To...** The Task List box appears, as shown in Figure 1-18.

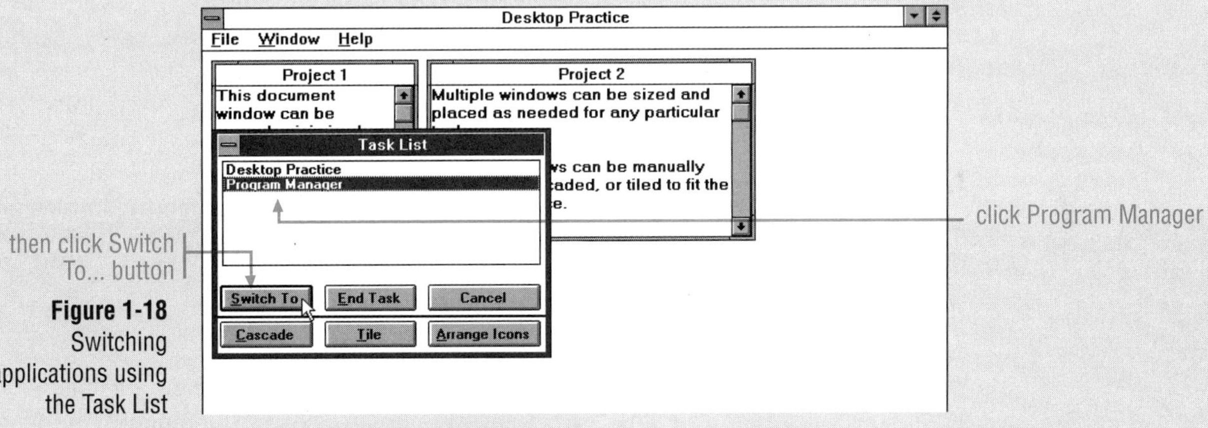

Figure 1-18
Switching applications using the Task List

❹ Click the **Program Manager option** from the list, then click the **Switch To button** to select the Program Manager. As a result the Program Manager reappears on the bottom half of your screen.

❺ If it is not already maximized, click the **maximize button** on the Program Manager window so both applications (Program Manager and Desktop Practice) are maximized.

The Program Manager window is active and "on top" of the Desktop Practice window. To view the Desktop Practice window, you will need to switch application windows again. You could switch tasks using the mouse, as we did in the last set of steps, or you can use the keyboard to quickly cycle through the tasks and activate the one you want. Let's use the keyboard method for switching windows this time, instead of using the Task List.

To switch to the Desktop Practice window using the keyboard:

1. Hold down **[Alt]** and continue holding it down while you press **[Tab]**. Don't release the Alt key yet! On the screen you should see a small rectangle that says "Desktop Practice."

   TROUBLE? Don't worry if you accidentally let go of the Alt key too soon. Try again. Press [Alt][Tab] until the "Desktop Practice" rectangle reappears.

2. Release the Alt key. Now the maximized Desktop Practice window is open.

When a window is maximized, it is easy to forget what's behind it. If you forget what's on the desktop, call up the Task List using the Control menu or use [Alt][Tab] to cycle through the tasks.

Organizing Document Windows

Think of document windows as subwindows within an application window. Because document windows do not have menu bars, the commands relating to these windows are selected from the menu bar of the application window. For example, you can use the Tile command in the Window menu to arrange windows so they are as large as possible without any overlap. The advantage of tiled windows is that one window won't cover up important information. The disadvantage of tiling is that the more windows you tile, the smaller each tile becomes and the more scrolling you will have to do.

You can use the Cascade command in the Window menu to arrange windows so they are all a standard size, they overlap each other, and all title bars are visible. Cascaded windows are often larger than tiled windows and at least one corner is always accessible so you can activate the window. Try experimenting with tiled and cascading windows. The desktop organizational skills you will learn will help you arrange the applications on your desktop so you can work effectively in the Windows multi-tasking environment.

Closing a Window

You close a window when you have finished working with a document or when you want to exit an application program. The steps you follow to close a document window are the same as those to close an application window. Let's close the Desktop Practice window.

To close the Desktop Practice application window:

1. Click the **Control-menu box** on the Desktop Practice window.
2. Click **Close** as shown in Figure 1-19 on the following page. The Desktop Practice window closes and you see the Program Manager window on the desktop.

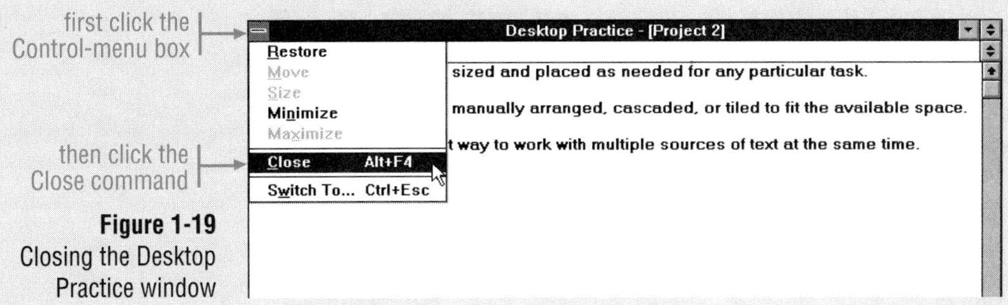

Figure 1-19
Closing the Desktop Practice window

Using Windows to Specify Tasks

In Windows, you issue instructions called **commands** to tell the computer what you want it to do. Windows applications provide you with lists of commands called **menus**. Many applications also have a ribbon of icons called a **toolbar**, which provides you with command shortcuts. Let's launch the Menu Practice application to find out how menus and toolbars work.

To launch the Menu Practice application:

❶ If the CTI WinApps window is not open, double-click its group icon at the bottom of the Program Manager window.

❷ Double-click the **Menu Practice** icon to open the Menu Practice window. See Figure 1-20.

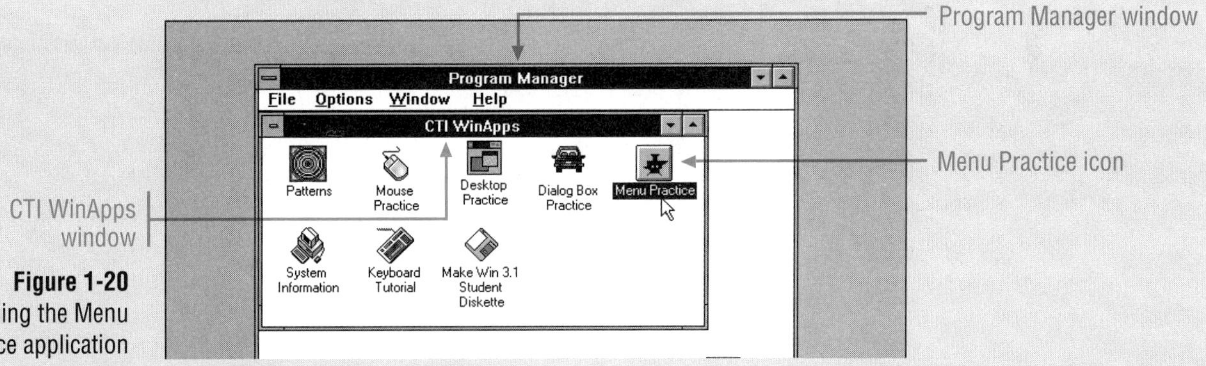

Figure 1-20
Launching the Menu Practice application

❸ Click the **maximize button** (the one with the triangle point up) for the Menu Practice window. The maximized Menu Practice window is shown in Figure 1-21 on the following page.

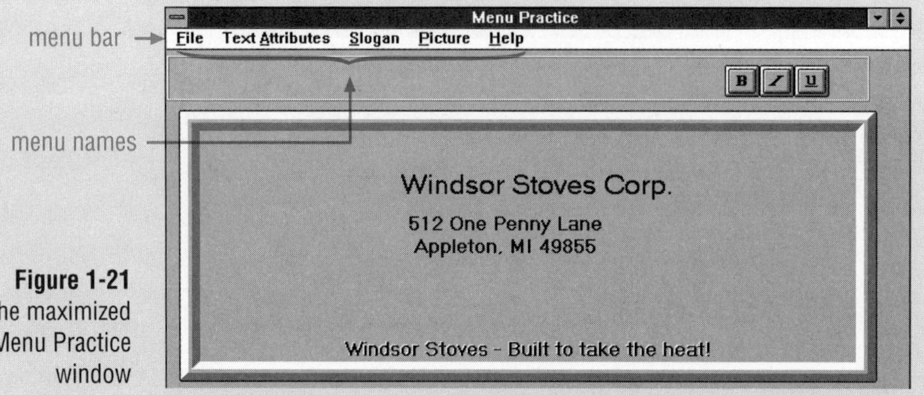

Figure 1-21
The maximized Menu Practice window

Opening and Closing Menus

Application windows, but not document windows, have menu bars such as the one shown in Figure 1-21. The menu bar contains menu names such as File, Text Attributes, Slogan, Picture, and Help. Let's practice opening and closing menus.

To open a menu:

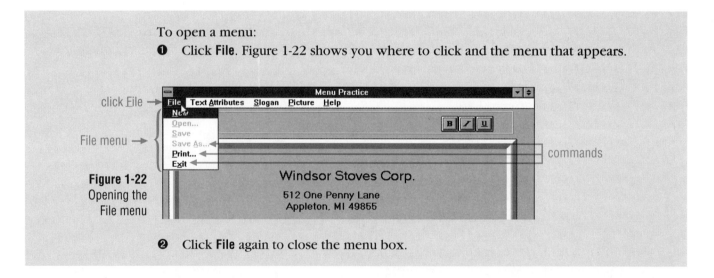

❶ Click **File**. Figure 1-22 shows you where to click and the menu that appears.

Figure 1-22
Opening the File menu

❷ Click **File** again to close the menu box.

When you click a menu name, the full menu drops down to display a list of commands. The commands on a menu are sometimes referred to as **menu items**.

Menu Conventions

The commands displayed on the Windows menus often include one or more **menu conventions**, such as check marks, ellipses, shortcut keys, and underlined letters. These menu conventions provide you with additional information about each menu command.

A check mark in front of a menu command indicates that the command is in effect. Clicking a checked command will remove the check mark and deactivate the command. For example, the Windsor Stoves logo currently has no graphic because the Show Picture command is not active. Let's add a picture to the logo by activating the Show Picture command.

To add or remove a check mark from the Show Picture command:

1. Click **Picture**. Notice that no check mark appears next to the Show Picture command.
2. Click **Show Picture**. The Picture menu closes, and a picture of a stove appears.
3. Click **Picture** to open the Picture menu again. Notice that a check mark appears next to the Show Picture command because you activated this command in Step 2.
4. Click **Show Picture**. This time clicking Show Picture removes the check mark and removes the picture.

Another menu convention is the use of gray, rather than black, type for commands. Commands displayed in gray type are sometimes referred to as **grayed-out commands**. Gray type indicates that a command is not currently available. The command might become available later, when it can be applied to the task. For example, a command that positions a picture on the right or left side of the logo would not apply to a logo without a picture. Therefore, the command for positioning the picture would be grayed out until a picture was included with the logo. Let's explore how this works.

To explore grayed-out commands:

1. Click **Picture**. Figure 1-23 shows the Picture menu with two grayed-out choices.

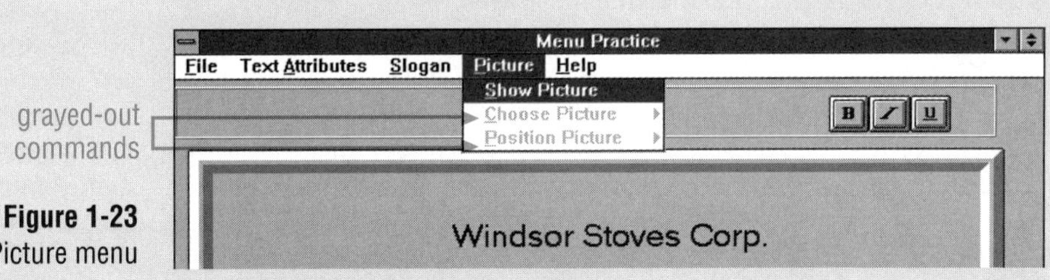

Figure 1-23
The Picture menu

2. Click the grayed-out command **Position Picture**. Although the highlight moves to this command, nothing else happens because the command is not currently available. You cannot position the picture until a picture is displayed.
3. Now click **Show Picture**. The Picture menu closes, and a picture is added to the logo.
4. Click **Picture**. Now that you have opened the Picture menu again, notice that the Choose Picture and Position Picture commands are no longer grayed out.

A **submenu** provides an additional set of command choices. On your screen the Choose Picture and Position Picture commands each have triangles next to them. A triangle is a menu convention that indicates a menu has a submenu. Let's use the submenu of the Position Picture command to move the stove picture to the right of the company name.

To use the position Picture submenu:

1. Click **Position Picture**. A submenu appears with options for left or right. In Figure 1-24 on the following page, the picture is to the left of the company name.

Figure 1-24
Viewing a submenu

❷ Click **Right**. Selecting this submenu command moves the picture to the right of the company name.

Some menu conventions allow you to use the menus without a mouse. It is useful to know how to use these conventions because, even if you have a mouse, in some situations it might be faster to use the keyboard.

One keyboard-related menu convention is the underlined letter in each menu name. If you wanted to open a menu using the keyboard, you would hold down the Alt key and then press the underlined letter. Let's open the Text Attributes menu using the keyboard.

To open the Text Attributes menu this way:

❶ Look at the menu name for the Text Attributes menu. Notice that the A is underlined.

❷ Press **[Alt][A]**. The Text Attributes menu opens.

TROUBLE? Remember from the Keyboard Tutorial that the [Alt][A] notation means to hold down the Alt key and press A. Don't type the brackets and don't use the Shift key to capitalize the A.

You can also use the keyboard to highlight and activate commands. On your screen the Bold command is highlighted. You use the arrow keys on the keyboard to move the highlight. You activate highlighted commands by pressing [Enter]. Let's use the keyboard to activate the Underline command.

To choose the Underline command using the keyboard:

❶ Press [↓] two times to highlight the Underline command.

❷ Press **[Enter]** to activate the highlighted command and underline the company name. Now look at the B, I, and U buttons near the upper-right corner of the screen. The U button has been "pressed" or activated. This button is another control for underlining. You'll find out how to use these buttons later.

Previously you used the Alt key in combination with the underlined letter in the menu title to open a menu. You might have noticed that each menu command also has an underlined letter. Once a menu is open, you can activate a command by pressing the underlined letter—there is no need to press the Alt key.

To activate the Italic command using the underlined letter:

❶ Press **[Alt][A]**. This key combination opens the Text Attributes menu. Next, notice which letter is underlined in the Italic command.

❷ Press **[I]** to activate the Italic command. Now the company name is italicized as well as underlined.

Look at the menu in Figure 1-25. Notice the Ctrl+B to the right of the Bold command. This is the key combination, often called a **shortcut key**, that can be used to activate the Bold command even if the menu is not open. The Windows Ctrl+B notation means the same thing as [Ctrl][B] in these tutorials: hold down the Control key and, while holding it down, press the letter B. When you use shortcut keys, don't type the + sign and don't use the Shift key to capitalize. Let's use a shortcut key to boldface the company name.

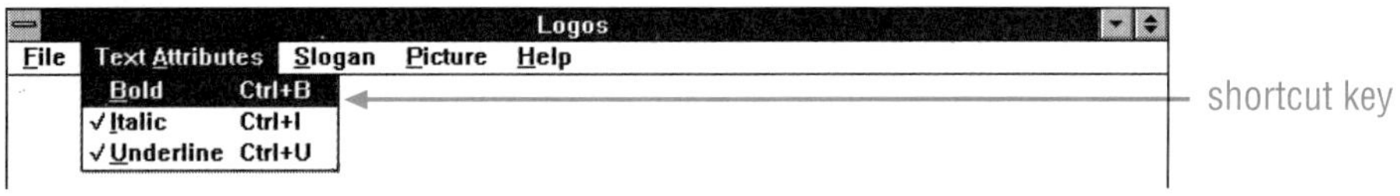

Figure 1-25
The Text Attributes menu

To Boldface the company name using a shortcut key:

❶ Press **[Ctrl][B]** and watch the company name appear in boldface type.

The **ellipsis (...)** menu convention means that when you select a command with three dots next to it, a dialog box will appear. A **dialog box** requests additional details about how you want the command carried out. We'll use the dialog box for the Choose Slogan command to change the company slogan.

To use the Choose Slogan dialog box:

❶ Click **Slogan**. Notice that the Choose Slogan command is followed by an ellipsis.

❷ Click **Choose Slogan...** and study the dialog box that appears. See Figure 1-26. Notice that this dialog box contains four sets of controls: the "Use Slogan" text box, the "Slogan in Bold Letters" check box, the "Slogan 3-D Effects" control buttons, and the OK and Cancel buttons. The "Use Slogan" text box displays the current slogan.

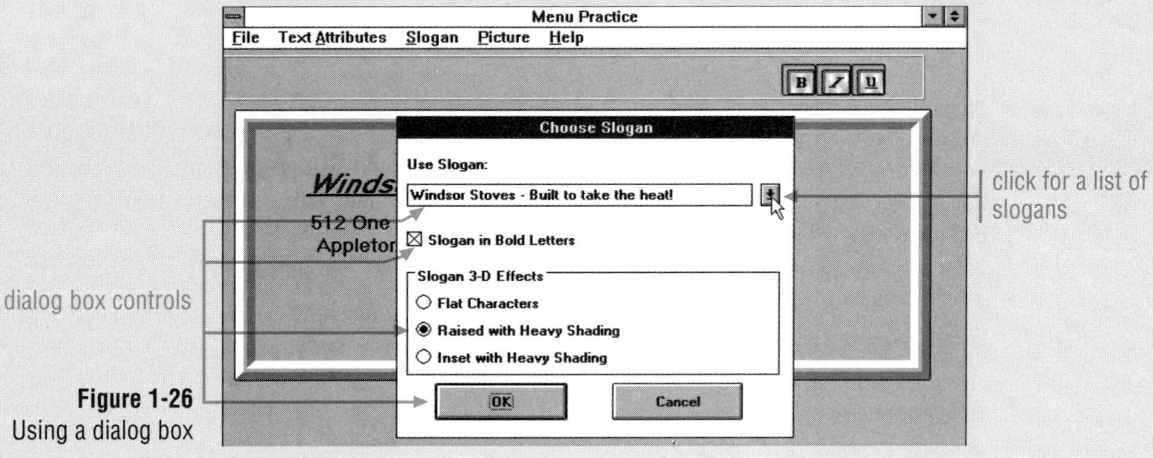

Figure 1-26
Using a dialog box

3. Click the **down arrow button** on the right of the slogan box to display a list of alternative slogans.
4. Click the slogan **Windsor Stoves - Built to last for generations!**
5. Click the **OK button** and watch the new slogan replace the old.

You have used the Menu Practice application to learn how to use Windows menus, and you have learned the meaning of the Windows menu conventions. Next we'll look at dialog box controls.

Dialog Box Controls

Figure 1-27 shows a dialog box with a number of different controls that could be used to specify the requirements for a rental car. **Command buttons** initiate an immediate action. A **text box** is a space for you to type in a command detail. A **list box** displays a list of choices. A drop-down list box appears initially with only one choice; clicking the list box arrow displays additional choices. **Option buttons**, sometimes called radio buttons, allow you to select one option. **Check boxes** allow you to select one or more options. A **spin bar** changes a numeric setting.

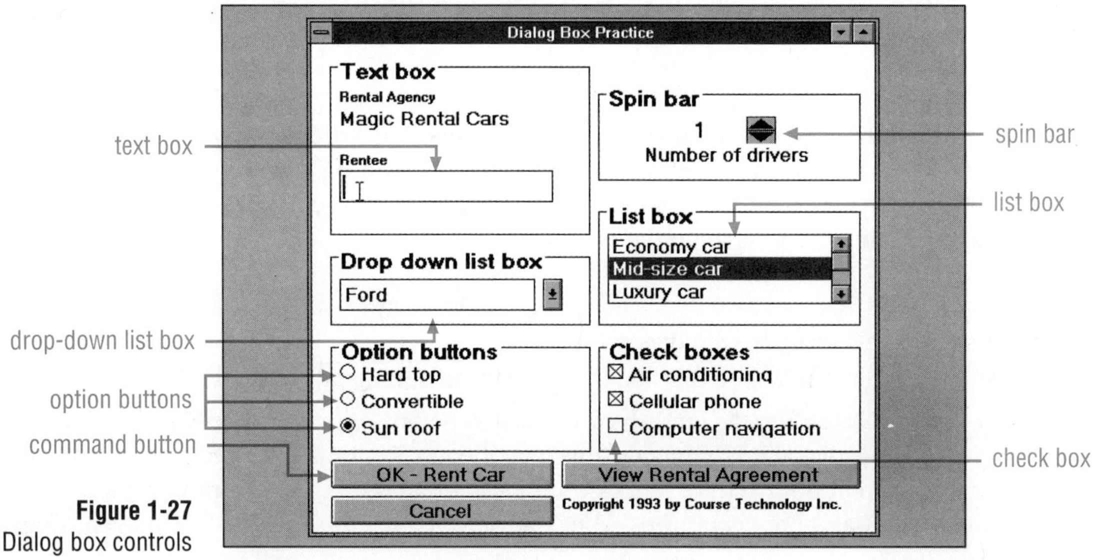

Figure 1-27
Dialog box controls

Windows uses standard dialog boxes for tasks such as printing documents and saving files. Most Windows applications use the standard dialog boxes, so if you learn how to use the Print dialog box for your word processing application, you will be well on your way to knowing how to print in any application. As you may have guessed, the rental car dialog box is not a standard Windows dialog box. It was designed to illustrate the variety of dialog box controls.

Let's see how the dialog box controls work. First, we will use a text box to type text. The Choose Slogan dialog box for the Menu Practice application has a text box that will let us change the slogan on the Windsor Stoves Corp. logo.

To activate the Use Slogan text box:

❶ Click **Slogan** to open the Slogan menu.

❷ Click **Choose Slogan...** and the Choose Slogan dialog box appears.

❸ Move the pointer to the text box and notice that it changes to an **I-bar** shape for text entry. See Figure 1-28.

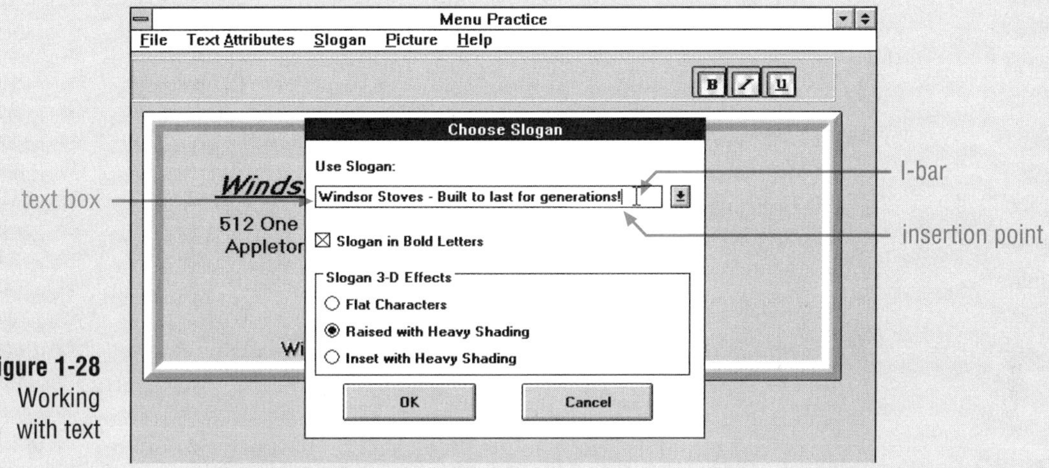

Figure 1-28 Working with text

❹ Click the **left mouse button** to activate the text box. A blinking bar called an **Insertion point** indicates that you can type text into the box. Also notice that all the text is highlighted.

❺ Press **[Del]** to erase the highlighted text of the old slogan.

When you work with a dialog box, be sure to set all the components the way you want them *before* you press the Enter key or click the OK button. Why? Because the Enter key, like the OK button, tells Windows that you are finished with the entire dialog box. Now let's type a new slogan in the text box and change the slogan 3-D effect.

To type a new slogan in a text box:

❶ Type **Quality is our Trademark!** but don't press [Enter], because while this dialog box is open, you are also going to change the slogan 3-D effect.

TROUBLE? If you make a typing mistake, press [Backspace] to delete the error, then type the correction.

❷ Look at the Slogan 3-D Effects list. Notice that the current selection is Raised with Heavy Shading.

❸ Click **Inset with Heavy Shading**.

❹ Click the **OK button** and then verify that the slogan and the 3-D effect have changed.

TROUBLE? If you are working on a monochrome system without the ability to display shade of gray, you may not be able to see the 3-D effect.

Using the Toolbar

A **toolbar** is a collection of icons that provides command shortcuts for mouse users. The icons on the toolbar are sometimes referred to as buttons. Generally the options on the toolbar duplicate menu options, but they are more convenient because they can be activated by a single mouse click. The toolbar for the Menu Practice application shown in Figure 1-29 has three buttons that are shortcuts for the Bold, Italic, and Underline commands. In a previous exercise you underlined, boldfaced, and italicized the company name using the menus. As a result the B, U, and I buttons are activated. Let's see what they look like when we deactivate them.

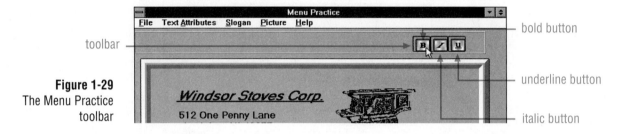

Figure 1-29 The Menu Practice toolbar

To change the type style using the toolbar:

1. Click B to remove the boldface.
2. Click I to turn off italics.
3. Click U to turn off underlining.
4. Click B to turn on boldface again.

You might want to spend a few minutes experimenting with the Menu Practice program to find the best logo design for Windsor Stoves Corp. When you are finished, close the Menu Practice window.

To close the Menu Practice window:

1. Click the **Control-menu box**.
2. Click **Close**. The Menu Practice program closes and returns you to Windows Program Manager.

You have now learned about Windows menus, dialog boxes and toolbars. In the next section, you will survey the Paintbrush application, experiment with tools, and access on-line help.

Using Paintbrush to Develop Your Windows Technique

After you have learned the basic Windows controls, you will find that most Windows *applications* contain similar controls. Let's launch the Paintbrush application and discover how to use it.

To launch the Paintbrush application:

1. Be sure the Program Manager window is open. If it is not open, use the skills you have learned to open it.
2. You should have an Accessories icon or an Accessories window on the desktop. If you have an Accessories group icon on the desktop, double-click it to open the Accessories group window.

   TROUBLE? If you don't see the Accessories icon or window, click the Window menu on the Program Manager menu bar. Look for Accessories in the list. If you find Accessories in this list, click it. If you do not find Accessories, ask your technical support person for help.

3. Double-click the **Paintbrush icon** to launch the Paintbrush application. Your screen will look similar to the one in Figure 1-30.

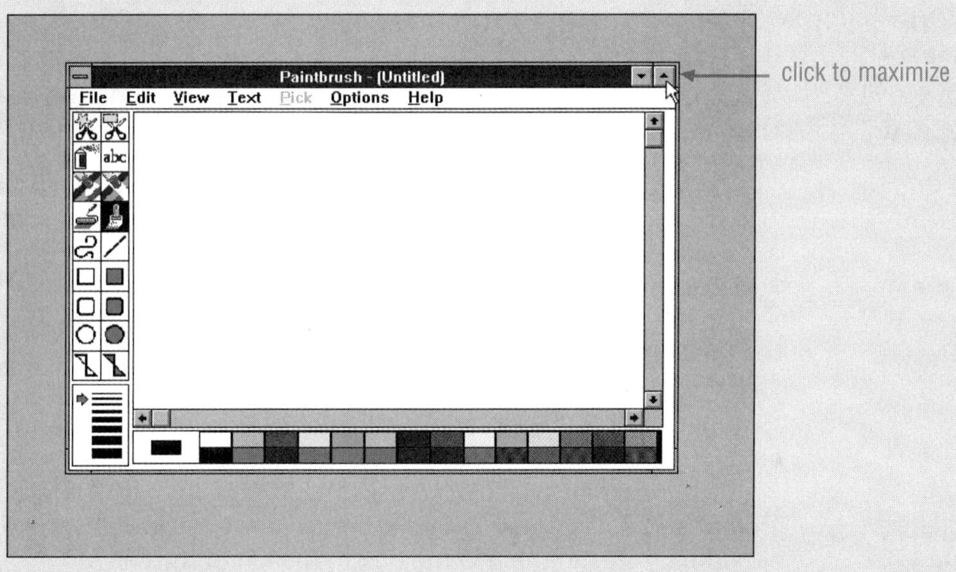

Figure 1-30
The Paintbrush window

4. Click the Paintbrush window **maximize button** so you will have a large drawing area.

Surveying the Paintbrush Application Window

Whether you are using a reference manual or experimenting on your own, your first step in learning a new application is to survey the window and familiarize yourself with its components.

Look at the Paintbrush window on your screen and make a list of the components you can identify. If you have not encountered a particular component before, try to guess what it might be.

Now refer to Figure 1-31 on the following page, which labels the Paintbrush window components.

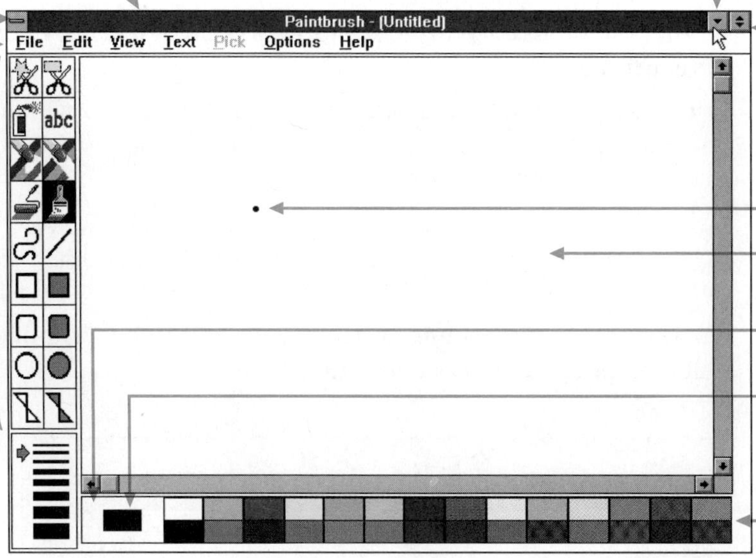

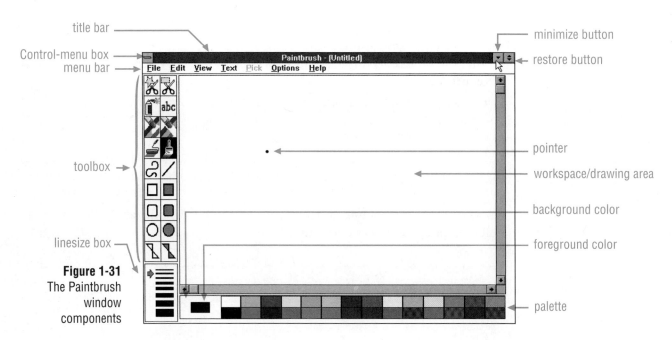

Figure 1-31
The Paintbrush window components

The darkened title bar shows that the Paintbrush window is activated. The resizing buttons are in the upper-right corner, as usual. Because there is a restore button and because the window takes up the entire screen, you know that the window is maximized. The Control-menu box is in the upper-left corner, and a menu bar lists seven menus.

On the left side of the window are a variety of icons. This looks similar to the toolbar you used when you created the logo, only it has more icons, which are arranged vertically. The Windows manual refers to this set of icons as the **toolbox**.

Under the toolbox is a box containing lines of various widths. This is the **linesize box**, which you use to select the width of the line you draw.

At the bottom of the screen is a color **palette**, which you use to select the foreground and background colors. The currently selected colors for the foreground and background are indicated in the box to the left of the palette.

The rectangular space in the middle of the window is the drawing area. When the pointer is in the drawing area, it will assume a variety of shapes, depending on the tool you are using.

Experimenting with Tools

The icons on toolbars might be some of the easiest Windows controls, but many people are a little mystified by the symbols used for some of the tools. Look at the icons in the Paintbrush toolbox and try to guess their use.

You can often make good guesses, when you know what the application does. For example, you probably guessed that the brush tool shown in Figure 1-32 is used for drawing a picture. However, you might not be able to guess how the brush and the roller tools differ.

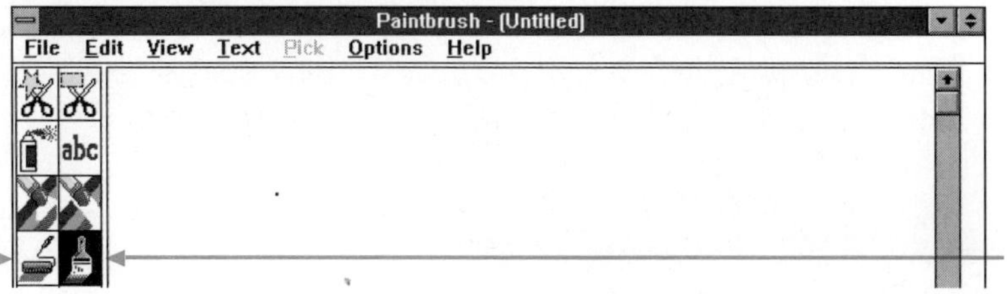

Figure 1-32
The paint roller and brush icons

If you can make some reasonable guess about how a tool works, it's not a bad idea to try it out. Can you write your name using the paintbrush tool? Let's try it.

To use the brush tool:

1. Locate and click the **brush tool** in the toolbox. The brush tool becomes highlighted, indicating that it is now the selected tool.
2. Move the pointer to the drawing area. Notice that it changes to a small dot.
3. Move the pointer to the place where you want to begin writing your name.

When the left mouse button is down, the brush will paint. When you release the mouse button, you can move the pointer without painting.

4. Use the mouse to control the brush as you write your name. Don't worry if it looks a little rough. Your "John Hancock" might look like the one in Figure 1-33.

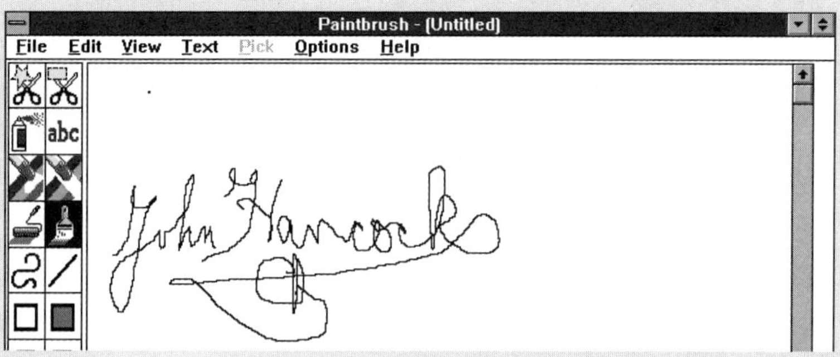

Figure 1-33
Your "John Hancock"

You will recall that we were curious about the difference between the brush and the paint roller. Let's experiment with the paint roller next.

To try the paint roller:

1. Click the **paint roller** tool.
2. Position the pointer in the upper-left corner of the drawing area and click. What happened?!

Did you get a strange result? Don't panic. This sort of thing happens when you experiment. Still, we probably should find out a little more about how to control the roller. To do this, we'll use the Paintbrush Help facility.

Using Help

Most Windows applications have an extensive on-line Help facility. A **Help facility** is an electronic reference manual that contains information about an application's menus, tools, and procedures. Some Help facilities also include **tutorials**, which you can use to learn the application.

There are a variety of ways to access Help, so people usually develop their own technique for finding information in it. We'll show you one way that seems to work for many Windows users. Later you can explore on your own and develop your own techniques.

When you use Help, a Help window opens. Usually the Help window overlays your application. If you want to view the problem spot and the Help information at the same time, it is a good idea to organize your desktop so the Help and application windows are side by side.

To access Help and organize the desktop:

❶ Click **Help**. A Help menu lists the Help commands.

❷ Click **Contents** to display a Paintbrush Help window similar to the one in Figure 1-34.

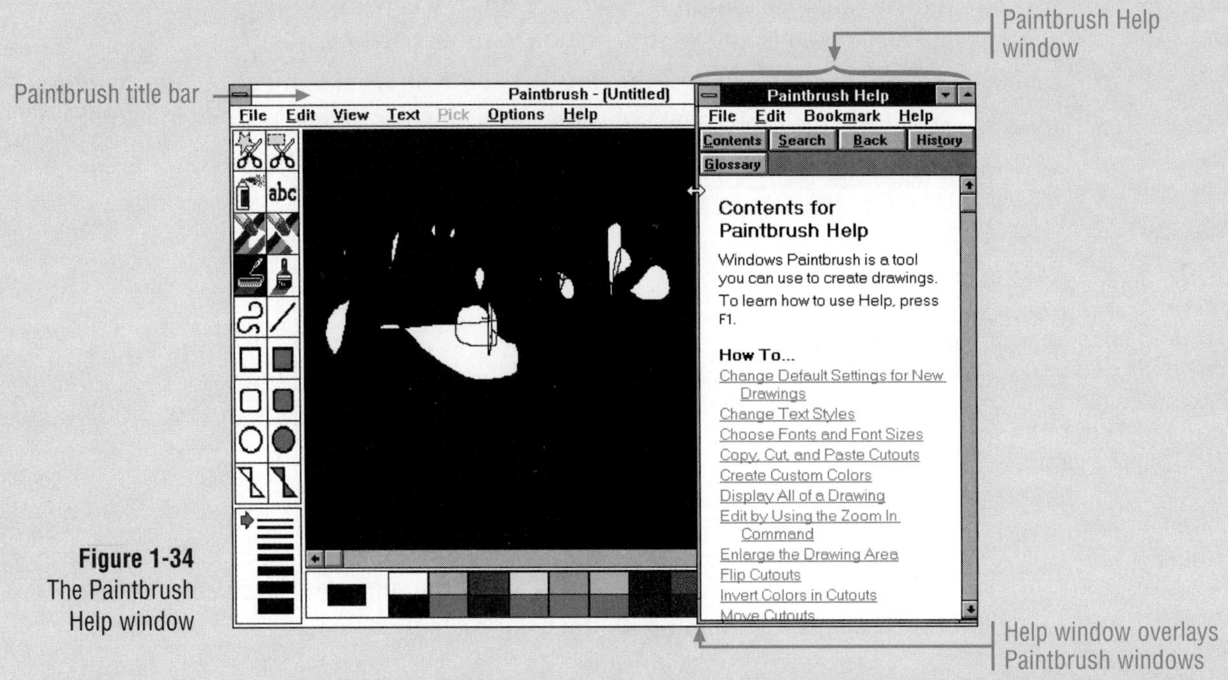

Figure 1-34
The Paintbrush Help window

❸ If the Paintbrush Help window is not the same size and shape as the one in Figure 1-34, drag the corners of the Help window until it looks like the one in the figure.

The Paintbrush application window is partially covered by the Help window. We need to fix that.

❹ Click the **Paintbrush title bar** to activate the Paintbrush window.

❺ Click the **restore button** to display the window borders and corners.

❻ Drag the corners of the Paintbrush application until your screen resembles the one in Figure 1-35 on the following page.

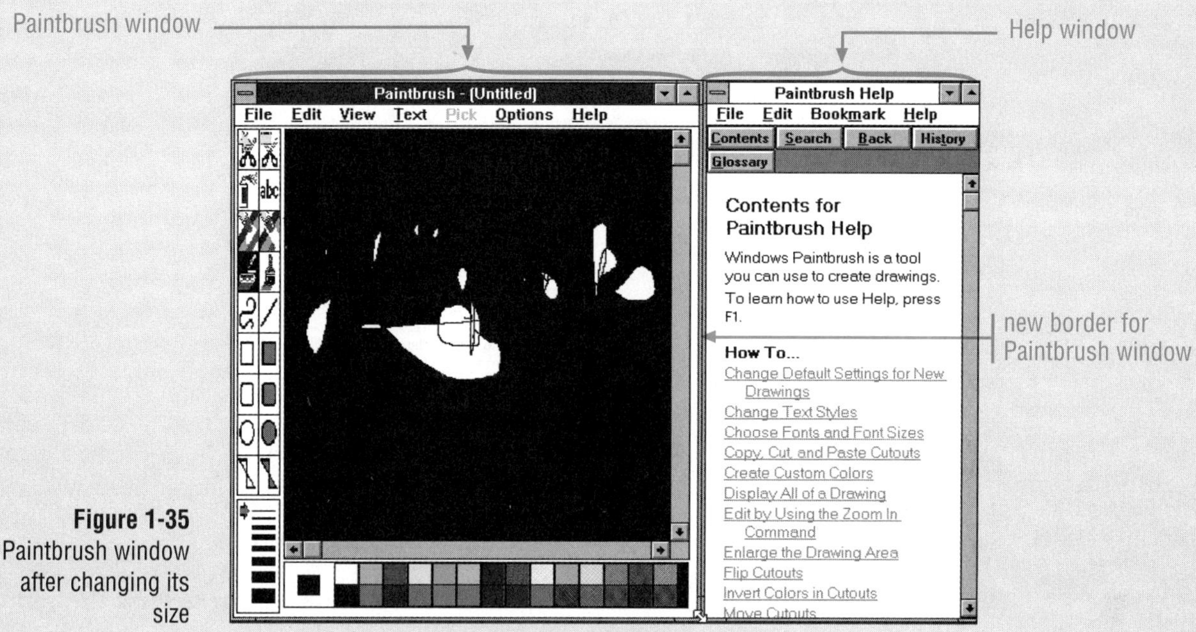

Figure 1-35
Paintbrush window after changing its size

Now that the windows are organized, let's find out about the roller tool. The Paintbrush Help window contains a Table of Contents, which is divided into three sections: How To, Tools, and Commands.

The **How To** section is a list of procedures that are explained in the Help facility. Use this section when you want to find out how to do something. The **Tools** section identifies the toolbar icons and explains how to use them. The **Commands** section provides an explanation of the commands that can be accessed from the menu bar.

To find information about the paint roller tool on the Help facility:

❶ Use the scroll box to scroll down the text in the Help window until you see the Tools section heading.

❷ Continue scrolling until the Paint Roller option comes into view.

❸ Position the pointer on the Paint Roller Option. Notice that the pointer changes to a pointing hand, indicating that Paint Roller is a clickable option.

❹ Click the **left mouse button**. The Help window now contains information about the paint roller, as shown in Figure 1-36 on the following page.

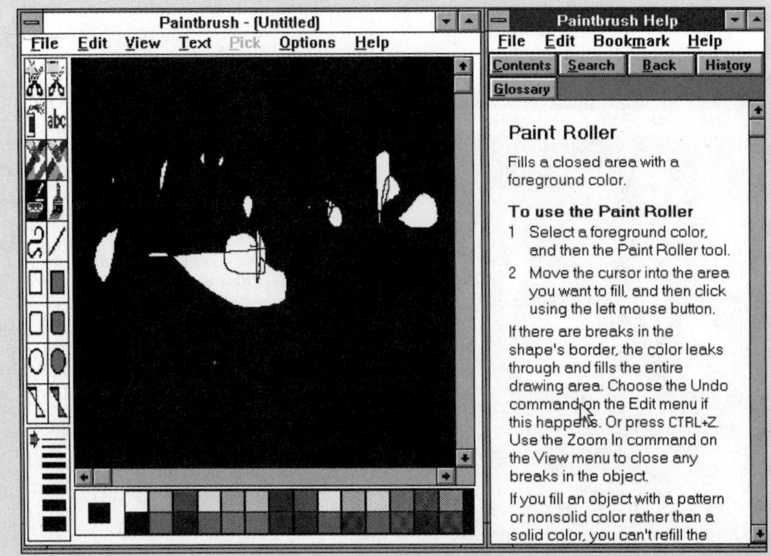

Figure 1-36
Paint Roller Help

❺ Read the information about the Paint Roller, using the scroll bar to view the entire text.

What did you learn about the paint roller? The first item you likely discovered is that the paint roller is used to fill an area. Well, it certainly did that in our experiment. It filled the entire drawing area with the foreground color, black. Next you might have noted that the first step in the procedure for using the paint roller is to select a foreground color. In our experiment, it would have been better if we selected some color other than black for the fill. Let's erase our old experiment so we can try again.

To start a new painting:

❶ Click **File** on the Paintbrush menu bar (not on the Help menu bar) to open the File menu.

❷ Click **New**, because you want to start a new drawing. A dialog box asks, "Do you want to save current changes?"

❸ Click the **No button** to clear the drawing area, because you don't want to save your first experiment.

Now you can paint your name and then use the roller to artistically fill areas. When you have finished experimenting, exit the Paintbrush application.

To exit Paintbrush:

❶ Click the **Control-menu box** and then click **Close**.

❷ In response to the prompt "Do you want to save current changes?" click the **No button**. The Paintbrush window closes, which also automatically closes the Help window.

You've covered a lot of ground. Next, it's time to learn how to exit Windows.

Exiting Windows

You might want to continue directly to the Questions and Tutorial Assignments. If so, stay in Windows until you have completed your work, then follow these instructions for exiting Windows.

To exit Windows:

1. Click the **Control-menu box** in the upper-left of the Program Manager window.
2. Click **Close**.
3. When you see the message "This will end your Windows session," click the **OK button**.

■ ■ ■

Steve congratulates you on your Windows progress. You have learned the terminology associated with the desktop environment and the names of the controls and how to use them. You have developed an understanding about desktop organization and how to arrange the application and document windows so you will use them most effectively. You have also learned to use menus, dialog boxes, toolbars and Help.

Questions

1. GUI is an acronym for graphical user Interface
2. A group window contains which of the following?
   a. application icons
   b. document icons
   c. program-item icons
   d. group icons
3. What is one of the main purposes of the Program Manager?
   a. to organize your diskette
   b. to launch applications
   c. to create documents
   d. to provide the Help facility for applications
4. Which mouse function is used as a shortcut for more lengthy mouse or keyboard procedures?
   a. pointing
   b. clicking
   c. dragging
   d. double-clicking
5. To change the focus to an icon, you ________________ it.
   a. close
   b. select
   c. drag
   d. launch

6. What is another name for document windows?
   a. child windows
   b. parent windows
   c. application windows
   d. group windows
7. In Figure 1-37 each window component is numbered. Write the name of the component that corresponds to the number.

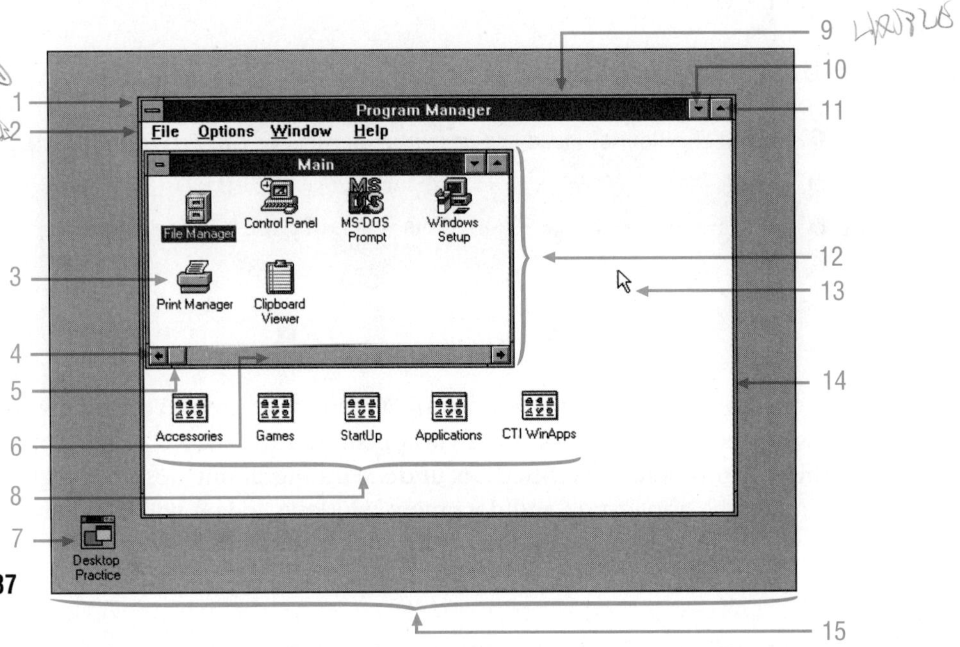

Figure 1-37

8. In Windows terminology you ______________ a window when you want to get it out of the way temporarily but leave the application running.
9. You ___CLOSE___ a window when you no longer need to have the application running.
10. The ________________ provides you with a way to switch between application windows.
    a. Task List
    b. program-item icon
    c. Window menu
    d. maximize button
11. How would you find out if you had more than one application running on your desktop?
12. ________________ refers to the capability of a computer to run more than one application at the same time.
13. Which menu provides the means to switch from one document to another?
    a. the File menu
    b. the Help menu
    c. the Window menu
    d. the Control menu
14. Describe three menu conventions used in Windows menus.

E 15. The flashing vertical bar that marks the place your typing will appear is ___I BAR___.

E 16. If you have access to a Windows reference manual such as the *Microsoft Windows User's Guide*, look for an explanation of the difference between group icons, program-item icons, and application icons. For your instructor's information, write down the name of the reference, the publisher, and the page(s) on which you found this information. If you were writing a textbook for first-time Windows users, how would you describe the difference between these icons?

E 17. Copy the definition of "metaphor" from any standard dictionary. For your instructor's information, write down the dictionary name, the edition, and the page number. After considering the definition, explain why Windows is said to be a "desktop metaphor."

Tutorial Assignments

If you exited Windows at the end of the tutorial, launch Windows and do Assignments 1 through 15. Write your answers to the questions in Assignments 1, 2, 3, 4, 5, 9, 10, 11, 12, 13, and 15. Also fill out the table in Assignment 7.

1. Close all applications except the Program Manager and shrink all the group windows to icons. What are the names of the group icons on the desktop?
2. Open the Main window. How many program-item icons are in this window?
3. Open the Accessories window. How many program-item icons are in this window?
4. Open, close, and change the dimensions of the windows so your screen looks like Figure 1-38.
   a. How many applications are now on the desktop?
   b. How did you find out how many applications are on the desktop?

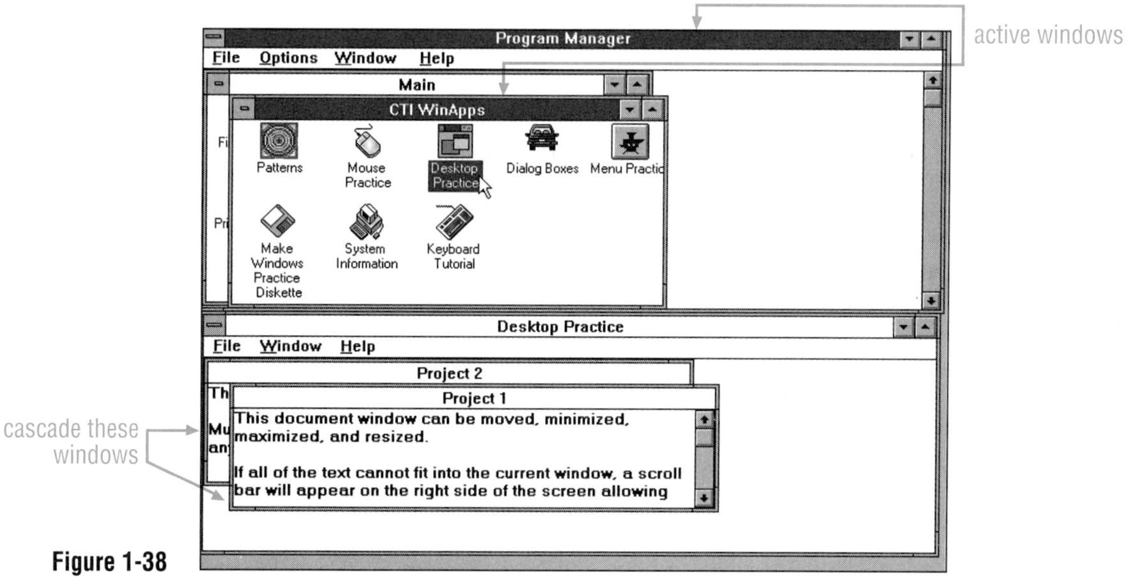

Figure 1-38

5. Open, close, and change the dimensions of the windows so your screen looks like Figure 1-39 on the following page. After you're done, close the Desktop Practice window using the fewest mouse clicks. How did you close the Desktop Practice window?

Open the CTI WinApps window and do Assignments 6 through 8.

Figure 1-39

6. Double-click the System Information icon.
7. Using the information displayed on your screen, fill out the following table:

CPU Type:	
Available Memory:	
Number of Diskette Drives:	
Capacity of Drive A:	
Capacity of Drive B:	
Horizontal Video Resolution:	
Vertical Video Resolution:	
Screen Colors or Shades:	
Network Type:	
DOS Version:	
Windows Version:	
Windows Mode:	
Windows Directory:	
Windows Free Resources:	
Available Drive Letters:	
Hard Drive Capacities:	

8. Click the Exit button to return to the Program Manager.

Launch the Mouse Practice application and do Assignments 9 through 14.

9. What happens when you drag the letter to the file cabinet?
10. What happens when you double-click the mouse icon located in the lower-left corner of the desktop?
11. What happens when you click an empty check box? What happens when you click a check box that contains an "X"?
12. Can you select both option buttons at the same time?
13. What happens when you click "Item Fourteen" from the list?
14. Exit the Mouse Practice.

Launch the Desktop Practice and do Assignments 15 through 17.

15. What is the last sentence of the document in the Project 2 window?
16. Close the Desktop Practice window.
17. Exit Windows.

T U T O R I A L 2

Effective File Management

Using the File Manager

OBJECTIVES

In this tutorial you will:

- Open and close the File Manager
- Format and make your student disk containing practice files
- Change the current drive
- Identify the components of the File Manager window
- Create directories
- Change the current directory
- Move, rename, delete, and copy files
- Make a disk backup
- Learn how to protect your data from hardware failures

CASE **A Professional Approach to Computing at Narraganset Shipyard** Ruth Sanchez works at the Narraganset Shipyard, a major government defense contractor. On a recent business trip to Washington, DC, Ruth read a magazine article that convinced her she should do a better job of organizing the files on her computer system. The article pointed out that a professional approach to computing includes a plan for maintaining an organized set of disk-based files that can be easily accessed, updated, and secured.

Ruth learns that the Windows File Manager can help to organize her files. Ruth has not used the File Manager very much, so before she begins to make organizational changes to the valuable files on her hard disk, she decides to practice with some sample files on a disk in drive A.

In this Tutorial, you will follow the progress of Ruth's File Manager practice and learn how to use Windows to manage effectively the data stored in your computer.

Files and the File Manager

A **file** is a named collection of data organized for a specific purpose and stored on a floppy disk or a hard disk. The typical computer user has hundreds of files.

The Windows File Manager provides some handy tools for organizing files. Ruth's first step is to launch the File Manager. Let's do the same.

To launch the File Manager:

1. Launch Windows.
2. Compare your screen to Figure 2-1. Use the skills you learned in Tutorial 1 to organize your desktop so only the Program Manager window and the Main window are open.

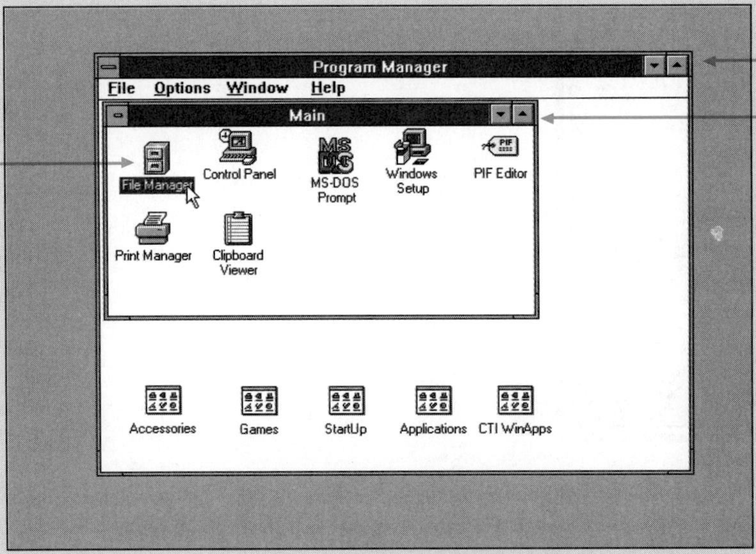

Figure 2-1
Launching the File Manager

3. Double-click the **File Manager icon** to launch the File Manager program and open the File Manager window.
4. If the File Manager window is not maximized, click the **maximize button**.
5. Click **Window**, then click **Tile**. You should now have one child window on the desktop. See Figure 2-2a on the following page. Don't worry if the title of your child window is not the same as the one in the figure.

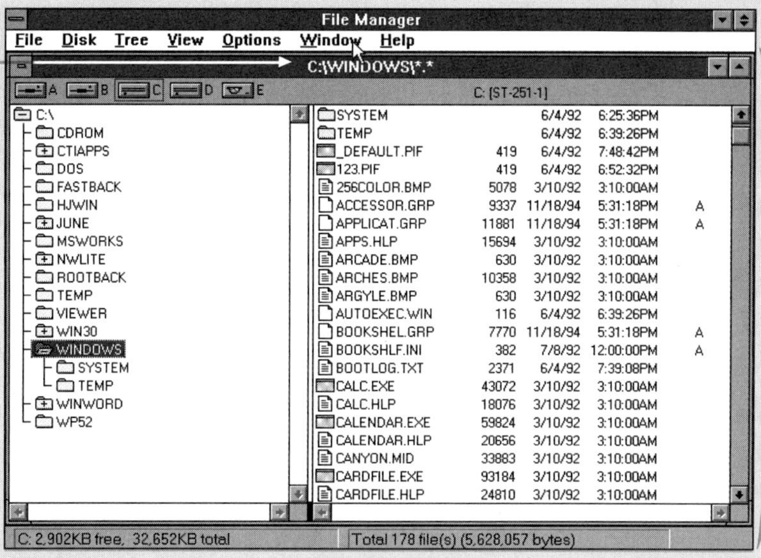

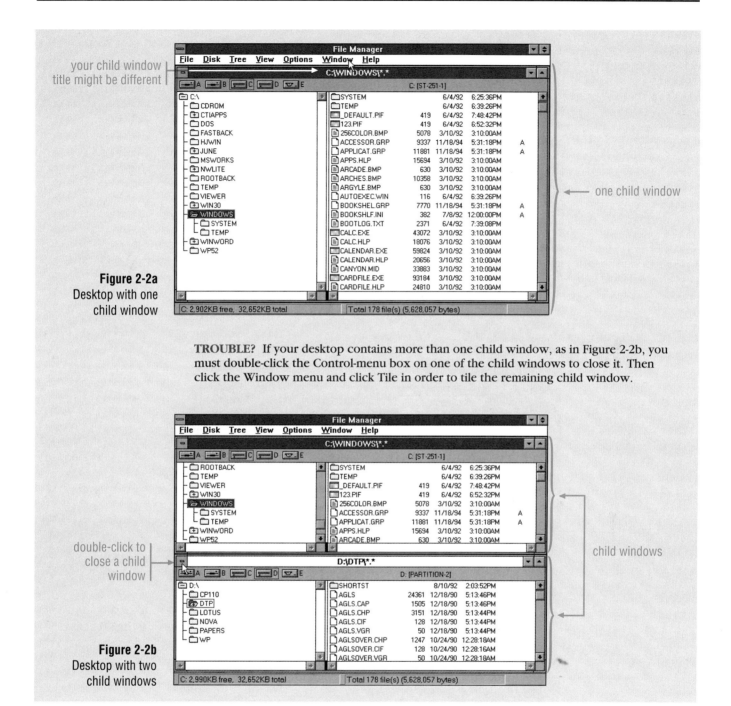

Figure 2-2a
Desktop with one child window

TROUBLE? If your desktop contains more than one child window, as in Figure 2-2b, you must double-click the Control-menu box on one of the child windows to close it. Then click the Window menu and click Tile in order to tile the remaining child window.

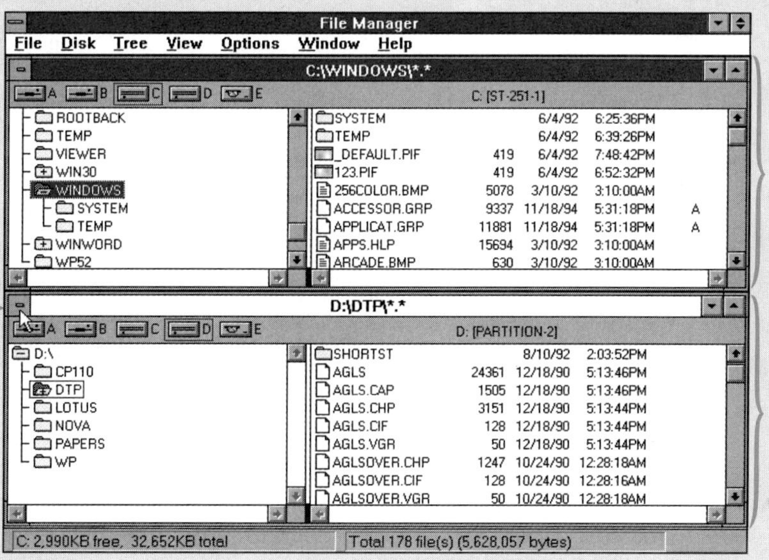

Figure 2-2b
Desktop with two child windows

Ruth decides to check her File Manager settings, which affect the way information is displayed. By adjusting your File Manager settings to match Ruth's, your computer will display screens and prompts similar to those in the Tutorial. *If you do not finish this tutorial in one session, remember to adjust the settings again when you begin your next session.*

To adjust your File Manager settings:

❶ Click **Tree**. Look at the command "Indicate Expandable Branches." See Figure 2-3. If no check mark appears next to this command, position the pointer on the command and click. If you see the check mark, go to Step 2.

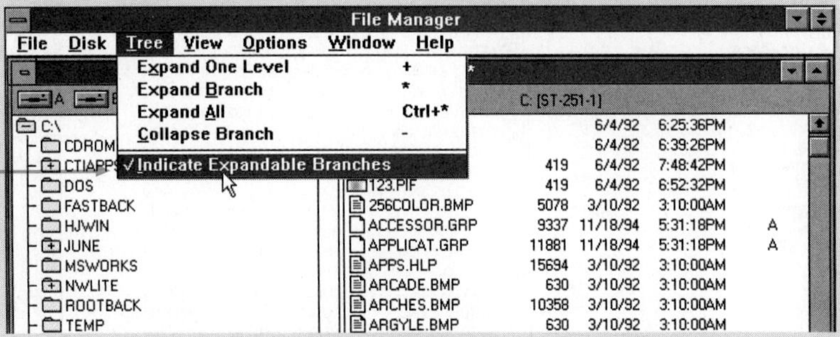

be sure this command is checked

Figure 2-3
File Manager settings: Tree

❷ Click **View**. Make any adjustments necessary so that the settings are the same as those in Figure 2-4.

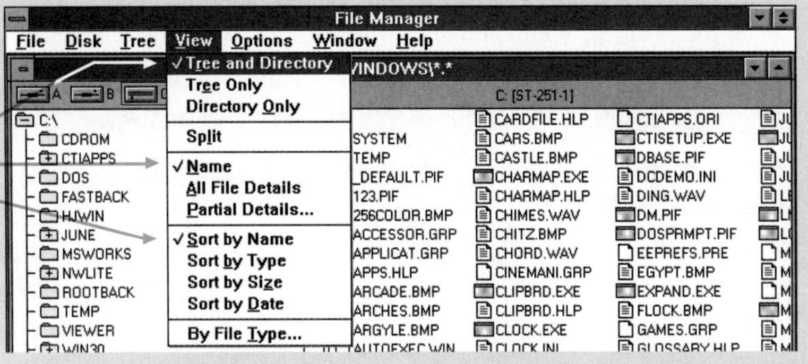

be sure these commands are checked

Figure 2-4
File Manager settings: View

TROUBLE? When you click a command to change the check mark, the menu closes. To change another command in the menu or to confirm your changes, you need to click the View menu again.

❸ Click **Options** and then click **Confirmation...**. Referring to Figure 2-5, make any adjustments necessary so that all the check boxes contain an X, then click the **OK button**.

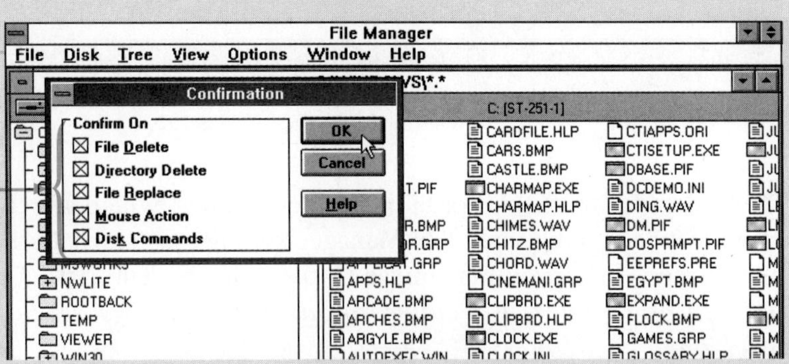

be sure each box contains "X"

Figure 2-5
File Manager settings: Confirmation

❹ Click **Options** again and then click **Font**. Make any adjustments necessary so your font settings match those in Figure 2-6 on the following page. Click the **OK button** whether or not you changed anything in this dialog box.

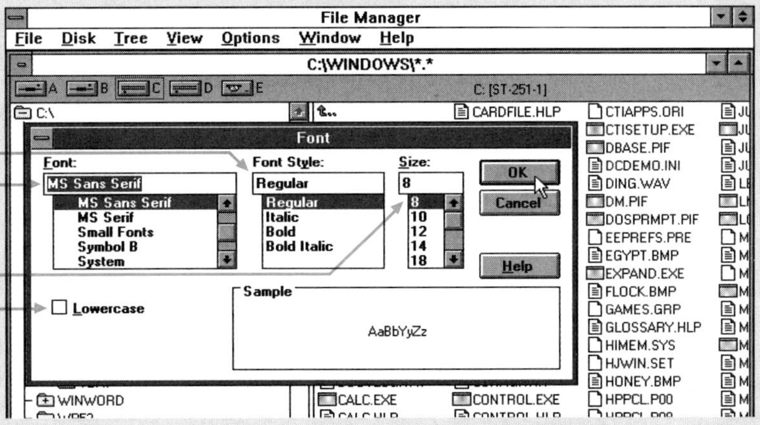

Figure 2-6
File Manager settings: Font

❺ Click **Options** again. Make any adjustments necessary so that the settings are the same as those in Figure 2-7. If no adjustments are necessary, click **Options** again to close the menu.

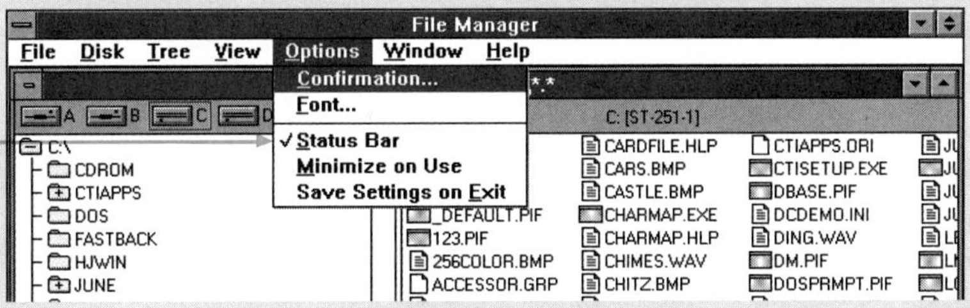

Figure 2-7
File Manager settings: Status Bar

Formatting a Disk

Next, Ruth needs to format the disks she will use for her File Manager practice. Disks must be formatted before they can be used to store data. Formatting arranges the magnetic particles on the disks in preparation for storing data. You need to format a disk when:

- you purchase a new disk
- you want to recycle an old disk that you used on a non-IBM-compatible computer
- you want to erase all the old files from a disk

Pay attention when you are formatting disks. *The formatting process erases all the data on the disk*. If you format a disk that already contains data, you will lose all the data. Fortunately, Windows will not let you format the hard disk or network drives using the Format Disk command.

To complete the steps in this Tutorial you need two disks of the same size and density. You may use blank, unformatted disks or disks that contain data you no longer need. *The following steps assume that you will format the disks in drive A. If you want to use drive B for the formatting process, substitute drive B for drive A* in Steps 3, 4, and 6.

To format the first disk:

❶ Make sure your disk is *not* write-protected. On a 5.25-inch disk the write-protect notch should *not* be covered. On a 3.5-inch disk the hole on the left side of the disk should be *closed*.

2. Write your name, course title, and course meeting time on an adhesive disk label. For the title of the disk, write Student Disk (Source Disk). Apply this label to one of the disks you are going to format. If you are using a 3.5-inch disk, do not stick the label on any of the metal parts.

3. Put this disk into drive A. If your disk drive has a door or a latch, secure it. See Figure 2-8.

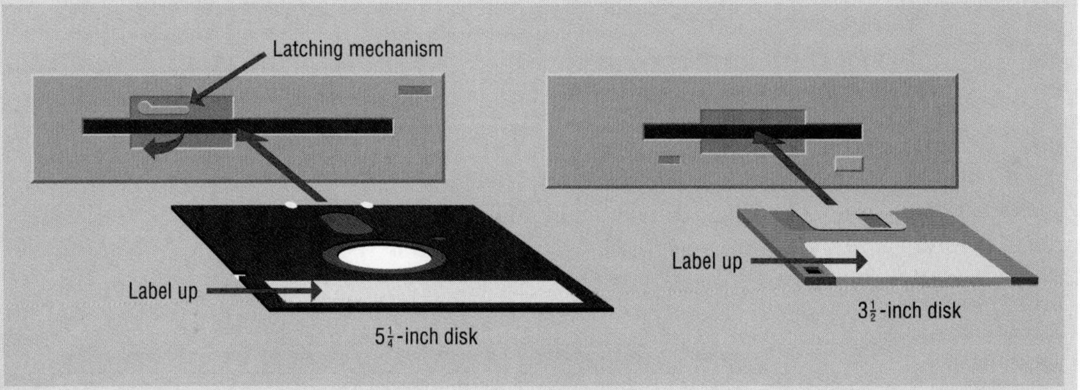

Figure 2-8
Inserting your disk

4. Click **Disk** and then click **Format Disk...**. A Format Disk dialog box appears. See Figure 2-9. If the Disk In box does not indicate Drive A, click the [↓] (down-arrow) button on this box, then click the Drive A option.

be sure these settings are correct

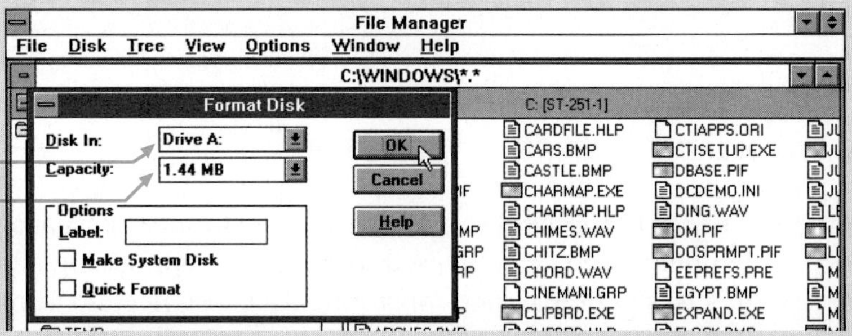

Figure 2-9
Format Disk dialog box

5. Look at the number displayed in the Capacity box. If you are formatting a disk that cannot store the displayed amount of data, click the [↓] (down-arrow) button at the right side of the Capacity box and then click the correct capacity from the list of options provided.

TROUBLE? How can you determine the capacity of your disk? The chart in Figure 2-10 (on the next page) will help you. If you still are not sure after looking at the figure, ask your technical support person.

Diskette size	Diskette density	Diskette capacity
51/4-inch	DD	360K
51/4-inch	HD	1.2MB
31/2-inch	DD	720K
31/2-inch	HD	1.44MB

Figure 2-10
Disk capacities

6. Click the **OK button**. The Confirm Format Disk dialog box appears with a warning. Read it. Look at the drive that is going to carry out the format operation (drive A). Be sure this is the correct drive. Double-check the disk that's in this drive to be sure it is the one you want to format.
7. Click the **Yes button**. The Formatting Disk dialog box keeps you updated on the progress of the format.
8. When the format is complete, the Format Complete dialog box reports the results of the format and asks if you'd like to format another disk. See Figure 2-11.

bytes available are same as bytes of total disk space

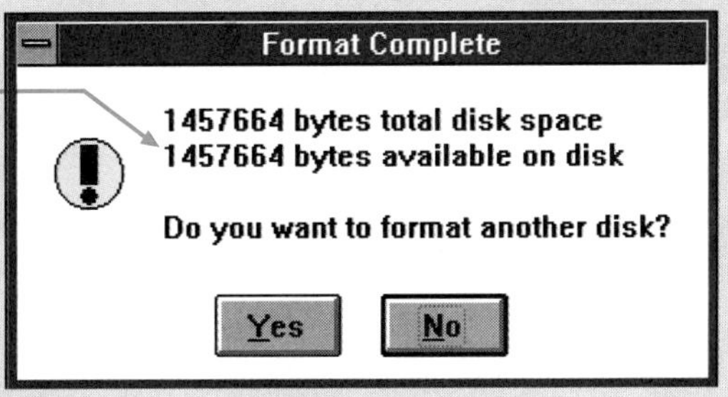

Figure 2-11
Format results: all sectors OK

Let's format your second floppy disk:

1. Click the **Yes button** after you review the formatting results.
2. Remove your Student disk from drive A.
3. Write your name, course title, and course meeting time on the label for the second disk. For the title of this disk write Backup (Destination Disk). Apply this label to your second disk and place this disk in drive A.
4. Be sure the **Disk In box** is set to drive A and the capacity is set to the capacity of your disk. (Remember to substitute B here if you are formatting your disk in drive B.)
5. Click the **OK button** to accept the settings. When you see the Confirm Format Disk dialog box, check to be sure you have the correct disk in the correct drive.
6. Click the **Yes button** to confirm that you want to format the disk. When the format is complete, review the format results.
7. You do not want to format another disk, so click the **No button** when the computer asks if you wish to format another disk.
8. *Remove the backup disk from drive A.* You will not need this backup disk until later.

Preparing Your Student Disk

Now that Ruth has formatted her disks, she is going to put some files on one of them to use for her file management exploration. To follow Ruth's progress, you must have copies of her files. A collection of files has been prepared for this purpose. You need to transfer them to one of your formatted disks.

To transfer files to your Student Disk:

1. Place the disk you labeled Student Disk (Source Disk) in drive A.

The File Manager window is open, but you need to go to the Program Manager window to launch the application that will transfer the files.

❷ Hold down **[Alt]** and continue to press **[Tab]** until Program Manager appears in the box, then release both keys. Program Manager becomes the active window.

❸ If the CTI WinApps window is not open, double-click the **CTI WinApps group icon**. If the CTI WinApps window is open but is not the active window, click it. Your screen should look similar to Figure 2-12.

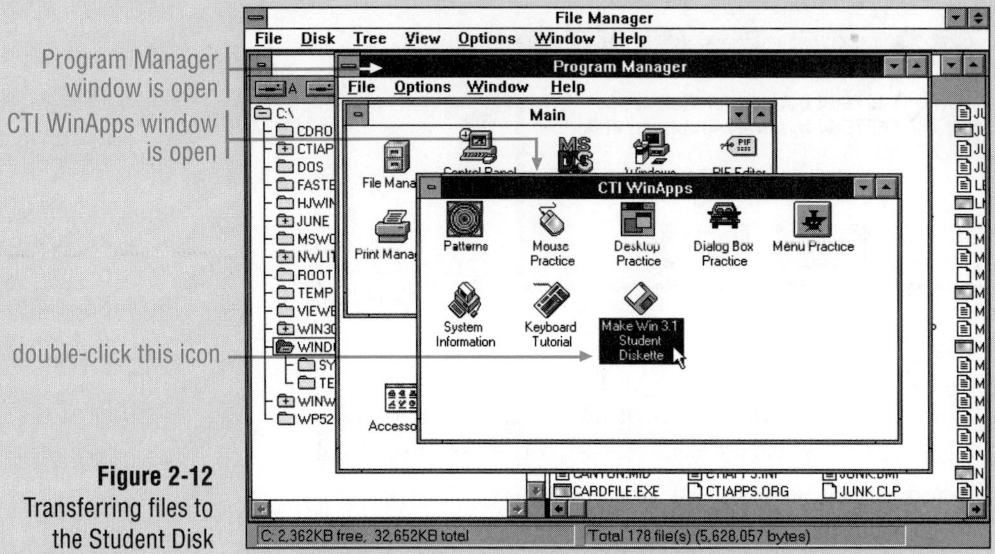

Figure 2-12
Transferring files to the Student Disk

❹ Double-click the **Make Win 3.1 Student Disk icon**. A dialog box appears.

❺ Make sure the drive that is selected in the dialog box corresponds to the drive that contains your disk (drive A or drive B), then click the **OK button**. It will take 30 seconds or so to transfer the files to your disk.

❻ Click the **OK button** when you see the message "24 files copied successfully!"

❼ Double-click on the **CTI WinWorks Apps Control-menu box** to close the window.

Now the data files you need should be on your Student Disk. To continue the Tutorial, you must switch back to the File Manager.

To switch back to the File Manager:

❶ Hold down **[Alt]** and press **[Tab]** until a box with File Manager appears. Then release both keys.

Finding Out What's on Your Disks

Ruth learned from the article that the first step toward effective data management is to find out what's stored on her disks. To see what's on your Student Disk, you will need to be sure your computer is referencing the correct disk drive.

Changing the Current Drive

Each drive on your computer system is represented by a **drive icon** that tells you the drive letter and the drive type. Figure 2-13 shows the drive types represented by these icons.

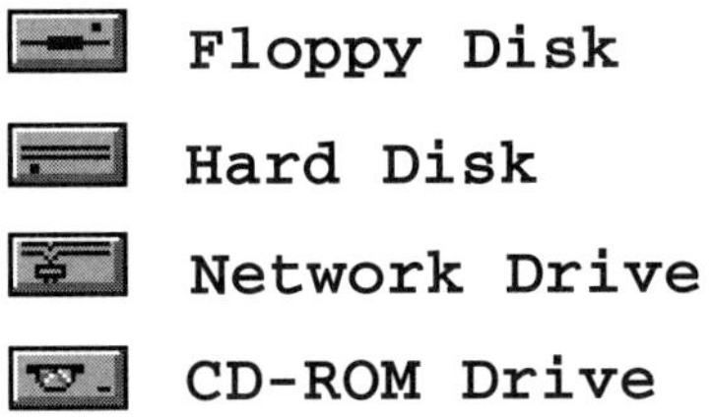

Figure 2-13
Drive icons

Near the top of the File Manager window, a **drive icon ribbon** indicates the drives on your computer system. See Figure 2-14. Your screen may be different because the drive icon ribbon on your screen reflects your particular hardware configuration.

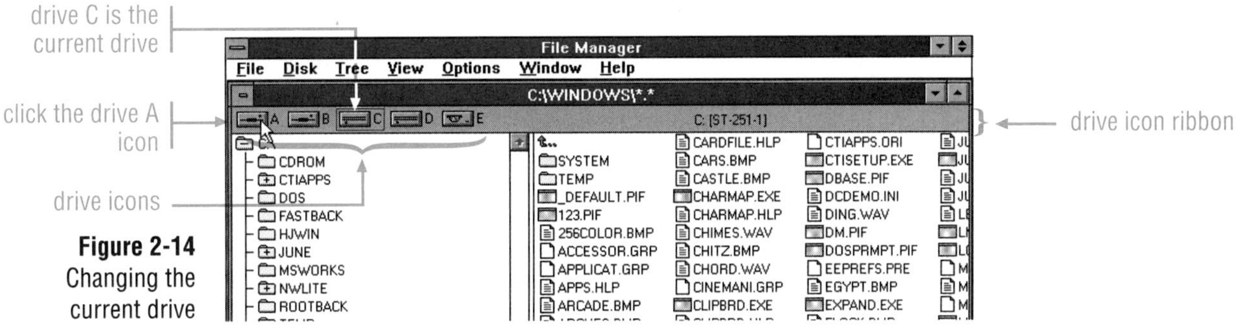

Figure 2-14
Changing the current drive

Your computer is connected to a number of storage drives or devices, but it can work with only one drive at a time. This drive is referred to as the **current drive** or **default drive**. You must change the current drive whenever you want to use files or programs that are stored on a different drive. The drive icon for the current drive is outlined with a rectangle. In Figure 2-14, the current drive is C.

To work with Ruth's files, you must be sure that the current drive is the one in which you have your Student Disk. *For this Tutorial we'll assume that your Student Disk is in drive A. If it is in drive B, substitute "drive B" for "drive A" in the rest of the steps for this Tutorial.*

Follow the next set of steps to change the current drive, if your current drive is not the one containing your Student Disk.

To change the current drive to A:

❶ Be sure your Student Disk is in drive A.

❷ Click the **drive A icon**. Drive A becomes the current drive. See Figure 2-15 on the following page.

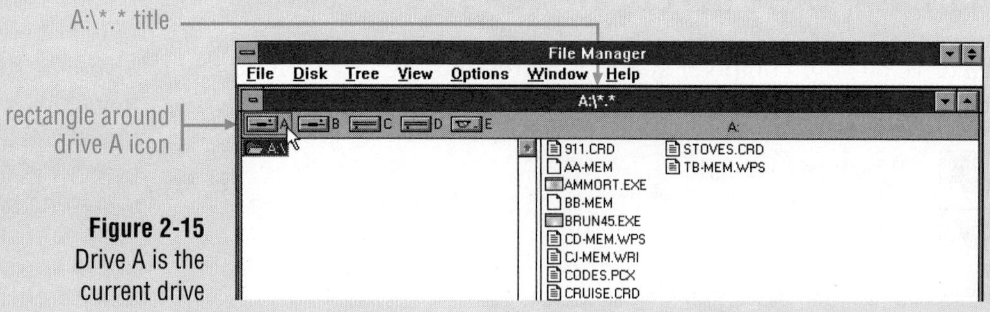

Figure 2-15
Drive A is the current drive

After you make drive A the current drive, your screen should look similar to Figure 2-15. Don't worry if everything is not exactly the same as the figure. Just be sure you see the A:*.* window title and that there is a rectangle around the drive A icon (or the drive B icon if drive B contains your floppy disk).

The File Manager Window

The components of the File Manager window are labeled in Figure 2-16. Your screen should contain similar components.

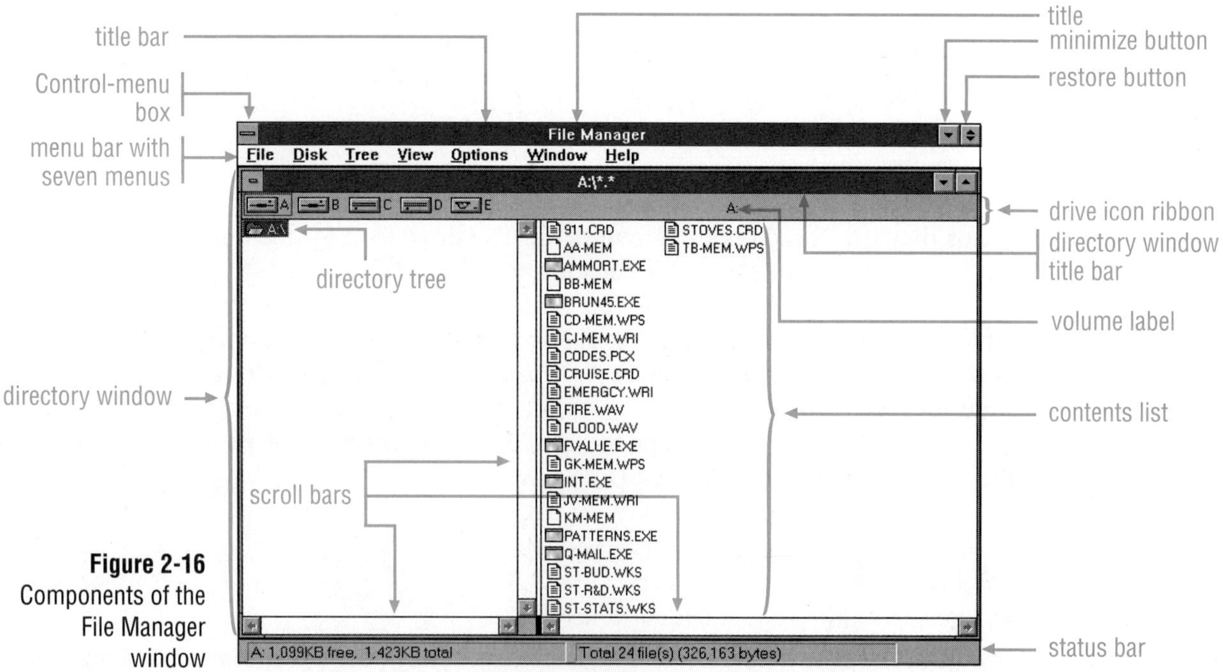

Figure 2-16
Components of the File Manager window

The top line of the File Manager window contains the Control-menu box, the title bar, the title, and the resizing buttons. The File Manager menu bar contains seven menus.

Inside the File Manager window is the **directory window**, which contains information about the current drive. The title bar for this window displays the current drive, in this case, A:*.*. This window has its own Control-menu box and resizing buttons.

Below the directory window title bar is the drive icon ribbon. On this line, the drive letter is followed by a volume label, if there is one. A **volume label** is a name you can assign to your disk during the format process to help you identify the contents of the disk. We did not assign a volume label, so the area after the A: is blank. Why is there a colon after the drive letter? Even though the colon is not displayed on the drive icons, when you type in a drive letter, you must always type a colon after it. The colon is a requirement of the DOS operating system that Windows uses behind the scenes to perform its file management tasks.

At the bottom of the screen, a status bar displays information about disk space. Remember that a byte is one character of data.

Notice that the directory window is split. The left half of the directory window displays the **directory tree**, which illustrates the organization of files on the current drive. The right half of the directory window displays the **contents list**, which lists the files on the current drive. Scroll bars on these windows let you view material that doesn't fit in the current window.

The Directory Tree

A list of files is called a **directory**. Because long lists of files are awkward to work with, directories can be subdivided into smaller lists called **subdirectories**. The organization of these directories and subdirectories is depicted in the directory tree.

Suppose you were using your computer for a small retail business. What information might you have on your disk, and how would it be organized? Figure 2-17 shows the directory tree for a hard disk (drive C) of a typical small business computer system.

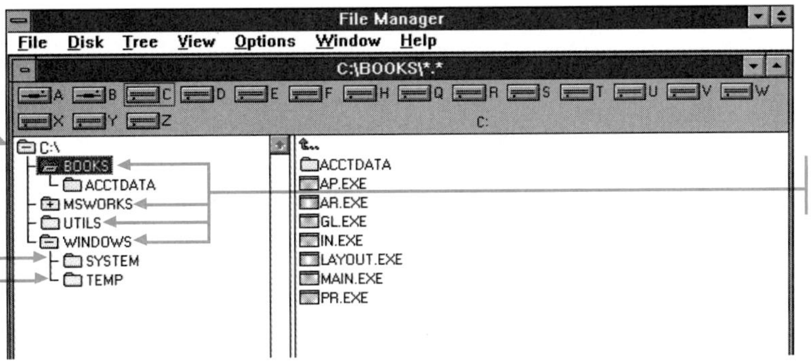

Figure 2-17
A directory tree

At the top of the directory tree is the **root directory**, called C:\ . The root directory is created when you format a disk and is indicated by a backslash after the drive letter and colon. Arranged under the root directory are the subdirectories BOOKS, MSWORKS, UTILS, and WINDOWS.

Directories other than the root directory can have subdirectories. In Figure 2-17 you can see that the BOOKS directory has a subdirectory called ACCTDATA. The WINDOWS directory contains two subdirectories, SYSTEM and TEMP. MSWORKS also has some subdirectories, but they are not listed. You'll find out how to expand the directory tree to display subdirectories later in the this tutorial.

Windows uses directory names to construct a path through the directory tree. For example, the path to ACCTDATA would be C:\BOOKS\ACCTDATA. To trace this path on Figure 2-17, begin at the root directory C:\, follow the line leading to the BOOKS directory, then follow the line leading to the ACCTDATA directory.

Each directory in the directory tree has a **file folder icon**, which can be either open or closed. An open file folder icon indicates the **active** or **current directory**. In Figure 2-17 the current directory is BOOKS. Only one directory can be current on a disk at a time.

Now look at the directory tree on your screen. The root directory of your Student Disk is called A:\. The file folder icon for this directory is open, indicating that this is the current directory. Are there any subdirectories on your disk?

The answer is no. A:\ has no subdirectories because its file folder icon does not contain a plus sign or a minus sign. A plus sign on a folder indicates that the directory can be expanded to show its subdirectories. A minus sign indicates that the subdirectories are currently being displayed. A file folder icon without a plus or a minus sign has no subdirectories.

Organizing Your Files

Ruth's disk, like your Student Disk, contains only one directory, and all her files are in that directory. As is typical of a poorly organized disk, files from different projects and programs are jumbled together. As Ruth's disk accumulates more files, she will have an increasingly difficult time finding the files she wants to use.

Ruth needs to organize her disk. First, she needs to make some new directories so she has a good basic structure for her files.

Creating Directories

When you create a directory, you indicate its location on the directory tree and specify the new directory name. The directory you create becomes a subdirectory of the current directory, which is designated by an open file folder. Directory names can be up to eight characters long.

Your Student Disk contains a collection of memos and spreadsheets that Ruth has created for a project code named "Stealth." Right now, all of these files are in the root directory. Ruth decides that to improve the organization of her disk, she should place her memos in one directory and the Stealth spreadsheets in another directory. To do this, she needs to make two new directories, MEMOS and STEALTH.

To make a new directory called MEMOS:

❶ Click the **file folder icon** representing the root directory of drive A. Figure 2-18 shows you where to click. This highlights the root directory A:\, making it the current directory.

click the A:\ file folder

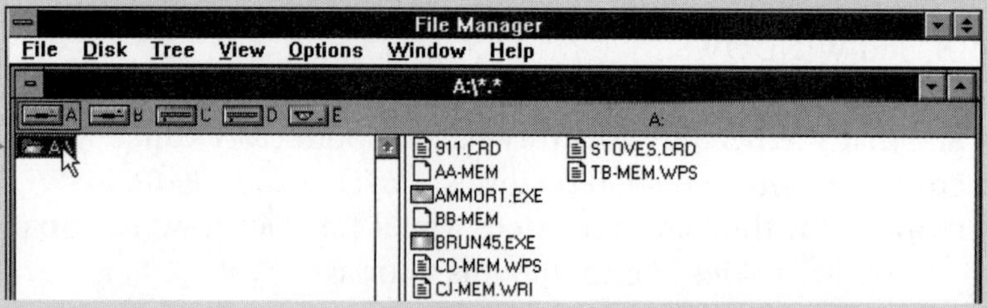

Figure 2-18
Creating a new directory

❷ Click **File**, then click **Create Directory...**. The Create Directory dialog box indicates that the current directory is A:\ and displays a text box for the name of the new directory.

❸ In the text box, type **MEMOS**, then click the **OK button**. It doesn't matter whether you type the directory name in uppercase or lowercase letters.

As a result, your screen should look like Figure 2-19. A new directory folder labeled MEMOS is now a subdirectory of A:\. The A:\ file folder now displays a minus sign to indicate that it has a subdirectory and that the subdirectory is displayed.

A:\ file folder displays minus sign

MEMOS subdirectory

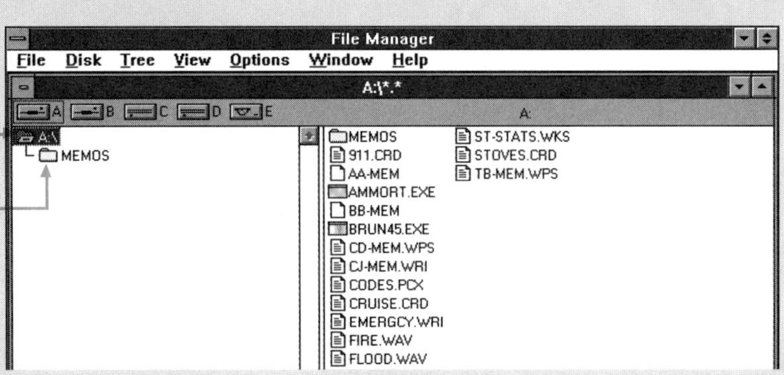

Figure 2-19 The new subdirectory

TROUBLE? If you do not see the minus sign on the A:\ file folder, click Tree, then click Indicate Expandable branches.

Next Ruth will make a directory for the spreadsheets. She wants her directory tree to look like the one in Figure 2-20a, not the one in Figure 2-20b.

Figure 2-20a SHEETS is a subdirectory of A:\

Figure 2-20b SHEETS is a subdirectory of MEMOS

The spreadsheet directory should be a subdirectory of the root, *not* of MEMOS.

To make a directory for spreadsheets:

1. Click the **directory folder icon for A:**.
2. Click **File**, then click **Create Directory...**.
3. In the text box type **SHEETS**, then click the **OK button**.
4. Make sure that your newly updated directory tree resembles the one in Figure 2-20a. There should be two directories under A:\ — MEMOS and SHEETS.

TROUBLE? If your directory tree is structured like the one in Figure 2-20b, use your mouse to drag the SHEETS directory icon to the A:\ file folder icon.

Now Ruth's disk has a structure she can use to organize her files. It contains three directories: the root A:\, MEMOS, and SHEETS. Each directory can contain a list of files. Ruth is happy with this new structure, but she is not sure what the directories contain. She decides to look in one of the new directories to see what's there.

Changing Directories

When you change directories, you open a different directory folder. If the directory contains files, they will be displayed in the contents list.

First, Ruth wants to look in the MEMOS directory.

To change to the MEMOS directory:

❶ Click the **MEMOS directory file folder icon**.

Notice that the A:\ file folder icon is closed and the MEMOS file folder icon is open, indicating that the MEMOS directory is now current.

Look at the status line at the bottom of your screen. The left side of the status line shows you how much space is left on your disk. The right side of the status line tells you that no files are in the current directory, that is, in the MEMOS directory. This makes sense. You just created the directory, and haven't put anything in it.

❷ Click the **A:\ file folder icon** to change back to the root directory.

Expanding and Collapsing Directories

Notice on your screen that the A:\ file folder icon has a minus sign on it. As you know, the minus sign indicates that A:\ has one or more subdirectories and that those subdirectories are displayed. To look at a simplified directory tree, you would **collapse** the A:\ directory. You would **expand** a directory to redisplay its subdirectories. Ruth wants to practice expanding and collapsing directories.

To expand and then collapse a directory:

❶ Double-click the **A:\ file folder icon** to collapse the directory. As a result the MEMOS and SHEETS branches of the directory tree are removed and a plus sign appears on the A:\ file folder icon.

❷ Double-click the **A:\ file folder icon** again. This time the directory expands, displaying the MEMOS and SHEETS branches. Notice the minus sign on the A:\ file folder icon.

The Contents List

The **contents list** on the right side of the desktop contains the list of files and subdirectories for the current directory. On your screen the directory tree shows that A:\ is the current directory. The status bar shows that this directory contains 26 files and subdirectories. These files are listed in the contents list. Ruth recalls that she had to follow a set of rules when she created the names for these files. Let's find out more about these rules, since you will soon need to create names for your own files.

Filenames and Extensions

A **filename** is a unique set of letters and numbers that identifies a program, document file, directory, or miscellaneous data file. A filename may be followed by an **extension**, which is separated from the filename by a period.

The rules for creating valid filenames are as follows:

- The filename can contain a maximum of eight characters.
- The extension cannot contain more than three characters.
- Use a period only between the filename and the extension.
- Neither the filename nor extension can include any spaces.
- Do not use the following characters: / [ ] ; = " \ : | ,
- Do not use the following names: AUX, COM1, COM2, COM3, COM4, CON, LPT1, LPT2, LPT3, PRN, or NUL.

Ruth used the letters ST at the beginning of her spreadsheet filenames so she could remember that these files contain information on project Stealth. Ruth used the rest of each filename to describe more about the file contents. For example, ST-BUD is the budget for project Stealth, ST-R&D is the research and development cost worksheet for the project, and ST-STATS contains the descriptive statistics for the project. Ruth's memos, on the other hand, begin with the initials of the person who received the memo. She used MEM as part of the filename for all her memos. For example, the file CJMEM.WRI contains a memo to Charles Jackson.

The file extension usually indicates the category of information a file contains. We can divide files into two broad categories, program files and data files. **Program files** contain the programming code for applications and systems software. For example, the computer program that makes your computer run the WordPerfect word processor would be classified as a program file. Program files are sometimes referred to as **executable files** because the computer executes, or performs, the instructions contained in the files. A common filename extension for this type of file is .EXE. Other extensions for program files include .BAT, .SYS, .PIF, and .COM. In the contents list, program files are shown with a **program file icon**, like the one you see next to the file PATTERNS.EXE on your screen and in Figure 2-21.

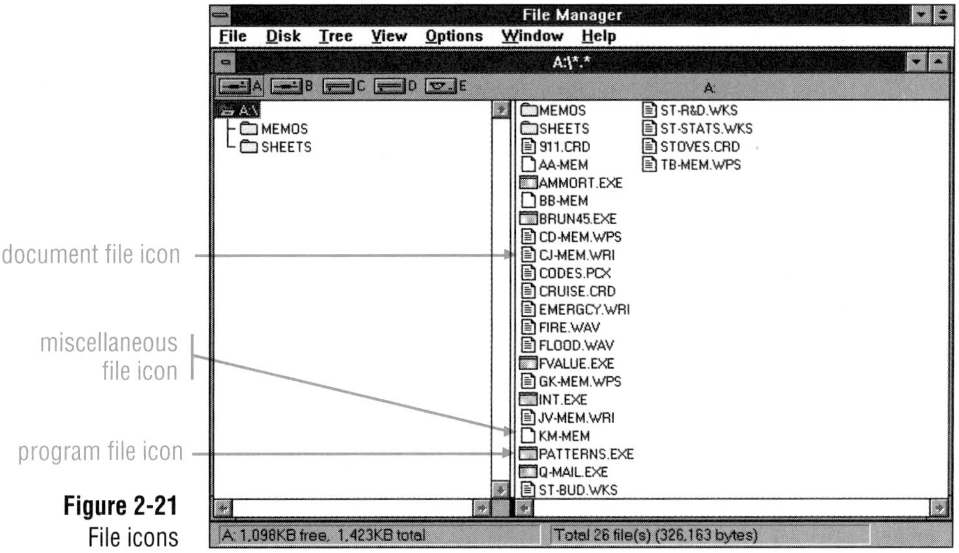

Figure 2-21
File icons

The second file category is data files. **Data files** contain the information with which you work: the memos, spreadsheets, reports, and graphs you create using applications such as word processors and spreadsheets. The filename extension for a data file usually indicates which application was used to create the file. For example, the file CD-MEM.WPS was created using the Microsoft Works word processor, which automatically puts the extension .WPS on any file you create with it. The use of .WPS as the standard extension for Works word processing documents creates an association between the application and the documents you create with it. Later, when you want to make modifications to your documents, Works can find them easily by looking for the .WPS extension.

Data files you create using a Windows application installed on your computer are shown in the contents list with a **document file icon** like the one you see next to CD-MEM.WPS on your screen. Data files you create using a non-Windows application or a Windows application that is not installed on your computer are shown in the contents list with a **miscellaneous file icon** like the one you see next to AA-MEM on your screen. AA-MEM was created using a non-Windows word processor.

Now that you have an idea of the contents for each of Ruth's files, you will be able to help her move them into the appropriate directory.

Moving Files

You can move files from one disk to another. You can also move files from one directory to another. When you move a file, the computer copies the file to its new location, then erases it from the original location. The File Manager lets you move files by dragging them on the screen or by using the File Manager menus.

Now that Ruth has created the MEMOS and SHEETS directories, the next step in organizing her disk is to put files in these directories. She begins by moving one of her memo files from the root directory A:\ to the MEMOS subdirectory. She decides to move JV-MEM.WRI first.

To move the file JV-MEM.WRI from A:\ to the MEMOS subdirectory:

1. Position the pointer on the filename JV-MEM.WRI and click the mouse button to select it. On the left side of the status bar, the message "Selected 1 file(s) (1,408 bytes)" appears.
2. Press the mouse button and hold it down while you drag the file icon to the MEMOS file folder in the directory tree.
3. When the icon arrives at its target location, a box appears around the MEMOS file icon. Release the mouse button. Figure 2-22 on the following page illustrates this procedure.

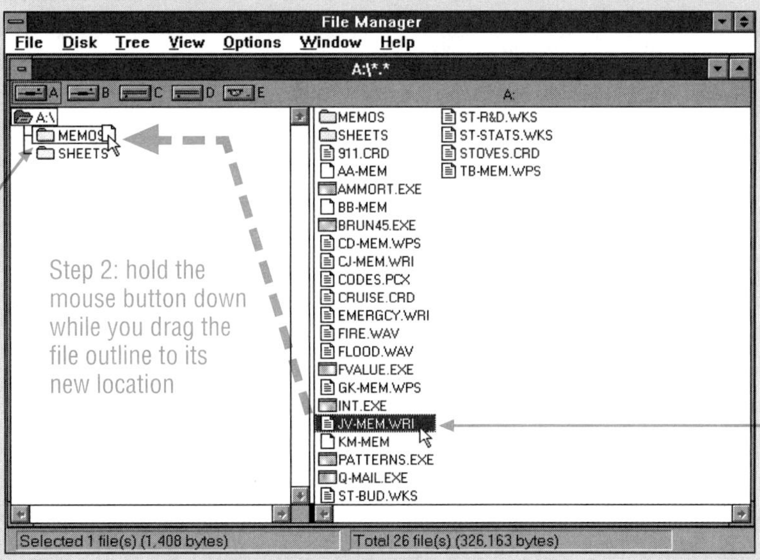

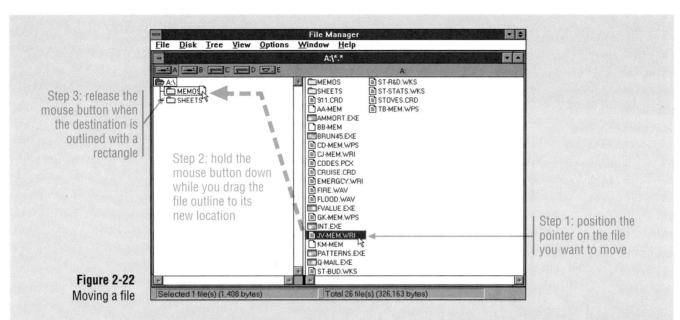

Figure 2-22
Moving a file

4. Click the **Yes button** in response to the message "Are you sure you want to move the selected files or directories to A:\MEMOS?" A Moving... dialog box may flash briefly on your screen before the file is moved. Look at the contents list on the right side of the screen. The file JV-MEM.WRI is no longer there.

Ruth wants to confirm that the file was moved.

5. Single click the **MEMOS file folder icon** in the directory tree on the left side of the screen. The file JV-MEM.WRI should be listed in the contents list on the right side of the screen.

   TROUBLE? If JV-MEM.WRI is not in the MEMOS subdirectory, you might have moved it inadvertently to the SHEETS directory. You can check this by clicking the SHEETS directory folder. If the file is in SHEETS, drag it to the MEMOS directory folder.

6. Click the **A:\file folder icon** to display the files in the root directory again.

Ruth sees that several memos are still in the root directory. She could move these memos one at a time to the MEMOS subdirectory, but she knows that it would be more efficient to move them as a group. To do this, she'll first select the files she wants to move. Then, she will drag them to the MEMOS directory.

To select a group of files:

1. The directory A:\ should be selected on your screen and the files in this directory should be displayed in the right directory window. If this is not the case, click the directory icon for A:\.
2. Click the filename **CD-MEM.WPS** to select it.
3. Hold down **[Ctrl]** while you click the next filename you want to add to the group, **CJMEM.WRI**. Now two files should be selected. Ruth wants to select two more files.
4. Hold down **[Ctrl]** while you click **GK-MEM.WPS**.
5. Hold down **[Ctrl]** while you click **TB-MEM.WPS**. Release **[Ctrl]**. When you have finished selecting the files, your screen should look similar to Figure 2-23 on the following page. Notice the status bar message, "Selected 4 file(s) (4,590 bytes)."

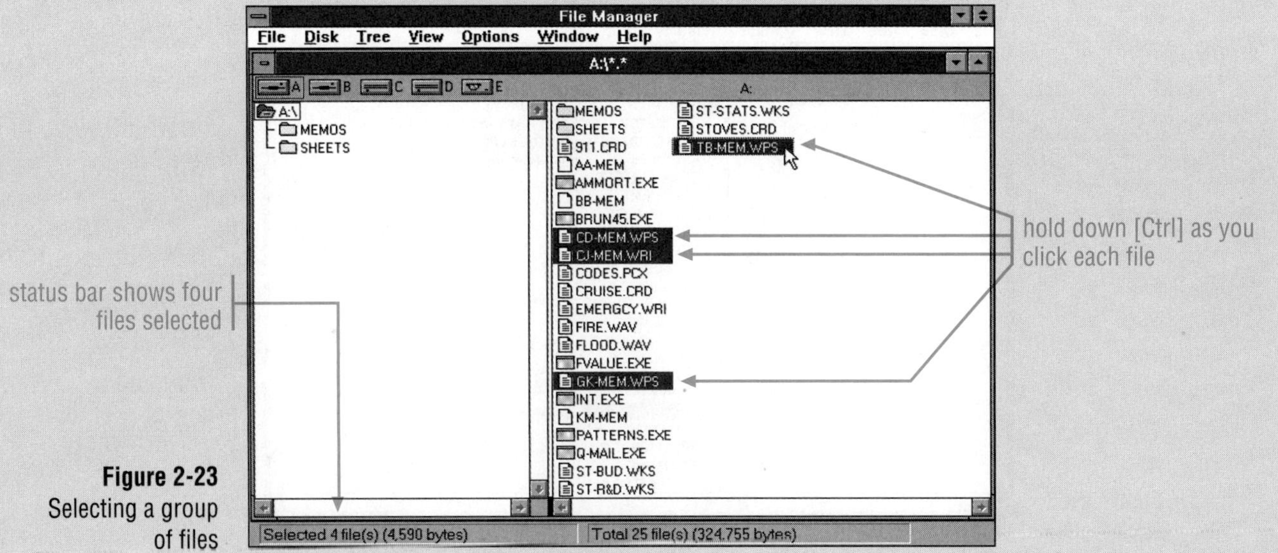

Figure 2-23
Selecting a group of files

TROUBLE? If you click a file that you do not want to add to the group, hold down [Ctrl] and click that filename again. This will deselect that one file and remove the highlighting.

Now that Ruth has selected the files she wants to move, she can drag them to their new location.

To move a group of files:

❶ Position the pointer on any one of the highlighted filenames.

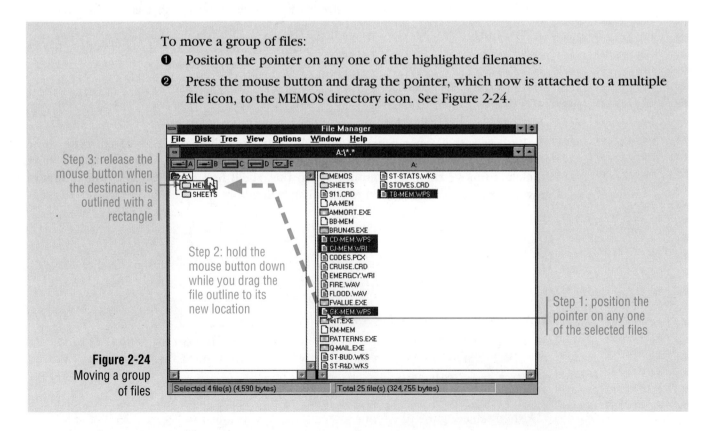

❷ Press the mouse button and drag the pointer, which now is attached to a multiple file icon, to the MEMOS directory icon. See Figure 2-24.

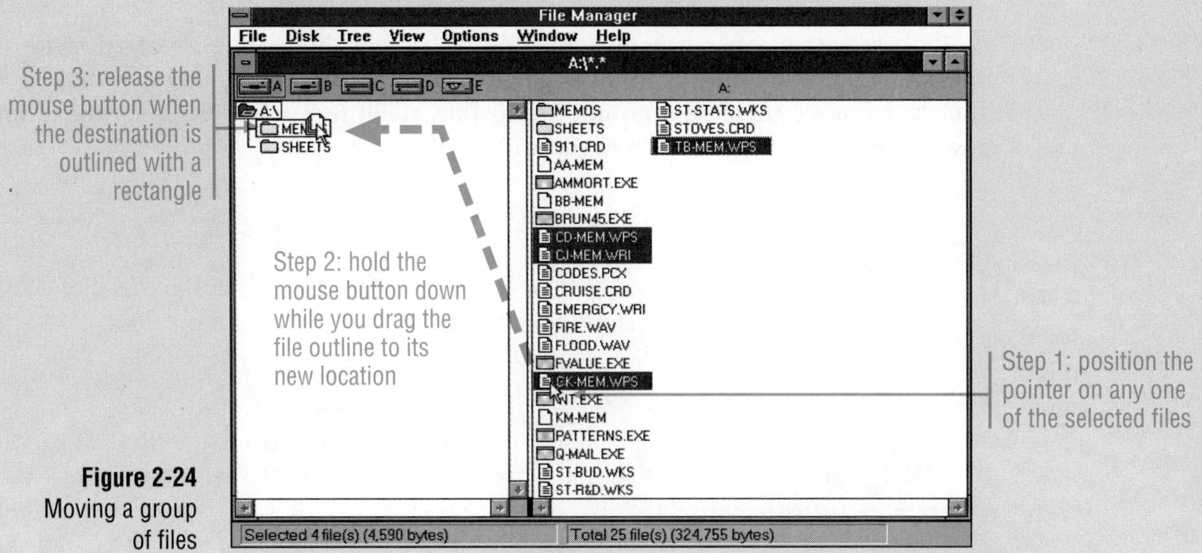

Figure 2-24
Moving a group of files

❸ When the you move the file icon onto the MEMOS directory, a box will outline the directory icon. Release the mouse button. The Confirm Mouse Operation dialog box appears.

❹ Click the **Yes button** to confirm that you want to move the files. After a brief period of activity on your disk drive, the contents list for the A:\ directory is updated and should no longer include the files you moved.

❺ Click the **MEMOS directory icon** to verify that the group of files arrived in the MEMOS directory.

❻ Click the **A:\ directory icon** to once again display the contents of the root directory.

Renaming Files

You may find it useful to change the name of a file to make it more descriptive of the file contents. Remember that Windows uses file extensions to associate document files with applications and to identify executable programs, so when you rename a file you should not change the extension.

Ruth looks down the list of files and notices ST-BUD.WKS, which contains the 1994 budget for project Stealth. Ruth knows that next week she will begin work on the 1995 budget. She decides that while she is organizing her files, she will change the name of ST-BUD.WKS to ST-BUD94.WKS. When she creates the budget for 1995, she will call it ST-BUD95.WKS so it will be easy to distinguish between the two budget files.

To change the name of ST-BUD.WKS to ST-BUD94.WKS:

❶ Click the filename **ST-BUD.WKS**.

❷ Click **File**, then click **Rename**. See Figure 2-25. The Rename dialog box shows you the current directory and the name of the file you are going to rename. Verify that the dialog box on your screen indicates that the current directory is A:\ and that the file you are going to rename is ST-BUD.WKS.

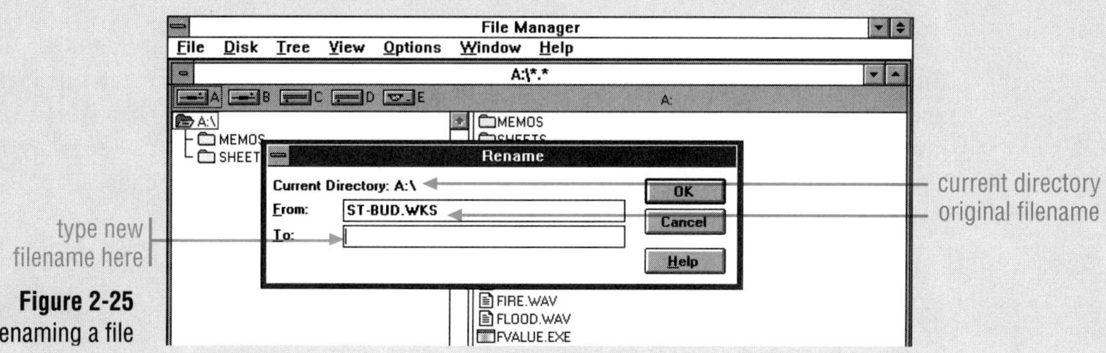

Figure 2-25
Renaming a file

TROUBLE? If the filename is not ST-BUD.WKS, click the Cancel button and go back to Step 1.

❸ In the To text box type **ST-BUD94.WKS** (using either uppercase or lowercase letters.

❹ Click the **OK button**.

❺ Check the file listing for ST-BUD94.WKS to verify that the rename procedure was successful.

Deleting Files

When you no longer need a file, it is good practice to delete it. Deleting a file frees up space on your disk and reduces the size of the directory listing you need to scroll through to find a file. A well-organized disk does not contain files you no longer need.

Ruth decides to delete the ST-STATS.WKS file. Although this file contains some statistics about the Stealth project, Ruth knows by looking at the file's date that those statistics are no longer current. She'll receive a new file from the Statistics department next week.

To delete the file ST-STATS.WKS:

1. Click the filename **ST-STATS.WKS**.
2. Click **File**, then click **Delete**. The Delete dialog box shows you that the file scheduled for deletion is in the A:\ directory and is called ST-STATS.WKS. See Figure 2-26.

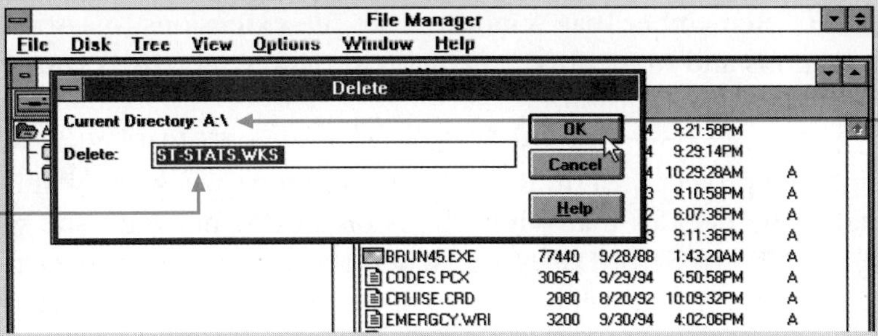

Figure 2-26
Deleting a file

TROUBLE? If the filename ST-STATS.WKS is not displayed in the Delete dialog box, click the Cancel button and go back to Step 1.

3. Click the **OK button**. The Confirm File Delete dialog box appears. This is your last chance to change your mind before the file is deleted.
4. Click the **Yes button** to delete the file. Look at the contents list to verify that the file ST-STATS.WKS has been deleted.

After using a floppy disk in drive A to experiment with the File Manager, Ruth feels more confident that she can use the File Manager to organize her hard disk. However, she feels slightly uncomfortable about something else. Ruth just learned that one of her co-workers lost several days worth of work when his computer had a hardware failure.

Ruth resolves to find out more about the problems that can cause data loss so she can take appropriate steps to protect the data files on her computer.

Data Backup

Ruth's initial research on data loss reveals that there is no totally fail-safe method to protect data from hardware failures, human error, and natural disasters. She does discover, however, some ways to reduce the risk of losing data. Every article Ruth reads emphasizes the importance of regular backups.

A **backup** is a copy of one or more files, made in case the original files are destroyed or become unusable. Ruth learns that Windows provides a Copy command and a Copy Disk command that she can use for data backup. Ruth decides to find out how these commands work, so she refers to the *Microsoft Windows User's Guide* which came with the Microsoft Windows 3.1 software. She quickly discovers that the Copy and Copy Disk commands are in the Windows File Manager.

To prepare the File Manager for data backup:

1. If you are returning from a break, launch Windows if it is not currently running. Be sure you see the Program Manager window.
2. Relaunch the File Manager if necessary. Make sure your Student Disk is in drive A.

   TROUBLE? If you want to use drive B instead of drive A, substitute "B" for "A" in any steps when drive A is specified.

3. Click the File Manager **maximize button** if the File Manager is not already maximized.
4. If necessary, click the **drive A icon** on the drive ribbon to make drive A the default drive.
5. Click **View** and be sure that a check mark appears next to All File Details.
6. Click **Window**, then click **Tile**. As a result, your desktop should look similar to Figure 2-27. Don't worry if your list of directories and files is different from the one shown in the figures.

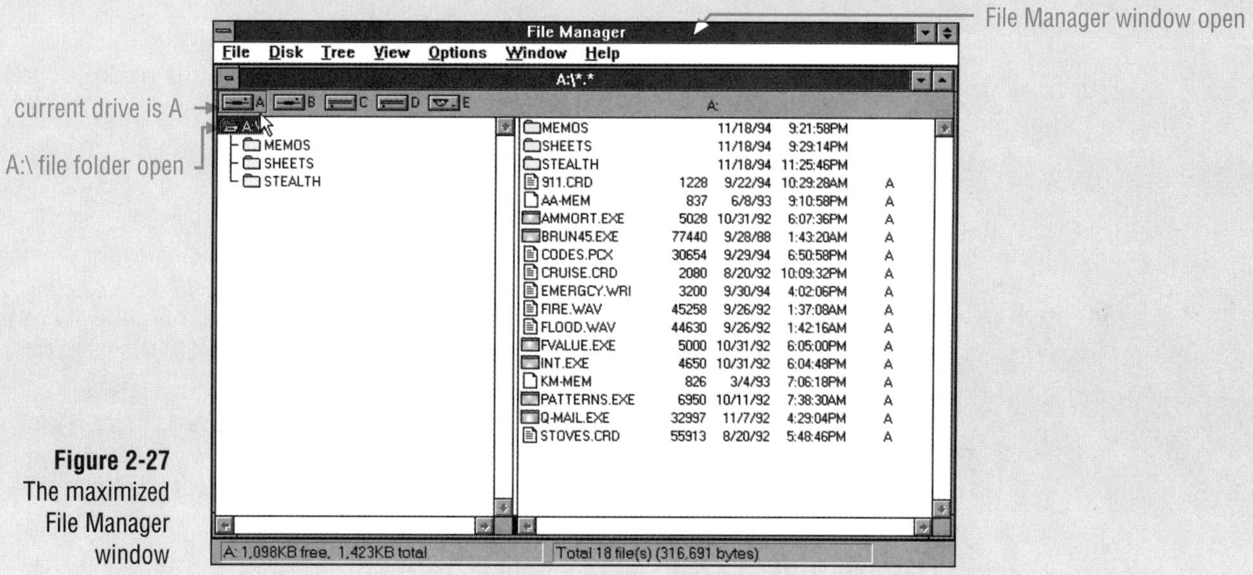

Figure 2-27
The maximized File Manager window

Now that Ruth has the File Manager window set-up, she decides to practice with the Copy command first.

The Copy Command

The Copy command duplicates a file in a new location. When the procedure has been completed, you have two files, your original and the copy. The additional copy of the file is useful for backup in case your original file develops a problem and becomes unusable.

The Copy command is different from the Move command, which you used earlier. The Move command deletes the file from its old location after moving it. When the move is completed, you have only one file.

If you understand the terminology associated with copying files, you will be able to achieve the results you want. The original location of a file is referred to as the **source**. The new location of the file is referred to as the **destination** or **target**.

You can copy one file or you can copy a group of files. In this Tutorial you will practice moving one file at a time. You can also copy files from one directory to another or from one disk to another. The disks you copy to and from do not need to be the same size. For backup purposes you would typically copy files from a hard disk to a disk.

Copying Files Using a Single Disk Drive

Ruth has been working on a spreadsheet called ST-BUD94.WKS for an entire week, and the data on this spreadsheet are critical for a presentation she is making tomorrow. The file is currently on a disk in drive A. Ruth will sleep much better tonight if she has an extra copy of this file. But Ruth has only one floppy disk drive. To make a copy of a file from one floppy disk to another, she must use her hard disk as a temporary storage location.

First, she will copy the file ST-BUD94.WKS to her hard disk. Then she will move the file to another floppy disk. Let's see how this procedure works.

To copy the file ST-BUD94.WKS from the source disk to the hard disk:

❶ Make sure your Student Disk is in drive A. Be sure you also have the backup disk you formatted earlier in the tutorial.

❷ Find the file ST-BUD94.WKS. It is in the root directory .

❸ Click the filename **ST-BUD94.WKS**.

❹ Click **File**, then click **Copy**.

TROUBLE? If you see a message that indicates you cannot copy a file to drive C, click the OK button. Your drive C has been write-protected, and you will not be able to copy ST-BUD94.WKS. Read through the copying procedure and resume doing the steps in the section entitled "Making a Disk Backup."

❺ Look at the ribbon of drive icons at the top of your screen. If you have an icon for drive C, type **C:** in the text box of the Copy dialog box. If you do not have an icon for drive C, ask your technical support person which drive you can use for a temporary destination in the file copy process, then type the drive letter.

❻ Confirm that the Copy dialog box settings are similar to those in Figure 2-28, then click the **OK button**. The file is copied to the root directory of drive C (or to the directory your technical support person told you to use).

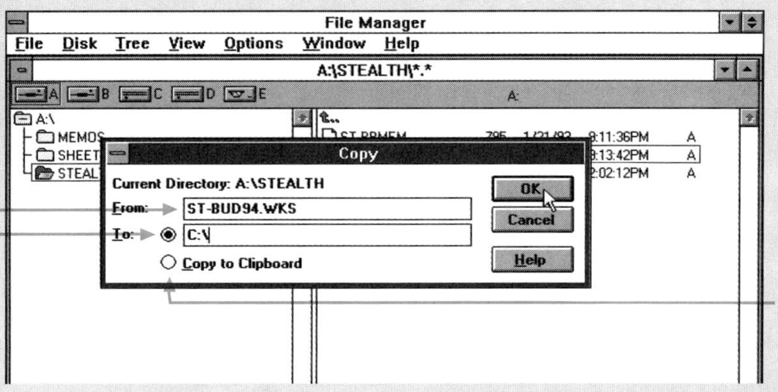

Figure 2-28 Copying ST-BUD94.WKS to drive C

TROUBLE? If a dialog box appears and prompts you to verify that you want to replace the existing file, click the Yes button. This message appeared because another student left the ST-BUD94.WKS file on the hard disk.

After the file has been copied to the hard disk, Ruth needs to switch disks. She will take her original disk out of drive A and replace it with the disk that will receive the copy of the ST-BUD94.WKS file. After Ruth switches disks, she must tell the File Manager to **refresh** the directory tree and the contents list so they show the files and directories for the disk that is now in the drive.

To switch disks and refresh the contents list:

1. Remove your Student Disk from drive A.
2. Put your Backup Disk in drive A.
3. Click the **drive A icon** on the drive ribbon to refresh the contents list. The directory tree will contain only the A:\ folder, because your backup disk does not have the directories you created for your original Student Disk.

Now let's look for the copy of ST-BUD94.WKS that is on drive C.

To locate the new copy of ST-BUD94.WKS:

1. Click the **drive C icon** (or the drive your technical support person told you to use).
2. Click the **C:\ file folder icon** (or the directory your technical support person told you to use).
3. If necessary, use the scroll bar on the side of the content list to find the file ST-BUD94.WKS in the contents list.

Now you need to move the file from the hard disk to the backup disk in drive A. You must use Move instead of Copy so you don't leave the file on your hard disk.

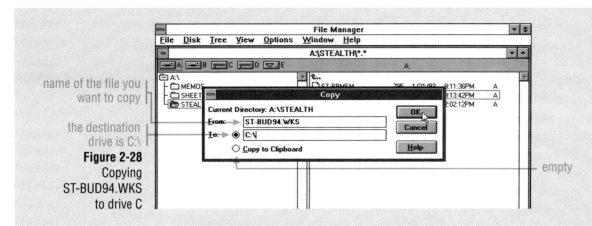

To move the new file copy to drive A:

1. Click the filename **ST-BUD94.WKS**.
2. Click **File**, then click **Move**. (Don't use Copy this time.) A Move dialog box appears.
3. Type **A:** in the text box.
4. Click the **OK button**. As a result, ST-BUD94.WKS is moved to the disk in drive A.
5. Click the **drive A icon** on the drive ribbon to view the contents list for the Backup disk. Verify that the file ST-BUD94.WKS is listed.
6. Remove the Backup disk from drive A.
7. Insert the **Student Disk** in drive A and click the **drive A icon** in the drive ribbon to refresh the contents listing.

Now you and Ruth have completed the entire procedure for copying a file from one disk to another on a single floppy disk system. In her research, Ruth also has discovered a Windows command for copying an entire disk. She wants to practice this command next.

Making a Disk Backup

The Windows Copy Disk command makes an exact duplicate of an entire disk. All the files and all the blank sectors of the disk are copied. If you have files on your destination disk, the Copy Disk command will erase them as it makes the copy so that the destination disk will be an exact duplicate of the original disk.

When you use the Copy Disk command, both disks must have the same storage capacity. For example, if your original disk is a 3.5-inch high-density disk, your destination disk also must be 3.5-inch high-density disk. For this reason, you cannot use the Copy Disk command to copy an entire hard disk to a floppy disk. If your computer does not have two disk drives that are the same size and capacity, the Copy Disk command will work with only one disk drive. When you back up the contents of one disk to another disk using only one disk drive, files are copied from the source disk into the random access memory (RAM) of the computer.

RAM is a temporary storage area on your computer's mother board which usually holds data and instructions for the operating system, application programs, and documents you are using. After the files are copied into RAM, you remove the source disk and replace it with the destination disk. The files in RAM are then copied onto the destination disk. If you don't have enough RAM available to hold the entire contents of the disk, only a portion of the source disk contents are copied during the first stage of the process, and the computer must repeat the process for the remaining contents of the disk.

Ruth wants to practice using the Copy Disk command to make a backup of a disk. She is going to make the copy using only one disk drive because she can use this procedure on both her computer at home, which has one disk drive, and her computer at work, which has two different-sized disk drives.

While Ruth makes a copy of her disk, let's make a backup of your Student Disk. After you learn the procedure, you'll be responsible for making regular backups of the work you do for this course. You should back up your disks at least once a week. If you are working on a particularly critical project, such as a term paper or a thesis, you might want to make backups more often.

To make a backup copy of your Student disk:

1. Be sure your Student Disk is in drive A and that you have the disk you labeled Backup handy. If you want to be very safe, write-protect your source disk before continuing with this procedure. Remember, to write-protect a 5.25-inch disk, you place a tab over the write-protect notch. On a 3.5-inch disk you open the write-protect hole.
2. Click **Disk**, then click **Copy Disk...**. Confirm that the Copy Disk dialog box on your screen looks like the one in Figure 2-29. The dialog box should indicate that "Source In" is A: and "Destination In" is A:. If this is not the case, click the appropriate down-arrow button and select A: from the list. When the dialog box display is correct, click the **OK button**.

both the source and the destination should be A:

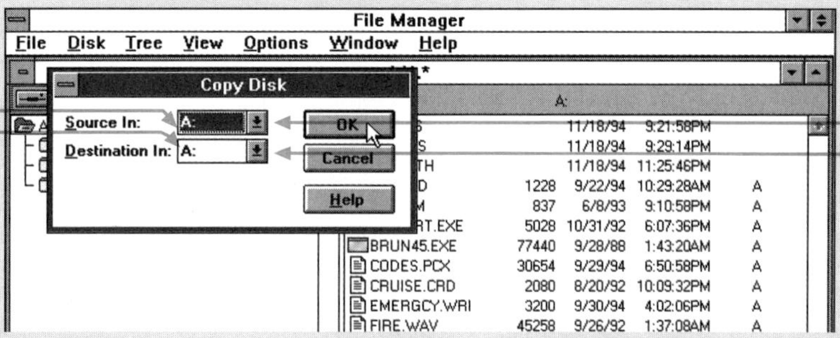

use these buttons to change settings

Figure 2-29 Copy Disk settings

3. The Confirm Copy Disk dialog box reminds you that this operation will erase all data from the destination disk. It asks, "Are you sure you want to continue?"
4. Click the **Yes button**. The next dialog box instructs you to "Insert source disk." Your source disk is the Student Disk and it is already in drive A.
5. Click the **OK button**.

After a flurry of activity, the computer begins to copy the data from drive A into RAM. The Copying Disk dialog box keeps you posted on its progress.

6. Eventually another message appears, telling you to "Insert destination disk." Take your Student Disk out of drive A and replace it with the disk you labeled Backup.
7. Click the **OK button**. The computer copies the files from RAM to the destination disk.

Depending on how much internal memory your computer has, you might be prompted to switch disks twice more. Carefully follow the dialog box prompts, remembering that the *source* disk is your Student Disk and the *destination* disk is your Backup disk.

8. When the Copy Disk operation is complete, the Copying Disk dialog box closes. If you write-protected your Student Disk in Step 1, you should unprotect it now; otherwise you won't be able to save data to the disk later.

As a result of the Copy Disk command, your Backup disk should be an exact duplicate of your Student Disk.

Ruth has completed her exploration of file management. Now, Ruth decides to finish for the day. If you are not going to proceed directly to the Tutorial Assignments, you should exit the File Manager.

To exit the File Manager:

1. Click the File Manager **Control-menu box**.
2. Click **Close**.
3. If you want to exit Windows, click the **Program Manager Control-menu box**, then click **Close**, and finally click the **OK button**.

■ ■ ■

Questions

1. Which one of the following is not a characteristic of a file?
   a. It has a name.
   b. It is a collection of data.
   c. It is the smallest unit of data.
   d. It is stored on a device such as a floppy disk or a hard disk.
2. What process arranges the magnetic particles on a disk in preparation for data storage?
3. In which one of the following situations would formatting your disk be the least desirable procedure?
   a. You have purchased a new disk.
   b. You have difficulty doing a spreadsheet assignment, and you want to start over again.
   c. You want to erase all the old files from a disk.
   d. You want to recycle an old disk that was used on a non-IBM-compatible computer.
4. If the label on your 3.5 inch diskette says HD, what is its capacity?
   a. 360K
   b. 720K
   c. 1.2MB
   d. 1.44MB
5. The disk drive that is indicated by a rectangle on the drive ribbon is called the ______________ drive or the ____________ drive.
6. Refer to the File Manager window in Figure 2-30 on the following page. What is the name of each numbered window component?

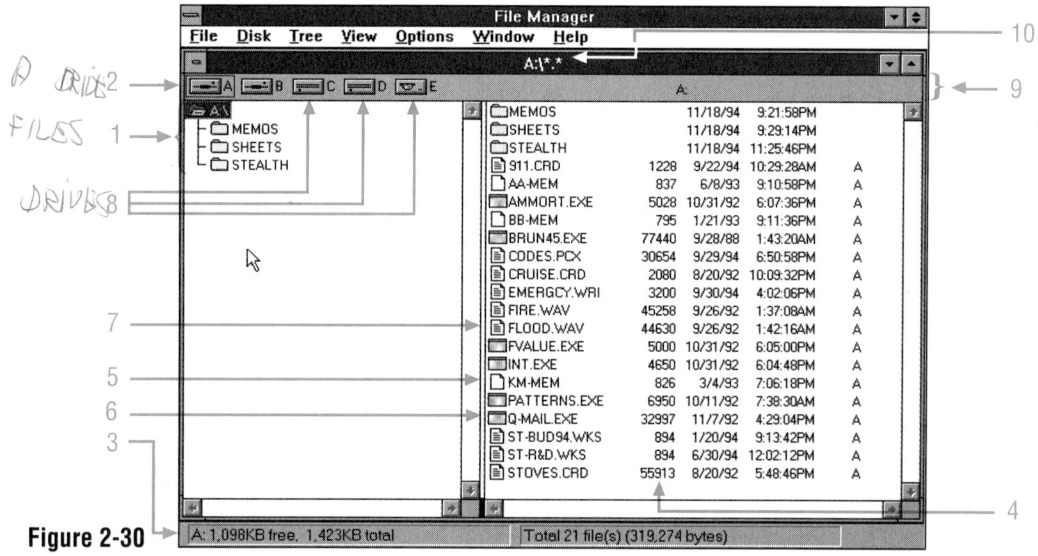

Figure 2-30

7. What is the directory that is automatically created when a disk is formatted?
8. What does a plus sign on a directory file folder icon indicate?
   a. The subdirectories are currently being displayed.
   b. The directory can be expanded.
   c. There are files in the directory.
   d. There are no subdirectories for this directory.
9. Indicate whether each of the following filenames is a valid or not valid Windows filename. If a filename is not valid, explain what is wrong.
   a. EOQ.WKS
   b. STATISTICS.WKS
   c. NUL.DOC
   d. VB-LET.DOC
   e. M
   f. M.M
   g. 92.BUD
   h. LET03/94
   i. CON.BMP
   d. Escape key

Tutorial Assignments

Launch Windows if necessary. Write your answers to Assignments 5, 6, 7, 8, 9, 11, 12, 13, and 14.

1. Move the two Microsoft Works spreadsheet files (.WKS extension) from the root directory to the SHEETS directory of your Student Disk.
2. You have a memo called BB-MEM that is about project Stealth. Now you need to change the filename to reflect the contents of the memo.
   a. Change the name to ST-BBMEM.
   b. Move ST-BBMEM into the MEMOS directory.
3. Create a directory called STEALTH under the root directory of your Student Disk. After you do this, your directory tree should look like Figure 2-30.
4. Now consolidate all the Stealth files.
   a. Move the file ST-BBMEM from the MEMOS directory to the STEALTH directory.

b. Move the files ST-BUD94.WKS and ST-R&D.WKS from the SHEETS directory to the STEALTH directory.

5. After doing Assignment 4, draw a diagram of your directory tree.
6. Make a list of the files that you now have in the MEMOS directory.
7. Make a list of the files that are in the SHEETS directory.
8. Make a list of the files that are in the STEALTH directory.
9. Describe what happens if you double-click the A:\ file folder icon.

E 10. Click to open the View menu and make sure the All File Details command has a check mark next to it.

E 11. Use the View menu to sort the files by date. What is the oldest file on your disk? (Be sure to look at all directories!)

E 12. Use the View menu to sort the files by type. Using this view, name the last file in your root directory contents list.

E 13. Use the View menu to sort the files by size. What is the name of the largest file on your Student Disk?

E 14. Change the current drive to C:, or, if you are on a network, to one of the network drives.

a. Draw a diagram of the directory tree for this disk.

b. List the filename of any files with .SYS, .COM, or .BAT extensions in the root directory of this disk.

c. Look at the file icons in the contents list of the root directory. How many of the files are program files? Document files? Miscellaneous data files?

d. Review the file organization tips that were in the article Ruth read. Write a short paragraph evaluating the organizational structure of your hard disk or network drive.

Windows Tutorials Index

M

O

P

R

S

T

U

V

W

TASK REFERENCE

BRIEF MICROSOFT WINDOWS 3.1

Italicized page numbers indicate the first discussion of each task.

TASK	MOUSE	MENU	KEYBOARD
GENERAL / PROGRAM MANAGER			
Change dimensions of a window *WIN 15*	Drag border or corner	Click , Size	Alt spacebar, S
Click *WIN 7*	Press mouse button, then release it		
Close a window *WIN 18*	Double-click	Click , Close	Alt spacebar, C or Alt F4
Double-click *WIN 8*	Click left mouse button twice		
Drag *WIN 9*	Hold left mouse button down while moving mouse		
Exit Windows *WIN 33*	Double-click Program Manager , click OK	Click Program Manager , Close, OK	Alt spacebar, C, Enter, or Alt F4, Enter
Help *WIN 30*		Click Help	F1 or Alt H
Launch Windows *WIN 4*			Type win and press Enter
Maximize a window *WIN 14*	Click	Click , Maximize	Alt spacebar, X
Minimize a window *WIN 14*	Click	Click , Minimize	Alt spacebar, N
Open a group window *WIN 10*	Double-click group icon	Click icon, click Restore	Ctrl F6 to group icon, Enter
Restore a window *WIN 14*	Click	Click , Restore	Alt spacebar, R
Switch applications *WIN 16*		Click , Switch To...	Alt Tab or Ctrl Esc
Switch documents *WIN 28*	Click the document	Click Window, click name of document	Alt W, press number of document

TASK REFERENCE

BRIEF MICROSOFT WINDOWS 3.1

Italicized page numbers indicate the first discussion of each task.

TASK	MOUSE	MENU	KEYBOARD
FILE MANAGER			
Change current/default drive *WIN 45*	Click on drive icon ribbon	Click Disk, Select Drive...	[Alt] [D], [S] or [Ctrl] [drive letter]
Change current/default directory *WIN 50*	Click		Press arrow key to directory
Collapse a directory *WIN 50*	Double-click	Click Tree, Collapse Branch	[-]
Copy a file *WIN 58*	Hold [Ctrl] down as you drag the file	Click the filename, click File, Copy	[F8]
Create a directory *WIN 48*		Click File, Create Directory	[Alt] [F], [E]
Delete a file *WIN 56*		Click the filename, click File, Delete	Click the filename, press [Del], [Enter]
Diskette copy/backup *WIN 61*		Click Disk, Copy Disk...	[Alt] [D], [C]
Exit File Manager *WIN 62*	Double-click File Manager	Click , Close	[Alt] [F4]
Expand a directory *WIN 50*	Double-click	Click Tree, Expand Branch	[*]
Format a diskette *WIN 41*		Click Disk, Format Disk...	[Alt] [D], [F]
Launch File Manager *WIN 38*	Double-click File Manager	Press arrow key to File Manager then click File, Open	Press arrow key to File Manager then press [Enter]
Make Student Diskette *WIN 43*	Double-click Make Win 3.1 Student Diskette	Press arrow key to Make Win 3.1 Student Diskette then click File, Open	Press arrow key to Make Win 3.1 Student Diskette then press [Enter]
Move a file *WIN 52*	Drag file to new directory	Click File, Move	[F7]
Rename a file *WIN 55*		Click File, Rename	[Alt] [F], [N]
Select multiple files *WIN 53*	Hold [Ctrl] down and click filenames	Click File, Select Files...	[Alt] [F], [S]

TASK REFERENCE

BRIEF MICROSOFT WINDOWS 3.1

Italicized page numbers indicate the first discussion of each task.

TASK	MOUSE	MENU	KEYBOARD
APPLICATIONS			
Exit application *WIN 33*	Double-click application	Click , Close	Alt F4
Launch application *WIN 10*	Double-click application icon	Press arrow key to icon, click File, Open	Press arrow key to icon, Enter

Introductory Microsoft Access® 2.0 for Windows™ Tutorials

Read This Before You Begin

To the Student

To use this book, you must have a Student Disk. Your instructor will either provide you with one or ask you to make your own by following the instructions in the section "Your Student Disk" in Tutorial 1. See your instructor or technical support person for further information. If you are going to work through this book using your own computer, you need a computer system running Microsoft Windows 3.1 and Microsoft Access 2.0, and a Student Disk. *You will not be able to complete the tutorials and exercises in this book using your own computer until you have a Student Disk.*

To the Instructor

Making the Student Disk To complete the tutorials in this book, your students must have a copy of the Student Disk. To relieve you of having to make multiple Student Disks from a single master copy, we provide you with the CTI WinApps Setup Disk, which contains an automatic Student Disk generating program. Once you install the Setup Disk on a network or standalone workstation, students can easily make their own Student Disks by double-clicking the "Make Access 2.0 Student Disk" icon in the CTI WinApps icon group. Double-clicking this icon transfers all the data files students will need to complete the tutorials, Tutorial Assignments, and Case Problems to a high-density disk in drive A or B. If some of your students will use their own computers to complete the tutorials and exercises in this book, they must first get the Student Disk. The section called "Your Student Disk" in Tutorial 1 provides complete instructions on how to make the Student Disk.

Installing the CTI WinApps Setup Disk To install the CTI WinApps icon group from the Setup Disk, follow the instructions inside the disk envelope that was bundled with your book. By adopting this book, you are granted a license to install this software on any computer or computer network used by you or your students.

README File A README.TXT file located on the Setup Disk provides additional technical notes, troubleshooting advice, and tips for using the CTI WinApps software in your school's computer lab. You can view the README.TXT file using any word processor you choose.

System Requirements

The minimum software and hardware requirements for your computer system are as follows:

- Microsoft Windows Version 3.1 or later on a local hard drive or a network drive.
- A 386 or higher processor with a minimum of 6 MB RAM (8 MB RAM or more is strongly recommended).
- A mouse supported by Windows 3.1.
- A printer supported by Windows 3.1.
- A VGA 640 × 480 16-color display is recommended; an 800 × 600 or 1024 × 768 SVGA, VGA monochrome, or EGA display is acceptable.
- 19 MB free hard disk space.
- Student workstations with at least 1 high-density 3.5-inch disk drive.
- If you wish to install the CTI WinApps Setup Disk on a network drive, your network must support Microsoft Windows.

Introduction to Database Concepts and Access

Planning a Special Magazine Issue

OBJECTIVES

In this tutorial you will:

- Learn terms used with databases
- Launch and exit Access
- Identify the components of Access windows
- Open and close an Access database
- Open and close Access objects
- View an Access table using a datasheet and a form
- Print an Access table
- Use the Access Help system

CASE

Vision Publishers Brian Murphy is the president of Vision Publishers, which produces five specialized monthly magazines from its Chicago headquarters. Brian founded the company in March 1970 when he began publishing *Business Perspective*, a magazine featuring articles, editorials, interviews, and investigative reports that are widely respected in the financial and business communities. Using the concept, format, style, and strong writing of *Business Perspective* as a model, Brian began *Total Sports* in 1975, *Media Scene* in 1978, *Science Outlook* in 1984, and *Travel Vista* in 1987. All five magazines are leaders in their fields and have experienced consistent annual increases in circulation and advertising revenue.

Brian decides to do something special to commemorate the upcoming 25th anniversary of *Business Perspective* and schedules a meeting with four key employees of the magazine. At the meeting are Judith Rossi, managing editor; Harold Larson, marketing director; Elena Sanchez, special projects editor; and Helen Chung, print production director. After reviewing alternatives, they agree that they will create a special 25th-anniversary issue of *Business Perspective*. The issue will include several articles reviewing the past 25 years of the magazine and of the business and financial worlds during those years. Most of the special issue, however, will consist of articles from previous issues, a top article from each year of the magazine's existence. They expect to sign up many advertisers for the issue and to use it as an incentive bonus gift for new and renewing subscribers.

Brian instructs Judith to select past articles, Elena to plan for the special issue, Harold to contact advertisers and plan the marketing campaign, and Helen to prepare the production schedule. Brian will decide on the concept for the new articles and will communicate assignments to the writers.

Judith begins her assignment by using the Vision Publishers database that contains all articles ever published in the five magazines. From this Access for Windows 2.0 database, Judith will scan the articles from *Business Perspective* and select the top articles.

Elena will also use Access for Windows 2.0 for her assignment. Once Judith and Brian determine which articles will be in the special issue, Elena will use Access for Windows 2.0 to store information about the selected business articles and their writers.

In this tutorial, you will follow along as Judith completes her task. You will also learn about databases and how to use the features of Access for Windows 2.0 to view and print your data.

Using the Tutorials Effectively

The tutorials will help you learn about Access for Windows 2.0. They are designed to be used at your computer. Begin by reading the text that explains the concepts. Then when you come to the numbered steps, follow the steps on your computer. Read each step carefully and completely before you try it.

As you work, compare your screen with the figures in the tutorials to verify your results. Don't worry if your screen display differs slightly from the figures. The important parts of the screen display are labeled in each figure. Just be sure you have these parts on your screen.

Don't worry about making mistakes; that's part of the learning process. **TROUBLE?** paragraphs identify common problems and explain how to get back on track. You complete the steps in a **TROUBLE?** paragraph *only* if you are having the problem described.

After you read the conceptual information and complete the steps, you can do the exercises found at the end of each tutorial in the sections entitled "Questions," "Tutorial Assignments," and "Case Problems." The exercises are carefully structured to help you review what you learned in the tutorials and apply your knowledge to new situations.

When you are doing the exercises, refer back to the Reference Window boxes. These boxes, which are found throughout the tutorials, provide you with short summaries of frequently used procedures. You can also use the Task Reference at the end of the tutorials; it summarizes how to accomplish tasks using the mouse, the menus, and the keyboard.

Before you begin the tutorials, you should know how to use the menus, dialog boxes, Help facility, Program Manager, and File Manager in Microsoft Windows. Course Technology, Inc. publishes two excellent texts for learning Windows: *A Guide to Microsoft Windows 3.1* and *An Introduction to Microsoft Windows 3.1*.

From this point on, the tutorials refer to Access for Windows 2.0 simply as Access.

Your Student Disk

To complete the tutorials and exercises in this book, you must have a Student Disk. The Student Disk contains all the practice files you need for the tutorials, the Tutorial Assignments, and the Case Problems. If your technical support person or instructor provides you with your Student Disk, you can skip this section and go to the section "Introduction to Database Concepts." If your instructor asks you to make your own Student Disk, follow the steps in this section.

To make your Student Disk, you need:

- a blank, formatted, high-density 3.5-inch disk
- a computer with Microsoft Windows 3.1, Microsoft Access 2.0, and the CTI WinApps icon group installed on it

If you are using your own computer, the CTI WinApps icon group will not be installed on it. Before you proceed, you must go to your school's computer lab and find a computer with the CTI WinApps icon group installed on it. Once you have made your own Student Disk, you can use it to complete all the tutorials and exercises in this book on any computer you choose.

To make your Access 2.0 Student Disk:

❶ Launch Windows and make sure the Program Manager window is open.

TROUBLE? The exact steps you follow to launch Microsoft Windows 3.1 might vary depending on how your computer is set up. On many computer systems, type WIN then press [Enter] to launch Windows. If you don't know how to launch Windows, ask your instructor or technical support person.

❷ Label your formatted disk "Access 2.0 Student Disk" and place it in drive A.

TROUBLE? If your computer has more than one disk drive, drive A is usually on top or on the left. If your Student Disk does not fit into drive A, then place it in drive B and substitute "drive B" anywhere you see "drive A" in the tutorial steps.

❸ Look for an icon labeled "CTI WinApps" like the one in Figure 1-1, or a window labeled "CTI WinApps," like the one in Figure 1-2 on the following page.

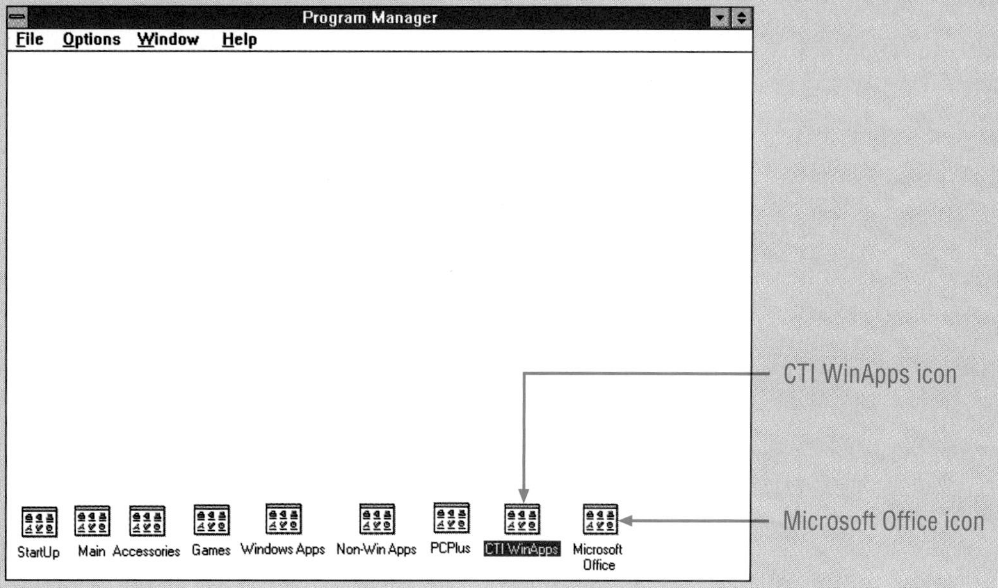

Figure 1-1
The CTI WinApps icon

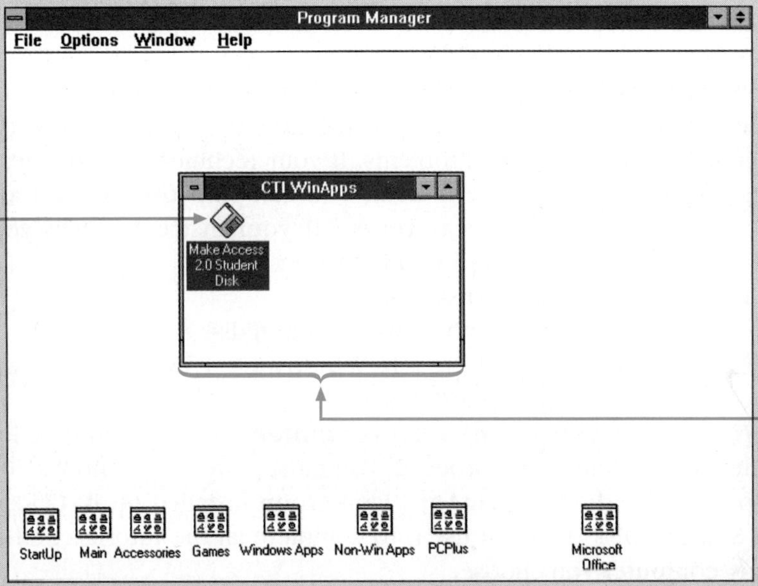

Figure 1-2
Making your Access Student Disk

TROUBLE? If you can't find anything labeled "CTI WinApps," the CTI software might not be installed on your computer. If you are in a computer lab, ask your instructor or technical support person for assistance. ***If you are using your own computer***, you will not be able to make your Student Disk. To make it, you need access to the CTI WinApps icon group, which is, most likely, installed on your school's lab computers. Ask your instructor or technical support person for further information on where to locate the CTI WinApps icon group. Once you create your Student Disk, you can use it to complete all the tutorials and exercises in this book on any computer you choose.

4. If you see an icon labeled "CTI WinApps," double-click it to open the CTI WinApps group window. If the CTI WinApps window is already open, go to Step 5.

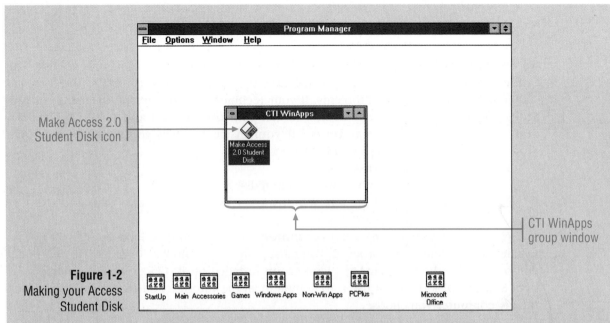

5. Double-click the icon labeled "Make Access 2.0 Student Disk." The Make Access 2.0 Student Disk window opens. See Figure 1-3.

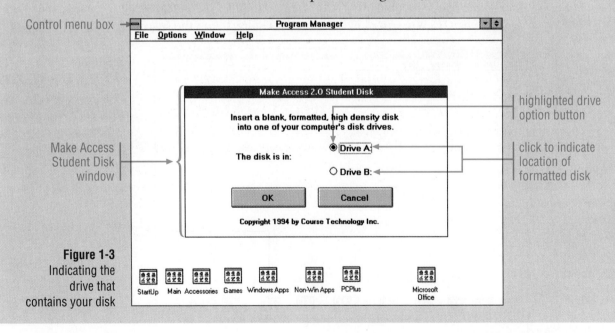

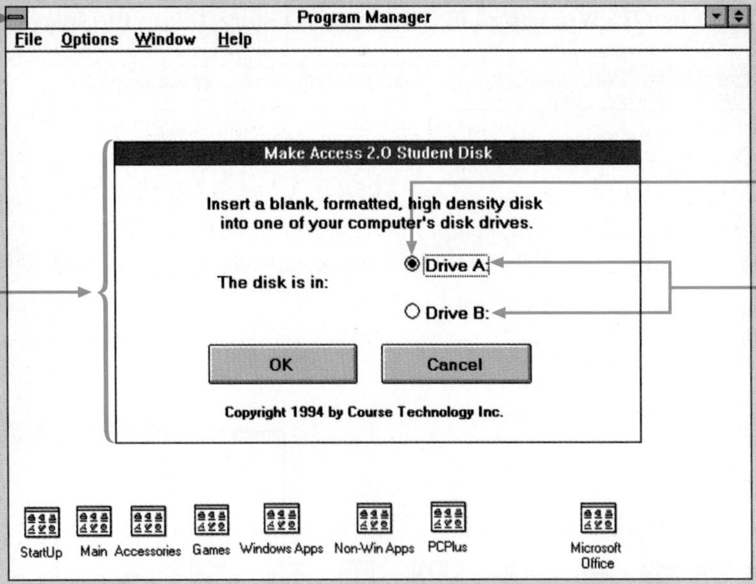

Figure 1-3
Indicating the drive that contains your disk

6. Make sure the drive that contains your formatted disk corresponds to the drive option button that is highlighted in the dialog box on your screen.
7. Click the **OK button** to copy the practice files to your formatted disk.
8. When the copying is complete, a message indicates the number of files copied to your disk. Click the **OK button**.
9. To close the CTI WinApps window, double-click the **Control menu box** on the CTI WinApps window.

Introduction to Database Concepts

Before you work along with Judith on her Vision Publishers assignment, you need to understand a few key terms and concepts associated with databases.

Organizing Data

Data is a valuable resource to companies. At Vision Publishers, for example, writers' names and payments and past magazine article titles and publication dates are data of great value. Organizing, creating, storing, maintaining, retrieving, and sorting such data are important activities that lead to the display and printing of information useful to a company.

When you plan to create and store new types of data either manually or on a computer, you follow a general three-step procedure:

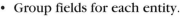

- Identify the individual fields.
- Group fields for each entity.
- Store the field values for each record.

You first identify the individual fields. A **field** is a single characteristic of an entity. An **entity** is a person, place, object, event, or idea. Article title and article length are examples of two fields that Vision Publishers tracks for the entity magazine articles. The company also tracks the fields of writer name and writer address for the entity writers. A field is also called a **data element**, **data item**, or **attribute**.

You next group together all fields for a specific entity into a structure called a **table**. Among its many tables, Vision Publishers has a MAGAZINE ARTICLES table and a WRITERS table, as shown in Figure 1-4. The MAGAZINE ARTICLES table has fields named Article Title, Magazine Issue, Magazine Name, and Article Length. The WRITERS table has fields named Writer Name, Writer Address, and Phone Number. By identifying the fields for each entity and organizing them into tables, you have created the physical structure for your data.

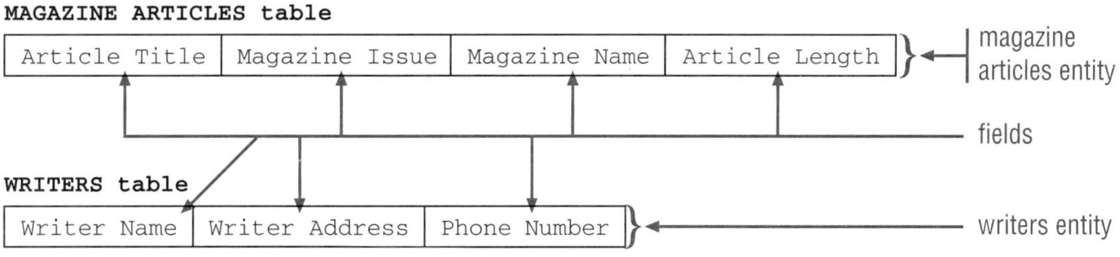

Figure 1-4 Fields organized in two tables

Your final step is to store specific values for the fields of each table. The specific value, or content, of a field is called the **field value**. In the MAGAZINE ARTICLES table, for example, the first set of field values for Article Title, Magazine Issue, Magazine Name, and Article Length are, respectively, Trans-Alaskan Oil Pipeline Opening, 1977 JUL, Business Perspective, and 803 (Figure 1-5). This set of field values is called a **record**. Each separate stored magazine article is a separate record. Nine records are shown in Figure 1-5; each row of field values is a record.

MAGAZINE ARTICLES table

Article Title	Magazine Issue	Magazine Name	Article Length
Trans-Alaskan Oil Pipeline Opening	1977 JUL	Business Perspective	803
Raging Bull	1980 NOV	Media Scene	1642
Farm Aid Abuses	1978 APR	Business Perspective	1866
Herbert A. Simon Interview	1978 DEC	Business Perspective	1811
U.S. Boycotts Moscow Olympics	1980 APR	Total Sports	1137
Alternative Energy Sources	1980 JUN	Business Perspective	2085
Windfall Tax on Oil Profits	1980 APR	Business Perspective	1497
Canada's Railroads	1987 MAR	Travel Vista	1681
Toyota and GM Joint Venture	1983 MAR	Business Perspective	1682

fields

records

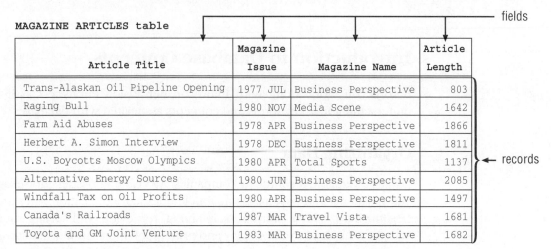

Figure 1-5
Data organization for a table of magazine articles

Databases and Relationships

A collection of related tables is called a **database**, or a **relational database**. Two related tables at Vision Publishers, for example, are the WRITERS table and the MAGAZINE ARTICLES table. Sometimes you might want information about writers and the articles they wrote. To obtain this information you must have a way to connect records from the WRITERS table to records from the MAGAZINE ARTICLES table. You connect the records from the separate tables through a **common field** that appears in both tables. Each record in the MAGAZINE ARTICLES table has a field named Writer ID, which is also a field in the WRITERS table (Figure 1-6). For example, Leroy W. Johnson is the third writer in the WRITERS table and has a Writer ID field value of J525. This same Writer ID field value, J525, appears in the first and third records of the MAGAZINE ARTICLES table. Leroy W. Johnson is therefore the writer of these two articles. Tables are also often called **relations**, because records can be connected to form relationships between tables.

MAGAZINE ARTICLES table

Article Title	Magazine Issue	Magazine Name	Article Length	Writer ID
Trans-Alaskan Oil Pipeline Opening	1977 JUL	Business Perspective	803	J525
Raging Bull	1980 NOV	Media Scene	1642	S253
Farm Aid Abuses	1978 APR	Business Perspective	1866	J525
Herbert A. Simon Interview	1978 DEC	Business Perspective	1811	C200
U.S. Boycotts Moscow Olympics	1980 APR	Total Sports	1137	R543
Alternative Energy Sources	1980 JUN	Business Perspective	2085	S260
Windfall Tax on Oil Profits	1980 APR	Business Perspective	1497	K500
Canada's Railroads	1987 MAR	Travel Vista	1681	H655
Toyota and GM Joint Venture	1983 MAR	Business Perspective	1682	S260

common field

foreign key

two articles by Leroy W. Johnson

primary key

WRITERS table

Writer ID	Writer Name	Phone Number	Last Contact Date	Freelance?
C200	Kelly Cox	(204)783-5415	11/14/82	Yes
H655	Maria L. Hernandez	(916)669-6518	4/9/94	No
J525	Leroy W. Johnson	(209)895-2046	1/29/91	Yes
K500	Chong Kim	(807)729-5364	5/19/94	No
R543	Adam Reynolds	(211)457-9811	10/30/88	No
S253	Myra Schneider	(819)534-6785	2/28/89	No
S260	Wilhelm Seeger	(306)423-0932	12/24/93	Yes

Figure 1-6
Database relationship between tables for magazine articles and writers

Each Writer ID value in the WRITERS table must be unique, so that we can distinguish one writer from another and identify the writer of specific articles in the MAGAZINE ARTICLES table. We call the Writer ID field the primary key of the WRITERS table. A **primary key** is a field, or a collection of fields, whose values uniquely identify each record in a table.

When we include a primary key from one table in a second table to form a relationship between the two tables, we call it a **foreign key** in the second table. For example, Writer ID is the primary key in the WRITERS table and is a foreign key in the MAGAZINE ARTICLES table. Although the primary key Writer ID has unique values in the WRITERS table, the same field as a foreign key in the MAGAZINE ARTICLES table does not have unique values. The Writer ID values J525 and S260, for example, each appear in two records in the MAGAZINE ARTICLES table. Each foreign key value, however, must match one of the field values for the primary key in the other table. Each Writer ID value in the MAGAZINE ARTICLES table, for instance, appears as a Writer ID value in the WRITERS table. The two tables are related, enabling us to tie together the facts about magazine articles with the facts about writers.

Relational Database Management Systems

To manage its databases, a company purchases a database management system. A **database management system (DBMS)** is a software package that lets us create databases and then manipulate data in the databases. Most of today's database management systems, including Access, are called relational database management systems. In a **relational database management system**, data is organized as a collection of tables. These tables are formally called relations, which is how the term relational databases originated.

A relationship between two tables in a relational DBMS is formed through a common field. A relational DBMS controls the physical databases on disk storage by carrying out data creation and manipulation requests. Specifically, a relational DBMS has the following functions (Figure 1-7 summarizes these functions):

- It allows you to create database structures containing fields, tables, and table relationships.
- It lets you easily add new records, change field values in existing records, and delete records.
- It contains a built-in query language, which lets you obtain immediate answers to the questions you ask about your data.
- It contains a built-in report generator, which lets you produce professional-looking, formatted, hardcopy reports from your data.
- It provides protection of databases through security, control, and recovery facilities.

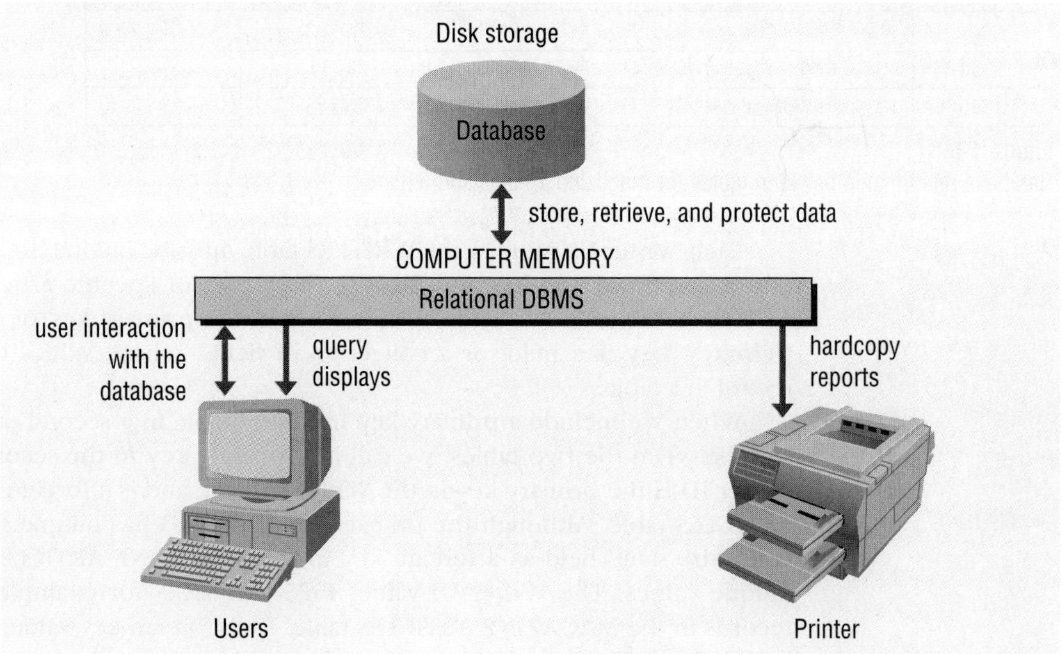

Figure 1-7
A relational database management system

A company like Vision Publishers additionally benefits from a relational DBMS because it allows several people working in different departments to share the same data. More than one person can enter data into a database, and more than one person can retrieve and analyze data that was entered by others. For example, Vision Publishers keeps only one copy of the WRITERS table, and all employees use it to satisfy their specific needs for writer information.

Finally, unlike other software tools, such as spreadsheets, a DBMS can handle massive amounts of data and can easily form relationships among multiple tables. Each Access database, for example, can be up to 1 gigabyte in size and can contain up to 32,768 tables.

Launching and Exiting Access

Access, marketed by Microsoft Corporation, is rapidly becoming one of the most popular relational DBMSs in the Windows environment. For the rest of this tutorial, you will learn to use Access as you work with Judith Rossi on her project.

You first need to learn how to launch Access, so let's launch Access from the Program Manager window.

To launch Access:

❶ Make sure you have created your copy of the Access Student Disk. The Microsoft Office group icon should be visible in the Program Manager window, as you saw in Figure 1-1.

TROUBLE? If you don't have a group icon labeled Microsoft Office, then look for a group icon labeled Microsoft Access and use it instead. If you do not have either of these group icons, ask your technical support person or instructor for help finding the proper icon. Perhaps Access has not been installed on the computer you are using. If you are using your own computer, make sure you have installed the Access software.

TROUBLE? If you don't have a Student Disk, then you need to get one. Your instructor will either give you one or ask you to make your own by following the steps earlier in this tutorial in the section called "Your Student Disk." See your instructor for information.

❷ Double-click the **Microsoft Office group icon** in the Program Manager window. The Microsoft Office group window opens. See Figure 1-8.

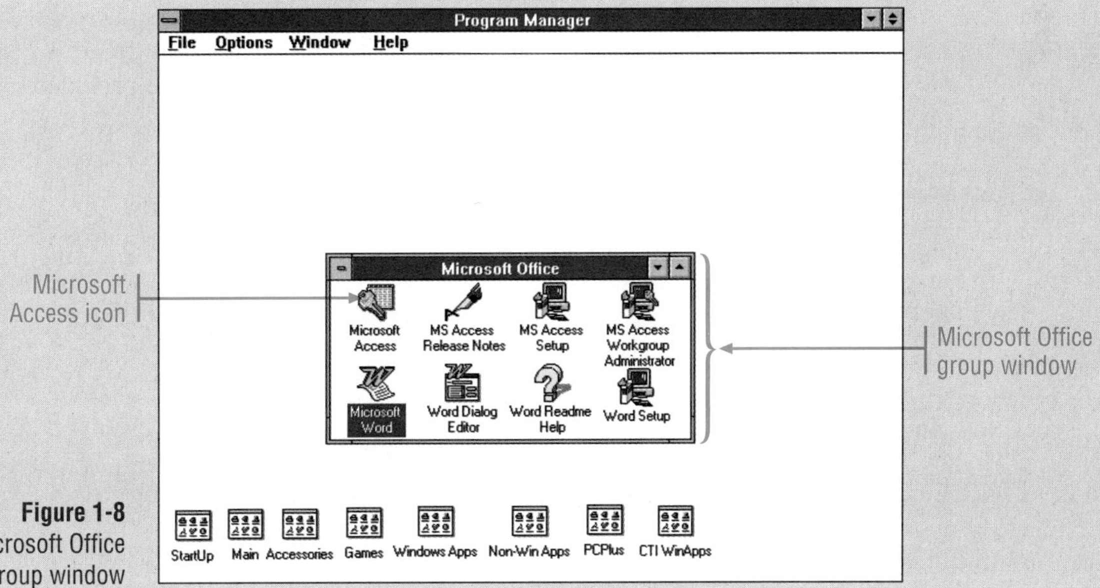

Figure 1-8
The Microsoft Office group window

❸ Double-click the **Microsoft Access icon** in the Microsoft Office group window. After a short pause, the Access copyright information appears in a message box and remains on the screen until Access is ready for use. See Figure 1-9.

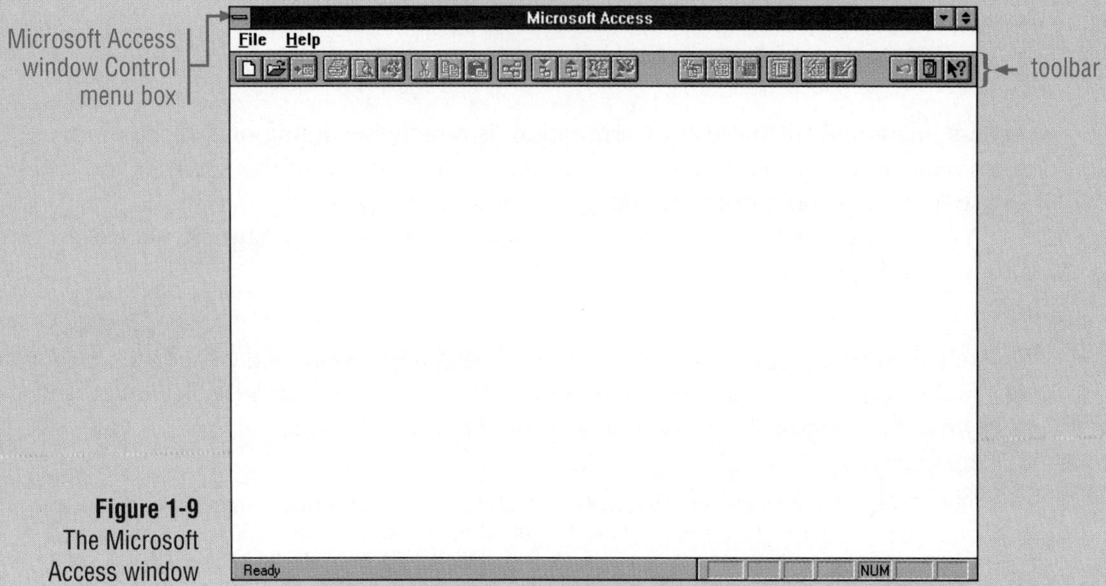

Figure 1-9
The Microsoft Access window

Access is now loaded into your computer's memory. Although Judith wants to work with an existing database, it's always a good idea to know how to exit a software package when you first start working with it. In case you need to end your working session with the package to do something else or if you want to start all over again, you should feel comfortable that you can exit the package at any time.

The Reference Window called "Exiting Access" lists the general steps for exiting Access. Don't try these steps now. Just read the Reference Window to get a general idea of what you are going to do. Specific steps for you to follow will be provided in the next section of numbered steps.

REFERENCE WINDOW

Exiting Access

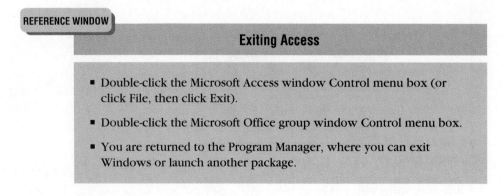

- Double-click the Microsoft Access window Control menu box (or click File, then click Exit).
- Double-click the Microsoft Office group window Control menu box.
- You are returned to the Program Manager, where you can exit Windows or launch another package.

Practice exiting Access by completing the following set of steps. You can exit Access almost any time, no matter what you are doing, by following these steps. If you ever try to exit Access and find you cannot, your active window is likely to be an open dialog box. An open dialog box will prevent you from immediately exiting Access. Simply cancel the dialog box, and you will then be able to exit Access.

To exit Access:

1. Double-click the Microsoft Access window **Control menu box** (or click **File**, then click **Exit**).
2. Double-click the Microsoft Office group window **Control menu box** to close it. You are returned to the Program Manager.

After exiting Access, you should follow the steps to launch Access when you continue with the next section of the tutorial.

Opening a Database

To select the anniversary issue articles, Judith will work with an existing database, so her first step is to open that database. When you want to use a database that was previously created, you must first open it. When you open a database, a copy of the database file is transferred into the random access memory (RAM) of your computer and becomes available for your use. You can then view, print, modify, or save it on your disk.

REFERENCE WINDOW

Opening a Database

- Click the Open Database button on the toolbar in the Microsoft Access window. The Open Database dialog box appears.
- Change the drive and directory information, if necessary, to the disk location of the database.
- Scroll through the File Name list box until the database name appears and then click it. The name appears in the File Name text box.
- Click OK or press [Enter] to accept the changes in the Open Database dialog box.

You open a database by using the Open Database button on the toolbar. The **toolbar buttons** on the toolbar represent common operations you perform with your database. For example, the Help button is used to ask for help about Access tasks. When you switch to different windows in Access, both the toolbar and menu bar change to provide you with the appropriate common operations relevant to that window.

When you first view the toolbar, you will probably be unsure of the function associated with each toolbar button. Fortunately, when you stop the mouse pointer on a toolbar button, Access displays a ToolTip under the button and a description of the button in the status bar at the bottom of the screen. A **ToolTip** is a boxed caption showing the name of the indicated toolbar button.

Let's display the ToolTip for the Open Database button. If you exited Access earlier, launch Access before you follow the next step.

To display a ToolTip:

1. Move the mouse pointer to the toolbar and stop the pointer on the second button from the left. After a short pause, Access displays a ToolTip under the button and the button's description in the status bar. See Figure 1-10.

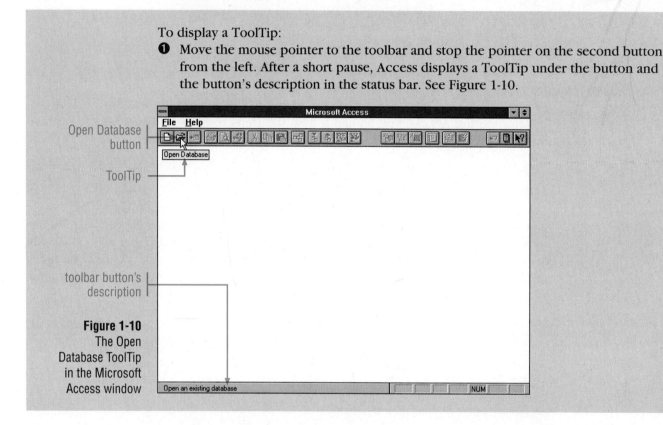

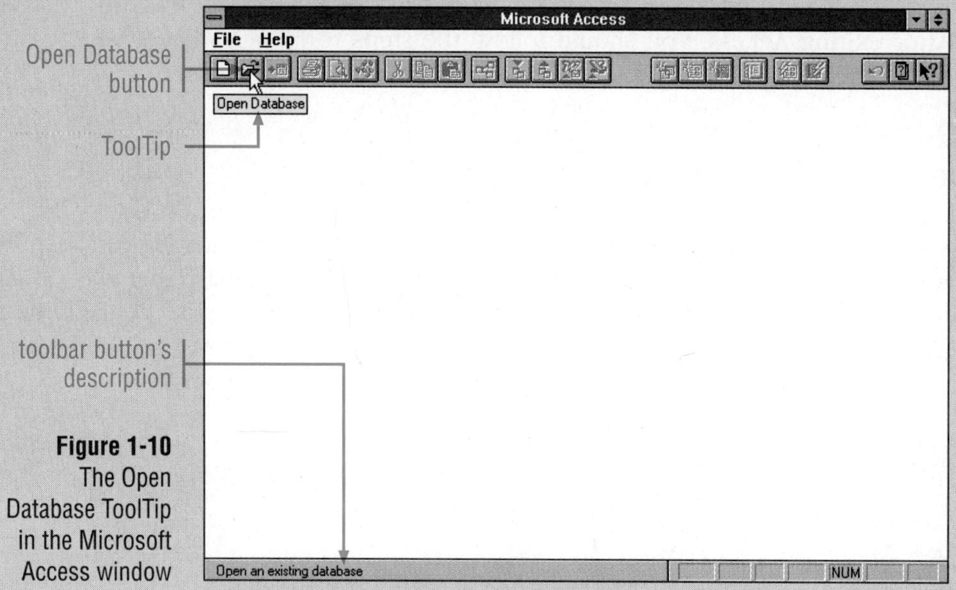

Figure 1-10 The Open Database ToolTip in the Microsoft Access window

Some toolbar buttons appear dimmed because they are not active now. They will become active later, after you have opened a database or taken some other action. You can spend a few moments stopping at each toolbar button to view its ToolTip and status bar description.

Let's now open the database for Vision Publishers.

To open an existing database:

1. Make sure your Access Student Disk is in the appropriate drive—either drive A or drive B.
2. Click the **Open Database button** in the Microsoft Access window. Access displays the Open Database dialog box. See Figure 1-11.

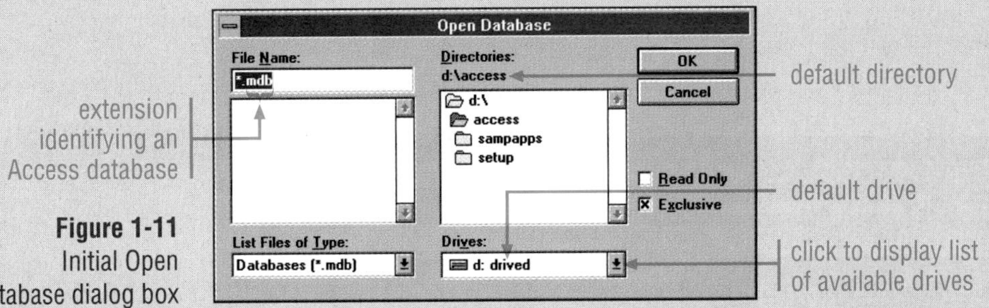

Figure 1-11 Initial Open Database dialog box

❸ Click the **down arrow button** on the right side of the Drives box. A list of available drives drops down. Click the letter of the drive in which you put your Student Disk. Notice that the Directories section of the dialog box also changes as you change your selection in the drop-down Drives box.

❹ Click **vision.mdb** in the File Name list box. The name of the selected file now appears in the File Name text box. See Figure 1-12.

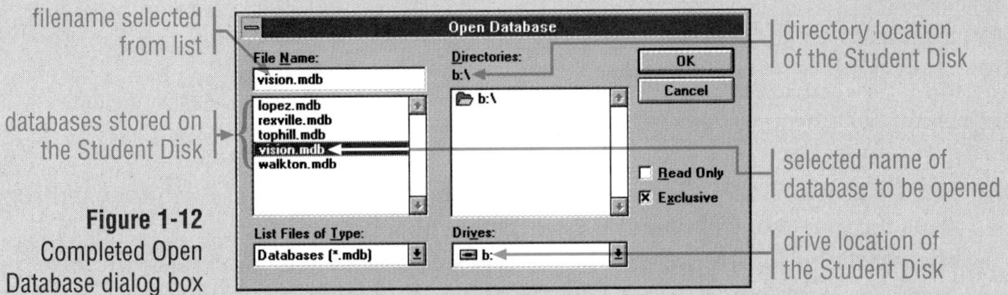

Figure 1-12 Completed Open Database dialog box

TROUBLE? If you can't find a file named vision.mdb, check that the Drives box indicates the location of your Student Disk. If the Drives box shows the correct drive, perhaps you are using the wrong disk in the drive. Check your disk to be sure it's your Student Disk. If it is the correct disk, check with your technical support person or instructor. If it is not the correct disk, place the correct Student Disk in the drive and resume your work from Step 3.

❺ Click the **OK button** to let Access know you have completed the Open Database dialog box. Access opens the Vision.mdb database and displays the Database window.

After opening the Vision Publishers database, Judith checks the window on the screen to familiarize herself with her options. After making this check she will begin her assignment for Brian. Judith wants to review magazine article titles to select past articles for the special edition of *Business Perspective*.

The Database Window

After a database is opened, Access displays the Database window. Because you have experience with the Windows graphical user interface (GUI), you already recognize these components of the Database window: the Microsoft Access window Control menu box, the title bar, the Microsoft Access window sizing buttons, the menu bar, the toolbar, the toolbar buttons, the Database window Control menu box, the Database window sizing buttons, the status bar, and the Microsoft Access window. These are labeled in blue in Figure 1-13 on the following page. Components of the Database window that are new to you appear in red in Figure 1-13.

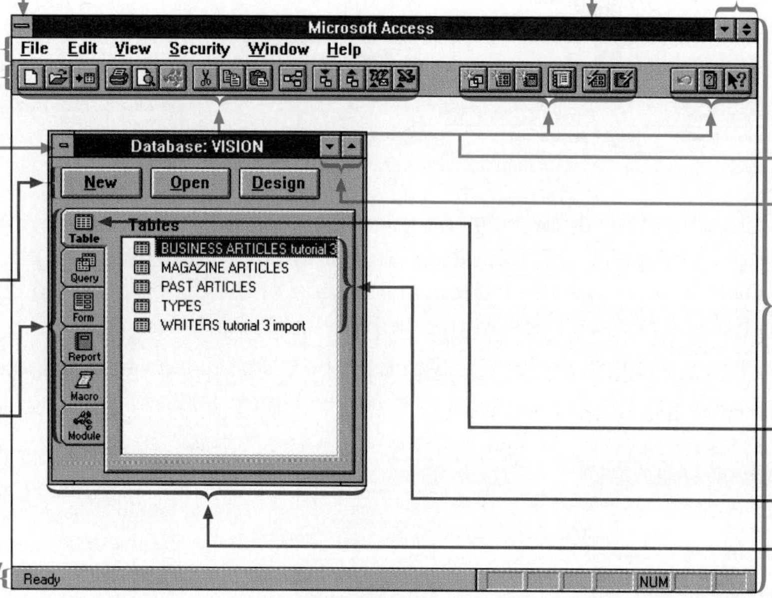

Figure 1-13
The Database window

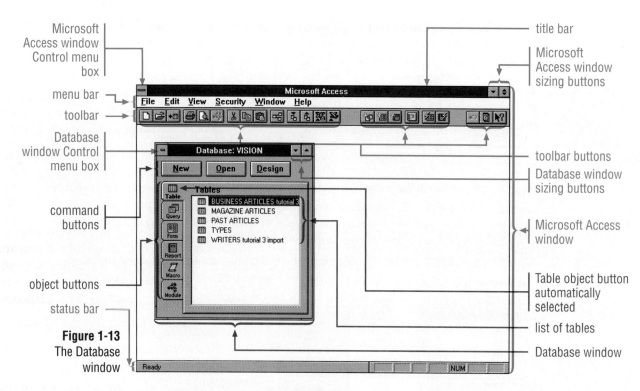

- The Database window appears on top of the Microsoft Access window and represents the main control center for working with a database.
- The object buttons represent the six types of objects you can create for an Access database. Unlike most other DBMSs, Access stores each database in a single file. The database contains all the tables you define for it, along with all queries, forms, reports, macros, and modules; these collectively are the objects that make up the database. Each separate query and each separate report, for example, is a separate object so that, if Vision Publishers has three tables, five queries, and four reports in a database, Access treats them as 12 separate objects.

You already know what a table is, so let's consider the other five objects. You use the built-in Access query language to create a query (or question) about data from your tables. For example, if Judith needs to find records from the MAGAZINE ARTICLES table for a specific writer she can use a query for this purpose. You use a form to store, display, and view records from your tables. For example, Judith can create a form for others to use that displays one record at a time from the WRITERS table. You use a report to print data from tables in a customized format. For example, Brian might need a printed list that shows all writer information; a report can be used to generate this list. A **macro** is a saved list of operations to be performed on data. Access carries out the operations when you run the macro. Judith can use a macro, for example, to open a special form automatically whenever someone opens the company database. Finally, Access has a built-in programming language called Access Basic. A **module** is a set of one or more Access Basic programmed procedures. Vision Publishers uses a module, for example, to calculate payments to its writers for the articles they write.

- The three command buttons represent the major operations performed on tables. You can create a new table by clicking the New button. For an existing table, click the Open button to view table records or click the Design button to change the table structure.
- Notice that the Table object button is automatically selected when you first open a database, and a list of available tables for the database appears. When you click one of the other object buttons, that object button becomes the one that is selected; a list of available objects of that type then appears.

Viewing and Printing a Table

Now that you have opened a database and familiarized yourself with the components of the Database window, you are ready to view and print an existing Access table. If you are interested in looking up information from a small number of records in a table, you usually view them on the screen. However, if you need information from a large number of records or need to present the information to other people, you usually print a hardcopy of the table.

Datasheet View Window

Vision Publishers has a table named MAGAZINE ARTICLES that contains data about all the magazine articles published by the company. Judith opens this table to start her selection of top articles from *Business Perspective* magazine.

REFERENCE WINDOW

Opening the Datasheet View Window for a Table

- Scroll through the Tables list box until the table name appears and then click it.
- Click the Open command button.

Let's open the MAGAZINE ARTICLES table for Vision Publishers.

To open the Datasheet View window for the MAGAZINE ARTICLES table:

1. Click **MAGAZINE ARTICLES**, then click the **Open command button**. The Datasheet View window for the MAGAZINE ARTICLES table appears on top of the previous windows. See Figure 1-14 on the following page.

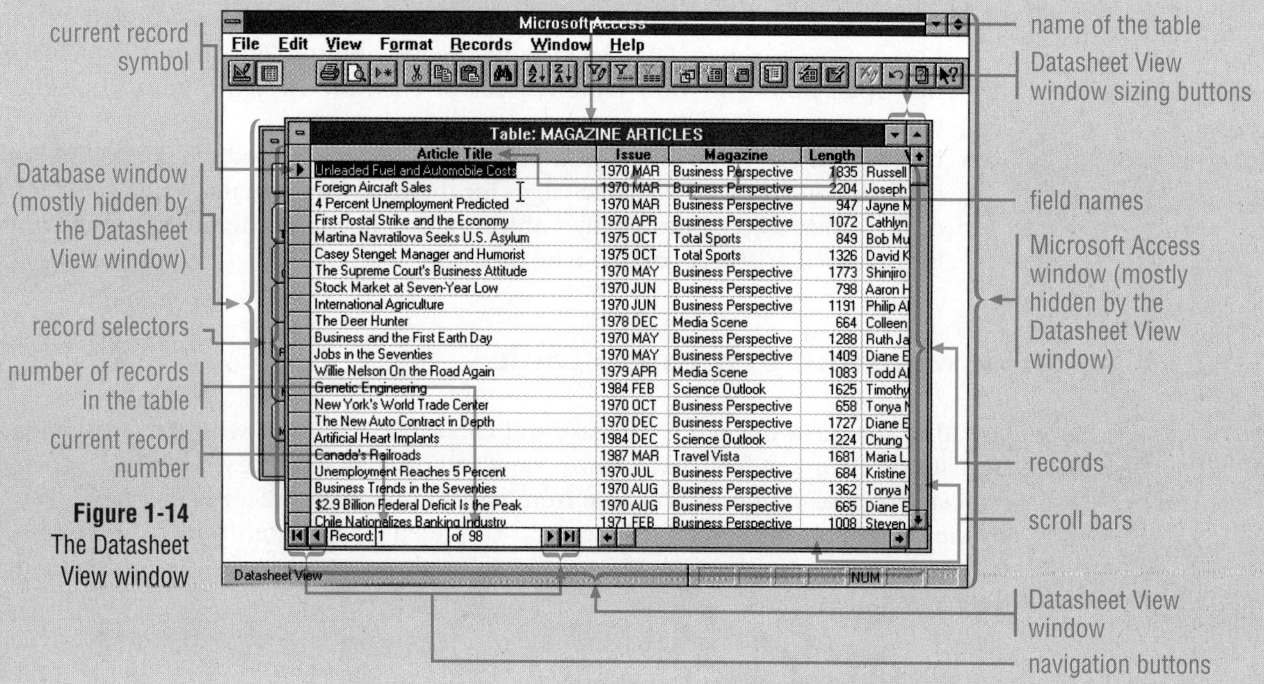

Figure 1-14
The Datasheet View window

The **Datasheet View window** shows a table's contents as a **datasheet** in rows and columns, similar to a spreadsheet. Each row is a separate record in the table, and each column contains the field values for one field from the table. Each column is headed by a field name. When you first open a datasheet, Access automatically selects the first field value in the first record for processing. Notice that this field is highlighted and that a darkened triangle symbol, called the current record symbol, appears in the record selector to the left of the first record. The **current record symbol** identifies the currently selected record. If you move your mouse pointer over any field value, it changes to I. If you then click the I on a field value in another row, that field value becomes the currently selected field. Although the entire field value is not highlighted, the insertion point stays where you clicked, the new record becomes the current record, and the current record number, between the navigation buttons at the bottom of the screen, changes. Practice clicking the I on different fields and records and notice the changes that occur in the datasheet.

Although the MAGAZINE ARTICLES table has only five fields, the Datasheet View window isn't large enough to display the entire writer name field. Similarly, you see only the first group of records from the table. One way to see different parts of a table is to use the vertical and horizontal scroll bars and arrows on the right and bottom of the datasheet. Practice clicking these scroll bars and arrows to become comfortable with their use.

Using the lower-left navigation buttons is another way to move vertically through the records. From left to right respectively, the **navigation buttons** advance the selected record to the first record, the previous record, the next record, and the last record in the table (Figure 1-15). The current record number appears between the two pairs of navigation buttons, as does the total number of records in the table. Practice clicking the four navigation buttons and notice the changes that occur in the datasheet, in the current record number, and in the placement of the current record symbol.

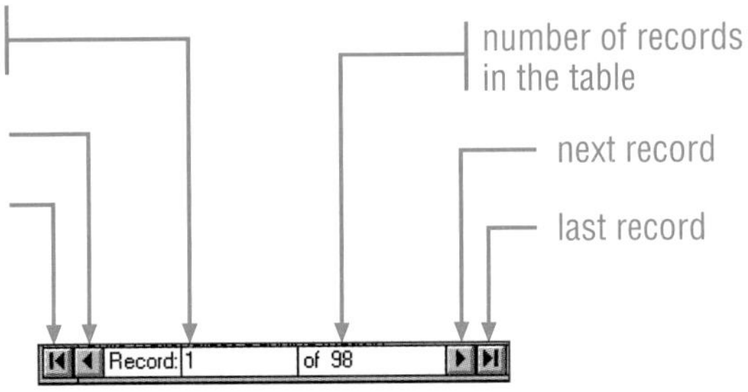

Figure 1-15
Navigation buttons

Judith decides to print the records from the first datasheet page of the table to study their contents more closely, but first she maximizes the Datasheet View window.

To maximize the Datasheet View window:

❶ Click the **maximize button** for the Datasheet View window to expand the window. See Figure 1-16. Notice that a restore button replaces the minimize and maximize buttons and that the table title appears in the Access title bar.

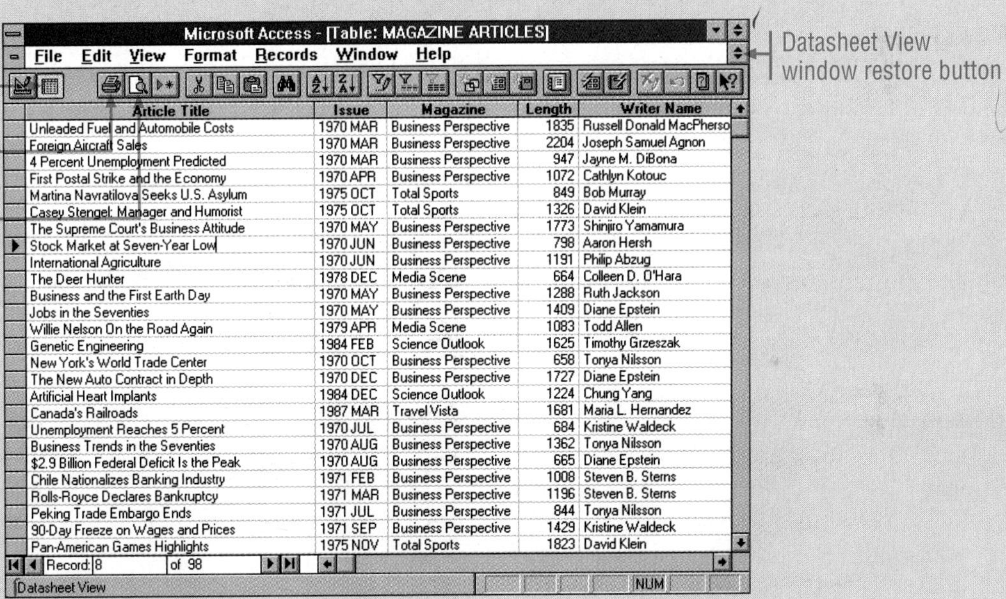
Datasheet View button selected
Print button
Print Preview button
Datasheet View window restore button
Microsoft Access - [Table: MAGAZINE ARTICLES]
File Edit View Format Records Window Help
Article Title
Issue
Magazine
Length
Writer Name
Unleaded Fuel and Automobile Costs 1970 MAR Business Perspective 1835 Russell Donald MacPherso
Foreign Aircraft Sales 1970 MAR Business Perspective 2204 Joseph Samuel Agnon
4 Percent Unemployment Predicted 1970 MAR Business Perspective 947 Jayne M. DiBona
First Postal Strike and the Economy 1970 APR Business Perspective 1072 Cathlyn Kotouc
Martina Navratilova Seeks U.S. Asylum 1975 OCT Total Sports 849 Bob Murray
Casey Stengel: Manager and Humorist 1975 OCT Total Sports 1326 David Klein
The Supreme Court's Business Attitude 1970 MAY Business Perspective 1773 Shinjiro Yamamura
Stock Market at Seven-Year Low 1970 JUN Business Perspective 798 Aaron Hersh
International Agriculture 1970 JUN Business Perspective 1191 Philip Abzug
The Deer Hunter 1978 DEC Media Scene 664 Colleen D. O'Hara
Business and the First Earth Day 1970 MAY Business Perspective 1288 Ruth Jackson
Jobs in the Seventies 1970 MAY Business Perspective 1409 Diane Epstein
Willie Nelson On the Road Again 1979 APR Media Scene 1083 Todd Allen
Genetic Engineering 1984 FEB Science Outlook 1625 Timothy Grzeszak
New York's World Trade Center 1970 OCT Business Perspective 658 Tonya Nilsson
The New Auto Contract in Depth 1970 DEC Business Perspective 1727 Diane Epstein
Artificial Heart Implants 1984 DEC Science Outlook 1224 Chung Yang
Canada's Railroads 1987 MAR Travel Vista 1681 Maria L. Hernandez
Unemployment Reaches 5 Percent 1970 JUL Business Perspective 684 Kristine Waldeck
Business Trends in the Seventies 1970 AUG Business Perspective 1362 Tonya Nilsson
$2.9 Billion Federal Deficit Is the Peak 1970 AUG Business Perspective 665 Diane Epstein
Chile Nationalizes Banking Industry 1971 FEB Business Perspective 1008 Steven B. Sterns
Rolls-Royce Declares Bankruptcy 1971 MAR Business Perspective 1196 Steven B. Sterns
Peking Trade Embargo Ends 1971 JUL Business Perspective 844 Tonya Nilsson
90-Day Freeze on Wages and Prices 1971 SEP Business Perspective 1429 Kristine Waldeck
Pan-American Games Highlights 1975 NOV Total Sports 1823 David Klein
Record: 8 of 98
Datasheet View
NUM

Figure 1-16
Maximized Datasheet View window

TROUBLE? If your datasheet is not maximized, you probably clicked the Datasheet View window minimize button or one of the Microsoft Access window sizing buttons instead. Use the appropriate sizing button to restore your screen to its previous condition, and then refer to Figure 1-14 for the location of the Datasheet View window maximize button.

You might have noticed that one toolbar button, the Datasheet View button is selected, as shown in Figure 1-16. You can click the Datasheet View button to switch to the Datasheet View window of your table whenever you see this button on the toolbar. To the right of the Datasheet View button are the Print and Print Preview buttons. You click the Print Preview button whenever you want to review the appearance of a datasheet on screen before you print a hardcopy of it. Use the **Print button** instead, if you want to print a hardcopy without reviewing it on screen.

REFERENCE WINDOW

Printing a Hardcopy of a Datasheet

- Click the Print Preview button on the toolbar to display the Print Preview window. Click the Print button on the toolbar. The Print dialog box appears.
- Select the Copies box if you want to change the number of copies you want to print.
- Click Pages in the Print Range section if your want to print only a portion of your datasheet. Specify the beginning page in the range in the From box and the ending page in the range in the To box.
- Click All in the Print Range section if you want to print all the pages in your datasheet.
- Click the OK button or press [Enter].

Let's print preview Judith's datasheet and then print its first page.

To print preview and print a datasheet:

1. Click the **Print Preview button** on the toolbar. The Print Preview window appears. See Figure 1-17.

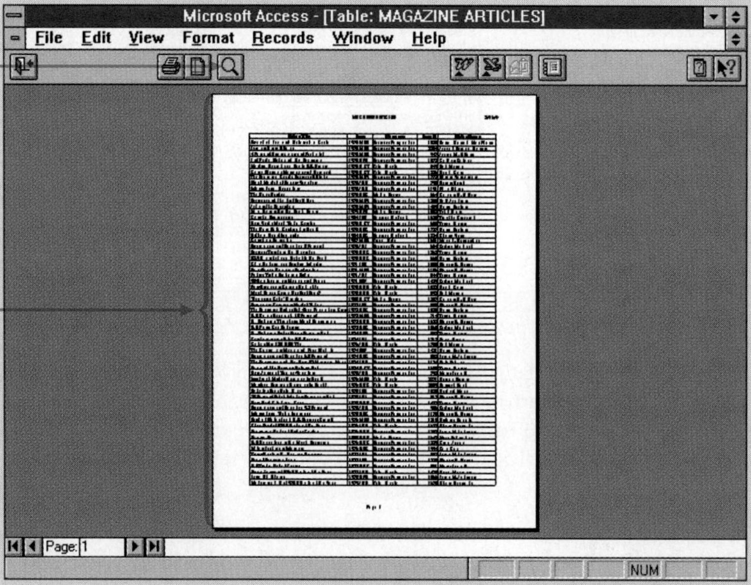

Figure 1-17 Initial Print Preview window

When you move the mouse pointer over the datasheet page, it changes to the magnifier pointer. You can click the magnifier or click the toolbar Zoom button to see a close-up of the datasheet page. Judith decides to preview a close-up of the page.

❷ Click the **Zoom button** [Zoom icon], or click the [magnifier pointer] when it is positioned over the miniaturized page. A close-up of the page appears. See Figure 1-18. Depending on whether you clicked the [Zoom icon] or the [magnifier pointer], your screen might differ from the illustration.

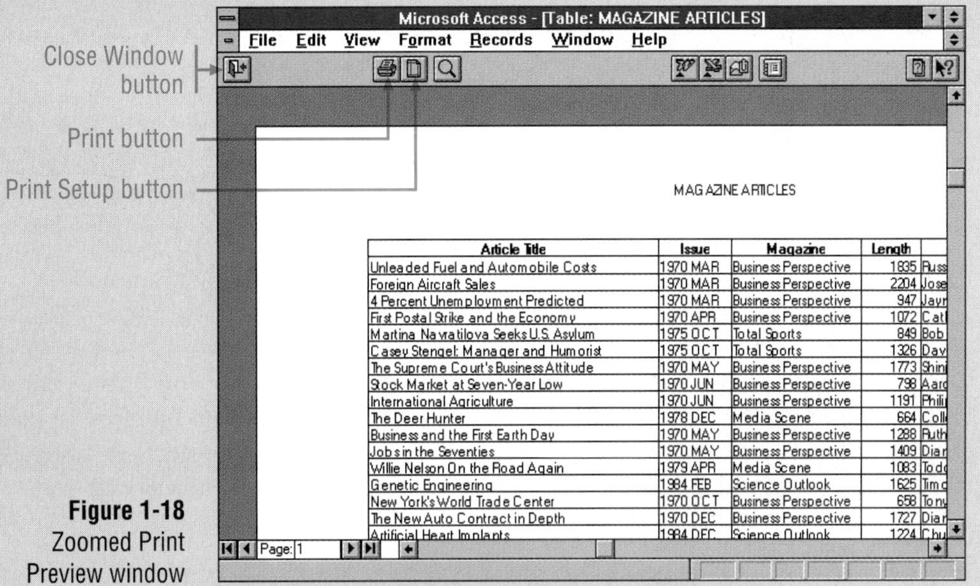

Figure 1-18
Zoomed Print Preview window

If you click the [Zoom icon] or the [magnifier pointer] a second time, the page returns to its original miniaturized view. Practice clicking the [Zoom icon], the [magnifier pointer], and the navigation buttons. When you are done practicing, you are ready to print the datasheet page.

❸ Make sure your printer is on-line and ready to print. Click the **Print button** [Print icon] on the toolbar. The Print dialog box appears. See Figure 1-19. Check the Printer section of the dialog box to make sure your printer is selected.

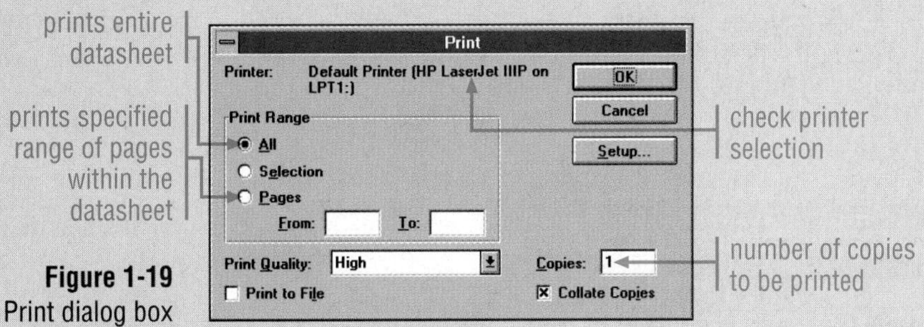

Figure 1-19
Print dialog box

TROUBLE? If the correct printer is not selected, click the Setup... button in the Print dialog box, select the correct printer from the Specified Printer list, and click the OK button.

❹ Because you want to print just the first datasheet page, click the **Pages option button**, type **1**, press **[Tab]**, type **1**, and click the **OK button**. A dialog box appears to inform you that your datasheet page is being sent to the printer. See Figure 1-20 on the following page.

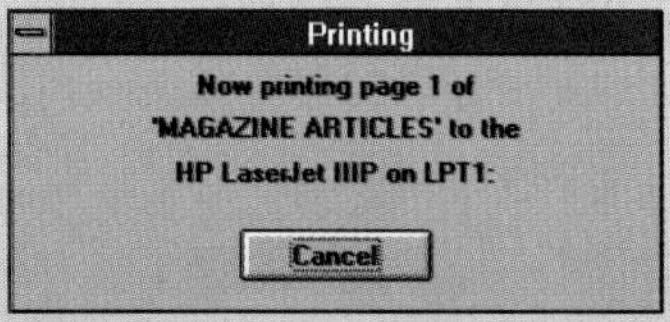

Figure 1-20 Printing dialog box

5. After the dialog box disappears, click the **Close Window button** in the Print Preview window toolbar to return to the Datasheet View window.

   TROUBLE? If your document hasn't printed yet, check the print status in the Windows Print Manager by pressing [Alt][Tab] until the Print Manager title bar appears, and then release. Remove your document from the print queue before returning to your datasheet and then print the first datasheet page again. If it still doesn't print, check with your technical support person or instructor.

Judith is ready to close the Datasheet View window. Whenever you finish your work with a particular window, you should close the window. This frees up memory, speeds up processing, and removes unnecessary clutter from your screen. Any object—a table using a datasheet, a query, a form, a report, a macro, or a module—is closed in a similar way.

REFERENCE WINDOW

Closing an Object Window

- Double-click the object window Control menu box (or click File, then click Close).

Let's close the Datasheet View window you have been using.

To close the Datasheet View window (or other object window):

1. Click **File** to open the File menu. See Figure 1-21.

Datasheet View window Control menu box

Close window command

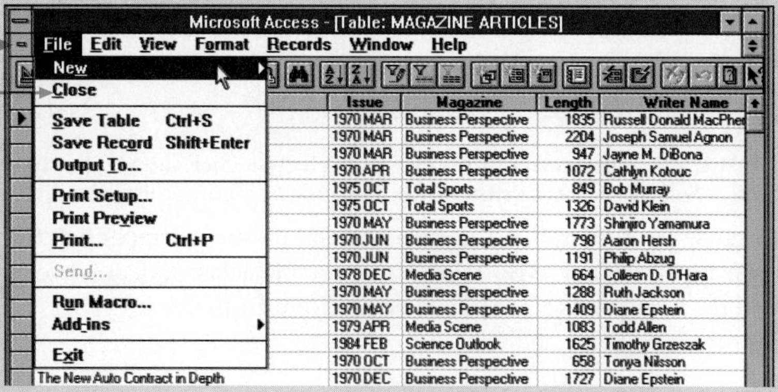

Figure 1-21 Closing the Datasheet View window

❷ Click **Close**. Access closes the Datasheet View window and returns you to the Database window. See Figure 1-22. Because you previously maximized the Datasheet View window, the Database window now appears maximized.

Form object button

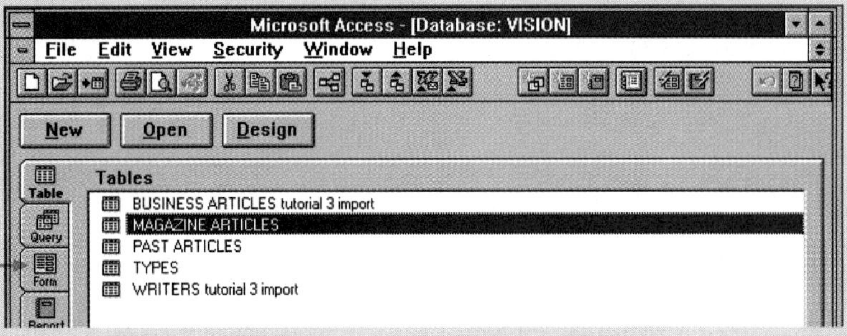

Figure 1-22
Maximized Database window

TROUBLE? If Access displays a message box asking if you want to save changes, click the No button. You accidentally changed the datasheet and do not want to save the modified version in your table.

If you want to take a break and resume the tutorial at a later time, you can exit Access by double-clicking the Microsoft Access window Control menu box in the upper-left corner of the screen. When you resume the tutorial, place your Student Disk in the appropriate drive and launch Access. Open the database vision.mdb, maximize the Database window, and then continue working on the next section of the tutorial.

■ ■ ■

Form View Window

Judith now opens an existing form to view the records from the MAGAZINE ARTICLES table. A form gives you a customized view of data from a database. You use a form, for example, to view one record from a table at a time, to view data in a more readable format, or to view related data from two or more tables. The way you open a form is similar to the way you opened a datasheet and the way you open all other database objects.

REFERENCE WINDOW

Opening a Form

- Click the Form object button.
- Scroll through the Forms list box until the form name appears and then click it.
- Click the Open command button.

Let's now open the form named Magazine Articles.

To open a form:

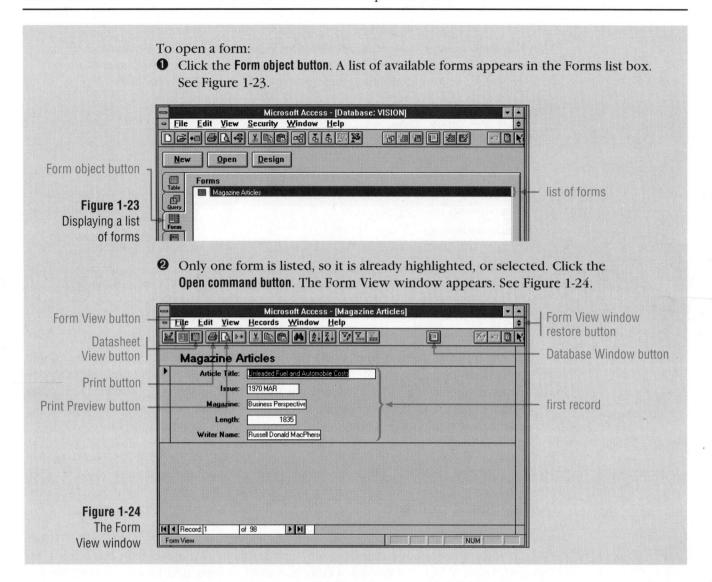

❶ Click the **Form object button**. A list of available forms appears in the Forms list box. See Figure 1-23.

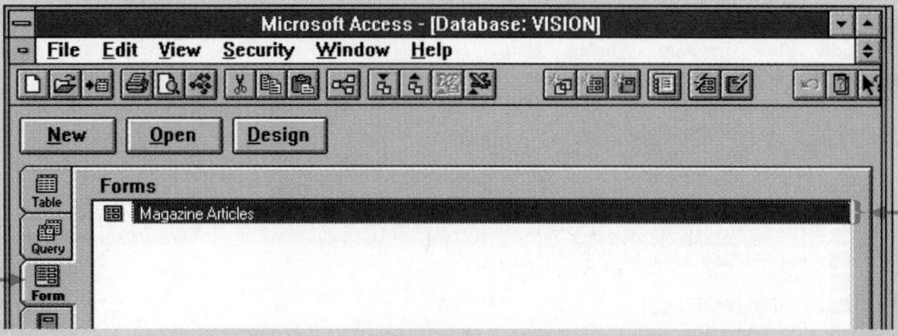

Figure 1-23 Displaying a list of forms

❷ Only one form is listed, so it is already highlighted, or selected. Click the **Open command button**. The Form View window appears. See Figure 1-24.

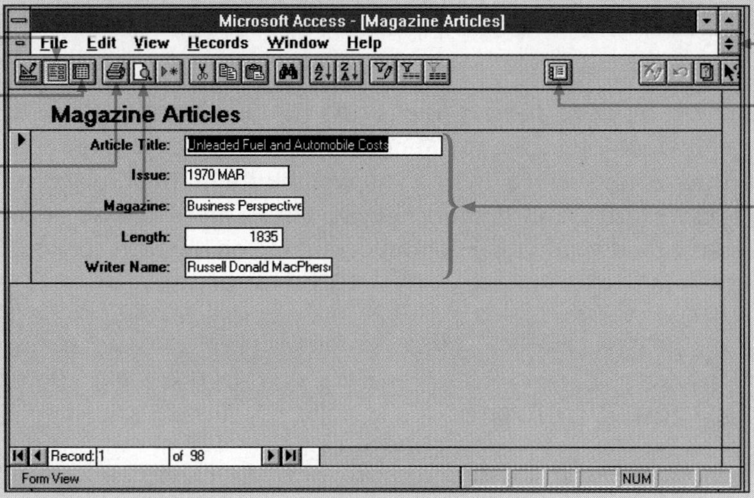

Figure 1-24 The Form View window

The **Form View window** shows a table's contents in a customized format, usually one record at a time. The form, as shown in Figure 1-24, displays all five fields from the MAGAZINE ARTICLES table vertically, one record at a time. Each field has a label on the left and a boxed field value on the right. The label is the field name.

Some of the same window components you saw in the Datasheet View window also appear in the Form View window and have the same functions. Notice the location of the Form View window restore button and the navigation buttons. Practice clicking the navigation buttons and clicking different field values. Then notice the changes that occur in the form.

You should also practice clicking the Datasheet View and Form View toolbar buttons. Clicking the Datasheet View button switches you from the Form View window to the Datasheet View window. Clicking the Form View button switches you from the Datasheet View window to the Form View window.

Judith prints the first page of records from the Form View window but does not first use the Print Preview option. Access prints as many form records as can fit on a printed page. The steps you follow to print from the Form View window are similar to the steps you followed when you printed from the Datasheet View window.

To print a form page:

1. Before continuing, be sure you are in the Form View window with the first record appearing in a maximized window. Click the **Print button** on the toolbar. The Print dialog box appears.
2. Make sure your printer is on-line and ready to print. Check the Printer section of the dialog box to make sure the correct printer is selected. Click the **Pages option button**, type **1**, press **[Tab]**, type **1**, and then click the **OK button**. A dialog box informs you that your datasheet page is being sent to the printer. After the dialog box disappears, Access returns you to the Form View window.

Closing a Database

Judith is done working on both the form and the database, so she closes the database. She could close the Form View window, as she previously closed the Datasheet View window, and then close the database. However, whenever you close a database without closing the Form View window or any other open object window, Access automatically closes all open windows before closing the database.

REFERENCE WINDOW

Closing a Database

- Click the Database Window button in an open object window to make the Database window visible and make it the active window.
- Double-click the Database window Control menu box.

Let's close the Vision Publishers database that you have been using.

To close a database:

1. Click the **Database Window button** on the toolbar to activate the Database window on top of a smaller-sized Form View window. See Figure 1-25.

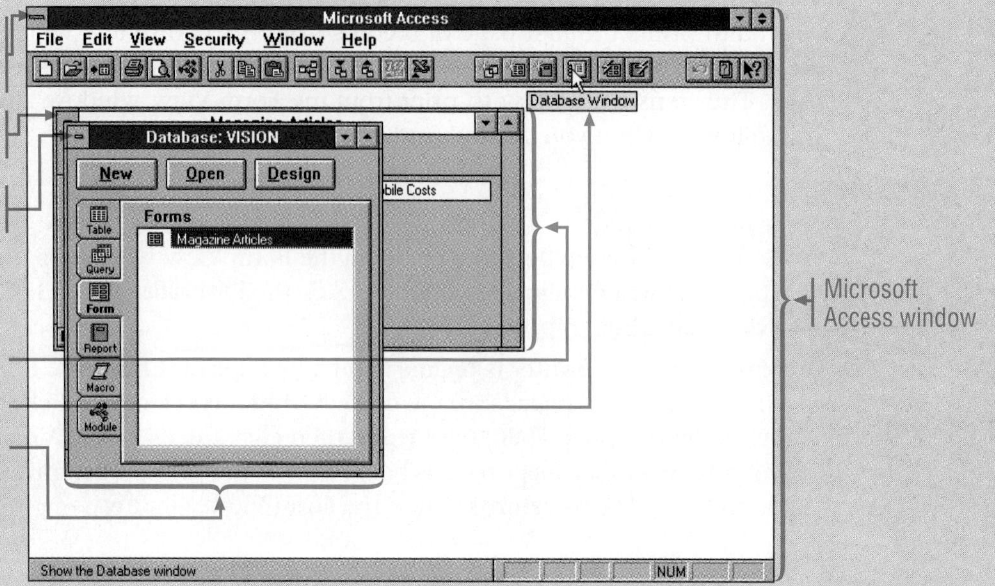

Figure 1-25 Activating the Database window

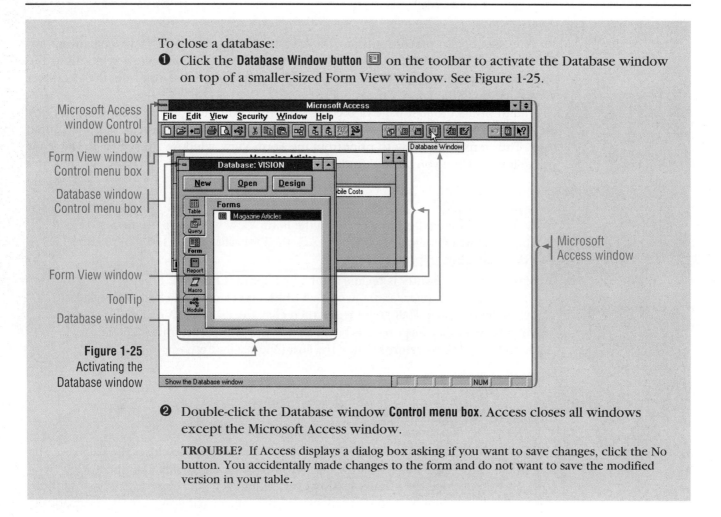

2. Double-click the Database window **Control menu box**. Access closes all windows except the Microsoft Access window.

   TROUBLE? If Access displays a dialog box asking if you want to save changes, click the No button. You accidentally made changes to the form and do not want to save the modified version in your table.

Getting Help

While you are using Access on your computer, there might be times when you are puzzled about how to complete a task. You might also need to clarify a definition or Access feature or investigate more advanced Access capabilities. You can use Access's Help system to give you on-line information about your specific questions. There are four ways you can get on-line help as you work: by using the Help Contents, the Search feature, the Glossary feature, or the context-sensitive Help system. Let's practice using the Access Help system.

Starting Help and Using the Help Contents

Judith has some questions about moving the toolbar and about shortcut menus and uses the Access Help system to find answers. One way to use the Access Help system is to click Help and then click Contents.

To start Help:

❶ Click **Help** and then click **Contents**. The Microsoft Access Help window becomes the active window and displays the Microsoft Access Help Contents topic. See Figure 1-26.

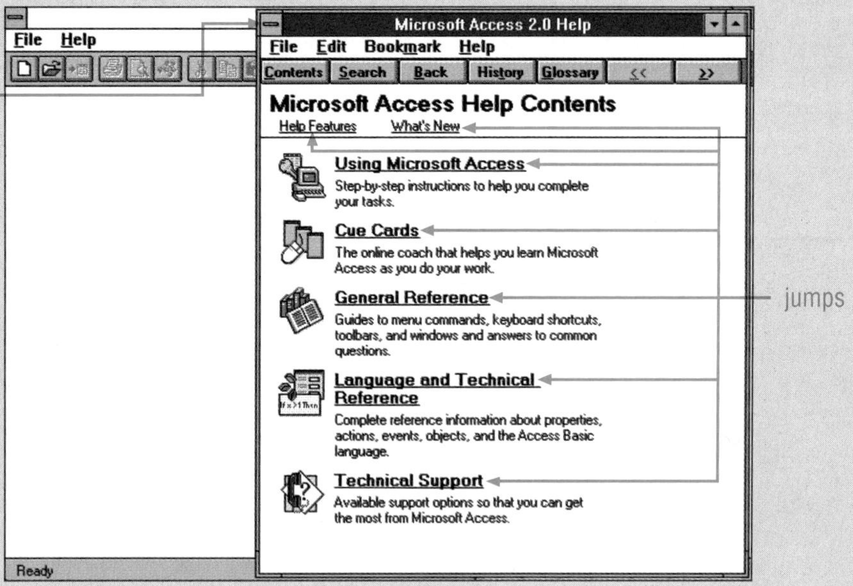

Figure 1-26 The Microsoft Access Help window

TROUBLE? If the size or position of your Microsoft Access Help window is different from what is shown in the illustration, don't worry. Continue with the tutorial.

The underlined words and topics in the Microsoft Access Help window serve as a top-level table of contents. You can get detailed information on each of these words or topics by clicking one of the words or topics. The mouse pointer changes to 👆 when you move it over any of the words or topics. Underlined words or topics are called jumps. A **jump** provides a link to other Help topics or to more information or a definition about the current word or topic.

Judith wants to find out how to use Help and decides that clicking Help on the Microsoft Access Help menu bar might tell her how to do this.

To get help on using Access Help:

❶ Press **[F1]** while the Microsoft Access Help window is active (or click **Help** within the Microsoft Access Help window, then click **How to Use Help**). See Figure 1-27 on the following page. Judith wants more information about the scroll bar jump.

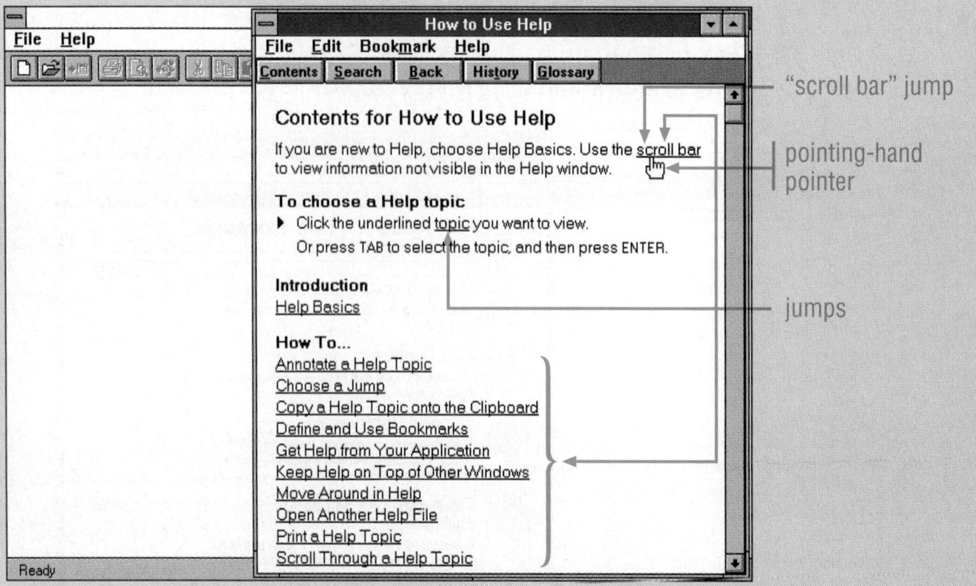

Figure 1-27
The How to Use Help window

❷ Click the words **scroll bar** when the mouse pointer changes to ☝ over them. Access Help displays a description of the term. See Figure 1-28. The pointer changes back to ↖.

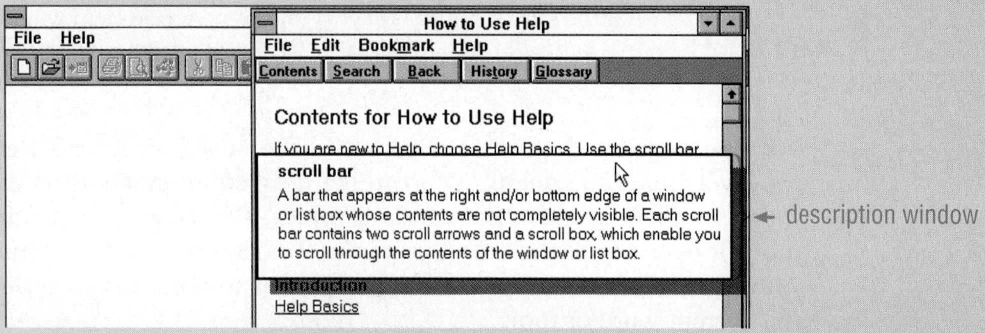

Figure 1-28
Description of "scroll bar"

TROUBLE? If you get the message "Help topic does not exist," you might not have the complete Access Help system installed on your system. Ask your technical support person or instructor for assistance.

❸ Click the words **scroll bar** again. The description window disappears.

❹ Read the material under the heading Contents for How to Use Help. Use the scroll bar to view the entire topic.

Judith sees the Search for a Help Topic jump as she scrolls through Contents for How to Use Help and decides to view that jump.

To view the Contents for How to Use Help jump:

1. Find and click the jump **Search for a Help Topic**.
2. Read the information under Search for a Help Topic, using the scroll bar to view the entire topic.

Using the Search feature of Help appears to be what Judith needs to use to get answers to her questions. Because the How to Use Help window is active, however, she must switch back to the Microsoft Access Help window before she can use the Search feature. If she does not switch back, she will be searching for Help topics rather than Access topics.

To return to the Microsoft Access Help window:

1. Click the **Back button** in the Help button bar two times. Notice that the title bar changes to Microsoft Access 2.0 Help.

Using Search

Having read about the Search feature in Access Help, Judith uses that feature to search for information about moving toolbars.

To use the search feature in Access Help:

1. Click the **Search button** on the Help button bar. The Search dialog box appears. See Figure 1-29.

insertion point in text box

list of Help topics

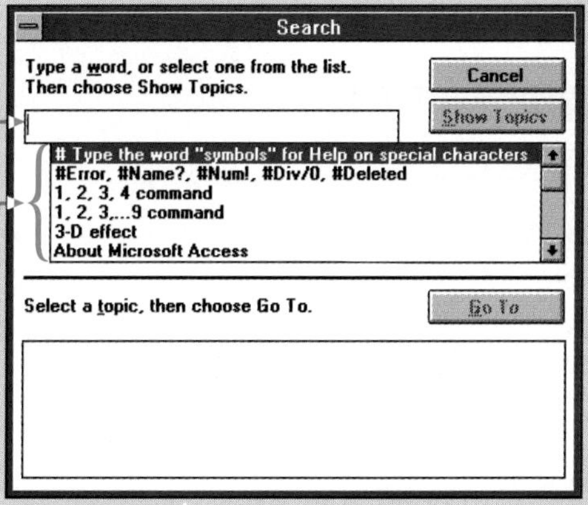

Figure 1-29 The Search dialog box

2. Type **m** in the text box. The list of topics shown changes to those topics starting with *m*.
3. Type **oving t** after the *m* in the text box. The list of topics shown changes to those starting with the letters "moving t" and the topic moving toolbars is visible in the list box.
4. Click **moving toolbars** in the list box and then click the **Show Topics button**. See Figure 1-30 on the following page.

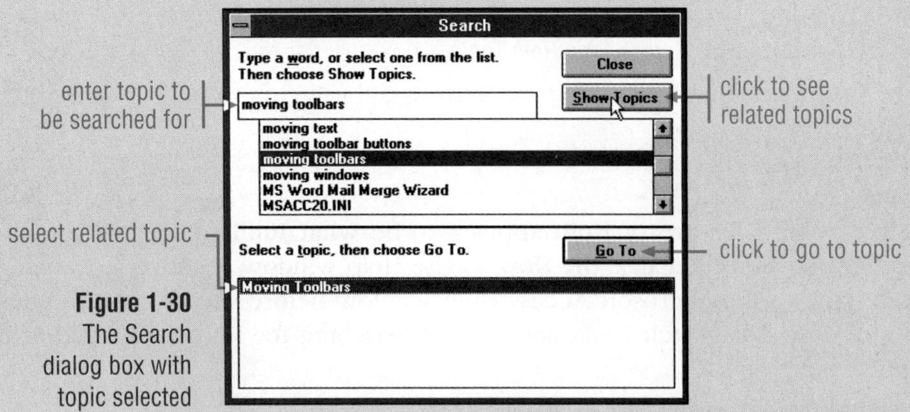

Figure 1-30 The Search dialog box with topic selected

❺ Click the **Go To button** or press **[Enter]**. The Moving Toolbars topic appears. Read the information under Moving Toolbars, using the scroll bar to view the entire topic.

Judith has the answers she needs to her questions about moving toolbars and next looks up the definition of the term Shortcut menu in the glossary.

Using the Glossary

The Glossary contains Access terms and their definitions. Judith uses the Glossary feature to read the definition of Shortcut menu.

To use the Glossary feature in Access Help:

❶ Click the **Glossary button** on the Help button bar. The Glossary topic appears. See Figure 1-31.

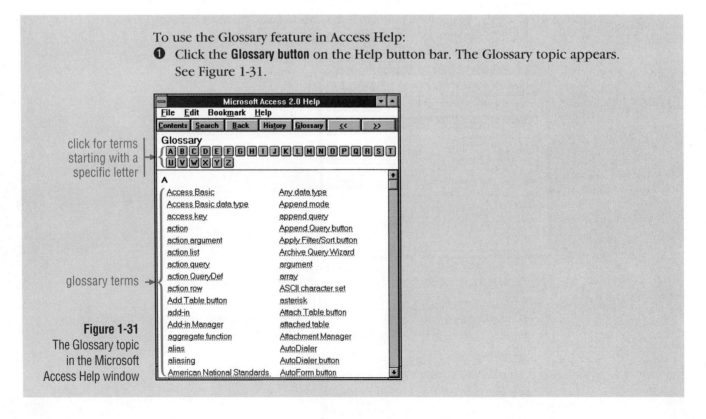

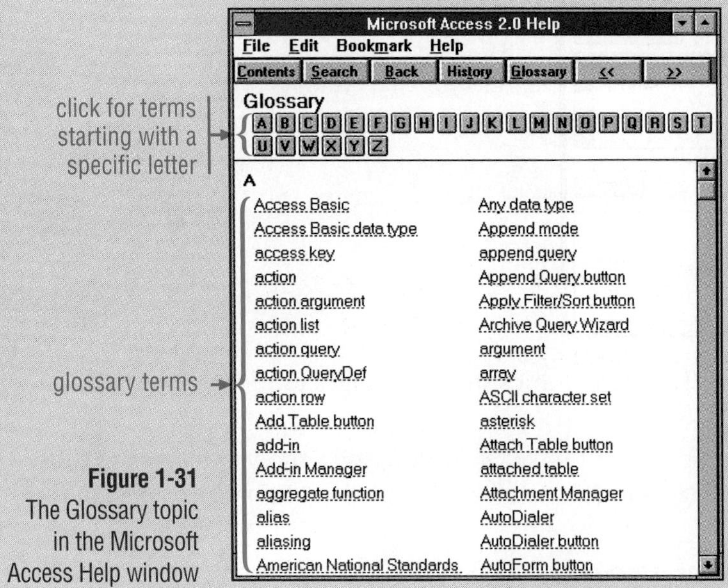

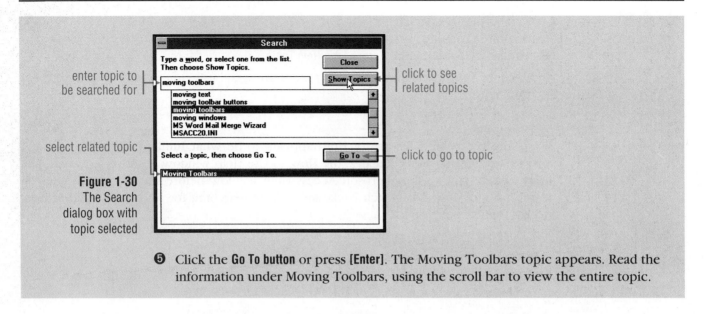

Figure 1-31 The Glossary topic in the Microsoft Access Help window

❷ Click the **S button**. Access displays the beginning of the list of terms beginning with the letter S.

❸ Scroll until the term Shortcut menu appears. Click the words **Shortcut menu**. Access displays the corresponding definition window. Read the definition.

❹ Click the words **shortcut menu** again. The definition window disappears.

Judith has the answers to her questions and is ready to exit Help.

To exit Help:

❶ Double-click the Microsoft Access Help **Control menu box**. The Help window closes.

Using Context-Sensitive Help

When you start Help by pressing [F1] instead of using the Help menu, the Microsoft Access Help window you see is **context sensitive**, which means that Access displays information that is relevant to the window or operation that is active when you start Help. If you want Help information about a particular component of an Access window, click the Help button on the toolbar instead of pressing [F1]. The mouse pointer changes to ?, which is the Help pointer. You then click the ? on the window component you want information about, and Help opens a window specific to that component.

Judith learns more about the Access toolbar by clicking the Help button.

To use context-sensitive Help on a specific window component:

❶ Click the **Help button** on the toolbar. The mouse pointer changes to ?. See Figure 1-32.

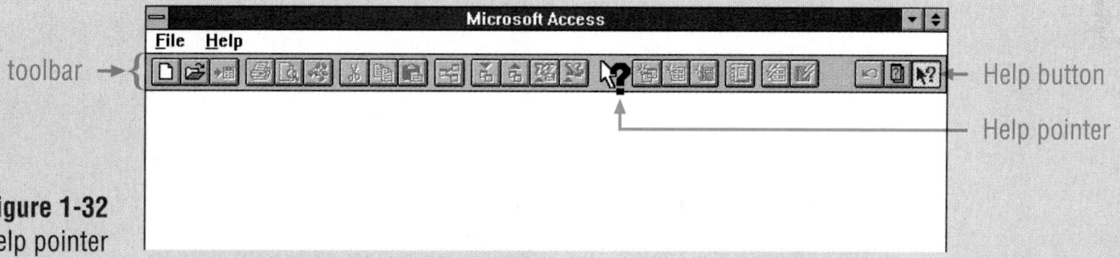

Figure 1-32
Help pointer

❷ Do not click any of the toolbar buttons. Instead, click anywhere else in the toolbar with the Help pointer. Help opens the Database Window Toolbar topic window. See Figure 1-33 on the following page.

jump with dashed underline

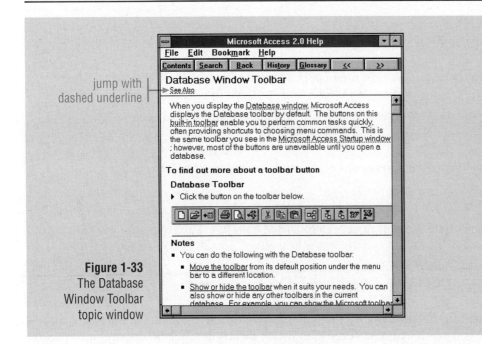

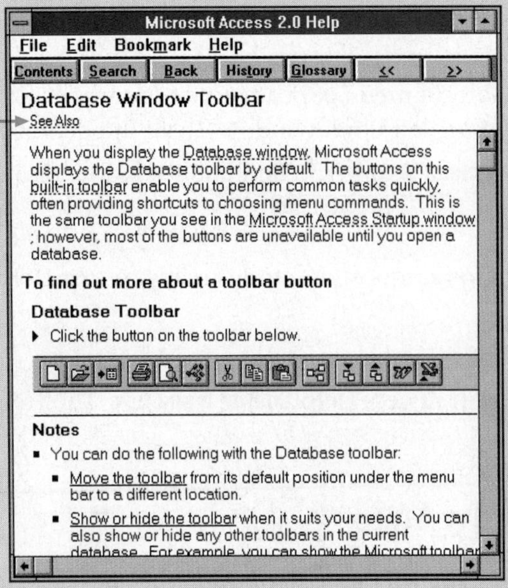

Figure 1-33
The Database Window Toolbar topic window

Judith notices the See Also jump, wonders what it means, and clicks it.

To view the See Also jump:

❶ Click the words **See Also**. Access Help displays a window containing other topics that are related to the Database Window Toolbar topic. See Figure 1-34.

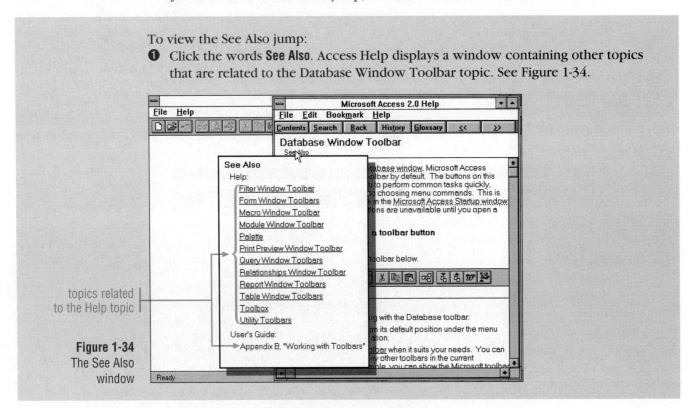

topics related to the Help topic

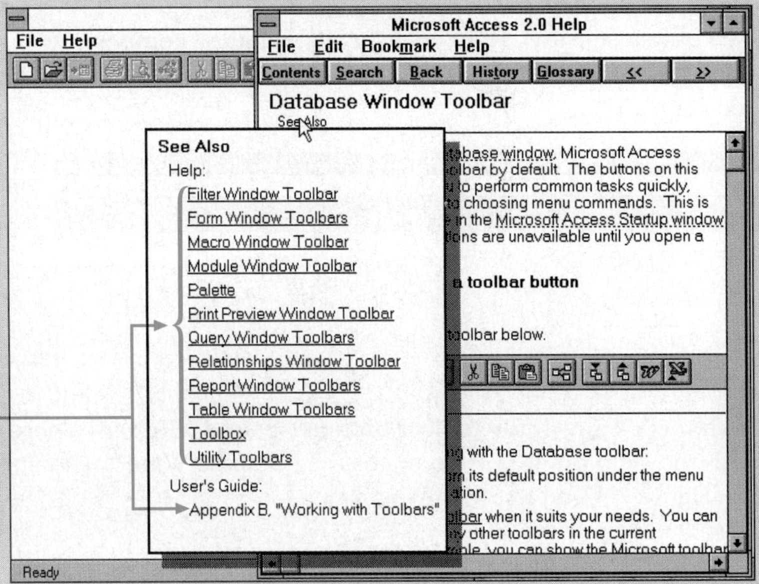

Figure 1-34
The See Also window

Her curiosity satisfied, Judith is done using Help and follows up by experimenting with Shortcut menus and moving the toolbar.

Shortcut Menus

As described in the Help glossary, a **Shortcut menu** contains a list of commands that relate to the object you click. To display a Shortcut menu window, you position the mouse pointer on a specific object or area and click the right mouse button. Using a Shortcut menu is often faster than using a menu or toolbar button.

Judith closes the Help window, opens the Vision database, and then displays a Shortcut menu.

To exit Help and open a database:

❶ Click the words **See Also** to close the jump window.

❷ Double-click the Microsoft Access Help **Control menu box** to close the Help window.

❸ Open the vision.mdb database.

Judith now opens the Shortcut menu for the table objects.

To display a Shortcut menu:

❶ Move the mouse pointer into the Database window and position it just below the last table listed.

❷ Click the right mouse button. Access displays the Shortcut menu. See Figure 1-35.

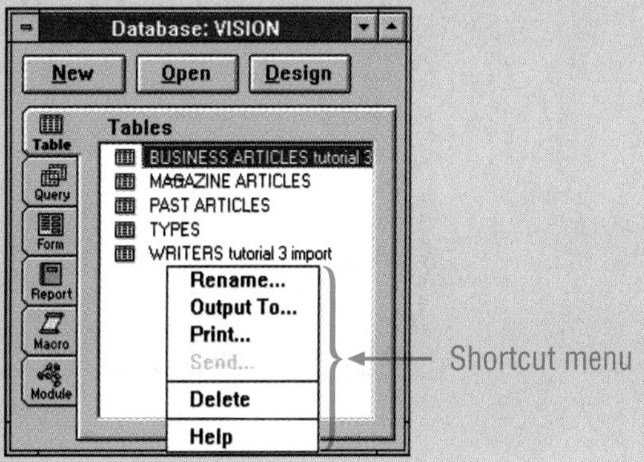

Figure 1-35
The Shortcut menu

If you select a Shortcut menu command, it applies to the highlighted table. Judith does not want to select a command, so she closes the Shortcut menu.

To close a Shortcut menu:

❶ Click the right mouse button again to close the Shortcut menu.

TROUBLE? If the Shortcut menu does not disappear, move the mouse pointer slightly outside the Shortcut menu and click the right mouse button again.

Judith experiments moving the toolbar to a different location on the screen.

Moving the Toolbar

The default location for the toolbar is just below the menu bar at the top of the screen. Most Windows software packages position the toolbar in the same location, so you do not usually want to move the toolbar to a different location on the screen. If you launch Access and find the toolbar in a location other than the default location, however, you should know how to move it back to its default location.

To move the toolbar to a different location:

1. Click anywhere in the toolbar's background but not on a toolbar button.
2. Click again in the toolbar's background and drag the toolbar to the bottom of the screen. As you drag the toolbar, the toolbar outline shows where the toolbar will be positioned if you release the mouse button. Release the mouse button when the toolbar is positioned as shown in Figure 1-36.

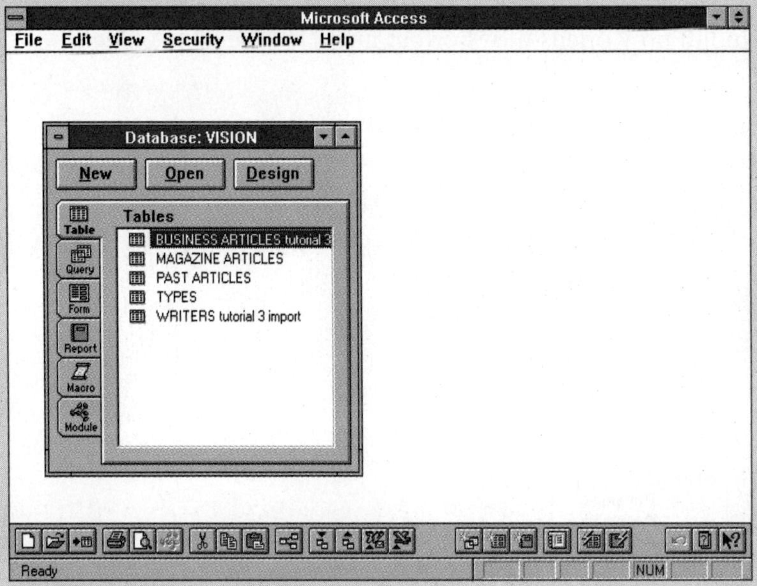

Figure 1-36 The toolbar at the bottom of the screen

Judith next moves the toolbar back to its default location. Although she could repeat the steps she previously used, Judith uses a command on the View menu instead.

To move the toolbar to its default location:

1. Click **View** and then click **Toolbars...** to display the Toolbars dialog box. See Figure 1-37.

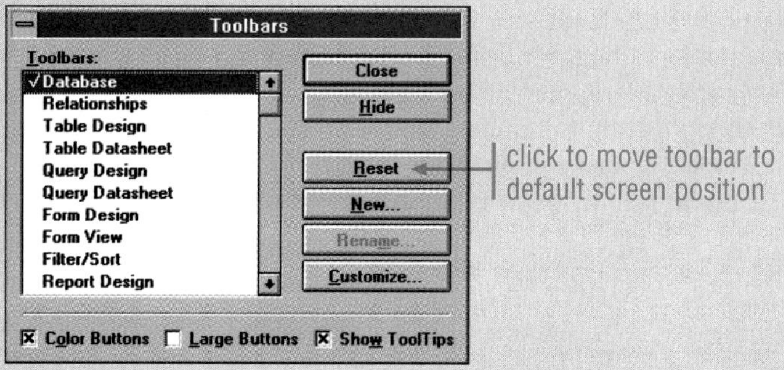

Figure 1-37 The Toolbars dialog box

❷ Be sure that Database is checked in the Toolbars list box and then click the **Reset button**. Access displays a dialog box that asks if you are sure you want to reset all changes to the toolbar.

❸ Click the **OK button** to close the dialog box. Access moves the toolbar back to its default location.

❹ Click the **Close button** in the Toolbars dialog box.

Judith is done experimenting with Access and exits Access.

To exit Access:

❶ Double-click the Microsoft Access window **Control menu box** to exit Access. Double-click the Microsoft Office group window **Control menu box** to close it. You are returned to the Program Manager.

■ ■ ■

Judith has completed her initial assignment. In the next tutorial she will meet with Brian to give him her business article selections.

Questions

1. What three steps should you generally follow when you plan to create and store a new type of data?
2. What are fields and entities, and how are they related?
3. How do you form a relationship between two tables?
4. What are the differences between a primary key and a foreign key?
5. Describe what a DBMS is designed to do.
6. What is a ToolTip?
7. What are the six different objects you can create for an Access database?
8. What do the columns and rows of a datasheet represent?

9. To which record do you advance when you use each of the four navigation buttons?
10. Which open object, the table or form object, allows you to switch between datasheet view and form view?
11. Where in Access do you find jumps, and what purpose do they serve?
12. Explain the steps for using context-sensitive Help.

Use the data in Figure 1-38 to answer Questions 13 through 18.

CHECKING ACCOUNTS table

Account Number	Name	Balance
2173	Theodore Lamont	842.27
4519	Beatrice Whalley	2071.92
8005	Benjamin Hoskins	1132.00

CHECKS table

Account Number	Check Number	Date	Amount
4519	1371	10/22/95	45.00
4519	1372	10/23/95	115.00
2173	1370	10/24/95	50.00
4519	1377	10/27/95	60.00
2173	1371	10/29/95	20.00

Figure 1-38

13. How many fields are in the CHECKING ACCOUNTS table?
14. Name the fields in the CHECKS table.
15. How many records are in the CHECKS table?
16. What is the primary key of the CHECKING ACCOUNTS table?
17. **E** What is the primary key of the CHECKS table?
18. **E** Which table has a foreign key, and what is the field name of the foreign key?

Use the Access Help feature to answer Questions 19 through 21.

19. **E** When you use the Close command on the File menu, do you need to save the changes to your data first?
20. **E** You can use the navigation buttons to move from one record to another. How can you move to a specific record number in datasheet view or form view?
21. **E** How can you print a Help topic?

Tutorial Assignments

Launch Access, open the Vision.mdb database on your Student Disk, and do the following:

1. Open the MAGAZINE ARTICLES table in the Datasheet View window.
2. Print preview the datasheet.
3. Print the last page of the datasheet.
4. Close the Datasheet View window.
5. Open the Magazine Articles form.
6. Print preview the form. What is the page number of the last page?
7. Print the last two pages of the form.
8. **E** Use Access Help with the following active windows: the Database window, the Datasheet View window, and the Print Preview window. Describe the differences you see in each situation in the initial Microsoft Access Help window.

T U T O R I A L 2

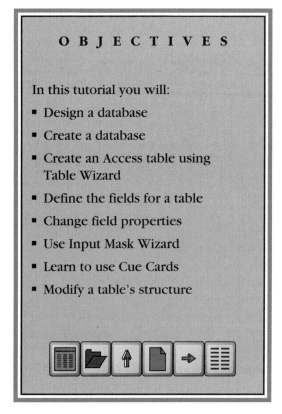

Creating Access Tables

Creating the WRITERS Table at Vision Publishers

OBJECTIVES

In this tutorial you will:

- Design a database
- Create a database
- Create an Access table using Table Wizard
- Define the fields for a table
- Change field properties
- Use Input Mask Wizard
- Learn to use Cue Cards
- Modify a table's structure

CASE

Vision Publishers Brian Murphy, Judith Rossi, and Elena Sanchez meet to exchange ideas about the cover design and article layout for the 25th-anniversary issue of *Business Perspective*. Because Elena will coordinate all production phases of the special issue, she will be in contact with writers, editors, and marketing. First, she concentrates on creating a table of all the writers.

From Judith, Elena needs information about the articles from past issues, specifically, the article title, the issue of *Business Perspective* in which the article appeared, the length of the article, and the writer name. Because she will need to phone all the writers to tell them about their inclusion in the special issue, she also needs each writer's phone number.

Brian reminds Elena that only freelancers will need to be paid for reprints of their articles. In her database design, Elena will need to indicate if the writer is a freelancer and, if so, what the reprint payment amount is.

After scanning the articles, Elena remarks that the 25 articles were written by only 13 writers and Chong Kim wrote four of them. Brian points out that the writer of "Cola Advertising War" is a different Chong Kim, so Elena realizes that a writer name is not unique. She will need to identify the writer of each article with a unique writer ID. The data that Elena recorded during the meeting is shown in Figure 2-1.

article title	writer phone number
issue of Business Perspective	is the writer a freelancer?
length of article	freelancer reprint payment amount
writer name	writer ID

Figure 2-1
Elena's data requirements

Elena knows from her previous work with databases that, before she can create her database tables on the computer, she must first design the database.

Database Design Guidelines

A database management system can be a useful tool, but only if you first carefully design your database to represent your data requirements accurately. In database design, you determine the fields, tables, and relationships needed to satisfy your data and processing requirements. Some database designs can be complicated because the underlying data requirements are complex. Most data requirements and their resulting database designs are much simpler, however, and these are the ones we will consider in the tutorials.

When you design a database, you should follow these guidelines:

- Identify all fields needed to produce the required information. For example, Elena needs information for contacting writers and for planning a magazine layout, so she listed the fields that would satisfy those informational requirements (Figure 2-1).
- Identify the entities involved in the data requirements. Recall that an entity is a person, place, object, event, or idea for which you want to store and process data. Elena's data requirements, for example, involve two entities, articles and writers. Entities usually become the names for the tables in a database.
- Group fields that describe each entity. Recall that fields are characteristics, or attributes, of entities, so it's logical to group together the characteristics of an entity. An entity and the fields that describe that entity represent a table in your database. Elena has articles and writers as entities, and she groups the fields for them under each entity name, as shown in Figure 2-2. So far, Elena's database design has an ARTICLES table and a WRITERS table.

ARTICLES	WRITERS
article title	writer ID
issue of Business Perspective	writer name
length of article	writer phone number
	is the writer a freelancer?
	freelancer reprint payment amount

Figure 2-2
Elena's fields describing each entity

- Determine each table's primary key. Recall that a primary key uniquely identifies each record in a table. Although a primary key is not mandatory in Access, it's usually a good idea to have one for each table. Without a primary key, selecting the proper record can be a problem. For example, Elena has decided to include a writer ID to identify uniquely each writer because she needs to distinguish between the two writers named Chong Kim. At this point, however, Elena does not have a primary key for the ARTICLES table. No field in the table is guaranteed to have unique field values. Even a combination of these fields cannot be guaranteed to be unique. Elena delays a final decision on a primary key for the ARTICLES table until later in the database design process.
- Include a common field in related tables. You use the common field to link one table logically with another table. For example, in the ARTICLES table Elena includes writer ID, which is the primary key for the WRITERS table. When she views a record in the ARTICLES table, writer ID serves as a foreign key. She uses the foreign key value to find the one record in the WRITERS table having that field value as a primary key. This process allows Elena to know who wrote which article. She can also find all articles written by a writer; she uses the writer ID value for that writer and searches the ARTICLES table for all articles with that writer ID value.
- Avoid data redundancy. **Data redundancy** occurs when you store the same data in more than one place. With the exception of common fields to relate tables, you should avoid redundancy. Figure 2-3 shows a correct database design for an ARTICLES table and a WRITERS table with no redundancy. The Writer ID field serves as the common field to link the two tables.

ARTICLES table

Article Title	Issue of Business Perspective	Article Length	Writer ID
Trans-Alaskan Oil Pipeline Opening	1977 JUL	803	J525
Farm Aid Abuses	1978 APR	1866	J525
Herbert A. Simon Interview	1978 DEC	1811	C200
Alternative Energy Sources	1980 JUN	2085	S260
Windfall Tax on Oil Profits	1980 APR	1497	K500
Toyota and GM Joint Venture	1983 MAR	1682	S260

WRITERS table

Writer ID	Writer Name	Writer Phone Number	Freelancer?	Reprint Payment Amount
C200	Kelly Cox	(204)783-5415	Yes	$100
J525	Leroy W. Johnson	(209)895-2046	Yes	$125
K500	Chong Kim	(807)729-5364	No	$0
S260	Wilhelm Seeger	(306)423-0932	Yes	$250

Figure 2-3
Correct database design with no redundancy

Data redundancy wastes storage space. Data redundancy can also cause inconsistencies, if, for instance, you type a field value one way in one table and a different way in the same table or in a second table. Figure 2-4 on the following page shows two examples of incorrect database design. Both designs illustrate data redundancy and the resulting waste of storage space and problem of inconsistent field values.

ARTICLES table

Article Title	Issue of Business Perspective	Article Length	Writer ID	Writer Name	Writer Phone Number	Freelancer?	Reprint Payment Amount
Trans-Alaskan Oil Pipeline Opening	1977 JUL	803	J525	Leroy W. Johnson	(209)895-2046	Yes	$125
Farm Aid Abuses	1978 APR	1866	J525	Renee Berris	(209)895-2046	Yes	$125
Herbert A. Simon Interview	1978 DEC	1811	C200	Kelly Cox	(204)783-5415	Yes	$100
Alternative Energy Sources	1980 JUN	2085	S260	Wilhelm Seeger	(306)423-0932	No	$0
Windfall Tax on Oil Profits	1980 APR	1497	K500	Chong Kim	(807)729-5364	No	$0
Toyota and GM Join Venture	1983 MAR	1682	S260	Wilhelm Seeger	(306)423-0932	Yes	$250

inconsistent data

redundancy

version 1: all data stored in one table

ARTICLES table

Article Title	Issue of Business Perspective	Article Length	Writer ID	Writer Name
Trans-Alaskan Oil Pipeline Opening	1977 JUL	803	J525	Leroy Johnson
Farm Aid Abuses	1978 APR	1866	J525	Leroy W. Jonson
Herbert A. Simon Interview	1978 DEC	1811	C200	Kellie Kox
Alternative Energy Sources	1980 JUN	2085	S260	Wilhelm Seeger
Windfall Tax on Oil Profits	1980 APR	1497	K500	Chong Kim
Toyota and GM Join Venture	1983 MAR	1682	S260	Wilhelm Seeger

inconsistent data

version 2: Writer Name redundant in ARTICLES table

WRITERS table

Writer ID	Writer Name	Writer Phone Number	Freelancer?	Reprint Payment Amount
C200	Kelly Cox	(204)783-5415	Yes	$100
J525	Leroy W. Johnson	(209)895-2046	Yes	$125
K500	Chong Kim	(807)729-5364	No	$0
S260	Wilhelm Seeger	(306)423-0932	Yes	$250

redundancy

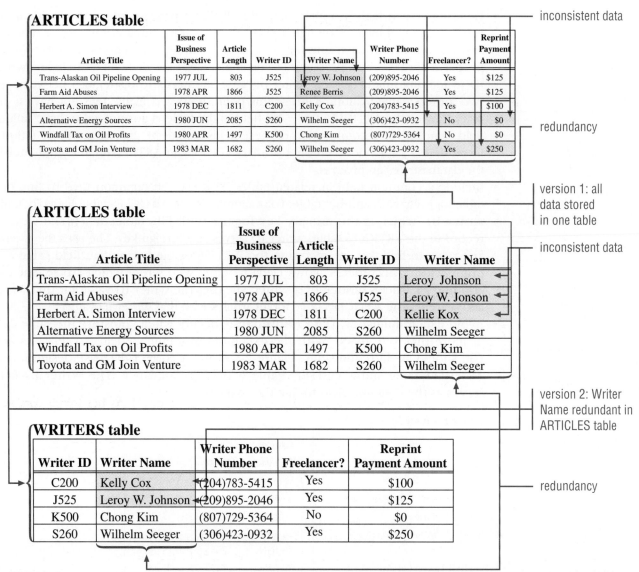

Figure 2-4
Incorrect database designs with redundancy

- Determine the properties of each field. You need to describe to the DBMS the **properties**, or characteristics, of each field, so that the DBMS knows how to store, display, and process the field. These properties include the field name, the field's maximum number of characters or digits, the field's description or explanation, and other field characteristics. For example, Elena notes that Length of Article is a field name, which has a maximum of four digits. You will learn more details about field properties later in this tutorial.

A diagram depicting the database design guidelines is shown in Figure 2-5.

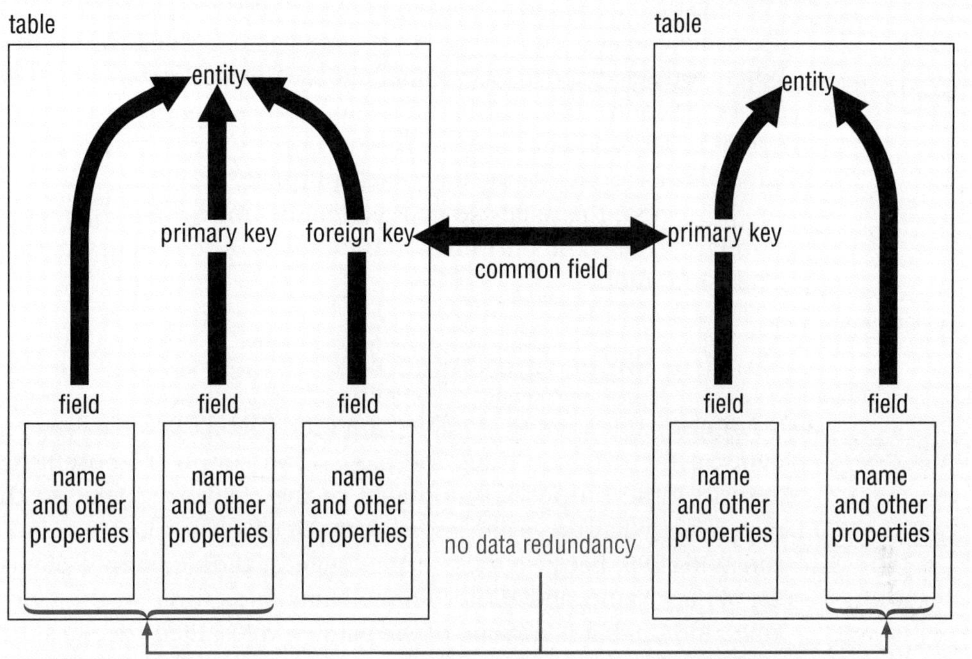

Figure 2-5
Database design guidelines

Keeping the database design guidelines in mind, Elena develops her initial database design, as shown in Figure 2-6.

<u>ARTICLES table</u>	<u>WRITERS table</u>
Article Title	Writer ID—primary key
Issue of Business Perspective	Writer Name
Length of Article	Writer Phone Number
Writer ID—foreign key	Is the Writer a Freelancer?
	Freelancer Reprint Payment Amount

Figure 2-6
Elena's initial database design

Guidelines for Creating an Access Table

In addition to following the database design guidelines, you must follow rules imposed by Access when you create a database. These rules apply to naming a database, naming fields and objects, and defining the properties of fields and objects. Rather than discuss all the property definition rules, let's initially consider the naming rules and three field-property rules.

Naming Databases

You must name each database you create. Access stores the database as a file on disk with the name you choose. You use that same name in the future when you open the database. When you select a database name, choose a descriptive name that will remind you of the database's purpose or contents. Vision Publishers' database is named Vision because it contains the company's data. Elena chooses for her new database the name Issue25, which is descriptive of the database's purpose.

In Access, the database name contains up to eight characters and must conform to standard DOS conventions for filenames. Access automatically adds the filename extension .mdb.

Naming Fields and Objects

You must name each field, table, and other object in a database. Access then stores these items in the database using the names you supply. Choose a field or object name that describes the purpose or contents of the field or object, so that later you can easily remember what the name represents. Elena names her two tables BUSINESS ARTICLES and WRITERS, because these names suggest their contents. Similarly, she chooses Writer ID, Writer Name, and Writer Phone Number as three of the field names in the WRITERS table. Although it is not one of the naming rules, Elena decides that identifying her critical tables might be easier if she uses a convention of all uppercase letters for table names and an appropriate mix of uppercase and lowercase for field names and the names of other database objects.

One set of rules applies to the naming of fields and objects:

- They can be up to 64 characters long.
- They can contain letters, numbers, spaces, and special characters except a period, exclamation mark, and square brackets.
- They must not start with a space.

Assigning Field Descriptions

When you define a field, you can assign an optional description for the field. If you choose a descriptive field name, you probably do not need to supply a description. Because, for example, Elena selected the descriptive field names Writer Name and Writer Phone Number, she does not plan to enter a description for these fields. For the Writer ID field in the BUSINESS ARTICLES table, however, Elena plans to assign the description "foreign key."

The field description can be up to 255 characters long. If you enter a description, choose one that explains the purpose or usage of the field.

Assigning Field Data Types

You must assign a data type for each field. The **data type** determines what field values you can enter for that field and what other properties the field will have. For example, Elena's Length of Article field is a number, so she tells Access that the field has the number data type. Access will allow Elena to enter only numbers as values for the field and will enable her to perform calculations on the field values.

In Access, you assign one of the following eight data types to each field:

- The **text data type** allows field values containing letters, digits, spaces, and special characters. Text fields can be up to 255 characters long. You should assign the text data type to fields in which you will store names, addresses, and descriptions, and to fields containing digits that are not used in calculations. Elena, for example, assigns the text data type to the Writer ID field; the Writer Name field; and the Writer Phone Number field, which contains digits not used in calculations.
- The **memo data type**, like the text data type, allows field values containing letters, digits, spaces, and special characters. Memo fields, however, can be up to 64,000 characters long and are used for long comments or explanations. Elena does not plan to assign the memo data type to any of her fields.
- The **number data type** limits field values to digits, an optional leading sign (+ or –), and an optional decimal point. Use the number data type for fields that you will use in calculations, except calculations involving money. Elena assigns the number data type to the Length of Article field in the BUSINESS ARTICLES table.
- The **date/time data type** allows field values containing valid dates and times only. Usually you enter dates in mm/dd/yy format, where mm is a two-digit month, dd is a two-digit day of the month, and yy are the last two digits of the year. This data type also permits other date formats and a variety of time formats. When using this data type, you can perform calculations on dates and times and you can sort them. The number of days between two dates, for example, can be determined. Elena does not assign the date/time data type to any of her fields.
- The **currency data type** allows field values similar to those for the number data type. Unlike calculations with number data type decimal values, calculations performed using the currency data type match to the penny exactly. Elena assigns the currency data type to the Freelancer Reprint Payment Amount field in the WRITERS table.
- The **counter data type** consists of integers that are values automatically controlled by Access. Access enters a value of 1 for the field in the first record of a table and adds 1 for each successive record's field value. This guarantees a unique field value, so that such a field can serve as a table's primary key. Elena does not assign the counter data type to any of her fields.
- The **yes/no data type** limits field values to yes and no entries. Use this data type for fields that indicate the presence or absence of a condition, such as whether an order has been filled, or if an employee is eligible for the company dental plan. Elena assigns the yes/no data type to the Is the Writer a Freelancer? field in the WRITERS table.
- The **OLE object data type** allows field values that are created in other software packages as objects, such as photographs, video images, graphics, drawings, sound recordings, voice-mail messages, spreadsheets, and word processing documents. **OLE** is an acronym for object linking and embedding. You can either import the object or link to the object, but you cannot modify it in Access. Elena does not assign the OLE object data type to any of her fields.

Assigning Field Sizes

The **field size** property defines a field value's maximum storage size for text and number fields only. The other data types have no field size property, because their storage size is either a fixed, predetermined amount or is variable, as shown in Figure 2-7 on the following page. You should still document every field's maximum size, however, so that you allow enough room for it on entry screens and on reports and other outputs, without wasting space.

Data Type	Storage Size
Text	1 to 255 bytes 50 bytes default
Memo	64,000 maximum exact size depends on field value
Number	1 to 8 bytes 8 bytes default
Date/Time	8 bytes
Currency	8 bytes
Counter	4 bytes
Yes/no	1 bit
OLE object	1 gigabyte maximum exact size depends on object size

Figure 2-7
Data type storage sizes

A text field has a default field size of 50 characters. You set its field size by entering a number in the range 1 to 255. You select the field size for a number field from the five choices of byte, integer, long integer, double, and single, as shown in Figure 2-8. Double is the default field size for a number field.

Field Size	Storage Size (Bytes)	Number Type	Field Values Allowed
Byte	1	Integer	0 to 255
Integer	2	Integer	-32,768 to 32,767
Long Integer	4	Integer	-2,147,483,648 to 2,147,483,647
Double	8	Decimal	15 significant digits
Single	4	Decimal	7 significant digits

Figure 2-8
Number data type field size

Elena's Writer ID field is a text field that is always exactly four characters long, so she documents its field size as 4. Writer Name is also a text field, but each field value varies in size. After studying the different field values, she finds that a field size of 25 will accommodate the largest field value for the Writer Name field. In a similar fashion, Elena determines the field size for the other fields in her database.

Creating an Access Table

Before you create a database and its objects on the computer, you should spend time carefully documenting your data requirements. You must understand, and accurately represent, the structure of each table in the database.

Planning the Table Structure

Now that you have learned the guidelines for designing databases and creating Access tables, you are ready to work with Elena to create the Issue25 database. Elena first develops the structure of the WRITERS and BUSINESS ARTICLES tables. For each field, she documents the field name and its data type, input/display field size, and description (Figure 2-9).

	Data Type	Input/Display Field Size	Description
WRITERS table			
Writer ID	text	4	primary key
Writer Name	text	25	
Writer Phone Number	text	14	(999) 999-9999 format
Is the Writer a Freelancer?	yes/no	3	
Freelancer Reprint Payment Amount	currency	4	$250 maximum
BUSINESS ARTICLES table			
Article Title	text	44	
Issue of Business Perspective	text	8	
Length of Article	number	4	integer field size
Writer ID	text	4	foreign key

Figure 2-9
Elena's table structures for the WRITERS and BUSINESS ARTICLES tables

With the exception of some new information, the file structures for these two tables are consistent with the planning Elena has done so far. The five fields in the WRITERS table are Writer ID, Writer Name, Writer Phone Number, Is the Writer a Freelancer? and Freelancer Reprint Payment Amount. The four fields in the BUSINESS ARTICLES table are Article Title, Issue of Business Perspective, Length of Article, and Writer ID. Six of these nine fields are text fields, while Is the Writer a Freelancer? is a yes/no field, Freelancer Reprint Payment Amount is a currency field, and Length of Article is a number field.

Elena needs to choose field sizes only for text and number fields. However, she decides that documenting the maximum field sizes for all data types will help her plan how many positions each field requires for input and for screen and report display. For this purpose, she includes a column labeled Input/Display Field Size. Freelancers will receive $250 at most for their articles, so she plans a field size of four for the Freelancer Reprint Payment Amount currency field.

Finally, she adds descriptions for Length of Article to remind her of its field size, for Writer Phone Number to specify its format, and for Freelancer Reprint Payment Amount to document its format and size.

Creating a Database

Having completed the planning for her table structures, Elena creates the database named Issue25. When you create a database, you give it a unique eight-character name that conforms to standard DOS conventions for filenames. Access stores the database by that name as a file on disk with an .mdb extension. A new Access database uses 64KB of disk space. Most of this is used when you add your first fields, tables, and other objects. As your database grows in size and needs more disk storage, Access increases its size in 32KB increments.

REFERENCE WINDOW

Creating a Database

- Click the New Database button on the toolbar. The New Database dialog box appears.
- With the File Name text box highlighted, type the name of the database you want to create. Do not press [Enter] yet.
- Change the drive and directory information, if necessary.
- Click the OK button or press [Enter] to accept the changes in the New Database dialog box.

Let's create the Issue25 database. If you have not done so, launch Access before you follow the next set of steps.

To create a database:

1. Click the **New Database button** on the toolbar in the Microsoft Access window. Access displays the New Database dialog box. See Figure 2-10. The File Name text box highlights the default name, db1.mdb.

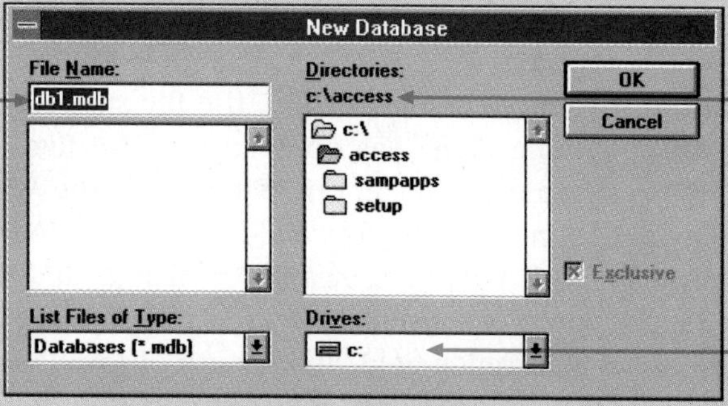

Figure 2-10 Initial New Database dialog box

2. Type **issue25** in the File Name text box. Click the **down arrow button** on the right side of the Drives box. A list of available drives drops down. Click the letter of the drive in which you put your Student Disk. See Figure 2-11. Your drive might be different.

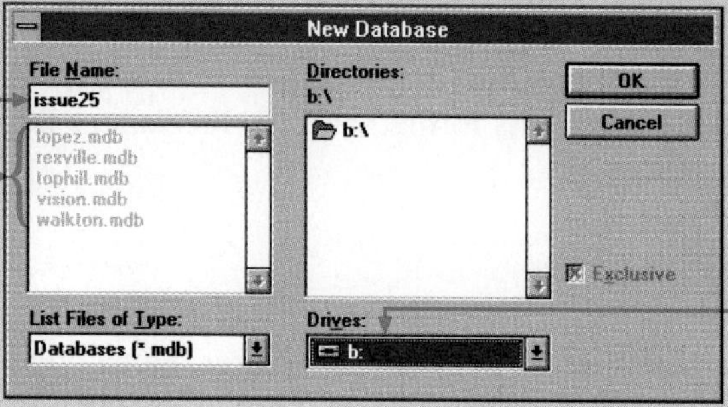

Figure 2-11 Completed New Database dialog box

TROUBLE? If the contents of the File Name text box do not show issue25, the text box might not have been highlighted when you began typing. If this is the case, highlight the contents of the text box and retype issue25.

❸ Click the **OK button** to let Access know you have completed the New Database dialog box. Access creates the Issue25 database, adding the extension .mdb, and opens the Database window. See Figure 2-12. Because this is a new database, no tables appear in the Tables list box.

click to create a new table

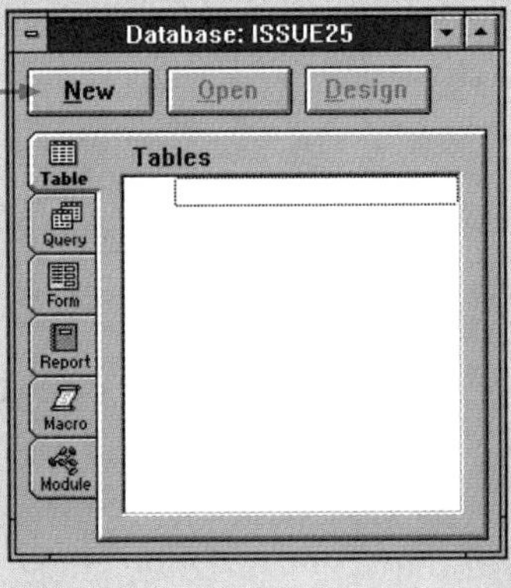

Figure 2-12 The Database window for a new database

Creating the Table Structure with Table Wizard

Having created her new database, Elena's next step is to create the WRITERS table structure. Creating a table structure consists of creating a table and defining the fields for the table. Therefore, Elena will create the WRITERS table and define its fields: Writer ID, Writer Name, Writer Phone Number, Is the Writer a Freelancer? and Freelancer Reprint Payment Amount.

In Access, you can keyboard the fields for a table or use Table Wizard to automate the table creation process. A **Wizard** is an Access tool that helps you create objects such as tables and reports by asking you a series of questions and then creating the objects based on your answers. **Table Wizard** asks you questions about your table and then creates the table based on your answers. Whether you use Table Wizard or keyboard the table fields, you can change a table's design after it is created.

Elena uses Table Wizard to create the WRITERS table.

To activate Table Wizard:

❶ Click the **New command button** in the Database window. Access displays the New Table dialog box. See Figure 2-13.

click to use Table Wizard to create a table

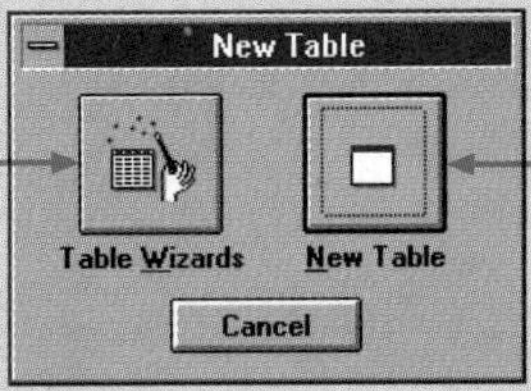

click to create your own table

Figure 2-13 The New Table dialog box

❷ Click the **Table Wizards button**. The first Table Wizard dialog box appears. See Figure 2-14 on the following page.

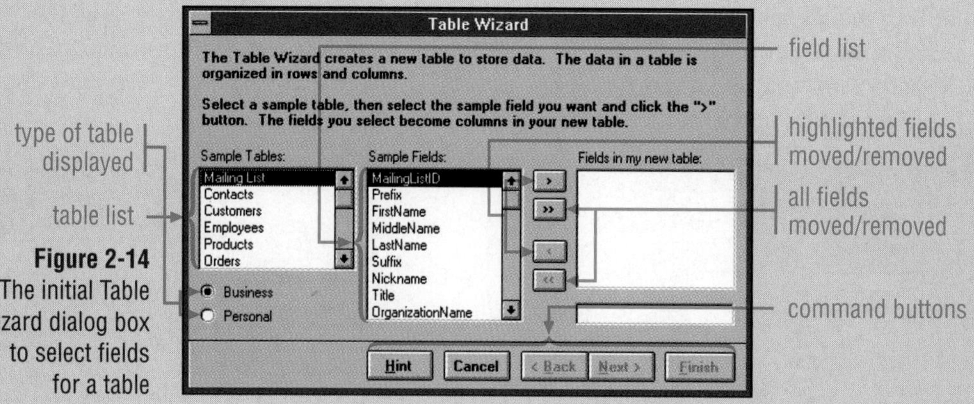

Figure 2-14
The initial Table Wizard dialog box to select fields for a table

In the first Table Wizard dialog box, you select the fields for your table from sample fields in dozens of sample tables. The sample tables include those for business and personal use; simply click the Business or Personal radio button to display the corresponding list of sample tables. Scroll through the Sample Tables list until you find an appropriate table and then select fields to add to your table from the Sample Fields list. If necessary, you can select fields from more than one table. Do not be concerned about selecting field names that exactly match the ones you need because you can change the names later. Instead, select fields that seem like they have the general properties you need for your fields. If a field's properties do not exactly match, you can change the properties later.

You select fields in the order you want them to appear in your table. If you want to select fields one at a time, highlight a field by clicking it, and then click the > button. If you want to select all the fields, click the >> button. The fields appear in the list box on the right as you select them. If you make a mistake, click the << button to remove all the fields from the list box on the right or highlight a field and click the < button to remove fields one at a time.

At the bottom of each Table Wizard dialog box is a set of command buttons. These command buttons allow you to move quickly to other Table Wizard dialog boxes, to cancel the table creation process, and to display hints. You can display a hint for a Table Wizard dialog box by clicking the Hint command button. After reading the hint, click OK to remove the hint and continue with your work.

Elena selects fields from the Mailing List sample table to create the WRITERS table.

To select fields for a new table:

1. If Mailing List is not highlighted in the Sample Tables list box, click it, so that it is highlighted. Click **MailingListID** in the Sample Fields list box and then click the **> button**. Access places MailingListID into the list box on the right as the first field in the new table.

2. In order, select LastName, HomePhone, MembershipStatus, and DuesAmount for the WRITERS table by clicking the field name in the Sample Fields list box, scrolling as needed, and then clicking the **> button**.

Elena has selected all the fields she needs for her table, so she continues through the remaining Table Wizard dialog boxes to finish creating the WRITERS table.

To finish creating a table using Table Wizard:

1. Click the **Next > button**. Access displays the second Table Wizard dialog box.
2. Type **WRITERS** in the text box and then click the **radio button** beside "Set the primary key myself." See Figure 2-15.

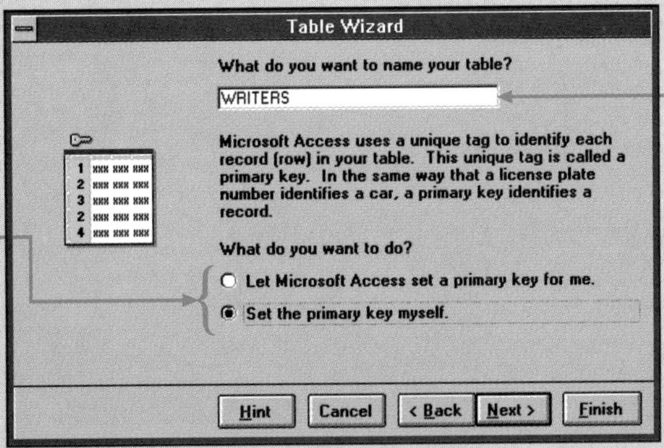

Figure 2-15 Choosing a table name and primary key option

3. Click the **Next > button**. Access displays the third Table Wizard dialog box.
4. Let MailingListID remain in the text box at the top of the dialog box and click the **bottom radio button**, so that the primary key will contain "Numbers and/or letters I enter when I add new records." You have now selected MailingListID as the primary key for the table. See Figure 2-16.

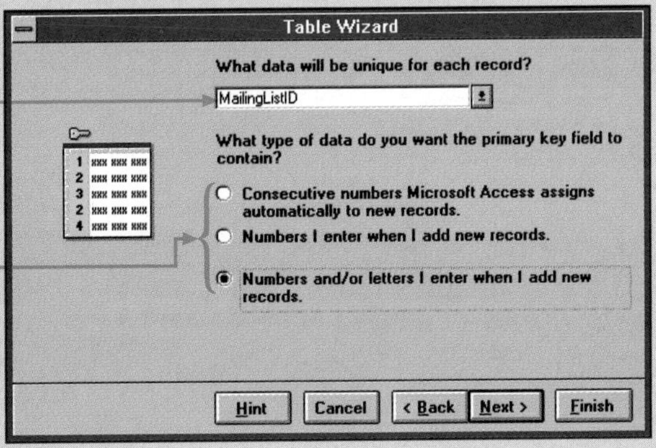

Figure 2-16 Choosing a primary key

5. Click the **Next > button**. Access displays the final Table Wizard dialog box.

Elena needs to change the field names and other field properties for the sample fields inserted into the WRITERS table by Table Wizard, so that they agree with her table design. To make these changes she must modify the table design. First, she must exit Table Wizard.

To exit Table Wizard:

1. Be sure that the "Modify the table design" radio button is on and that the Cue Cards box at the bottom is unchecked. See Figure 2-17 on the following page.

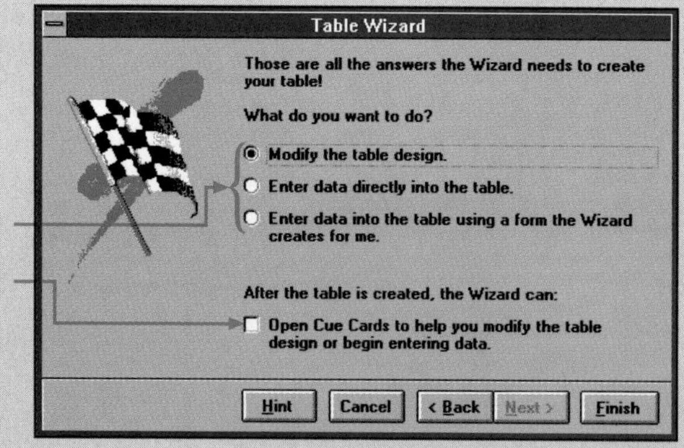

Figure 2-17
The final Table Wizard dialog box

❷ Click the **Finish button**. Access closes the final Table Wizard dialog box and opens the Table Design View window. See Figure 2-18.

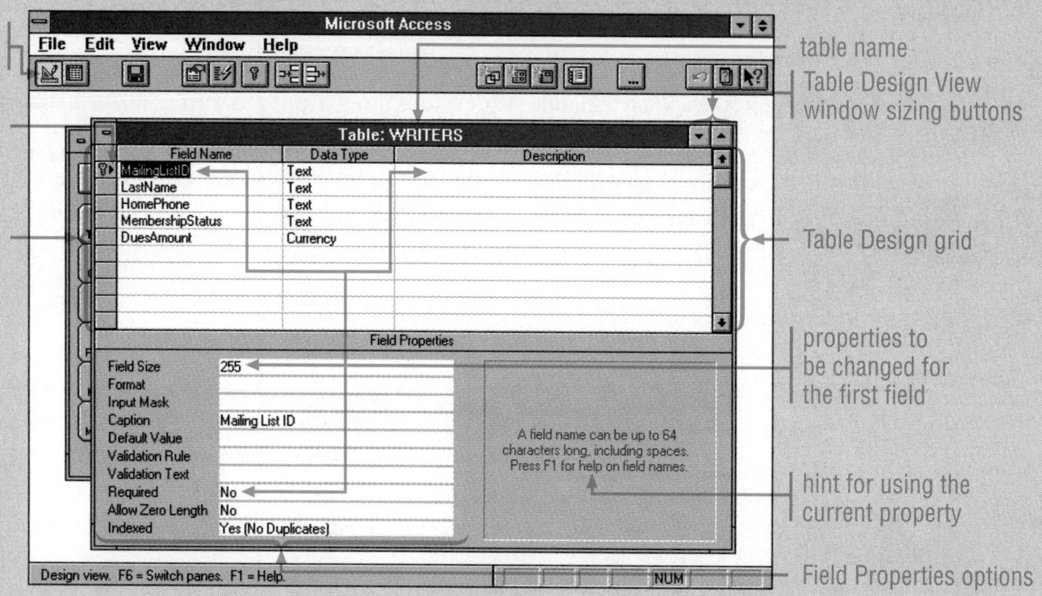

Figure 2-18
The Table Design View window

Changing the Sample Field Properties

You use the Table Design View window to define or modify a table structure or the properties for the fields in a table. If you create a table without using Table Wizard, you enter the fields and their properties for your table directly in this window.

Initially, the Design View button on the toolbar is selected, the table name appears in the Table Design View window title bar, the first field name is highlighted, and the current row symbol is positioned in the first row selector of the Table Design grid. When you click a row selector, Access highlights the entire row and moves the current row symbol to that row. If you click a field name, data type, or description for a different field, Access moves the current row symbol to that row but does not highlight the entire row.

A hint for using the current property appears in the lower-right corner of the Table Design View window. As you press [Tab] or click a different property, the hint changes to define or explain the new property. If the hint does not answer your questions about the property, press [F1] for a full explanation.

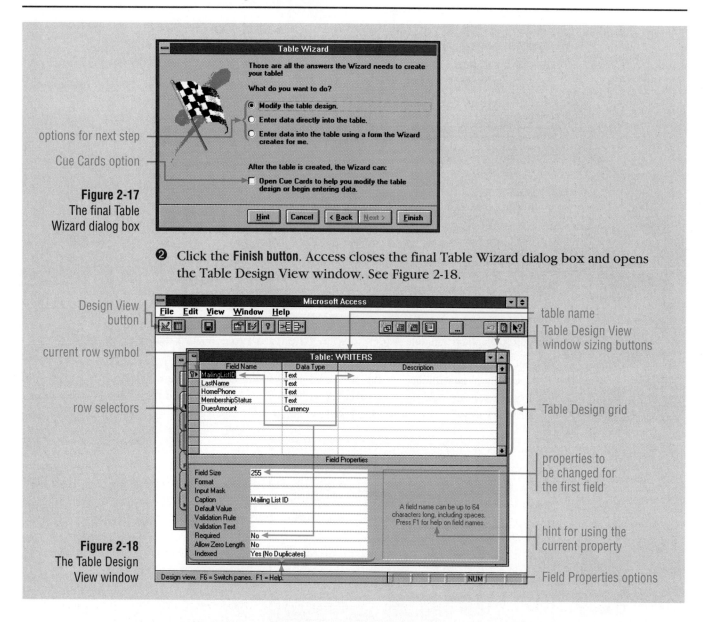

The field name, data type, and description field properties appear in the top half of the Table Design View window. In the Field Properties sheet, which appears in the lower-left corner of the window, you view and change other properties for the current field. For example, in the property sheet you can change the size of a text field or the number of decimal places for a number field. The Field Properties displayed are appropriate for the data type of the currently selected field.

For the first field, Elena changes the field name to Writer ID, the Field Size property to 4, the Required property to Yes, and adds "primary key" as a description.

To change the first field's properties:

1. If MailingListID is not highlighted in the first row of the Field Name column, double-click it. Then type **Writer ID** to replace the highlighted MailingListID and press **[Tab]** twice to move the I to the Description box.
2. Type **primary key** as the Description for the first field.
3. Double-click **255** in the Field Size property box to highlight it and then type **4**.
4. Click **Mailing List ID** in the Caption property box, press **[F2]** to highlight it, and then press **[Del]** to delete it.
5. Click anywhere in the **Required property text box** and then click the **down arrow button** that appears in that box to display the Required list box. Click **Yes** in the Required list box to choose that as the property value.

Setting the **Required property** to Yes for a field means you must enter a value in the field for every record in the table. Every primary-key field should have the Required property set to Yes, so that each record has a unique value. Fields other than a primary key usually have the Required property set to No, which is the default value.

The Caption property allows you to use a **caption**, which is text that replaces the default field name in the datasheet column heading box and in the label on a form. Elena deletes all Caption property values because they do not represent the new field names she will use.

Elena next changes some of the properties for each of the remaining fields in the WRITERS table. If you make a mistake in typing a field name or description value, click that box, press [F2] to select the entire property value, and retype the value.

To change the properties of the remaining fields:

1. Double-click **LastName** in the second row's Field Name text box and type **Writer Name**. Double-click **50** in the Field Size property box to highlight it and then type **25**. Finally, click **Last Name** in the Caption property box, press **[F2]** to highlight it, and then press **[Del]** to delete it.
2. Double-click **HomePhone** in the third row's Field Name text box and type **Writer Phone Number**. Press **[Tab]** twice and type **(999) 999-9999 format** in the Description text box. Double-click **30** in the Field Size property box to highlight it and then type **14**. Finally, click **Home Phone** in the Caption property box, press **[F2]** to highlight it, and then press **[Del]** to delete it.
3. Double-click **MembershipStatus** in the fourth row's Field Name text box and type **Is the Writer a Freelancer?** Press **[Tab]** and then click the **down arrow button** in the Data Type text box to display the Data Type list box. See Figure 2-19 on the following page.

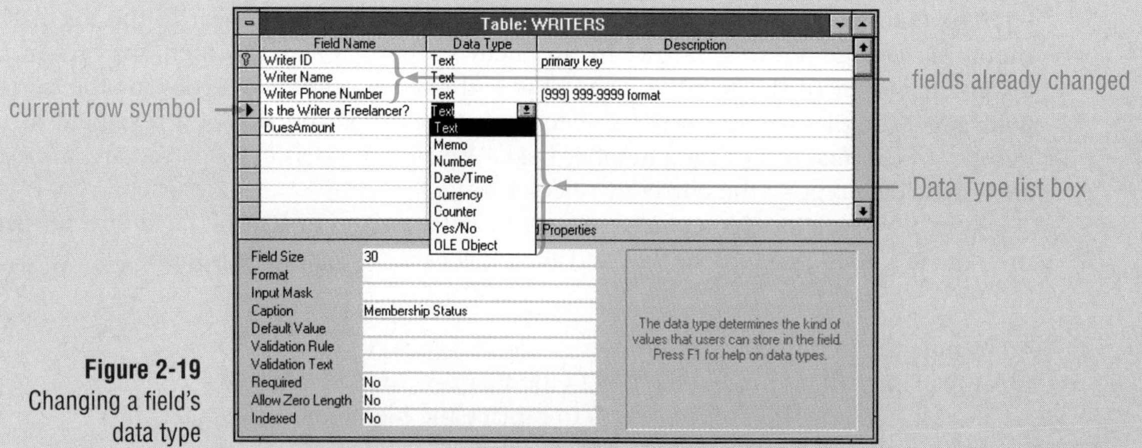

Figure 2-19 Changing a field's data type

4. Click **Yes/No** in the Data Type list box to choose that data type. Click **Membership Status** in the Caption property box, press **[F2]** to highlight it, and then press **[Del]** to delete it.

5. Double-click **DuesAmount** in the fifth row's Field Name text box, type **Freelancer Reprint Payment Amount**, press **[Tab]**, and then type **cu** in the Data Type box. "Currency" replaces the "cu" you typed in the Data Type box.

6. Press **[Tab]**, and then type **$250 maximum** to enter the field's Description property. Click **Dues Amount** in the Caption property box, press **[F2]** to highlight it, and then press **[Del]** to delete it. See Figure 2-20.

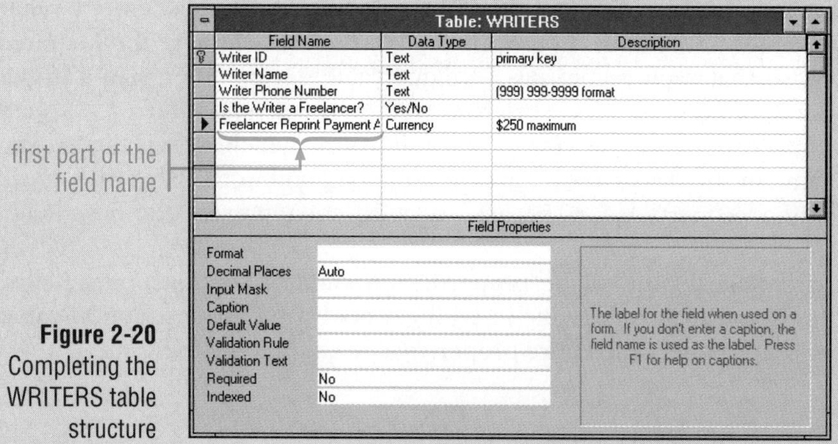

Figure 2-20 Completing the WRITERS table structure

Instead of selecting a field's data type by clicking one of the choices in the Data Type list box, you can type the entire data type in the field's Data Type box. Alternatively, type just the first character—or the first two characters for currency and counter—of the data type to select that data type.

Field names can be up to 64 characters long. However, the Field Name text box is not wide enough to show an entire long name. Freelancer Reprint Payment Amount is an example of a long field name.

Saving the Table Structure

Elena has finished defining and changing the WRITERS table structure, so she saves the table. When you first create a table, you save the table with its field definitions to add the table structure permanently to your database. If you use Table Wizard, Access saves your table before you switch to the Table Design View window. Elena saves the table, so that her field property changes are retained in the database.

To save a table:

1. Click the **Save button** on the toolbar. Access saves the WRITERS table on your Student Disk.

Switching to the Datasheet View Window

Once you have defined a table, you can view the table in either the Table Design View window or the Datasheet View window. Use the Table Design View window to view or change a table's fields, and use the Datasheet View window to view or change the field values and records stored in a table. Even though she has not yet entered field values and records in the WRITERS table, Elena displays the WRITERS table in the Datasheet View window. She wants to study the datasheet to determine if she needs to make further changes to the table structure.

To switch from the Table Design View window to the Datasheet View window:

1. Click the **Datasheet View button** on the toolbar. Access displays the Datasheet View window for the WRITERS table. See Figure 2-21.

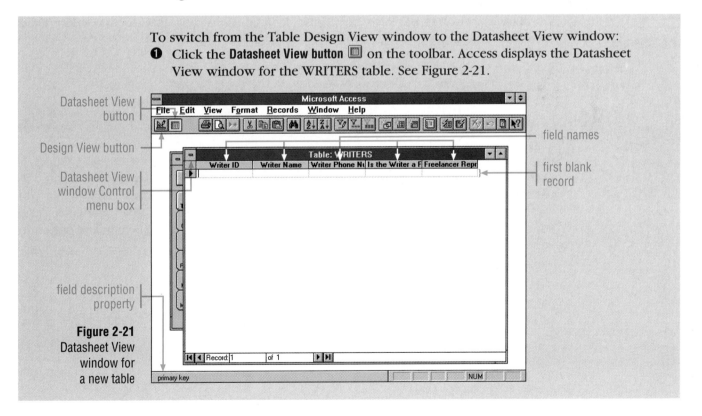

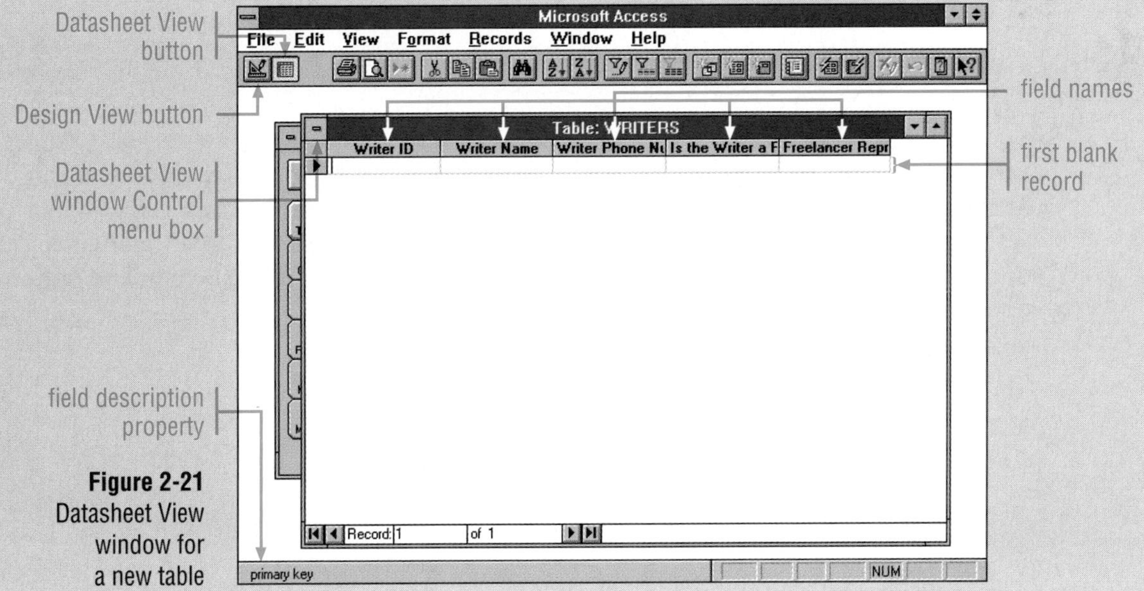

Figure 2-21 Datasheet View window for a new table

Elena notices that the description property for Writer ID appears in the status bar. Also, the first record has no field values. Thus, no records exist for the new WRITERS table. This is correct because Elena has not yet entered field values in the table.

Elena sees two problems in the Datasheet View window of the WRITERS table that she wants to correct. First, the field names Writer Phone Number, Is the Writer a Freelancer? and Freelancer Reprint Payment Amount are only partially displayed, and their field value boxes are wider than they need to be to accommodate the field values that will be entered. Second, the Writer Name field value box is too narrow to display the entire field value.

Printing a Datasheet

Before making any changes, Elena prints the datasheet for the WRITERS table, so that she can refer to it when she makes the field changes to correct the problems she discovered.

To print the datasheet:

1. Click the **Print button** on the toolbar to open the Print dialog box.
2. Check the Printer section of the Print dialog box to make sure your computer's printer is selected. Click the **OK button** to initiate printing. After the message box disappears, Access returns you to the Datasheet View window.

Elena switches back to the Table Design View window to make her field property changes.

To switch from the Datasheet View window to the Table Design View window:

1. Click the **Design View button** on the toolbar. Access again displays the Table Design View window for the WRITERS table.

If you want to take a break and resume the tutorial at a later time, you can exit Access by double-clicking the Microsoft Access window Control menu box. When you resume the tutorial, place your Student Disk in the appropriate drive, launch Access, open the Issue25 database on your Student Disk, and click the Design command button to open the Table Design View window for the WRITERS table.

■ ■ ■

Changing Field Properties

The first changes Elena makes are to shorten the field names for Writer Phone Number and Is the Writer a Freelancer? The field name for Freelancer Reprint Payment Amount is also too wide to fit in the datasheet column heading box. Rather than change the field name, however, Elena uses its Caption property to replace the default field name in the datasheet column heading box and in the label on a form. You use the Caption property to display a shorter version of a longer, more descriptive table field name.

Changing Field Names and Entering Captions

Let's change the names for the fields Writer Phone Number and Is the Writer a Freelancer?

To change a table field name in the Table Design View window:

❶ Double-click **Number** in the Field Name box for Writer Phone Number to highlight it. Press **[Backspace]** twice to leave Writer Phone as the new field name.

❷ Click anywhere in the Field Name box for Is the Writer a Freelancer? and then press **[F2]** to highlight the entire field name.

❸ Type **Freelancer** to make it the new field name.

Suppose you make a change that you immediately realize is a mistake. You can click the **Undo button** on the toolbar to cancel your change. Not all changes can be undone; the Undo button is dimmed in those cases.

Let's make a field name change to Writer Name that we will immediately undo.

To undo a change:

❶ Click anywhere in the Field Name box for Writer Name and then press **[F2]** to select the entire field name. Type **Amount**, which becomes the new field name.

❷ Click the **Undo button**. Access restores the previous field name, Writer Name.

Having completed her field name changes, Elena enters a caption for Freelancer Reprint Payment Amount.

To enter a caption:

❶ Click anywhere in the Field Name box for Freelancer Reprint Payment Amount. The current row symbol moves to the Freelancer Reprint Payment Amount row, and the Field Properties options apply to this current field. Click the **Caption text box** and then type **Amount**. See Figure 2-22.

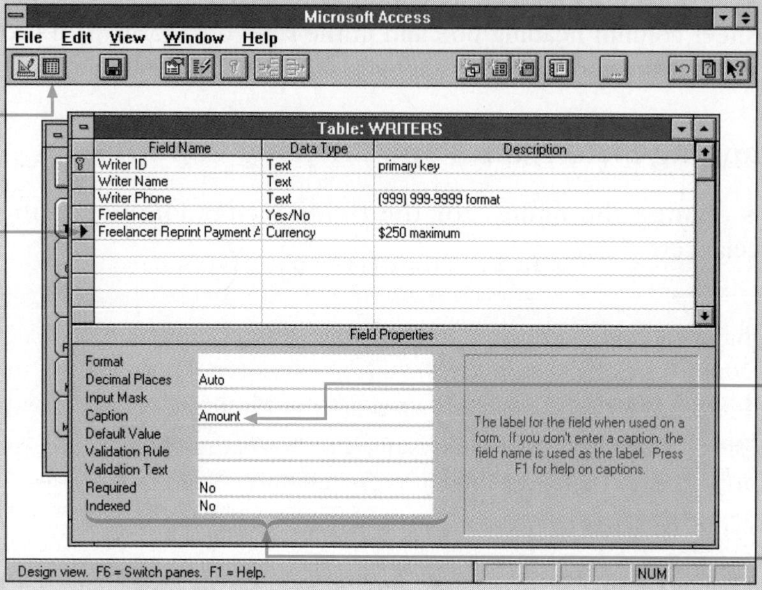

Figure 2-22
Entering a Caption property for a field

Elena switches to the Datasheet View window to review the effects of the changes she's made so far.

To switch to the Datasheet View window:

❶ Click the **Datasheet View button** on the toolbar. Access displays the "Save now?" dialog box. See Figure 2-23.

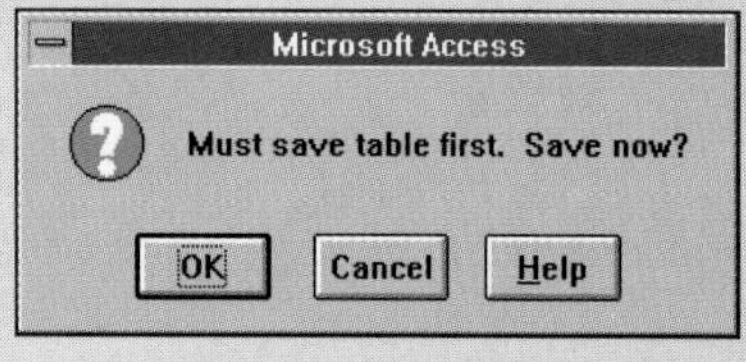

Figure 2-23
The "Save now?" dialog box

Access makes your table structure changes permanent only when you take action to save the changes or to close the Table Design View window. Switching to the Datasheet View window first involves closing the Table Design View window, so Access displays the dialog box to ask you about saving your table changes. If you want to keep the Table Design View window open and continue making table structure changes, click the **Cancel button**. If you would rather switch to the Datasheet View window, you need to save your changes first.

❷ Click the **OK button**. Access saves your table structure changes, closes the Table Design View window, and opens the Datasheet View window. See Figure 2-24.

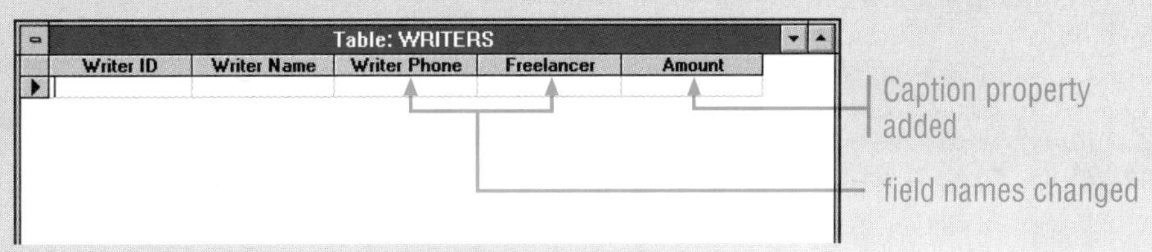

Figure 2-24 Reviewing file structure changes in the Datasheet View window

Elena reviews the changes she has made to the WRITERS table structure. The two new field names, Writer Phone and Freelancer, appear; and the Amount caption replaces the Freelancer Reprint Payment Amount field name. Elena is still bothered by the column widths in some of the fields in the datasheet, so she changes them.

Resizing Columns in a Datasheet

There are often several ways to accomplish a task in Access. For example, you can close a database by double-clicking the Database window Control menu box; by clicking File and then clicking Close Database; or by pressing and holding [Alt] and then pressing [F], then releasing both keys, and then pressing [C]. Elena has been choosing the simplest and fastest method to accomplish her tasks and has not spent time experimenting with alternative methods. However, Elena has never resized datasheet columns before, so she wants to practice three different techniques.

Let's first resize a datasheet column using the Format menu.

To resize datasheet columns using the Format menu:

❶ Click anywhere in the **Writer ID column**, click **Format**, and then click **Column Width...**. Access opens the Column Width dialog box. See Figure 2-25. Access has automatically selected the default, standard column width of 18.8 positions and has checked the Standard Width check box.

Figure 2-25 The Column Width dialog box

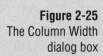

❷ Type **11** and then click the **OK button**. The Column Width dialog box disappears, and Access resizes the Writer ID column from 18.8 to 11 positions.

Changing a datasheet column width does not change the field size for the table field. The standard column width of 18.8 positions is approximately 1" wide on the screen. The actual number of characters you can place in a column depends on the typeface and font size you are using. Elena chooses not to change the typeface and font size.

Elena resizes the Writer Name field with a second resizing method, which uses the mouse pointer to drag the column's right edge. To resize this way, you must first position the mouse pointer in the field's **column selector**, which is the gray box that contains the field name at the top of the column. A column selector is also called a **field selector**.

To resize datasheet columns using the mouse pointer to drag the column's right edge:

1. Move the mouse pointer to the right edge of the Writer Name column selector until it changes to ✢. See Figure 2-26.

Figure 2-26
Resizing columns using the resizing pointer

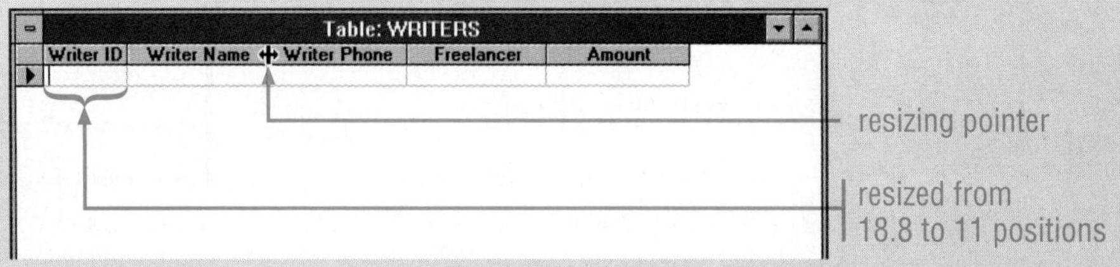

2. Click-and-drag the pointer to the right until the column width is approximately twice its original size.
3. Release the mouse button to complete the resizing of the Writer Name field.

   TROUBLE? Be sure that all five fields are still visible in the Datasheet View window. If not, you can repeat the previous steps to make the column narrower.

Elena tries a third technique—the best-fit column width method—to resize the Freelancer and Amount columns. When you use the **best-fit column width** method, Access automatically resizes the column to accommodate its largest value, including the field name at the top of the column. To use this method, you position the mouse pointer at the right edge of the column selector for the field and, when the mouse pointer changes to ✢, double-click the left mouse button. Access then automatically resizes the column. (A fourth method for resizing columns is to use the Best Fit button in the Column Width dialog box, but Elena does not experiment with this method.)

For both best-fit methods, you can resize two or more adjacent columns at the same time. Simply move the mouse pointer to the column selector of the leftmost of the fields. When the pointer changes to ↓, click-and-drag it to the column selector of the rightmost field and then release the mouse button. You then double-click the ✢ at the right edge of the column selector for the rightmost field.

To resize datasheet columns using the best-fit column width method:

1. Move the mouse pointer to the Freelancer column selector. When it changes to ↓, click the left mouse button, drag the pointer to the right to the Amount column selector, and then release the mouse button. Both columns are now highlighted.
2. Move the mouse pointer to the right edge of the Amount column selector. When it changes to ✢, double-click the left mouse button. Access automatically resizes both columns to their best fits. See Figure 2-27.

Figure 2-27
Four columns resized

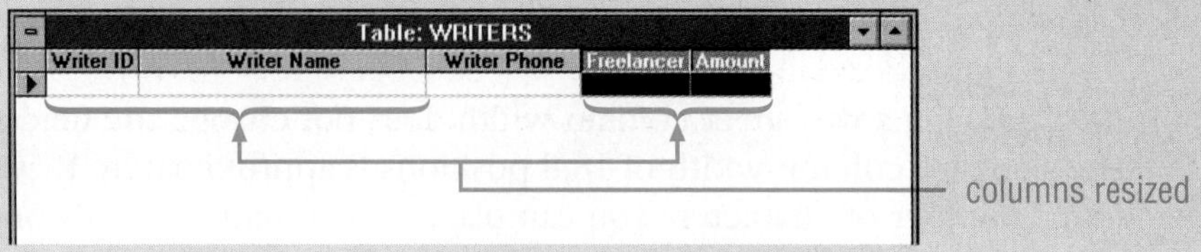

For her final set of table structure changes, Elena assigns a default value to the Freelancer field, eliminates the decimal places in the Amount field, and adds an input mask to the Writer Phone field. These changes must be made in the Table Design View window, so Elena first switches from the Datasheet View window.

Assigning Default Values

With a few exceptions, Elena knows which writers are freelancers and which are staff writers. To be safe, Elena will assume that the exceptions are freelancers until she finds out for sure. She assigns the default value Yes to the Freelancer field, which means each writer will have the value Yes in the Freelancer field unless it is changed individually to No.

To assign a default value:

1. Click the **Design View button** on the toolbar to switch to the Table Design View window.
2. Click anywhere in the **Freelancer field row** to make it the current field, click the Field Properties **Default Value text box**, and then type **Yes**. See Figure 2-28.

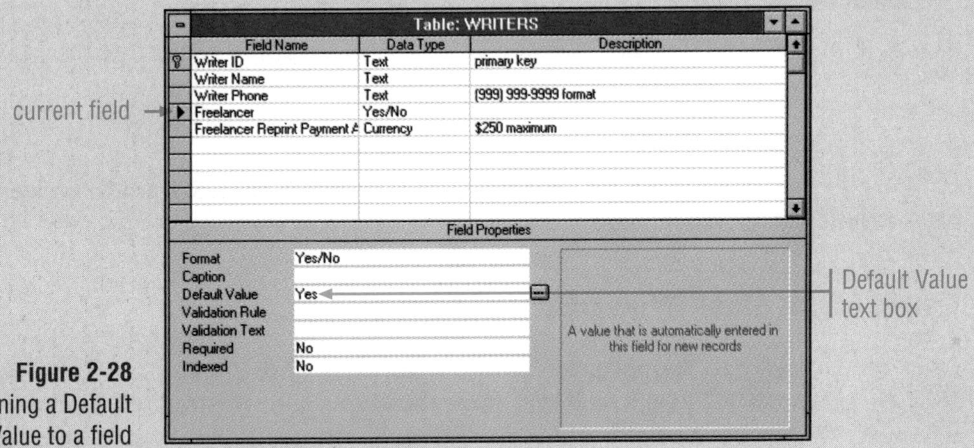

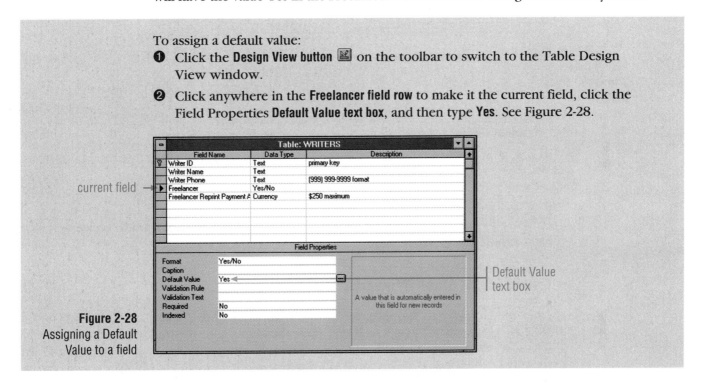

Figure 2-28
Assigning a Default Value to a field

Elena's next table structure change is to eliminate the decimal places in the Freelancer Reprint Payment Amount field.

Changing Decimal Places

Vision Publishers pays freelancers at most $250 for reprint rights to their articles. Some freelancers will be paid less, but in all cases, a whole dollar amount will be paid. Elena changes the Freelancer Reprint Payment Amount field to show only whole dollar amounts. To do this, she modifies the Decimal Places property for the field.

To change the number of decimal places displayed:

1. Click anywhere in the **Freelancer Reprint Payment Amount field row** to make it the current field and to display its Field Properties options.
2. Click the **Decimal Places text box**, and then click the **down arrow button** that appears in the box. Access displays the Decimal Places list box. See Figure 2-29.

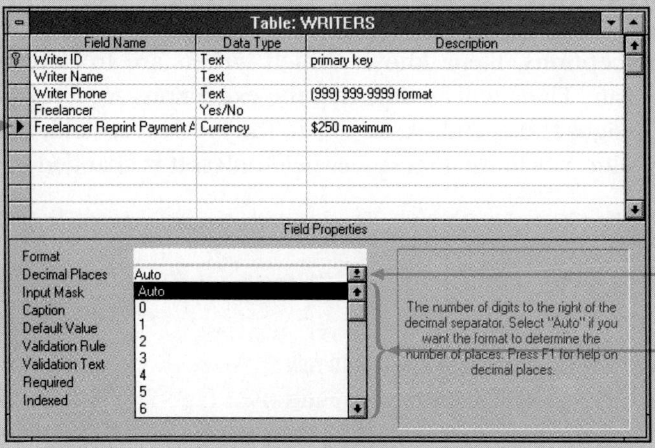

Figure 2-29
Changing the default Decimal Places field property

3. Click the **0** in the Decimal Places list box. The Decimal Places list box disappears, and 0 is now the value for the Decimal Places field property.

For the final table structure change, Elena uses Input Mask Wizard to create an input mask for the Writer Phone field.

Using Input Mask Wizard

One standard way to format a telephone number is with parentheses, a space, and a hyphen—as in (917) 729-5364. If you want these special formatting characters to appear whenever Writer Phone field values are entered, you need to create an input mask. An **input mask** is a predefined format you use to enter data in a field. An easy way to create an input mask is to use **Input Mask Wizard**, which is an Access tool that guides you in creating a predefined format for a field. To start Input Mask Wizard, click the text box for the Input Mask property and then click either the Build button that appears to the right of the text box or the Build button on the toolbar. You use the **Build button** to start a builder or wizard, which are Access tools to help you perform a task.

Let's use Input Mask Wizard to create an input mask for the Writer Phone field.

To start Input Mask Wizard:

1. Click anywhere in the **Writer Phone field row** to make it the current field and to display its Field Properties options.
2. Click the **Input Mask text box**. A Build button appears to the right of the Input Mask text box. See Figure 2-30.

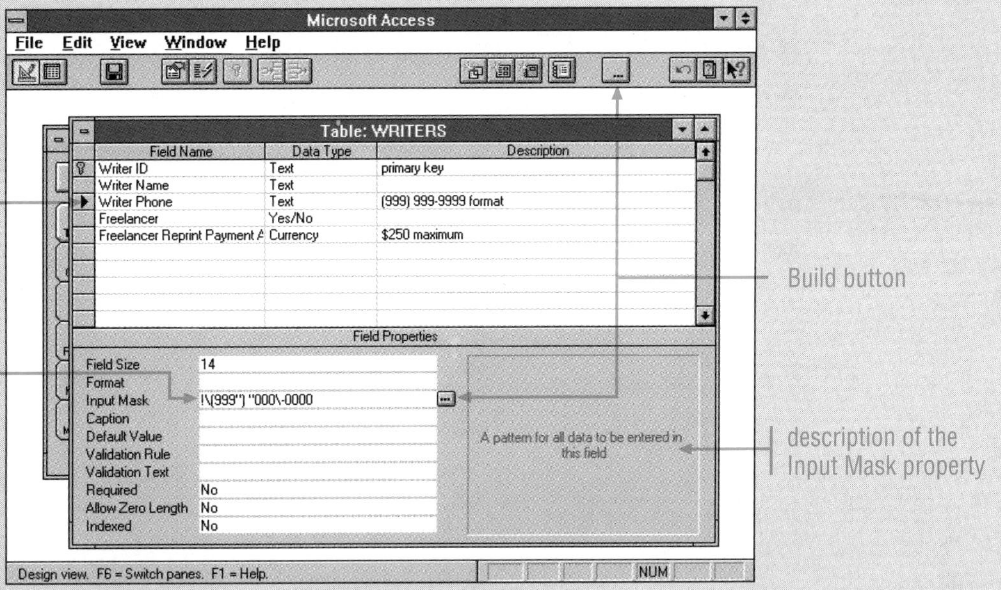

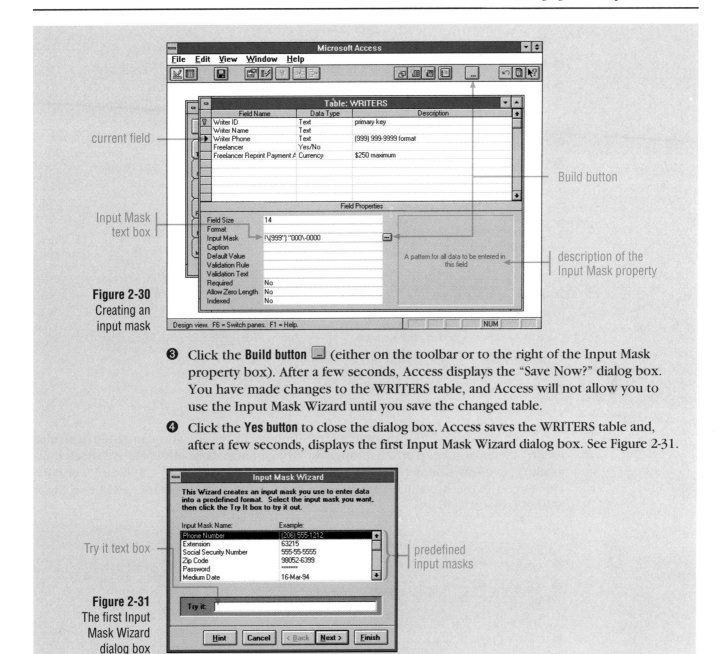

Figure 2-30 Creating an input mask

❸ Click the **Build button** (either on the toolbar or to the right of the Input Mask property box). After a few seconds, Access displays the "Save Now?" dialog box. You have made changes to the WRITERS table, and Access will not allow you to use the Input Mask Wizard until you save the changed table.

❹ Click the **Yes button** to close the dialog box. Access saves the WRITERS table and, after a few seconds, displays the first Input Mask Wizard dialog box. See Figure 2-31.

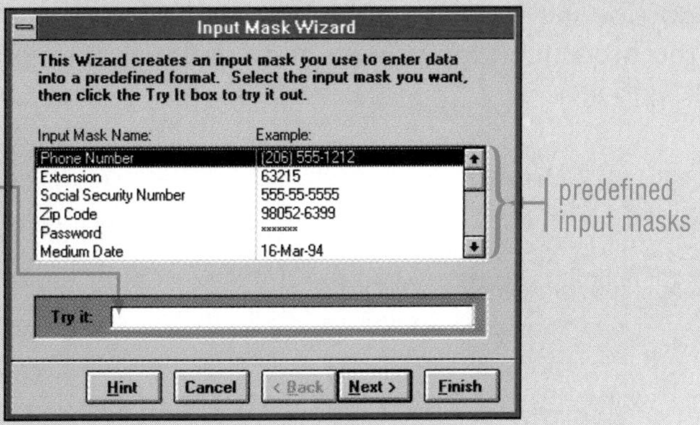

Figure 2-31 The first Input Mask Wizard dialog box

You scroll through the Input Mask Name list box, select the input mask you want, and then enter representative values to experiment with the input mask. Elena selects the Phone Number input mask for the Writer Phone field.

To select an input mask:

1. If necessary, click **Phone Number** in the Input Mask Name list box to highlight it.
2. Click **Try it** and then type **9** in the Try it text box. Access displays (9__) ___-____ in the Try it text box. The underscores are placeholder characters that are replaced as you type.
3. Type **876543210** to complete the sample entry.
4. Click the **Next > button**. Access displays the second Input Mask Wizard dialog box. See Figure 2-32.

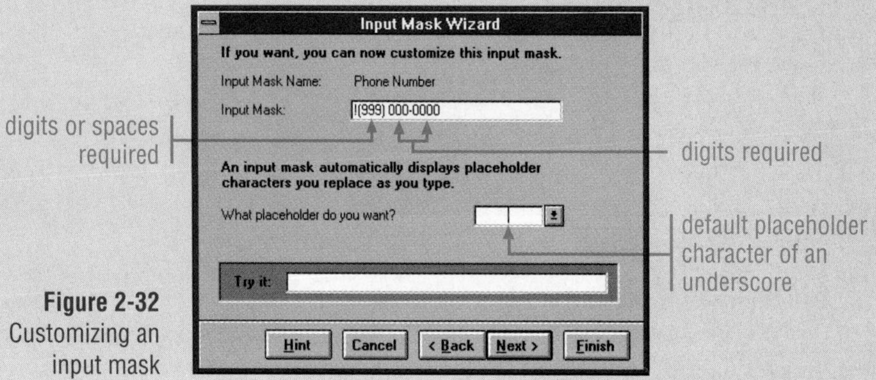

Figure 2-32
Customizing an input mask

When you have more experience creating input masks, you can modify, or customize, the input mask. You can change the default underscore placeholder character, for example, to a space or one of the following special characters: #, @, !, $, %, or *. For now, Elena accepts the predefined input mask and continues through the remaining Input Mask Wizard dialog boxes.

To finish an input mask:

1. Click the **Next > button**. Access displays the third Input Mask Wizard dialog box.
2. Click the **top radio button**, so that you store the data "With the symbols in the mask, like this: (206) 555-1212." Then click the **Next > button**. Access displays the final Input Mask Wizard dialog box.
3. Click the **Finish button**. Access ends Input Mask Wizard and displays the newly created input mask for Writer Phone.

Elena is done with her initial work on the WRITERS table structure, so she exits Access.

To exit Access after changing a table structure:

1. Double-click the Microsoft Access window **Control menu box**. A dialog box asks, "Save changes to Table 'WRITERS'?"
2. Click the **Yes button** to save your changes to the WRITERS table structure. Access saves the table structure changes, closes all windows, and then exits to Windows.

Selecting the Primary Key

As Elena thinks about her Issue25 database later that day, she can't remember if she made Writer ID the primary key of the WRITERS table. Although Access does not require that tables have a primary key, Elena knows that choosing a primary key has several advantages.

- Based on its definition, a primary key does serve to identify uniquely each record in a table. For example, Elena is using Writer ID to distinguish one writer from another when both have the same name.
- Access does not allow duplicate values in the primary key field. If Elena already has a record with N425 as the field value for Writer ID, Access prevents her from adding another record with this same field value in the Writer ID field. Preventing duplicate values ensures the uniqueness of the primary key field.
- Access enforces entity integrity on the primary key field. **Entity integrity** means that every record's primary key field must have a value. If you do not enter a value for a field, you have actually given the field what is known as a **null value**. You cannot give a null value to the primary key field; Access will not store the record for you unless you've entered a field value in the primary-key field.
- Access displays records in primary key sequence when you view a table in the Datasheet View window or the Form View window. If you enter records in no specific order, you are ensured that you will later be able to work with them in a more meaningful, primary key sequence.
- Access responds faster to your requests for specific records based on the primary key.

To verify that Writer ID is the primary key of the WRITERS table, Elena launches Access, opens the Issue25 database, and then opens the WRITERS table in the Table Design View window.

To open a table in the Table Design View window:

1. Launch Access.
2. Open the Issue25 database.
3. WRITERS should be highlighted in the Tables list box, so click the **Design button**. Access opens the Table Design View window for the WRITERS table. See Figure 2-33.

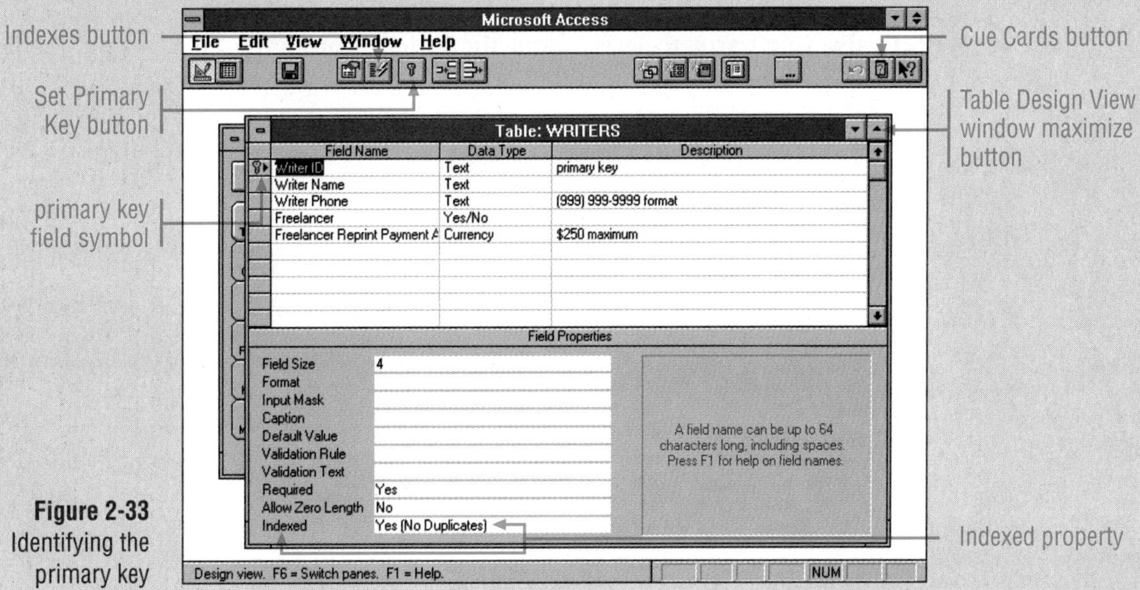

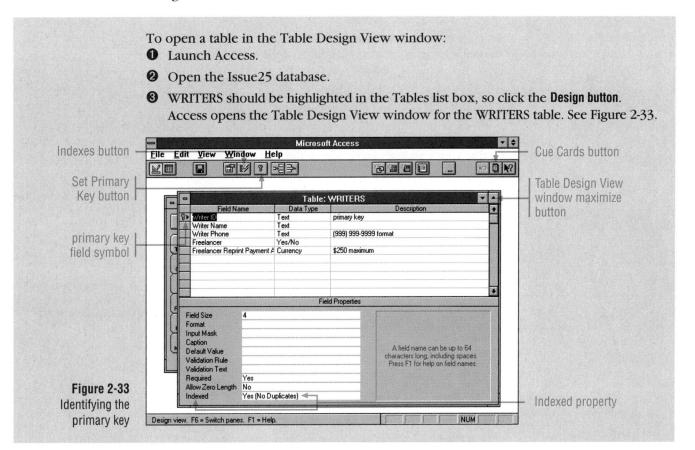

Figure 2-33
Identifying the primary key

Writer ID is highlighted and has the current row symbol in its row selector because Writer ID is the current field. Elena sees a key symbol to the left of the current row symbol. Access uses the key symbol as a **primary key field symbol** to identify the table's primary key. To change the primary key to another field, click the other field's row selector and then click the Set Primary Key button on the toolbar; Access will move the primary-key field symbol to that other field. If the primary key consists of two or more fields, hold down [Ctrl], click the row selector for each field, and then click the Set Primary Key button. Access will move the primary-key field symbol to all selected fields.

Elena sees the toolbar Indexes button to the left of the Set Primary Key button and the Indexed property as one of the Field Properties options. Elena uses Cue Cards to learn more about indexes.

Using Cue Cards and Creating Indexes

The Access Help system contains a Cue Cards feature. **Cue Cards** are interactive Access tutorials that remain visible to help you while you do the most common database tasks. They provide examples, guidance, and shortcuts to Access Help information.

REFERENCE WINDOW

Opening and Using Cue Cards

- Click the Cue Cards button on the toolbar. The Cue Cards window appears.
- Click the Cue Cards option you want to use.
- As each successive display appears, read the coaching information, and then click the option button of your choice. Continue until you have the information you need.
- When you finish using the Cue Cards, double-click the Cue Cards window Control menu box to close the Cue Cards window.

Let's use Cue Cards to learn about the Indexes property. First, maximize the Table Design View window so that the Cue Cards hide less of the window.

To maximize a window and open Cue Cards:

1. Click the Table Design View window **maximize button**.
2. Click the **Cue Cards button** on the toolbar to open the Cue Cards window. See Figure 2-34 on the following page.

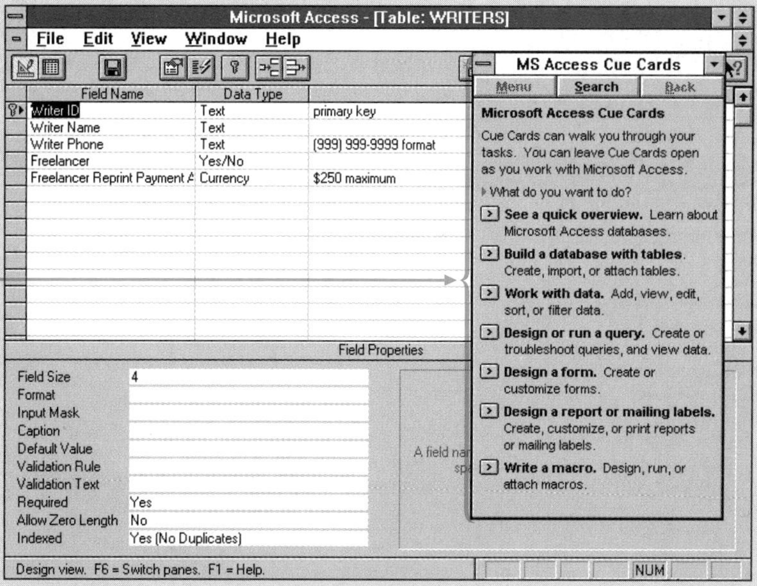

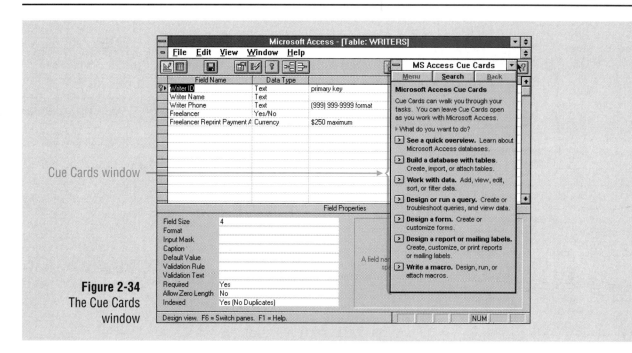

Figure 2-34
The Cue Cards window

The Cue Cards window appears as an active window. Although normally only one window at a time is active, the Table Design View window is now also an active window. You can perform tasks in either window. If you switch from the Table Design View window to another Access window and from the current Cue Cards window to another Cue Cards window, both new windows will become active windows.

Review the displayed Cue Cards options. If you have time, you might want to investigate the Cue Cards topic called "See a quick overview." If you do, be sure to complete the topic so that you return to the Cue Cards window shown in Figure 2-34 before continuing with the tutorial.

Elena wants guidance working with table indexes, so she first chooses the Cue Cards topic "Build a database with tables" and then makes the appropriate choices on subsequent Cue Cards windows.

To open a Cue Cards topic:

1. Click the **Build a database with tables button** to open the Cue Cards Build a Database with Tables window. See Figure 2-35.

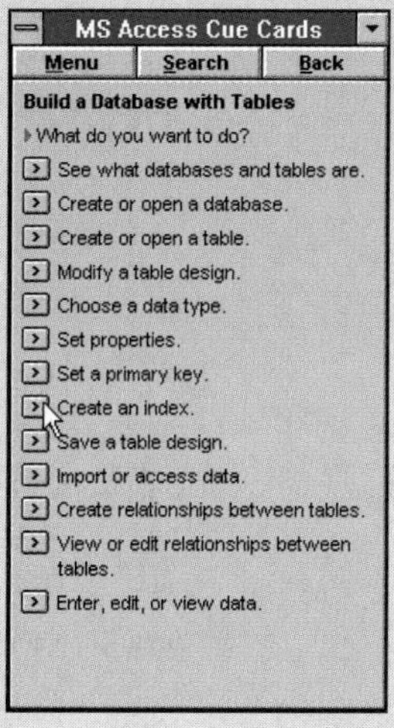

Figure 2-35
The Cue Cards Build a Database with Tables window

❷ Click the **Create an index button** to see the next Cue Cards window.

❸ Carefully read the contents of each Cue Cards window, then click the **Next button** in each Cue Cards window until you reach the last Cue Cards window in the sequence. See Figure 2-36.

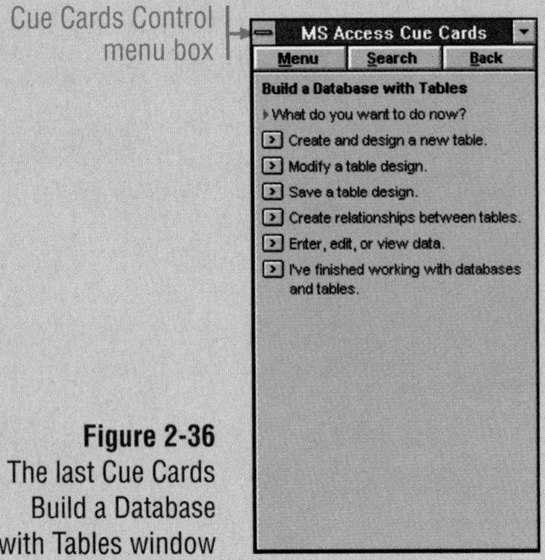

Figure 2-36
The last Cue Cards Build a Database with Tables window

❹ Double-click the Cue Cards **Control menu box** to close the Cue Cards feature.

Elena has learned that Access automatically creates and maintains an index for the primary key field. An **index**, in this case, is a list of primary-key values and their corresponding record numbers. For a primary-key field, the index cannot have duplicate values. The index adds to the database disk storage requirements and takes time to maintain as you add and delete records. These are two disadvantages of having a primary key and its corresponding index for a table, but they are insignificant compared with the many advantages of an index. You cannot index fields that have the data types memo, yes/no, and OLE object, but this restriction should never be a problem.

You can also create indexes for other selected table fields. Do so to improve processing speed if you think you will often sort or find records based on data in those fields. However, each index requires extra disk space and additional processing time when records are added, changed, or deleted in the table.

Elena views the indexes that currently exist for the WRITERS table by using the Indexes button on the toolbar.

To display the indexes for a table:

❶ Click the **Indexes button** on the toolbar. Access displays the Indexes window. See Figure 2-37.

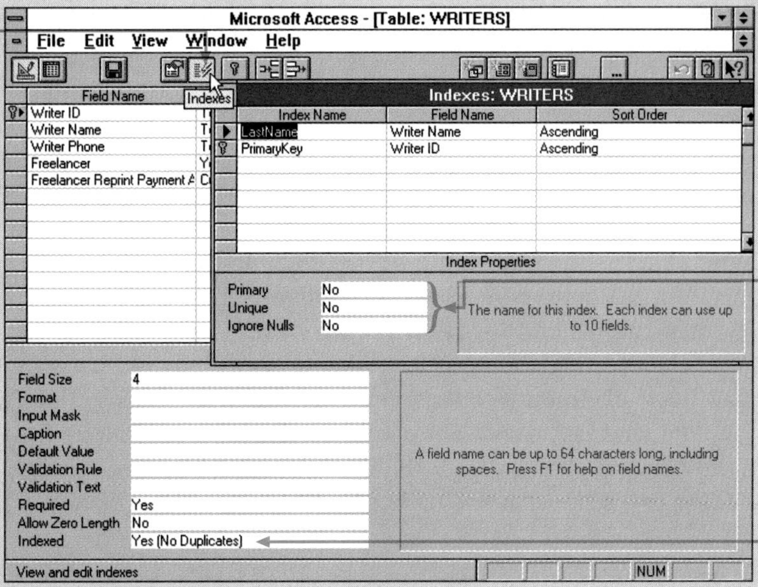

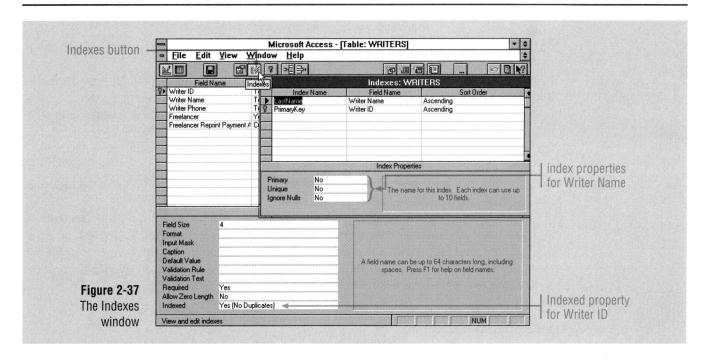

Figure 2-37 The Indexes window

Two indexes appear in the Indexes window: one for the primary-key field of Writer ID and a second one for the Writer Name field. How was the second index created? Recall that you used Table Wizard to create the WRITERS table. When you select Table Wizard fields, you also select all their predefined properties. One of the fields you selected was LastName, which had "Yes (Duplicates OK)" as the value for its Indexed property. When you changed LastName to Writer Name, the field retained this Indexed property value.

Elena doesn't think she needs an index for Writer Name, so she deletes the index. If she ever needs an index for this field in the future, she can add it back by using the Indexes window or the Indexed property for Writer Name.

To delete an index:

❶ Position the mouse pointer in the first row of the Indexes window with the Index Name LastName and click the right mouse button. Access displays the Shortcut menu.

❷ Using the left mouse button, click **Delete Row**. Access deletes the index for Writer Name from the Indexes window.

❸ Click the **Indexes button** on the toolbar to close the Indexes window.

If you want to take a break and resume the tutorial at a later time, you can exit Access by double-clicking the Microsoft Access window Control menu box and then clicking Yes in the dialog box that asks if you want to save your table changes. When you resume the tutorial, place your Student Disk in the appropriate drive, launch Access, open the Issue25 database on your Student Disk, and open the Table Design View window for the WRITERS table.

Modifying the Structure of an Access Table

Elena learns that Vision Publishers has a writer contact list containing each writer's name, phone number, and last contact date. Because Vision Publishers has not contacted some writers for many years, Elena decides that she should add a field named Last Contact Date to her WRITERS table. She will contact those writers who have a reasonably current date before she tries to track down those who wrote articles for the company many years ago.

When Elena shows Brian the WRITERS table she is developing, he realizes that he can use this information to contact writers and asks for a list of all the WRITERS table information arranged alphabetically by writer last name.

After the meeting, Elena realizes she has a problem with giving Brian this information. She had been planning to enter names in the Writer Name field in the regular order of first, middle, and last name. She needs to change her strategy for the Writer Name field. Her solution is to change the WRITERS table structure by deleting the Writer Name field and adding two fields that she names Last Name and First Name.

Deleting a Field

After meeting with Brian, Elena makes her table structure modifications to the WRITERS table. She first deletes the Writer Name field.

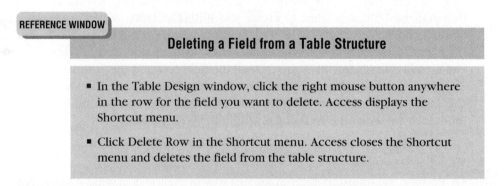

REFERENCE WINDOW

Deleting a Field from a Table Structure

- In the Table Design window, click the right mouse button anywhere in the row for the field you want to delete. Access displays the Shortcut menu.
- Click Delete Row in the Shortcut menu. Access closes the Shortcut menu and deletes the field from the table structure.

Let's delete the Writer Name field from the WRITERS table.

To delete a field from a table structure:

❶ Move the mouse pointer to the row for the Writer Name field and click the right mouse button. Access displays the Shortcut menu. See Figure 2-38.

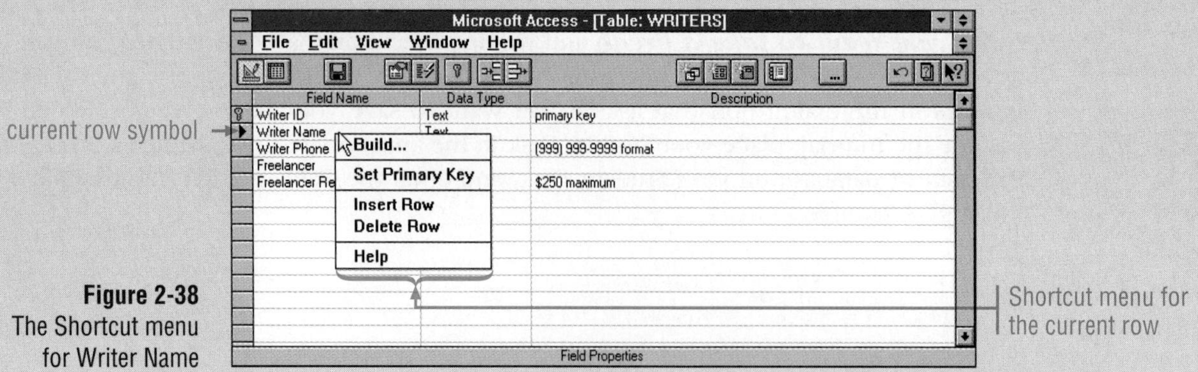

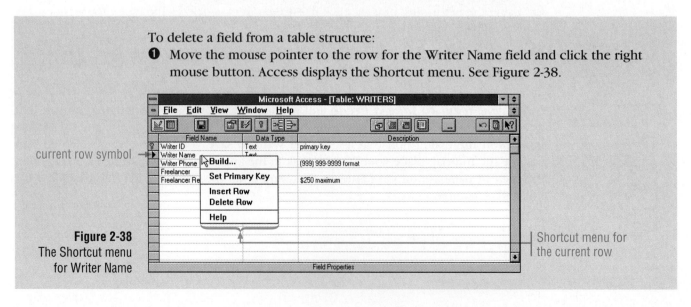

Figure 2-38 The Shortcut menu for Writer Name

❷ Click **Delete Row** in the Shortcut menu. Access deletes the Writer Name field from the WRITERS table structure. The row where Writer Name had been positioned is also deleted.

TROUBLE? If you deleted the wrong field, immediately click the Undo button. The field you deleted reappears. You should repeat the deletion steps from the beginning for the correct field.

Adding a Field

The order of fields in the Table Design window determines the order of the fields in the Datasheet View window. Therefore, Elena decides that the two new fields, Last Name and First Name, should be positioned right after the Writer ID row. Then she will position the third new field, Last Contact Date, between the Writer Phone and Freelancer rows.

REFERENCE WINDOW

Adding a Field to a Table Structure

- In the Table Design window, open the Shortcut menu by clicking the right mouse button anywhere in the row that will end up below the field you are adding. If the new field is to be added to the end of the table, click the Field Name column for the first blank row and skip the next step.
- Click Insert Row in the Shortcut menu. Access inserts a blank row.
- Define the new field by entering a field name, data type, and optional description in the new row.

Let's add the three fields to the WRITERS table.

To add a field to a table structure:

❶ Click the right mouse button anywhere in the **Writer Phone row**. Above this row you want to insert two blank rows in preparation for adding two fields. Access displays the Shortcut menu.

❷ Click **Insert Row** in the Shortcut menu. Access adds a blank row between the Writer ID and Writer Phone rows and closes the Shortcut menu.

❸ Because you need to add two rows, click the right mouse button anywhere in the **Writer Phone row** and then click **Insert Row** in the Shortcut menu to insert the second blank row. See Figure 2-39.

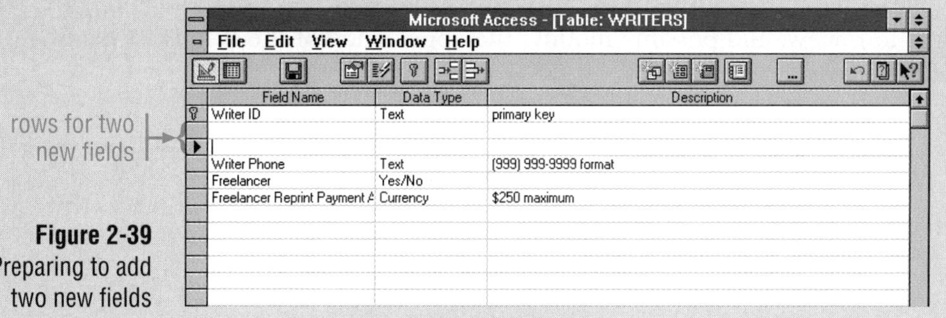

Figure 2-39
Preparing to add two new fields

❹ Click the Field Name box for the first of the two new rows. To define the Last Name field, type **Last Name**, press **[Tab]**, and highlight the 50 in the Field Size box. Then type **15** and click the Field Name box for the second of the two new rows.

❺ To define the First Name field, type **First Name**, press **[Tab]**, highlight the 50 in the Field Size box, and then type **15**. See Figure 2-40.

new fields

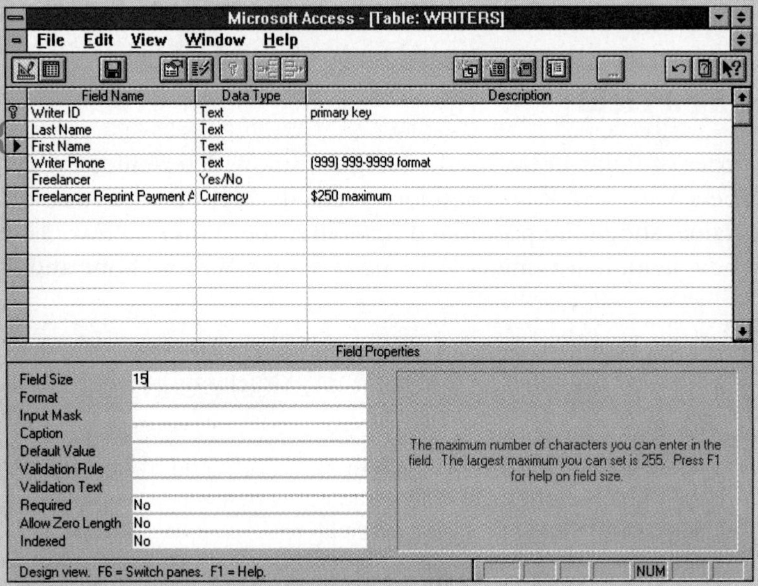

Figure 2-40
Completing the field addition process

❻ After adding Last Name and First Name, Elena next adds Last Contact Date to the WRITERS table. Click the right mouse button anywhere in the Freelancer row and then click **Insert Row** in the Shortcut menu to insert a row between the Writer Phone and Freelancer rows. Access places the insertion point in the Field Name box of the new row.

❼ Type **Last Contact Date**, press **[Tab]**, type **d**, and then press **[Tab]**. See Figure 2-41. Last Contact Date is a date/time field.

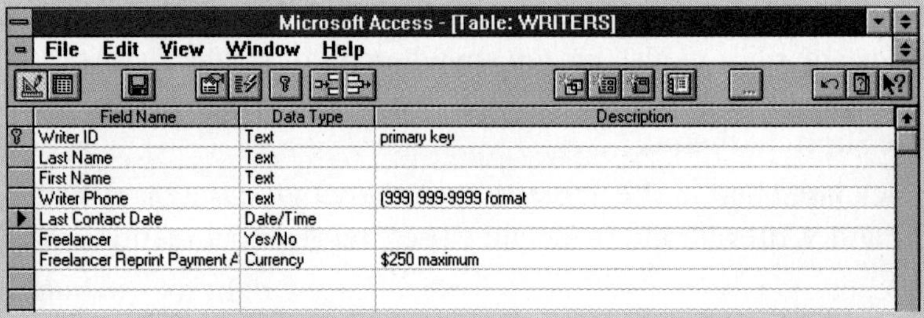

Figure 2-41
Last Contact Date field added

Elena has now defined the WRITERS table structure. Once again, however, she wants to review, and possibly modify, the appearance of the WRITERS datasheet before exiting Access.

To review and modify a datasheet:

❶ Click the **Datasheet View button** . The "Save now?" dialog box appears.

❷ Click the **OK button**. Access displays the Datasheet View window. The Last Name and First Name fields appear to the right of the Writer ID field, and Last Contact Date is to the right of Writer Phone. The one change you should make is to widen the column for Last Contact Date so the whole field name will be visible.

❸ Resize the column for Last Contact Date so that the entire field name appears in the heading box. See Figure 2-42.

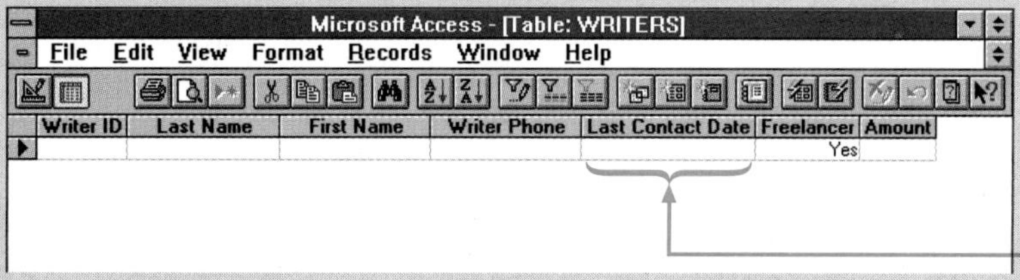

Figure 2-42 The final Datasheet View window for the WRITERS table

❹ Double-click the Microsoft Access window **Control menu box**, and then click the **Yes button** in the "Save layout changes to table 'WRITERS'" dialog box to save your table changes and exit Access.

■ ■ ■

Elena has defined the WRITERS table structure and refined the table's datasheet. In the next tutorial, Elena will add data to the WRITERS table.

Questions

1. What two types of keys represent a common field when you form a relationship between tables?
2. What is data redundancy?
3. Which Access names must conform to standard DOS conventions for filenames?
4. Which Access field property can be up to 255 characters long?
5. What are the eight Access data types?
6. Which data type could automatically serve as a table's primary key because Access itself fills in each field value to guarantee uniqueness?
7. Which data types have the Field Size property?
8. What is a caption?
9. Describe three different ways to select a field's data type.
10. When is it appropriate to use the Undo button?
11. Describe three different ways to resize a datasheet column.
12. What is an input mask?
13. Explain entity integrity.
14. What are Cue Cards?
15. When is it possible to have two active windows?

E 16. Using Cue Cards for information on the technique, explain how to move a field in the Table Design View window.

E 17. Using Cue Cards for information, document for your instructor the tips for choosing a data type.

E 18. Use the "Work with data" Cue Cards to describe a method for rearranging columns in a datasheet while the Datasheet View window is active.

Tutorial Assignments

Elena creates the BUSINESS ARTICLES table structure, as shown in Figure 2-43.

BUSINESS ARTICLES table	Data Type	Input/Display Field Size	Description
Article Title	text	44	
Issue of Business Perspective	text	8	yyyy mmm format
Length of Article	number	4	Integer field size
Writer Name	text	25	

Figure 2-43

Launch Access, open the Issue25.mdb database on your Student Disk, and do the following:

1. Create a new table without using Table Wizard. Use Figure 2-43 to define these properties, as appropriate, for each of the four fields in the table: field name, data type, description, and field size. For the number data type field, use the Description column in Figure 2-43 to set its Field Size property.
2. Save the table with the name BUSINESS ARTICLES. Do not select a primary key.
3. Switch to the Datasheet View window and resize columns so that the entire field name can be read in the column heading for every field.
4. Print the datasheet for the table.
5. In the Table Design View window, change the field name Length of Article to Article Length. For the field Issue of Business Perspective, add the Caption property Issue. Resize the columns, if necessary, for these two fields in the Datasheet View window.
6. Print the datasheet for the table.
7. Delete the field Writer Name from the table structure.
8. Add a four-character text field named Writer ID to the end of the table. For a description, enter "foreign key."
9. Change the data type of the field Issue of Business Perspective to date/time.
10. Add a three-character text field named Type between the Article Length and Writer ID fields. For this new field, enter the description "article type" and the Default Value BUS, which represents a business article.
11. Resize columns, as necessary, in the Datasheet View window.
12. Print the datasheet for the table.

E 13. Switch the order of the Article Length and Type columns in the datasheet, using the "Work with data" Cue Cards for guidance. Do not switch their order in the table structure. Print the datasheet for the table.

E 14. Using Cue Cards for guidance, move the field named Type in the Table Design View window so that it follows the field named Article Title. Print the datasheet for the table and then close the Issue25 database.

Case Problems

1. Walkton Daily Press Carriers

Grant Sherman, circulation manager of the Walkton Daily Press, wants a better way to keep track of the carriers who deliver the newspaper. Grant meets with Robin Witkop, one of the newspaper's computer experts, to discuss what can be done to improve his current tracking system.

Robin reviews Grant's informational needs and recommends that she design a database to keep track of carriers and their outstanding balances. Grant agrees and, after obtaining her manager's approval, Robin designs a database that has two tables: CARRIERS and BILLINGS. Robin first creates the CARRIERS table structure, as shown in Figure 2-44.

CARRIERS table

Field Name	Data Type	Input/Display Field Size	Description
Carrier ID	counter	3	primary key; unique carrier identification number
Carrier First Name	text	14	
Carrier Last Name	text	15	
Carrier Phone	number	8	Long Integer field size
Carrier Birthdate	date/time	8	

Figure 2-44

Launch Access and do the following:

1. Create a new database on your Student Disk with the name Press.
2. Create a new table without using Table Wizard. Use Figure 2-44 to define these properties, as appropriate, for each of the five fields in the table: field name, data type, and description. Define the Field Size property for only the text and number fields, using the Description column in Figure 2-44 to set the Field Size property for the number field.
3. Select Carrier ID as the table's primary key.
4. Save the table with the name CARRIERS.
5. Switch to the Datasheet View window and resize columns so that the entire field name can be read in the column heading for every field.
6. Print the datasheet for the table.
7. In the Table Design View window, change the field name Carrier Birthdate to Birthdate. Add the Caption property First Name for the field Carrier First Name. Add the Caption property Last Name for the field Carrier Last Name. Resize the columns, if necessary, for the fields in the Datasheet View window.
8. Print the datasheet for the table.
9. E Using Cue Cards for guidance, move the field named Carrier Last Name in the Table Design View window so that it follows the field named Carrier ID. Print the datasheet for the table and then close the Datasheet View window.

Robin next creates the BILLINGS table structure, as shown in Figure 2-45.

BILLINGS table

Field Name	Data Type	Input/Display Field Size	Description
Route ID	text	4	primary key
Carrier ID	number	3	Long Integer field size; carrier assigned to the route; foreign key
Balance Amount	currency	5	outstanding balance due from the carrier

Figure 2-45

Launch Access, if necessary, and do the following:

10. Open the database named Press.mdb on your Student Disk.
11. Create a new table without using Table Wizard. Use Figure 2-45 to define these properties, as appropriate, for each of the three fields in the table: field name, data type, and description. Define the Field Size property for only the text and number fields, using the Description column in Figure 2-45 to set the Field Size property for the number field.
12. Select Route ID as the primary key and then save the table with the name BILLINGS.
13. Switch to the Datasheet View window and resize columns so that the entire field name can be read in the column heading for every field.
14. Print the datasheet for the table.
15. In the Table Design View window, add the Caption property Balance for the field Balance Amount, and change the Decimal Places property for the field Balance Amount from Auto to 2. Resize the columns, if necessary, for the fields in the Datasheet View window.
16. Print the datasheet for the table and then close the Press database.

2. Lopez Used Cars

Maria and Hector Lopez own a chain of used-car lots throughout Texas. They have used a computer in their business for several years to handle their payroll and normal accounting functions. Their phenomenal expansion, both in the number of used-car locations and the number of used cars handled, forces them to develop a database to track their used-car inventory. They design a database that has two tables: USED CARS and LOCATIONS. They first create the USED CARS table structure, as shown in Figure 2-46.

USED CARS table

Field Name	Data Type	Input/Display Field Size	Description
Vehicle ID	text	5	primary key
Manufacturer	text	13	
Model	text	15	
Class Type	text	2	code for the type of sedan, van, truck, and so on; foreign key
Transmission Type	text	3	code for type of transmission; foreign key
Year	number	4	Integer field size
Cost	currency		
Selling Price	currency		
Location Code	text	2	lot location within the state; foreign key

Figure 2-46

Launch Access and do the following:

1. Create a new database on your Student Disk with the name Usedcars.
2. Create a new table without using Table Wizard. Use Figure 2-46 to define these properties, as appropriate, for each of the nine fields in the table: field name, data type, and description. Define the Field Size property for only the text and number fields, using the Description column in Figure 2-46 to set the Field Size property for the number field.

3. Select Vehicle ID as the table's primary key.
4. Save the table with the name USED CARS.
5. Switch to the Datasheet View window and resize columns so that the entire field name can be read in the column heading for every field. Maximize the Datasheet View window, and continue to resize columns until you can see all column headings on the screen at one time.
6. Print the datasheet for the table.
7. In the Table Design View window, change the field name Class Type to Class. Add the Caption property Transmission for the field Transmission Type and the Caption property Location for the field Location Code. Resize the columns, if necessary, for the fields in the Datasheet View window.
8. Print the datasheet for the table.
9. **E** Using Cue Cards for guidance, move the field named Location Code in the Table Design View window so that it follows the field named Year. Print the datasheet for the table and then close the Datasheet View window.

Hector and Maria next create the LOCATIONS table structure, as shown in Figure 2-47.

LOCATIONS table

Field Name	Data Type	Input/Display Field Size	Description
Location Code	text	2	primary key
Location Name	text	15	
Manager Name	text	25	

Figure 2-47

Launch Access, if necessary, and do the following:

10. Open the database named Usedcars.mdb on your Student Disk.
11. Create a new table without using Table Wizard. Use Figure 2-47 to define these properties, as appropriate, for each of the three fields in the table: field name, data type, description, and field size.
12. Select Location Code as the primary key and then save the table with the name LOCATIONS.
13. Switch to the Datasheet View window and resize columns so that the entire field name can be read in the column heading for every field.
14. Print the datasheet for the table and then close the Usedcars database.

3. Tophill University Student Employment

Olivia Tyler is an administrative assistant in the Student Employment office of the Financial Aid department at Tophill University. She is responsible for tracking the companies that have announced part-time jobs for students. She keeps track of each available job and the person to contact at each company. Olivia had previously relied on student workers to do the paperwork, but reductions in the university budget have forced her department to reduce the number of part-time student workers. As a result, Olivia's backlog of work is increasing. After discussing the problem with her supervisor, Olivia meets with Lee Chang, a database analyst on the staff of the university computer center.

Lee questions Olivia in detail about her requirements and suggests that he could develop a database to reduce her workload. He designs a database that has two tables: JOBS and EMPLOYERS. He first creates the JOBS table structure, as shown in Figure 2-48 on the following page.

JOBS table

Field Name	Data Type	Input/Display Field Size	Description
Job Order	counter	5	primary key; unique number assigned to the job position
Employer ID	text	4	foreign key
Job Title	text	30	
Wage	currency	6	rate per hour
Hours	number	2	Integer field size; hours per week

Figure 2-48

Launch Access and do the following:

1. Create a new database on your Student Disk with the name Parttime.
2. Create a new table without using Table Wizard. Use Figure 2-48 to define these properties, as appropriate, for each of the five fields in the table: field name, data type, and description. Define the Field Size property for only the text and number fields, using the Description column in Figure 2-48 to set the Field Size property for the number field.
3. Select Job Order as the table's primary key.
4. Save the table with the name JOBS.
5. Switch to the Datasheet View window and resize columns so that the entire field name can be read in the column heading for every field.
6. Print the datasheet for the table.
7. In the Table Design View window, change the field name Hours to Hours/Week. Add the Caption property Job# for the field Job Order and the Caption property Wages for the field Wage. Resize the columns, if necessary, for the fields in the Datasheet View window.
8. Print the datasheet for the table.
9. **E** Using Cue Cards for guidance, move the field named Hours/Week in the Table Design View window so that it follows the field named Job Order. Print the datasheet for the table and then close the Datasheet View window.

Lee next creates the EMPLOYERS table structure, as shown in Figure 2-49.

EMPLOYERS table

Field Name	Data Type	Input/Display Field Size	Description
Employer ID	text	4	primary key
Employer Name	text	40	
Contact Name	text	25	
Contact Phone	text	8	999-9999 format

Figure 2-49

Launch Access, if necessary, and do the following:

10. Open the database named Parttime.mdb on your Student Disk.
11. Create a new table without using Table Wizard. Use Figure 2-49 to define these properties, as appropriate, for each of the four fields in the table: field name, data type, description, and field size.
12. Select Employer ID as the primary key and then save the table with the name EMPLOYERS.
13. Switch to the Datasheet View window and resize columns so that the entire field name can be read in the column heading for every field.
14. Print the datasheet for the table and then close the Parttime database.

4. Rexville Business Licenses

Chester Pearce works as a clerk in the town hall in Rexville, North Dakota. He has just been assigned responsibility for maintaining the licenses issued to businesses in the town. He learns that the town issues over 30 different types of licenses to over 1,500 businesses, and that most licenses must be renewed annually by March 1.

The clerk formerly responsible for the processing gives Chester the license information in two full boxes of file folders. Chester has been using a computer to help him with his other work, so he designs a database to keep track of the town's business licenses. When he completes his database design, he has two tables to create. One table, named LICENSES, contains data about the different types of business licenses the town issues. The second table, named BUSINESSES, contains data about all the businesses in town. Chester first creates the LICENSES table structure, as shown in Figure 2-50.

LICENSES table

Field Name	Data Type	Input/Display Field Size	Description
License Type	text	2	primary key
License Name	text	60	license description
Basic Cost	currency	4	cost of the license

Figure 2-50

Launch Access and do the following:

1. Create a new database on your Student Disk with the name Buslic.
2. Create a new table without using Table Wizard. Use Figure 2-50 to define these properties, as appropriate, for each of the three fields in the table: field name, data type, and description. Define the Field Size property for the text fields only.
3. Select License Type as the table's primary key.
4. Save the table with the name LICENSES.
5. Switch to the Datasheet View window and resize columns so that the entire field name can be read in the column heading for every field.
6. Print the datasheet for the table.
7. In the Table Design View window, change the field name License Name to License Description. Add the Caption property License Code for the field License Type. Change the Decimal Places property of the field Basic Cost from Auto to 0. Resize the columns, if necessary, for the fields in the Datasheet View window.
8. Print the datasheet for the table and then close the Datasheet View window.

Chester next creates the BUSINESSES table structure, as shown in Figure 2-51.

BUSINESSES table

Field Name	Data Type	Input/Display Field Size	Description
Business ID	counter	4	primary key; unique number assigned to a business
Business Name	text	35	official business name
Street Number	number	4	business street number; Integer field size
Street Name	text	25	
Proprietor	text	25	business owner name
Phone Number	text	8	999-9999 format

Figure 2-51

Launch Access, if necessary, and do the following:

9. Open the database named Buslic.mdb on your Student Disk.
10. Create a new table without using Table Wizard. Use Figure 2-51 to define these properties, as appropriate, for each of the six fields in the table: field name, data type, description, and field size. Define the Field Size property for only the text and number fields, using the Description column in Figure 2-51 to set the Field Size property for the number field.
11. Select Business ID as the primary key and then save the table with the name BUSINESSES.
12. Switch to the Datasheet View window and resize columns so that the entire field name can be read in the column heading for every field.
13. Print the datasheet for the table.
14. In the Table Design View window, add the Caption property Street# for the field Street Number. Resize the columns, if necessary, for the fields in the Datasheet View window.
15. Print the datasheet for the table.

E 16. Using Cue Cards for guidance, move the field named Phone Number in the Table Design View window so that it follows the field named Street Name. Print the datasheet for the table and then close the Buslic database.

T U T O R I A L 3

Maintaining Database Tables

Maintaining the WRITERS Table at Vision Publishers

O B J E C T I V E S

In this tutorial you will:

- Add and change data in a table
- Move the insertion and selection points
- Change table structure and datasheet properties
- Delete records from a table
- Import data
- Delete and rename a table
- Find field values in a table
- Replace data in a table
- Sort records in a datasheet
- Print table documentation
- Back up and compact a database

CASE

Vision Publishers Special projects editor Elena Sanchez meets with the production staff of Vision Publishers to set the schedule for the special 25th-anniversary issue of *Business Perspective*. After the meeting, she plans the work she needs to do with the WRITERS table. Because Elena has already created the WRITERS table structure, she is ready to enter the writers' data.

Based on her prior experience working with databases, Elena decides to enter only three records into the WRITERS table. Then she will review the table structure and the datasheet. If she finds a difference between a field's values and its definition, she will change the table structure to correct the problem. For example, if Elena defined the field size for a text field as 25 characters and finds some field values as large as 30 characters, she can change the field size to 30. Elena might also need to change the table's datasheet. For example, if a field's column is too narrow to show the entire field value, she can resize the datasheet column to make it wider.

Elena plans to confirm her list of writers and articles for the special magazine issue with president Brian Murphy and managing editor Judith Rossi before entering the remaining records into the WRITERS table. Finally, Elena will examine the WRITERS table records and correct any errors she finds. Elena takes her written plan, as shown in Figure 3-1, to her computer and starts her work with the WRITERS table.

WRITERS table task list:
- Enter complete information for three writers
- Change the table structure, if necessary
- Change the table datasheet, if necessary
- Confirm the WRITERS table data
- Enter complete information for remaining writers
- Correct errors

Figure 3-1
Elena's task list for the WRITERS table

Updating a Database

Elena built the table structure for the WRITERS table by defining the table's fields and their properties. Before the Issue25 database can provide useful and accurate information, however, Elena must update the database. **Updating a database**, or **maintaining a database**, is the process of adding, changing, and deleting records in database tables to keep them current and accurate.

Recall that the first step in creating a database is carefully planning the contents of the table structures. Similarly, the first step in updating a database is planning the field and record modifications that are needed. For example, preparing a task list of modifications was Elena's first step in updating the WRITERS table. In this tutorial, you will learn how to update the tables in a database.

Adding Records

When you initially create a database, adding records to the tables is the first step in updating a database. You also add records whenever you encounter new occurrences of the entities represented by the tables. At Vision Publishers, for example, an editorial assistant adds one record to the MAGAZINE ARTICLES table for each article in a new issue of one of its five magazines.

Using the Datasheet to Enter Data

In Tutorial 1 you used the Datasheet View window to view a table's records. You can also use a table's datasheet to update a table by adding, changing, and deleting its records. As her first step in updating the Issue25 database, for example, Elena adds to the WRITERS table the three records shown in Figure 3-2. She uses the WRITERS table datasheet to enter these records.

Figure 3-2
The first three WRITERS table records

WRITERS table data

	Writer ID	Last Name	First Name	Writer Phone	Last Contact Date	Freelancer	Amount
Record 1:	N425	Nilsson	Tonya	(909) 702-4082	7/9/77	No	$0
Record 2:	S260	Seeger	Wilhelm	(706) 423-0932	12/24/93	Yes	$350
Record 3:	S365	Sterns	Steven B.	(710) 669-6518	12/13/84	No	$0

Let's add the same three records to the WRITERS table. If you have not done so, place your Student Disk in the appropriate drive, launch Access, open the Issue25 database on your Student Disk, maximize the Database window, click the WRITERS table, and then click the Open command button. The Datasheet View window appears, and the insertion point is at the beginning of the Writer ID field for the first record.

To add records in a table's datasheet:

❶ Type **N425**, which is the first record's Writer ID field value, and press **[Tab]**. Each time you press **[Tab]**, the insertion point moves to the right to the next field in the record.

❷ Continue to enter the field values for all three records shown in Figure 3-2. For the Writer Phone field values, type the digits only. Access automatically supplies the parentheses, spaces, and hyphens from the field's input mask. If the value for the Freelancer field is the default value Yes, simply press **[Tab]** to accept the displayed value and move to the next field. Press **[Tab]** to move from the Amount field in the first two rows to the start of the next record, but do not press **[Tab]** after typing the Amount field for the third record. See Figure 3-3.

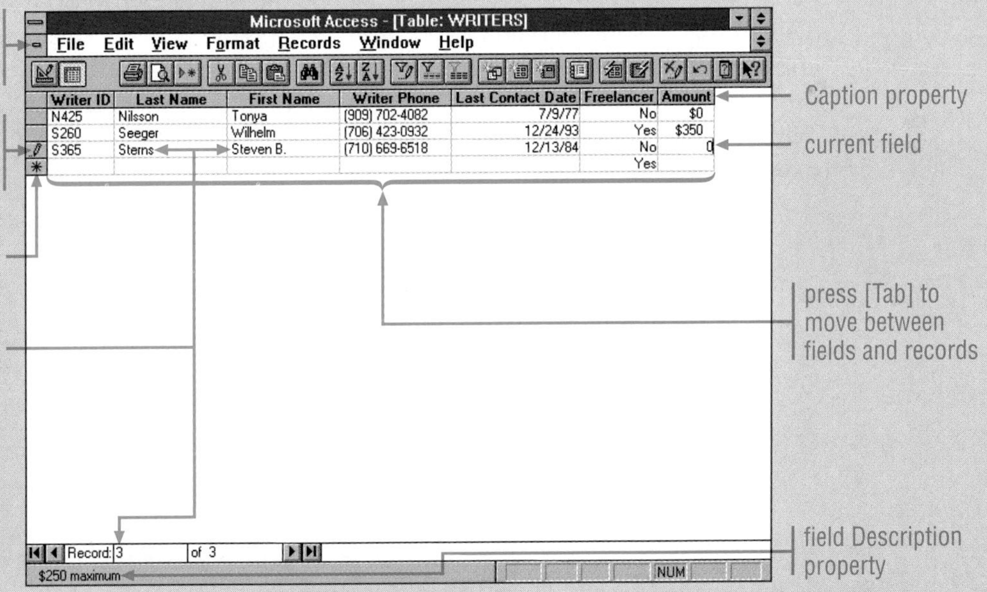

Figure 3-3
The WRITERS table datasheet with the first three records entered

TROUBLE? If you enter any field value incorrectly, double-click the field value to highlight it and retype the field value correctly to replace it.

Two new symbols appear in the record selectors for rows three and four. The pencil symbol in the third row indicates that you have made changes to the current record and have not yet saved the changes. The asterisk symbol in the fourth row shows you the next row available for entering a new record.

TROUBLE? If the pencil symbol and the asterisk symbol do not appear exactly as shown in Figure 3-3, the insertion point might be in the fourth row. If the current record symbol (a black, right-facing triangle) appears in the record selector for row four, then just observe these two new symbols the next time you make a change. If the pencil symbol and asterisk symbol appear in the fourth and fifth rows, then you should double-click the Datasheet View window Control menu box and click the OK button two times to close the datasheet and return to the Database window. Then click the WRITERS table and click the Open command button to redisplay the datasheet.

Elena has completed her first task, so she continues with the next two tasks on her list.

Changing a Field's Properties

Elena's next two tasks are to change the WRITERS table structure and the table datasheet if changes are needed. Because all field values and field names fit in their datasheet boxes, Elena does not need to change the datasheet. If a datasheet column were too narrow to display the entire field name and all the field values, however, Elena could resize the column for that field to widen it.

The value $350 in the Amount field for the second record catches Elena's eye, because the field's description in the status bar reads "$250 maximum." Elena realizes that $250 is a maximum for each reprinted article and not a maximum value for the field. She changes the field description in the Table Design View window to "$250 maximum per article." Elena also reassesses the field name Freelancer Reprint Payment Amount and decides that Amount would be a shorter, acceptable table field name. This table structure change makes the field name and the field caption the same, so Elena deletes the Caption property for the field. All these changes are field definition changes that are made in the Table Design View window. You can add fields to a table and modify field properties even after you have added data to the table.

To change properties for a field:

1. Click the **Design View button** to close the datasheet and open the Table Design View window.
2. To change the description for the field, click the right end of the Description box for Freelancer Reprint Payment Amount, press **[Spacebar]**, and then type **per article**.
3. To change the field's name, click anywhere in the Field Name box for Freelancer Reprint Payment Amount, press **[F2]** to highlight the entire field name, and then type **Amount**.
4. To delete the field's Caption property, double-click **Amount** in the Caption text box, click the right mouse button in the same text box to open the Shortcut menu, and then click **Cut** in the Shortcut menu.

Now that she has changed field properties, Elena meets with Judith to discuss the list of articles for the special issue.

Changing Records

During the meeting with Judith, Elena notices some differences between the preliminary and final lists of writers for the special issue. First, Tonya Nilsson, who is one of the three writers she just added to the WRITERS table, is a freelancer and will be paid $450 for her two reprint articles. Elena entered Nilsson as a staff writer, so she needs to change both the Freelancer and Amount fields for Nilsson. Elena also added Steven B. Sterns to the WRITERS table, and he does not appear in the final list. Thus, Elena needs to delete his record from the table.

Changing Field Values

Elena's next task is to change the two field values for Tonya Nilsson in the WRITERS table datasheet. The field values for Freelancer and for Amount are to be Yes and $450, respectively. The Table Design View window for the WRITERS table should still be displayed on the screen, so Elena first opens the WRITERS table datasheet.

To change field values in a datasheet:

1. Click the **Datasheet View button** and then click the **OK button** in the "Save now?" dialog box.
2. Double-click **No** in the Freelancer column for the first record, type **yes**, press **[Tab]**, and then type **450**. See Figure 3-4. Both field values in the first record are now correctly changed. Access changed the entered value "yes" to "Yes."

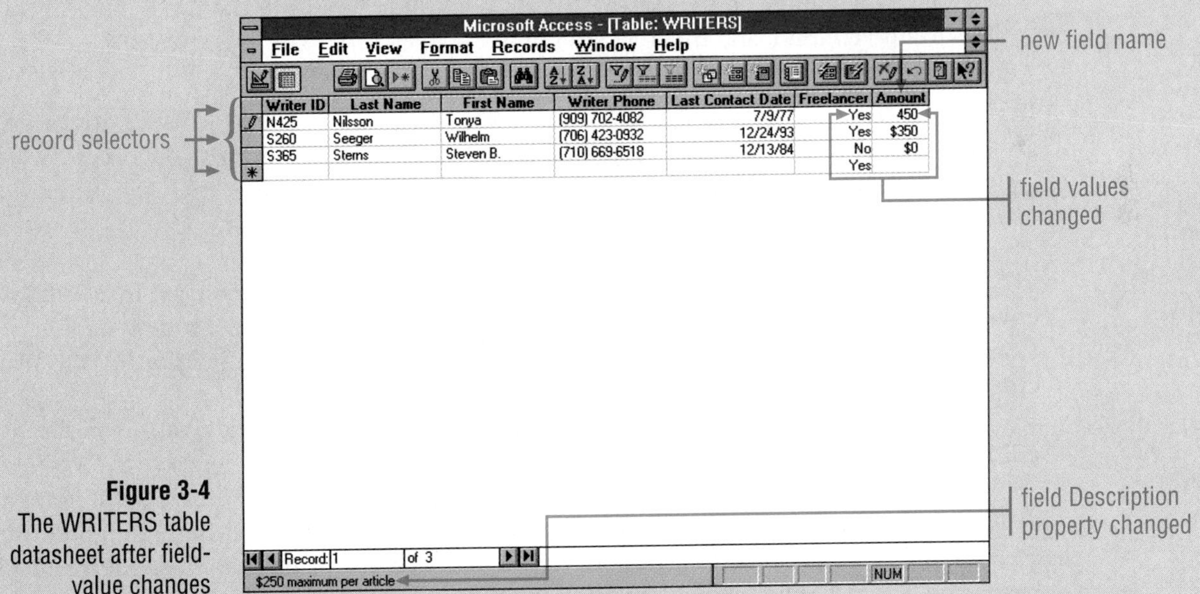

Figure 3-4
The WRITERS table datasheet after field-value changes

3. Press **[Tab]**; the dollar symbol appears in front of the field value 450 as the insertion point moves to the start of the next row.

Access saves the changes you make to the current record whenever you move to a different record. Thus, your data is kept current as you make changes, and you do not need to worry about losing your changes if a hardware or software problem occurs.

Using the Mouse and Keyboard

You use the mouse to move through the fields and records in a datasheet or to make changes to field values. The mouse techniques you use include those for movement, selection, and placement. To move to a specific record in the Datasheet View window, for example, you click combinations of the scroll bars and arrows on the right and at the bottom, the navigation buttons on the lower-left, and the record selectors on the left. Also, clicking a record selector when the pointer appears as ➡ selects an entire row, and clicking a field name box when the pointer appears as ⬇ selects an entire column. You can also select entire field values by clicking the ⇖ that appears when you position the mouse pointer near the left side of a field-value box. Finally, when the pointer changes to I, clicking a field-value box makes that row the current record and places the insertion point at that field-value position.

Let's practice these mouse techniques on the WRITERS datasheet that you are now viewing.

To change the location of the selection and insertion points using a mouse:

1. Click the **Last Record navigation button** ▶| to highlight the Writer ID field value in the third, or last, record. The third row becomes the current record.
2. Click the record selector for the first row when the pointer changes to ➡. Access highlights the entire first record.
3. Click the **Writer Phone field-name box** when the pointer changes to ⬇. Access highlights the entire fourth column.
4. Position the pointer on the left side of the field-value box for Wilhelm in the First Name column, and then click when it changes to ⇖. The entire field value is highlighted, and the second row becomes the current record.
5. Position the I between the 1 and the 3 in the third record's Last Contact Date field value and click. The insertion point appears there, and the third row becomes the current record.

Most Access keyboard techniques are also compatible with those used in a Windows environment, but Access has some keyboard techniques that might be new to you. For example, Access handles navigation and selection through a combination of the usual cursor-movement keystrokes and the [F2] key.

The **[F2] key** is a toggle that you use to switch between navigation mode and editing mode.

- In **navigation mode**, Access highlights, or selects, an entire field value. If you type while you are in navigation mode, your typed entry replaces the highlighted field value. Using a cursor-movement key when you are in navigation mode results in the field value being highlighted in the new location.
- In **editing mode**, you can replace or insert characters in a field-value box based on the position ofthe insertion point. You press [Ins] to switch between replacement and insertion, which is the default. When you are replacing characters, the right side of the status bar at the bottom of the screen displays the letters OVR, which is an abbreviation for "overtype," and one character is highlighted. The character you type replaces the highlighted character. When you are inserting characters, the right side of the status bar displays spaces, and the insertion point blinks between characters. The character you type is inserted between the characters.

The navigation-mode and editing-mode keyboard movement techniques are shown in Figure 3-5. They allow numerous selection and insertion-point movement possibilities. You can perform moves that involve two keys by holding down the first key and pressing the second key. You will find, however, that using the mouse is faster than using the keyboard. Use Figure 3-5 for reference or if you want to practice some of the keyboard movement techniques.

Press	To Move the Selection Point in Navigation Mode	To Move the Insertion Point in Editing Mode
[Left Arrow]	Left one field value at a time	Left one character at a time
[Right Arrow] or [Tab] or [Enter]	Right one field value at a time	Right one character at a time
[Home]	Left to the first field value in the record	Before the first character in the field value
[End]	Right to the last field value in the record	After the last character in the field value
[Up Arrow] or [Down Arrow]	Up or down one record at a time	Up or down one record at a time and switch to navigation mode
[Pg Up]	To previous screen	To previous screen and switch to navigation mode
[Pg Dn]	To next screen	To next screen and switch to navigation mode
[Ctrl] [Left Arrow] or [Ctrl] [Right Arrow]	Left or right one field value at a time	Left or right one word at a time
[Ctrl] [Up Arrow] or [Ctrl] [Down Arrow]	To first or last record	Before the first character or after the last character in the field
[Ctrl] [PgUp]	Left to first field value in the record	Before the first character in the field value
[Ctrl] [PgDn]	Right to the last field value in the record	After the last character in the field value
[Ctrl] [Home]	To the first field value in the first record	Before the first character in the field value
[Ctrl] [End]	To the last field value in the last record	After the last character in the field value

Figure 3-5
Navigation-and editing-mode keyboard movement techniques

When you are in editing mode, Access supports the usual Windows keyboard deletion techniques, as shown in Figure 3-6 on the following page. If you are in navigation mode, however, using any of the deletion keystrokes causes Access to delete the entire selection.

Press	To Delete
[Del]	The character to the right of the insertion point
[Backspace]	The character to the left of the insertion point
[Ctrl] [Del]	Text from the insertion point to the end of the word
[Ctrl] [Backspace]	Text from the insertion point to the beginning of the word

Figure 3-6
Keyboard deletion techniques in editing mode

Let's practice these deletion techniques in editing mode.

To use the keyboard deletion techniques in editing mode:

1. If you have moved the cursor, click between the 1 and the 3 in the third record's Last Contact Date field-value box to place the insertion point there and to switch to editing mode. Press **[Del]** to remove the 3 and then press **[Backspace]** to remove the 1.
2. Press **[Ctrl][Backspace]** to remove the 12/ and then press **[Ctrl][Del]** to remove the /84. The field value should now be null.
3. To restore the original field value, click the **Undo Current Field/Record button** on the toolbar. Access highlights the entire field value and switches from editing mode to navigation mode.

Changing Datasheet Properties

Elena has completed her initial changes to the WRITERS table. Before continuing with her next task, however, Elena changes the datasheet font to a larger size. Because you can create tables with dozens of fields, Access uses the default font MS Sans Serif and the default font size 8 for screen display. The small font size allows Access to display more data on the screen than it could with a larger font size. If your table has few fields, you can make the data easier to read by choosing a larger font size.

REFERENCE WINDOW

Changing a Datasheet's Font Properties

- Open the Format menu.
- Click Font... to open the Font dialog box.
- Select the font from the Font list box.
- Select the font style from the Font Style list box.
- Select the font size from the Size list box.
- Click the Underline check box if you want to select this special effect.
- A sample of the font characteristics appears in the Sample box as options are chosen. Click the OK button to accept the changes in the Font dialog box.

Let's change the font size for the WRITERS datasheet.

To change the datasheet font size:

❶ Click **Format**, and then click **Font...** to display the Font dialog box. See Figure 3-7.

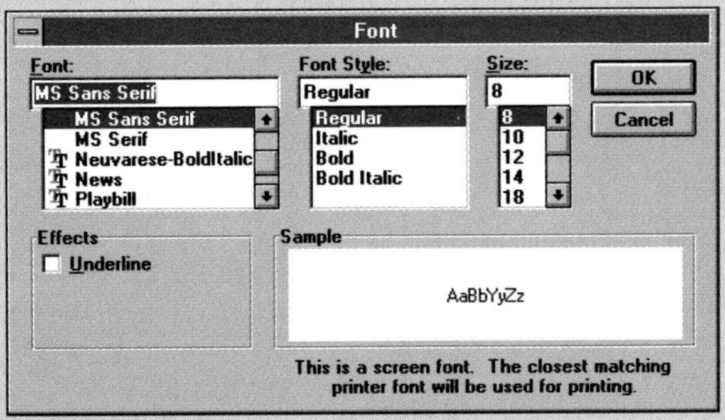

Figure 3-7 The Font dialog box

❷ Click **10** in the Size list box. The Sample box changes to show the larger font size.

❸ Click the **OK button** to accept the font size change. The Font dialog box disappears, and the datasheet displays the selected font size in place of the original default size.

Access automatically increases the row height to accommodate the larger font size. You can change the row height using the Format menu, but it is usually better to let Access make row height adjustments automatically.

Now that Elena has changed the datasheet font size, she notices that several of the field name boxes no longer display the field names in their entirety. She resizes the datasheet column widths for all the datasheet fields.

To resize datasheet column widths:

❶ Use the Format menu, the mouse pointer, or the best-fit column width method to resize datasheet columns until each field-name box displays the entire field name. Fit the entire datasheet on the screen by narrowing some column widths, if necessary. See Figure 3-8.

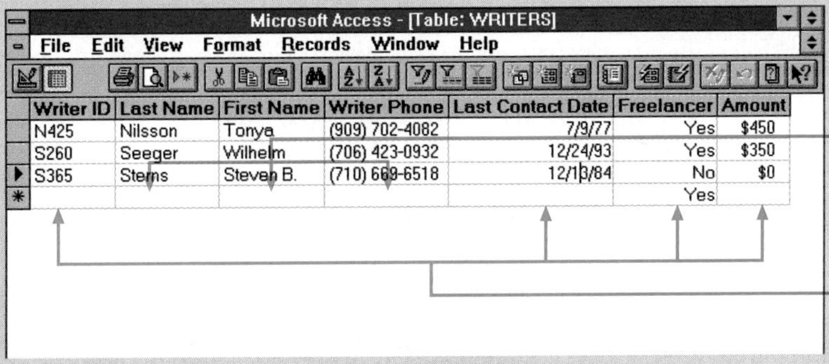

Figure 3-8 The datasheet after column width changes

Deleting Records

Elena needs to make one last update to the WRITERS table. Steven B. Sterns should not be included in the final list of writers for the special anniversary issue, so Elena deletes his record from the table.

REFERENCE WINDOW

Deleting Records from a Table

- Click the record selector of the record you want to delete. If you want to delete two or more consecutive records, click the record selector of the first record and hold the mouse button, while dragging the ➡ to the last record selector of the group, and then release.
- Click the right mouse button in the record selector to display the Shortcut menu.
- Click Cut in the Shortcut menu. The "Delete record" dialog box appears.
- Click the OK button to delete the record or records.

Let's delete the third record from the WRITERS datasheet and then close the datasheet.

To delete a datasheet record and close a datasheet:

❶ Click the record selector for the third record. Access highlights the entire third row.

❷ Click the right mouse button in the record selector for the third record. Access displays the Shortcut menu.

❸ Click **Cut** in the Shortcut menu. Access displays the "Delete record" dialog box. See Figure 3-9. The current record indicator is positioned in the third row's record selector, and all field values (except default values) in the third record have disappeared.

Datasheet View window Control menu box

current record to be deleted

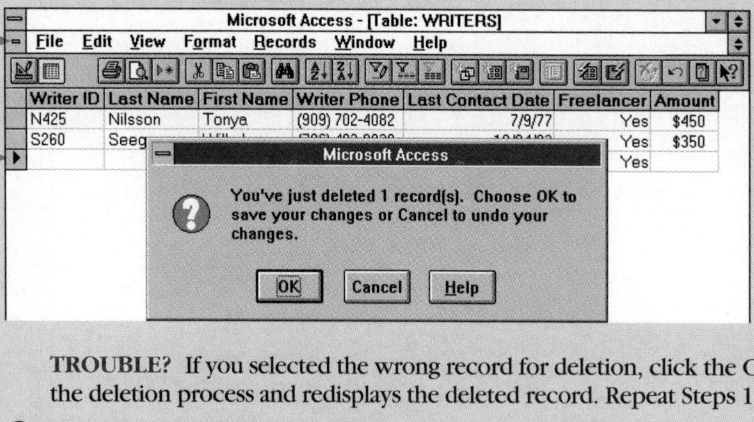

Figure 3-9
The "Delete record" dialog box

TROUBLE? If you selected the wrong record for deletion, click the Cancel button. Access ends the deletion process and redisplays the deleted record. Repeat Steps 1 and 2 for the third record.

❹ Click the **OK button**. Access deletes the third record from the WRITERS table.

❺ Double-click the Datasheet View window **Control menu box**. Access displays the message "Save layout changes to Table 'WRITERS'?"

❻ Click the **Yes button**. The dialog box disappears, and then the datasheet disappears. The Database window becomes the active window.

If you want to take a break and resume the tutorial at a later time, you can exit Access by double-clicking the Microsoft Access window Control menu box. When you resume the tutorial, place your Student Disk in the appropriate drive, launch Access, open the Issue25 database on your Student Disk, and maximize the Database window.

■ ■ ■

Importing Data

After Elena finishes deleting the table record, she asks Judith to help her add the remaining writers to the WRITERS table. While Judith and Brian were selecting the final articles for the special anniversary issue, Judith was also maintaining a database table containing data about the selected writers. If they use Access to transfer writers' data from Judith's database to Elena's database, Elena will save time and will be sure that the data is accurate.

Judith first verifies that she has all the fields Elena needs for the WRITERS table and finds that their table structures are compatible. Judith will show Elena how to import this special table from the Vision database to the Issue25 database.

Importing data involves copying data from a text file, spreadsheet, or database table into a new Access table. You can also import objects from another Access database into an open database. You can import data from Access tables; from spreadsheets, such as Excel and Lotus 1-2-3; from database management systems, such as Paradox, dBASE, and FoxPro; and from delimited text and fixed-width text files. Importing existing data, as shown in Figure 3-10, saves you time and eliminates potential data-entry errors.

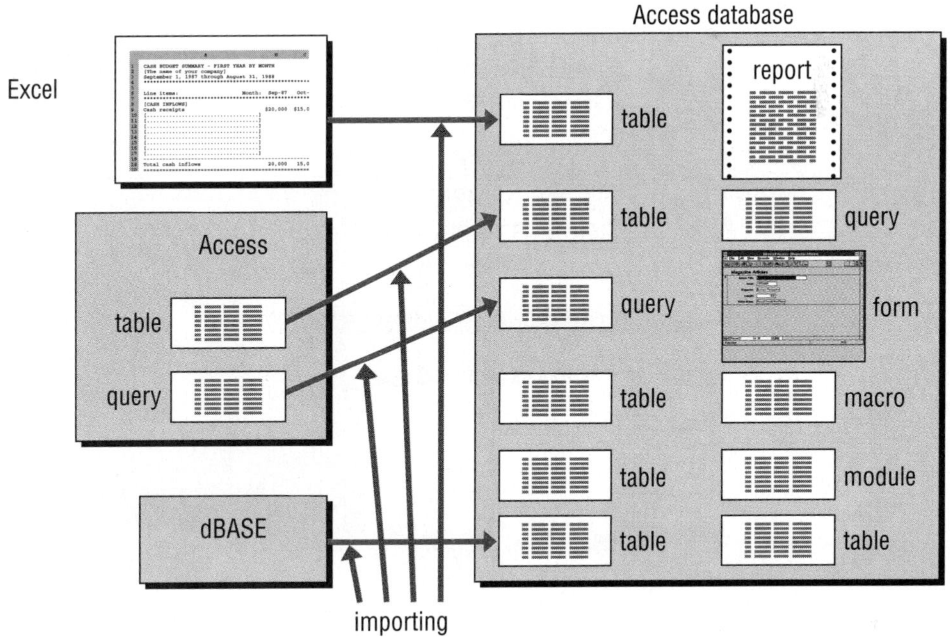

Figure 3-10
Importing data

REFERENCE WINDOW

Importing an Access Table

- Click the toolbar Import button (or click File, and then click Import...). The Import dialog box appears.
- Select Microsoft Access in the Data Source list box, and then click the OK button. The Import dialog box disappears, and the Select Microsoft Access Database dialog box appears.
- Select the drive and directory combination that has the database containing the table you want to import. From the File Name list box, select the database name.
- Click the OK button to accept your selections and close the dialog box. Access displays the Import Objects dialog box.
- Select Tables in the Object Type list box, select the desired table name from the Objects list box, click the Structure and Data option button, and then click the Import button to complete your selections. If you want to import only the table structure and not the table's records, click the Structure Only option button instead of the Structure and Data option button.
- Access imports the table and displays the "Successfully Imported" dialog box.
- Click the OK button in the dialog box, and then click Close in the Import Objects dialog box. Access adds the imported table name to the Tables list box in the Database window.

Let's import the table named "WRITERS tutorial 3 import" from the Vision database to your Issue25 database. Be sure that the Issue25 database is open and the active Database window is maximized.

To import an Access table:

1. Click the **Import button** on the toolbar. Access displays the Import dialog box. See Figure 3-11.

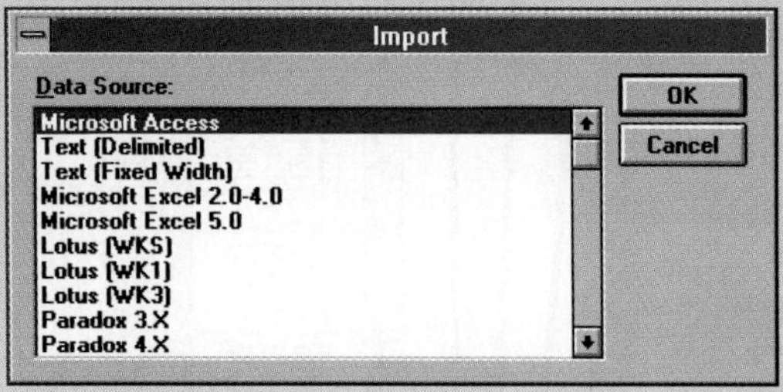

Figure 3-11 The Import dialog box

❷ If necessary, click **Microsoft Access** in the Data Source list box to highlight it; then click the **OK button**. The dialog box disappears, and Access displays the Select Microsoft Access Database dialog box.

❸ In the Drives drop-down list box, select the drive that contains your Student Disk. Next, scroll down the File Name list box and click **vision.mdb**. See Figure 3-12.

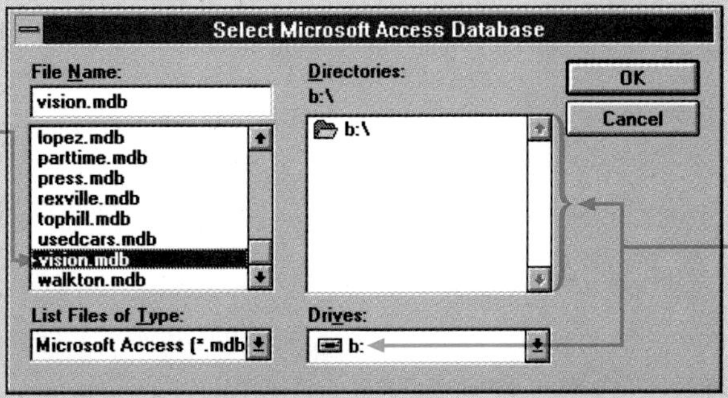

Figure 3-12 The Select Microsoft Access Database dialog box

❹ Click the **OK button**. The dialog box disappears, and Access displays the Import Objects dialog box. See Figure 3-13.

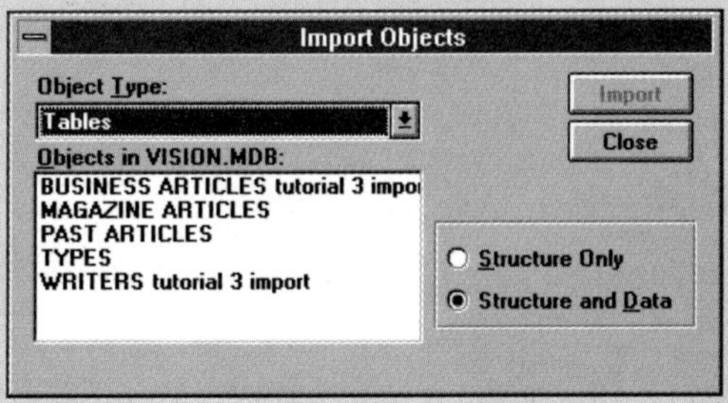

Figure 3-13 The Import Objects dialog box

❺ The Tables selection should be highlighted in the Object Type list box. If not, then click **Tables** in the drop-down list box. Next, click **WRITERS tutorial 3 import** in the Objects in VISION.MDB list box, click the **Structure and Data button**, and then click the **Import button**. Access imports the table, and displays the "Successfully Imported" dialog box on top of the Import Objects dialog box.

❻ Click the **OK button** in the "Successfully Imported" dialog box to close the dialog box, and then click the **Close button** in the Import Objects dialog box. The dialog box disappears.

❼ The Database window now displays the new table in the Tables list box. If you want, you can open this new table to view its 14 records, but do not update any of the records. When you are done viewing the records, close the table by double-clicking the Datasheet View window Control menu box.

Deleting a Table

Because the "WRITERS tutorial 3 import" table contains the records she needs, Elena no longer needs the WRITERS table. She deletes this table.

REFERENCE WINDOW

Deleting a Table

- In the Database window, click the table that you want to delete.
- Click the right mouse button to open the Shortcut menu.
- Click Delete. The "Delete Table" dialog box appears.
- Click the OK button. The "Delete Table" dialog box disappears, and Access deletes the table. When the active Database window appears, it does not list the table you just deleted.

Let's delete the WRITERS table.

To delete a table:

❶ Click the **WRITERS** table and then click the **WRITERS** table again with the right mouse button. Access displays the Shortcut menu.

❷ Click **Delete**. The "Delete Table" dialog box appears. See Figure 3-14.

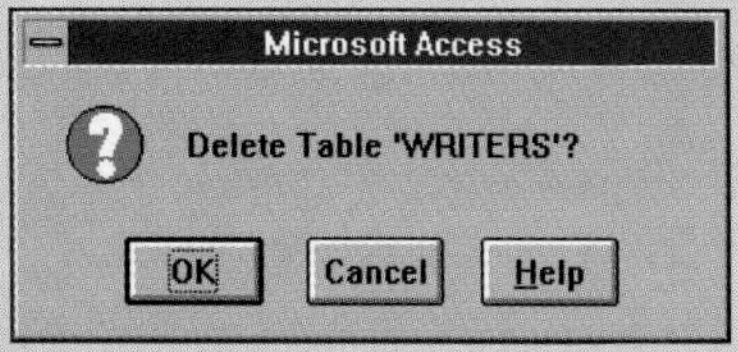

Figure 3-14
The "Delete Table" dialog box

❸ Click the **OK button**. The dialog box disappears, and the WRITERS table no longer appears in the Tables list box.

Renaming a Table

Elena renames the "WRITERS tutorial 3 import" table to WRITERS.

To rename a table:

❶ Click **WRITERS tutorial 3 import** in the Tables list box and then click **WRITERS tutorial 3 import** again with the right mouse button. Access displays the Shortcut menu. See Figure 3-15.

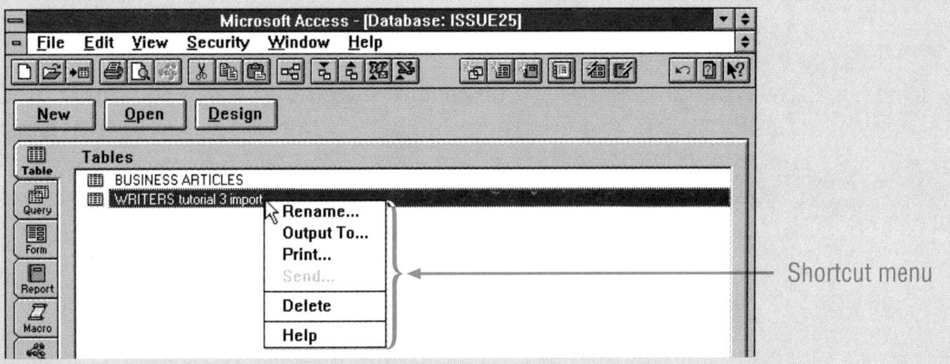

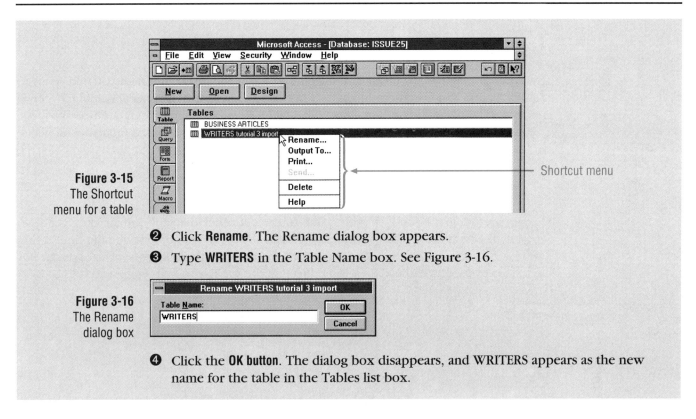

Figure 3-15 The Shortcut menu for a table

❷ Click **Rename**. The Rename dialog box appears.

❸ Type **WRITERS** in the Table Name box. See Figure 3-16.

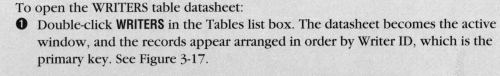

Figure 3-16 The Rename dialog box

❹ Click the **OK button**. The dialog box disappears, and WRITERS appears as the new name for the table in the Tables list box.

Elena next reviews the imported records in the WRITERS table by opening the datasheet.

To open the WRITERS table datasheet:

❶ Double-click **WRITERS** in the Tables list box. The datasheet becomes the active window, and the records appear arranged in order by Writer ID, which is the primary key. See Figure 3-17.

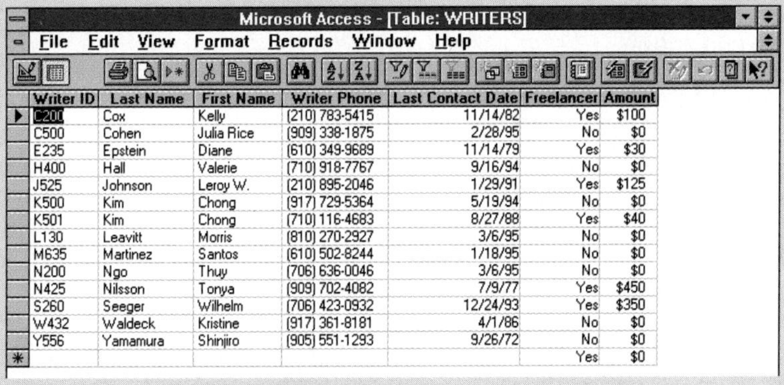

Writer ID	Last Name	First Name	Writer Phone	Last Contact Date	Freelancer	Amount
C200	Cox	Kelly	(210) 783-5415	11/14/82	Yes	$100
C500	Cohen	Julia Rice	(909) 338-1875	2/28/95	No	$0
E235	Epstein	Diane	(610) 349-9689	11/14/79	Yes	$30
H400	Hall	Valerie	(710) 918-7767	9/16/94	No	$0
J525	Johnson	Leroy W.	(210) 895-2046	1/29/91	Yes	$125
K500	Kim	Chong	(917) 729-5364	5/19/94	No	$0
K501	Kim	Chong	(710) 116-4683	8/27/88	Yes	$40
L130	Leavitt	Morris	(810) 270-2927	3/6/95	No	$0
M635	Martinez	Santos	(610) 502-8244	1/18/95	No	$0
N200	Ngo	Thuy	(706) 636-0046	3/6/95	No	$0
N425	Nilsson	Tonya	(909) 702-4082	7/9/77	Yes	$450
S260	Seeger	Wilhelm	(706) 423-0932	12/24/93	Yes	$350
W432	Waldeck	Kristine	(917) 361-8181	4/1/86	No	$0
Y556	Yamamura	Shinjiro	(905) 551-1293	9/26/72	No	$0
					Yes	$0

Figure 3-17 The WRITERS datasheet with newly imported records

To open a table's datasheet from the Database window, you click the table name and then click the Open command button. You can also open a datasheet by double-clicking the table name. Because the second method is faster, you will use it in future tutorials.

Finding and Replacing Data in a Datasheet

Even though records are physically stored on disk in the order in which you add them to a table, Access displays them in primary-key sequence in the datasheet. Finding a record in the WRITERS table based on a specific Writer ID value, therefore, is a simple process. Because of the small size of the WRITERS table, finding records based on a specific value for another field is also relatively simple.

Finding Data

Finding records based on a specific value for a field other than the primary key is not so simple when you are working with larger tables. You can spend considerable time trying to locate the records and can easily miss one or more of them in your visual search. For these situations, you can use the Find button on the toolbar to help your search.

REFERENCE WINDOW

Finding Data in a Table

- Click anywhere in the field column you want to search.
- Click the Find button on the toolbar.
- In the Find What box, type the field value you want to find.
- To find field values that entirely match a value, select Match Whole Field in the Where box.
- To find a match between a value and any part of a field's value, select Any Part of Field in the Where box.
- To find a match between a value and the start of a field's value, select Start of Field in the Where box.
- To search all fields for the search value, click the All Fields option button.
- To find matches with a certain pattern of lowercase and uppercase letters, click the Match Case option box.
- Click the Up option button if you want the search to go from the current record to earlier records in the table, rather than down, which is the default.
- Click the Find First button to have Access begin the search at the top of the table, or click the Find Next button to begin the search at the current record. If a match is found, Access scrolls the table and highlights the field value.
- Click the Find Next button to continue the search for the next match. Access displays the "End of records" dialog box if the search began at a record other than the first and it reaches the last record without finding a match. Click the Yes button to continue searching from the first record.
- Click the Close button to stop the search operation.

Let's search the WRITERS table for phone numbers that have a 909 area code.

To find data in a table:

❶ Click the **Writer Phone box** for the fourth record.

❷ Click the **Find button** on the toolbar. Access displays the Find dialog box. See Figure 3-18.

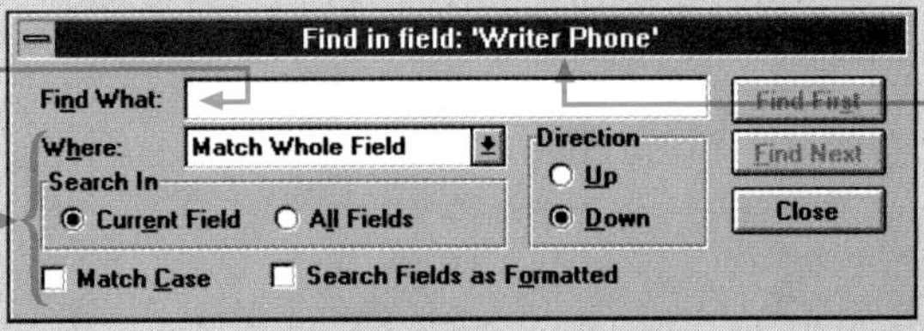

Figure 3-18
The Find dialog box

❸ Type the search value **909** in the Find What text box. The left parenthesis, which is the first character of the Writer Phone field, is part of the input mask and not part of the field value. Therefore, searching for 909 at the start of the field is the same as searching for 909 area codes.

❹ Click the **down arrow button** in the Where drop-down list box, and then click **Start of Field** to restrict the search to the first three digits of the Writer Phone field. To start the search, click the **Find Next button**. Access finds a match in the 11th record. Record 11 is displayed as the current record number at the bottom of the screen between the navigation buttons, and the field value is hidden behind the dialog box. See Figure 3-19.

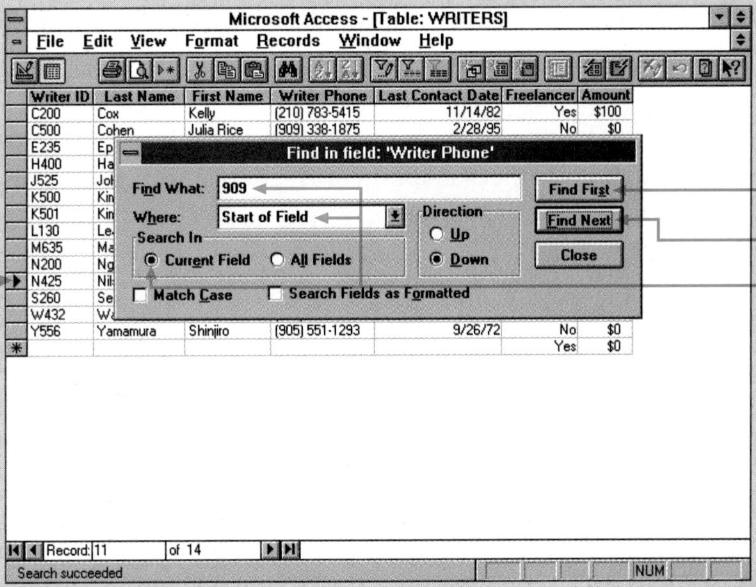

Figure 3-19
Completed Find dialog box

TROUBLE? If the second record becomes the current record instead of the 11th record, you did not click the Writer Phone box for the fourth record in Step 1. Click the Close button in the Find dialog box and repeat your work starting with Step 1.

The Find dialog box remains open and hides a portion of the datasheet. You can move the dialog box so that it covers less critical parts of the datasheet.

To move a dialog box:

1. Click the Find dialog box **title bar** and hold down the mouse button.
2. Drag the dialog box outline to the lower-right corner of the screen and release the mouse button. See Figure 3-20.

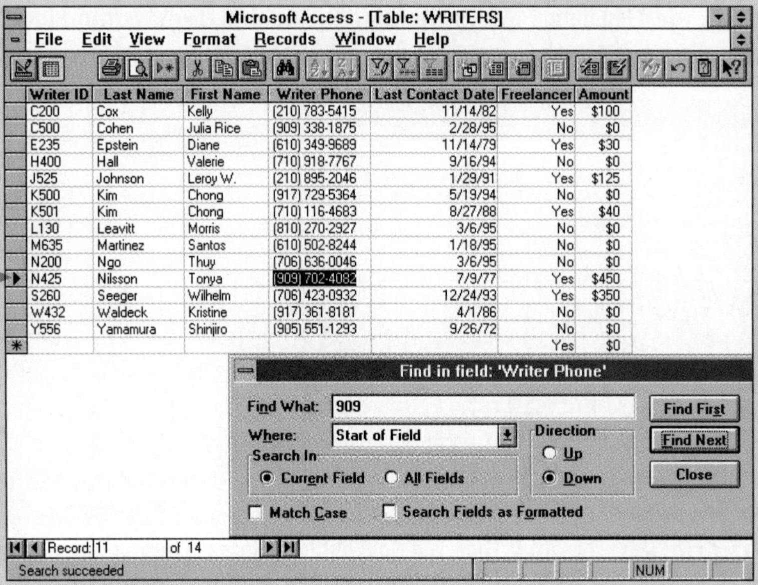

current record completely in view

Figure 3-20
The Find dialog box repositioned

You can now see the entire record found by the Find operation. To find other records that match the search criterion, you continue by again clicking the Find Next button.

To continue a Find operation:

1. Click the **Find Next button**. Access reaches the end of the table without finding a match and displays the "End of records" dialog box.
2. Click the **Yes button** to continue the search from the beginning of the table. Access finds a match in the second record and highlights the entire Writer Phone field value.
3. Click the **Close button** in the Find dialog box. The Find dialog box disappears.

You can use the standard DOS wildcard characters in the Find What text box. Use an asterisk (*) to represent any sequence of characters, and use a question mark (?) to represent any single character. You can also use the number symbol (#) to represent any single digit.

Replacing Data

While verifying the WRITERS data, Judith and Elena notice that the digits 909 appear only in the area code portion of the Writer Phone field. If they need to search for records having a 909 area code again that day, they will not need to restrict the search to the start of the field. They also notice that the two records with 909 area codes should have 905 area codes instead. Elena corrects these values by using the Replace option on the Edit menu. You use the Replace option to find a specific value in your records and replace that value with another value.

REFERENCE WINDOW

Replacing Data in a Table

- Click anywhere in the field column in which you want to replace data.
- Click Edit and then click Replace....
- In the Find What box, type the field value you want to find.
- Type the replacement value in the Replace With box.
- To search all fields for the search value, click the All Fields option button.
- To find field values that entirely match a value, click the Match Whole Field option box.
- To find matches with a certain pattern of lowercase and uppercase letters, click the Match Case option box.
- Click the Find Next button to begin the search at the current record. If a match is found, Access scrolls the table and highlights the field value.
- Click the Replace button to substitute the replacement value for the search value, or click the Find Next button to leave the highlighted value unchanged and to continue the search for the next match.
- Access displays the "End of records" dialog box if the replacement began at a record other than the first and it reaches the last record without finding its next match. Click the Yes button to continue searching from the first record.
- Click the Replace All button to perform the search and replace without stopping for confirmation of each replacement.
- Click the Close button to stop the replacement operation.

Let's search the WRITERS table and replace the 909 phone number area codes with 905.

To replace data in a table:

1. Click the **Writer Phone box** for the fifth record.
2. Click **Edit**, and then click **Replace....** Access displays the Replace dialog box. See Figure 3-21. Because you previously repositioned the Find dialog box, the Replace dialog box is similarly positioned. Your previous search value, 909, appears in the new Find What box.

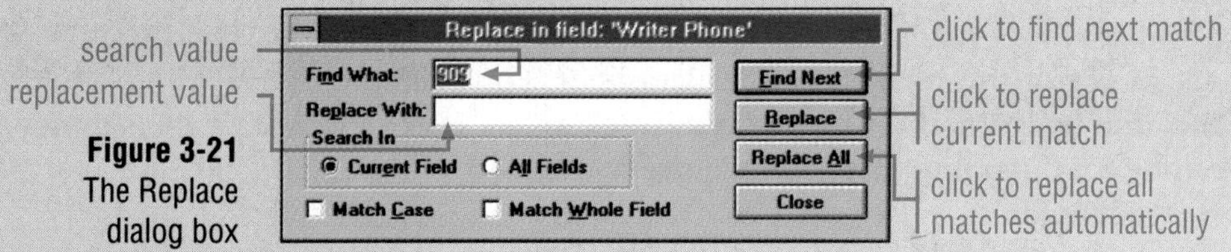

Figure 3-21 The Replace dialog box

3. Press **[Tab]** and then type **905** in the Replace With text box.
4. To start the replacement process, click the **Replace All button**. Access finds all 909 area codes in the table and replaces them with 905 area codes.

5. You might get one or more different "End of records" dialog boxes. For each one, click the **Yes button** or the **OK button**, as appropriate, to close the dialog box and continue the replace operation.
6. Access displays a dialog box that states: "You won't be able to undo this replace operation. Choose OK to continue or Cancel to undo the change(s) you just made." Access displays this message when more than one replacement occurs, because it cannot undo all the replacements it makes. When this message box appears, click the **OK button** to complete the replacement operation.
7. Click the **Close button** in the Replace dialog box.

   TROUBLE? If no replacement occurred, try repeating the preceding steps starting with Step 2. Be sure the Match Whole Field option is not checked in the Replace dialog box before Step 4.
8. Preview and print a copy of the datasheet, using the Print Preview button as you have done before.

   TROUBLE? If, in the printed copy, a field, such as Writer Phone, contains only parts of the field values, return to the Datasheet View window, resize the column, and reprint the datasheet. Also, if the printed copy takes up two pages, return to the Datasheet View window, resize columns to make them narrower, without hiding any of the field names or field values, and reprint the datasheet.

You can use the standard DOS wildcard characters in the Find What text box, but not in the Replace With text box.

Sorting Records in a Datasheet

Elena will be contacting the writers who are listed in the WRITERS datasheet. She feels she will be more successful reaching those writers having a recent contact date, so she wants to view the datasheet records arranged by the Last Contact Date field. Because the datasheet displays records in Writer ID, or primary-key, sequence, Elena needs to sort the records in the datasheet.

Sorting is the process of rearranging records in a specified order or sequence. Most companies sort their data before they display or print it because staff use the information in different ways according to their job responsibilities. For example, Brian might want to review writer information arranged by the Amount field because he is interested in knowing what the writers will be paid. On the other hand, Elena wants her information arranged by date of last contact because she will be calling the writers.

When you sort records in a datasheet, Access does not change the sequence of records in the underlying table. Only the records in the datasheet are rearranged according to your specifications.

To sort a table's records, you select the **sort key**, which is the field used to determine the order of the records in the datasheet. For example, Elena wants to sort the WRITERS data by last contact date, so the Last Contact Date field will be the sort key. Sort keys can be text, number, date/time, currency, counter, or yes/no fields, but not memo or OLE object fields.

You sort records in either ascending (increasing) or descending (decreasing) order. Sorting the WRITERS data in descending order by last contact date means that the record with the most recent date will be the first record in the datasheet. The record with the earliest, or oldest, date will be the last record in the datasheet. If the sort key is a number, currency, or counter field, ascending order means from lowest to highest numeric value; descending means the reverse. If the sort key is a text field, ascending order means alphabetical order beginning with A. Descending order begins with Z. For yes/no fields, ascending order means yes values appear first; descending order means no values appear first.

Sort keys can be unique or nonunique. Sort keys are **unique** if the value of the sort-key field for each record is different. The Writer ID field in the WRITERS table is an example of a unique sort key, because each writer has a different value in the ID field. Sort keys are **nonunique** if more than one record can have the same value for the sort key field. The Freelancer field in the WRITERS table is a nonunique sort key because more than one record has the same value (either yes or no).

When the sort key is nonunique, records with the same sort-key value are grouped together, but they are not in a specific order within the group. To arrange these grouped records in a specific order, you can specify a **secondary sort key**, which is a second sort-key field. The first sort-key field is called the **primary sort key**. Note that the primary sort key is not the same as the table's primary-key field. A table has at most one primary key, which must be unique, whereas any field in a table can serve as a primary sort key.

Quick Sorting a Single Field

The **Sort Ascending** and the **Sort Descending buttons** on the toolbar are called quick-sort buttons. **Quick sort buttons** allow you to sort records immediately, based on the selected field. You first select the column on which you want to base the sort and then click the appropriate quick sort button on the toolbar to rearrange the records in either ascending or descending order.

Elena uses the Sort Descending button to rearrange the records in descending order by the Last Contact Date field.

To quick sort records in a datasheet:

1. Click anywhere in the **Last Contact Date column** to establish that field as the current field.
2. Click the **Sort Descending button** on the toolbar. Access rearranges the records in descending order by last contact date. See Figure 3-22.

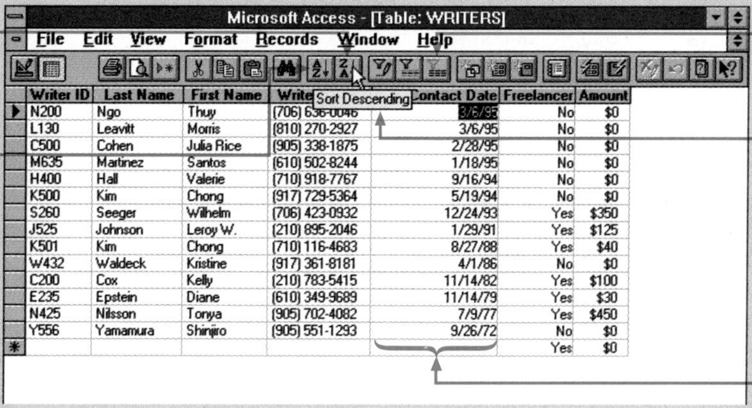

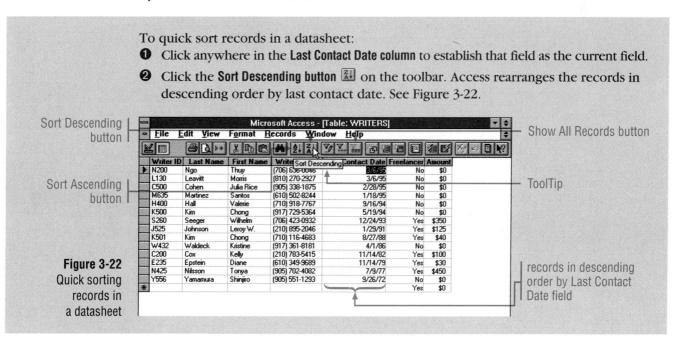

Figure 3-22
Quick sorting records in a datasheet

You can restore the records to their original Writer ID order by clicking the Show All Records button on the toolbar.

To restore records to their original order:

1. Click the **Show All Records button** on the toolbar. Access rearranges the records in ascending Writer ID order.

Quick Sorting Multiple Fields

Access allows you to quick sort a datasheet using two or more sort keys. The sort-key fields must be in adjacent columns in the datasheet. You highlight the columns, and Access sorts first by the first column and then by each other highlighted column in order from left to right. Because you click either the Sort Ascending or the Sort Descending button to perform a quick sort, each of the multiple sort-key fields is in either ascending or descending sort order.

Elena selects the adjacent fields Freelancer and Amount and performs an ascending-order quick sort.

To use multiple sort keys to quick sort records in a datasheet:

1. Click the **Freelancer field selector**, which is the gray box containing the field name at the top of the column, and, while holding down the mouse button, drag the ⬇ to the right until both the Freelancer and Amount columns are highlighted. Then release the mouse button.

2. Click the **Sort Ascending button** on the toolbar. Access rearranges the records to place them in ascending order by Freelancer and, when the Freelancer field values are the same, in ascending order by Amount. See Figure 3-23.

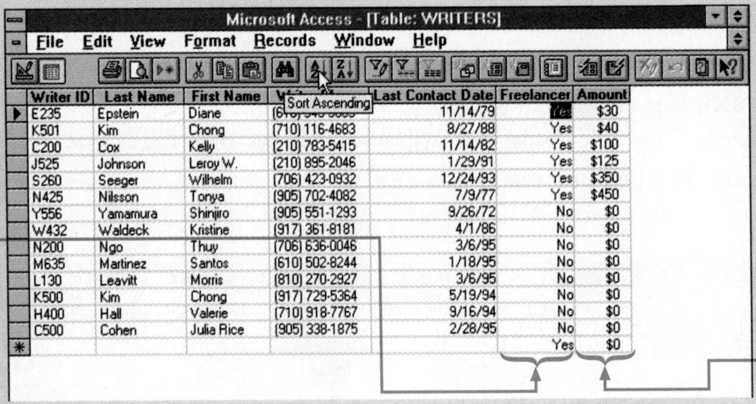

Figure 3-23
Datasheet quick sorted on two adjacent fields

Elena does a final review of the data in the WRITERS table and determines that she is finished with her updates. She next uses the Access Database Documentor for the WRITERS table.

Printing Table Documentation

Access has a **Database Documentor**, which you use to print the characteristics of a database or of selected database objects. For a table, Access prints the table fields and their properties.

Let's print the Access documentation for the WRITERS table.

To start the Database Documentor:

1. Double-click the Datasheet View window **Control menu box** to close the datasheet and activate the Database window.
2. Be sure the WRITERS table is highlighted in the Tables list box. Click **File** and then click **Print Definition...** to open the Print Table Definition dialog box. See Figure 3-24.

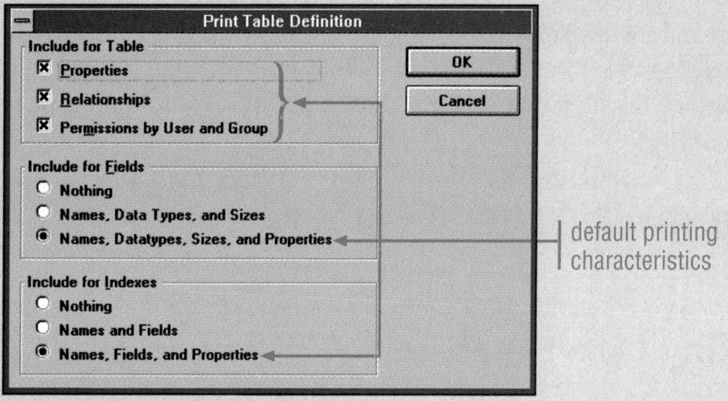

Figure 3-24
The Print Table Definition dialog box

The default characteristics for fields and indexes are fine. Because she has not yet defined any relationships or permissions for the WRITERS table, however, Elena turns off these check boxes.

To print table documentation:

1. Click the **Relationships check box** and the **Permissions by User and Group check box** so that these table characteristics do not print.

   TROUBLE? If your Print Table Definition dialog box looks different from Figure 3-24, just be sure that only the Properties box is checked and only the radio buttons shown are turned on.

2. Click the **OK button** to close the dialog box. After a short wait, Access opens the Print Preview window and displays the top of the first page of the documentation. See Figure 3-25 on the following page.

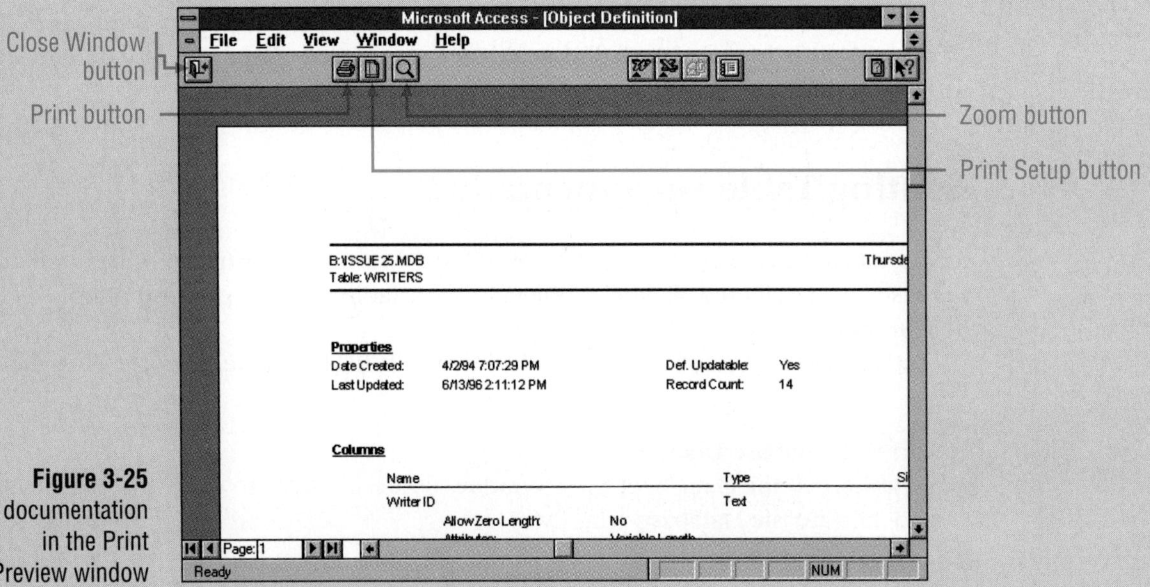

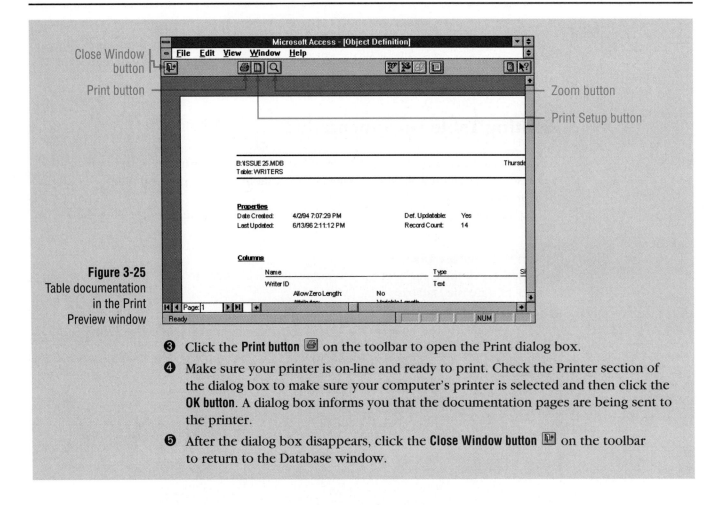

Figure 3-25
Table documentation in the Print Preview window

❸ Click the **Print button** on the toolbar to open the Print dialog box.

❹ Make sure your printer is on-line and ready to print. Check the Printer section of the dialog box to make sure your computer's printer is selected and then click the **OK button**. A dialog box informs you that the documentation pages are being sent to the printer.

❺ After the dialog box disappears, click the **Close Window button** on the toolbar to return to the Database window.

Backing Up a Database

Elena is done with her work on the WRITERS table. Before exiting Access, however, Elena backs up the Issue25 database. **Backing up** is the process of making a duplicate copy of a database on a different disk. Elena does this to protect against loss of or damage to the original database. If problems occur, she can simply use the backup database.

In Access, a database and all its objects are contained in a single file, so backing up an Access database consists of copying the database file from one disk to another disk. Before backing up a database file, however, you must close the database in Access.

Access does not have its own backup command, so you use the Windows File Manager to back up an Access database from one disk to another disk. If you have both a drive A and drive B, you copy the Issue25 database from the drive containing your Student Disk to the other drive. If you have a drive A but not a drive B, however, you copy the Issue25 database from your Student Disk in drive A to the hard disk. Next, you place a different disk, which serves as the backup disk, in drive A and move the database to it from the hard disk.

Let's back up the Issue25 database from your Student Disk to your backup disk.

To back up a database:

1. Double-click the Database window **Control menu box** to close the Issue25 database.
2. Switch to the Windows Program Manager without exiting Access using **[Alt] [Tab]**, and launch File Manager.
3. Copy the issue25.mdb file from your Student Disk to a backup disk, using the procedure appropriate for your disk configuration.
4. Exit File Manager.
5. Be sure that your Student Disk is in the same drive you've been using for your Access work.
6. Switch back to Access. The Access window is the active window.

Compacting a Database

Elena deleted a record from the WRITERS table during her updating work. She knows that, when records are deleted in Access, the space occupied by the deleted records does not become available for other records. The same is true if an object, such as a form or report, is deleted. To make the space available, you must compact the database. When you **compact a database**, Access removes deleted records and objects and creates a smaller version of the database. Unlike backing up a database, which you do to protect your database against loss or damage, you compact a database to make it smaller, thereby making more space available on your disk. Before compacting a database, you must close it.

REFERENCE WINDOW

Compacting a Database

- Close any database you are using, so that the Microsoft Access window is active.
- Click File, and then click Compact Database... to open the Database to Compact From dialog box.
- In the Drives list box and in the Directories list box, select the drive and directory that contain the database you want to compact.
- In the File Name list box, select the database you want to compact.
- Click the OK button. Access closes the Database to Compact From dialog box and opens the Database to Compact Into dialog box.
- In the Drives list box and in the Directories list box, select the drive and directory for the location of the compacted form of the database.
- Type the name you want to assign to the compacted form of the database.
- Click the OK button. The Database to Compact Into dialog box disappears, and Access starts compacting the database.
- If you use the same name for both the original and compacted database, Access displays the message "Replace existing file?" Click Yes to continue compacting the database.
- After the database compacting is complete, Access returns you to the Microsoft Access window.

Elena compacts the Issue25 database before exiting Access. Because she has just made a backup copy, she uses Issue25 as the compacted database name. You can use the same name, or a different name, for your original and compacted databases. If you use the same name, you should back up the original database first in case a hardware or software malfunction occurs in the middle of the compacting process.

Let's compact the Issue25 database and then exit Access.

To compact a database:

1. Click **File**, and then click **Compact Database....** Access displays the Database to Compact From dialog box. See Figure 3-26.

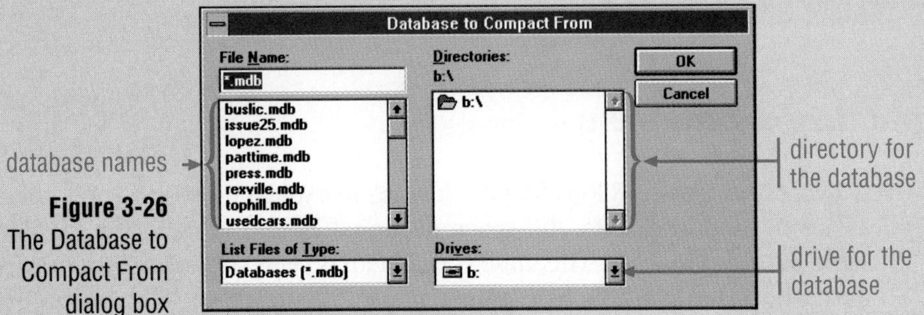

Figure 3-26 The Database to Compact From dialog box

2. In the Drives list box, select the drive that contains your Student Disk.
3. Click **issue25.mdb** in the File Name list box.
4. Click the **OK button**. The Database to Compact From dialog box disappears, and Access displays the Database to Compact Into dialog box. See Figure 3-27.

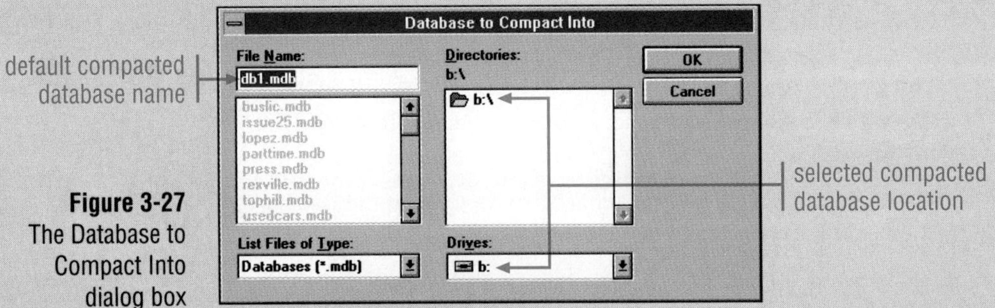

Figure 3-27 The Database to Compact Into dialog box

5. Type **issue25** in the File Name list box. Access will automatically supply an .mdb filename extension.
6. Click the **OK button**. The Database to Compact Into dialog box disappears, and Access displays the message "Replace existing file?"
7. Click the **Yes button**. Access closes the dialog boxes and compacts the database.
8. Double-click the Microsoft Access window **Control menu boxes** to exit Access.

■ ■ ■

Elena has finished updating the WRITERS table. In the next tutorial, she will use the Access query feature to answer questions about the data in the WRITERS table.

Questions

1. What operations are performed when you update a database?
2. What does a pencil symbol signify in a record selector? What does an asterisk symbol signify in a record selector?

E 3. You can use the Format menu to hide columns in a datasheet. Use the Access Help system to learn a reason for hiding columns in a datasheet.

4. When you make changes to a field value, what mode are you in when an entire field is highlighted? What mode do you change to if you then press [F2]?
5. When you change a datasheet's font size, what other datasheet property is automatically changed?

E 6. Use the Access Help system to document for your instructor the difference between exporting and importing.

7. In what sequence are records displayed in a datasheet?
8. When might you consider using a secondary sort key?
9. What is the Database Documentor?
10. How many different files do you copy when you back up one Access database?

E 11. Use Cue Cards to document for your instructor how to save changes to a record without moving to another record.

E 12. Use Cue Cards to find out which update operations you cannot undo.

13. What is the purpose of compacting a database?

Tutorial Assignments

Elena imports one of Judith's Vision database tables to replace her BUSINESS ARTICLES table in the Issue25 database. After importing the table, Elena adds, changes, and deletes data in the BUSINESS ARTICLES table.

Launch Access, open the Issue25 database on your Student Disk, maximize the Database window, and do the following:

1. Delete the BUSINESS ARTICLES table.
2. Import the "BUSINESS ARTICLES tutorial 3 import" table from the Vision database on your Student Disk.
3. Change the table name "BUSINESS ARTICLES tutorial 3 import" to BUSINESS ARTICLES.
4. Open the BUSINESS ARTICLES table. It should contain 23 records.
5. Print the BUSINESS ARTICLES datasheet.
6. Delete the third record, which is an article that appeared in a 1972 issue.
7. In the Type field, change the type of the 1988 article from LAW to POL.
8. Switch to the Table Design View window. Make the row for the Issue of Business Perspective field the current field, click in its Format property box, and start the Access Help system. Click Search..., type date/time, click the Show Topics button, click Format Property, and then click the Go To button. Next, click the Date/Time Data Types jump and read the explanation about the date/time format "yyyy mmm." Exit the Access Help system, switch back to the Datasheet View window, and observe the format of the field values in the Issue column.
9. Add the three new records shown in Figure 3-28 on the following page to the end of the BUSINESS ARTICLES table. Notice the format of the Issue field and enter the three new Issue field values in the exact same format.

BUSINESS ARTICLES table data

	Article Title	Type	Issue	Article Length	Writer ID
Record 1:	The Economy Under Sub-Zero Population Growth	BUS	1972 Dec	1020	E235
Record 2:	New York City Fiscal Crisis	POL	1975 Nov	1477	N425
Record 3:	Toyota and GM Joint Venture	INT	1983 Mar	1682	S260

Figure 3-28

10. Resize the datasheet columns so that all field names and field values appear on the screen.
11. Print the datasheet.
12. Back up the Issue25 database from your Student Disk to your backup disk.
13. Compact the Issue25 database using Issue25 as the File Name in the Database to Compact Into dialog box.

Case Problems

1. Walkton Daily Press Carriers

Robin Witkop has created a database to help Grant Sherman track newspaper carriers and their outstanding balances. Grant starts his maintenance of the CARRIERS table. He imports data to his database and then adds, changes, and deletes data to update the CARRIERS table.

Launch Access and do the following:

1. Open the Press database on your Student Disk and maximize the Database window.
2. Delete the CARRIERS table.
3. Import the "CARRIERS starting data" table from the Walkton database on your Student Disk.
4. Change the table name "CARRIERS starting data" to CARRIERS.
5. Open the CARRIERS table, which should contain 19 records.
6. Print the CARRIERS datasheet.
7. Delete the record that has a value of 10 in the Carrier ID field. This is the record for Joe Carrasco.
8. In the Last Name field of the record having a Carrier ID value of 11, change Thompson to Thomson.
9. Make the following changes to the record that has a Carrier ID value of 17, which is the record for Bradley Slachter: change the First Name field to Sean; change the Birthdate field value 3/4/79 to 3/14/79.
10. Add the two new records shown in Figure 3-29 to the end of the CARRIERS table. Because Access automatically controls fields that are assigned a counter data type, press [Tab] instead of typing a field value in the Carrier ID field.

CARRIERS table data

	Carrier ID	Last Name	First Name	Carrier Phone	Birthdate
Record 1:	20	Rivera	Nelia	281-3787	6/3/80
Record 2:	21	Hansen	Gunnar	949-6745	4/30/81

Figure 3-29

11. Resize the datasheet columns, if necessary, so that all field names and field values appear on the screen.
12. Print the datasheet.
13. Back up the Press database from your Student Disk to your backup disk.
14. Compact the Press database using Press as the File Name in the Database to Compact Into dialog box.

2. Lopez Used Cars

Maria and Hector Lopez have created a database to track their used-car inventory in the lots they own throughout Texas. They start their maintenance of the USED CARS table. They import data and then add, change, and delete data to update the USED CARS table.

Launch Access and do the following:

1. Open the Usedcars database on your Student Disk and maximize the Database window.
2. Delete the USED CARS table.
3. Import the "USED CARS starting data" table from the Lopez database on your Student Disk.
4. Change the table name "USED CARS starting data" to USED CARS.
5. Open the USED CARS table. It should contain 25 records.
6. Print the USED CARS datasheet.
7. Delete the record that has the value JT4AA in the Vehicle ID field. The record is for a Cadillac Fleetwood.
8. In the Cost field of the record having the Vehicle ID QQRT6, which is a Nissan 240SX, change $6700 to $6200. You might need to resize the column to see the entire field value.
9. Make the following changes to the record that has the Vehicle ID value AB7J8, which is an Acura Legend: change the Model field from Legend to Integra; change the Cost field value from $300 to $4300.
10. Add the two new records shown in Figure 3-30 to the end of the USED CARS table.

USED CARS table data

	Vehicle ID	Manufacturer	Model	Class	Transmision Type	Year	Location Code	Cost	Selling Price
Record 1:	MX8M4	Ford	Taurus Wagon	WM	L4	1992	P1	5225	6600
Record 2:	BY7BZ	Subaru	Justy	S2	M5	1991	H1	1900	2700

Figure 3-30

11. Resize the datasheet columns so that all field names and field values appear on the screen.
12. Print the datasheet. If some columns are too narrow to print all field names and values, or if more than one page is needed to print the datasheet, resize the datasheet columns and reprint the datasheet.
13. Back up the Usedcars database from your Student Disk to your backup disk.
14. Compact the Usedcars database using Usedcars as the File Name in the Database to Compact Into dialog box.

3. Tophill University Student Employment

Lee Chang has created a database to help Olivia Tyler track employers and their advertised part-time jobs for students. Olivia starts her maintenance of the JOBS table. She imports data to her database and then adds, changes, and deletes data to update the JOBS table.

Launch Access and do the following:

1. Open the Parttime database on your Student Disk and maximize the Database window.
2. Delete the JOBS table.
3. Import the "JOBS starting data" table from the Tophill database on your Student Disk.
4. Change the table name "JOBS starting data" to JOBS.
5. Open the JOBS table. It should contain 17 records.

6. Print the JOBS datasheet.
7. Resize the datasheet columns so that all field names and field values appear on the screen.
8. Delete the record that has a value of 16 in the Job# field. This record describes a position for a night stock clerk.
9. In the Job Title field of the record having a Job# value of 3, change Computer Analyst to Computer Lab Associate.
10. Make the following changes to the record that has a Job# value of 13, which is the record describing a position for an actuarial aide: change the Employer ID field to BJ93; change the Wage field value $8.40 to $9.25.
11. Add the two new records shown in Figure 3-31 to the end of the JOBS table. Because Access automatically controls fields that are assigned a counter data type, press [Tab] instead of typing a field value in the Job# field.

JOBS table data

	Job Order	Hours/Week	Employer ID	Job Title	Wage
Record 1:	18	21	ME86	Lab Technician	5.30
Record 2:	19	18	BJ92	Desktop Publishing Aide	5.80

Figure 3-31

12. Print the datasheet. If some columns are too narrow to print all field names and values, or if more than one page is needed to print the datasheet, resize the datasheet columns and reprint the datasheet.
13. Back up the Parttime database from your Student Disk to your backup disk.
14. Compact the Parttime database using Parttime as the File Name in the Database to Compact Into dialog box.

4. Rexville Business Licenses

Chester Pearce has created a database to help him track the licenses issued to businesses in the town of Rexville. Chester starts his maintenance of the BUSINESSES table. He imports data to his database and then adds, changes, and deletes data to update the BUSINESSES table.

Launch Access and do the following:

1. Open the Buslic database on your Student Disk and maximize the Database window.
2. Delete the BUSINESSES table.
3. Import the "BUSINESSES starting data" table from the Rexville database on your Student Disk.
4. Change the table name "BUSINESSES starting data" to BUSINESSES.
5. Open the BUSINESSES table. It should contain 12 records.
6. Print the BUSINESSES datasheet.
7. Change to the Table Design View window. Enter the Caption property value Bus ID for the Business ID field and the Caption property value Phone# for the Phone Number field.

8. Resize the datasheet columns so that all field names and field values appear on the screen.
9. Delete the record that has a value of 3 in the Business ID field. The content of the Business Name field for this record is Take a Chance.
10. In the Street Name field of the record having a Business ID value of 9, change West Emerald Street to East Emerald Street.
11. Make the following changes to the record that has a Business ID value of 8. The Business Name for this field reads Lakeview House. Change the Business Name field to Rexville Billiards; change the Street# field value 2425 to 4252.
12. Add the two new records shown in Figure 3-32 to the end of the BUSINESSES table. Because Access automatically controls fields that are assigned a counter data type, press [Tab] instead of typing a field value in the Business ID field.

BUSINESSES table data

	Business ID	Business Name	Street Number	Street Name	Phone Number	Proprietor
Record 1:	13	Kyle Manufacturing, Inc.	4818	West Paris Road	942-9239	Myron Kyle
Record 2:	14	Merlin Auto Body	2922	Riverview Drive	243-5525	Lester Tiahrt

Figure 3-32

13. Print the datasheet. If some columns are too narrow to print all field names and values, or if more than one page is needed to print the datasheet, resize the datasheet columns and reprint the datasheet.
14. Back up the Buslic database from your Student Disk to your backup disk.
15. Compact the Buslic database using Buslic as the File Name in the Database to Compact Into dialog box.

TUTORIAL 4

Querying Database Tables

OBJECTIVES

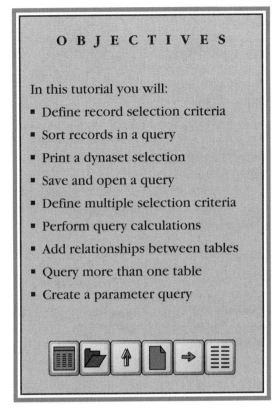

In this tutorial you will:

- Define record selection criteria
- Sort records in a query
- Print a dynaset selection
- Save and open a query
- Define multiple selection criteria
- Perform query calculations
- Add relationships between tables
- Query more than one table
- Create a parameter query

Querying the Issue25 Database at Vision Publishers

CASE

Vision Publishers At the next progress meeting on the special 25th-anniversary issue of *Business Perspective*, Brian Murphy, Elena Sanchez, Judith Rossi, and Harold Larson discuss the information each needs to obtain from the database. Brian asks for a list of the freelancers, their phone numbers, and the amounts owed to them. He also wants to know the total amount owed to freelancers, the dollar impact of giving all writers an extra $50, and the dollar impact of giving the extra money to freelancers versus staff writers.

Judith and Elena decide to develop writer contact lists based on specific area codes and the last dates the writers were contacted. Because Elena is starting the magazine layout process, she wants to see the article titles and lengths.

Harold plans to highlight the diversity of articles in his marketing campaign, so he needs a list of writers, article titles, and article types arranged by article type. Harold also wants to feature one or two writers in the marketing campaign, and the group decides that Valerie Hall and Wilhelm Seeger should be the featured writers. Elena agrees to get Harold the contact information for these two writers.

After further discussion, the group agrees on a list of questions (Figure 4-1) that they want Elena to answer. Elena will use Access's query capability to obtain the answers.

Answer these questions:

1. What are the names, phone numbers, and amounts owed for all writers?
2. What is the complete information on Valerie Hall?
3. What are the names, phone numbers, last contact dates, and amounts owed for all freelancers?
4. What is the contact information for writers with 706 area codes, for Valerie Hall and Wilhelm Seger, and for writers last contacted prior to 1994?
5. Who are the staff writers and who are the freelancers, arranged in order by last contact date?
6. Who are the freelancers last contacted prior to 1990?
7. What is the phone contact information for freelancers with 210 or 706 area codes?
8. What is the impact of giving all writers an extra $50? What would be the total cost and average cost per writer with and without the extra $50? What would be the total cost and average cost for freelancers versus staff writers with and without the extra $50?
9. What are the article titles, types, and lengths for each writer in order by article type?
10. What are the article titles and lengths and the writer names for a specific article type in order by article title?

Figure 4-1
Elena's questions about the Issue25 database

Using a Query

A **query** is a question you ask about the data stored in a database. Elena's list of questions about the Issue25 database are examples of queries. When you create a query, you tell Access which fields you need and what criteria Access should use to select records for you. Access shows you just the information you want, so you don't need to scan through an entire database for that information.

Access has a powerful query capability that can:

- display selected fields and records from a table
- sort records
- perform calculations
- generate data for forms, reports, and other queries
- access data from two or more tables

The specific type of Access query Elena will use to answer her questions is called a select query. A **select query** asks a question about the data stored in a database and returns an answer in a format that is the same as the format of a datasheet. When you create a select query, you phrase the question with definitions of the fields and records you want Access to select for you.

Access has a set of **Query Wizards** that ask you questions about your queries and then create queries based on your answers. You use Query Wizards for specialized, complex queries such as finding duplicate records in a table and copying table records to a new table. For common queries such as select queries, however, you do not use Query Wizards.

You use Access's Query Design window to create a select query. In the Query Design window you specify the data you want to see by constructing a query by example. Using **query by example (QBE)**, you give Access an example of the information you are requesting. Access then retrieves the information that precisely matches your example.

Access also allows you to create queries using Structured Query Language (SQL). **SQL**, which can be pronounced either "sequel" or "ess cue ell," is a powerful computer language used in querying, updating, and managing relational databases. When you create a QBE query, Access automatically constructs the equivalent SQL statement. Although you will not use SQL in this tutorial, you can view the SQL statement by switching from the Query Design window to the SQL View window.

Access has a set of Cue Cards you can use while working with queries. Although we will not use these Cue Cards in this tutorial, you might find they enhance your understanding of queries. At any time during this tutorial, therefore, select Design a Query from the Cue Card menu window to launch the appropriate Cue Cards.

Creating a Query

Before Elena creates her first query, she compares the tables in the Issue25 database against those in the Vision database. She finds some differences and determines that the tables containing data about articles and article types are more complete and accurate in the Vision database. She imports these tables from the Vision database to the Issue25 database to make her data accurate.

Let's import the same two tables, named PAST ARTICLES and TYPES, to the Issue25 database. Doing so will ensure that your tables are consistent with the remaining tutorials even if you have not accurately completed previous Tutorial Assignments. If you have not done so, place your Student Disk in the appropriate drive, launch Access, and open the Issue25 database on your Student Disk.

To import tables:

1. Import the PAST ARTICLES table from the Vision database on your Student Disk. Be sure that the Structure and Data option button in the Import Objects dialog box is selected.
2. Click the **OK button** to close the "Successfully Imported" dialog box. The Import Objects dialog box becomes the active window. Do not close this window because you can import the next table from the same database by continuing in this active window.
3. In the Import Objects dialog box, click **TYPES** in the Objects list box. Be sure that the Structure and Data option button is selected and click the **Import button**.
4. Click the **OK button** to close the "Successfully Imported" dialog box and then click the **Close button** to close the Import Objects dialog box. The two new tables now appear in the Database window.

Elena has very little experience working with queries, so she practices with the first few questions on her list. She will not save any queries until she completes her practice. Elena creates her first query using the WRITERS table. She must first open the Query Design window.

REFERENCE WINDOW

Opening the Query Design Window for a Single Table

- In the Tables list box of the Database window, click the table name that you will use for the query.
- Click the New Query button. The New Query dialog box appears.
- Click the New Query button to open the Query Design window.

Let's open the Query Design window for the WRITERS table.

To open the Query Design window:

❶ Click **WRITERS** in the Tables list box. See Figure 4-2.

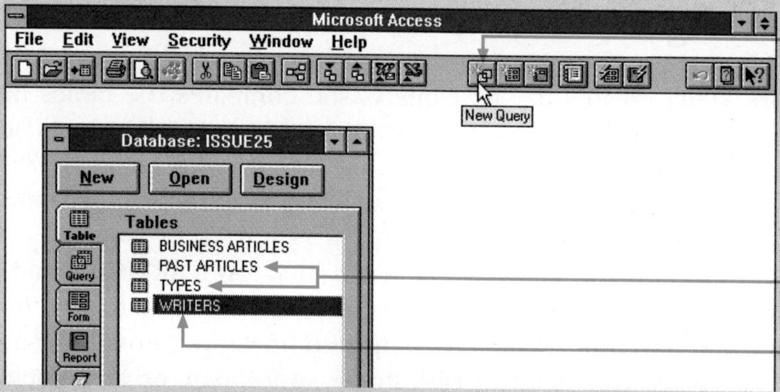

Figure 4-2 Database window showing imported tables PAST ARTICLES and TYPES

❷ Click the toolbar **New Query button** to open the New Query dialog box.

❸ Click the **New Query button** in the New Query dialog box. Access opens the Query Design window. See Figure 4-3.

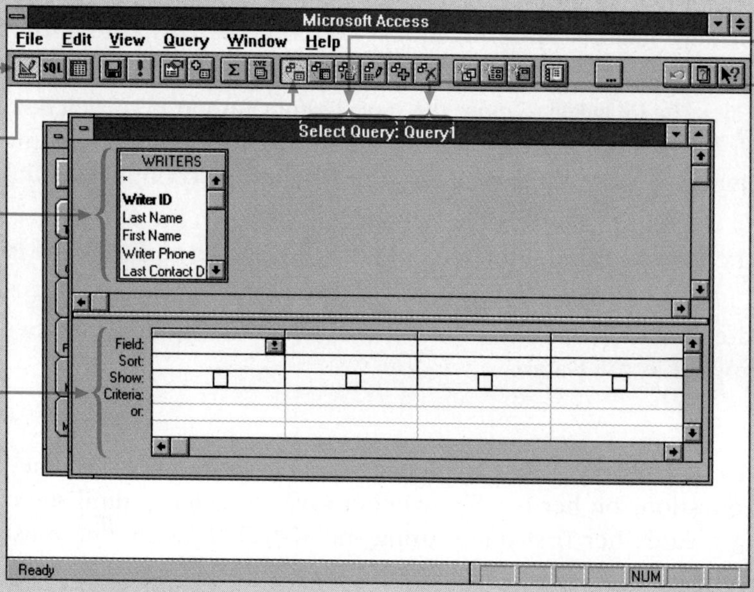

Figure 4-3 The Query Design window

The Query Design Window

The Query Design window contains the standard title bar, menu bar, toolbar, and status bar. On the toolbar, both the Design View and Select Query buttons are automatically selected to identify that you are in the Query Design window designing a select query. The title bar displays the query type, Select Query, and the default query name, Query1. You change the default query name to a more meaningful one when you save the query.

In addition to the standard window components, the Query Design window contains a field list and the QBE grid. The **field list**, in the upper-left part of the window, contains the fields for the table you are querying. The table name appears at the top of the list box. The fields are listed in the order in which they appear in the Table Design window. If your query needs fields from two or more tables, each table's field list appears in this upper portion of the Query Design window. You choose a field for your query by dragging its name from the field list to the QBE grid in the lower portion of the window.

In the **QBE grid**, you include the fields and record selection criteria for the information you want to see. Each column in the QBE grid contains specifications about a field you will use in the query.

If Elena's query uses all fields from the WRITERS table, she can choose one of three methods to transfer all the fields from the field list to the QBE grid. You use the three methods as follows:

- In the first method, you click and drag each field individually from the field list to the QBE grid. Use this method if you want the fields in your query to appear in an order that is different from that in the field list.
- In the second method, you double-click the asterisk in the field list. Access places WRITERS.* in the QBE grid. This signifies that the order of the fields will be the same in the query as it is in the field list. Use this method if the query does not need to be sorted or to have conditions for the records you want to select. The advantage of using this method is that you do not need to change the query if you add or delete fields from the underlying table structure. They will all automatically appear in the query.
- In the third method, you double-click the field list title bar to highlight all the fields. Click and drag one of the highlighted fields to the QBE grid. Access places each field in a separate column and arranges the fields in the order in which they appear in the field list. Use this method rather than the previous one if your query needs to be sorted or to have record selection criteria.

To help you understand the purpose and relationship of the field list and QBE grid better, let's create a simple query.

Adding All Fields Using the Asterisk Method

Elena's first query is to find the names, phone numbers, and amounts owed for all writers. She decides to use all the fields from the WRITERS table in her query.

To use the asterisk method to add all fields to the QBE grid:

❶ The insertion point should be in the QBE grid's first column Field box; if it is not, click that box. Double-click the **asterisk** in the WRITERS field list. Access places WRITERS.* in the QBE grid's first column Field box. See Figure 4-4.

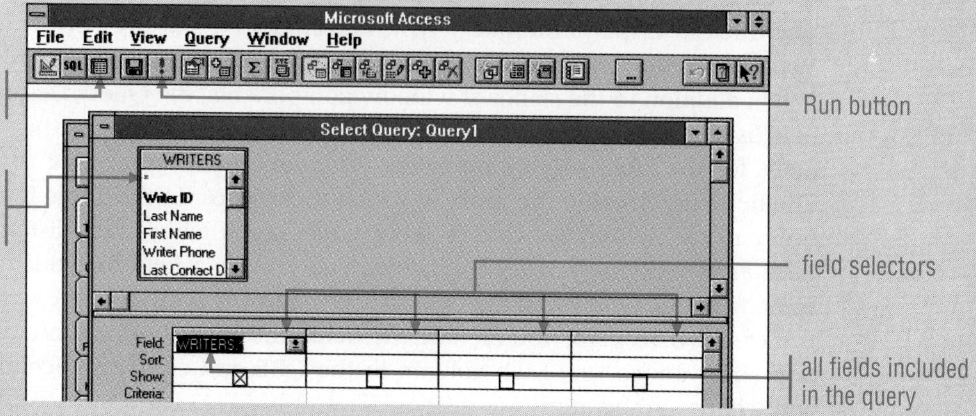

Figure 4-4
Adding all fields to a query with the asterisk method

While you are constructing a query, you can see the answer at any time by clicking the Run button or the Datasheet View button on the toolbar. In response, Access displays the **dynaset**, which is the set of fields and records that results from answering, or running, a query. Although a dynaset looks just like a table's datasheet and appears in the same Datasheet View window, the dynaset is temporary and its contents are based on the criteria you establish in the QBE grid. In contrast, the datasheet shows the permanent data in a table.

Elena views the dynaset for the query she just created.

To view a query's dynaset:

❶ Click the toolbar **Run button** [!]. Access displays the dynaset for the query. See Figure 4-5.

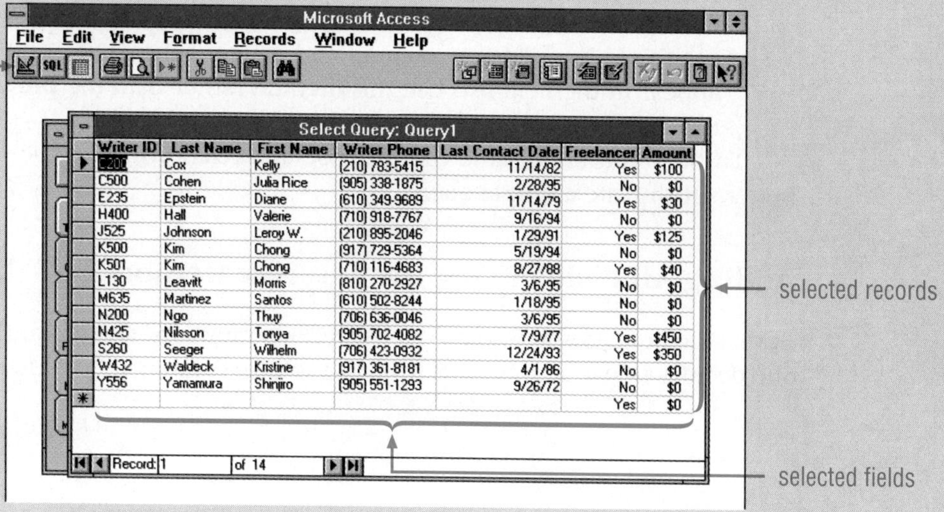

Figure 4-5
Dynaset displayed in the Datasheet View window

Viewing the WRITERS table datasheet would have produced the same results as shown in the dynaset because all the fields and records appear in the same order in both. Elena realizes that she did not ask the right question, which was to list just the writer names, phone numbers, and amounts. To change the query, Elena switches back to the Query Design window by clicking the Design View button.

Deleting a Field

You will rarely create a query to list all the fields from a table. More often, you will want to include some fields and exclude other fields. You might also want to rearrange the order of the included fields. Therefore, you seldom use the asterisk method to add all fields to a query. Let's remove WRITERS.* from the QBE grid in preparation for creating the correct first query.

To delete a field from the QBE grid:

1. Click the toolbar **Design View button** to switch to the Query Design window.
2. The field selectors are the gray bars above the Field row in the QBE grid. Move the pointer to the field selector for the first column. When the pointer changes to ↓, click to highlight or select the entire column.
3. Position the pointer again in the first column's field selector and click the right mouse button to display the Shortcut menu.
4. Click **Cut** in the Shortcut menu. The Shortcut menu disappears and the contents of the first QBE grid column are deleted.

Adding All Fields by Dragging

Elena uses another method to add all the fields to the QBE grid. She then deletes those fields she does not need.

To add all fields to the QBE grid by dragging:

1. Double-click the **title bar** of the WRITERS field list to highlight, or select, all the fields in the table. Notice that the asterisk in the first row of the field list is not highlighted.
2. Click and hold the mouse button anywhere in the highlighted area of the WRITERS field list.
3. Drag the pointer to the QBE grid's first column Field box. As you near the destination Field box, the pointer changes to . Release the mouse button in the Field box. Access adds each table field in a separate Field box, from left to right. See Figure 4-6 on the following page. You can use the QBE grid's horizontal scroll bars and arrows to see the fields that are off the screen.

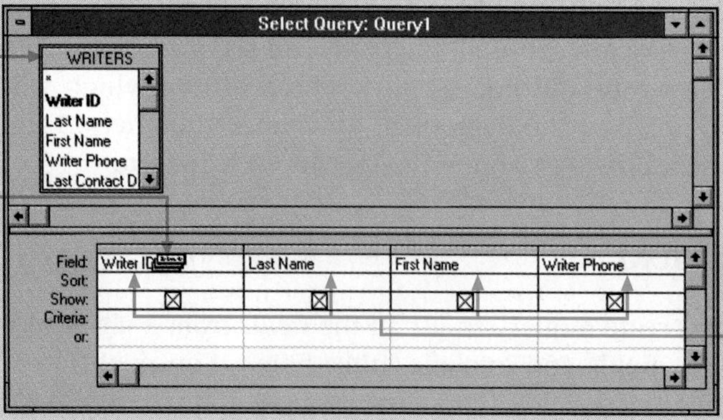

Figure 4-6
Adding all fields to a query by the dragging method

Moving a Field

Elena does not need the Writer ID, Last Contact Date, and Freelancer fields for her first query. She also thinks viewing the dynaset would be easier for everyone if the First Name field preceded the Last Name field. Elena deletes the three unneeded fields and then moves the First Name field.

To delete multiple fields from the QBE grid:

❶ Move the pointer to the Writer ID field selector in the QBE grid. When the pointer changes to ⬇, click to select the entire column. Position the pointer again in the Writer ID field selector and click the right mouse button to display the Shortcut menu.

❷ Click **Cut** in the Shortcut menu. The Shortcut menu disappears, and Access deletes the Writer ID column. The remaining fields shift one column to the left.

❸ If necessary, click the horizontal scroll bar's **right arrow button** once so that the Last Contact Date and Freelancer fields are visible in the QBE grid.

❹ Move the pointer to the Last Contact Date field selector. When the pointer changes to ⬇, click to select the entire column and, while holding the mouse button, drag the pointer to the right until the Freelancer field is also highlighted. Release the mouse button and click the right mouse button in either field selector to display the Shortcut menu.

❺ Click **Cut** in the Shortcut menu. The Shortcut menu disappears, and Access deletes the Last Contact Date and Freelancer columns. Access moves the Freelancer Reprint Payment Amount field to the column next to the Writer Phone field.

Elena next moves the First Name field to the left of the Last Name field.

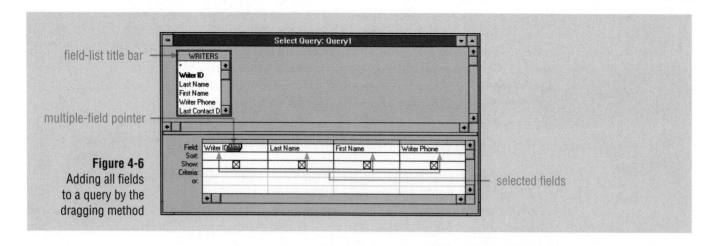

To move a field in the QBE grid:

1. If necessary, click the horizontal scroll bar's **left arrow button** once so that the Last Name field is visible in the QBE grid.
2. Click the **First Name field selector** to highlight the entire column. Click the **First Name field selector** again and drag the pointer, which appears as [pointer icon], to the left. When the pointer is anywhere in the Last Name column, release the mouse button. Access moves the First Name field to the left of the Last Name field. See Figure 4-7.

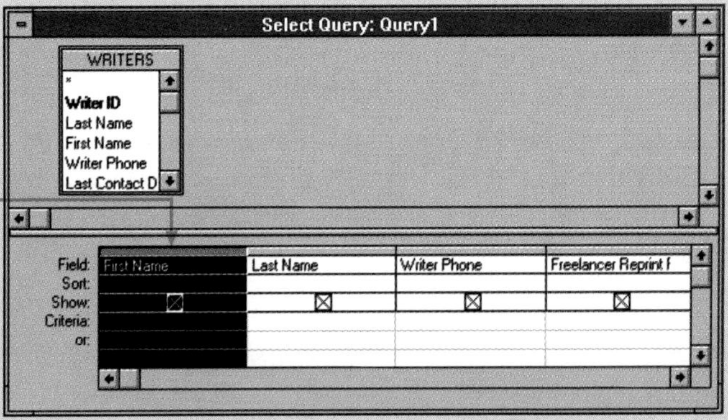

Figure 4-7 The QBE grid showing fields deleted and moved

TROUBLE? If the field does not move, you probably did not drag it far enough to the left. Repeat the move process to correct the problem.

Elena now views the dynaset for this query.

To view a dynaset for a query that uses a subset of the fields from a table:

1. Click the toolbar **Run button** [!]. Access displays the dynaset for the query. See Figure 4-8. The First Name field appears to the left of the Last Name field, and the three deleted fields do not appear in the dynaset.

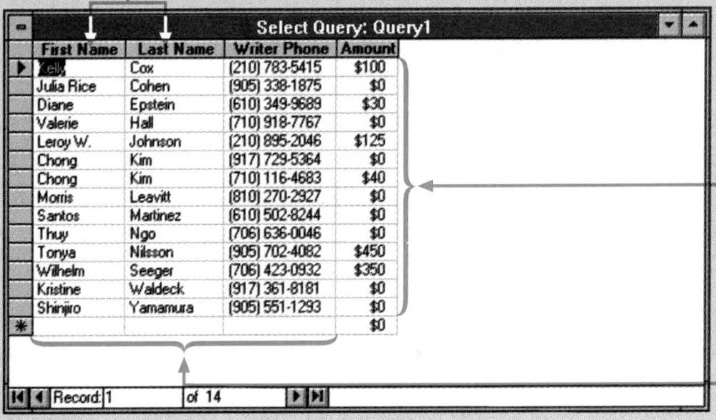

First Name	Last Name	Writer Phone	Amount
Kelly	Cox	(210) 783-5415	$100
Julia Rice	Cohen	(905) 338-1875	$0
Diane	Epstein	(610) 349-9689	$30
Valerie	Hall	(710) 918-7767	$0
Leroy W.	Johnson	(210) 895-2046	$125
Chong	Kim	(917) 729-5364	$0
Chong	Kim	(710) 116-4683	$40
Morris	Leavitt	(810) 270-2927	$0
Santos	Martinez	(610) 502-8244	$0
Thuy	Ngo	(706) 636-0046	$0
Tonya	Nilsson	(905) 702-4082	$450
Wilhelm	Seeger	(706) 423-0932	$350
Kristine	Waldeck	(917) 361-8181	$0
Shinjiro	Yamamura	(905) 551-1293	$0
*			$0

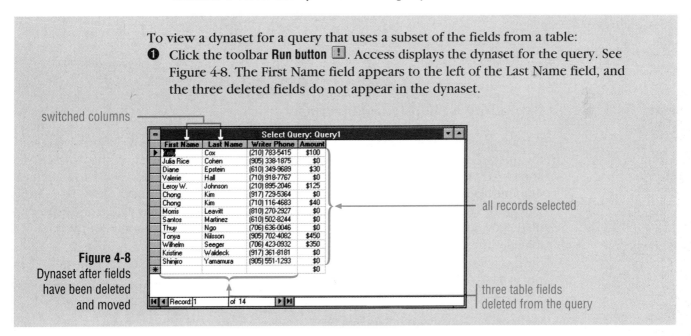

Figure 4-8 Dynaset after fields have been deleted and moved

Deleting and moving fields in the query and resulting dynaset has no effect on the underlying WRITERS table. All fields remain in the table in the order you specified in the table structure design. With queries, you can view information any way you want without being restricted by the table structure.

Inserting a Field

Elena does not need to see the Freelancer field in this first query, but she realizes that others might want the field to appear in the dynaset. She adds the Freelancer field to the QBE grid between the Writer Phone and Freelancer Reprint Payment Amount fields.

To insert a field in the QBE grid:

1. Click the toolbar **Design View button** to switch to the Query Design window.
2. Scroll the WRITERS field list and click **Freelancer**. The Freelancer field becomes the only highlighted field in the WRITERS field list.
3. Drag Freelancer from the field list to the Freelancer Reprint Payment Amount column in the QBE grid, where the cursor changes to , and then release. See Figure 4-9. The Freelancer field is positioned between the Writer Phone and Freelancer Reprint Payment Amount columns. You might need to scroll to the right to see the Freelancer Reprint Payment Amount column.

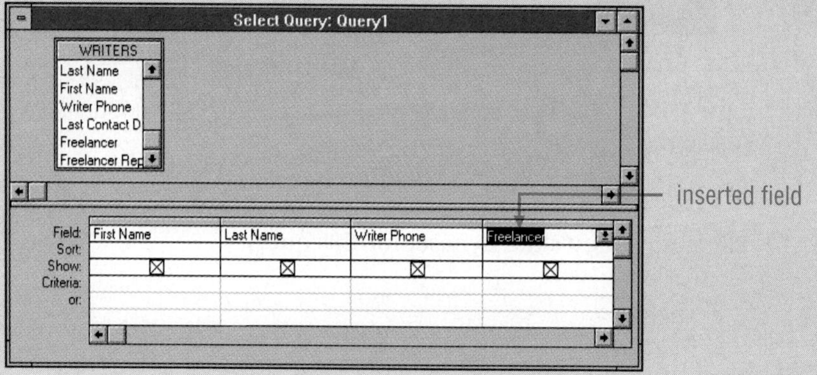

Figure 4-9
Inserting a field in the QBE grid

Excluding a Field from a Dynaset

When others at Vision Publishers use this query, they will simply run it. When Elena runs the query, however, she does not need the Freelancer field to appear in the dynaset. She knows the writers who are freelancers because they have values greater than zero in their Amount fields. Before she runs the query, she can click the Freelancer Show box in the QBE grid. This removes the × from the Show box and prevents the field from appearing in the dynaset. Clicking the Show box again puts the × back in the Show box and includes the field in the dynaset.

Let's use the Freelancer Show box to exclude and then include the Freelancer field in the dynaset.

To exclude and include a field in a dynaset:

1. Click the **Freelancer Show box** to remove the ×. Access will no longer show the Freelancer field in the dynaset.
2. Click the toolbar **Run button** to display the dynaset. The Freelancer field does not appear in the dynaset.
3. Click the toolbar **Design View button** to display the Query Design window.

❹ Click the **Freelancer Show box** to place the × back in the box. Access will now display the Freelancer field in the dynaset.

❺ Click the [!] to display the dynaset. The Freelancer field now appears in the dynaset.

❻ Click the [Design View] to return to the Query Design window.

Renaming Fields in a Query

Elena thinks that Phone Number would look better than Writer Phone as the dynaset column heading for this query. She could change the field name in the table structure. Instead, she renames the field in the Query Design window. You change a field name in the table structure when you want the change to be permanent and reflected throughout the database. Rename the field in the Query Design window when the name change is intended only for that query.

To rename a field in the Query Design window:

❶ Move the pointer to the beginning of the Field box in the QBE grid for Writer Phone. When the I appears on the left side of the W, click to position the insertion point there.

❷ Type **Phone Number:** to insert it before Writer Phone. See Figure 4-10. This name will now appear (without the colon) in the dynaset in place of the field name.

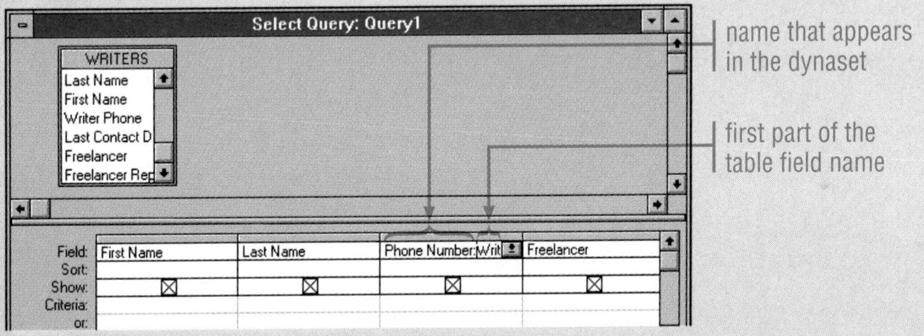

Figure 4-10 Renaming a field in a query

❸ Click the toolbar **Run button** [!]. Access displays the dynaset and shows Phone Number instead of Writer Phone.

TROUBLE? If you omit the colon, Access displays the Syntax error dialog box when you run the query. Click the OK button, insert the colon, and repeat step three.

❹ Click the toolbar **Design View button** [Design View] to switch back to the Query Design window.

After practicing with this query, Elena refers to her list of questions for her next task. She needs the Last Contact Date field for the next query, so she adds it to the QBE grid between the Phone Number and Freelancer fields.

To add a field to the QBE grid:

❶ Click **Last Contact Date** in the WRITERS field list.

❷ Drag Last Contact Date from the WRITERS field list to the Freelancer column in the QBE grid and then release the mouse button. The Last Contact Date field is now positioned between the Phone Number and the Freelancer columns.

Defining Record Selection Criteria

Elena's next few questions include showing the complete information on Valerie Hall, listing information on freelancers only, locating writers who have specific area codes, and finding which writers were last contacted prior to 1994. Unlike her first query, which selected some fields but all records from the WRITERS table, these questions ask Access to select specific records based on a condition.

A **condition** is a criterion, or rule, that determines which records are selected. For example, Elena wants records selected if they meet the condition that a writer is a freelancer. To define a condition for a field, you place in the QBE grid Criteria text box the condition for the field against which you want Access to match. To select only records for those writers who are freelancers, Elena can enter =Yes for the Freelancer field in the Criteria row of the QBE grid.

When you select records based on one condition, for a single field, you are using a **simple condition**. To form a simple condition, you enter a comparison operator and a value. A **comparison operator** asks Access to compare the relationship of two values and to select the record if the relationship is true. For example, the simple condition =Yes for the Freelancer field selects all records having Freelancer field values equal to Yes. The Access comparison operators are shown in Figure 4-11.

Operator	Meaning	Example
=	Equal to (optional, default operator)	="Hall"
<	Less than	<#1/1/94#
<=	Less than or equal to	<=100
>	Greater than	>"C400"
>=	Greater than or equal to	>=18.75
<>	Not equal to	<>"Hall"
Between...And	Between two values (inclusive)	Between 50 And 325
In ( )	In a list of values	In ("Hall", "Seeger")
Like	Matches a pattern that includes wildcards	Like "706*"

Figure 4-11
Access comparison operators

Simple conditions fit into the following categories. Do not be concerned about the details of the simple condition examples—they will be covered more thoroughly in the following sections.

- **Exact match**—selects records that have a value for the selected field exactly matching the simple condition value. To find information on freelancers, Elena will enter =Yes as the simple condition value.
- **Pattern match**—selects records that have a value for the selected field matching the pattern of the simple condition value. To find information on writers with 706 area codes, Elena will enter Like "706*" as the simple condition value.

- **List-of-values match**—selects records that have a value for the selected field matching one of two or more simple condition values. If Elena wants to obtain contact information for Valerie Hall and Wilhelm Seeger, she will enter In ("Hall","Seeger") as the simple condition value.
- **Non-matching value**—selects records that have a value for the selected field that does not match the simple condition value. To list contact information on writers having an area code other than 706, Elena will enter Not Like "706*" as the simple condition value.
- **Range-of-values match**—selects records that have a value for the selected field within a range specified in the simple condition. To find writers last contacted prior to 1994, Elena will enter <#1/1/94# as the simple condition value.

Using an Exact Match

Elena creates a query to select the complete information on Valerie Hall. She enters the simple condition ="Hall" in the Criteria text box for the Last Name field. When Elena runs the query, Access selects records that have the exact value Hall in the Last Name field. For text fields only, you need to use quotation marks around the condition value if the value contains spaces or punctuation. For text-field condition values without spaces or punctuation, the quotation marks are optional; Access inserts them automatically for you. Elena consistently uses the quotation marks for text-field condition values so that she will not accidentally omit them when they are required.

To select records that match a specific value:

1. Click the **Criteria text box** in the QBE grid for the Last Name field and then type **="Hall"**. See Figure 4-12. Access will select a record only if the Last Name field value matches Hall exactly. You can omit the equals symbol, because it is the default comparison operator automatically inserted by Access.

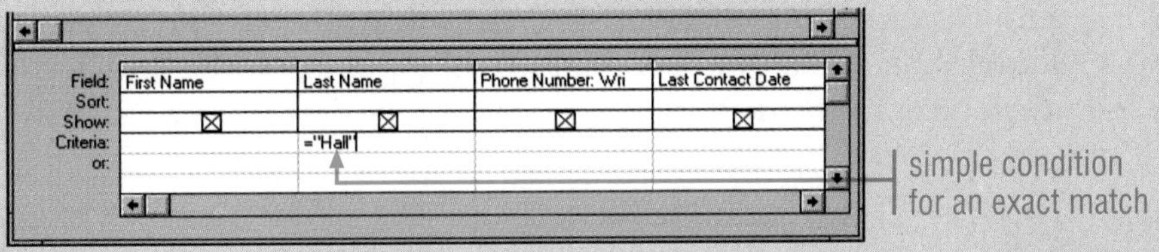

Figure 4-12 Record selection based on an exact match

2. Click the toolbar **Run button**. The dynaset appears, showing only the record for Valerie Hall.
3. Click the toolbar **Design View button** to switch back to the Query Design window.

Elena's third task is to create a query to show the names, phone numbers, last contact dates, and amounts owed for all freelancers. Before she continues her practice and enters the new condition in the QBE grid, she removes the previous condition.

To remove a previous condition from the QBE grid:

1. Click the **Criteria text box** for the Last Name field and press **[F2]** to highlight the entire condition.
2. Press **[Del]** and Access removes the previous condition.

Elena now enters the simple condition =Yes in the QBE grid for the Freelancer field. When she runs the query, Access selects records that have the value Yes for the Freelancer field.

To select records that match a specific value of a field with a yes/no data type:

1. If necessary, scroll to the right in the QBE grid to display the Freelancer column.
2. Click the **Criteria text box** in the QBE grid for the Freelancer field, and then type **=Yes** (note that you do not use quotation marks in a criterion for a yes/no data type).
3. Click the toolbar **Run button**. The dynaset appears and displays only records having the Freelancer field value Yes. See Figure 4-13.

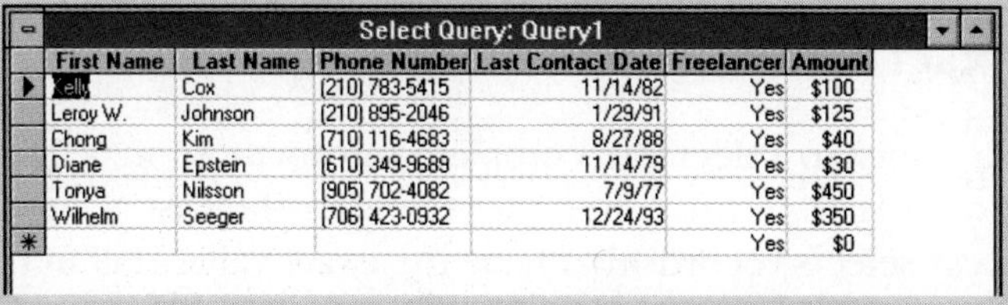

Select Query: Query1

First Name	Last Name	Phone Number	Last Contact Date	Freelancer	Amount
Kelly	Cox	(210) 783-5415	11/14/82	Yes	$100
Leroy W.	Johnson	(210) 895-2046	1/29/91	Yes	$125
Chong	Kim	(710) 116-4683	8/27/88	Yes	$40
Diane	Epstein	(610) 349-9689	11/14/79	Yes	$30
Tonya	Nilsson	(905) 702-4082	7/9/77	Yes	$450
Wilhelm	Seeger	(706) 423-0932	12/24/93	Yes	$350
				Yes	$0

Figure 4-13 Dynaset showing records with Yes in the Freelancer field

4. Click the toolbar **Design View button** to switch back to the Query Design window.

Using a Pattern Match

The fourth question on Elena's list is to find the contact information for writers with 706 area codes. She can do this using the Like comparison operator. The **Like comparison operator** selects records by matching field values to a specific pattern that includes one or more wildcard characters—asterisk (*), question mark (?), and number symbol (#).

Elena enters the simple condition Like "706*" for the Phone Number field. Access will select records that have a Phone Number field value containing 706 in positions one through three. Any characters can appear in the last seven positions of the field value. Because the Phone Number field has an input mask, the displayed placeholder characters are not part of the field value.

To select records that match a specific pattern:

1. Click the **Criteria text box** for the Freelancer field, press **[F2]** to highlight the entire condition, and then press **[Del]** to remove the previous condition.
2. Click the **Criteria text box** in the QBE grid for the Phone Number field and then type **Like "706*"**. See Figure 4-14. Note that Access will automatically add Like and the quotation marks to the simple condition if you omit them.

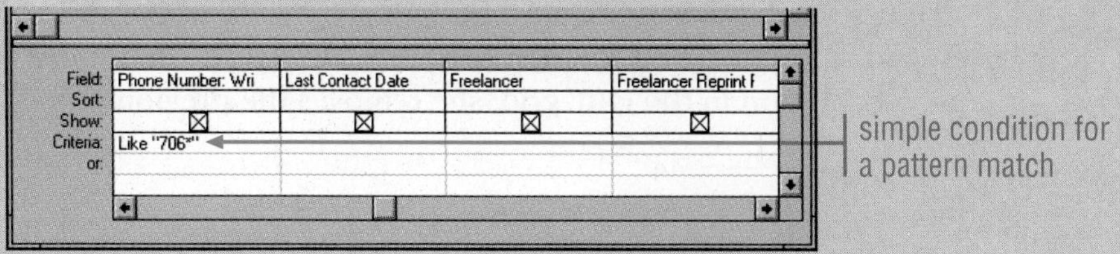

Figure 4-14 Record selection based on matching a specific pattern

❸ Click the toolbar **Run button** . The dynaset appears and displays the two records having the area code 706.

❹ Click the toolbar **Design View button** to switch back to the Query Design window.

Using a List-of-Values Match

Elena's next task is to find the contact information for Valerie Hall and Wilhelm Seeger. She uses the In comparison operator to create the condition. The **In comparison operator** allows you to define a condition with two or more values. If a record's field value matches one value from the list of values, Access selects that record.

Elena wants records selected if the Last Name field value is equal to Hall or to Seeger. These are the values she will use with the In comparison operator. The simple condition she enters is: In ("hall","Seeger"). Because matching is not case-sensitive, Hall and HALL and other variations will also match. Notice that when you make a list of values, you place them inside parentheses.

To select records having a field value that matches a value in a list of values:

❶ Click the **Criteria text box** for the Phone Number field, press **[F2]** to highlight the entire condition, and then press **[Del]** to remove the previous condition.

❷ Scroll left in the QBE grid if necessary to display the Last Name column. Click the **Criteria text box** for the Last Name field and then type **In ("hall","Seeger")**. See Figure 4-15.

Figure 4-15 Record selection based on matching field values to a list of values

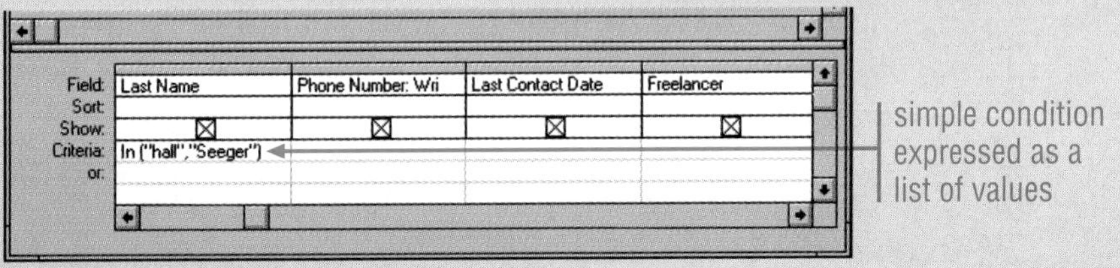

❸ Click the toolbar **Run button** . The dynaset appears and displays the two records having hall or Seeger in the Last Name field.

❹ Click the toolbar **Design View button** to switch back to the Query Design window.

Using a Non-Matching Value

Elena now needs to find all writers who do not have 706 area codes. She uses a combination of the Like comparison operator and the Not logical operator. The **Not logical operator** allows you to find records that do not match a value. If Elena wants to find all records that do not have Hall in the Last Name field, for example, her condition is Not ="Hall".

Elena enters the simple condition Not Like "706*" in the Phone Number field to select writers who do not have 706 area codes.

To select records having a field value that does not match a specific pattern:

1. Click the **Criteria text box** for the Last Name field, press **[F2]** to highlight the entire condition, and then press **[Del]** to remove the previous condition.
2. Click the **Criteria text box** for the Phone Number field and then type **Not Like "706*"**. See Figure 4-16. Access will select a record only if the Phone Number field value does not have a 706 area code.

Figure 4-16 Record selection based on not matching a specific pattern

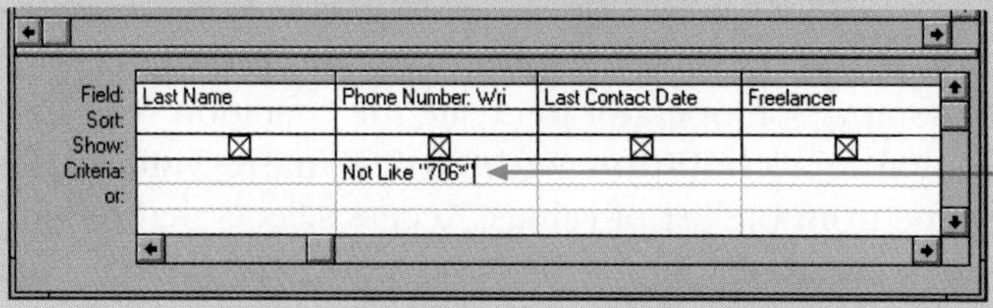

3. Click the toolbar **Datasheet View button**. The dynaset appears and displays only those records having a Phone Number field value that does not have a 706 area code.
4. Click the toolbar **Design View button** to switch back to the Query Design window.

Matching a Range of Values

Elena next finds all writers who were last contacted prior to 1994. She uses the less than (<) comparison operator with a date value of 1/1/94 and enters <#1/1/94# as the simple condition. Access will select records that have, in the Last Contact Date field, a date anywhere in the range of dates prior to January 1, 1994. You place date and time values inside number symbols (#). If you omit the number symbols, however, Access will automatically include them.

To select records having a field value in a range of values:

1. Click the **Criteria text box** for the Phone Number field, press **[F2]** to highlight the entire condition, and then press **[Del]** to remove the previous condition.
2. Click the **Criteria text box** for the Last Contact Date field and then type **<#1/1/94#**. See Figure 4-17. Access will select a record only if the Last Contact Date field value is in the range of dates prior to January 1, 1994.

Figure 4-17 Record selection based on matching a value to a range of values

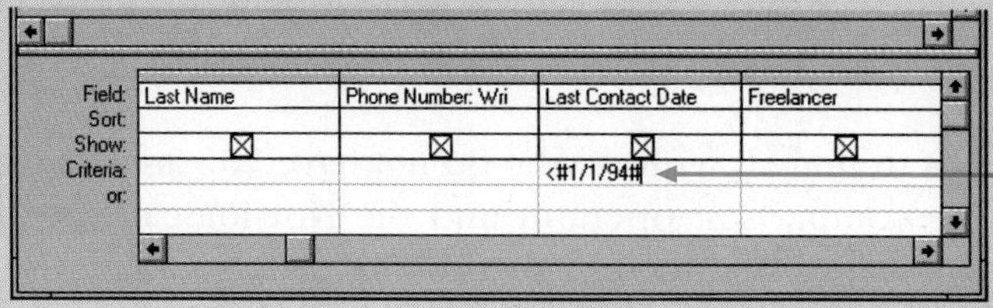

❸ Click the toolbar **Datasheet View button**. The dynaset appears and displays only those records having a Last Contact Date field value prior to 1994. See Figure 4-18.

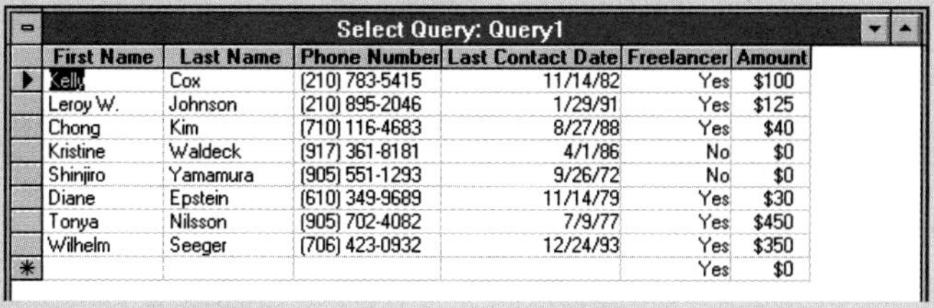

Select Query: Query1

First Name	Last Name	Phone Number	Last Contact Date	Freelancer	Amount
Kelly	Cox	(210) 783-5415	11/14/82	Yes	$100
Leroy W.	Johnson	(210) 895-2046	1/29/91	Yes	$125
Chong	Kim	(710) 116-4683	8/27/88	Yes	$40
Kristine	Waldeck	(917) 361-8181	4/1/86	No	$0
Shinjiro	Yamamura	(905) 551-1293	9/26/72	No	$0
Diane	Epstein	(610) 349-9689	11/14/79	Yes	$30
Tonya	Nilsson	(905) 702-4082	7/9/77	Yes	$450
Wilhelm	Seeger	(706) 423-0932	12/24/93	Yes	$350
				Yes	$0

Figure 4-18 Selected records for writers last contacted prior to 1994

❹ Click the toolbar **Design View button** to switch back to the Query Design window.

As Elena finishes her query, Harold stops by to remind her of a meeting with the marketing staff. Elena quickly closes the Query Design window without saving the query.

To close the Query Design window without saving the query:

❶ Double-click the Query Design window **Control menu box**. The "Save changes to Query 'Query1'?" dialog box appears. See Figure 4-19.

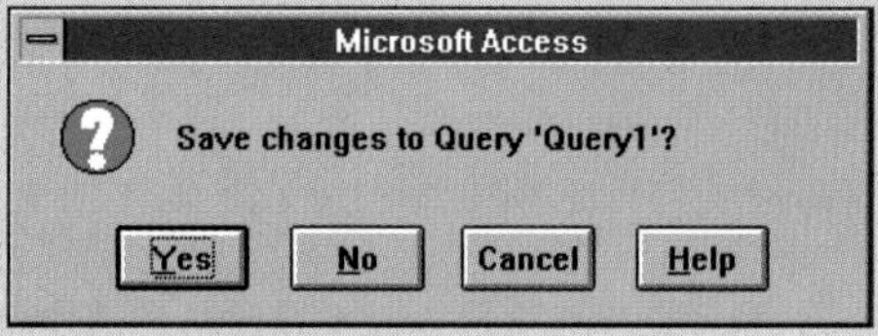

Figure 4-19 The "Save changes to Query 'Query1'?" dialog box

❷ Click the **No button**. Access closes the Query Design window without saving the query.

If you want to take a break and resume the tutorial at a later time, you can exit Access by double-clicking the Microsoft Access window Control menu box. When you resume the tutorial, place your Student Disk in the appropriate drive, launch Access, open the Issue25 database on your Student Disk, and click the WRITERS table.

■ ■ ■

Sorting Data

After the meeting, Elena resumes work on the Issue25 database queries. The next item on her list of questions asks for staff writers and freelancers in order by last contact date. Because the WRITERS table displays records in WRITER ID, or primary-key, sequence, Elena will need to sort records from the table to produce the requested information.

When you sort records from a table, Access does not change the sequence of records in the underlying table. Only the records in the dynaset are rearranged according to your specifications.

Sorting a Single Field

You sort records in an Access query by selecting one or more fields to be sort keys in the QBE grid. Elena chooses the Last Contact Date field to be the sort key for her next query. Because her last Access task was to return to the Database window, she first opens the Query Design window. Elena then adds all the fields from the WRITERS table to the QBE grid.

To start a new query for a single table:

1. Click the toolbar **New Query button** to open the New Query dialog box.
2. Click the **New Query button** in the New Query dialog box. Access opens the Query Design window.
3. Double-click the **title bar** of the WRITERS field list to highlight all the fields in the table.
4. Click and hold the mouse button anywhere in the highlighted area of the WRITERS field list.
5. Drag the pointer to the QBE grid's first column Field text box and release the mouse button when the pointer changes to . Access adds all the fields from the WRITERS table to separate boxes in the QBE grid.

Elena now selects the Last Contact Date field to be the sort key.

REFERENCE WINDOW

Selecting a Sort Key in the Query Window

- Click the Sort text box for the field designated as the sort key.
- Click the down arrow button on the right side of the Sort text box to display the Sort list.
- Click Ascending or Descending from the Sort list. The Sort list disappears, and Access displays the selected sort order in the Sort text box.

Elena decides a descending sort order for the Last Contact Date will be the best way to display the query results, and she now selects the sort key and its sort order. She does this by clicking the Sort text box for the last Contact Date column in the QBE grid. Access then displays a down arrow button on the right side of the text box. The text box has changed into a drop-down list box. Clicking the down arrow button displays the contents of the drop-down list box.

In most cases, you can use a quicker method to display the contents of the drop-down list box. If you click the text box near the right side, Access displays both the down arrow button and the contents of the drop-down list box.

To select a sort key and view a sorted dynaset:

1. If necessary, scroll right in the QBE grid to display the Last Contact Date column. Click the **Sort text box** in the QBE grid for the Last Contact Date field to position the insertion point there. A down arrow button appears on the right side of the Sort text box.
2. Click the **down arrow button** in the Sort text box. Access displays the Sort list. See Figure 4-20.

Figure 4-20
Specifying the sort order for the Last Contact Date field

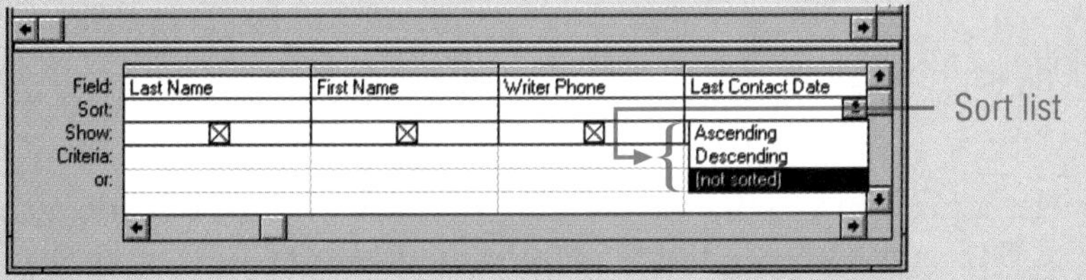

3. Click **Descending** in the Sort list. The Sort list disappears, and Descending appears in the Sort text box as the selected sort order.
4. Click the toolbar **Run button** [!]. The dynaset appears and displays all the fields of the WRITERS table and all its records in descending order by last contact date. See Figure 4-21. Notice that Writer Phone appears in the column heading box instead of Phone Number. Recall that Writer Phone is the table field name that appears in a dynaset unless you rename the field in the Query window.

Figure 4-21
Records sorted in descending order based on last contact date

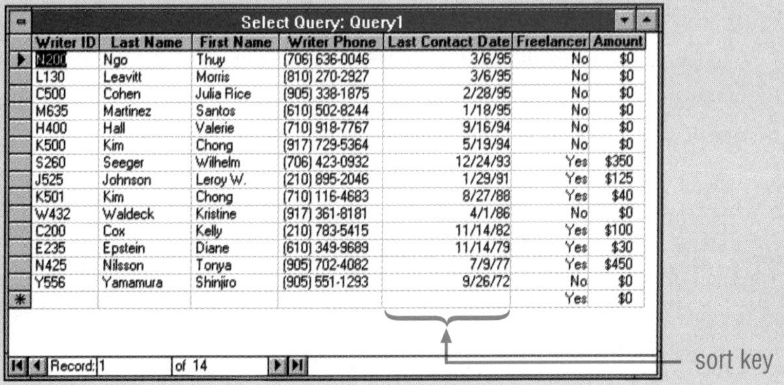

Select Query: Query1

Writer ID	Last Name	First Name	Writer Phone	Last Contact Date	Freelancer	Amount
N200	Ngo	Thuy	(706) 636-0046	3/6/95	No	$0
L130	Leavitt	Morris	(810) 270-2927	3/6/95	No	$0
C500	Cohen	Julia Rice	(905) 338-1875	2/28/95	No	$0
M635	Martinez	Santos	(610) 502-8244	1/18/95	No	$0
H400	Hall	Valerie	(710) 918-7767	9/16/94	No	$0
K500	Kim	Chong	(917) 729-5364	5/19/94	No	$0
S260	Seeger	Wilhelm	(706) 423-0932	12/24/93	Yes	$350
J525	Johnson	Leroy W.	(210) 895-2046	1/29/91	Yes	$125
K501	Kim	Chong	(710) 116-4683	8/27/88	Yes	$40
W432	Waldeck	Kristine	(917) 361-8181	4/1/86	No	$0
C200	Cox	Kelly	(210) 783-5415	11/14/82	Yes	$100
E235	Epstein	Diane	(610) 349-9689	11/14/79	Yes	$30
N425	Nilsson	Tonya	(905) 702-4082	7/9/77	Yes	$450
Y556	Yamamura	Shinjiro	(905) 551-1293	9/26/72	No	$0
					Yes	$0

Record: 1 of 14

Elena studies the dynaset, rereads the question that the new query is supposed to answer, and realizes that her sort is incorrect. The question (Who are the staff writers and who are the freelancers, arranged in order by last contact date?) requires two sort keys. Elena needs to select Freelancer as the primary sort key and Last Contact Date as the secondary sort key.

Sorting Multiple Fields

Access allows you to select up to 10 different sort keys. When you have two or more sort keys, Access first uses the sort key that is leftmost in the QBE grid. Therefore, you must arrange the fields you want to sort from left to right in the QBE grid with the primary sort key being the leftmost sort-key field.

The Freelancer field appears to the right of the Last Contact Date field in the QBE grid. Because the Freelancer field is the primary sort key, Elena must move it to the left of the Last Contact Date field.

To move a field in the QBE grid:

1. If necessary, click the toolbar **Design View button** to switch back to the Query Design window.
2. Click the QBE grid horizontal scroll bar **right arrow button** until the Last Contact Date and Freelancer fields are visible.
3. Click the **Freelancer field selector** to highlight the entire column.
4. Click the **Freelancer field selector** again and drag the pointer, which appears as , to the left. When the pointer is anywhere in the Last Contact Date column, release the mouse button. Access moves the Freelancer field one column to the left.

Elena previously selected the Last Contact Date field to be a sort key and it is still in effect. She now chooses the appropriate sort order for the Freelancer field. Elena wants staff writers to appear first in the query, and they are identified in the Freelancer field by a value of No. Thus, Elena uses descending sort order for the Freelancer field so that all No values appear first. The Freelancer field will serve as the primary sort key because it is to the left of the Last Contact Date field, which will be the secondary sort key.

To select a sort key:

1. Click the **Sort text box** in the QBE grid for the Freelancer field to position the insertion point there. A down arrow button appears on the right side of the Sort text box.
2. Click the **down arrow button** in the Sort text box. Access displays the Sort list.
3. Click **Descending** in the Sort list. The Sort list disappears, and Descending appears in the Sort text box as the selected sort order. See Figure 4-22.

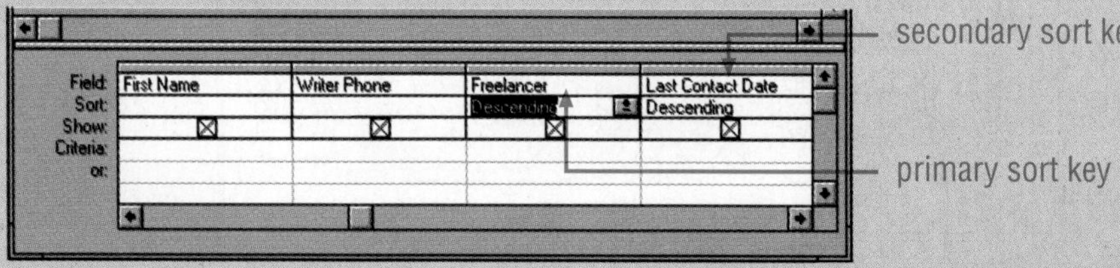

Figure 4-22 Sort orders specified for two fields

4. Click the toolbar **Run button**. The dynaset appears and displays all the fields of the WRITERS table and all its records, in descending order, based on the Freelancer field. Within the two groups of records that have the same Freelancer field value (No and Yes), the records are in descending order by last contact date. See Figure 4-23.

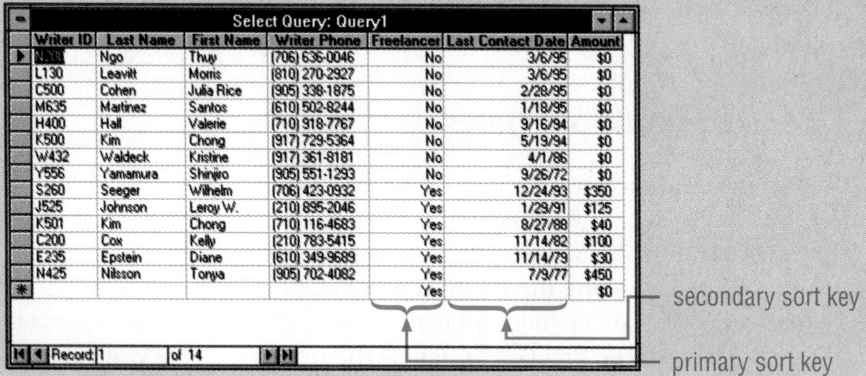
Select Query: Query1

Writer ID	Last Name	First Name	Writer Phone	Freelancer	Last Contact Date	Amount
N200	Ngo	Thuy	(706) 636-0046	No	3/6/95	$0
L130	Leavitt	Morris	(810) 270-2927	No	3/6/95	$0
C500	Cohen	Julia Rice	(905) 338-1875	No	2/28/95	$0
M635	Martinez	Santos	(610) 502-8244	No	1/18/95	$0
H400	Hall	Valerie	(710) 918-7767	No	9/16/94	$0
K500	Kim	Chong	(917) 729-5364	No	5/19/94	$0
W432	Waldeck	Kristine	(917) 361-8181	No	4/1/86	$0
Y556	Yamamura	Shinjiro	(905) 551-1293	No	9/26/72	$0
S260	Seeger	Wilhelm	(706) 423-0932	Yes	12/24/93	$350
J525	Johnson	Leroy W.	(210) 895-2046	Yes	1/29/91	$125
K501	Kim	Chong	(710) 116-4683	Yes	8/27/88	$40
C200	Cox	Kelly	(210) 783-5415	Yes	11/14/82	$100
E235	Epstein	Diane	(610) 349-9689	Yes	11/14/79	$30
N425	Nilsson	Tonya	(905) 702-4082	Yes	7/9/77	$450
*				Yes		$0

Figure 4-23 Dynaset sorted on two fields

Printing a Dynaset Selection

Next, Elena prints the dynaset. Rather than print the staff writers and freelancers together, however, she prints just the staff writers and then just the freelancers. Elena could change the query to select one group, run the query, print the dynaset, and then repeat the process for the other group. Instead, she selects one group in the dynaset, prints the dynaset selection, and then does the same for the other group. She uses this method because it is faster than changing the query.

To print a dynaset selection:

❶ Click the record selector for the first dynaset record and, while holding the mouse button, drag the pointer to the record selector of the last record that has a No value in the Freelancer field. Release the button. The group of records with Freelancer field values of No is highlighted. See Figure 4-24.

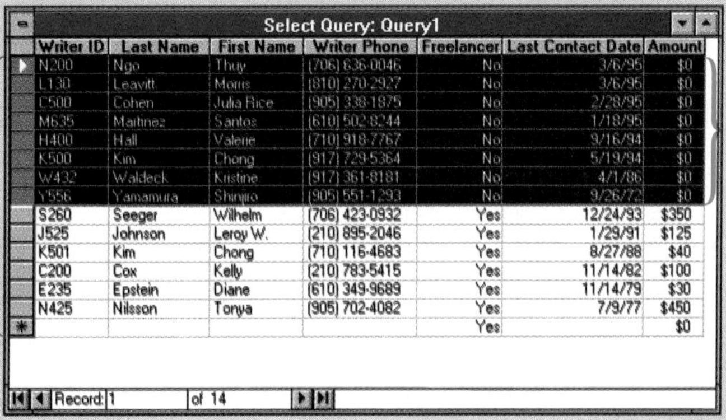

Writer ID	Last Name	First Name	Writer Phone	Freelancer	Last Contact Date	Amount
N200	Ngo	Thuy	(706) 636-0046	No	3/6/95	$0
L130	Leavitt	Morris	(810) 270-2927	No	3/6/95	$0
C500	Cohen	Julia Rice	(905) 338-1875	No	2/28/95	$0
M635	Martinez	Santos	(610) 502-8244	No	1/18/95	$0
H400	Hall	Valerie	(710) 918-7767	No	9/16/94	$0
K500	Kim	Chong	(917) 729-5364	No	5/19/94	$0
W432	Waldeck	Kristine	(917) 361-8181	No	4/1/86	$0
Y556	Yamamura	Shinjiro	(905) 551-1293	No	9/26/72	$0
S260	Seeger	Wilhelm	(706) 423-0932	Yes	12/24/93	$350
J525	Johnson	Leroy W.	(210) 895-2046	Yes	1/29/91	$125
K501	Kim	Chong	(710) 116-4683	Yes	8/27/88	$40
C200	Cox	Kelly	(210) 783-5415	Yes	11/14/82	$100
E235	Epstein	Diane	(610) 349-9689	Yes	11/14/79	$30
N425	Nilsson	Tonya	(905) 702-4082	Yes	7/9/77	$450
				Yes		$0

Figure 4-24
Dynaset records selected for printing

❷ Click the toolbar **Print button** to open the Print dialog box.

❸ Make sure your printer is on-line and ready to print.

❹ Check the Printer section of the Print dialog box to make sure that your computer's printer is selected.

❺ Click the **Selection radio button** to print just those records that are highlighted in the dynaset. See Figure 4-25.

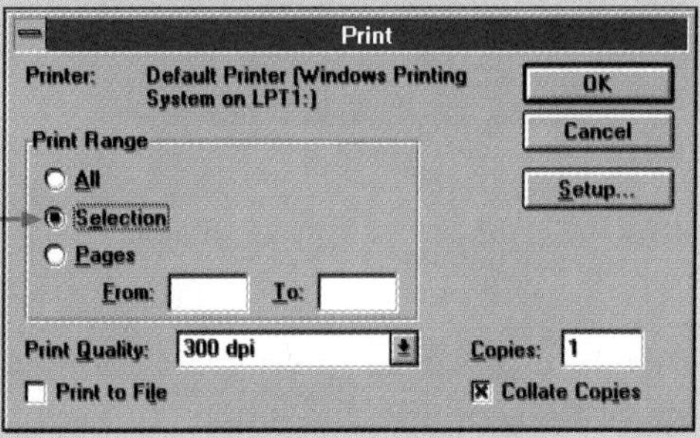

Figure 4-25
The Print dialog box

❻ Click the **OK button** to initiate printing. After the printing dialog box disappears, you are returned to the dynaset.

Saving a Query

Elena saves the query, so that she and others can open and run it again in the future.

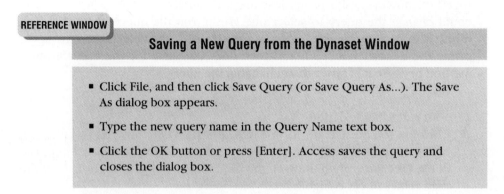

REFERENCE WINDOW

Saving a New Query from the Dynaset Window

- Click File, and then click Save Query (or Save Query As...). The Save As dialog box appears.
- Type the new query name in the Query Name text box.
- Click the OK button or press [Enter]. Access saves the query and closes the dialog box.

Elena saves the query using the name "WRITERS sorted by Freelancer, Last Contact Date."

To save a new query:

1. Click **File**, and then click **Save Query**. The Save As dialog box appears.

   TROUBLE? If the options in the File menu are Save and Save As..., then you are saving from the Query Design window. Click Save and continue with the next step.

2. Type **WRITERS sorted by Freelancer, Last Contact Date**.
3. Press **[Enter]**. The Save As dialog box disappears, and Access saves the query for later use.
4. Double-click the dynaset **Control menu box**. The dynaset disappears, and the Database window becomes the active window.
5. Click the **Query object button** and then click the **Database window maximize button**. Access displays the newly saved query in the Queries list box. See Figure 4-26.

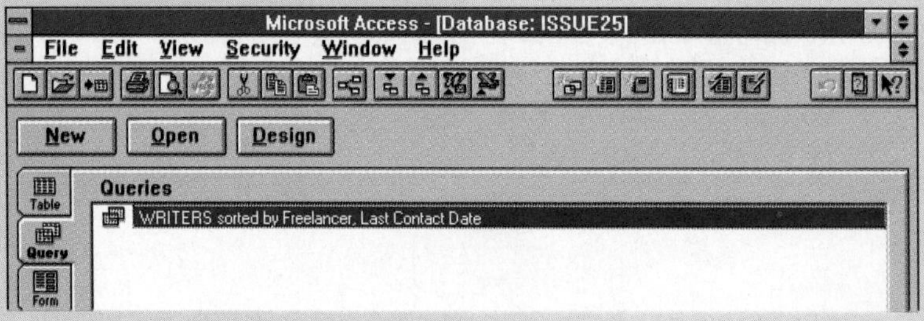

Figure 4-26
Query listed in the Database window

You can use a similar procedure to save a query from the Query Design window. In the Query Design window, the options on the File menu are Save and Save As.... If you try to close either the Query Design window or the dynaset without saving the query, Access displays a dialog box asking if you want to save the query. If you click Yes, Access displays the Save As dialog box.

If you want to take a break and resume the tutorial at a later time, you can exit Access by double-clicking the Microsoft Access window Control menu box. When you resume the tutorial, place your Student Disk in the appropriate drive, launch Access, open the Issue25 database on your Student Disk, maximize the Database window, and click the Query object button.

■ ■ ■

Opening a Query

Elena decides to use her saved query as a starting point for the next question on her list. She opens the saved query and then changes its design for the next query.

REFERENCE WINDOW

Opening a Saved Query

- Click the Query object button to display the Queries list box in the Database window.
- To view the query dynaset, either click the query name and then click the Open command button or double-click the left mouse button on the query name.
- Click the query name and then click the Design command button to open the Query Design window. You can change the query design in this window.

Let's open the Query Design window for the query saved with the name "WRITERS sorted by Freelancer, Last Contact Date."

To open a saved query to change its design:

1. If the Query object button is not selected, click it to display the Queries list box. The most recently saved query is highlighted in the Queries list box. In this case, there is only one saved query.
2. Click the **Design command button**. The Query Design window appears with the saved query on the screen.

Defining Multiple Selection Criteria

Elena's next task is to find all freelancers who were last contacted prior to 1990. This query involves two conditions.

Multiple conditions require you to use **logical operators** to combine two or more simple conditions. When you want a record selected only if two or more conditions are met, then you need to use the **And logical operator**. For an Access query, you use the And logical operator when you place two or more simple conditions in the same Criteria row of the QBE grid. If a record meets every one of the conditions in the Criteria row, then Access selects the record.

If you place multiple conditions in different Criteria rows, Access selects a record if at least one of the conditions is satisfied. If none of the conditions is satisfied, then Access does not select the record. This is known as the **Or logical operator**. The difference between the two logical operators is illustrated in Figure 4-27.

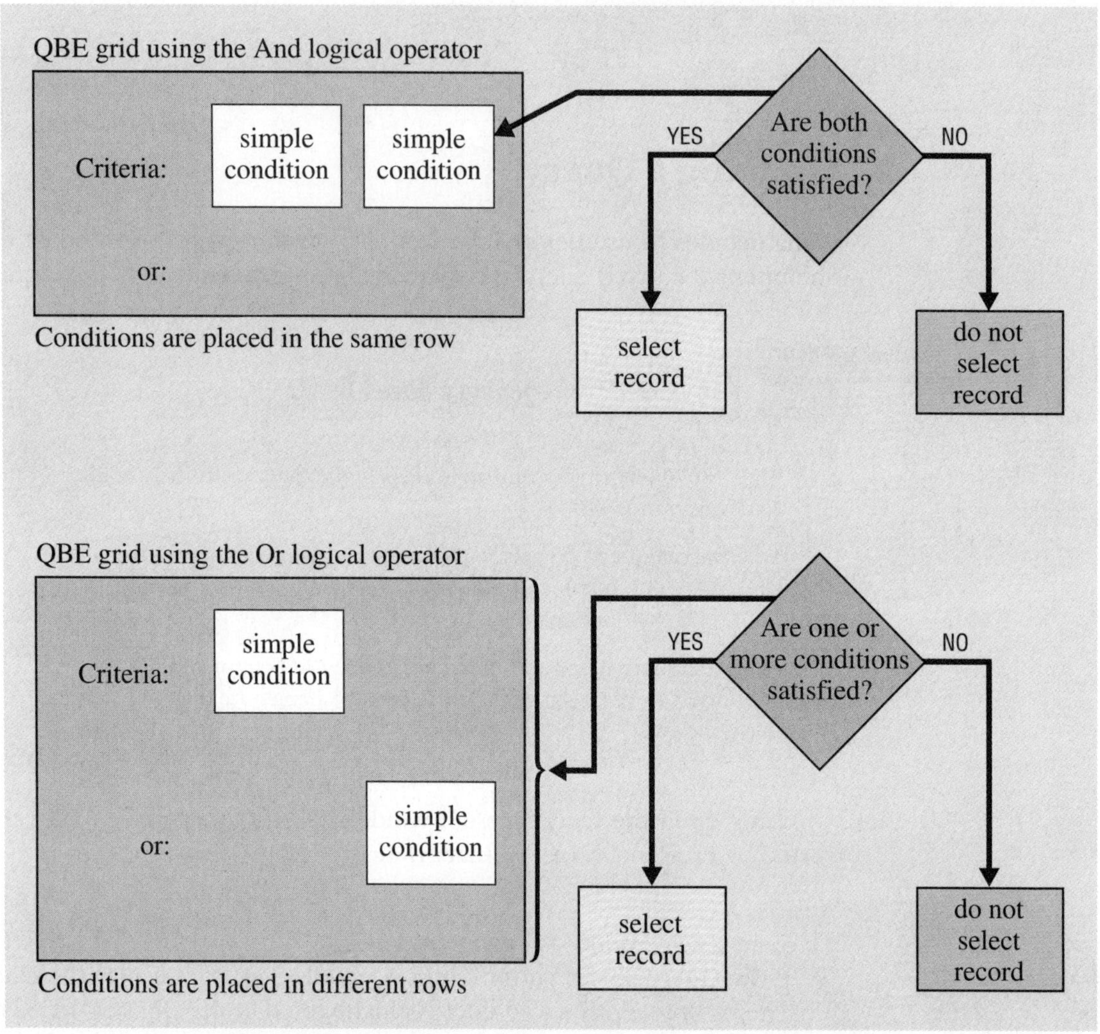

Figure 4-27
Logical operators And and Or for multiple selection criteria

The use of the word "and" in a question is usually a clue that you should use the And logical operator. The word "or" in a question usually means that you should use the Or logical operator.

The And Logical Operator

Elena will use the And logical operator and enter conditions for the Freelancer field and the Last Contact Date field in the same Criteria row. She will enter =Yes as the condition for the Freelancer field and <#1/1/90# as the condition for the Last Contact Date field. Because the conditions appear in the same Criteria row, Access selects records only if both conditions are met.

Elena's new query does not need sort keys, so Elena removes the sort keys for the Freelancer and Last Contact Date fields.

To remove sort keys from the QBE grid:

❶ Click the **Sort text box** in the Freelancer column and then click the **down arrow button**. Access displays the Sort list.

❷ Click **(not sorted)** in the Sort list. The Sort list disappears, and Access removes the sort order from the Sort text box.

❸ If necessary, scroll to the right in the QBE grid until the Last Contact Date column appears. Click the **Sort text box** in the Last Contact Date column and then click the **down arrow button**. Access displays the Sort list.

❹ Click **(not sorted)** in the Sort list. The Sort list disappears, and Access clears the sort order from the Sort text box.

Elena now enters the two conditions.

To select records using the And logical operator:

❶ Click the **Freelancer Criteria text box** and then type **=Yes**.

❷ Click the **Last Contact Date Criteria text box** and then type **<#1/1/90#**. See Figure 4-28. Access will select a record only if both conditions are met.

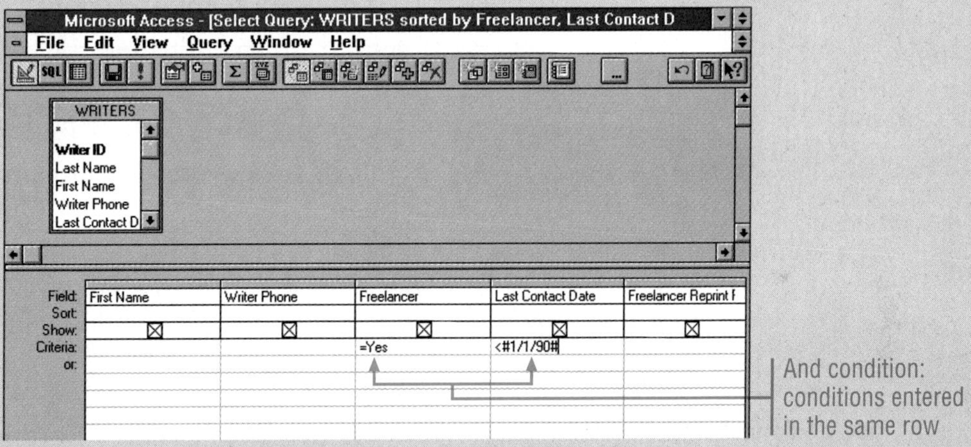

Figure 4-28 Criteria to find freelancers last contacted prior to 1990

❸ Click the toolbar **Run button**. The dynaset appears and displays only records for freelancers last contacted prior to 1990.

❹ Click the toolbar **Design View button** to switch back to the Query Design window.

The Or Logical Operator

Elena's next query asks for those writers who have 210 or 706 area codes. For this query, Elena uses the Or logical operator and enters conditions for the Writer Phone field in two different Criteria rows. She will enter Like "210*" in one row and Like "706*" in another row. Because the conditions appear in different Criteria rows, Access selects records if either condition is satisfied. The Or logical operator used in one field is similar to the In comparison operator.

To select records using the Or logical operator:

1. Move the pointer to the left side of the Criteria text box for the first column and click when the pointer changes to ➡. Access highlights the entire Criteria row.
2. Click the right mouse button in the first column's Criteria text box to display the Shortcut menu. Click **Cut** to remove the previous conditions from the QBE grid.

   TROUBLE? If the Shortcut menu does not appear, you clicked too far from the point where you originally clicked in Step 1. Repeat Step 1 and, without moving the mouse pointer, click the right mouse button once again.
3. Click the **Criteria text box** in the Writer Phone column and then type **Like "210*"**.
4. Click the **Criteria text box** below the one you just used and type **Like "706*"**. See Figure 4-29. Access will select a record if either condition is met.

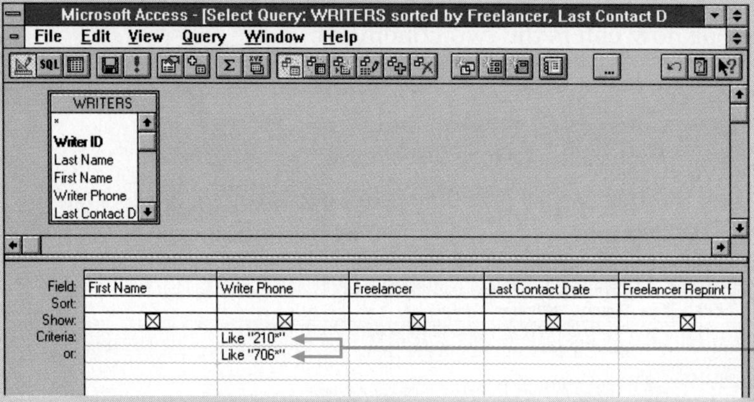

Figure 4-29 Criteria to find writers with 210 or 706 area codes

5. Click the toolbar **Run button** ❗. The dynaset appears and displays just those records for writers with 210 or 706 area codes.
6. Click the toolbar **Design View button** to switch back to the Query Design window.

Using And with Or

To make sure that she created the right query, Elena rechecks the question on her list and discovers she misread it. She really should be selecting records for freelancers who have 210 or 706 area codes. In other words, she really wants writers who are freelancers and have 210 area codes, or who are freelancers and have 706 area codes. To form this query, she needs to add the =Yes condition for the Freelancer field to both rows that already contain the Writer Phone conditions. Access will select a record if either And condition is met. Only freelancers will be selected, but only if their area codes are 210 or 706.

Elena adds the Freelancer conditions to the QBE grid to complete her new query.

To select records using the And logical operator with the Or logical operator:

1. Click the **Criteria text box** in the Freelancer column and then type **=Yes**.
2. Press [↓] and then type **=Yes**. See Figure 4-30. Access will select a record if either And condition is met.

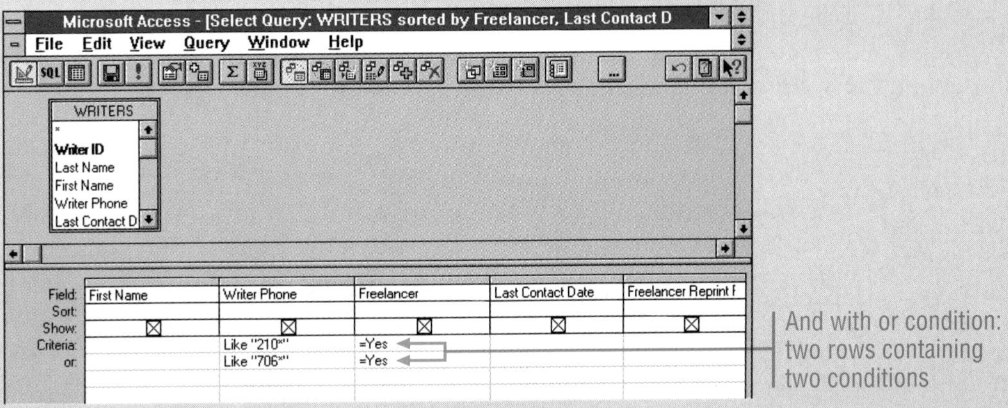

Figure 4-30 Criteria to find freelancers who have 210 or 706 area codes

3. Click the toolbar **Run button**. The dynaset appears and displays only records for freelancers with 210 or 706 area codes. See Figure 4-31.

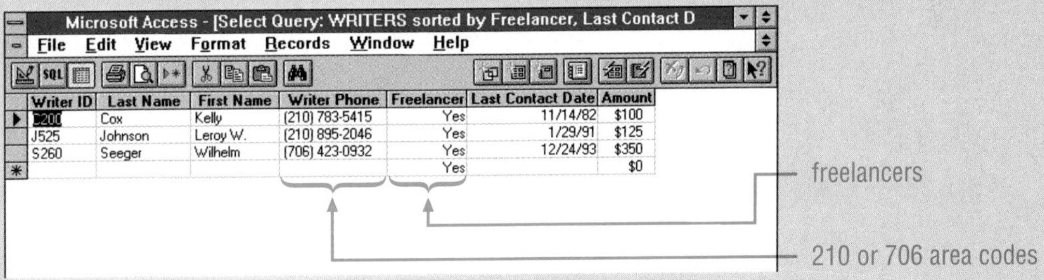

Figure 4-31 Results of a query to find freelancers who have 210 or 706 area codes

4. Click the toolbar **Design View button** to switch back to the Query Design window.

Performing Calculations

Elena's next task is to find the impact of giving all writers an extra $50. This query requires the addition of a calculated field in the QBE grid.

A **calculated field** is a new field that exists in a dynaset but does not exist in a database. The value of a calculated field is determined from fields that are in a database. You can define a calculated field in a query. When you run the query, Access determines the value for the calculated field. You perform your calculations using number, currency, or date/time fields from your database. Among the arithmetic operators you can use are those for addition (+), subtraction (–), multiplication (*), and division (/).

Using Calculated Fields

Elena creates a calculated field that adds 50 to the amount stored in the Freelancer Reprint Payment Amount field. Whenever a calculation includes a field name, you place brackets around the name to tell Access that the name is from your database. Elena's calculation, for example, will be expressed as [Freelancer Reprint Payment Amount]+50. Access supplies the default name Expr1 for your first calculated field, but you can change the name at any time. Elena uses Add50 as the name for the calculated field. Because the Field text box is too small to show the entire calculated field, Elena uses the Zoom box while she enters the calculated field. The **Zoom box** is a large text box for entering text or other values. You open the zoom box either by pressing [Shift][F2] or by using the Shortcut menu.

The new query will select all records in the WRITERS table, so Elena first removes the conditions in the two Criteria rows. At the same time, she decides to simplify the query by deleting three fields: Writer ID, Writer Phone, and Last Contact Date.

To remove conditions and delete fields from the QBE grid:

1. Move the pointer to the left side of the Criteria text box for the first column. The pointer changes to ➡. Click and, while holding the mouse button, drag the pointer down to the next row before releasing the mouse button. The two rows are highlighted. Click the right mouse button in either highlighted row to display the Shortcut menu and click **Cut** to remove the previous conditions from the QBE grid.
2. Scroll to make the Writer ID column visible. Move the pointer to the Writer ID field selector and then click it to highlight the entire column. Click the right mouse button in the Writer ID field selector to display the Shortcut menu and click **Cut** to delete the column.
3. In a similar manner, delete the Writer Phone and Last Contact Date columns in the QBE grid.

The QBE grid now contains four fields: Last Name, First Name, Freelancer, and Freelancer Reprint Payment Amount. Elena next adds the calculated field.

To add a calculated field to the QBE grid and run the query:

1. Click the right mouse button in the Field text box for the first unused column to open the Shortcut menu.
2. Click **Zoom...** to open the Zoom box.
3. Type **Add50:[Freelancer Reprint Payment Amount]+50**. See Figure 4-32.

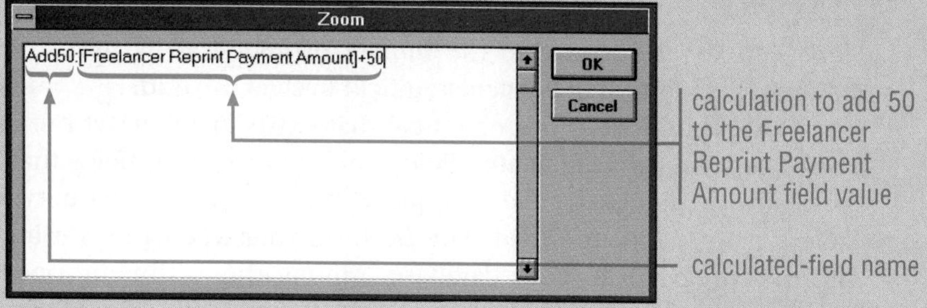

Figure 4-32 The Zoom box for entering long calculations

4. Click the **OK button**. The Zoom box disappears.

❺ Click the toolbar **Run button** [!]. The dynaset displays all records in the WRITERS table and includes the new calculated field. See Figure 4-33.

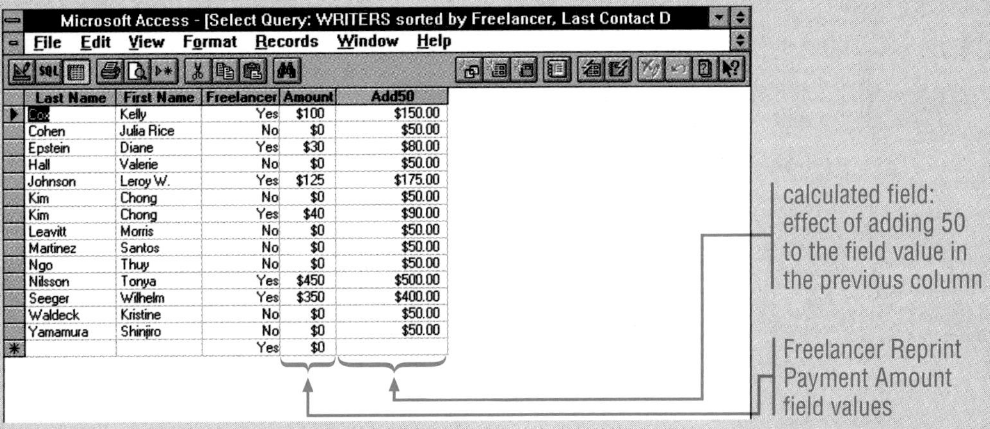

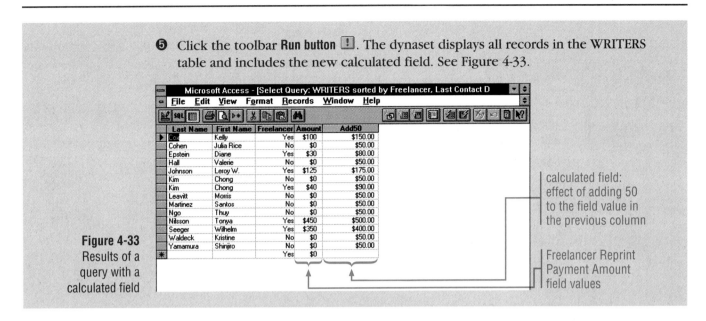

Figure 4-33
Results of a query with a calculated field

The calculated field values in the new Add50 column are $50 more than those in the Amount column, which is the Caption property name for the Freelancer Reprint Payment Amount field.

Using Record Calculations

Elena must now find both the total cost and the average cost per writer, with and without the extra $50. For this query, she uses aggregate functions. **Aggregate functions** perform arithmetic operations on the records in a database. The most frequently used aggregate functions are shown in Figure 4-34. Aggregate functions operate upon the records that meet a query's selection criteria. You specify an aggregate function for a specific field, and the appropriate operation applies to that field's values for the selected records.

Function	Meaning
Avg	Average of the field values for the selected records
Count	Number of records selected
Min	Lowest field value for the selected records
Max	Highest field value for the selected records
Sum	Total of the field values for the selected records

Figure 4-34
Frequently used aggregate functions

Elena uses the Sum and Avg aggregate functions for both the Freelancer Reprint Payment Amount field and for the calculated field she just created in her previous query. The Sum aggregate function gives the total of the field values, and the Avg aggregate function gives the average of the field values. Elena's query result will be a dynaset with one record displaying the four requested aggregate function values.

To use aggregate functions in the Query Design window, you click the toolbar Totals button. Access inserts a Total row between the Field and Sort rows in the QBE grid. You specify the aggregate functions you want to use in the Total row. When you run the query, one record appears in the dynaset with your selected aggregate function values. The individual table records themselves do not appear.

Elena does not need any fields other than the Freelancer Reprint Payment Amount field and the calculated field, so she deletes the Last Name, First Name, and Freelancer fields. She then restores the Query Design window to its smaller size.

To delete fields from the QBE grid:

1. Click the toolbar **Design View button** to switch back to the Query Design window.
2. If necessary, scroll to make the Last Name, First Name, and Freelancer fields visible. Move the pointer to the Last Name field selector. Then click to highlight the entire column, hold the mouse button, drag the pointer to the right until the First Name and Freelancer fields are also highlighted, and release the mouse button. Click the right mouse button in the field selector for one of these three fields to display the Shortcut menu, and click **Cut** to delete the three columns.

   TROUBLE? If the fields are not side by side, delete one column and then the others in separate steps.
3. Click the Query Design window **restore button**, which is on the right side of the menu bar.

Elena now has two fields left in the QBE grid: the Freelancer Reprint Payment Amount field and the Add50 calculated field. She needs two columns for each of these: one for a Sum aggregate function, and the other for an Avg aggregate function. The four columns will allow her to find the total cost and average cost per writer with and without the extra $50. She inserts a second copy of the Freelancer Reprint Payment Amount field in the QBE grid. She then renames the first Freelancer Reprint Payment Amount field AmountSum and the second AmountAvg. She likewise makes a second copy of the Add50 calculated field and renames the first one Add50Sum and the second Add50Avg.

First Elena adds the copy of the Freelancer Reprint Payment Amount field to the QBE grid and renames all three fields.

To add and rename fields in the QBE grid:

1. If necessary, scroll to the left to make both fields visible in the QBE grid. Click **Freelancer Reprint Payment Amount** in the WRITERS field list, drag it to the Add50 calculated field column in the QBE grid, and then release the mouse button. The three fields in the QBE grid, from left to right, are Freelancer Reprint Payment Amount, Freelancer Reprint Payment Amount, and Add50.
2. Click the beginning of the Field box for the first Freelancer Reprint Payment Amount field and type **AmountSum:**.
3. Click the beginning of the Field box for the second Freelancer Reprint Payment Amount field and type **AmountAvg:**.
4. Click just before the colon in the Field box for the Add50 calculated field and type **Sum**. The name of the calculated field is now Add50Sum.

Elena next selects aggregate functions for these three fields.

To select aggregate functions:

❶ Click the **Totals button** [Σ] on the toolbar. The Total row appears in the QBE grid.

❷ Click the **Total text box** for the AmountSum field and then click the **down arrow button** that appears. Click **Sum** in the Total list box.

❸ Click the **Total text box** for the AmountAvg field and then click the **down arrow button** that appears. Click **Avg** in the Total list box.

❹ Click the **Total text box** for the Add50Sum field and then click the **down arrow button** that appears. See Figure 4-35.

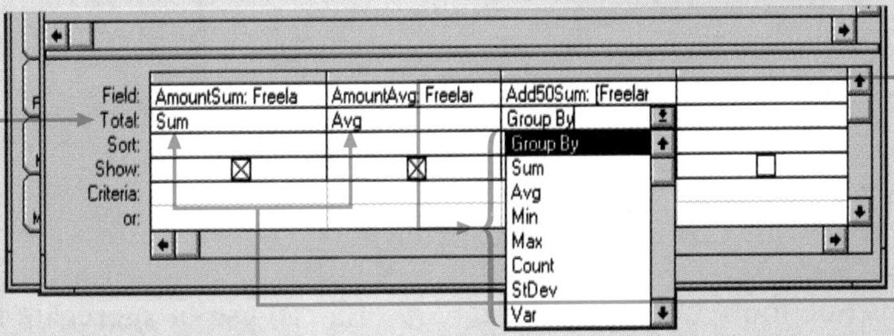

Figure 4-35 Aggregate function selection

❺ Click **Sum** in the Total list box.

Elena's last steps are to copy the calculated field, paste it to the fourth column, rename the new field Add50Avg, and change its Total text box to Avg.

To copy and paste a new calculated field with an aggregate function:

❶ Click the **Add50Sum field selector** to highlight the entire column.

❷ Click the right mouse button in the Add50Sum field selector to display the Shortcut menu and then click **Copy** to copy the column to the Clipboard.

❸ Click the **field selector** for the fourth column to highlight the entire column. Click the right mouse button in the fourth column's field selector to display the Shortcut menu and then click **Paste**. A copy of the third column appears in the fourth column.

❹ Highlight **Sum** in the Field text box for the fourth column and type **Avg**. The renamed field name is now Add50Avg.

❺ Click the **Total text box** for the Add50Avg column and then click the **down arrow button** that appears. Click **Avg** in the Total list box. See Figure 4-36.

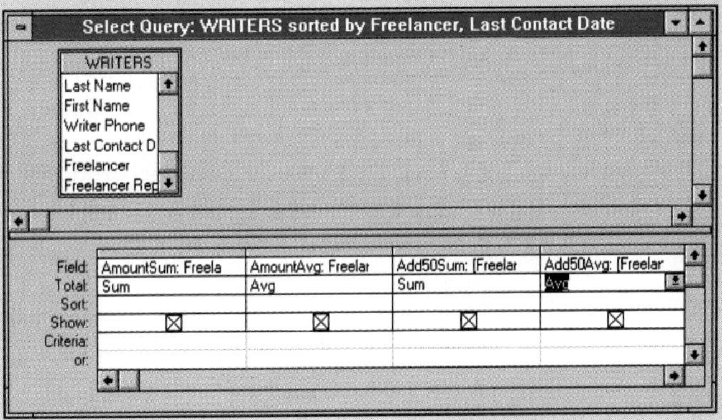

Figure 4-36 Calculating total cost and average cost per writer with and without an extra $50

As her final step, Elena views the query's dynaset.

To view a query dynaset:

1. Click the toolbar **Run button** . The dynaset appears and displays one record containing the four aggregate function values. See Figure 4-37.

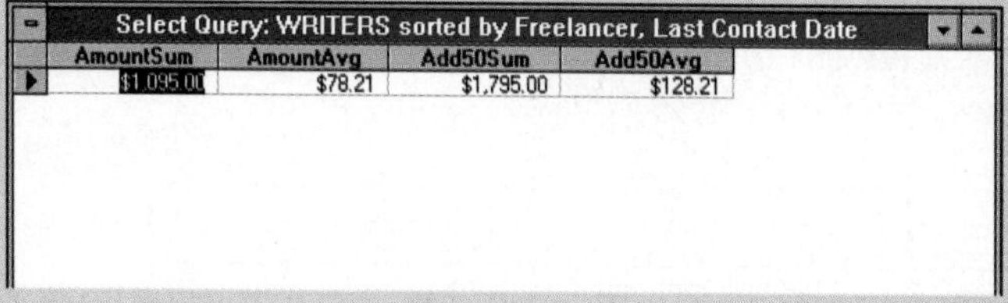

Figure 4-37 Results of a query using aggregate functions

Using Record Group Calculations

Elena has one more query to create requiring the use of aggregate functions. Brian wants to know the total cost and average cost for freelancers versus staff writers with and without the extra $50. This query is exactly like her previous query, except Elena needs to add the Freelancer field and assign the Group By operator to it.

The **Group By operator** combines records with identical field values into a single record. The Group By operator used with the Freelancer field results in two records: one record for the Yes field values, and the other for the No field values. Subtotals for each of the two records are created if you use aggregate functions.

Elena adds the Freelancer field to the QBE grid in the first column, assigns it the Group By operator, and views the dynaset for the revised query.

To add a field with the Group By operator and view the dynaset:

1. Click the toolbar **Design View button** to switch back to the Query Design window.
2. Click **Freelancer** in the WRITERS field list and drag it to the first QBE grid column. The Total text box for the field shows the Group By operator by default. See Figure 4-38.

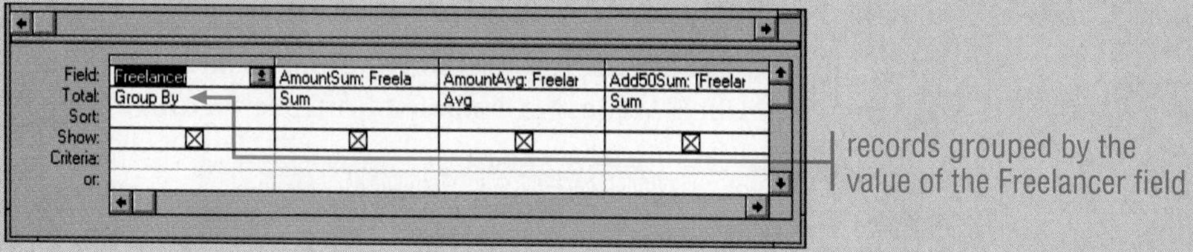

Figure 4-38 Query using aggregate functions on groups of records

3. Click the toolbar **Run button** . The dynaset appears and displays two records, each containing the four aggregate function values. See Figure 4-39.

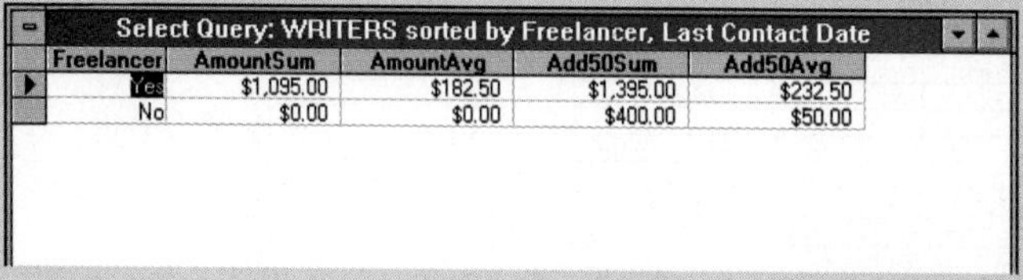

Figure 4-39 Results of a query using aggregate functions on groups of records

Elena has some phone calls to make, so she closes the dynaset without saving her latest queries.

To close a dynaset without saving the query:

1. Double-click the Datasheet View window **Control menu box**. The "Save changes to Query" dialog box appears.
2. Click the **No button**. Access closes the dialog box and then closes the dynaset without saving the query.

If you want to take a break and resume the tutorial at a later time, you can exit Access by double-clicking the Microsoft Access window Control menu box. When you resume the tutorial, place your Student Disk in the appropriate drive, launch Access, open the Issue25 database on your Student Disk, and click the Query object button.

■ ■ ■

Establishing Table Relationships

One of the most powerful features of a database management system is its ability to establish relationships between tables. You use a common field to relate, or link, one table with another table. The process of linking tables is often called performing a **join**. When you link tables with a common field, you can extract data from them as if they were one larger table. For example, Elena links the WRITERS and PAST ARTICLES tables by using the Writer ID field in both tables as the common field. She can then use a query to extract all the article data for each writer, even though the fields are contained in two separate tables. The WRITERS and PAST ARTICLES tables have a type of relationship called a one-to-many relationship. The other two types of relationships are the one-to-one relationship and the many-to-many relationship.

Types of Relationships

A **one-to-one relationship** exists between two tables when each record in one table has exactly one matching record in the other table. For example, suppose Elena splits the WRITERS table into two tables, as shown in Figure 4-40. These two tables have a one-to-one relationship. Both the WRITERS CONTACT table and the WRITERS PAYMENT table have Writer ID as the primary key. Writer ID is also the common field between the two tables. Each record in the WRITERS CONTACT table matches one record in the WRITERS PAYMENT table through the common field. The reverse is also true that each record in the WRITERS PAYMENT table matches one record in the WRITERS CONTACT table through the common field. You can query the data from the two tables as if they were one table by linking, or joining, the two tables on the common field. Unless you set criteria to limit the dynaset to specific records, the resulting dynaset contains the same number of records each table has and fields from both tables—but only the fields you need.

WRITERS CONTACT table

Writer ID	Last Name	First Name	Writer Phone	Last Contact Date
C200	Cox	Kelly	(210)783-5415	11/14/82
C500	Cohen	Julia Rice	(905)338-1875	2/28/95
E235	Epstein	Diane	(610)349-9689	11/14/79
H400	Hall	Valerie	(710)918-7767	9/16/94
J525	Johnson	Leroy W.	(210)895-2046	1/29/91
K500	Kim	Chong	(917)729-5364	5/19/94

WRITERS PAYMENT table

Writer ID	Freelancer	Amount
C200	Yes	$100
C500	No	$0
E235	Yes	$30
H400	No	$0
J525	Yes	$125
K500	No	$0

query dynaset

Last Name	First Name	Amount
Cox	Kelly	$100
Cohen	Julia Rice	$0
Epstein	Diane	$30
Hall	Valerie	$0
Johnson	Leroy W.	$125
Kim	Chong	$0

- common field and primary key
- fields from WRITERS CONTACT table
- fields from WRITERS PAYMENT table

Figure 4-40
One-to-one relationship

A **one-to-many relationship** exists between two tables when one record in the first table matches many records in the second table, but one record in the second table matches only one record in the first table. The relationship between the WRITERS CONTACT table and the PAST ARTICLES table, as shown in Figure 4-41 on the following page, is an example of a one-to-many relationship. Each record in the WRITERS CONTACT table matches many records in the PAST ARTICLES table. Valerie Hall's record in the WRITERS CONTACT table with a Writer ID of H400, for example, links to three records in the PAST ARTICLES table: "25% Tax Cut Bill Approved," "The BCCI Scandal Revealed," and "Computers in the Future." Many can also mean zero records or one record. There is no article listed for Leroy W. Johnson, for example. There is one article for Kelly Cox. Conversely, each record in the PAST ARTICLES table links to a single record in the WRITERS CONTACT table, with Writer ID used as the common field.

PAST ARTICLES table

common field as a foreign key

Article Title	Type	Issue	Article Length	Writer ID
The Economy Under Sub-Zero Population Growth	BUS	1972 Dec	1020	E235
Milton Friedman Interview	ITV	1976 Dec	1994	C200
Chrysler Asks U.S. For $1 Billion	POL	1979 Aug	975	K500
25% Tax Cut Bill Approved	LAW	1981 Aug	2371	H400
AT&T Antitrust Settlement	BUS	1982 Feb	1600	K500
Building Trade Outlook	BUS	1984 Apr	1437	K500
Reagan's $1.09 Trillion Budget	POL	1988 Mar	1798	C500
The BCCI Scandal Revealed	EXP	1991 Jul	2461	H400
Computers in the Future	TEC	1994 Jan	2222	H400

WRITERS CONTACT table

common field as a primary key

Writer ID	Last Name	First Name	Writer Phone	Last Contact Date
C200	Cox	Kelly	(210)783-5415	11/14/82
C500	Cohen	Julia Rice	(905)338-1875	2/28/95
E235	Epstein	Diane	(610)349-9689	11/14/79
H400	Hall	Valerie	(710)918-7767	9/16/94
J525	Johnson	Leroy W.	(210)895-2046	1/29/91
K500	Kim	Chong	(917)729-5364	5/19/94

query dynaset

Article Title	Issue	Last Name	First Name
The Economy Under Sub-Zero Population Growth	1972 Dec	Epstein	Diane
Milton Friedman Interwiew	1976 Dec	Cox	Kelly
Chrysler Asks U.S. For $1 Billion	1979 Aug	Kim	Chong
25% Tax Cut Bill Approved	1981 Aug	Hall	Valerie
AT&T Antitrust Settlement	1982 Feb	Kim	Chong
Building Trade Outlook	1984 Apr	Kim	Chong
Reagan's $1.09 Trillion Budget	1988 Mar	Cohen	Julia Rice
The BCCI Scandal Revealed	1991 Jul	Hall	Valerie
Computers in the Future	1994 Jan	Hall	Valerie

common field

fields from WRITERS CONTACT table

fields from PAST ARTICLES table

Figure 4-41
One-to-many relationship

For a one-to-many relationship, like a one-to-one relationship, you can query the data from the two tables as if they were one table by linking the two tables on the common field. The resulting dynaset can contain the same number of records as does the table that has the foreign key; this table is the table on the "many" side of the one-to-many relationship.

A **many-to-many relationship** exists between two tables when one record in the first table matches many records in the second table and one record in the second table matches many records in the first table. For example, suppose that an article was written by cowriters. The relationship between the WRITERS CONTACT and PAST ARTICLES tables would then be a many-to-many relationship, as shown in Figure 4-42. To handle this type of relationship, you first make sure that each table has a primary key. A counter field named Article ID needs to be added as a primary key to the PAST ARTICLES table, which did not have a primary key. Then you create a new table that has a primary key combining the primary keys of the other two tables. The WRITERS AND PAST ARTICLES table is created. Its primary key is Article ID *and* Writer ID. Each record in this new table represents one article and one of the article's writers. Even though an article ID and writer ID can appear more than once, each combination of article ID and writer ID is unique.

WRITERS CONTACT table

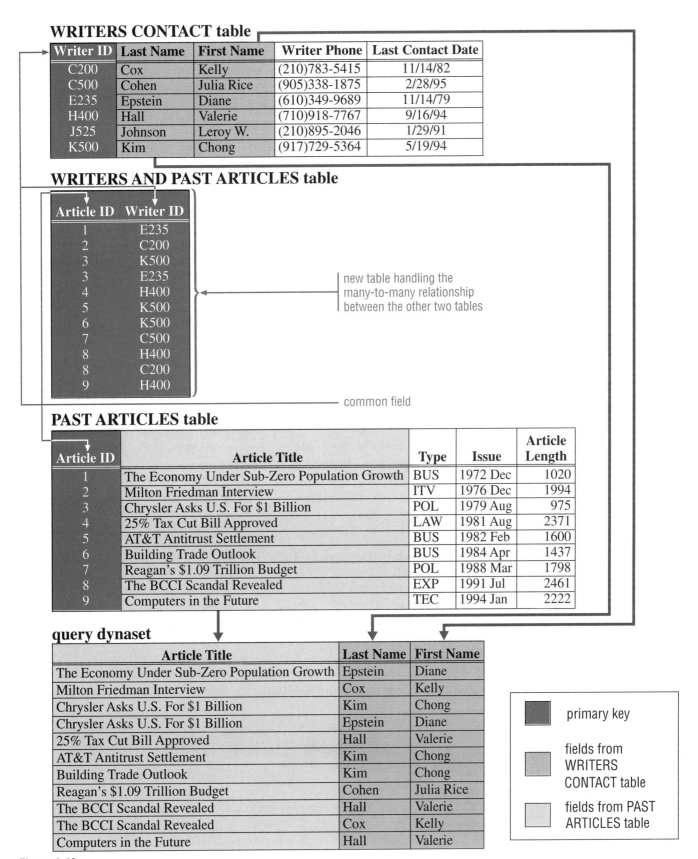

Writer ID	Last Name	First Name	Writer Phone	Last Contact Date
C200	Cox	Kelly	(210)783-5415	11/14/82
C500	Cohen	Julia Rice	(905)338-1875	2/28/95
E235	Epstein	Diane	(610)349-9689	11/14/79
H400	Hall	Valerie	(710)918-7767	9/16/94
J525	Johnson	Leroy W.	(210)895-2046	1/29/91
K500	Kim	Chong	(917)729-5364	5/19/94

WRITERS AND PAST ARTICLES table

Article ID	Writer ID
1	E235
2	C200
3	K500
3	E235
4	H400
5	K500
6	K500
7	C500
8	H400
8	C200
9	H400

new table handling the many-to-many relationship between the other two tables

common field

PAST ARTICLES table

Article ID	Article Title	Type	Issue	Article Length
1	The Economy Under Sub-Zero Population Growth	BUS	1972 Dec	1020
2	Milton Friedman Interview	ITV	1976 Dec	1994
3	Chrysler Asks U.S. For $1 Billion	POL	1979 Aug	975
4	25% Tax Cut Bill Approved	LAW	1981 Aug	2371
5	AT&T Antitrust Settlement	BUS	1982 Feb	1600
6	Building Trade Outlook	BUS	1984 Apr	1437
7	Reagan's $1.09 Trillion Budget	POL	1988 Mar	1798
8	The BCCI Scandal Revealed	EXP	1991 Jul	2461
9	Computers in the Future	TEC	1994 Jan	2222

query dynaset

Article Title	Last Name	First Name
The Economy Under Sub-Zero Population Growth	Epstein	Diane
Milton Friedman Interview	Cox	Kelly
Chrysler Asks U.S. For $1 Billion	Kim	Chong
Chrysler Asks U.S. For $1 Billion	Epstein	Diane
25% Tax Cut Bill Approved	Hall	Valerie
AT&T Antitrust Settlement	Kim	Chong
Building Trade Outlook	Kim	Chong
Reagan's $1.09 Trillion Budget	Cohen	Julia Rice
The BCCI Scandal Revealed	Hall	Valerie
The BCCI Scandal Revealed	Cox	Kelly
Computers in the Future	Hall	Valerie

primary key

fields from WRITERS CONTACT table

fields from PAST ARTICLES table

Figure 4-42
Many-to-many relationship

The many-to-many relationship between the WRITERS CONTACT and PAST ARTICLES tables has been changed into two one-to-many relationships. The WRITERS CONTACT table has a one-to-many relationship with the WRITERS AND PAST ARTICLES table, and the PAST ARTICLES table has a one-to-many relationship with the WRITERS AND PAST ARTICLES table.

For a many-to-many relationship, you can query the data from the tables as if they were one table by linking the tables on their common fields. For example, you link the WRITERS CONTACT and the WRITERS AND PAST ARTICLES tables on their common field, Writer ID, and you link the PAST ARTICLES and the WRITERS AND PAST ARTICLES tables on their common field, Article ID. The resulting dynaset can contain the same number of records as does the new table that you created—in this case, the WRITERS AND PAST ARTICLES table.

Access refers to the two tables that form a relationship as the primary table and the related table. The **primary table** is the one table in a one-to-many relationship, and the **related table** is the many table. In a one-to-one relationship, you can choose either table as the primary table and the other table as the related table.

When two tables are related, you can choose to enforce referential integrity rules. The **referential integrity** rules are:

- When you add a record to a related table, a matching record must already exist in the primary table.
- You cannot delete a record from a primary table if matching records exist in the related table, unless you choose to cascade deletes.

When you delete a record with a particular primary-key value from the primary table and choose to **cascade deletes**, Access automatically deletes from related tables all records having foreign-key values equal to that primary-key value. You can also choose to cascade updates. When you change a table's primary-key value and choose to **cascade updates**, Access automatically changes all related tables' foreign-key values that equal that primary-key value.

Let's see how to define relationships and choose referential integrity and cascade options in Access.

Adding a Relationship between Two Tables

When two tables have a common field, you can define the relationship between them in the Relationships window. The **Relationships window** illustrates the one-to-one and one-to-many relationships among a database's tables. In this window you can view or change existing relationships, define new relationships between tables, and rearrange the layout of the tables.

Elena defines the one-to-many relationship between the WRITERS and PAST ARTICLES tables. First, she opens the Relationships window.

To open the Relationships window:

1. Click the toolbar **Relationships button**. Access displays the Add Table dialog box on top of the Relationships window.
2. In the Add Table dialog box, double-click **WRITERS** and then double-click **PAST ARTICLES** in the Table/Query list box. Access adds both tables to the Relationships window.

3. Click the **Close button** in the Add Table dialog box. Access closes the Add Table dialog box and reveals the entire Relationships window. See Figure 4-43.

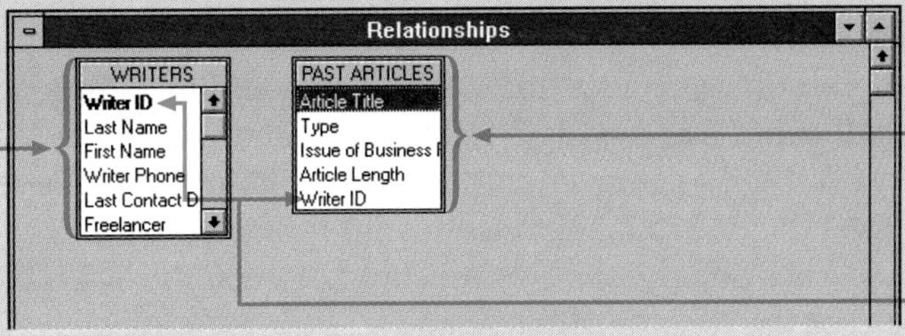

Figure 4-43
The Relationships window

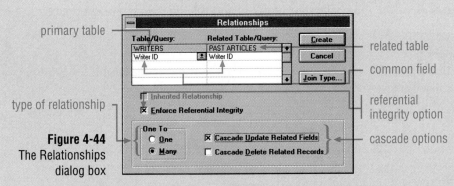

To form a relationship between the two tables, you drag the common field from one table to the other table. Specifically, you click the primary-key field in the primary table and drag it to the foreign-key field in the related table. Access then displays the Relationships dialog box, in which you select the relationship options for the two tables.

Elena drags Writer ID from the WRITERS table to the PAST ARTICLES table and then selects the relationship options in the Relationships dialog box.

To define a relationship between two tables:

1. Click **Writer ID** in the WRITERS table list and drag it to Writer ID in the PAST ARTICLES table list. When you release the mouse button, Access displays the Relationships dialog box.
2. Click the **Enforce Referential Integrity check box** to turn this option on. Access turns on the Many radio button in the One To list.
3. Click the **Cascade Update Related Fields check box** to turn this option on. See Figure 4-44. Do not turn on the Cascade Delete Related Records option.

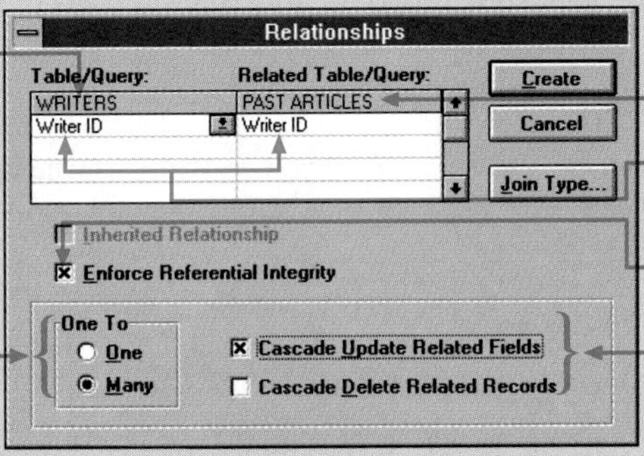

Figure 4-44
The Relationships dialog box

4. Click the **Create button**. Access saves the defined relationship between the two tables, closes the Relationships dialog box, and reveals the entire Relationships window. See Figure 4-45.

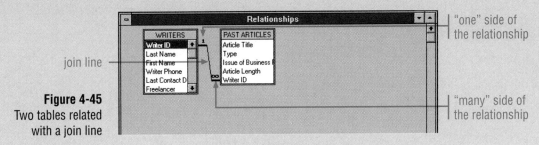

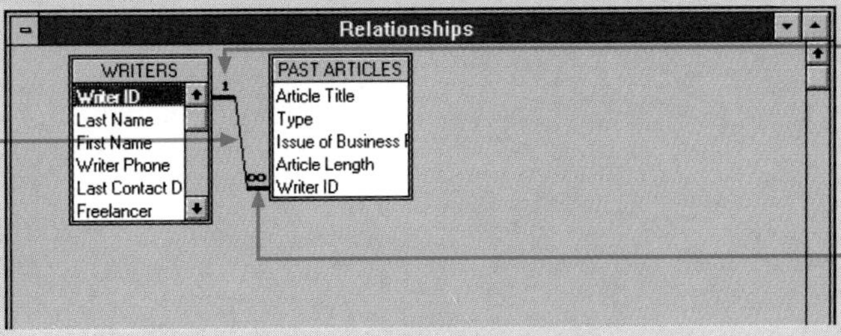

Figure 4-45
Two tables related with a join line

Notice the join line that connects the Writer ID fields common to the two tables. The **join line** shows you the common field between two tables. The common fields link (or join) the two tables, which have either a one-to-one or one-to-many relationship. The join line is bold at both ends; this signifies that you have chosen the option to enforce referential integrity. If you do not select this option, the join line is thin at both ends. The "one" side of the relationship has the digit 1 at its end, and the "many" side of the relationship has the infinity symbol (∞) at its end. Although the two tables are still separate tables, you have now defined the one-to-many relationship between them.

Now that she has defined the relationship between the WRITERS and PAST ARTICLES tables, Elena closes the Relationships window.

To close the Relationships window:

1. Double-click the Relationships window **Control menu box**. Access displays the "Save layout changes to 'Relationships'?" dialog box.
2. Click the **Yes button** to save the layout. Access closes the dialog box and the Relationships window and returns you to the Database window.

Elena can now build her next query, which requires data from both the WRITERS and PAST ARTICLES tables.

Querying More Than One Table

Elena's next query seeks the article titles, types, and lengths for each writer ordered by article type. This query involves fields from both the WRITERS and PAST ARTICLES tables and requires a sort.

Elena first opens the Query Design window and selects the two needed tables.

To start a query using two tables:

1. Be sure that the Query object button is selected in the Database window and then click the **New command button**. The New Query dialog box appears.
2. Click the **New Query button** in the dialog box. The Add Table dialog box appears on top of the Query Design window.
3. Double-click **WRITERS** and then double-click **PAST ARTICLES** in the Table/Query list box. Access displays the WRITERS and PAST ARTICLES field lists in the upper portion of the Query Design window.

❹ Click the **Close button**. The Add Table dialog box disappears. See Figure 4-46.

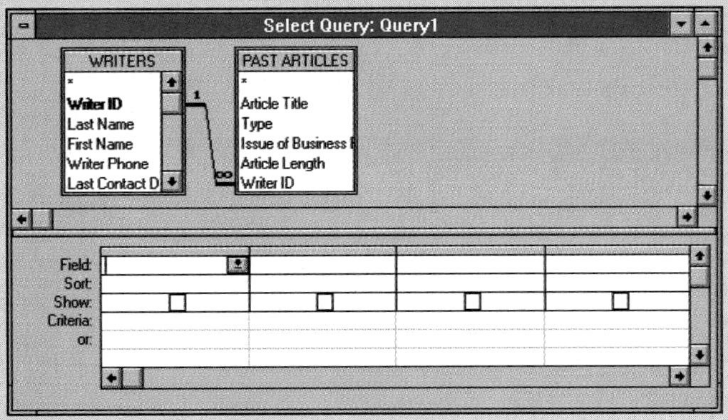

Figure 4-46
Two tables related with a join line in the Query Design window

Elena now defines the query. In the QBE grid she inserts the Article Title, Type, and Article Length fields from the PAST ARTICLES table. She inserts the Last Name and First Name fields from the WRITERS table. She then chooses ascending sort order for the Type field.

To define a query using two tables:

❶ Double-click **Article Title** in the PAST ARTICLES field list. Access places this field in the first column's Field text box.

❷ Double-click **Type** in the PAST ARTICLES field list. Access places this field in the second column's Field text box.

❸ Double-click **Article Length** in the PAST ARTICLES field list. Access places this field in the third column's Field text box.

❹ Double-click **Last Name** in the WRITERS field list. Access places this field in the fourth column's Field text box.

❺ Double-click **First Name** in the WRITERS field list. Access places this field in the fifth column's Field text box.

❻ Click the **Sort text box** for the Type field, and then click the **down arrow button** in the Sort text box. Access displays the Sort list.

❼ Click **Ascending** in the Sort list. The Sort list disappears, and Ascending appears in the Sort text box as the selected sort order.

Elena switches to the dynaset to verify her query.

To view a query dynaset:

1. Click the toolbar **Run button** [!]. The dynaset appears and displays the fields from the two tables.
2. Click the dynaset's **maximize button** to see all the fields and records. See Figure 4-47.

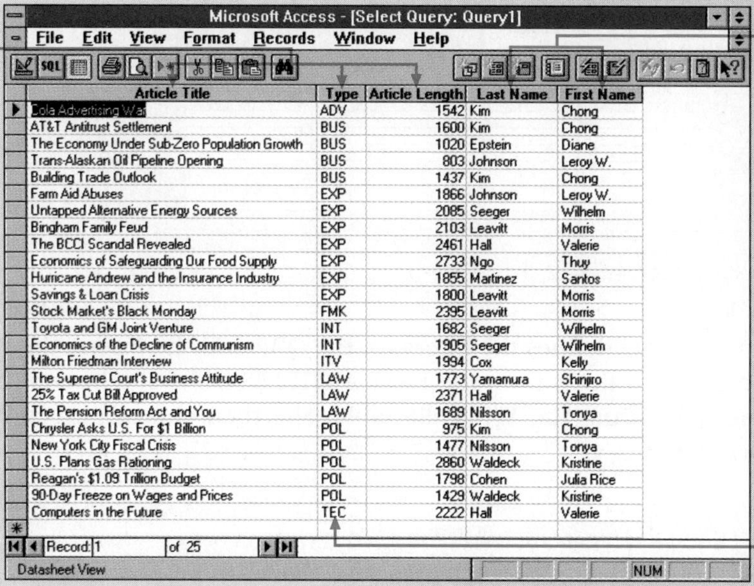

Article Title	Type	Article Length	Last Name	First Name
Cola Advertising War	ADV	1542	Kim	Chong
AT&T Antitrust Settlement	BUS	1600	Kim	Chong
The Economy Under Sub-Zero Population Growth	BUS	1020	Epstein	Diane
Trans-Alaskan Oil Pipeline Opening	BUS	803	Johnson	Leroy W.
Building Trade Outlook	BUS	1437	Kim	Chong
Farm Aid Abuses	EXP	1866	Johnson	Leroy W.
Untapped Alternative Energy Sources	EXP	2085	Seeger	Wilhelm
Bingham Family Feud	EXP	2103	Leavitt	Morris
The BCCI Scandal Revealed	EXP	2461	Hall	Valerie
Economics of Safeguarding Our Food Supply	EXP	2733	Ngo	Thuy
Hurricane Andrew and the Insurance Industry	EXP	1855	Martinez	Santos
Savings & Loan Crisis	EXP	1800	Leavitt	Morris
Stock Market's Black Monday	FMK	2395	Leavitt	Morris
Toyota and GM Joint Venture	INT	1682	Seeger	Wilhelm
Economics of the Decline of Communism	INT	1905	Seeger	Wilhelm
Milton Friedman Interview	ITV	1994	Cox	Kelly
The Supreme Court's Business Attitude	LAW	1773	Yamamura	Shinjiro
25% Tax Cut Bill Approved	LAW	2371	Hall	Valerie
The Pension Reform Act and You	LAW	1689	Nilsson	Tonya
Chrysler Asks U.S. For $1 Billion	POL	975	Kim	Chong
New York City Fiscal Crisis	POL	1477	Nilsson	Tonya
U.S. Plans Gas Rationing	POL	2860	Waldeck	Kristine
Reagan's $1.09 Trillion Budget	POL	1798	Cohen	Julia Rice
90-Day Freeze on Wages and Prices	POL	1429	Waldeck	Kristine
Computers in the Future	TEC	2222	Hall	Valerie

Figure 4-47
Results of a query using fields from two tables

TROUBLE? You should see 25 records in the dynaset. If you see none, then you probably did not import the PAST ARTICLES table correctly with the Data and Structure option. Save the query with the name Article Type Query. Delete the table and import it again. Then try running the query. If you see more than 25 records, then you created the relationship between the two tables incorrectly. Save the query with the name Article Type Query, repeat the steps for adding the relationship between the two tables, and then try running the query again.

Elena next saves this query and then closes the dynaset.

To save a new query:

1. Click **File**, and then click **Save Query As...** The Save As dialog box appears.
2. Type **Article Type Query**.
3. Click the **OK button**. The Save As dialog box disappears, and Access saves the query for later use.
4. Double-click the Datasheet View window **Control menu box**. The dynaset disappears, and the Database window becomes the active window and lists all saved queries alphabetically. See Figure 4-48.

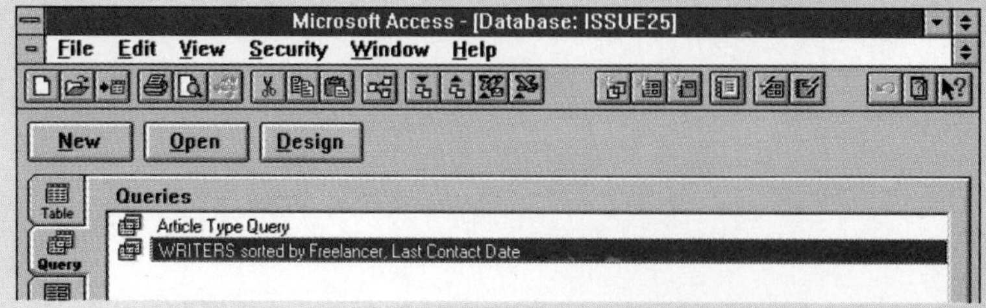

Figure 4-48
List of saved queries

Creating a Parameter Query

Elena's last query asks for the article titles and lengths and the writer names for a specific article type arranged by article title. She will use the PAST ARTICLES table for the Article Title, Article Length, and Type fields and the WRITERS table for the Last Name and First Name fields. Article Title will be the sort key and will have an ascending sort order. Because this query is similar to her last saved query, Elena will open the Article Type Query in the Query Design window and modify its design.

ADV for advertising, BUS for business, EXP for exposé, and POL for political are examples of specific article types. Elena can create a simple condition using an exact match for the Type field that she can change in the Query Design window every time she runs the query. Instead, Elena creates a parameter query.

For a **parameter query**, Access displays a dialog box and prompts you to enter your criteria, or parameters, when you run the query. Access then creates the dynaset just as if you had changed the criteria in the Query Design window.

REFERENCE WINDOW

Creating a Parameter Query

- Create a select query that includes all the fields that will appear in the dynaset. Also choose the sort keys and set the criteria that do not change when you run the query.
- Decide on the fields that will have prompts when you run the query. For each of them, type the prompt you want in the field's Criteria box and enclose the prompt in brackets.
- Highlight the prompt, but do not highlight the brackets. Click Edit and then click Copy to copy the prompt to the Clipboard.
- Click Query and then click Parameters... to open the Query Parameters dialog box.
- Press [Ctrl][V] to paste the contents of the Clipboard into the Parameter text box. Press [Tab] and select the field's data type.
- Click the OK button to close the Query Parameters dialog box.

Elena opens the query saved under the name Article Type Query in the Query Design window and changes its design.

To open a saved query and modify its design:

1. Be sure that the Database window is active and the Query object button is selected. Click **Article Type Query** in the Queries list box and then click the **Design command button** to open the Query Design window.
2. To remove the sort key for the Type field, click its Sort text box, click the **down arrow button**, and then click **(not sorted)**.
3. To add a sort key for the Article Title field, click its **Sort text box**, click the **down arrow button**, and then click **Ascending**.

Elena has completed the changes to the select query. She now changes the query to a parameter query.

To create a parameter query:

1. Click the **Criteria text box** for the Type field and type **[Enter an Article Type:]**. See Figure 4-49.

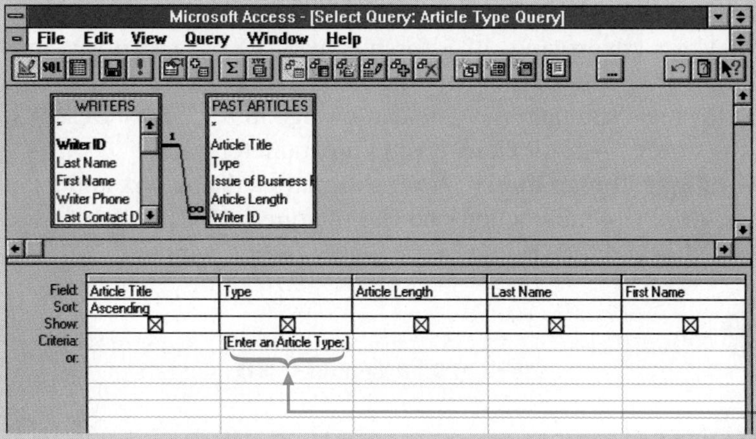

Figure 4-49 Entering a prompt for a parameter query

2. Highlight the prompt, including the colon, but do not highlight the brackets. The parameter query will not work unless "Enter an Article Type:" is exactly what you highlight. Click **Edit** and then click **Copy** to copy the prompt to the Clipboard.
3. Click **Query** and then click **Parameters...** to open the Query Parameters dialog box.
4. Press **[Ctrl][V]** to paste the prompt from the Clipboard into the Parameter text box and then press **[Tab]**. See Figure 4-50.

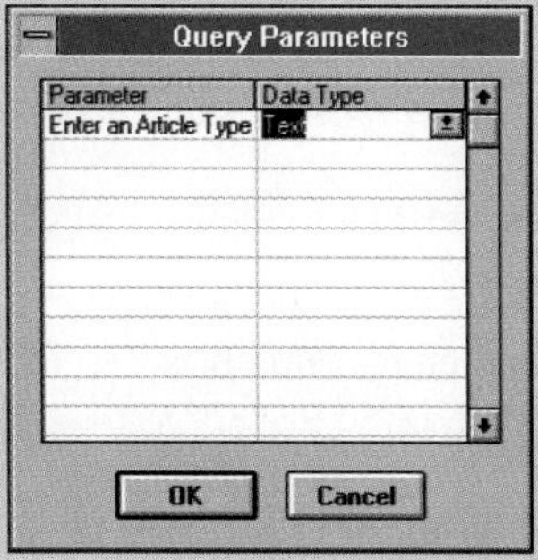

Figure 4-50 The Query Parameters dialog box

5. Your selection in the Data Type text box must be of the same data type as that of the Type field. Because the data type of the Type field is text, which is the default, click the **OK button** to close the Query Parameters dialog box.

Elena runs the parameter query, saves it with the name Article Type Parameter Query, and closes the dynaset. Elena wants to keep the saved version of the query named Article Type Query, as well as save the new parameter query. When she saves the parameter query, therefore, Elena uses the File menu's Save Query As... command instead of the Save Query command. If she were to use the Save Query command, Access would save the parameter query with the name Article Type Query after deleting the saved query.

To run and save a parameter query:

1. Click the toolbar **Run button**. The Enter Parameter Value dialog box appears with your prompt above the text box.
2. To see all the articles that are exposés, type **EXP** in the text box. See Figure 4-51.

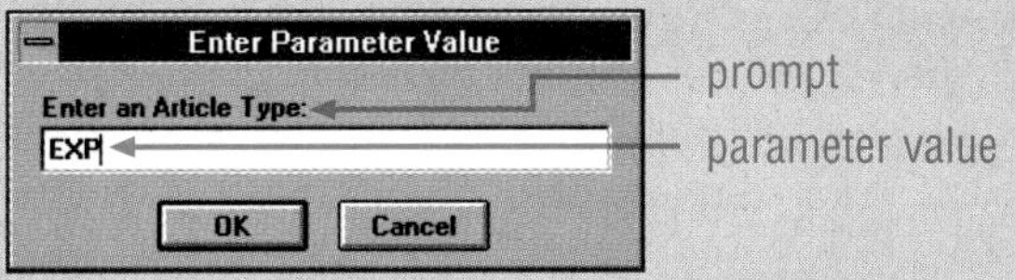

Figure 4-51 The Enter Parameter Value dialog box

3. Press **[Enter]**. Access runs the parameter query and displays the dynaset. See Figure 4-52. Only records of type EXP appear, and the records are in ascending order by the Article Title field.

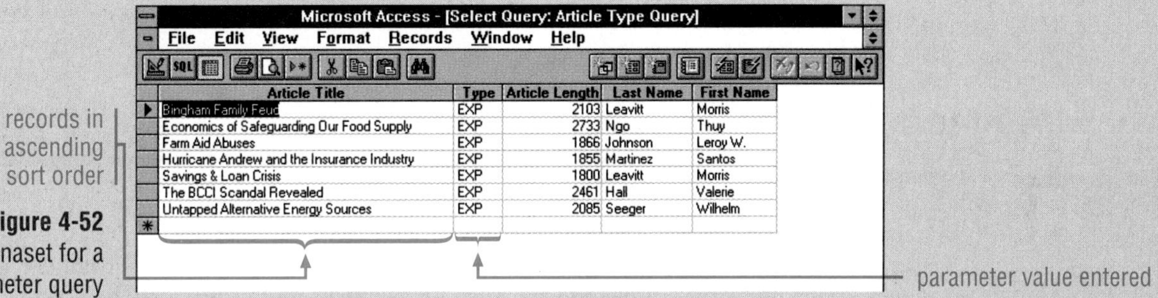

Figure 4-52 The dynaset for a parameter query

4. To save the query, click **File** and then click **Save Query As...**. The Save As dialog box appears showing the query name Article Type Query, which is the name of the previously saved query. Place the insertion point just in front of the letter Q, type **Parameter**, press **[Spacebar]**, and then press **[Enter]** to name the new query.
5. Double-click the Datasheet View window **Control menu box**. The dynaset disappears. The Database window becomes the active window and lists the newly saved query.

■ ■ ■

Elena exits Access and then schedules a meeting with her colleagues to review the results of her queries.

Questions

1. What is QBE?
2. What are three methods for adding all the fields from a table to the QBE grid?
3. What is a dynaset?
4. How do you exclude from a dynaset a field that appears in the QBE grid?
5. What are the two components of a simple condition?
6. What comparison operator is used to select records based on a specific pattern?
7. When do you use the In comparison operator?
8. How must you position the fields in the QBE grid when you have multiple sort keys?
9. When do you use logical operators?
10. What is a calculated field?

11. When do you use an aggregate function?
12. When do you use the Group By operator?
E 13. Look for an example of a one-to-many relationship and an example of a many-to-many relationship in a newspaper, magazine, or everyday situation you encounter. For each one, name the entities and select the primary keys and common fields.
14. What are the two referential integrity rules?
15. What does a join line signify?
16. When do you use a parameter query?
E 17. Use Cue Cards to document for your instructor four aggregate functions that do not appear in Figure 4-34.
E 18. Suppose you create a calculated field in the Query Design window by typing NewField:[Writer ID]+50. Writer ID is a text field from the table you are using in your query and it appears in the QBE grid. When you run the query, the calculated field does not appear in the dynaset. Why did this occur?
E 19. Suppose you want to print a dynaset selection, but the Selection option is dimmed out when the Print dialog box appears. What has caused this problem, and how do you correct it?

Tutorial Assignments

Elena creates several queries using the PAST ARTICLES table that she imported into the Issue25 database. Launch Access, open the Issue25 database on your Student Disk, maximize the Database window, click the PAST ARTICLES table, click the New Query button on the toolbar, and then click the New Query button in the New Query message box.

For each of the following questions, prepare an appropriate query in the Query Design window and print its entire dynaset. Whenever you use the Issue of Business Perspective field, rename it Issue. Whenever fields are listed in the question, display the fields in the order listed. Do not save any of the queries.

1. Which articles are of type BUS? Print all fields for this query.
2. What are the article titles and article lengths for all articles that have a length greater than 2103?
3. What are the article titles, article lengths, and writer IDs for all articles written by writers with writer IDs H400 or W432?
4. What are the article titles, article lengths, writer IDs, and issues for all articles published in *Business Perspective* in the 1980s?
5. What are the article lengths, article titles, writer IDs, and issues for all articles of type EXP that have a length less than 2100?
6. What are the article titles, writer IDs, and issues for all articles of type ITV or that were written by writer L130?
7. What are the article lengths, writer IDs, issues, types, and article titles for all articles that have a length less than 2000 and are of type BUS or LAW?
8. What are the article lengths, writer IDs, issues, types, and article titles for all articles that have a length less than 2000 and are of type BUS or LAW? Print in ascending order by length.
9. What are the article lengths, writer IDs, issues, types, and article titles for all articles in descending order by length?
10. What are the writer IDs, article titles, issues, types, and article lengths for all articles? Display the dynaset in ascending order with writer ID as the primary sort key and article length as the secondary sort key.
11. What are the article titles, writer IDs, issues, types, article lengths, and costs per article for all articles, based on a cost per article of three cents per word? Use the name CostPerArticle for the calculated field, assume that the Article Length field gives the number of words in the article, and use ascending sort order for the Article Length field.

12. What is the total cost, average cost, lowest cost, and highest cost for all articles? Assume that the Article Length field gives the number of words in an article and that the cost per article is three cents per word.
13. What is the total cost, average cost, lowest cost, and highest cost for all articles by type? Assume that the Article Length field gives the number of words in an article and that the cost per article is three cents per word.

E 14. Using the PAST ARTICLES and WRITERS tables, list the article titles, article types, issues, writer last names, and writer first names in ascending order by article length for all articles of type BUS, LAW, or POL. Do not print the Article Length field in the dynaset. Be sure that there is no Total row in the QBE grid.

15. Using the PAST ARTICLES and WRITERS tables, list the article titles, issues, writer last names, and writer first names in ascending order by article length for a selected article type. This query should be a parameter query.

Case Problems

1. Walkton Daily Press Carriers

Grant Sherman has created and updated his Press database and is now ready to query it. Launch Access and do the following:

1. Open the Press database on your Student Disk and maximize the Database window.
2. Delete the BILLINGS table.
3. Import the BILLINGS table from the Walkton database on your Student Disk.

Grant creates several queries using the CARRIERS table. For each of the following questions, prepare an appropriate query in the Query Design window and print its entire dynaset. Whenever you use one of the carrier name fields, rename it omitting the word "Carrier." Whenever fields are listed in the question, display the fields in the order listed.

4. What is all the carrier information on Ashley Shaub?
5. What is all the information on those carriers whose last names begin with the letter S?
6. What are the birthdates, phone numbers, first names, and last names of carriers born in 1981 or later?
7. What are the birthdates, phone numbers, last names, and first names of carriers whose phone numbers end with the digits 4 or 7?
8. What are the birthdates, carrier IDs, first names, and last names of those carriers born prior to 1980 who have a carrier ID either less than 5 or greater than 10?
9. What are the birthdates, carrier IDs, first names, last names, and phone numbers of all carriers in descending order by birthdate?

Close the dynaset to return to the Database window without saving your queries. Complete the following queries using the BILLINGS table.

E 10. What is the total, average, lowest, and highest balance amount for all carriers? Your four calculated fields should use the Balance Amount field as is. Note that Balance Amount is the table field name and Balance is the Caption property name.

E 11. What is the total, average, lowest, and highest balance amount, grouped by carrier?

12. Create a parameter query to display all the fields in the BILLINGS table based on a selected Carrier ID.

2. Lopez Used Cars

Maria and Hector Lopez have created and updated their Usedcars database and are now ready to query it. Launch Access and do the following:

1. Open the Usedcars database on your Student Disk and maximize the Database window.
2. Delete the LOCATIONS table.

3. Import the CLASSES, LOCATIONS, and TRANSMISSIONS tables from the Lopez database on your Student Disk.

Maria and Hector create several queries using the USED CARS table. For each of the following questions, prepare an appropriate query in the Query Design window and print its entire dynaset. Whenever fields are listed in the question, display the fields in the order listed. If a field has a Caption property, rename the field to match the name in the Query Design window.

4. What are the manufacturers, models, years, and selling prices for all cars?
5. What are the manufacturers, models, years, and selling prices for cars manufactured by Ford?
6. What are the manufacturers, models, years, costs, and selling prices for cars manufactured prior to 1989?
7. What are the manufacturers, models, years, costs, and selling prices for cars having a manufacturer that starts with the letter C or the letter N?
8. What are the manufacturers, models, classes, years, costs, and selling prices for cars manufactured prior to 1990 and having either an S2 or an S3 class?
9. What are the manufacturers, models, classes, years, costs, and selling prices for all cars in descending sequence by selling price?
10. Create a field that calculates the difference (profit) between the Selling Price and the Cost and name it Diff. What are the manufacturers, models, classes, years, costs, selling prices, and profits for all cars?

E 11. What is the total cost, total selling price, total profit, and average profit for all the cars?

E 12. What is the total cost, total selling price, total profit, and average profit grouped by year?

13. Create a parameter query to display all the fields from the USED CARS table based on a selected manufacturer.

Close the dynaset to return to the Database window without saving your query, and then complete the following problem.

E 14. Add a one-to-many relationship between the LOCATIONS and USED CARS tables using Location Code as the common field. Create a query to find the manufacturers, models, selling prices, location names, and manager names for all cars in descending sequence by manager name.

3. Tophill University Student Employment

Olivia Tyler has created and updated her Parttime database and is now ready to query it. Launch Access and do the following:

1. Open the Parttime database on your Student Disk and maximize the Database window.
2. Delete the EMPLOYERS table.
3. Import the EMPLOYERS table from the Tophill database on your Student Disk.

Olivia creates several queries using the JOBS table. For each of the following questions, prepare an appropriate query in the Query Design window and print its entire dynaset. Whenever fields are listed in the question, display the fields in the listed order. If a field has a Caption property, rename the field to match the name in the Query Design window.

4. What is all the job information on job order 7?
5. What is all the information on jobs having job titles that begin with Computer?
6. What are the job titles, hours per week, and wages of jobs paying wages greater than or equal to $7.05?
7. What are the job titles, hours per week, employer IDs, and wages of jobs requiring between 20 and 24 hours per week, inclusive?
8. What are the job titles, hours per week, employer IDs, and wages of jobs requiring between 20 and 24 hours per week, inclusive, and paying wages less than or equal to $6.75?

9. What are the job titles, hours per week, employer IDs, and wages of all jobs in order by ascending hours per week (the primary sort key) and by descending job title (the secondary sort key)?
10. Create a calculated field that is the product of hours per week and wage, and name it Weekly. What are the hours per week, wages, weekly wages, and job titles for all jobs?

E 11. What is the total, average, lowest, and highest weekly wage for all the jobs listed in the JOBS table?

E 12. What is the total, average, lowest, and highest weekly wage for all jobs grouped by employer ID?

13. Create a parameter query to display all the fields in the JOBS table based on a selected employer ID.

4. Rexville Business Licenses

Chester Pearce has created and updated his Buslic database and is now ready to query it. Launch Access and do the following:

1. Open the Buslic database on your Student Disk and maximize the Database window.
2. Delete the LICENSES table.
3. Import the LICENSES and ISSUED LICENSES tables from the Rexville database on your Student Disk.

Chester creates several queries using the BUSINESSES table. For each of the following questions, prepare an appropriate query in the Query Design window and print its entire dynaset. Whenever fields are listed in the question, display the fields in the listed order. If a field has a Caption property, rename the field to match the name in the Query Design window.

4. What is all the information for business ID 11?
5. What is all the information on those businesses that have the word "avenue" in the street-name field?
6. What are the business names, street numbers, street names, and proprietors for businesses having street numbers greater than 5100?
7. What are the business names, street numbers, street names, proprietors, and phone numbers for businesses having phone numbers starting 243 or 942?
8. What are the proprietors, business names, street numbers, street names, and phone numbers of all businesses in ascending sequence by business name?

Close the dynaset to return to the Database window without saving your query. Complete the following queries using the ISSUED LICENSES table.

E 9. What is the total amount, total count, and average amount for all issued licenses?

E 10. What is the total amount, total count, and average amount for all issued licenses grouped by license type?

11. Create a parameter query to display all the fields from the BUSINESSES table based on a selected business ID.

T U T O R I A L 5

Designing Forms

Creating Forms at Vision Publishers

OBJECTIVES

In this tutorial you will:

- Create forms using Form Wizards
- Save and open a form
- View and maintain data using forms
- Find and sort data in a form
- Select and sort records with a filter
- Design and create a custom form
- Use Control Wizards

CASE

Vision Publishers At the next Issue25 database meeting Brian Murphy, Judith Rossi, and Harold Larson are pleased when Elena Sanchez presents her query results. Everyone agrees that Elena should place the Issue25 database on the company network so that everyone can access and query the data.

Because some people seek information about a single writer, Elena creates a form to display one writer at a time on the screen. The form will be easier to read than a datasheet or dynaset and Elena can use the form to correct a writer's data.

Using a Form

A **form** is an object you use to maintain, view, and print records of data from a database. In Access, you can design your own form or use a Form Wizard to automate the form creation process. A **Form Wizard** is an Access tool that asks you a series of questions and then creates a form based on your answers. Whether you use a Form Wizard or design your own form, you can change a form's design after it is created.

Access has five different Form Wizards. Four of these Form Wizards are shown in Figure 5-1.

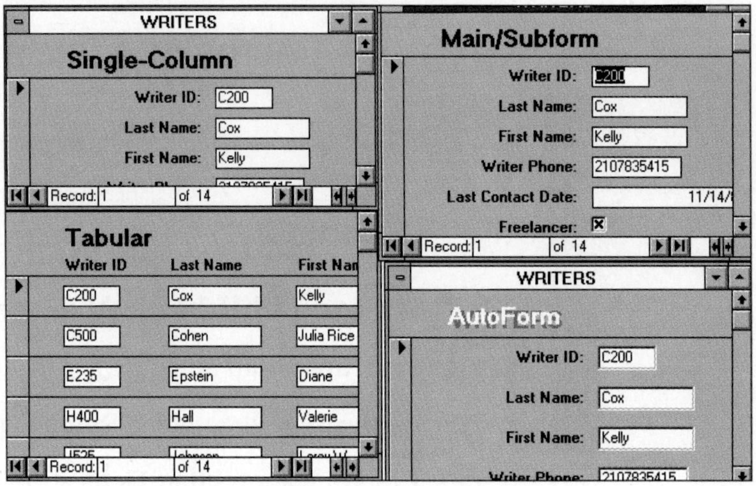

Figure 5-1
Four types of Form Wizards

- A **single-column form** displays the fields, one on a line, vertically on the form. Field values appear in boxes. Labels, which are the table field names, appear to the left of the field values.
- A **tabular form** displays multiple records and field values in a row-and-column format. Field values appear in boxes with the table field names as column headings.
- A **main/subform form** displays data from two or more related tables. One record from the primary table appears in single-column format in the main form at the top. Access displays one or more records in datasheet format from the related tables in the subforms at the bottom.
- An **AutoForm form** is a special single-column form that Access creates immediately without asking you further questions about the form's content and style. Access includes in the form all the fields from the underlying table or query.
- A **graph form** displays a graph of your designated data.

Each Form Wizard offers you a choice of five different form styles, as shown in Figure 5-2.

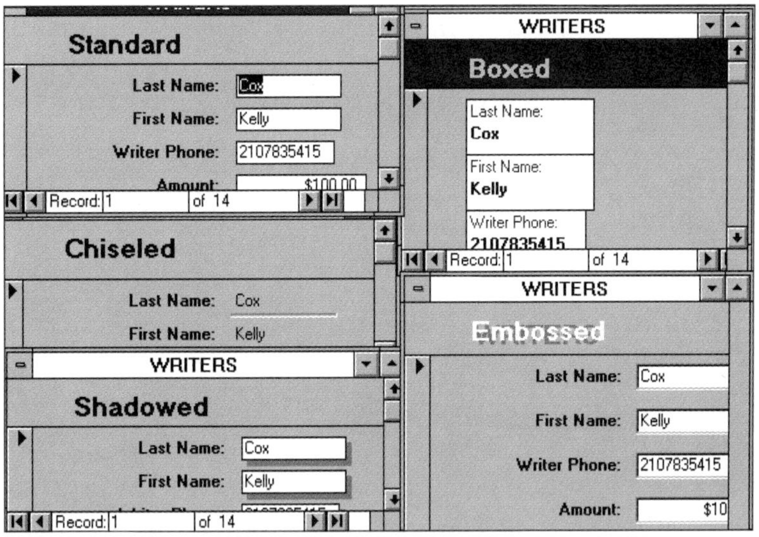

Figure 5-2
Form style options

- The **standard style** displays field values in white boxes on a light gray background.
- The **chiseled style** displays field values with sculpted underlines on a light gray background.
- The **shadowed style** is the same as the standard style with the addition of dark rectangles attached to the field-value boxes to give a shadowed, three-dimensional effect.
- The **boxed style** pairs field values and their labels inside white boxes on a light gray background with each label above its field value.
- The **embossed style** displays field values inside white boxes with a sunken, three-dimensional effect on a blue-green background.

Although you might find the last four styles to be more elegant, you should choose the standard style when you first begin working with forms. Some printers have problems printing colored forms, and changing a form's design by moving or resizing fields is easier when you use the standard style.

Access has a set of Cue Cards you can use while working with forms. Although we will not use these Cue Cards in this tutorial, you might find they enhance your understanding of forms. At any time during this tutorial, therefore, select Design a Form from the Cue Card menu window to launch the appropriate Cue Cards.

Creating Forms Using the AutoForm Wizard

The quickest way to create a form is to use the toolbar AutoForm button, which launches the AutoForm Wizard. When you click the **AutoForm button**, the AutoForm Wizard selects all the fields from the highlighted table or query in the Database window, creates a single-column form for these fields, and displays the form on the screen.

To create a form to display all the fields from the TYPES table, Elena uses the AutoForm button. If you have not done so, place your Student Disk in the appropriate drive, launch Access, and open the Issue25 database on your Student Disk.

To create a form using the AutoForm button:

1. Click **TYPES** in the Tables list box. Access will place the fields from the TYPES table, which is now highlighted, into the form it creates when you click the toolbar AutoForm button.
2. Locate on the toolbar. See Figure 5-3.

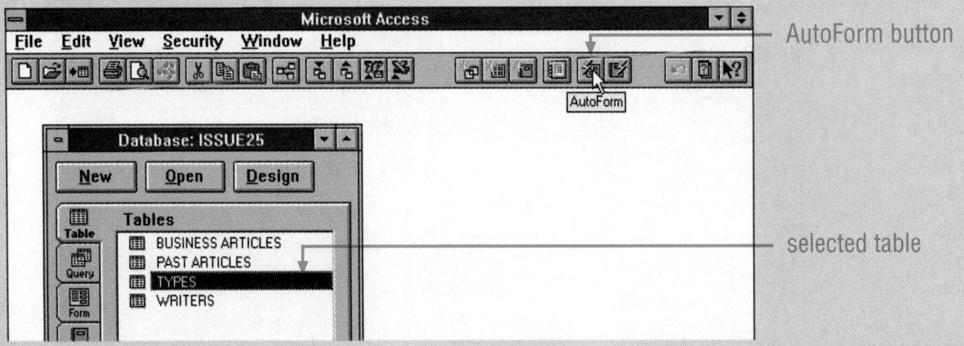

Figure 5-3
The toolbar AutoForm button

3. Click . Access constructs and displays a form that contains the two fields from the TYPES table. See Figure 5-4.

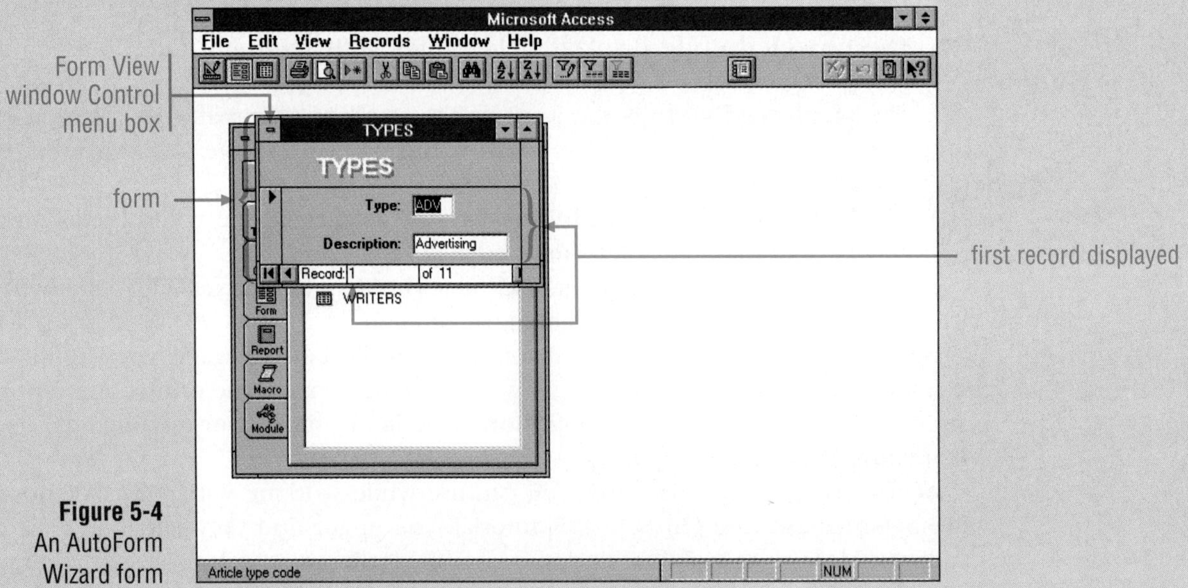

Figure 5-4
An AutoForm Wizard form

Access displays the first record from the TYPES table in the new form. If you want to view other records from the TYPES table, click the form navigation buttons or type a record number between the navigation buttons. You might need to resize the form to see all four navigation buttons.

Saving a Form

Elena saves the form so that she and others can use it for future work with data from the TYPES table. Elena saves the form, using the name TYPES form, and then closes the Form View window.

REFERENCE WINDOW

Saving a New Form

- Click File and then click Save Form As... Access opens the Save As dialog box.
- Type the new form name in the Form Name text box.
- Press [Enter] or click the OK button. Access saves the Form and closes the dialog box.

Let's save Elena's form.

To save and close a new form:

❶ Click **File**, and then click **Save Form As...**. The Save As dialog box appears.

❷ Type **TYPES form** in the Form Name text box.

❸ Press **[Enter]**. The Save As dialog box disappears, and Access saves the form.

❹ Double-click the Form View window **Control menu box**. The Form View window disappears, and the Database window becomes the active window.

❺ Click the **Form object button**. Access lists the newly saved form. See Figure 5-5.

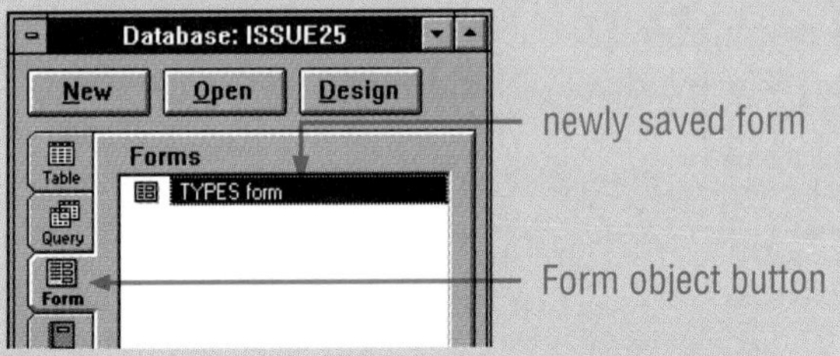

Figure 5-5
Listing a new form

Creating Forms Using Form Wizards

For her next form, Elena uses a Form Wizard to display data from the WRITERS table. She chooses to display all the fields from the table in a single-column form with the standard style.

Creating Single-Column Forms

Let's use a Form Wizard to create a single-column form type with the standard style.

To activate Form Wizards and select a form type:

❶ Click the toolbar **New Form button**. The New Form dialog box appears.

❷ Click the Select A Table/Query drop-down list box **down arrow button** to display the list of the Issue25 database tables and queries.

❸ Scroll through the Select A Table/Query drop-down list box and then click **WRITERS**. The drop-down list disappears and WRITERS appears highlighted in the box. See Figure 5-6.

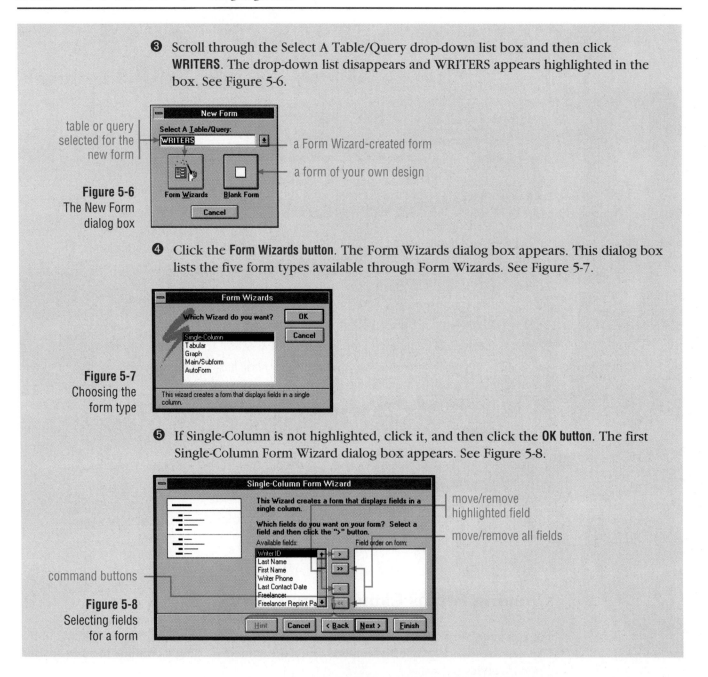

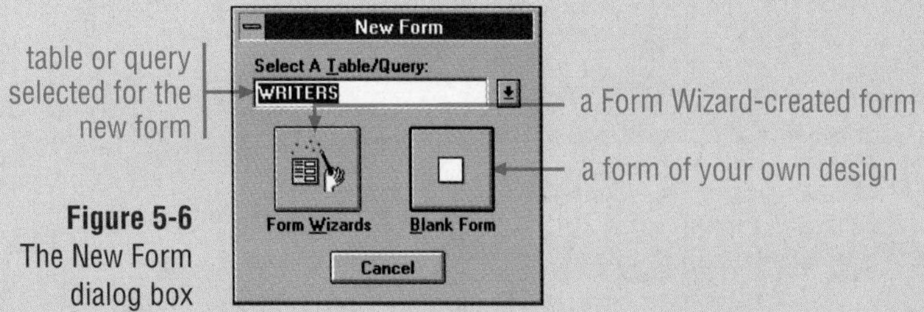

Figure 5-6
The New Form dialog box

❹ Click the **Form Wizards button**. The Form Wizards dialog box appears. This dialog box lists the five form types available through Form Wizards. See Figure 5-7.

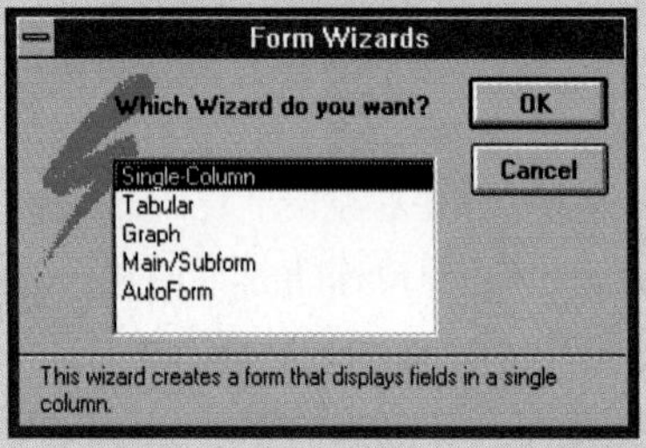

Figure 5-7
Choosing the form type

❺ If Single-Column is not highlighted, click it, and then click the **OK button**. The first Single-Column Form Wizard dialog box appears. See Figure 5-8.

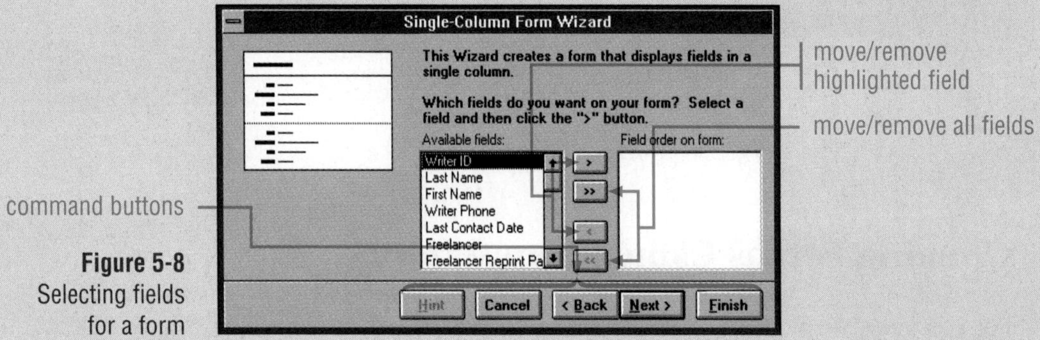

Figure 5-8
Selecting fields for a form

In this Single-Column Form Wizard dialog box, you select fields in the order you want them to appear on the form. If you want to select fields one at a time, highlight a field by clicking it, and then click the > button. If you want to select all fields, click the >> button. The selected fields move from the box on the left to the box on the right as you select them. If you make a mistake, click the << button to remove all fields from the box on the right or highlight a field and click the < button to remove fields one at a time.

Each Form Wizards dialog box displays command buttons on the bottom that allow you to move quickly to the other Form Wizards dialog boxes. You can go to the previous or next Form Wizards dialog box. You can also cancel the form creation process to return to the Database window; you can prematurely finish the form and accept the Form Wizards defaults for the remaining form options; and you can ask for hints about the Form Wizards options.

Elena wants her form to display all the fields from the WRITERS table in the order in which they appear in the table.

To finish creating a form using the Single-Column Form Wizards:

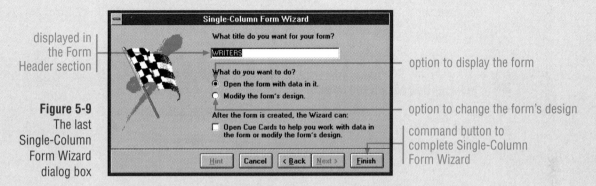

1. Click the **>> button**. Access removes all the fields from the box on the left and places them in the same order in the box on the right.
2. Click the **Next > button** to display the next Single-Column Form Wizard dialog box, in which you choose the form's style.
3. Click the **Standard radio button** and then click the **Next > button**. Access displays the final Single-Column Form Wizard dialog box and shows the table name as the default for the title that will appear in the Form Header section. Elena wants to use the default form title. See Figure 5-9.

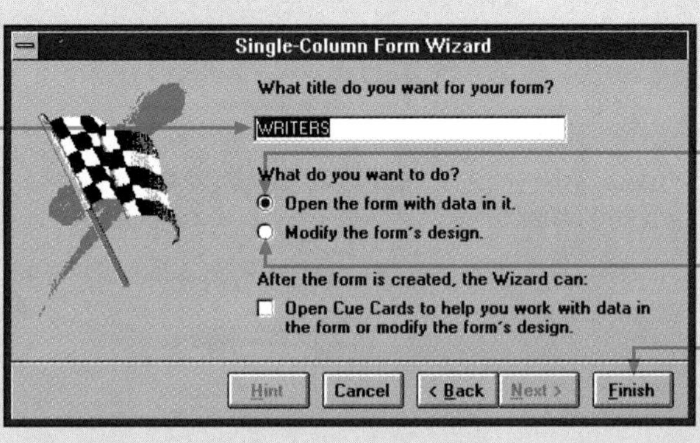

Figure 5-9 The last Single-Column Form Wizard dialog box

4. Click the **Finish button**. The Form View window opens and displays the completed form. See Figure 5-10.

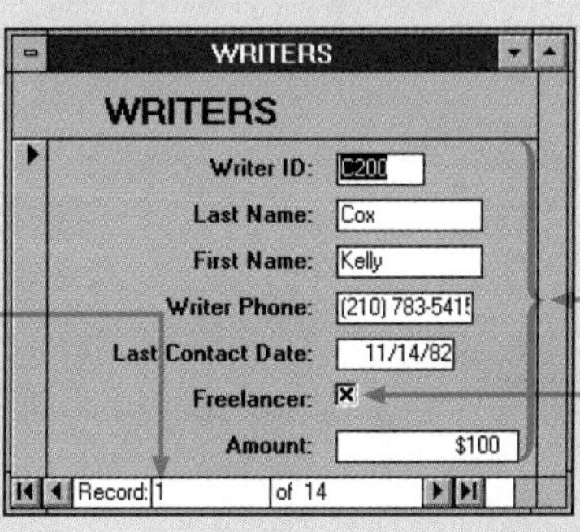

Figure 5-10 The completed form

Notice that Freelancer is a yes/no field and that Form Wizards automatically creates a check box for it. An empty check box indicates a value of No, and an × in the check box indicates a value of Yes.

Elena saves the form, using the name WRITERS form, and then closes the Form View window.

To save and close a new form:

1. Click **File**, and then click **Save Form As...**. The Save As dialog box appears.
2. Type **WRITERS form** in the Form Name text box.
3. Press **[Enter]**. The Save As dialog box disappears, and Access saves the form.
4. Double-click the Form View window **Control menu box**. The Form View window disappears, and the Database window becomes the active window.

Creating Main/Subform Forms

Elena next creates a form to show a specific writer and his or her articles. Elena will use this form to enter the writer and article data for the first two new articles written for the 25th-anniversary issue.

Because the main/subform form type allows you to work with data from two or more tables, Elena chooses this form type for her new form. The WRITERS table has a one-to-many relationship with the PAST ARTICLES table. Elena selects the WRITERS table for the main form because it is the primary table and the PAST ARTICLES table for the subform because it is the related table. Elena again uses a Form Wizard to create the form.

Because the Form object button is selected, Elena can create the new form by clicking either the toolbar New Form button or the New command button.

To activate Form Wizards and create a main/subform form type:

1. Click the **New command button**. The New Form dialog box appears.
2. Click the Select A Table/Query drop-down list box **down arrow button** to display the list of the Issue25 database tables and queries.
3. Scroll down the list and then click **WRITERS**. The drop-down list disappears and WRITERS appears highlighted in the box.
4. Click the **Form Wizards button**. The Form Wizards dialog box appears.
5. Click **Main/Subform** in the list box and then click the **OK button**. Access displays the first Main/Subform Wizard dialog box, in which you select the table or query for the subform. See Figure 5-11.

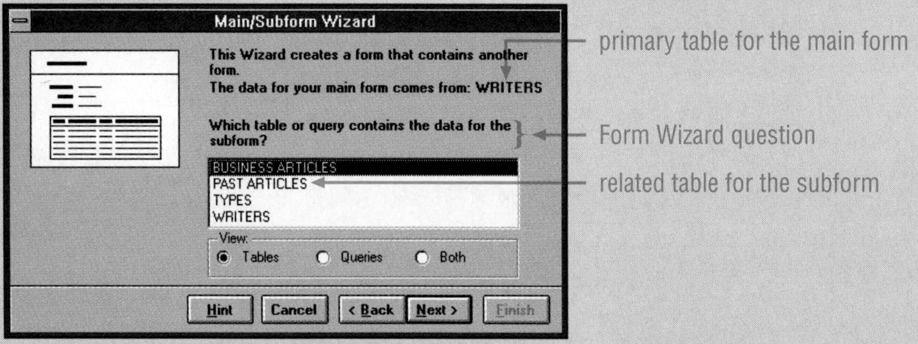

Figure 5-11 Selecting the subform table or query

6. Click **PAST ARTICLES** in the list box, and then click the **Next > button**. Access displays the next Main/Subform Wizard dialog box, in which you select the fields for the main form. Elena wants to display all the fields from the WRITERS table on the main form.
7. Click the **>> button** to select all fields and move them to the box on the right, and then click the **Next > button**. Access displays the next Main/Subform Wizard dialog box, in which you select the fields for the subform.

The Writer ID field will appear in the main form, so it is not needed in the subform. Otherwise, Elena wants to place all the fields from the PAST ARTICLES table on the subform.

To select the subform fields and a main/subform style:

1. Click the **>>button** to select all fields. If Writer ID is not highlighted in the box on the right, click it. Then click the **< button** to remove Writer ID from the box on the right. See Figure 5-12.

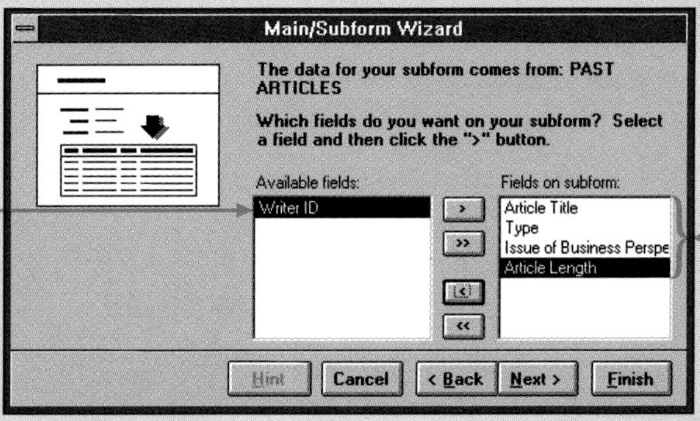

Figure 5-12
Selecting fields for a subform

2. Click the **Next > button**. Access displays the next Main/Subform Wizard dialog box, in which you select the form style.
3. Click the **Standard radio button** and then click the **Next > button**. Access displays the final Main/Subform Wizard window and shows the primary table name as the default form title.

Elena enters the form title WRITERS and PAST ARTICLES. This form title appears at the top of the form in the Form View window. The form itself is saved as two separate forms when you create a main/subform form type. You first save the subform and then you save the form/subform combination.

To title a form and save a subform:

1. Type **WRITERS and PAST ARTICLES**, and then click the **Finish button**. Access displays the "Save the subform" dialog box. You must save the subform before the Main/Subform Wizard can continue.
2. Click the **OK button**. The dialog box disappears, and the Save As dialog box appears.
3. Type **PAST ARTICLES subform** in the Form Name box and then press **[Enter]**. Access saves the subform and displays the completed main/subform window. See Figure 5-13.

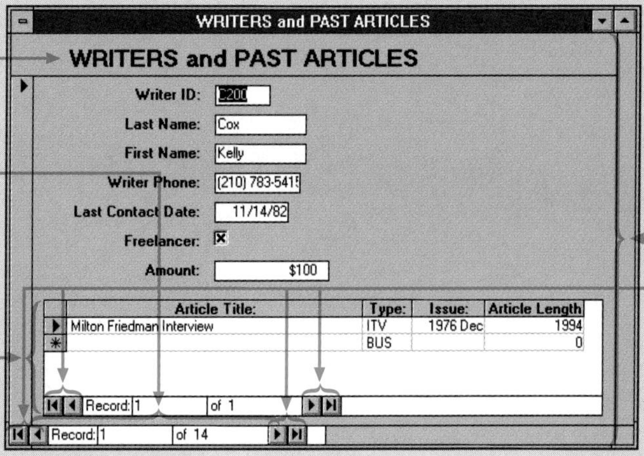

Figure 5-13
The completed main/subform form type

Access displays the fields from the first record in the WRITERS table in single-column format. The records in this main form appear in primary-key sequence. The writer Kelly Cox has one record in the PAST ARTICLES table that is shown at the bottom in datasheet format.

Elena wants to view the data for a writer who has more than one record in the PAST ARTICLES table. Two sets of navigation buttons appear at the bottom of the form. You use the top set of navigation buttons to select records from the related table in the subform and the bottom set to select records from the primary table in the main form.

To navigate to different main and subform records:

❶ Click the main form **Next Record button** ▶ three times. Access displays the record for Valerie Hall in the main form and her three articles in the subform.

❷ Click the subform ▶ once. Access changes the current record to the second article in the subform.

In addition to viewing data in a form and in a subform, you can also add, change, and delete field values and records. If a writer has four or more articles, Access adds a scroll bar on the right side of the subform.

Elena saves the main/subform combination using the name WRITERS and PAST ARTICLES form. This form name will appear in the Database window when you click the Form object button to display a list of the database's forms.

To save a new form/subform:

❶ Click **File**, and then click **Save Form As...**. The Save As dialog box appears.

❷ Type **WRITERS and PAST ARTICLES form**.

❸ Press **[Enter]**. The Save As dialog box disappears, and Access saves the form.

Maintaining Table Data Using a Form

Elena needs to make two field value changes to one of Valerie Hall's articles. Then she will add two new articles to the database. The database modifications involve three articles and three writers, as shown in Figure 5-14.

Action	Table	Record and Fields
Change	PAST ARTICLES	Article Title: The BBCI Scandal Revealed (by Valerie Hall) Issue: from 1991 Jul to 1991 Aug Article Length: from 2461 to 2779
Add	PAST ARTICLES	Article Title: Advertising Over the Past 25 Years (by Thuy Ngo) Type: ADV Issue: 1994 Dec Article Length: 3285
Add	WRITERS	Writer ID: L350 Last Name: Lawton First Name: Pat Writer Phone: (705) 677-1991 Last Contact Date: 9/4/94 Freelancer: No Amount: $0
	PAST ARTICLES	Article Title: Law Over the Past 25 Years (by Pat Lawton) Type: LAW Issue: 1994 Dec Article Length: 2834

Figure 5-14
Maintenance changes to the Issue25 database

To maintain table data using a form, you must know how to move from field to field and from record to record. The mouse movement, selection, and placement techniques to do this are the standard Windows techniques that you used in Tutorial 3. If you are maintaining data in a subform, the keyboard techniques are also the same as those described in Tutorial 3. For other form types, you use the same keyboard deletion techniques that you use in editing mode and the same data entry and editing shortcut keys. The form navigation and editing mode keyboard movement techniques, however, differ slightly, as shown in Figure 5-15 on the following page.

Press	To Move the Selection Point in Navigation Mode	To Move the Insertion Point in Editing Mode
[Left Arrow]	To the previous field value	Left one character at a time
[Right Arrow] or [Tab] or [Enter]	To the next field value	Right one character at a time
[Home]	To the first field value in the record	Before the first character in the field value
[End]	To the last field value in the record	After the last character in the field value
[Up Arrow] or [Down Arrow]	To the previous or next field value	The insertion point does not move
[PgUp]	To the same field value in the previous record	To the same field value in the previous record and switch to navigation mode
[PgDn]	To the same field value in the next record	To the same field value in the next record and switch to navigation mode
[Ctrl][Left Arrow] or [Ctrl][Right Arrow]	To the previous or next field value	Left or right one word at a time
[Ctrl][Up Arrow] or [Ctrl][Down Arrow]	To the same field value in the first or last record	Before the first character or after the last character in the field value
[Ctrl][PgUp]	To the same field value in the previous record	Before the first character in the field value
[Ctrl][PgDn]	To the same field in the next record	After the last character in the field value
[Ctrl][Home]	To the first value in the first record	Before the first character in the field value
[Ctrl][End]	To the first subform field value for the last main form record	After the last character in the field value

Figure 5-15
Form navigation and editing mode keyboard movement techniques

Elena first makes the two changes to one of Valerie Hall's articles. Because the article she wants to change is already selected, Elena just moves to the field values in the subform and changes them.

To change table field values using a form:

1. Press **[Tab]** twice. The Issue field value 1991 Jul is highlighted.
2. Double-click Jul and then type **Aug** as the changed month value for the Issue field.
3. Press **[Tab]** to move to and highlight the Article Length field.
4. Type **2779** as the changed field value for the Article Length field.

Elena next adds records to the Issue25 database. She first adds one article for Thuy Ngo. There is already a record for Thuy Ngo in the WRITERS table, record number 10.

To add a record in a subform:

1. Click the record number that is displayed between the main form navigation buttons **(4)** and then press **[F2]** to highlight the number. Type **10** and then press **[Enter]**. Thuy Ngo's record appears, and the Article Title field is selected in the subform.
2. Press **[Down Arrow]** once to move to the Article Title field for the next available record in the subform.
3. Type **Advertising Over the Past 25 Years**, press **[Tab]**, type **ADV**, press **[Tab]**, type **1994 Dec**, press **[Tab]**, type **3285**, and then press **[Tab]**. See Figure 5-16. Access has added this record to the PAST ARTICLES table for Thuy Ngo.

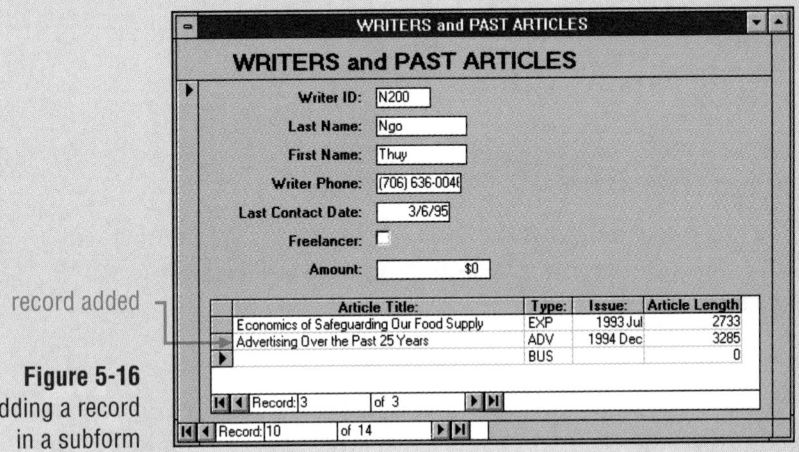

Figure 5-16
Adding a record in a subform

Elena's last change is to add one record to the WRITERS table and one record to the PAST ARTICLES table. To add a record to the WRITERS table, Elena navigates to the next available record in the table. You use the bottom set of navigation buttons to change which record Access displays in the main WRITERS form.

To add a new writer and a new article using a form:

1. Click the main form's **Last Record button**. Access displays the record for Shinjiro Yamamura in the main form and his one article in the subform.
2. Click the main form's **Next Record button**. Access moves to record 15 in the main form and to record 1 in the subform, clears all field values, and positions the insertion point in the subform's Article Title field.
3. Click the **field-value box** for the Writer ID field in the main form to position the insertion point there.
4. Type **L350**, press **[Tab]**, type **Lawton**, press **[Tab]**, type **Pat**, press **[Tab]**, type **7056771991**, press **[Tab]**, type **9/4/94**, and then press **[Tab]** to enter the first five field values. An ×, which indicates a value of Yes, appears in the Freelancer field value box.
5. Press **[Spacebar]** to change the Freelancer field value to No, and then press **[Tab]** to move to the Amount field.
6. Press **[Tab]**. Access saves the new record in the WRITERS table and positions the insertion point in the Article Title field in the subform.

7. Type **Law Over the Past 25 Years**, press **[Tab]**, type **LAW**, press **[Tab]**, type **1994 Dec**, press **[Tab]**, and then type **2834**. See Figure 5-17.

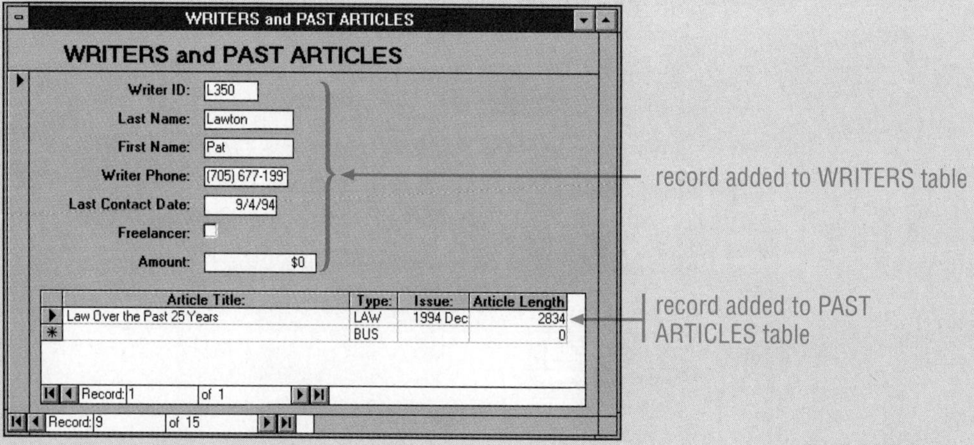

Figure 5-17 Adding records in a main form and a subform

8. Press **[Tab]**. Access saves the new record in the PAST ARTICLES table and positions the insertion point in the Article Title field for the next available record in the subform.

When you created the WRITERS and PAST ARTICLES form, you selected all fields from the WRITERS table for the main form. However, you did not select the Writer ID field for the subform. Because the Writer ID field is the common field between the two tables, Access uses the Writer ID field value from the main form when it saves the subform record in the PAST ARTICLES table.

Elena has completed her maintenance tasks, so she closes the Form View window and maximizes the Database window to see a list of the forms in the Issue25 database.

To close the Form View window and list the forms for a database:

1. Double-click the Form View window **Control menu box**. The Form View window disappears.
2. Click the Database window **maximize button**. Access displays a full list of the forms you created. See Figure 5-18.

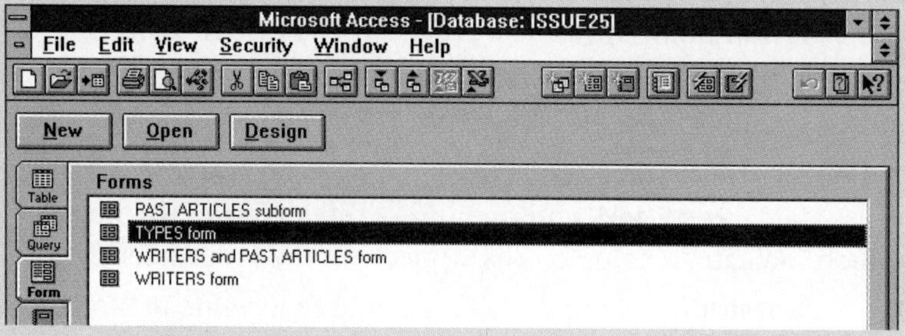

Figure 5-18 The Forms list in the Database window

If you want to take a break and resume the tutorial at a later time, you can exit Access by double-clicking the Microsoft Access window Control menu box. When you resume the tutorial, place your Student Disk in the appropriate drive, launch Access, open the Issue25 database on your Student Disk, maximize the Database window, and click the Form object button.

■ ■ ■

Finding and Sorting Records in a Form

Later that same day, Harold calls Elena to ask for the phone number of the freelance writer Chong Kim. Elena answers Harold's question by searching in the WRITERS and PAST ARTICLES form.

Using the Find Command

To find Chong Kim's phone number, Elena uses the toolbar Find button. Elena first opens the WRITERS and PAST ARTICLES form.

To open a form:

1. If it is not already selected, click **WRITERS and PAST ARTICLES form** in the Database window's Forms list box.
2. Click the **Open command button**. The Form View window that appears is maximized because you had maximized the Database window.

The left side of the toolbar in the Form View window has several buttons, as shown in Figure 5-19. You have already used some of these buttons. You will use the six buttons on the right side of Figure 5-19 in the next few steps of this tutorial.

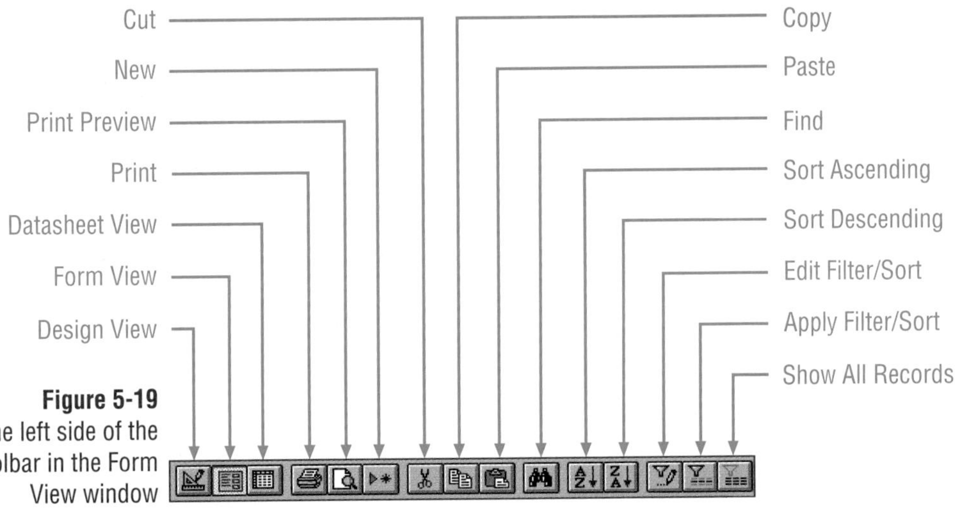

Figure 5-19 The left side of the toolbar in the Form View window

To find Chong Kim's record, Elena uses the Find button to search for a match on the Last Name field.

To find data in the Form View window:

❶ Click the main form's **field-value box** for the Last Name field to make it the search field for the Find command.

❷ Click the toolbar **Find button**. The Find dialog box appears.

❸ Click the title bar of the Find dialog box and drag the Find dialog box to the lower right to get a better view of the main form's field values and navigation buttons.

❹ Type **Kim** in the Find What text box, and then click the **Find First button** in the Find dialog box. Access finds the first Chong Kim and displays the sixth WRITERS table record. This Chong Kim is not a freelancer, so Elena searches for the next Chong Kim.

❺ Click the **Find Next button** in the Find dialog box. Access displays the next Chong Kim, whose record is the seventh WRITERS table record. His article is titled Cola Advertising War. This Chong Kim is a freelancer, so Elena has completed her search. She jots down the phone number.

❻ Click the **Close button**. The Find dialog box disappears.

Elena gives Chong Kim's phone number to Harold. Harold next asks Elena for the phone number and name of the writer with the oldest last contact date.

Quick Sorting in a Form

To find the writer with the oldest last contact date, Elena uses the toolbar Sort Ascending button to do a quick sort. She first selects the Last Contact Date field, so that the records will appear in the form in increasing order by this field.

To quick sort records in a form:

❶ Click the main form's **field-value box** for the Last Contact Date field to make it the selected field for the quick sort.

❷ Click the toolbar **Sort Ascending button**. Access displays the record for Shinjiro Yamamura, who has the earliest Last Contact Date field value, 9/26/72.

You can use the main form's Next Record navigation button to display the writer records, one at a time, in ascending order by last contact date. If you want Access to display the records in the default order by Writer ID, which is the primary key, click the toolbar's Show All Records button, and then use the navigation buttons.

Elena gives Shinjiro Yamamura's phone number to Harold. Harold next asks Elena for the phone numbers of all freelance writers.

Using a Filter

You use the Find command in a form when you want to see records that match a specific field value, and you use the quick sort buttons if you want Access to display all records in order by a single field. If you want Access to display selected records, display records sorted by two or more fields, or display selected records and sort them, you use a filter.

A **filter** is a set of criteria that describes the records you want to see in a form and their sequence. You enter record selection criteria in the Filter window in the same way you specify record selection criteria for a query. Elena wants to view only records for freelancers in her form, so she uses a filter to specify this criterion. Elena chooses a descending sort of the records based on the Last Contact Date field.

To open the Filter window and specify selection and sorting criteria:

1. Click the toolbar **Edit Filter/Sort button**. The Filter window appears.
2. Scroll the WRITERS field list to display the Freelancer field. Double-click **Freelancer** in the WRITERS field list. Access adds the Freelancer field to the second column of the Filter window grid. Because you selected the Last Contact Date field for the previous quick sort, it appears in the Filter window grid in the first column.
3. Click the **Criteria text box** in the Freelancer column and then type **Yes**.
4. Click the **Sort text box** in the Last Contact Date column, click the **down arrow button**, and click **Descending**. See Figure 5-20.

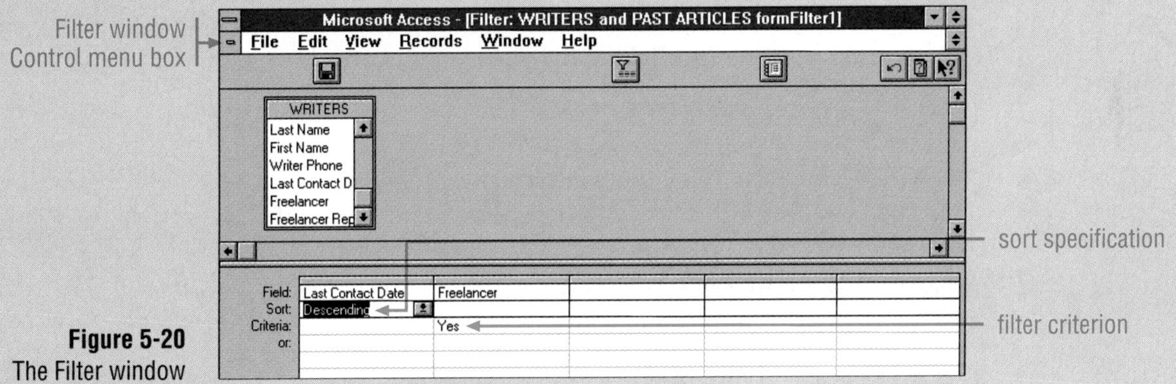

Figure 5-20
The Filter window

Elena has defined the filter; next she saves it as a query. By doing this, she can reuse the filter in the future by opening the saved query.

To save a filter as a query:

1. Click the toolbar **Save button**. The Save As Query dialog box appears.
2. Type **Freelancers and PAST ARTICLES** in the Query Name box and then press **[Enter]**. Access saves the filter as a query, and the Save As Query dialog box disappears.

Elena closes the Filter window and applies the filter. Applying the filter selects the records based on your selection criteria in the order specified by the sort criteria.

To close the Filter window and apply a filter:

1. Double-click the Filter window **Control menu box**. The Filter window disappears and Access displays the Form View window.

   TROUBLE? If you accidentally exit Access, launch Access, open the Issue25 database, maximize the Database window, click the Form object button, double-click the WRITERS and PAST ARTICLES form, click the Edit Filter/Sort button, click File, click Load From Query..., double-click Freelancers and PAST ARTICLES, and double-click the Filter window Control menu box. Then continue to Step 2.

2. Click the toolbar **Apply Filter/Sort button**. Access selects records based on the filter criteria and displays records in sort-key sequence. The record for Wilhelm Seeger is the first record to appear in the main form. His three articles appear in the subform.
3. Click the main form **Last Record button**. Access displays the record for Tonya Nilsson in the main form and her two articles in the subform.

The last record is record six. Because you view only the freelancer records when you apply the filter, you see only six of the 15 records in the table.

Elena gives Harold the phone numbers for all the freelancers. She then removes the filter. You remove a filter by clicking the Show All Records button on the toolbar.

To remove a filter:

1. Click the toolbar **Show All Records button**. Access displays the record from the WRITERS table with the lowest primary-key value. This is the record for Kelly Cox, who has a Writer ID of C200.
2. Click the main form **Last Record button**. Access displays the record from the WRITERS table with the highest primary key value. This is the record for Shinjiro Yamamura, who has a Writer ID of Y556.

When the filter is applied, Access displays one of the six records for freelancers from the WRITERS table. When you remove the filter, Access displays one of the 15 records stored in the WRITERS table.

Elena closes the Form View window and checks to be sure the filter was saved as a query.

To close the Form View window and view the query list:

1. Double-click the Form View window **Control menu box**. Access closes the Form View window and activates the Database window.
2. Click the **Query object button**. The Queries list box appears. See Figure 5-21.

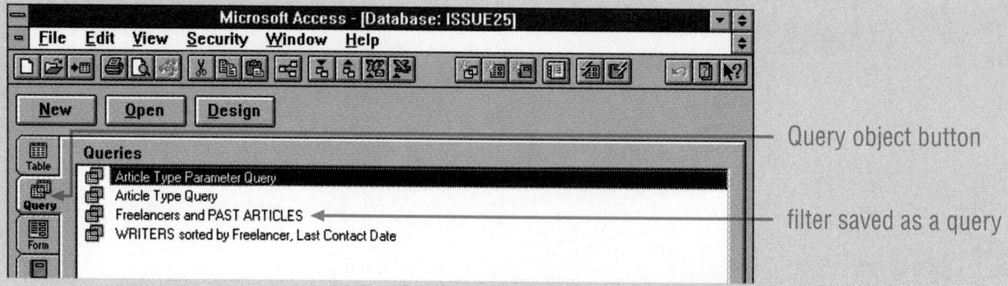

Figure 5-21 The Queries list box in the Database window

Elena wants to be sure she remembers how to apply a filter that she saved as a query. She opens the WRITERS and PAST ARTICLES form and applies the Freelancers and PAST ARTICLES query as a filter.

To apply a filter that was saved as a query:

1. Click the **Form object button** in the Database window and double-click **WRITERS and PAST ARTICLES form** in the Forms list box. The Form View window appears.
2. Click the toolbar **Edit Filter/Sort button**. Access displays the Filter window.
3. Click **File**, and then click **Load From Query....** The Applicable Filter dialog box appears. See Figure 5-22.

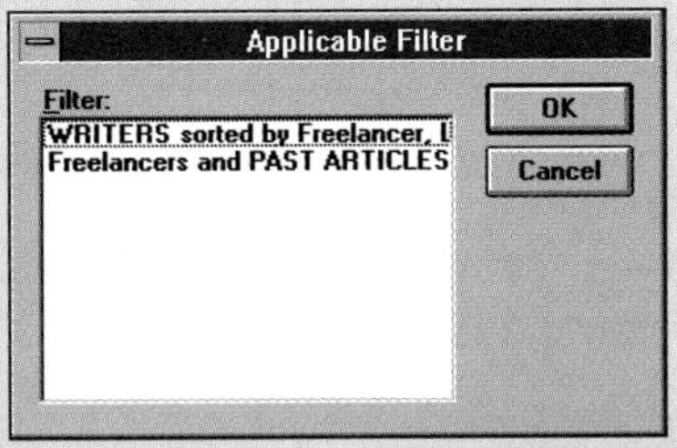

Figure 5-22
The Applicable Filter dialog box

4. Double-click **Freelancers and PAST ARTICLES**. The Applicable Filter dialog box disappears, and Access loads the saved query into the Filter grid.
5. Double-click the Filter window **Control menu box** to close the Filter window.
6. Click the toolbar **Apply Filter/Sort button**. Access applies the filter.
7. Click the main form **Last Record button**. Access displays the sixth freelancer record, which is for Tonya Nilsson.
8. Double-click the Form View window **Control menu box**. The Form View window disappears, and the Database window becomes the active window.

If you want to take a break and resume the tutorial at a later time, you can exit Access by double-clicking the Microsoft Access window Control menu box. When you resume the tutorial, place your Student Disk in the appropriate drive, launch Access, open the Issue25 database on your Student Disk, maximize the Database window, and click the Form object button.

■ ■ ■

Creating a Custom Form

Elena places the Issue25 database on the company network, and Harold, Judith, and Brian use it to answer their questions. The most popular query proves to be the Article Type Query, which lists the article title, type, and length, and the writer's first and last names. Harold tells Elena that he would like the option of viewing the same information in a form, and Elena designs a custom form based on the query.

If you modify a form created by a Form Wizard, or if you design and create a form without using a Form Wizard, you have developed a **custom form**. You might create a custom form, for example, to match a paper form, to display some fields side by side and others top to bottom, to highlight the form with color, or to add special buttons and list boxes.

Designing a Custom Form

Although Elena's custom form is relatively simple, she first designs the form's content and appearance on paper. Elena's finished design is shown in Figure 5-23.

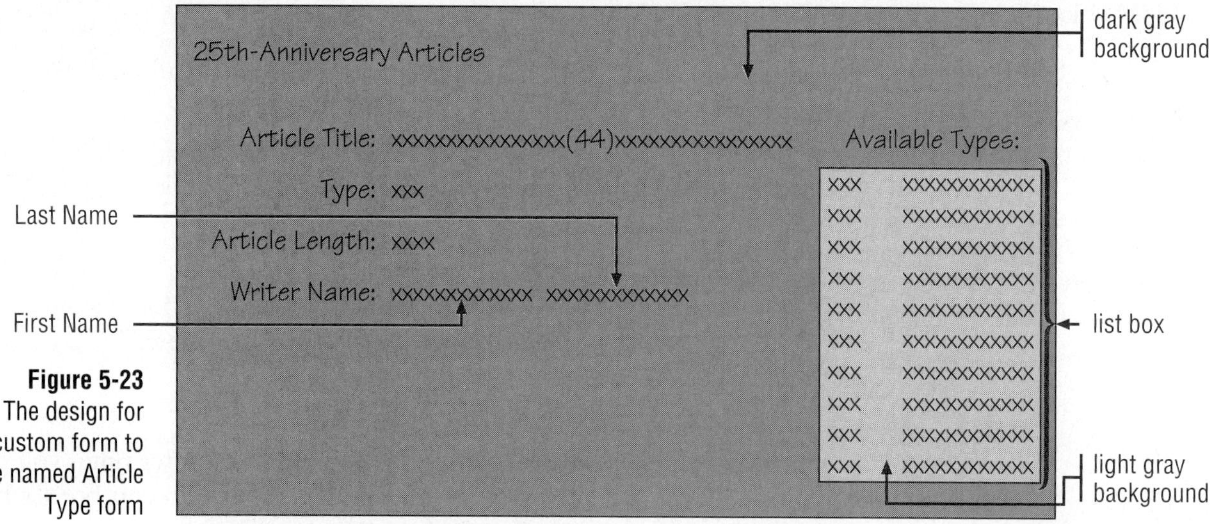

Figure 5-23
The design for the custom form to be named Article Type form

The title for the designed form is 25th-Anniversary Articles. The designed form displays all fields from the Article Type Query in single-column format, except for the writer's First Name and Last Name fields, which are side by side.

Each field value will appear in a text box and will be preceded by a label. Elena indicates the locations and lengths of each field value by a series of Xs. The three Xs that follow the Type field label indicate that the field value will be three characters wide.

Because many of her coworkers are unfamiliar with all the article type codes, a list box containing both the article types and their full descriptions will appear on the right. Elena plans to add background colors of light gray to the list box and dark gray to the rest of the form to make the form easier to read.

All the data Elena needs for her custom form is contained in the Article Type Query. Thus, unlike her previous Form Wizard forms that were based on tables, Elena will use a query to create the custom form and will use all the fields from the Article Type Query. This query obtains data from both the PAST ARTICLES and WRITERS tables and displays records in ascending order by Article Type. The form, which Elena plans to name Article Type form, will likewise display records in ascending Article Type.

The Form Design Window

You use the **Form Design window** to create and modify forms. To create the custom form, Elena creates a blank form based on the Article Type Query in the Form Design window.

To create a blank form in the Form Design window:

1. Click the toolbar **New Form button**. The New Form dialog box appears.
2. Click the Select A Table/Query drop-down list box **down arrow button**. Scroll if necessary, click **Article Type Query**, and then click the **Blank Form button**. The Form Design window appears. See Figure 5-24.

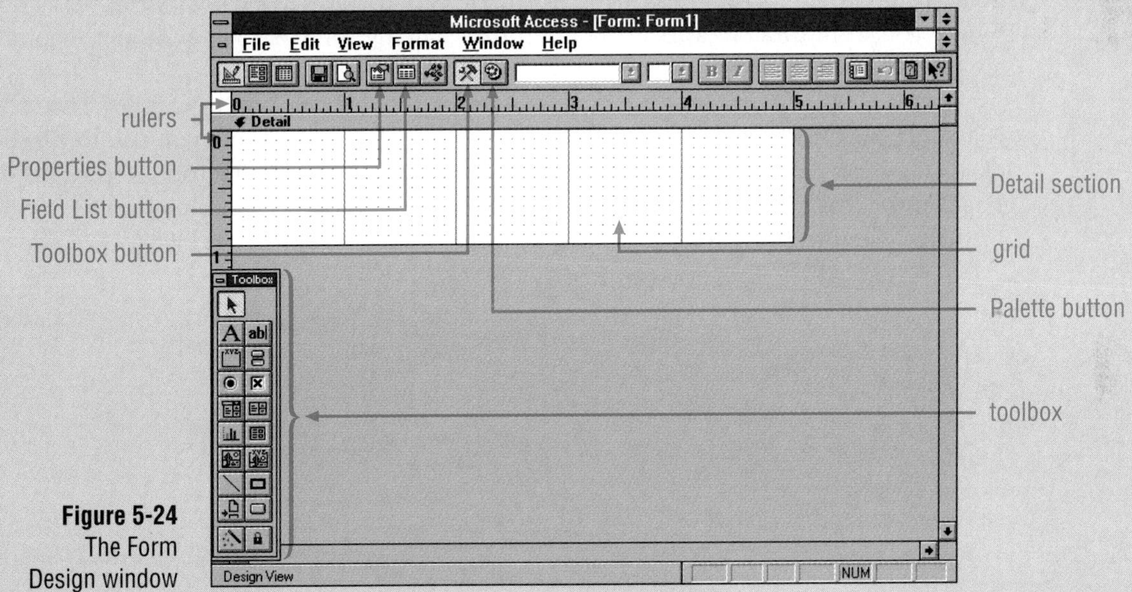

Figure 5-24
The Form Design window

TROUBLE? If the rulers, grid, or toolbox do not appear, click the View menu and then click Ruler, Grid, or Toolbox to display the missing component in the Form Design window. A check mark appears in front of these View menu commands when the components are displayed in the Form Design window. If the grid is still invisible, see your technical support person or instructor for assistance. If the Palette appears in the Form Design window, click the toolbar Palette button to close it until later in the tutorial. If the toolbar Properties button is selected, click it to close the property sheet.

The Form Design window contains four new components and four new toolbar buttons. The new components are the rulers, the Detail section, the grid, and the toolbox; the new toolbar buttons are the Properties button, the Field List button, the Toolbox button and the Palette button.

The **rulers** show the horizontal and vertical dimensions of the form and serve as a guide to the placement of controls on the form. A **control** is a graphical object, such as a text box, a list box, a rectangle, or a command button, that you place on a form or a report to display data, perform an action, or make the form or report easier to read and use. Access has three types of controls: bound controls, unbound controls, and calculated controls. A **bound control** is linked, or bound, to a field in the underlying table or query. You use a bound control to display or update a table field value. An **unbound control** is not linked to a field in the underlying table or query. You use an unbound control to display text, such as a form title or instructions, or to display graphics and pictures from other applications. If you use an unbound control to display text, the unbound control is called a **label**. You can have a label relate to a bound control—a field-name label and a field-value text box can be paired as a bound control, for example. A **calculated control** displays a value calculated from data from one or more fields.

When you want to create a bound control, click the toolbar **Field List button** to display a list of fields available from the underlying table or query. You click and drag fields from the field list box to the Form Design window, placing the bound controls where you want them to appear on the form. Clicking the Field List button a second time closes the field list box.

To place other controls on a form, you use the tool buttons on the toolbox. The **toolbox** is a specialized toolbar containing buttons that represent the tools you use to place controls on a form or a report. When you hold the mouse pointer on a tool, Access displays a ToolTip for that tool. If you want to show or hide the toolbox, click the toolbar **Toolbox button**. A summary of the tools available in the toolbox is shown in Figure 5-25.

Icon	Tool Name	Control Purpose on a Form or Report
	Select objects	Select, move, size, and edit controls
	Label	Display text, such as a title or instructions; an unbound control
	Text Box	Display a label attached to a text box that contains a bound control or a calculated control
	Option Group	Display a group frame containing toggle buttons, option buttons, or check boxes; can use Control Wizards to create
	Toggle Button	Signal if a situation is true (button is selected or pushed down) or false
	Option Button	Signal if a situation is true (black dot appears in the option button's center) or false; also called a radio button
	Check Box	Signal if a situation is true (× appears in the check box) or false
	Combo Box	Display a drop-down list box, so that you can either type a value or select a value from the list; can use Control Wizards to create
	List Box	Display a list of values from which you can choose one value; can use Control Wizards to create
	Graph	Display a graph that can be editd with Microsoft Graph; uses Graph Wizard
	Subform/Subreport	Display both a main form or report from a primary table and a subform or subreport form a related table
	Object Frame	Display a picture, graph, or other OLE object that is stored in an Access database table
	Bound Object Frame	Display a picture, graph, or other OLE object that is stored in an Access database table
	Line	Display a horizontal, vertical, or diagonal line
	Rectangle	Display a rectangle
	Page Break	Mark the start of a new screen or printed page
	Command Button	Display a command button that runs a macro or calls an Access Basic event procedure when the button is clicked; can use Control Wizards to create
	Control Wizards	When selected, activates Control Wizards for certain other toolbox tools
	Tool Lock	Keeps a toolbox tool selected when clicked after target tool is selected; clicking another toolbox tool deactivates

Figure 5-25
Summary of tools available in the toolbox for a form or a report

To open and close the property sheet for a selected control, a section of the form, or the entire form, click the toolbar **Properties button**. You use the **property sheet** to modify the appearance, behavior, and other characteristics of the overall form, a section of a form, or the controls on a form. For example, you can change a control's size or position on the form. The properties shown in the property sheet differ depending on the type of control selected.

When you click the toolbar Palette button, you open or close the Palette. You use the **Palette** to change the appearance and color of a form and its controls. **Appearance** options are normal, raised, or sunken. Colors can be chosen for text, background, and borders from a color palette. You can also use the Palette to control the thickness of lines drawn on the form.

The **Detail section**, which appears in white in the Form Design window, is the area in which you place the fields, labels, and most other controls for your form. You can change the default Detail section size, which is 5" wide by 1" high, by dragging the edges. The **grid** consists of the dots that appear in the Detail section. These dots help you to position controls precisely on a form.

You can add four other sections to a form by clicking the Format menu. The other four sections are the Form Header, Form Footer, Page Header, and Page Footer. Use the **Form Header** and **Form Footer sections** for information such as titles, dates, and instructions that you want to appear only at the top or bottom of a form on the screen or in print. Use the **Page Header** and **Page Footer sections** for information such as column headings or page numbers that you want to appear at the top or bottom of each page in a printed form.

Adding Fields to a Form

Elena's first task in the Form Design window is to add bound controls to the form Detail section for all the fields from the Article Type Query. When you add a bound control to a form, Access adds a label and, to its right, a field-value text box. You create a bound control by selecting one or more fields from the field list box and dragging them to the form. You select a single field by clicking the field. You select two or more fields by holding down [Ctrl] and clicking each field, and you select all fields by double-clicking the field-list title bar.

Because Elena wants to place all the fields from the field list box on the form, she adds bound controls to the form Detail section for all the fields in the field list.

To add bound controls for all the fields in the field list:

1. Click the toolbar **Field List button**. The field list box appears.
2. Double-click the **field-list title bar** to select all the fields in the field list. Access highlights the field list box.
3. Click anywhere in the highlighted area of the field list box and drag to the form's Detail section. Release the mouse button when the pointer is positioned at the top of the Detail section and at the 1.25" mark on the horizontal ruler. Access adds bound controls for the five selected fields. Each bound control consists of a text box and, to its left, an attached label. See Figure 5-26.

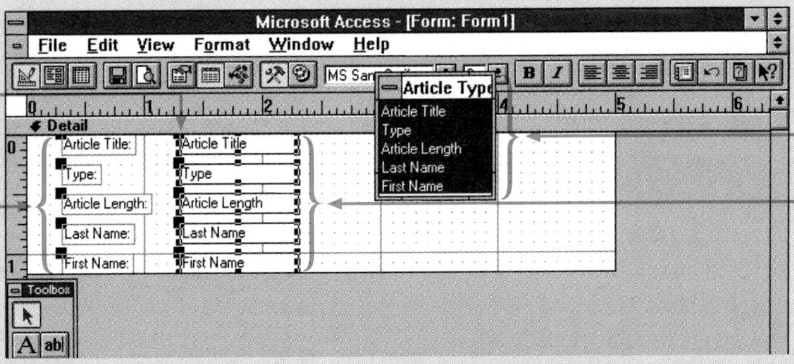

Figure 5-26
Adding text boxes and attached labels as bound controls to a form

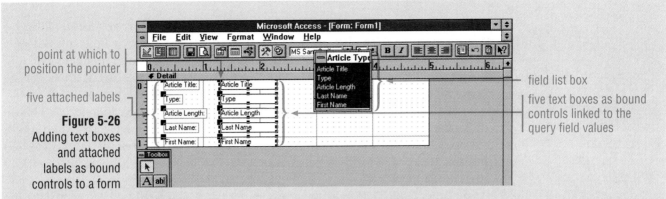

TROUBLE? If you did not position the bound controls properly in the Detail section, you can click the Undo button immediately to delete the text boxes and labels from the Detail section. Repeat the click and drag operation to position the bound controls.

Performing operations in the Form Design window might seem awkward for you at first. With practice you will become comfortable with creating a custom form. Remember that you can always click the Undo button immediately after you make a form adjustment that has undesired results.

Selecting, Moving, and Deleting Controls

Five text boxes now appear in a column in the form Detail section. Each text box is a bound control linked to a field in the underlying query and has an attached label box to its left. Because she is done with the field list box, Elena closes it by clicking the Field List button. Elena next compares the form Detail section with her design and arranges the Last Name and First Name text boxes side by side to agree with her form design, as shown in Figure 5-23.

To close the field list box and select a single bound control:

1. Click the toolbar **Field List button** to close the field list box.
2. Two boxes in the Detail section have Last Name inside them. The box on the left is the label box, and the box on the right is the field-value text box. Click in the gray area outside the Detail section to deselect any previous selection and then click the Last Name **field-value text box**. Move handles appear on the field-value text box and its attached label box; in addition, sizing handles appear, but only on the field-value text box. See Figure 5-27.

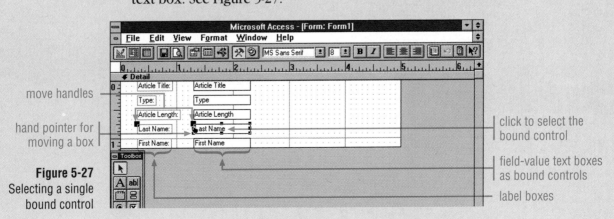

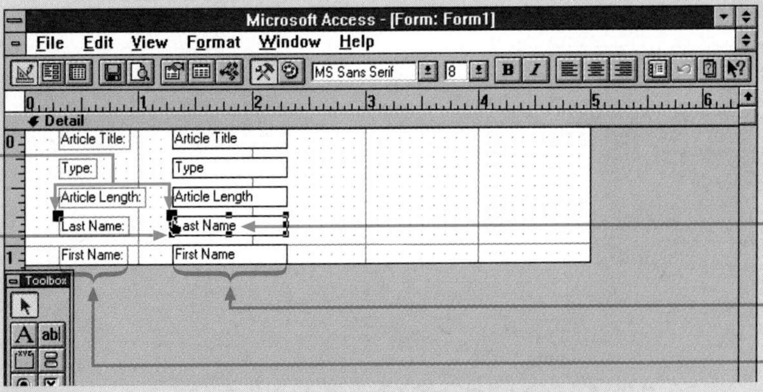

Figure 5-27
Selecting a single bound control

You can move a field-value text box and its attached label box together. To move them, place the pointer anywhere on the border of the field-value text box, but not on a move handle or a sizing handle. When the pointer changes to , drag the field-value text box and its attached label box to the new location. As you move the boxes, their outline moves to show you the changing position.

You can also move either the field-value text box or its label box individually. If you want to move the field-value text box but not its label box, for example, place the pointer on the text box's move handle. When the pointer changes to , drag the field-value text box to the new location. You use the label box's move handle in a similar way to move just the label box.

You can also delete a field-value text box and its attached label box or delete just the label box. To delete both boxes together, click inside the field-value text box to select both boxes, click the right mouse button inside the text box to open its Shortcut menu, and then click Cut on the menu. To delete just the label box, perform the same steps, clicking inside the label box instead of the field-value text box.

Elena moves the Last Name field-value text box to the right without moving its label box. She moves the First Name field-value text box (without its label box) up beside the Last Name box. Then she deletes the First Name label box.

To move field-value text boxes and delete labels:

1. Move the pointer to the Last Name field-value text box move handle. When the mouse pointer changes to , drag the text box horizontally to the right, leaving enough room for the First Name field-value text box to fit in its place. An outline of the box appears as you change its position to guide you in the move operation. Be sure to take advantage of the grid dots in the Detail section to position the box outline.

   TROUBLE? If you move the box incorrectly, click the Undo button immediately and then repeat the step.

2. Click the **field-value text box** for the First Name field and then move the pointer to its move handle. When the mouse pointer changes to , drag the box up to the position previously occupied by the Last Name field-value text box.

3. Click the **label box** for the First Name field to select it. Click the First Name **label box** with the right mouse button to open its Shortcut menu and click **Cut**. The First Name label box disappears. See Figure 5-28.

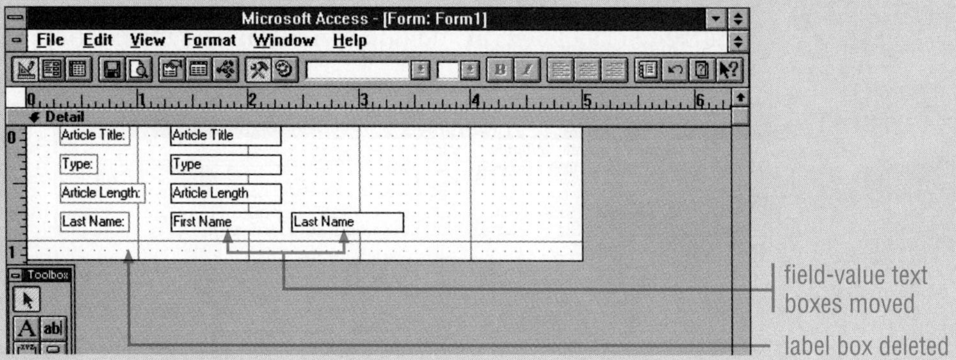

Figure 5-28 Moving field-value text boxes and deleting a label box

Resizing a Control

Elena notices that the Article Title field-value text box is too small to contain long titles, so she resizes it.

You use the seven sizing handles to resize a control. Moving the pointer over a sizing handle changes the pointer to a two-headed arrow; the pointer's direction differs depending on the sizing handle you use. When you drag the sizing handle you resize the control. Thin lines appear, which guide you as you drag the control. You can also resize a label box by selecting the label and using the sizing handles that appear.

Let's resize the Article Title field-value text box by stretching it to the right.

To resize a field-value text box:

1. Click the **field-value text box** for the Article Title field to select it. Move handles and sizing handles appear.
2. Move the pointer to the right side of the box over the middle handle. The pointer changes to ↔.
3. Drag the right border horizontally to the right until the right edge is just past the 3.75" mark on the horizontal ruler. The text box will now accommodate longer Article Title field values.

Changing a Label's Caption and Resizing a Label

Elena now compares the form to her design and notices that she needs to change the name in the Last Name label box to Writer Name. Elena uses the label's property sheet to change the label's Caption property.

To change the Caption property for a label:

1. Click in an unoccupied area of the grid to deselect all the control boxes.
2. Click the Last Name **label box** to select it.
3. Click the toolbar **Properties button** . The property sheet for the Last Name label appears.
4. Click the **Caption text box** in the property sheet and then press **[F2]** to select the entire value. See Figure 5-29 on the following page.

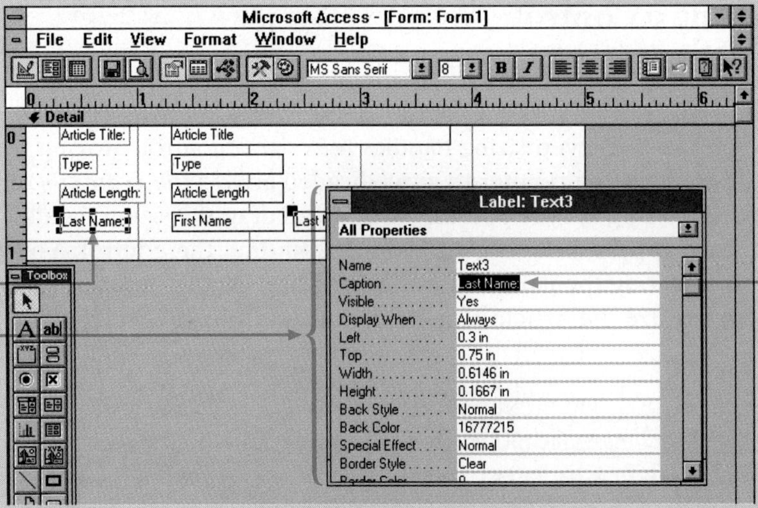

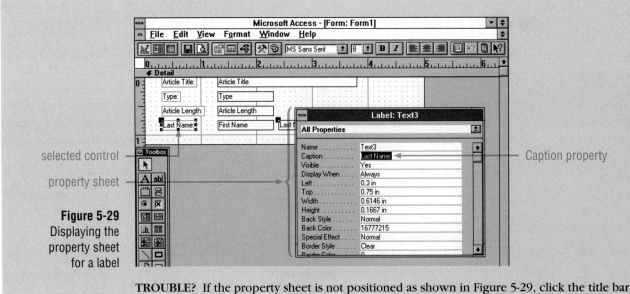

Figure 5-29 Displaying the property sheet for a label

TROUBLE? If the property sheet is not positioned as shown in Figure 5-29, click the title bar of the property sheet and drag the property sheet to the position shown. If some of the property values on your screen differ from those shown in the figure, do not be concerned. Property values will be different if you completed prior operations in a slightly different way.

❺ Type **Writer Name:**. Be sure to type a colon at the end of the caption.

❻ Click to close the property sheet. The label box contents change from Last Name: to Writer Name:.

Only part of the new caption is visible in the label box, so Elena resizes the label box.

To resize a label box:

❶ The Writer Name **label box** is still the selected control, so move the pointer to the left side of the control over the middle handle. When the pointer changes to ↔, drag the left border horizontally to the left one entire set of grid dots. You might need to try a few times to get it right. If you change the vertical size of the box by mistake, just click the Undo button and try again.

Aligning Labels

Elena next notices that the top three label boxes are left-justified; that is, they are aligned on their left edges. She wants all four label boxes aligned on their right edges. This is an individual preference on her part. Some people prefer left justification for the labels and others prefer right justification. To align several label boxes on the right simultaneously, you must first select all the label boxes by clicking inside each label box while holding down [Shift]. In the following steps be sure you select the label boxes only. If you select the field-value text boxes by mistake, click Undo.

To align all label boxes on the right:

❶ While pressing and holding **[Shift]**, click each of the remaining label boxes so that all four are selected, and then release [Shift].

❷ Click any one of the selected label boxes with the right mouse button to display the Shortcut menu.

❸ Click **Align** in the Shortcut menu to open the Align list box, and then click **Right**. Access aligns the label boxes on their right edges. See Figure 5-30.

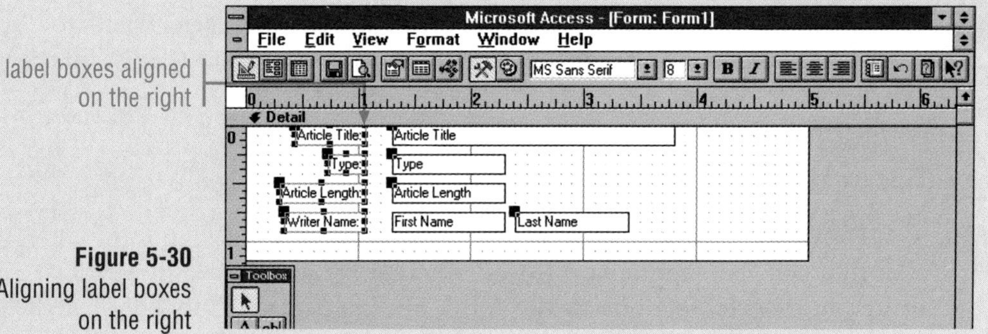

Figure 5-30
Aligning label boxes on the right

Viewing a Form in the Form View Window

Before Elena makes further changes in the Form Design window, she switches to the Form View window to study her results. The first three buttons on the left of the toolbar allow you to switch at any time among the Form Design, Form View, and Datasheet View windows. When you create a form, you should periodically check your progress in the Form View window. You might see adjustments you want to make on your form in the Form Design window.

Let's switch to the Form View window.

To switch to the Form View window:

❶ Click the toolbar **Form View button** . Access closes the Form Design window and opens the Form View window. See Figure 5-31.

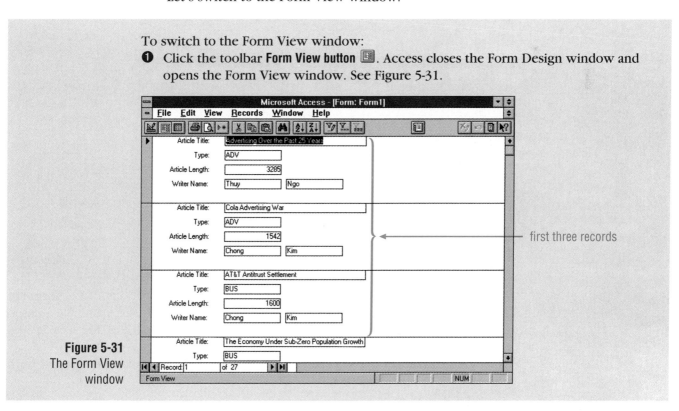

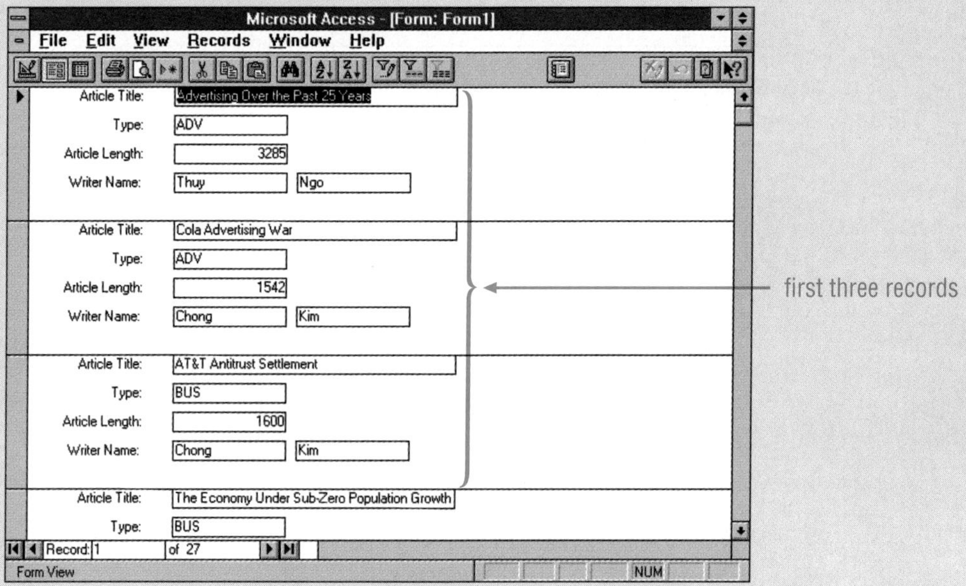

Figure 5-31
The Form View window

Your form uses the Article Type Query to sort the records in ascending order by the Type Field. Access displays the first three records from the query and part of the fourth record. You can use the scroll bars and navigation buttons to view other records from the query on the form.

Elena sees some adjustments she wants to make to her design. By default, Access displays as many form records as it can on the screen at one time. Elena wants to display only one record at a time. She also needs to add a form title and add the list box for the article types and descriptions.

Using Form Headers and Footers

Elena next adds a title to the form so that others can easily identify the form when they see it. To do this, she chooses the Form Header/Footer command from the Format menu to add header and footer sections to the form. She then places the title in the Form Header section and deletes the Form Footer section by decreasing its height to zero.

The Form Header and Footer sections allow you to add titles, instructions, command buttons, and other information to your form. You add the Form Header and Footer as a pair. If your form needs one of them but not the other, decrease the height of the unwanted one to zero. This is a way you delete any section on a form.

Elena adds the Form Header and Footer sections to the form.

To add Form Header and Footer sections to a form:

1. Click the toolbar **Design View button**. Access closes the Form View window and opens the Form Design window.
2. Click **Format**, and then click **Form Header/Footer**. Access inserts a Form Header section above the Detail section and a Form Footer section below the Detail section. See Figure 5-32.

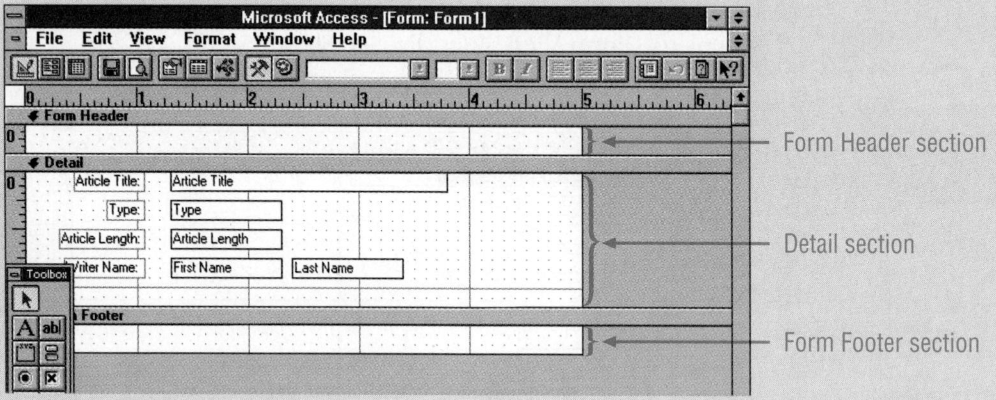

Figure 5-32 Adding the Form Header and Form Footer sections

When you change the width of one section of a form, all sections of the form are affected—the sections all have the same width. Each section, however, can have a different height. You change the width of a form by dragging the right edge of any section, and you change the height of a section by dragging its bottom edge.

Elena deletes the Form Footer section by dragging its bottom edge upward until it disappears.

To delete a Form Footer section:

1. Move the pointer to the bottom edge of the Form Footer section. When the pointer changes to ‡, click and drag the bottom edge upward until it disappears. Even though the words Form Footer remain, the white area defining the section is gone and the section will not appear in the form.

Elena now adds the form title to the Form Header section with the toolbox Label tool. You use the toolbox **Label tool** to add an unbound control to a form or report for the display of text, such as a title or instructions.

To add a label to a form:

1. Click the toolbox **Label tool** A.
2. Move the pointer into the Form Header section. As you move the pointer into the form, the pointer changes to +A. See Figure 5-33. Position the pointer as shown in Figure 5-33.

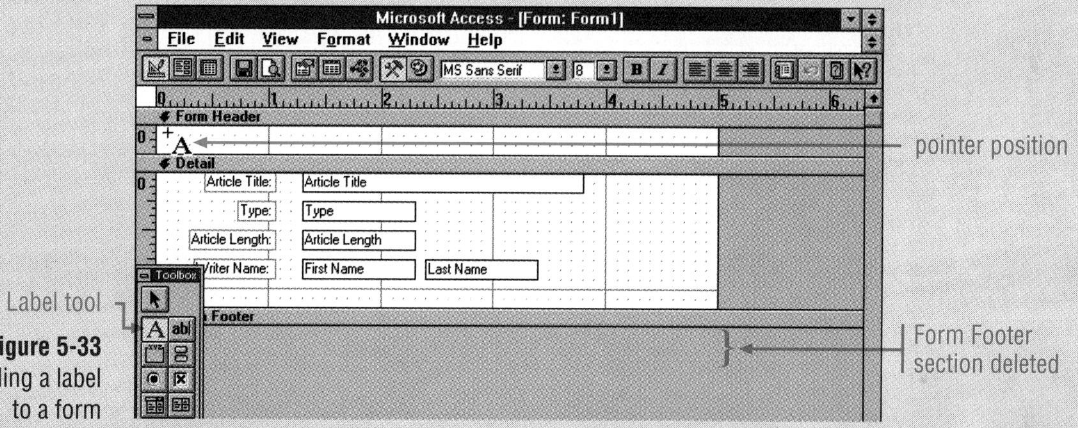

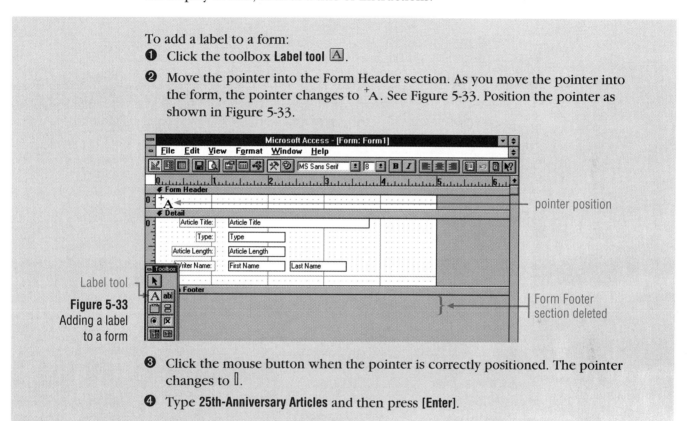

Figure 5-33 Adding a label to a form

3. Click the mouse button when the pointer is correctly positioned. The pointer changes to I.
4. Type **25th-Anniversary Articles** and then press **[Enter]**.

Adding a List Box Using Control Wizards

Because many of her coworkers are unfamiliar with the various article type codes, Elena adds a list box to the form's Detail section. The list box will display all the article types and their full descriptions from the TYPES table. A **list box** is a control that displays a list of values. You can use a list box when a field, such as the Type field, contains a limited set of values. The list box eliminates the need to remember all the Type field values. When you click one of the list box values, Access replaces the form's Type field value with the value you clicked. Thus, you can eliminate the need to keyboard a Type field-value. When you add a list box to a form, Access by default adds a label box to its left.

You use the toolbox List Box tool to add a list box to a form. Depending on whether the toolbox Control Wizards tool is selected, you can add a list box with or without using Control Wizards. A **Control Wizard** is an Access tool that asks you a series of questions and then creates a control on a form or report based on your answers. Access offers Control Wizards for the toolbox Combo Box tool, List Box tool, Option Group tool, and Command Button tool.

Elena will use the List Box Wizard to add the list box for the article types and descriptions. Before she adds the list box, Elena increases the width and the height of the Detail section to make room for the list box. She first moves the toolbox, so that it is out of the way.

To move the toolbox and resize the Detail section:

1. Click the **toolbox title bar** and drag it to the right to the ruler 1" mark.
2. Drag the right edge of the Detail section to the horizontal ruler's 6" mark.
3. Drag the bottom edge of the Detail section to the vertical ruler's 2.25" mark.
4. Drag the **toolbox title bar** to the lower-right corner of the screen. See Figure 5-34.

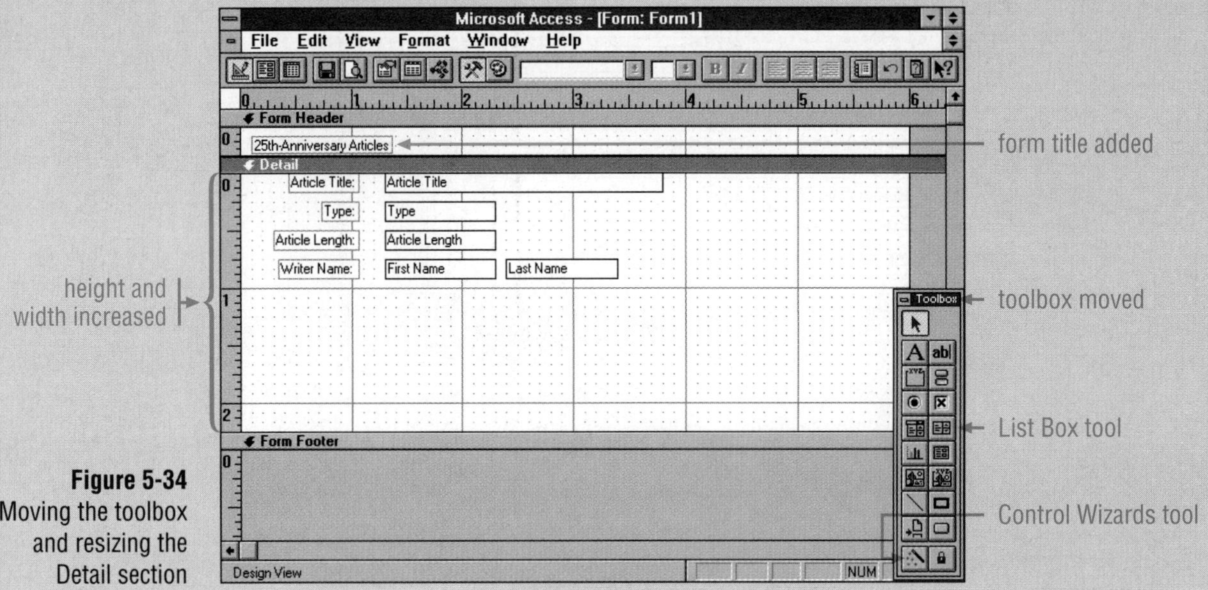

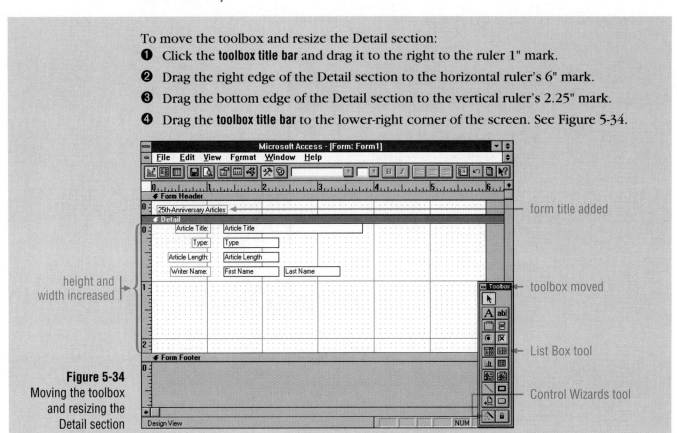

Figure 5-34
Moving the toolbox and resizing the Detail section

Elena adds a list box to the Detail section using the List Box Wizard.

To activate the List Box Wizard:

1. Click the toolbox **Control Wizards tool**.
2. Click the toolbox **List Box tool**. As you move the pointer away from the toolbox, the pointer changes to +. See Figure 5-35.

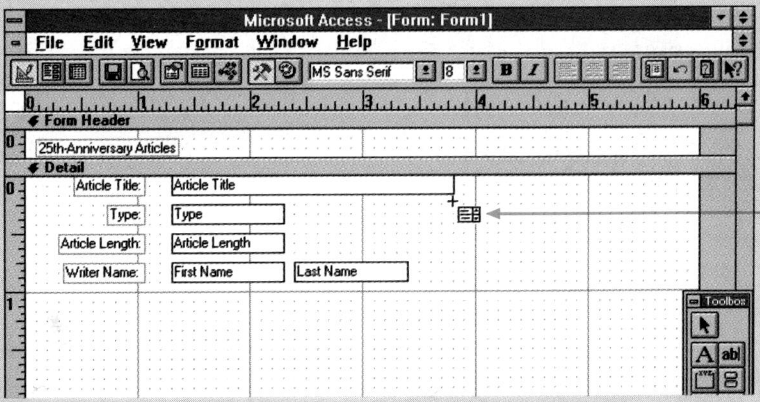

Figure 5-35
Positioning a list box

❸ Click when the list box pointer is positioned as shown in Figure 5-35. After a few seconds, the first List Box Wizard dialog box appears.

Elena tells the List Box Wizard to display two fields from the TYPES table: the Type field and the Description field. She also uses the List Box Wizard dialog box to size the two fields' column widths and to add the label Article Types.

To add a list box using the List Box Wizard:

❶ The TYPES table will supply the values for the list box, so click the **top radio button**, which is labeled "I want the list box to look up the values in a table or query." Then click the **Next > button**. The second List Box Wizard dialog box appears.

❷ Click **TYPES** as the source table for the list box and then click the **Next > button**. The third List Box Wizard dialog box appears.

❸ Because you want both the Type and Description fields to appear in the list box, click the **>> button** to select both fields and then click the **Next > button**. The fourth List Box Wizard dialog box appears.

❹ For both columns, double-click the right edge of each column selector to get the best column fit and then click the **Next > button**. The fifth List Box Wizard dialog box appears.

❺ If Type is not highlighted, click it to select it. Then click the **Next > button**. The sixth List Box Wizard dialog box appears.

❻ Because you want to be able to select a Type field value from the list box and store it in the form's Type field-value text box, click the bottom radio button, which is labeled "Store that value in this field:." Next, click the **down arrow button**, click **Type**, and then click the **Next > button**. The seventh and final List Box Wizard dialog box appears.

7. For a label, type **Article Types:** in the text box and then click the **Finish button**. Access closes the List Box Wizard dialog box and displays the completed list box in the Detail section of the form. See Figure 5-36.

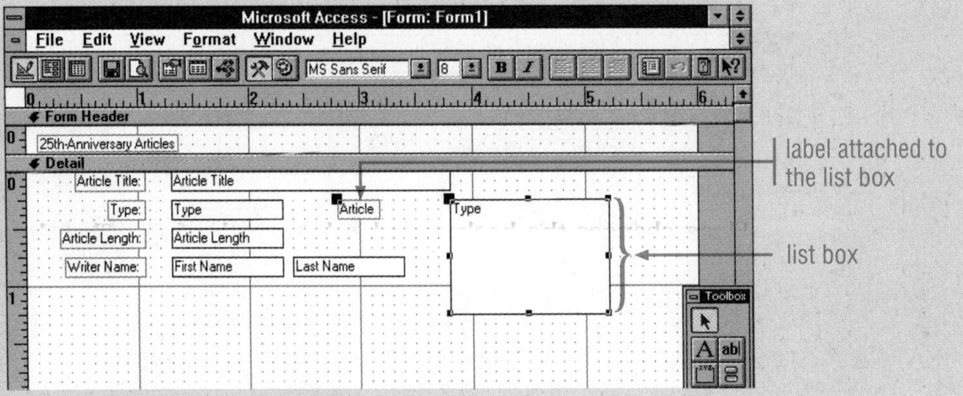

Figure 5-36 Adding a list box to a form

The attached label appears to the left of the list box. Elena resizes the label and then moves it above the list box.

To resize and move a label:

1. Click the label box attached to the list box to select it.
2. Click **Format**, click **Size,** and then click **to Fit.** The label's entire caption is now visible.
3. Click and drag the **label box's move handle** to position the label box above the list box. See Figure 5-37.

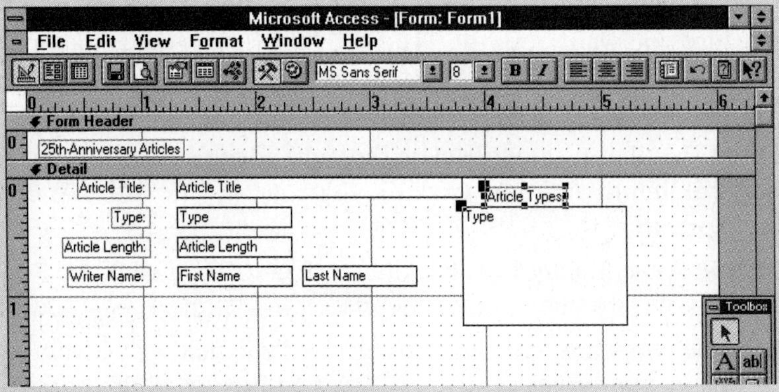

Figure 5-37 Resizing and moving a label

Adding Background Colors to a Form

Elena's final tasks are to add background colors to the list box and to the Form Header and Detail sections and to change the form property sheet to display a single record at a time. The Default View property for a form, Continuous Forms, displays as many records as possible on a form. To show a single record on a form, you change the Default View property to Single Form.

To display a single record at a time on a form:

1. Click anywhere in the area below the Form Footer bar. This action makes the form itself the selected control.
2. Click the toolbar **Properties button** to display the property sheet for the form.
3. Click the **Default View box** in the property sheet, click the **down arrow button**, and then click **Single Form**.
4. Click to close the property sheet.

Elena changes the background colors on the form. She changes the list box background to light gray and the background of the Detail and Form Header sections to a darker gray.

REFERENCE WINDOW

Adding Colors to a Form

- Click the control you want to color.
- Click the toolbar Palette button to display the Palette.
- Select the appearance, color, or other special effect from the Palette.
- Click the Palette button to close the Palette.

Let's change the colors of the list box and the two form sections.

To change the colors of a list box and the form sections:

1. Click the list box to select it.
2. Click the toolbar **Palette button** to display the Palette. See Figure 5-38.

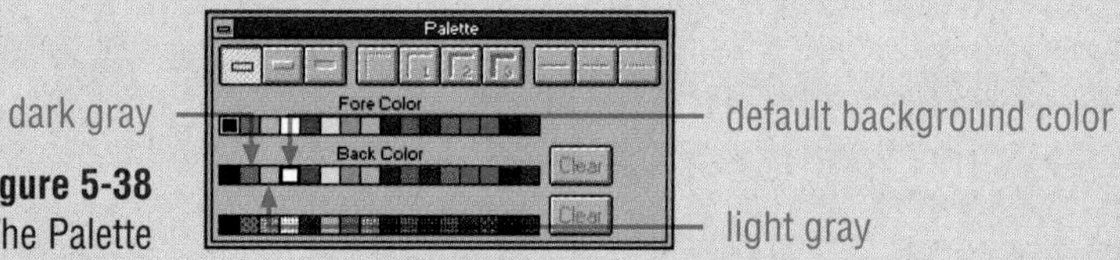

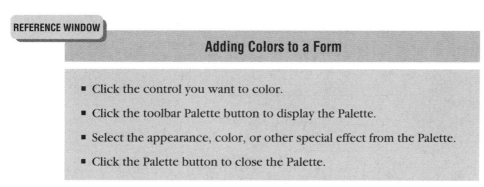

Figure 5-38
The Palette

3. Click the **light gray color box** on the Back Color line. This is the third box from the left.
4. Click the Detail section, but do not click any of the controls in that section. This makes the Detail section the selected control.
5. Click the **dark gray color box** on the Back Color line. This is the second box from the left.
6. Click the Form Header section, but do not click the label box. This makes the Form Header section the selected control.

❼ Click the **dark gray color box** on the Back Color line again. See Figure 5-39.

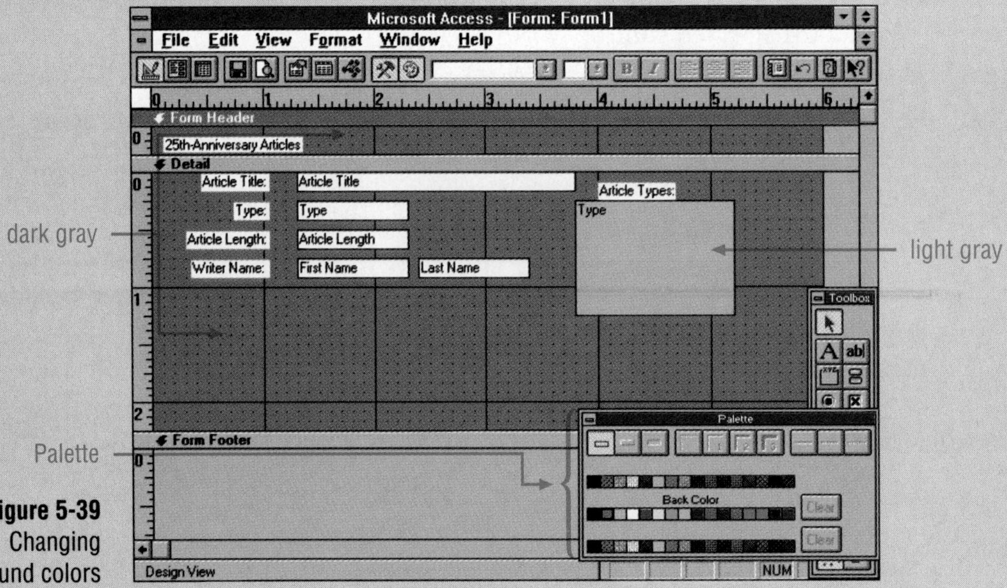

Figure 5-39 Changing background colors

❽ Click [button] to close the Palette.

Making Final Revisions to a Custom Form

Elena switches to the Form View window to review the custom form. She wants to see if there are any further changes she needs to make to the form.

To switch to the Form View window to review a custom form:

❶ Click the toolbar **Form View button** [button]. Access closes the Form Design window and opens the Form View window. See Figure 5-40.

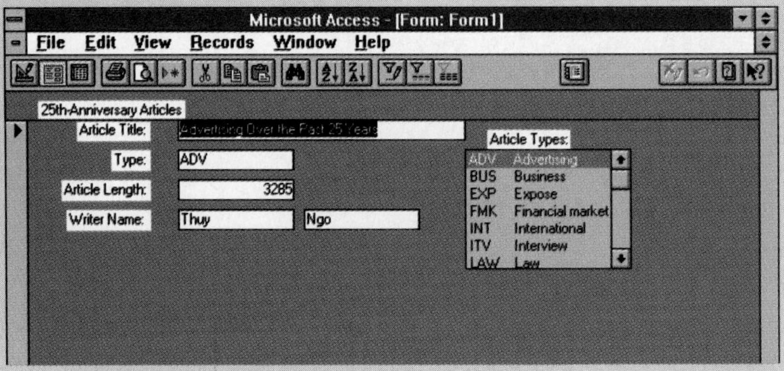

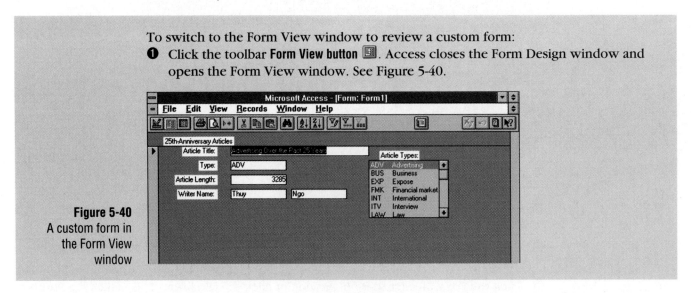

Figure 5-40 A custom form in the Form View window

Elena sees that the list box is not tall enough to show the entire list of article types and descriptions. She switches back to the Form Design window to resize the list box.

To switch to the Form Design window and resize a list box:

1. Click the toolbar **Design View button**. Access closes the Form View window and opens the Form Design window.
2. Click the list box to select it. Drag the middle sizing handle on the bottom border to the 2.00" mark on the vertical ruler to increase the height of the list box. Switch back and forth between the Form View window and the Form Design window until the list box is large enough to show all the article types. See Figure 5-41.

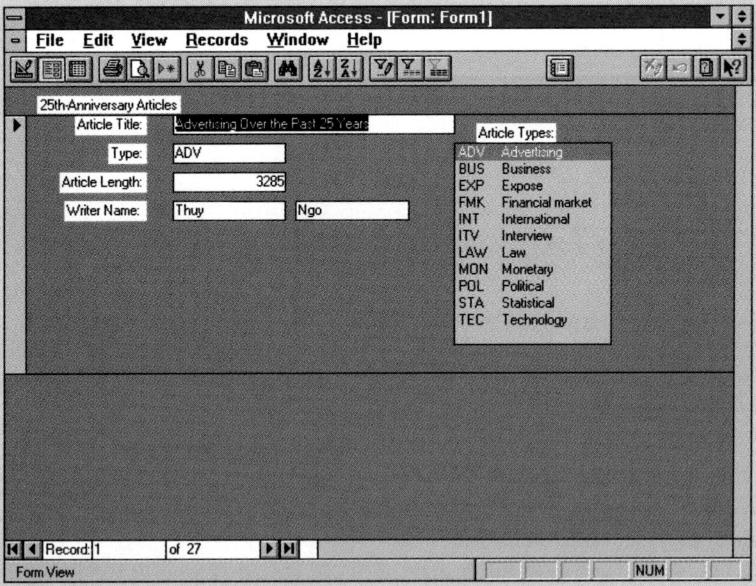

Figure 5-41 The final version of a custom form in the Form View window

3. When you have completed the custom form, switch to the Form Design window to view the form's final design. See Figure 5-42.

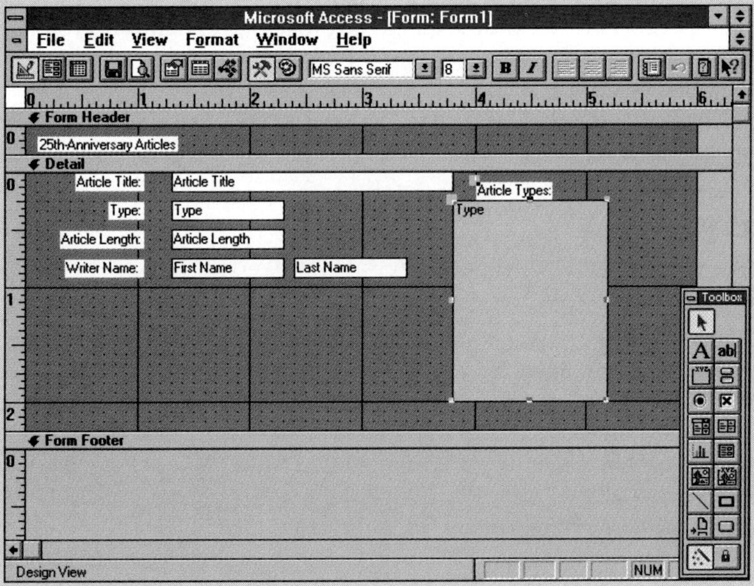

Figure 5-42 The final version of a custom form in the Form Design window

Elena saves the custom form, naming it Article Type form, and closes the Form Design window.

To save a custom form and close the Form Design window:

1. Click the toolbar **Save button** . The Save As dialog box appears.
2. Type **Article Type form** and then press **[Enter]**. Access saves the custom form.
3. Double-click the Form Design window **Control menu box**. Access closes the Form Design window and activates the Database window.

■ ■ ■

Elena now has five forms displayed in the Forms list box. Having completed her work with forms for the Issue25 database, Elena exits Access.

Questions

1. What type of Form Wizard form displays data from two related tables?
2. Which Form Wizard style should you select when you first start working with forms?
3. What is the quickest way to create a form?
4. How does a Form Wizard display the value for a yes/no field?
5. What formats do Form Wizards use to display records in a main/subform form?
6. How many sets of navigation buttons appear in a main/subform form, and what does each set control?
7. When should you use a filter instead of the Find button or the quick sort buttons?
8. If you want to reuse a filter in the future, you save the filter as what type of object?
9. What is the difference between a bound and an unbound control?
10. What five different sections can a form have?
11. How do you move a control and its label together, and how do you move each separately?
12. How do you change a label name?
13. What form property do you change so that Access displays a single record at a time?

Tutorial Assignments

Elena uses a Form Wizard to create a form named PAST ARTICLES form for the Issue25 database. Launch Access, open the Issue25 database on your Student Disk, and do the following:

1. Use Form Wizards to create a single-column form type with the standard style based on the PAST ARTICLES table. Select all the fields from the table in the order in which they are stored in the table, and use the default form title PAST ARTICLES.
2. Open the Form View window and then print the first page.
3. Change the form's design so that the Article Length text box and its attached label box are to the right of, and on the same line as, the Issue field.
4. Move the Writer ID text box and its attached label box up to the position previously occupied by the Article Length bound control.
5. Change the Caption property for the Article Length label box to Length followed by a colon.
6. Resize the Article Title text box so that the field value for each record is completely displayed.

7. Verify your design changes in the Form View window by navigating through all records.
8. Print the first page.
9. Save the form, using the name PAST ARTICLES form, and close the form window on your screen.

Elena next creates a custom form and names it PAST ARTICLES by Issue and Length form. Use the Issue25 database on your Student Disk to do the following:

10. Create a query by selecting the PAST ARTICLES and WRITERS tables and selecting the following fields in the order given here: Article Title, Type, Issue of Business Perspectives, Article Length, Last Name, and First Name. Rename the Issue of Business Perspectives field simply Issue. Then sort the records based on Issue as the primary sort key in descending order and Article Length as the secondary sort key in ascending order. Print the entire dynaset for this query. Finally, save the query, naming it ARTICLES sorted by Issue, Length, and close the active window to activate the Database window.
11. Create a custom form by selecting the query named ARTICLES sorted by Issue, Length and then clicking the Blank Form button.
12. Add all the fields from the query named ARTICLES sorted by Issue, Length to the Detail section and print the first page of the form.
13. Change the Caption property for the Article Length label box to Length, right align all the label boxes, resize the Article Title text box so that the field-value for each record is completely displayed, and print the first page of the form.
14. Move the First Name text box to the right of, and on the same line as, the Last Name text box; delete the First Name label; change the Caption property for the Last Name label to Writer Name; resize the Writer Name label; and print the first page of the form.
15. **E** Use the Format menu's to Fit option under the Size command for the five labels and then right align all the labels. Print the first page of the form.
16. **E** Change the form width to 4.5" and then move the Issue text box and its attached label to the right of, and on the same line as, the Type field. Move all the lines that follow the Type and Issue fields up to eliminate blank lines. If necessary, right align all the labels that appear on the left of the form and then left align the field-value text boxes to their immediate right. Print the first page of the form.
17. **E** Add Form Header and Footer sections; delete the Form Footer section; add to the Form Header section the form title PAST ARTICLES by Issue, Length; change the height of the Detail section to 3"; and print the first page of the form.
18. **E** Use the List Box Wizard to create a list box to display all the article types and their descriptions. Position the list box under all the fields. Use the TYPES table for the list box, and display both table fields. Add the label Types to the form and position it just to the left of the list box. Resize the list box to display all types and descriptions. Finally, change the form's Default View to Single Form, and then print the first and last pages of the form.
19. Save the form as PAST ARTICLES by Issue and Length form.

Case Problems

1. Walkton Daily Press Carriers

Grant Sherman uses a Form Wizard to create a form for his Press database. Launch Access, open the Press database on your Student Disk, and do the following:

1. Use Form Wizards to create a single-column form type with the standard style based on the CARRIERS table. Select all the fields from the table in the order in which they are stored in the table. Use the form title CARRIERS data.
2. Open the Form View window and then print the second page.

3. Save the form with the name CARRIERS form and close the form window on your screen.

Grant creates a custom form named CARRIERS by Name, Route ID form. Use the Press database on your Student Disk to do the following:

4. Create a query by selecting the BILLINGS and CARRIERS tables. Create a join line for the Carrier ID fields and select these fields in the order given here: Carrier Last Name, Carrier First Name, Carrier Phone, Route ID, and Balance Amount. Rename the Balance Amount field simply Balance, and then sort the records based on Carrier Last Name as the primary sort key in ascending order and on Route ID as the secondary sort key in ascending order. Print the entire dynaset for this query. Finally, save the query, naming it CARRIERS sorted by Name, Route ID. Close the active window to activate the Database window.
5. **E** Create a custom form by selecting the query named CARRIERS sorted by Name, Route ID and then clicking the Blank Form button.
6. **E** To the Detail section of the form, add all the fields from the query named CARRIERS sorted by Name, Route ID. Print the first page of the form.
7. **E** Move the Carrier Last Name text box without its attached label to the right on the same line, leaving room to move the Carrier First Name text box from the line below up in front of it. Then move the Carrier First Name text box without its attached label up between the Carrier Last Name label box and the Carrier Last Name text box. Delete the Carrier First Name label box, change the Caption property for the Carrier Last Name label box to Carrier Name, resize the Carrier Name label box to accommodate the shorter caption, and print the first page of the form.
8. **E** Move the Carrier Phone text box and its attached label up one line, and move the Route ID text box and its attached label up one line. Move the Balance text box and its attached label to the right of, and on the same line as, the Route ID bound control. Print the first page of the form.
9. Move the Balance label to the right, so that it is closer to its attached text box.
10. Right align all the labels on the left side of the form.
11. Change the form's Default View to Single Form and change the Detail section background color to blue-green (third color from the right in the Back Color row of the Palette).
12. Add Form Header and Footer sections. Add to the Form Header section the form title CARRIERS by Name and Route ID. Add to the Form Footer section the label Press Database, and print the first page of the form.
13. Save the form as CARRIERS by Name, Route ID form.

2. Lopez Used Cars

Hector Lopez uses a Form Wizard to create a form for his Usedcars database. Launch Access, open the Usedcars database on your Student Disk, and do the following:

1. Use Form Wizards to create a single-column form type with the standard style based on the USED CARS table. Select all the fields from the table in the order in which they are stored in the table. Use the form title USED CARS data.
2. Open the Form View window and then print the first two pages.
3. Save the form with the name USED CARS form and close the form window on your screen.

Maria Lopez creates a custom form, naming it USED CARS by Manufacturer and Model form. Use the Usedcars database on your Student Disk to do the following:

4. Create a query by selecting the CLASSES, LOCATIONS, USED CARS, and TRANSMISSIONS tables. You need join lines between the two Transmission Type fields, between the two Location Code fields, and between Class Type and Class. If any of these join lines are not shown, then create them. Select these fields in the order given here: Manufacturer, Model, Class Description, Transmission Desc, Year, Location Name, Manager Name, Cost, and Selling Price. Sort the records based on Manufacturer as the primary sort key in ascending order and on Model as the secondary sort key in ascending order. Print the entire dynaset for this query. Finally, save the query, naming it USED CARS by Manufacturer, Model.
5. **E** Create a custom form by selecting the query named USED CARS by Manufacturer, Model and then clicking the Blank Form button.
6. **E** Add to the Detail section all the fields from the query named USED CARS by Manufacturer, Model. Print the fourth page of the form.
7. **E** Resize the field-value text boxes, as necessary, so that, in the Form View window, all the field values for each record are completely displayed without unnecessary extra space. Navigate through the records in the Form View window to be sure the box sizes are correct. The Class Description and Transmission Desc text boxes should be widened, for example, and the Year, Cost, and Selling Price text boxes should be narrowed.
8. **E** Change the form's Default View to Single Form and then change the width of the Detail section to 5.75" and its height to 3.75".
9. Move the Model text box and its attached label to the right of, and on the same line as, the Manufacturer bound control. Then move the Model text box to the left to be one grid dot away from its related label.
10. Move the Year text box and its attached label to the right of, and on the same line as, the Model bound control. Then move the Year label to the right to be one grid dot away from its related text box.
11. Move the Manager Name text box and its attached label to the right of, and on the same line as, the Location Name bound control.
12. Move the Selling Price text box and its attached label to the right of, and on the same line as, the Cost bound control.
13. Eliminate blank lines by moving text boxes and their attached labels up, and then print the fourth page of the form.
14. Change the Captions properties for these labels: Class Description to Class, Transmission Desc to Trans, and Location Name to Location.
15. **E** Apply the Format menu's to Fit option under the Size command for the labels on the left side of the form, right align these labels, and then print the fourth page of the form.
16. **E** Use the List Box Wizard to add two list boxes to the form—one for class types and descriptions and one for location codes and names. Position the list boxes side by side below all the control boxes in the Detail Section, placing the one containing class types and descriptions on the left. For the class list box, use the CLASSES table, display both table fields, and enter Classes for the label. For the location list box, use the LOCATIONS table, display the Location Code and Location Name fields, and enter Locations as the label. Resize and move the labels and list boxes to display as much of each record and as many records as possible.
17. **E** Print the fourth page of the form.
18. Save the form as USED CARS by Manufacturer and Model form.

3. Tophill University Student Employment

Olivia Tyler uses a Form Wizard to create a form for her Parttime database. Launch Access, open the Parttime database on your Student Disk, and do the following:

1. Use Form Wizards to create a main/subform form type with the standard style based on the EMPLOYERS table as the primary table for the main form and the JOBS table as the related table for the subform. Select all the fields from the EMPLOYERS table in the order in which they are stored in the table. Select all the fields from the JOBS table, except for the Employer ID field, in the order in which they are stored in the table. Use the form title EMPLOYERS and JOBS data.
2. Open the Form View window, save the subform with the name JOBS subform, and then print the first page.
3. Save the form as EMPLOYERS and JOBS form and close the form window on your screen.

Olivia creates a custom form named JOBS by Employer and Job Title form. Use the Parttime database on your Student Disk to do the following:

E 4. Create a query by selecting the EMPLOYERS and JOBS tables and, if necessary, create a join line for the Employer ID fields. Select all the fields from the EMPLOYERS table in the order in which they are stored in the table, and then select these fields from the JOBS table in the order given here: Hours/Week, Job Title, and Wage. Sort the records based on Employer Name as the primary sort key in ascending order and on Job Title as the secondary sort key in ascending order. Print the entire dynaset for this query. Finally, save the query, naming it JOBS sorted by Employer, Job Title.

E 5. Create a custom form by selecting the query named JOBS sorted by Employer, Job Title and then clicking the Blank Form button.

E 6. Add all the fields from the query named JOBS sorted by Employer, Job Title to the Detail section and then print the first page of the form.

E 7. Resize the Employer Name and Job Title text boxes and print the first page of the form.

8. Right align all the labels.
9. Change the form's Default View to Single Form, change the Detail section background color to light gray (third color from the left in the Back Color row on the Palette), and then print the first page of the form.
10. Add Form Header and Footer sections, add to the Form Header section the form title JOBS by Employer and Job Title, add to the Form Footer section the label Parttime Database, and print the first page of the form.
11. Save the form as JOBS by Employer and Job Title form.

4. Rexville Business Licenses

Chester Pearce uses a Form Wizard to create a form for his Buslic database. Launch Access, open the Buslic database on your Student Disk, and do the following:

1. Use Form Wizards to create a single-column form type with the standard style based on the BUSINESSES table. Select all the fields from the table in the order in which they are stored in the table. Use the form title BUSINESSES data.
2. Open the Form View window and then print the first two pages.
3. Save the form as BUSINESSES form and close the form window on your screen.

Chester"creates a custom form, naming it BUSINESSES by License Type and Business Name form. Use the Buslic database on your Student Disk to do the following:

E 4. Create a query by selecting the BUSINESSES, ISSUED LICENSES, and LICENSES tables and, if necessary, create join lines for the Business ID fields and the License Type fields. Select all the fields, except the Business ID field, from the BUSINESSES table in the order in which they are stored in the table; select the License Number, License Type, Amount, and Date Issued fields (in the order given here) from the ISSUED LICENSES table; and then select the License

Description and Basic Cost fields from the LICENSES table. Rename the License Description field simply License. Sort the records based on License Type as the primary sort key in ascending order and on Business Name as the secondary sort key in ascending order, but do not show the License Type field in the dynaset. Print the entire dynaset for this query. Finally, save the query, naming it BUSINESSES sorted by License Type, Business Name.

E 5. Create a custom form by selecting the query named BUSINESSES sorted by License Type, Business Name and then clicking the Blank Form button.

E 6. Add all the fields from the query named BUSINESSES sorted by License Type, Business Name to the Detail section and then print the first page of the form.

7. Resize the Business Name and License text boxes, and print the first page of the form.

8. Right align all the labels.

9. Change the form's Default View to Single Form, change the Detail section background color to blue-green (third color from the right in the Back Color row on the Palette), and then print the first page of the form.

E 10. Add Form Header and Footer sections, add to the Form Header section the form title BUSINESSES by License Type and Business Name, add to the Form Footer section the label Buslic Database, and print the first page of the form.

11. Save the form as BUSINESSES by License Type and Business Name form.

T U T O R I A L 6

Creating Reports

Creating a Marketing Report at Vision Publishers

O B J E C T I V E S

In this tutorial you will:

- Create reports using Report Wizards
- Open and save a report
- Design and create a custom report
- Modify report controls and properties

CASE

Vision Publishers Harold Larson plans a meeting with several advertisers in New York for the special 25th-anniversary issue of *Business Perspective*. He asks Elena Sanchez to produce a report of all the articles and authors to help him describe their contents to potential advertisers.

Using a Report

A **report** is a formatted hardcopy of the contents of one or more tables from a database. Although you can print data from datasheets, queries, and forms, reports allow you the greatest flexibility for formatting hardcopy output. Reports can be used, for example, to print membership lists, billing statements, and mailing labels.

The Sections of a Report

Figure 6-1 shows a sample report produced from the Issue25 database.

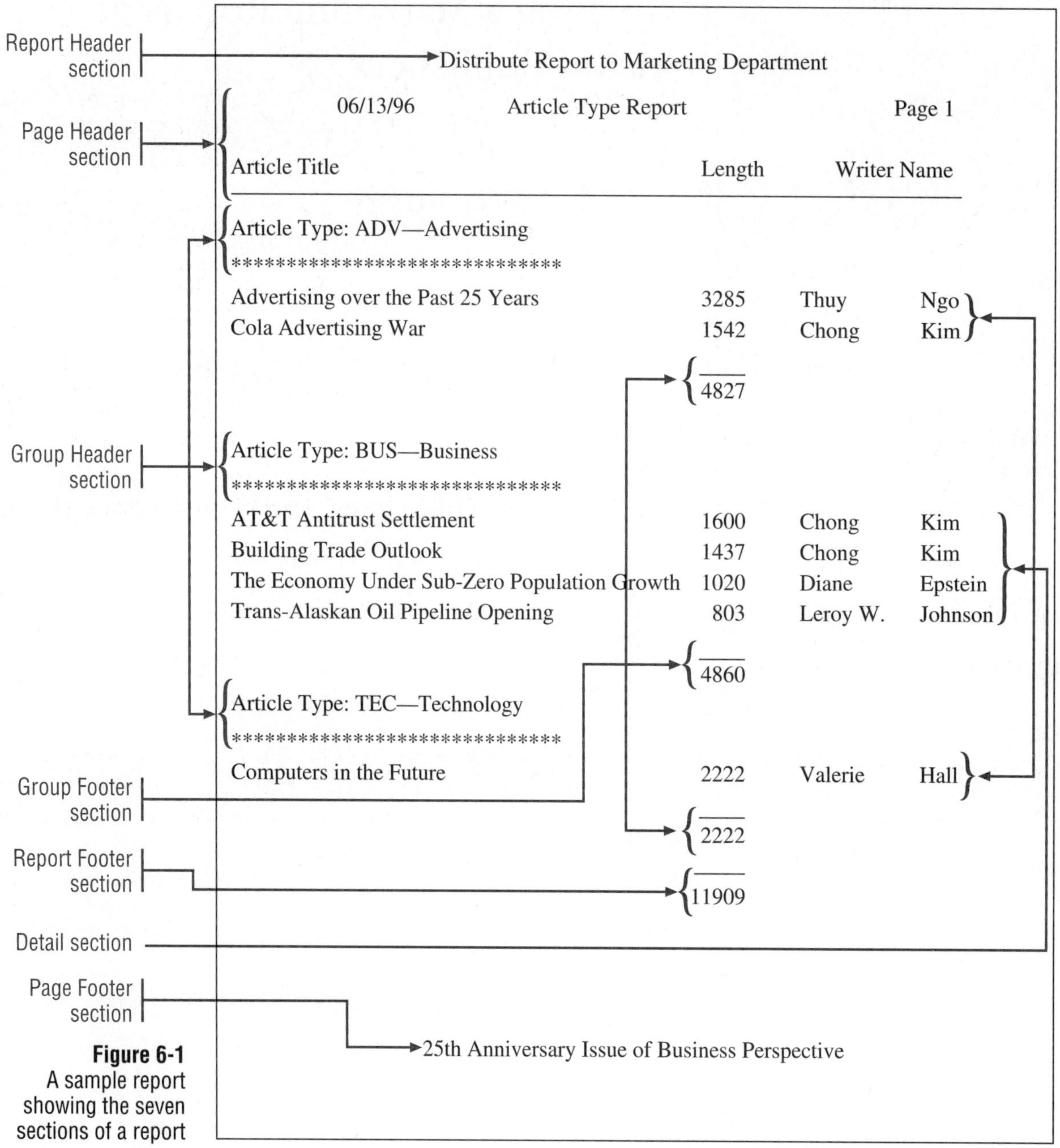
Report Header section
Distribute Report to Marketing Department
Page Header section
06/13/96
Article Type Report
Page 1
Article Title
Length
Writer Name
Article Type: ADV—Advertising
****
Advertising over the Past 25 Years 3285 Thuy Ngo
Cola Advertising War 1542 Chong Kim
4827
Group Header section
Article Type: BUS—Business
****
AT&T Antitrust Settlement 1600 Chong Kim
Building Trade Outlook 1437 Chong Kim
The Economy Under Sub-Zero Population Growth 1020 Diane Epstein
Trans-Alaskan Oil Pipeline Opening 803 Leroy W. Johnson
4860
Article Type: TEC—Technology
****
Computers in the Future 2222 Valerie Hall
Group Footer section
2222
Report Footer section
11909
Detail section
Page Footer section
25th Anniversary Issue of Business Perspective

Figure 6-1
A sample report showing the seven sections of a report

The report is divided into **sections**. Each Access report can have seven different sections, which are described in Figure 6-2. You do not need to use all seven report sections in a report. When you design your report, you determine which sections to use and what information to place in each section.

Report Section	Description
Report Header	Appears once at the beginning of a report. Use it for report titles, company logos, report introductions, and cover pages.
Page Header	Appears at the top of each page of a report. Use it for column headings, report titles, page numbers, and report dates. If your report has a Report Header section, it precedes the first Page Header section.
Group Header	Appears once at the beginning of a new group of records. Use it to print the group name and the field value that all records in the group have in common. A report can have up to 10 grouping levels.
Detail	Appears once for each record in the underlying table or query. Use it to print selected fields from the table or query and to print calculated values.
Group Footer	Appears once at the end of a group of records. It is usually used to print totals for the group.
Report Footer	Appears once at the end of the report. Use it for report totals and other summary information.
Page Footer	Appears at the bottom of each page of a report. Use it for page numbers and brief explanations of symbols or abbreviations. If your report has a Report Footer section, it precedes the Page Footer section on the last page of the report.

Figure 6-2
Descriptions of Access report sections

Elena has never created an Access report, so she first familiarizes herself with the Report Wizards tool.

Using Report Wizards

In Access, you can create your own report or use Report Wizards to create one for you. **Report Wizards** ask you a series of questions about your report requirements and then create a report based on your answers. Whether you use Report Wizards or create your own report, you can change a report design after it is created.

Access has seven different Report Wizards. Six of these Report Wizards are shown in Figure 6-3 on the following page.

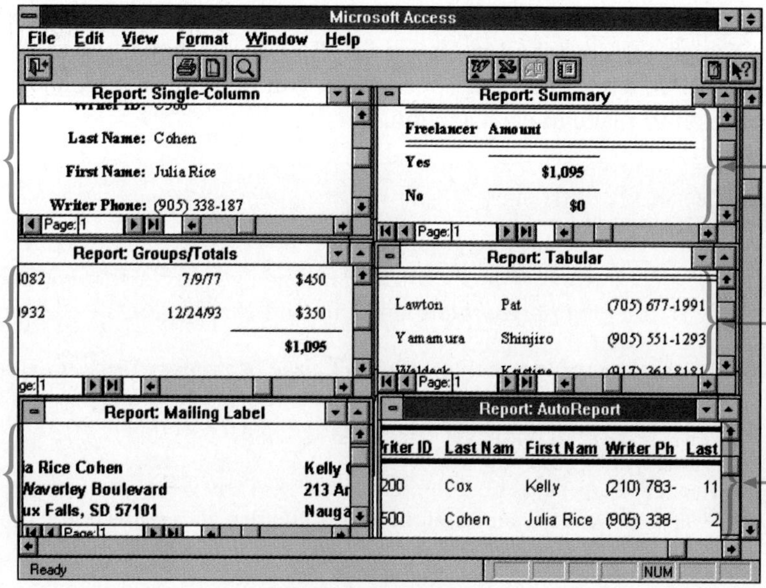

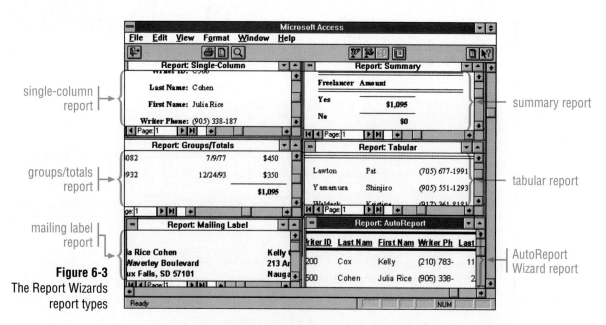

Figure 6-3
The Report Wizards report types

- A **single-column report** prints the fields, one to a line, vertically on the report. Table field names appear as labels to the left of the field values.
- A **groups/totals report** prints record and field values in a row-and-column format with the table field names used as column heads. You can group records according to field values and calculate totals for each group and for all groups. For example, Elena might create a groups/totals report that shows freelancers and then staff writers, with total payment amounts for freelancers, for staff writers, and for all writers.
- A **mailing label report** prints names and addresses that are positioned to fit your company's mailing label forms.
- A **summary report** organizes data into groups and prints both a subtotal for each group and a grand total for all the groups in a tabular format. No detail lines appear in a summary report.
- A **tabular report** prints field values in columns with field names at the top of each column. Each row is a separate record. It is like a groups/totals report, but does not contain totals.
- An **AutoReport Wizard report** is a single-column report of all the fields in the selected table or query. Access automatically produces an AutoReport without asking you questions.
- An **MS Word Mail Merge report** allows you to merge data from a table or query to a Microsoft Word for Windows 6.0 document. You can use the merged data to create form letters or envelopes, for example.

Report Wizards offer you a choice of three different report styles, as shown in Figure 6-4. The main difference between the **executive style** and the **presentation style** is the font in which the report is printed. The executive style uses the serif Times New Roman font, and the presentation style uses the sans serif Arial font. Use either style for the majority of your reports; they both produce easy-to-read text with ample open space. Because it packs more information into a page, the **ledger style** is suitable for long, detailed reports, such as financial reports, especially when they are intended for internal use.

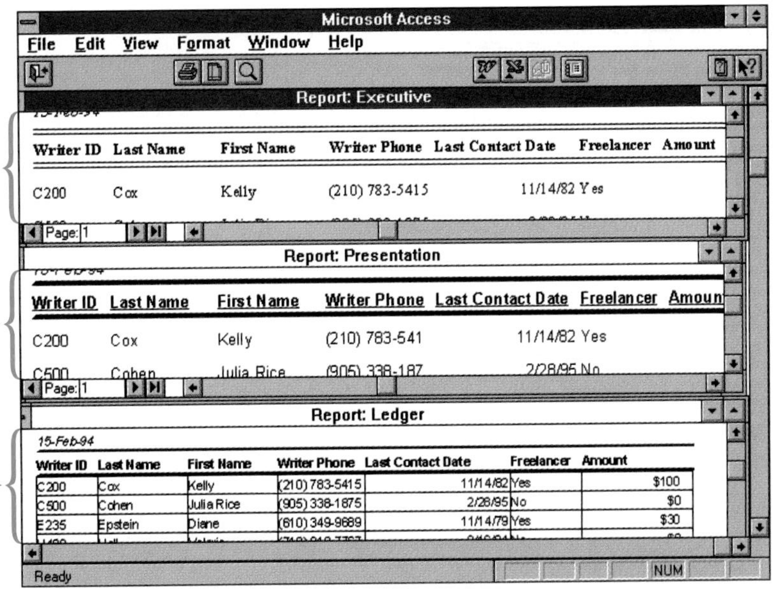

Figure 6-4
The Report Wizards report styles

Access has a set of Cue Cards you can use while working with reports. Although we will not use these Cue Cards in this tutorial, you might find they enhance your understanding of reports. At any time during this tutorial, select Design a Report or Mailing Labels from the Cue Card menu window to launch the appropriate Cue Cards.

Creating a Report Using the AutoReport Wizard

The quickest way to create a report is to use the toolbar AutoReport button, which launches the **AutoReport Wizard**. The AutoReport Wizard selects all the fields from the highlighted table or query in the Database window, creates a single-column report for these fields, and displays the report on the screen in the Print Preview window.

Elena uses the AutoReport Wizard to create a report containing all the fields from the TYPES table. If you have not done so, place your Student Disk in the appropriate drive, launch Access, and open the Issue25 database on your Student Disk.

To create a report using the AutoReport button:

❶ Click **TYPES** in the Tables list box. Access will place the fields from the TYPES table, which is now highlighted, into the report it creates when you click the toolbar AutoReport button.

❷ Click on the toolbar. Access creates a report that contains the two fields from the TYPES table and displays the report in the Print Preview window.

❸ You can use the vertical scroll bar buttons and the navigation buttons on the Print Preview window to view the entire report. See Figure 6-5 on the following page.

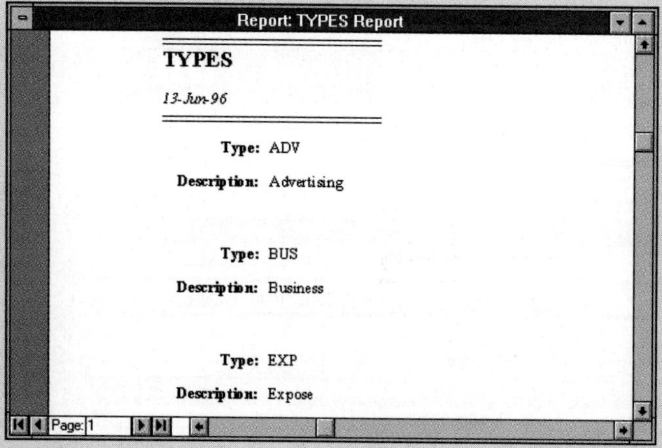

Figure 6-5
An AutoReport Wizard report in the Print Preview window

Saving a Report

After viewing the first several lines of the report based on the TYPES table in the Print Preview screen, Elena saves the report so that she and others can print it whenever they need an updated copy. She saves the report using the name TYPES Report and then closes the Print Preview window.

To save and close a new report:

1. Click **File** and then click **Save As...**. The Save As dialog box appears.
2. Type **TYPES Report** in the Report Name text box and then press **[Enter]**. The Save As dialog box disappears, and Access saves the report.
3. Double-click the Print Preview window **Control menu box**. The report disappears, and the Database window becomes the active window.

Creating Reports Using Report Wizards

Elena next uses Report Wizards to create a report containing all the fields from the WRITERS table. Because she wants space on the report to make notes, she chooses the single-column report type and the presentation style.

Creating Single-Column Reports

Let's use Report Wizards to create a single-column report in the presentation style.

To activate Report Wizards and select a report type:

1. Locate the toolbar New Report button. It is to the right of the New Form button and to the left of the Database Window button.
2. Click. The New Report dialog box appears. Click the Select A Table/Query **down arrow button** to display the list of the Issue25 database tables and queries. Scroll through the list if necessary and click **WRITERS** in the drop-down list box.

❸ Click the **Report Wizards button**. The first Report Wizards dialog box appears. See Figure 6-6. This dialog box displays the list of report types available through Report Wizards.

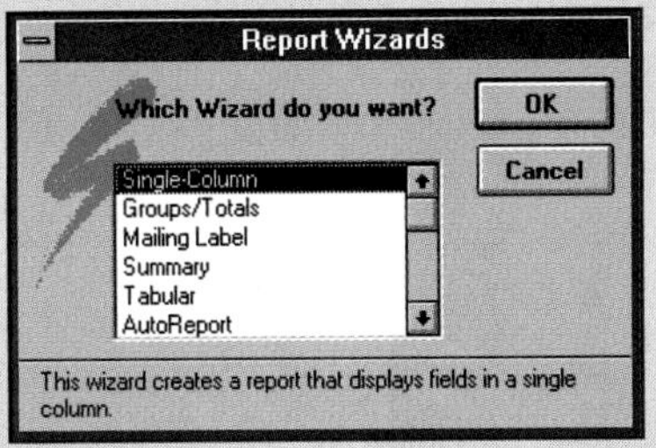

Figure 6-6
Choosing the report type

❹ If it is not already highlighted, click **Single-Column**, and then click the **OK button**. The first Single-Column Report Wizard dialog box appears.

In the first Single-Column Report Wizard dialog box, you select fields in the order you want them to appear on the report. Elena wants the report to contain all the fields in the WRITERS table in the order in which they appear in the table, and she wants Freelancer to be the primary sort key and Last Contact Date to be the secondary sort key. She will include the report title WRITERS by Last Contact Date Within Freelancer.

To finish creating a report using the Single-Column Report Wizard:

❶ Click the >> **button**. Access removes all the fields from the box on the left and places them in the same order in the box on the right.

❷ Click the **Next > button**. The second Single-Column Report Wizard dialog box appears. In this dialog box, you select the primary and secondary sort keys.

❸ Click **Freelancer** and then click the > **button**. Access moves the Freelancer field to the list box on the right, designating the Freelancer field as the primary sort key. Click **Last Contact Date** and then click the > **button**. Access moves the Last Contact Date field under the Freelancer field in the list box on the right, designating it as the secondary sort key. See Figure 6-7.

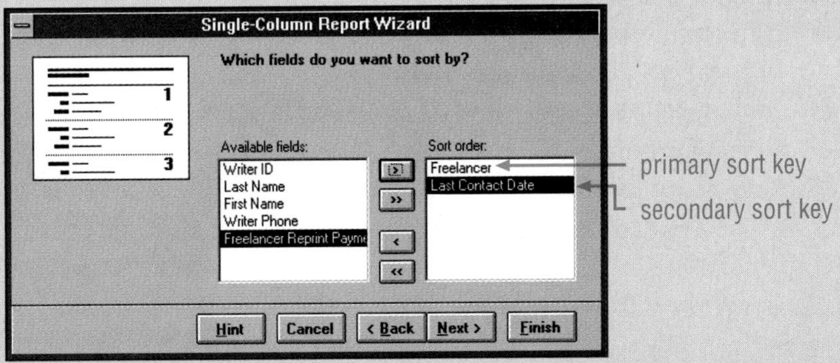

Figure 6-7
Selecting sort keys for a report

❹ Click the **Next > button**. The third Single-Column Report Wizard dialog box appears. In this dialog box, you choose the style for your report.

❺ If it is not already selected, click the **Presentation radio button**; then click the **Next > button**. Access displays the final Single-Column Report Wizard dialog box and shows the table name WRITERS as the default report title.

❻ To change the default report title that will appear at the beginning of the report, type **WRITERS by Last Contact Date Within Freelancer**. See Figure 6-8.

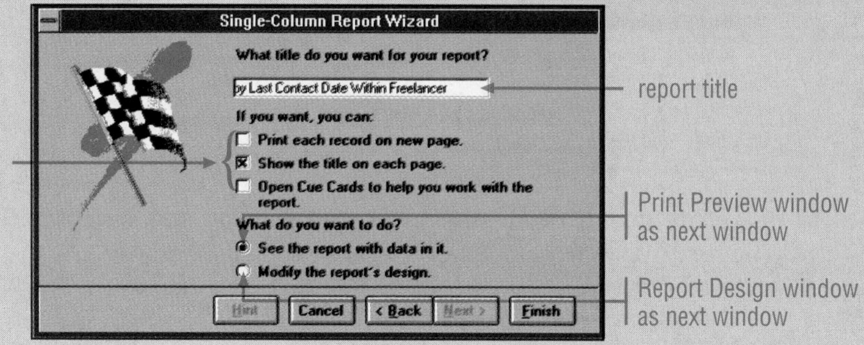

Figure 6-8 The last Single-Column Report Wizard dialog box

The three check boxes in the last Report Wizard dialog box let you do the following:

- Print each record on a new page
- Change the report title that prints once at the beginning of each report to a page title that prints on the top of each page
- Use Cue Cards

Printing the report title on each page is usually preferred, so make sure that the first and third boxes are unchecked and the second box is checked.

Previewing a Report

Now that she has made her report selections, Elena checks the overall report layout. She views the new report in the Print Preview window to see what the report will look like when it's printed.

To view a report in the Print Preview window:

❶ In the last Report Wizard dialog box, be sure that only the middle check box is checked and the top radio button is on.

❷ Click the **Finish button**. The Print Preview window opens, and Access displays the new report.

❸ Click the Print Preview window **maximize button**. See Figure 6-9.

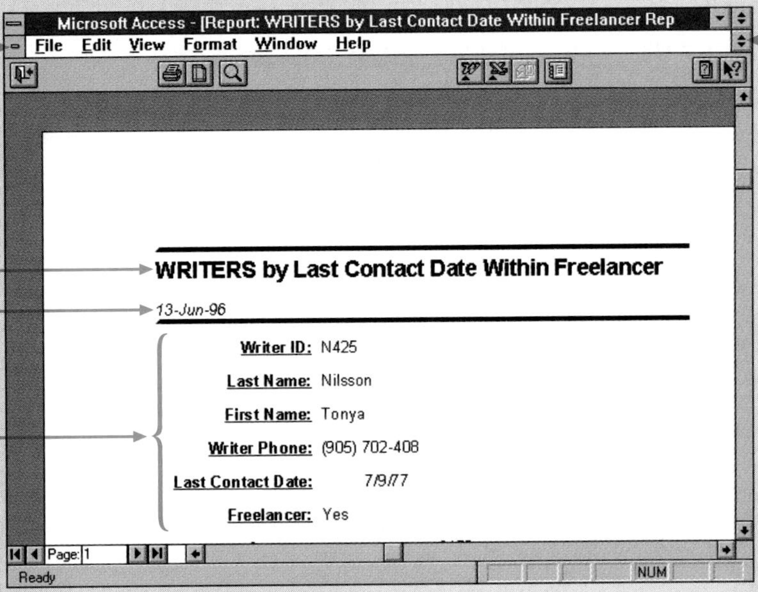

Figure 6-9 The completed report in the Print Preview window

Access displays the report title and current date at the top of the report page. These are preceded and followed by lines that serve to separate this section visually from the rest of the report page.

Below the title section, the record for the freelance writer having the earliest Last Contact Date in the WRITERS table appears as the first record on the report. You can use the vertical scroll bar and the navigation buttons to view the other records in the report.

Printing a Report

Next, Elena prints the first page of the report from the Print Preview window as a sample.

To print the first page of a report from the Print Preview window:

1. Make sure your printer is on line and ready to print. Click the toolbar **Print button** to open the Print dialog box.
2. Check the Printer section of the Print dialog box to make sure your computer's printer is selected.
3. Click the **Pages button** to choose the range of pages to print.
4. Type **1** in the From box, press **[Tab]**, and then type **1** in the To box.
5. Press **[Enter]** to initiate printing. After a printing dialog box appears briefly and then disappears, Access prints the first page of the report and returns you to the Print Preview window.

Elena saves the report as WRITERS by Last Contact Date Within Freelancer Report and then closes the Print Preview window.

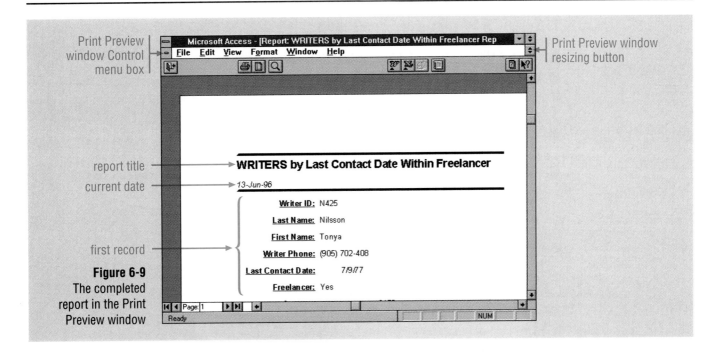

To save and close a new report:

1. Click **File**, and then click **Save As....** The Save As dialog box appears.
2. Type **WRITERS by Last Contact Date Within Freelancer Report** in the Report Name text box and then press **[Enter]**. The Save As dialog box disappears, and Access saves the report.
3. Double-click the Print Preview window **Control menu box**. The report disappears, and the Database window becomes the active window.
4. Click the **Report object button**. Access lists the two reports that have been created and saved. See Figure 6-10.

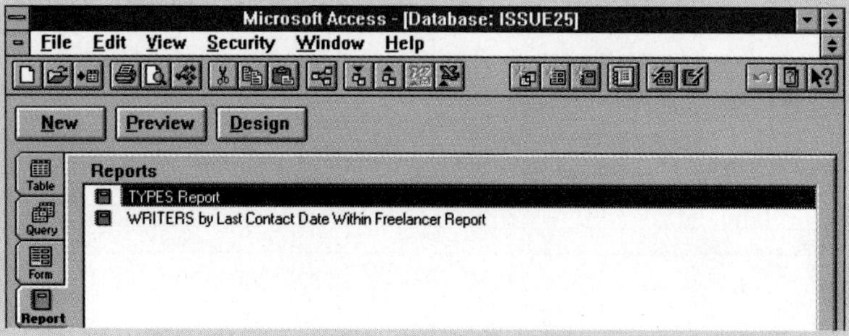

Figure 6-10
List of reports

Creating a Groups/Totals Report

After viewing, printing, and saving the single-column report, Elena decides that a groups/totals report of the same data would be more useful to her and her colleagues. A **group** is a set of records that share common values for one or more fields. Grouping records is a way for you to organize and sequence printed information. When you use a groups/totals report, you can select up to three different grouping fields. The first grouping field is the primary sort key, and any subsequent grouping fields are secondary sort keys.

Elena groups her report using the Freelancer field. This means that all the freelancer records will be printed first, then all the staff writer records. Because Access can print headers before each group and footers after each group, Elena's report includes a **Group Header section** that introduces each group and a **Group Footer section** that concludes each group. The Group Header section prints the value of the Freelancer field, and the Group Footer section prints the total of the Amount field values for the group. Elena's report also has a **Report Footer section** to print the grand total of the Amount field values for both groups.

When you create a groups/totals report, Access asks you to choose a grouping method for each grouping field. A **grouping method** uses either an entire field value or a portion of a field value upon which to base the record grouping process. **Normal grouping** uses the entire field value to group records and is the default grouping method. You can also base groups on a portion of a grouping field. For a date/time field, for example, you can group records based on the year, quarter, month, week, day, hour, or minute portions of the grouping field. For number or currency fields, you can group based on 10s, 50s, 100s, 500s, 1000s, 5000s, or 10000s. For text fields, you can group on the first character, first two characters, first three characters, first four characters, or first five characters. Because yes/no fields have just two values, normal grouping is the only possible option for them.

Elena again uses Report Wizards to create this report. Because the Report object button is selected, Elena can start creating the new report by clicking either the toolbar New Report button or the New command button.

To activate Report Wizards and create a groups/totals report:

1. Click the **New command button**. The New Report dialog box appears. Click the Select A Table/Query **down arrow button** to display the list of the Issue25 database tables and queries and scroll until WRITERS appears. Click **WRITERS** in the list box.
2. Click the **Report Wizards button**. Access displays the first Report Wizards dialog box, in which you select the report type.
3. Click **Groups/Totals** in the list box, and then click the **OK button**. Access displays the first Group/Totals Report Wizard dialog box, in which you select the fields for the report. Elena wants the report to contain all the WRITERS table fields in the order in which they appear in the table.
4. Click the **>> button**. Access removes all the fields from the box on the left and places them in the same order in the box on the right.
5. Click the **Next > button**. Access displays the second Group/Totals Report Wizard dialog box, in which you choose the grouping field. Elena groups the records from the WRITERS table by the Freelancer field.
6. Click **Freelancer** in the Available fields list box, and then click the **> button** to move it to the list box on the right. See Figure 6-11.

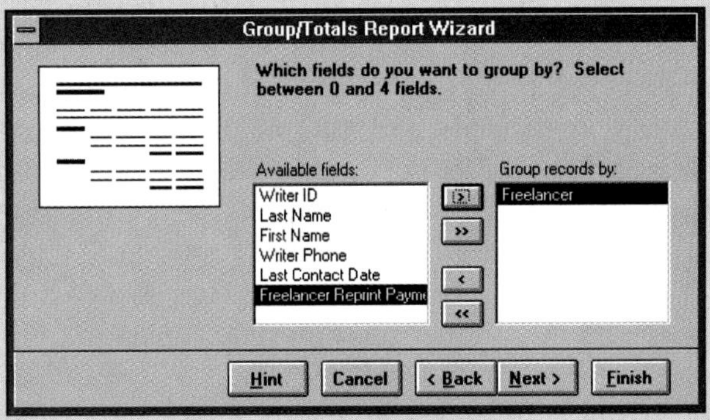

Figure 6-11
Selecting a field on which to group a report

7. Click the **Next > button**. Access displays the third Group/Totals Report Wizard dialog box, in which you select the grouping method. The only grouping choice for the yes/no Freelancer field is Normal. See Figure 6-12.

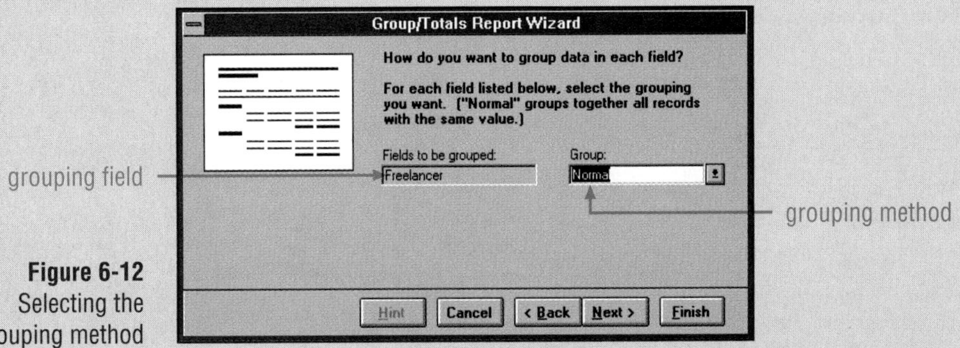

Figure 6-12
Selecting the grouping method

8. Click the **Next > button**. Access displays the next Group/Totals Report Wizard dialog box, in which you choose the report's sort keys.

Elena chooses Last Contact Date to be a sort key. Because the Freelancer field is a grouping field, Access uses it as the primary sort key and uses Last Contact Date as the secondary sort key.

To choose a report sort key:

1. Click **Last Contact Date** in the Available fields list box, and then click the **> button** to move it to the list box on the right.
2. Click the **Next > button**. Access displays the next Group/Totals Report Wizard dialog box, in which you choose the report style.
3. If it is not already selected, click the **Executive button**, and then click the **Next > button**. Access displays the final Group/Totals Report Wizard dialog box and shows the table name WRITERS as the default title that will appear at the beginning of the report. Elena changes the default report title.
4. Type **WRITERS With Freelancer Group Totals.**

In the final Group/Totals Report Wizard dialog box, Access displays three check boxes. Access uses the first check box, "See all the fields on one page," for reports that have too many columns to fit on one page using the standard column widths. If the box is checked, Access narrows the report columns so that all the fields can fit on one page. If the box is unchecked, Access prints multiple pages for groups of columns. You should check this option box unless you have so many fields that they cannot be read clearly when printed on one page.

Use the other two check boxes if you want to print percentages of the totals for each report group or if you want to use Cue Cards. Elena makes sure that the first box is checked and the other two are unchecked and then opens the Print Preview window to preview the report.

To finish and preview a groups/totals report:

1. Be sure that, in the final Group/Totals Report Wizard dialog box, the first check box is checked and the other two check boxes are unchecked. See Figure 6-13.

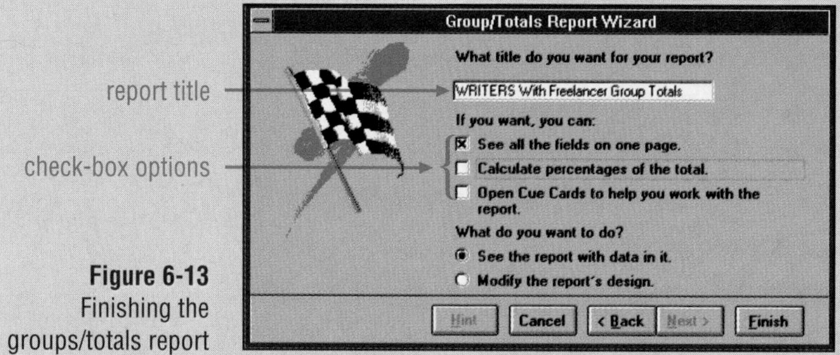

Figure 6-13
Finishing the groups/totals report

2. Click the **Finish button**. The Print Preview window opens, and Access displays the groups/totals report.

❸ Click the Print Preview window **maximize button**, click the **right arrow scroll button** three times, and then click the **down arrow scroll button** three times. See Figure 6-14.

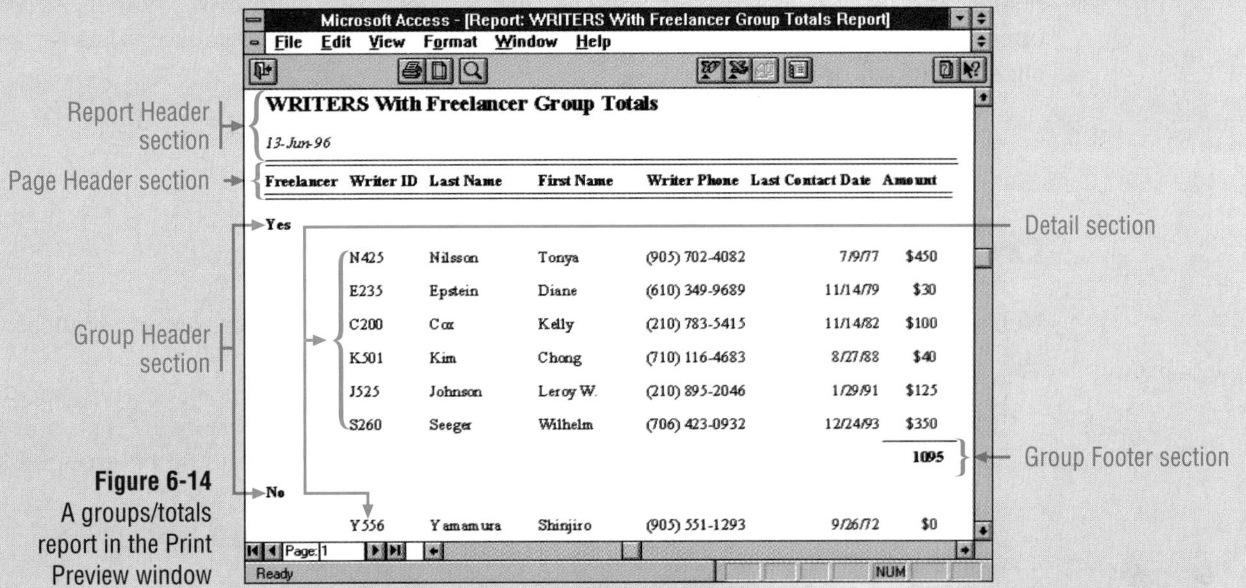

Figure 6-14
A groups/totals report in the Print Preview window

TROUBLE? If your screen display differs slightly from the one shown in Figure 6-14, click the scroll buttons to adjust your screen display.

Elena previews the rest of the report by using the down arrow scroll button.

To preview the end of a groups/totals report:

❶ Click the **down arrow scroll button** until you see the bottom of the first page of the report. If you do not see the grand totals at the end of the report, click the navigation **Next Record button** ▶ and click the **up arrow scroll button** until the grand totals are in view.

As she previews the report, Elena notices that it contains each of the seven different sections that a report can contain. Elena saves the groups/totals report and closes the Print Preview window.

To save and close a new report:

❶ Double-click the Print Preview window **Control menu box**. The "Save changes to 'Report1'" dialog box appears.

❷ Click the **Yes button**. The Save As dialog box appears.

❸ Type **WRITERS With Freelancer Group Totals Report** and then press **[Enter]**. The Save As dialog box disappears, Access saves the report, and the Database window becomes the active window.

If you want to take a break and resume the tutorial at a later time, you can exit Access by double-clicking the Microsoft Access window Control menu box. When you resume the tutorial, place your Student Disk in the appropriate drive, launch Access, open the Issue25 database on your Student Disk, maximize the Database window, and click the Report object button.

■ ■ ■

Creating a Custom Report

Elena and Harold discuss his report requirements and decide that the report should contain the following:

- A Detail section that lists the title, type, and length of each article, and the name of each writer. Records should appear in ascending order based on Type and in descending order based on Article Length, and the records should be grouped by the Type field value
- A Page Header section that shows the current date, report title, page number, and column headings for each field
- A Group Footer section that prints subtotals of the Article Length field for each Type group
- A Report Footer section that prints the grand total of the Article Length field

From her work with Report Wizards, Elena knows that Access places the report title and date in the Report Header section and the page number in the Page Footer section. Harold prefers all three items at the top of each page, so Elena needs to place that information in the Page Header section. To do this, Elena will create a custom report.

If you modify a report created by Report Wizards or if you design and create your own report, you have produced a **custom report**. You should create a custom report whenever Report Wizards cannot automatically create the specific report you need.

Designing a Custom Report

Before she creates the custom report, Elena designs the report's contents and appearance. Elena's completed design is shown in Figure 6-15.

The report title is Article Type Report. Descriptive column heads appear at the bottom of the Page Header section. The Page Header section also contains the current date and page number on the same line as the report title.

Elena indicates the locations and lengths of the field values by a series of X's. The three X's under the Type field label indicate that the field value will be three characters wide. The Type field value will appear only with the first record of a group.

The subtotals for each group and an overall total will appear in the report. The Article Length is the only field for which totals will appear.

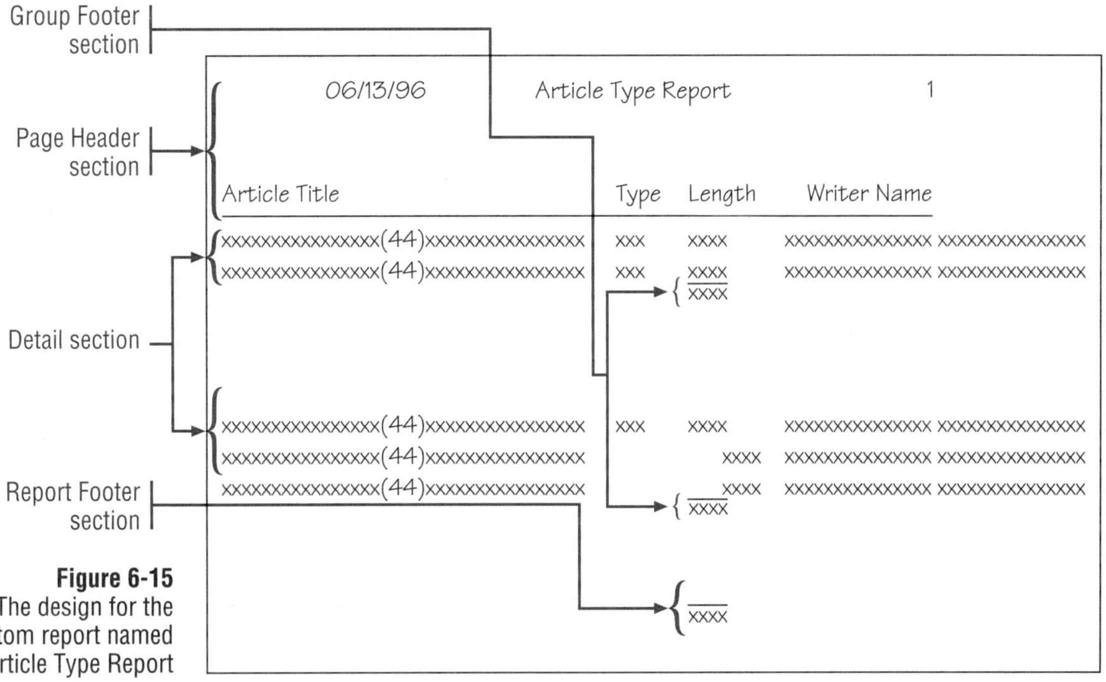

Figure 6-15
The design for the custom report named Article Type Report

Elena's report design contains four different report sections: the Page Header section, the Detail section, the Group Footer section, and the Report Footer section. Her report will not include Report Header, Group Header, or Page Footer sections.

The data for a report can come from either a single table or from a query based on one or more tables. Because Elena's report will contain data from the WRITERS and PAST ARTICLES tables, Elena must use a query for this report. She will use the Article Type Query because it contains the fields she needs from the two tables.

The Report Design Window

Elena could use Report Wizards to create a report based on the Article Type Query and then modify the report to match her report design. Report Wizards would construct the majority of the report, so Elena would save time and reduce the possibility for errors. However, Elena creates her custom report without using Report Wizards so that she can control the precise placement of fields and labels and become more skilled at constructing reports. Elena's first step is to create a blank report in the Report Design window. You use the **Report Design window** to create and modify reports.

REFERENCE WINDOW

Creating a Blank Report

- Click the toolbar New Report button. The New Report dialog box appears.
- Select the table or query you want to use for the new report and then click the Blank Report button. Access opens the Report Design window.

Elena creates a blank report based on the Article Type Query and opens the field list box.

To create a blank report in the Report Design window and open the field list box:

1. Click the toolbar **New Report button** to open the New Report dialog box.
2. Click the Select A Table/Query **down arrow button** to display the list of the Issue25 database tables and queries.
3. Click **Article Type Query** and then click the **Blank Report button**. The Report Design window appears.
4. Click the toolbar **Field List button**. The field list box appears. See Figure 6-16.

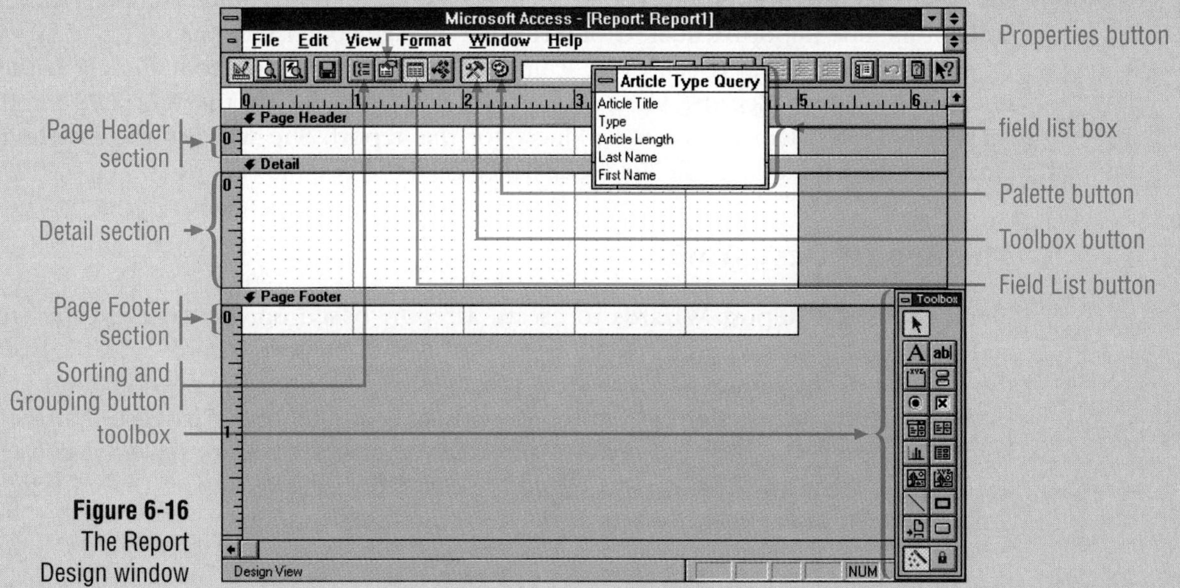

Figure 6-16 The Report Design window

TROUBLE? If the rulers, grid, or toolbox do not appear, click the View menu and then click Ruler, Grid, or Toolbox to display the missing component in the Report Design window. A check mark appears in front of these View menu commands when the components are displayed in the Report Design window. If the grid is still invisible, see your technical support person or instructor for assistance. If the Palette appears, click the View menu and then click Palette to close the Palette.

The Report Design window has several components in common with the Form Design window. The toolbar for both windows has a Properties button, a Field List button, and a Palette button. Both windows also have horizontal and vertical rulers, a grid, and a toolbox.

The Report Design window displays one new toolbar button, the Sorting and Grouping button. Recall that for a form you use a filter to display records in a specific order. In reports, you use the **Sorting and Grouping button** to establish sort keys and grouping fields. A maximum of 10 fields can serve as sort keys, and any number of them can also be grouping fields.

Unlike the Form Design window, which initially displays only the Detail section on a blank form, the Report Design window displays a Page Header section and a Page Footer section in addition to the Detail section. Reports often contain these sections, so Access automatically includes them in a blank report.

Adding Fields to a Report

Elena's first task is to add bound controls to the report Detail section for all the fields from the Article Type Query. You use bound controls to print field values from a table or query on a report. You add bound controls to a report the same way you added them to a form. In fact, every task you accomplished in the Form Design window is done in a similar way in the Report Design window.

To add bound controls for all the fields in the field list:

❶ If the toolbox Control Wizards tool is selected, click it to deselect it.

❷ Double-click the **field list title bar** to highlight all the fields in the Article Type Query field list.

❸ Click anywhere in the highlighted area of the field list and drag to the report Detail section. Release the mouse button when the is positioned at the top of the Detail section and at the 1.25" mark on the horizontal ruler. Access resizes the Detail Section and adds bound controls for the five selected fields. Each bound control consists of a text box and, to its left, an attached label. See Figure 6-17. Notice that the text boxes align at the 1.25" mark.

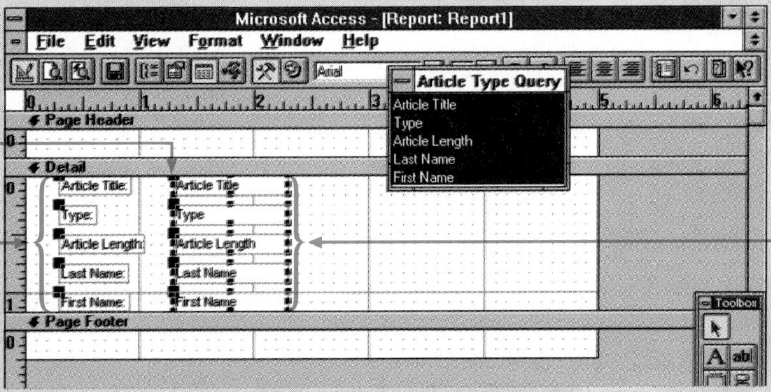

Figure 6-17 Adding bound controls to a report

TROUBLE? If you did not position the bound controls properly in the Detail section, click the Undo button immediately and then repeat the drag operation.

Performing operations in the Report Design window will become easier with practice. Remember, you can always click the Undo button immediately after you make a report design change that has undesired results.

You can also click the toolbar Print Preview button at any time to view your progress on the report and return to the Report Design window by clicking the toolbar Close Window button in the Print Preview window.

Selecting, Moving, Resizing, and Deleting Controls

Five text boxes now appear in a column in the Detail section. Each text box is a bound control linked to a field in the underlying query and has an attached label box to its left. Because she is done with the field list box, Elena closes it by clicking the toolbar Field List button. Elena next compares the report Detail section with her design and moves all the label boxes to the Page Header section. She then repositions the label boxes and text boxes so that they agree with her report design, shown in Figure 6-15.

To close the field list and move all label boxes to the Page Header section:

1. Click the toolbar **Field List button** to close the field list.
2. Click anywhere in the Page Footer section to deselect the five text boxes and their attached label boxes. While pressing and holding **[Shift]**, click each of the five label boxes in the Detail section. This action selects all the label boxes in preparation for cutting them from the Detail section and pasting them in the Page Header section.
3. With the positioned inside any one of the selected label boxes click the right mouse button to display the Shortcut menu.
4. Click **Cut** in the Shortcut menu. Access deletes the label boxes from the Detail section and places them in the Windows Clipboard. See Figure 6-18.

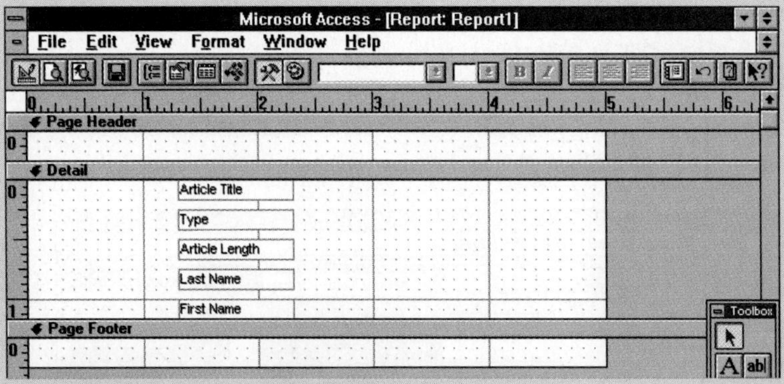

Figure 6-18 Label boxes cut from the Detail Section

TROUBLE? If you selected both the label boxes and the text boxes, click Undo and try again, selecting only the label boxes.

5. Click anywhere in the Page Header section, click the right mouse button in the Page Header section to open the Shortcut menu, and then click **Paste**. Access resizes the Page Header section and pastes all the label boxes from the Windows Clipboard into that section. See Figure 6-19.

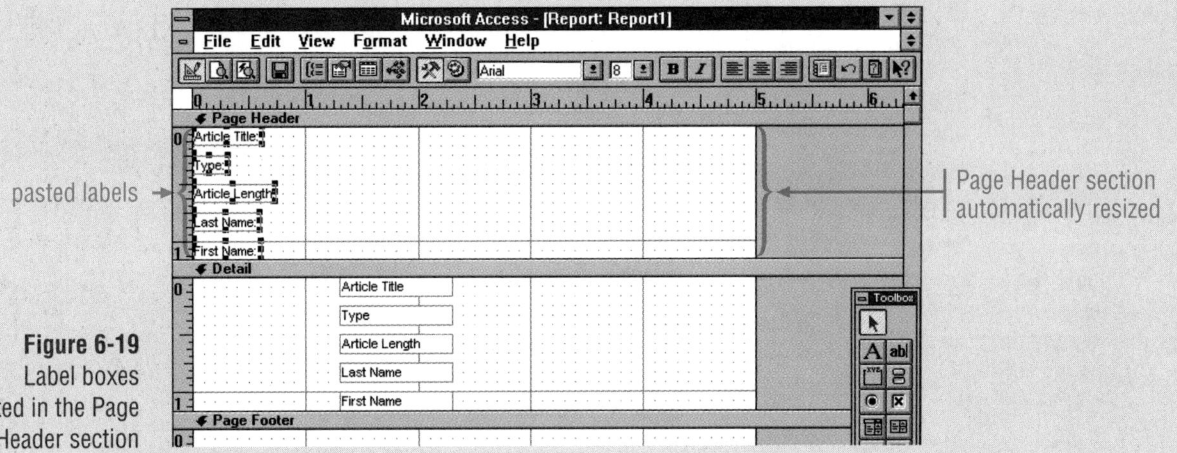

Figure 6-19 Label boxes pasted in the Page Header section

Moving the label boxes has unlinked them from their attached text boxes. You can now select and move either a label box or a text box, but not both at once.

Elena needs to reposition the text boxes and label boxes. She first drags the Article Title text box to the left into the corner of the Detail section and resizes it. She then moves and resizes the other four text boxes and resizes the Detail section.

To move and resize text boxes and resize the Detail section:

❶ Click the Article Title field-value **text box** in the Detail section, move the pointer to the move handle in the upper-left corner of the field-value text box, and click and drag the ☝ to the upper-left corner of the Detail section.

❷ Next, move the pointer to the middle sizing handle on the right side of the Article Title field-value text box. When the pointer changes to ↔, drag the right border horizontally to the right to the 2.5" mark on the horizontal ruler. See Figure 6-20.

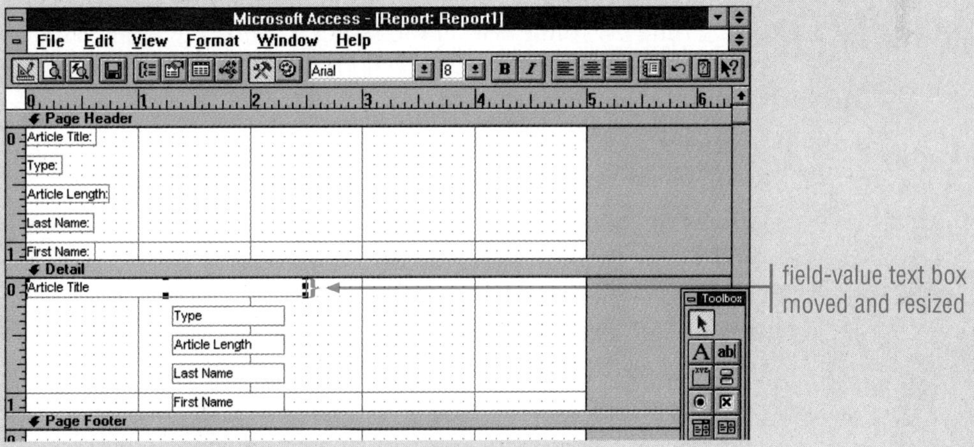

Figure 6-20 Moving and resizing a field-value text box

❸ Select each of the other four field-value text boxes in the Detail section, and move and resize them separately, following the report design. See Figure 6-21.

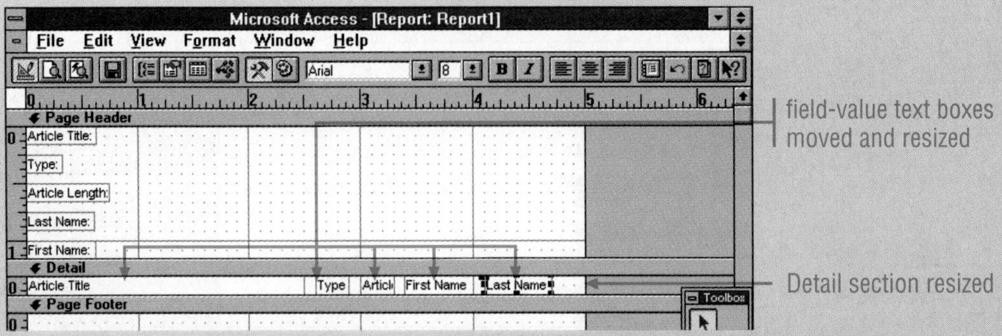

Figure 6-21 After moving and resizing all the field-value text boxes

❹ Move the pointer to the bottom edge of the Detail section. When the pointer changes to ‡, drag the bottom edge upward to align with the bottom of the field-value text boxes. See Figure 6-21. When the Detail section height is the same as the text-box height, the lines in the Detail section of the report will be single spaced.

TROUBLE? If Access widens the report too much while you are moving and resizing the text boxes, wait until you are finished with these operations and then reduce the width of the report. To reduce the report's width, start by moving the pointer to the right edge of the Detail section. When the pointer changes to ✛, drag the right edge to the left to narrow the report's width to 5".

Elena deletes the First Name label and changes the Caption property for all other labels in the Page Header section. She changes the Last Name Caption property to Writer Name and the Article Length Caption property to Length. She also deletes the colons in the Caption properties for the Article Title label and the Type label.

To delete a label and change label Caption properties:

❶ Click the First Name **label box** to select it. Click the First Name **label box** with the right mouse button to open the Shortcut menu and then click **Cut**. The First Name **label box** disappears.

❷ Click the Last Name **label box** to select it, and then click the toolbar **Properties button** ▣. The property sheet for the Last Name label appears.

❸ Click the **Caption text box** in the property sheet, press **[F2]** to select the entire value, and then type **Writer Name**.

❹ Click the Article Length **label box** to select it. The property sheet changes to show the properties for the Article Length field. Click the **Caption text box** in the property sheet, press **[F2]**, and then type **Length**.

❺ Click the Type **label box** to select it. Click near the end of the **Caption text box** in the property sheet and press **[Backspace]** to remove the colon from the caption.

❻ Click the Article Title **label box** to select it. Click near the end of the **Caption text box** in the property sheet and press **[Backspace]** to remove the colon from the caption.

❼ Click ▣ to close the property sheet.

After checking her report design, Elena resizes the Length and Writer Name label boxes and rearranges the label boxes in the Page Header section.

To resize and move labels:

❶ Click in an unoccupied area of the grid to deselect the Article Title **label box**. While holding **[Shift]**, click the Length **label box** and then click the Writer Name **label box** to select them.

❷ Click **Format**, click **Size**, and then click **to Fit**. Access resizes the two label boxes to fit around the captions. See Figure 6-22.

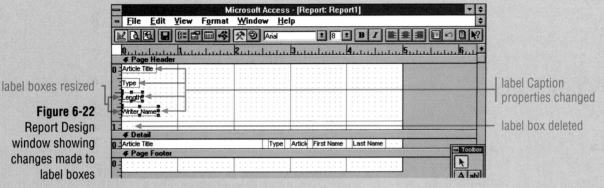

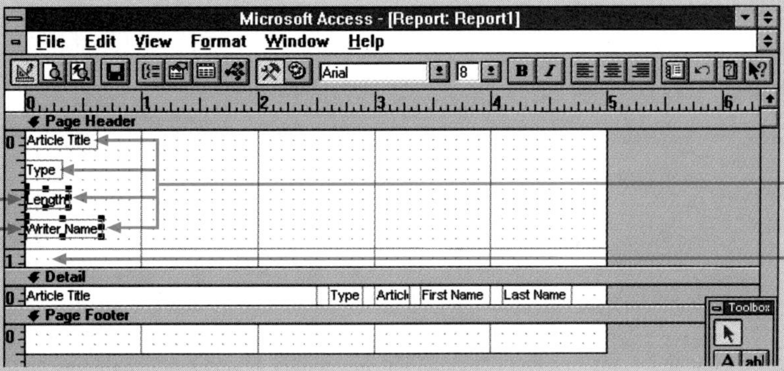

Figure 6-22 Report Design window showing changes made to label boxes

❸ Individually select and move each of the label boxes in the Page Header section, following the report design. See Figure 6-23.

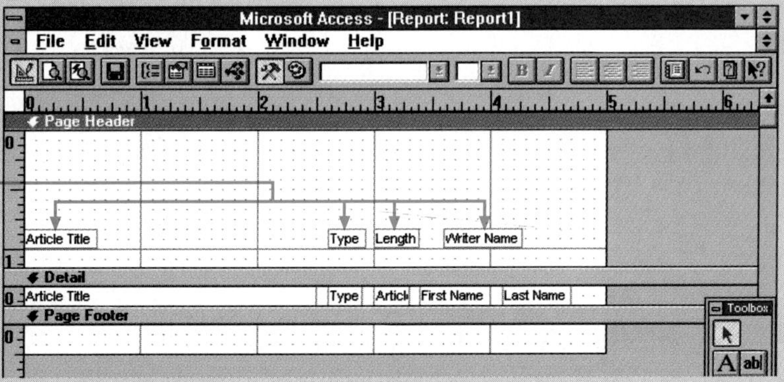

Figure 6-23 Label boxes positioned above their field-value text boxes

Adding a Title, Date, and Page Number to a Report

Elena's report design includes the title Article Type Report. She places this report title in the Page Header section using the toolbox Label tool.

To add a report title to the Page Header section:

❶ Click the toolbox **Label tool** A.

❷ Move the pointer into the Page Header section. As you move the pointer into the report, the pointer changes to $^{+}$A. Click the mouse button when the pointer's plus symbol (+) is positioned at the top of the Page Header section at the 2" mark on the horizontal ruler. The pointer changes to I.

❸ Type **Article Type Report** and then press **[Enter]**. See Figure 6-24.

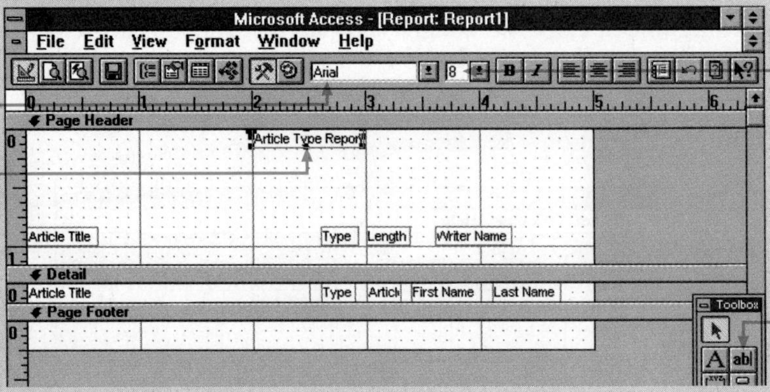

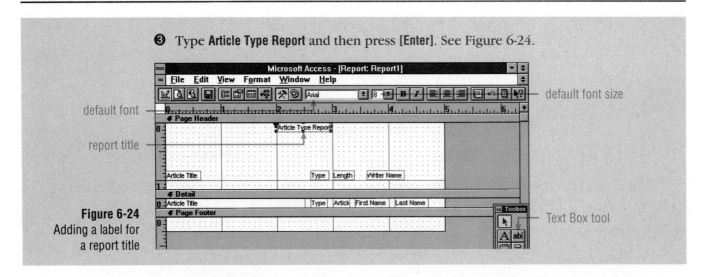

Figure 6-24
Adding a label for a report title

Elena increases the report title font size from 8, the default, to 10 (the default typeface is Arial), and adds a text box to the Page Header section. Here she will insert the Date function. You use the toolbar **Text Box tool** to add a text box with an attached label to a report or form. Text boxes are mostly used to contain bound controls or calculated controls. You use the **Date function**, which is a type of calculated control, to print the current date on a report. Let's do this now.

To change font size and use the Text Box tool to add the Date function:

❶ Click the Font Size **down arrow button** and click **10**. Access changes the font size of the report title from 8 to 10. The text box is now too small to display the entire report title. The text box needs to be resized and recentered in the Page Header section.

❷ Resize the height and width of the report title **text box**, so that the entire report title is visible. Next, move the report title text box one grid mark to the left, so it is centered in the Page Header section.

❸ Click the toolbar **Text Box tool** abl. Move the pointer into the Page Header section. As you move the pointer into the report, the pointer changes to +abl. Click the mouse button when the pointer's plus symbol is positioned at the top of the Page Header section just to the right of the .75" mark on the horizontal ruler. Access adds a text box with an attached label box to its left. Inside the text box is the description Unbound.

❹ Click the Unbound **text box**, type **=Date()**, and then press **[Enter]**. See Figure 6-25.

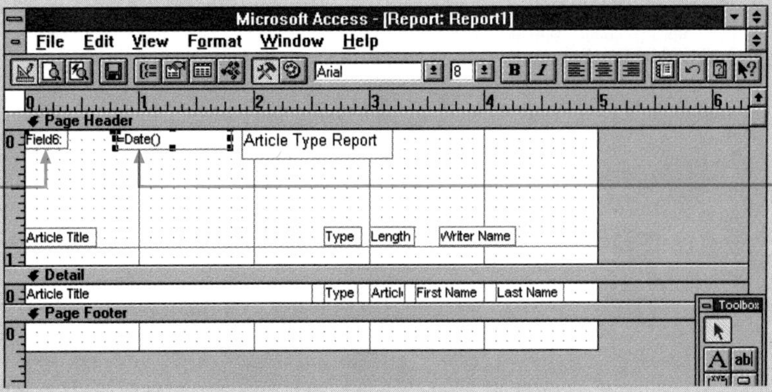

Figure 6-25
Adding the current date to a report

TROUBLE? If your text box and attached label box are too close together, resize and reposition the text box using Figure 6-25 as a guide. Also, the attached label box on your screen might have a Caption other than Field6. This causes no problem.

When Access prints your report, the current date replaces the Date function you entered in the Unbound text box. Because a current date in a Page Header section does not usually need a label, Elena deletes the label box. She then changes the Date text box to font size 10 and moves it to the upper-left corner of the Page Header section. Finally, Elena uses the Text Box tool to add the Page property to the upper-right corner of the Page Header section. The **Page property** automatically prints the correct page number on each page of a report.

To finish formatting the current date and add a page number in the Page Header section:

1. Click the Date **label box**, which is located in the upper-left corner of the Page Header section. Click the Date **label box** with the right mouse button to open the Shortcut menu and then click **Cut** to delete the label.
2. Click the Date **text box** and then drag its move handle to the upper-left corner of the Page Header section.
3. Click the Font Size **down arrow button** and click **10** to change the font size of the Date text box.
4. Click the toolbox **Text Box tool** [abl]. Move the pointer into the Page Header section. The mouse pointer changes to +[abl]. Click the mouse button when the pointer's plus symbol is positioned at the top of the Page Header section at the 4.5" mark on the horizontal ruler. Access adds an Unbound text box with an attached label box to its left.
5. Click the label box with the right mouse button to open the Shortcut menu, and then click **Cut**. The label box disappears.
6. Click the Unbound text box, type **=Page**, press **[Enter]**, click the Font Size **drop-down list box down arrow button**, and then click **10**. See Figure 6-26 on the following page.

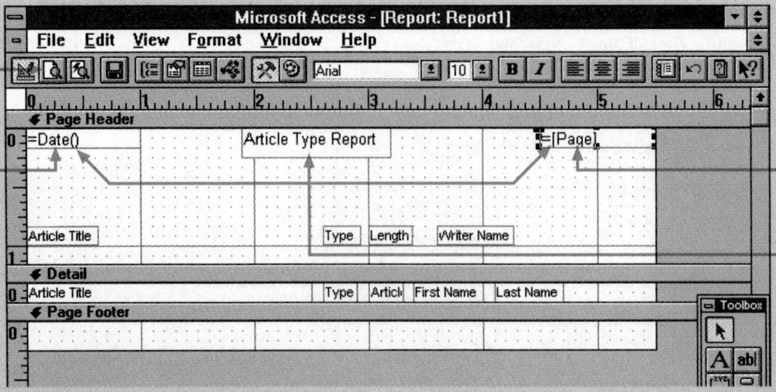

Figure 6-26
Date function and Page property added to the Report Design Window

❼ Move the mouse pointer to the middle sizing handle on the right side of the Page text box. The pointer changes to ↔. Click and drag to the left to the 5" mark on the horizontal ruler.

❽ Move the mouse pointer to the right edge of the Page Header section. When the pointer changes to ✥, click and drag to the left to the 5" mark on the horizontal ruler.

Elena switches to the Print Preview window. She wants to check the report against her design.

To view a report in the Print Preview window:

❶ Click the toolbar **Print Preview button** to open the Print Preview window. See Figure 6-27.

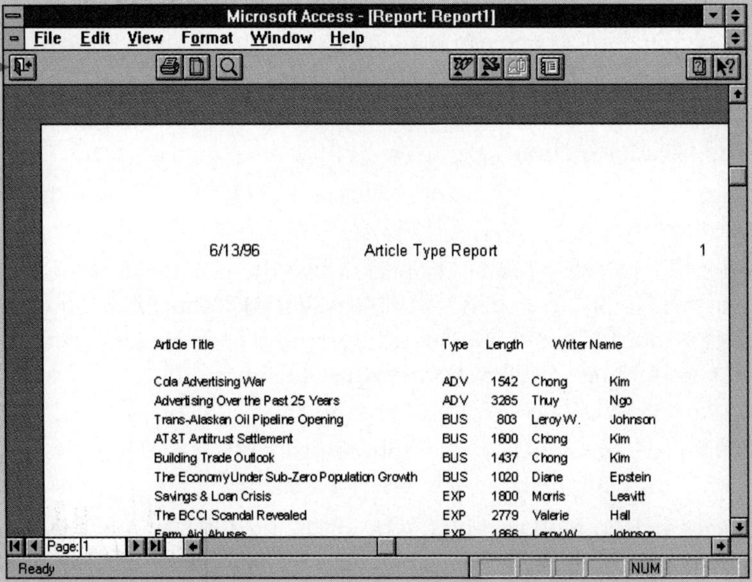

Figure 6-27
A custom report in the Print Preview window

TROUBLE? If your report shows a gap between the first and second records in the Detail section, you need to reduce the height of the Detail section. The bottom of the Detail section should align with the bottom of the text boxes in that section. Reduce the height during the next series of steps.

Adding Lines to a Report

Elena adds a horizontal line to the Page Header section below the column heads. Before doing this, she repositions the column heading labels just below the report title line and decreases the height of the Page Header section.

To move labels and decrease the Page Header section height:

1. Click the toolbar **Close Window button** to return to the Report Design window.
2. While pressing and holding **[Shift]**, click each of the four label boxes in the Page Header section to select them. Click one of the label boxes when the pointer changes to and drag the label boxes straight up so they are positioned just below the report title. Position the labels so that the top of each label box is at the .25" mark on the vertical ruler.

   TROUBLE? If the label boxes do not move, the Page text box is probably selected along with the label boxes. Click in any unoccupied portion of the Page Header section to deselect all boxes, then repeat Step 2.
3. Move the pointer to the bottom edge of the Page Header section. When the pointer changes to ‡, drag the bottom edge upward to reduce the height of the Page Header section. Align the bottom edge with the grid marks that are just below the .5" mark on the vertical ruler.

Elena now adds a medium-thick horizontal line to the bottom of the Page Header section. You use the **toolbox Line tool** to add a line to a report or form.

To add a line to a report:

1. Click the toolbox **Line tool** . Move the pointer into the Page Header section; the pointer changes to +\. Position the Pointer's plus symbol at the left edge of the Page Header section and at the .5" mark on the vertical ruler.

   TROUBLE? If the toolbox is too low for you to see the Line tool, drag the toolbox title bar straight up until the Line tool is visible.
2. Click and hold the mouse button, drag a horizontal line from left to right ending just after the 4.25" mark on the horizontal ruler, and then release the mouse button.
3. To increase the thickness of the line, click the toolbar **Properties button** . The property sheet appears. The Border Width property controls the line's width, or thickness.
4. Click the **Border Width text box** in the property sheet, click the **down arrow button** that appears, and then click **3 pt**. The line's width increases. See Figure 6-28 on the following page.

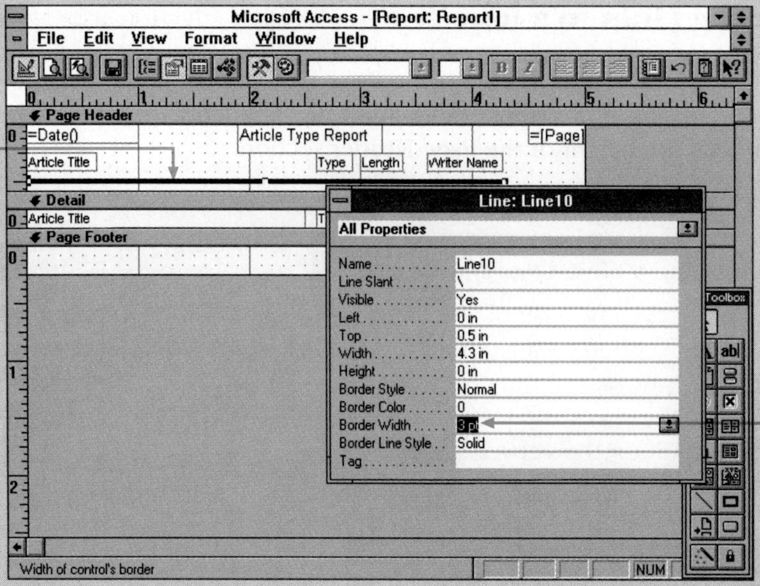

Figure 6-28 Changing the width of a line

❺ Click [button] to close the property sheet.

Elena has finished her design of the Page Header section. She next chooses the sort fields and the grouping field for the report.

Sorting and Grouping Data in a Report

Elena wants Access to print records in ascending order based on the Type field and to print subtotals for each set of Type field values. Thus, the Type field is both the primary sort key and the grouping field. Elena wants the records within a Type to be printed in descending order based on the Article Length field. This makes Article Length the secondary sort key. Because Elena does not want subtotals for each Article Length value, Article Length is not a grouping field.

You use the toolbar **Sorting and Grouping button** to select sort keys and grouping fields. Each report can have up to 10 sort fields, and any of the 10 sort fields can also be grouping fields.

To select sort keys and grouping fields:

❶ Click the toolbar **Sorting and Grouping button** [button]. The Sorting and Grouping dialog box appears.

❷ Click the **down arrow button** in the first Field/Expression box in the Sorting and Grouping dialog box and then click **Type**. Ascending is the default sort order in the Sort Order box.

❸ Click anywhere in the second Field/Expression box in the Sorting and Grouping dialog box, click the **down arrow button** that appears, and then click **Article Length**. Ascending, the default sort order, needs to be changed to Descending in the Sort Order box.

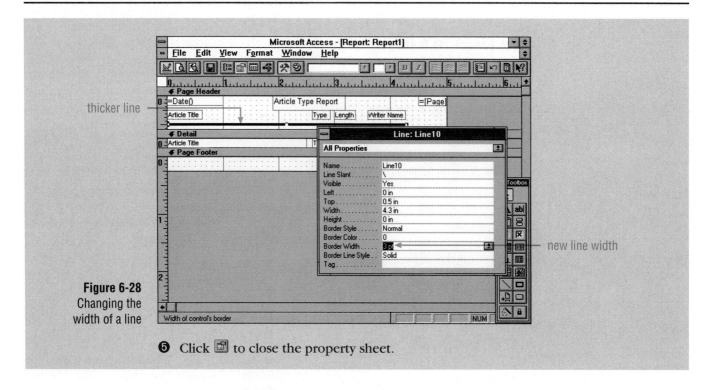

❹ Click anywhere in the second Sort Order box, click the **down arrow button** that appears, and then click **Descending**. See Figure 6-29.

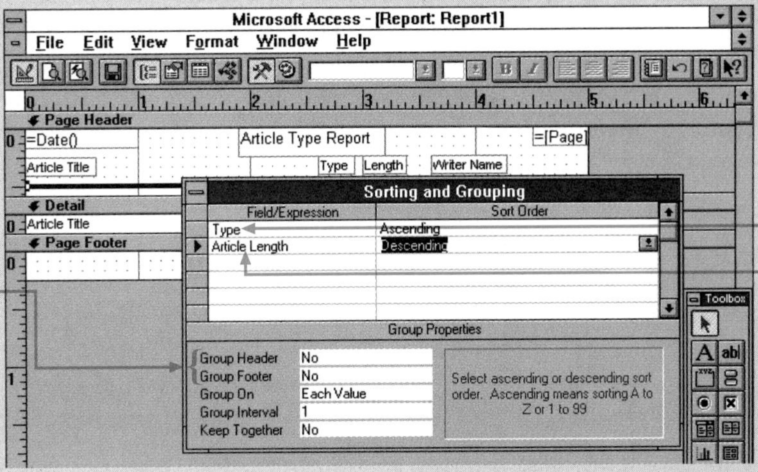

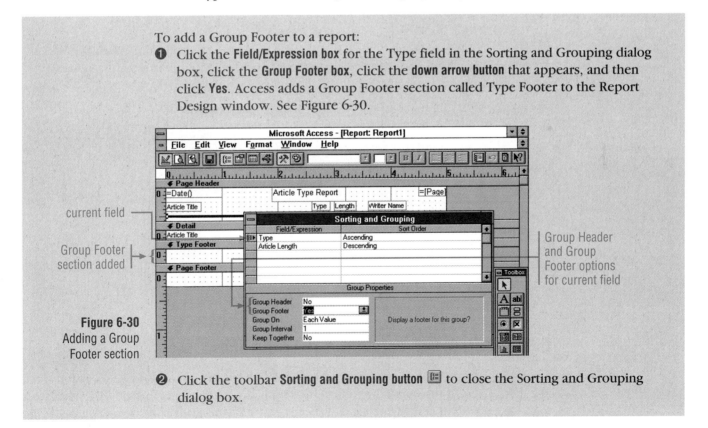

Figure 6-29
The Sorting and Grouping dialog box

Elena notices that adding the two sort keys did not cause any new sections to be added to the report. To add a Group Footer, she must choose the Group Footer option for the Type field in the Sorting and Grouping dialog box.

To add a Group Footer to a report:

❶ Click the **Field/Expression box** for the Type field in the Sorting and Grouping dialog box, click the **Group Footer box**, click the **down arrow button** that appears, and then click **Yes**. Access adds a Group Footer section called Type Footer to the Report Design window. See Figure 6-30.

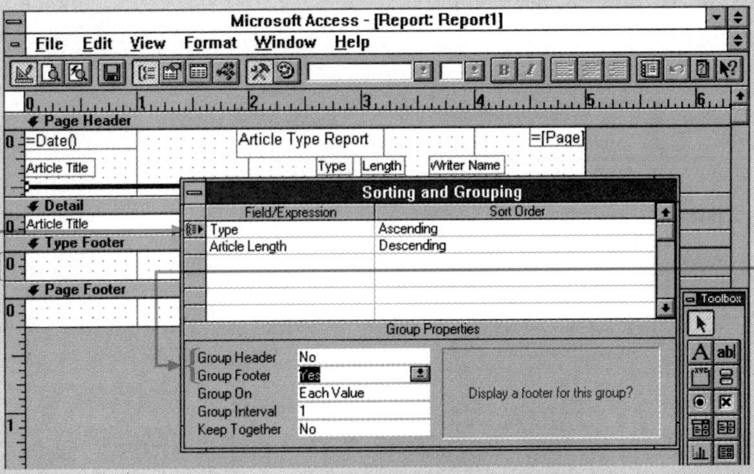

Figure 6-30
Adding a Group Footer section

❷ Click the toolbar **Sorting and Grouping button** to close the Sorting and Grouping dialog box.

Adding a Report Header and Footer

Elena compares her progress against her report design again and sees that she is almost done. She next adds a Report Footer section to her report. To add this new section, Elena adds the Report Header and Footer sections to the report. Because she does not need the Report Header section, she deletes it. She also deletes the Page Footer section that was automatically included when the Report Design window was opened.

REFERENCE WINDOW

Adding Report Header and Footer Sections

- Click Format, then click Report Header/Footer. Access adds a Report Header section and a Report Footer section to the report.

Let's add Report Header and Footer sections to the report and then delete the Page Footer section.

To add and delete sections from a report:

1. Click **Format** and then click **Report Header/Footer**. Access creates a Report Header section at the top of the report and a Report Footer section at the bottom of the report.
2. Move the pointer to the bottom edge of the Report Header section. When the pointer changes to ‡, drag the bottom edge upward until the section disappears. Repeat this process for the Page Footer section. See Figure 6-31.

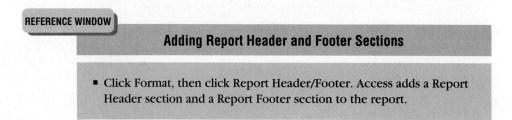

sections resized to zero

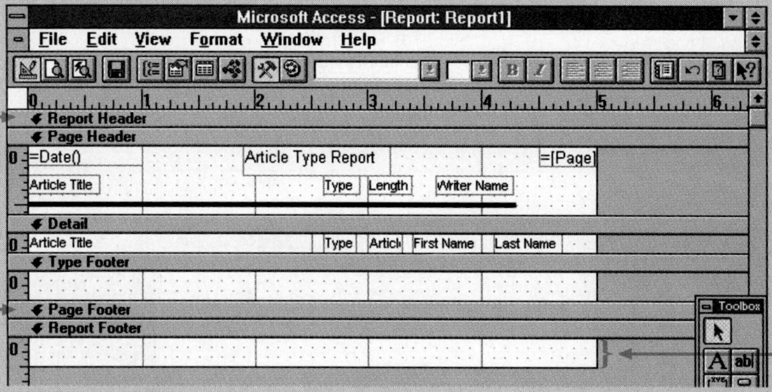

Report Footer section added

Figure 6-31 Adding and deleting report sections

Calculating Group Totals and Overall Totals

Elena wants the report to print subtotals for each Type group and an overall grand total. She adds calculations to produce these totals for the Article Length field. To calculate a total for a group of records or for all records, you use the **Sum function**. You place the Sum function in a Group Footer section to print a group total and in the Report Footer section to print an overall total. The format for the Sum function is =Sum([field name]). When you enter the function, you replace "field name" with the name of the field you want to sum. Use the toolbox Text Box tool to create appropriate text boxes in the footer sections.

In the Type Footer and Report Footer sections, Elena adds text boxes, deletes the attached labels for both, and adds the Sum function to each text box. She also draws lines above each Sum function so that the totals will be visually separated from the Detail section field values.

To add text boxes to footer sections and delete labels:

1. Increase the height of the Type Footer section so that you see four rows of grid dots, and increase the height of the Report Footer section so that you see three rows of grid dots.
2. Click the toolbox **Text Box tool**. Move the pointer into the Type Footer section. Click the mouse button when the pointer's plus symbol is positioned in the second row of grid lines and vertically aligned with the right edge of the Type field-value text box. Access adds a text box with an attached label box to its left.
3. Click. Move the pointer into the Report Footer section. Click the mouse button when the pointer's plus symbol is positioned in the second row of grid lines and vertically aligned with the right edge of the Type field-value text box. Access adds a text box with an attached label box to its left. See Figure 6-32.

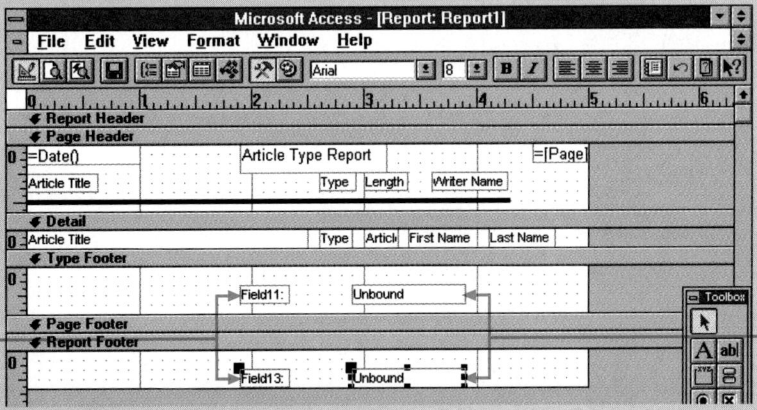

Figure 6-32
Adding text boxes in footer sections

4. Click anywhere in the Type Footer section, outside both boxes to deselect all boxes.
5. While you press and hold **[Shift]**, click the label box in the Type Footer section, and then click the label box in the Report Footer section. You have selected both boxes.
6. Click either label box with the right mouse button to open the Shortcut menu and then click **Cut**. The two label boxes disappear.

Elena now adds the Sum function to the two footer section text boxes.

To add the Sum function to calculate group and overall totals:

1. Click the text box in the Type Footer section, type **=Sum([Article Length])**, and then press **[Enter]**. The text box in the Type Footer section needs to be narrower.
2. Click the middle **sizing handle** on the right side of the text box and drag it to the left until the right edge of the box lines up with the right edge of the Article Length field-value text box in the Detail section.

❸ Click the text box in the Report Footer section, type **=Sum([Article Length])**, and then press **[Enter]**. See Figure 6-33.

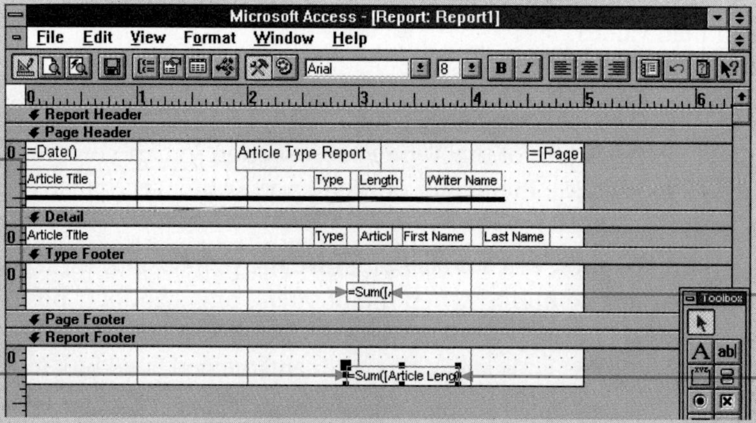

Figure 6-33
Adding a group total and overall total

❹ To resize the text box in the Report Footer section, click the middle **sizing handle** on the right side of the text box and drag it to the left until the right edge of the box lines up with the right edge of the Article Length field-value text box in the Detail section.

Elena next adds lines above each Sum function.

To add lines above totals:

❶ Click the toolbox **Line tool** . Move the pointer into the Type Footer section; the pointer changes to +\. Position the pointer's plus symbol in the top row of grid lines and vertically align it with the right edge of the Type field-value text box in the Detail section above.

❷ Click and hold the mouse button, and drag a horizontal line to the right until the right end of the line is below the right edge of the Article Length field-value text box.

❸ Repeat Steps 1 and 2 for the Report Footer section. See Figure 6-34.

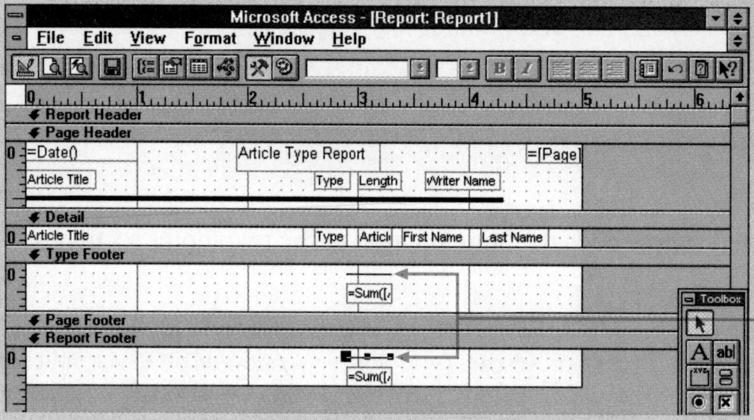

Figure 6-34
Adding horizontal lines above group and overall totals

Elena's report is almost finished. There is, however, still one change she can make to improve its appearance.

Hiding Duplicate Values in a Group Report

Elena's final change is to display the Type value only in the first record in a group. Within a group, all Type field values are the same, so if you display only the first one, you simplify the report and make it easier to read.

To hide duplicate values:

1. Click the Type **text box** in the Detail section and then click the toolbar **Properties button**. The property sheet for the Type field appears.
2. If necessary, scroll through the property sheet, then click the **Hide Duplicates text box** in the property sheet, click the **down arrow button**, and click **Yes**. See Figure 6-35.

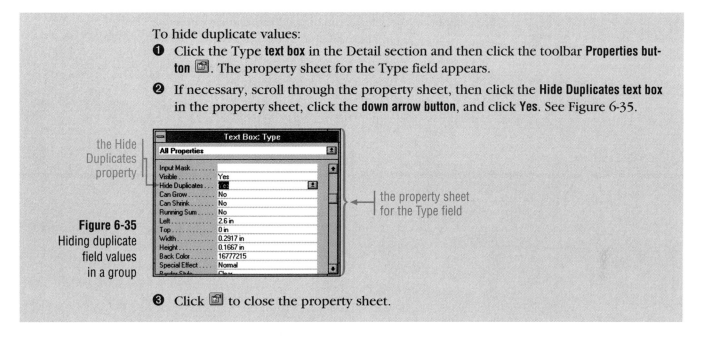

the Hide Duplicates property

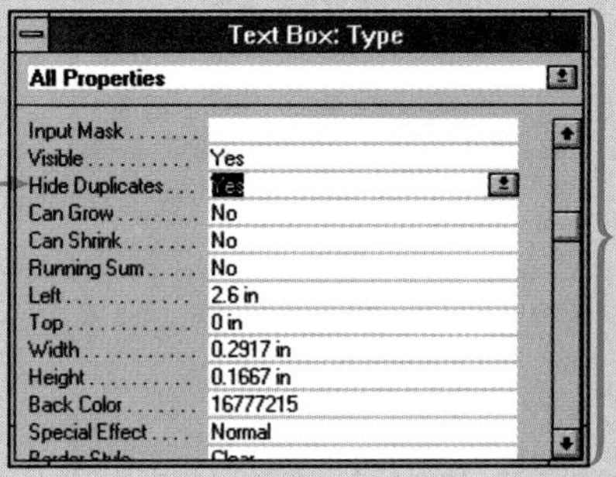

the property sheet for the Type field

Figure 6-35 Hiding duplicate field values in a group

3. Click the Properties button to close the property sheet.

Elena views the report in the Print Preview window and then saves the report.

To view and save a report:

1. Click the toolbar **Print Preview button**. Access displays the first page of the report. See Figure 6-36.

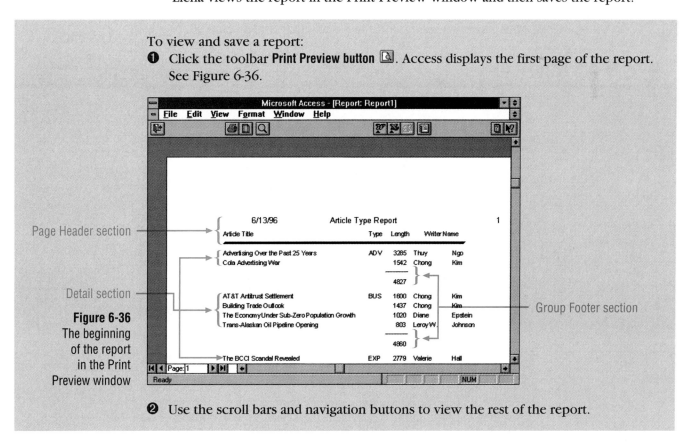

Page Header section

Detail section

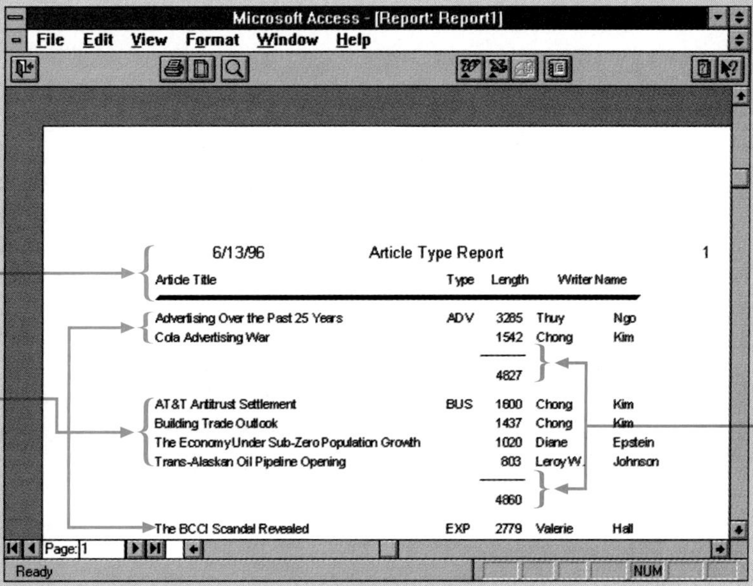

Group Footer section

Figure 6-36 The beginning of the report in the Print Preview window

2. Use the scroll bars and navigation buttons to view the rest of the report.

3. Double-click the Print Preview window **Control menu box**. The "Save changes to 'Report1'" dialog box appears.
4. Click the **Yes button**. The dialog box disappears, and Access displays the Save As dialog box.
5. Type **Article Type Report** in the Report Name text box and then press **[Enter]**. Access saves the custom report, closes the dialog box, and activates the Database window.

■ ■ ■

Elena exits Access and brings her report to Harold.

Questions

1. What are the seven Access report sections, and when is each printed?
2. What types of reports can the Report Wizards tool create?
3. What three different styles does Report Wizards offer you?
4. What is a group?
5. What is normal grouping?
6. What is a custom report?
7. When do you use the toolbox Text Box tool?
8. What do you type in a text box to tell Access to print the current date?
9. What do you type in a text box to tell Access to print the page number?
10. How do you add a Report Footer section to a report without adding a Report Header section?
11. Why might you want to hide duplicate values in a group report?

Tutorial Assignments

Elena uses Report Wizards to create a report named PAST ARTICLES Report for the Issue25 database. Launch Access, open the Issue25 database on your Student Disk, and do the following:

1. Use Report Wizards to create a groups/totals report based on the PAST ARTICLES table. Use the executive style for the report. Select all the fields from the table in the order in which they are stored in the table, group the records by Writer ID, select Normal grouping, select no sort key fields, check the "Calculate percentages of the total" box, and enter PAST ARTICLES Report as the report title.
2. Display the report in the Print Preview window and then print the last report page.
3. Save the report, naming it PAST ARTICLES Report, and return to the Database window.

Elena next creates a custom report. Use the Issue25 database on your Student Disk to do the following. Use the report shown in Figure 6-14 as a basis for your report design.

E 4. Create a blank report using the WRITERS table.

E 5. Include in your report these sections: Page Header, Freelancer Header, Detail, Freelancer Footer, Page Footer, and Report Footer.

E 6. In the Page Header section at the beginning of the first line, enter Freelancer Group Totals as the report title. Enter the current date at the beginning of the second line. Position the labels under these lines, as shown in Figure 6-14. Add a single line, instead of a double line, below the column heads line. Do not place any lines above the column heads or above the report title.

E 7. Use Freelancer for the grouping field. There are no sorting fields in this report. In the Freelancer Header section, include the Freelancer field value.

E 8. In the Detail section, include the field values, as shown in Figure 6-14.

E 9. In the Freelancer Footer section, include the group total for the Amount field.

E 10. In the Page Footer section, include a page number aligned with the right edge of the Amount field.

E 11. In the Report Footer section, include the overall total for the Amount field.

E 12. When you finish creating the report, print the entire report.

E 13. Save the report, naming it Freelancer Group Totals Report, and then exit Access.

Case Problems

1. Walkton Daily Press Carriers

Grant Sherman uses Report Wizards to create a report for his Press database. Launch Access, open the Press database on your Student Disk, and do the following:

1. Use Report Wizards to create a groups/totals report in the executive style based on the CARRIERS table. Select all the fields from the table in the order in which they are stored in the table. Do not select a grouping field, sort by Carrier ID, do not check the "Calculate percentages of the total" box, and enter CARRIERS Report as the report title.
2. Display the report in the Print Preview window and then print the entire report.
3. Save the report, naming it CARRIERS Report, then close the Print Preview window, and return to the Database window.

Grant next modifies the design of this report. Open the newly created CARRIERS Report in the Report Design window and do the following:

4. In the Report Footer section, delete the two Sum function text boxes, delete the two sets of double lines, and delete the Report Footer section.
5. Click the Print Preview button to display the report and then print the entire report.
6. Save the report, naming it CARRIERS Report #2, and return to the Database window.

Grant next creates a custom report. Use the Press database on your Student Disk to do the following:

E 7. Create a blank report using the query named Carriers sorted by Name, Route ID.

E 8. Sketch a design for the report based on the requirements described in the next five steps, and then create the report following these same steps.

E 9. Include in your report these sections: Page Header, Detail, Group Footer, and Report Footer.

E 10. In the Page Header section at the beginning of the first line, enter CARRIERS sorted by Name, Route ID Report as the report title. Enter the current date at the beginning of the second line and the page number at the end of the second line. Position under these elements a row of column heads with these labels: Last Name, First Name, Carrier Phone, Route ID, and Balance. Add a single horizontal line under the column heads.

E 11. In the Detail section, include the field values for Last Name, First Name, Carrier Phone, Route ID, and Balance. Hide duplicates for the Last Name, First Name, and Carrier Phone fields.

E 12. In the Group Footer section, print the group total for the Balance field. Select Last Name as the primary sort key, and use this field as a grouping field. Select Route ID as the secondary sort key, but do not use it as a grouping field. Choose ascending sort order for each sort key.

E 13. In the Report Footer section, print the overall total for the Balance field.

E 14. When you finish creating the report, print the entire report.

E 15. Save the report, naming it CARRIERS sorted by Name and Route ID Report, and then exit Access.

2. Lopez Used Cars

Maria Lopez uses Report Wizards to create a report for her Usedcars database. Launch Access, open the Usedcars database on your Student Disk, and do the following:

1. Use Report Wizards to create a groups/totals report in the executive style based on the USED CARS table. Select all the fields from the table in the order in which they are stored in the table. Do not select a grouping field, sort by Year, do not check the "Calculate percentages of the total" box, and enter USED CARS by Year as the report title.
2. Display the report in the Print Preview window and then print the entire report.
3. Save the report, naming it USED CARS by Year Report, and return to the Database window.

Maria next modifies the design of this report. Open the newly created report named USED CARS by Year Report in the Report Design window and do the following:

4. In the Report Footer section, delete the Sum function text box for the Year field, and delete its set of double lines.
5. Click the Print Preview button to display the report and then print the entire report.
6. Save the report, naming it USED CARS by Year Report #2, and return to the Database window.

Maria next creates a custom report. Use the Usedcars database on your Student Disk and do the following:

E 7. Create a blank report using the USED CARS table.

E 8. Sketch a design for the report based on the requirements described in the next five steps, and then create the report following these same steps.

E 9. Include in your report these sections: Page Header, Detail, Group Footer, and Report Footer.

E 10. In the Page Header section at the beginning of the first line, enter USED CARS sorted by Manufacturer, Model, Year as the report title. Enter the current date at the beginning of the second line and the page number at the end of the second line. Position under these elements a row of column heads with these labels: Manufacturer, Model, Year, Cost, and Selling Price. Add a single horizontal line under the column heads.

E 11. In the Detail section, include the field values for Manufacturer, Model, Year, Cost, and Selling Price. Hide duplicates for the Manufacturer field.

E 12. In the Group Footer section, print the group total for the Cost and Selling Price fields. Select Manufacturer as the primary sort key and as the grouping field. Select Model, and then Year, as the secondary sort keys, but do not use them as grouping fields. Choose ascending sort order for each sort key.

E 13. In the Report Footer section, print the overall totals for the Cost and Selling Price fields.

E 14. When you finish creating the report, print the entire report.

E 15. Save the report, naming it USED CARS by Manufacturer, Model, and Year Report, and then exit Access.

3. Tophill University Student Employment

Olivia Tyler uses Report Wizards to create a report for her Parttime database. Launch Access, open the Parttime database on your Student Disk, and do the following:

1. Use Report Wizards to create a groups/totals report in the executive style based on the JOBS table. Select all the fields from the table in the order in which they are stored in the table. Do not select a grouping field, sort by Job Order, do not check the "Calculate percentages of the total" box, and enter JOBS as the report title.
2. Display the report in the Print Preview window and then print the entire report.
3. Save the report, naming it JOBS Report, and return to the Database window.

Olivia next modifies the design of this report. Open the newly created JOBS Report in the Report Design window and do the following:

4. In the Report Footer section, delete the three Sum function text boxes, delete the three sets of double lines, and delete the Report Footer section.
5. Click the Print Preview button to display the report and then print the entire report.
6. Save the report, naming it JOBS Report #2, and return to the Database window.

Olivia next creates a custom report. Use the Parttime database on your Student Disk to do the following:

E 7. Create a blank report using the query named JOBS sorted by Employer, Job Title.

E 8. Sketch a design for the report based on the requirements described in the next four steps, and then create the report following these same steps.

E 9. Include in your report a Page Header section and a Detail section.

E 10. In the Page Header section at the beginning of the first line, enter JOBS sorted by Employer, Job Title as the report title. Enter the current date at the beginning of the second line and the page number at the end of the second line. Position under these elements a row of column heads with these labels: Employer Name, Hours/Week, Job Title, and Wages. Add a single horizontal line under the column heads.

E 11. In the Detail section, include the field values for Employer Name, Hours/Week, Job Title, and Wages. Hide duplicates for the Employer Name field.

E 12. Select Employer Name as the primary sort key and Job Title as the secondary sort key. Do not select a grouping field. Choose ascending sort order for each sort key.

E 13. When you finish creating the report, print the entire report.

E 14. Save the report, naming it JOBS sorted by Employer and Job Title Report, and then exit Access.

4. Rexville Business Licenses

Chester Pearce uses Report Wizards to create a report for his Buslic database. Launch Access, open the Buslic database on your Student Disk, and do the following:

1. Use Report Wizards to create a groups/totals report in the executive style based on the BUSINESSES table. Select all the fields from the table in the order in which they are stored in the table. Do not select a grouping field, sort by Business Name, do not check the "Calculate percentages of the total" box, and enter BUSINESSES Report as the report title.

2. Display the report in the Print Preview window and then print the entire report.
3. Save the report, naming it BUSINESSES Report, and return to the Database window.

Chester next modifies the design of this report. Open the newly created BUSINESSES Report in the Report Design window and do the following:

4. In the Report Footer section, delete the Sum function text box for the two fields, delete the two sets of double lines, and delete the Report Footer section.
5. Click the Print Preview button to display the report and then print the entire report.
6. Save the report, naming it BUSINESSES Report #2, and then return to the Database window.

Chester next creates a custom report. Use the Buslic database on your Student Disk to do the following:

E 7. Create a blank report using the query named BUSINESSES sorted by License Type, Business Name.

E 8. Sketch a design for the report based on the requirements described in the next five steps, and then create the report following these same steps.

E 9. Include in your report these sections: Page Header, Detail, Group Footer, and Report Footer.

E 10. In the Page Header section at the beginning of the first line, enter BUSINESSES sorted by License Type, Business Name as the report title. Enter the current date at the beginning of the second line and the page number at the end of the second line. Position under these elements a row of column heads with these labels: License, Basic Cost, Business Name, and Amount. Add a single horizontal line under the column heads.

E 11. In the Detail section, include the field values for License (do not use License Number), Basic Cost, Business Name, and Amount. Hide duplicates for the License and Basic Cost fields.

E 12. In the Group Footer section, print the group total for the Amount field. Select License as the primary sort key and as the grouping field. Select Business Name as the secondary sort key, but do not use it as a grouping field. Choose ascending sort order for each sort key.

E 13. In the Report Footer section, print the overall totals for the Amount field.

E 14. When you finish creating the report, print the entire report.

E 15. Save the report, naming it BUSINESSES sorted by License Type and Business Name Report, and then exit Access.

Microsoft® Access 2.0 for Windows® Intermediate Tutorials

Read This Before You Begin

To the Student

To use these tutorials, you must have Student Disks. Your instructor will either provide you with them or ask you to make your own by following the instructions in the section "Making Your Student Disks" below. See your instructor or technical support person for further information. If you are going to work through this book using your own computer, you need a computer system running Microsoft Windows 3.1 and Microsoft Access 2.0, and Student Disks. *You will not be able to complete the tutorials and exercises in this book using your own computer until you have Student Disks.*

Making Your Student Disks Before you start the tutorials, you need to make Student Disks containing the practice files you need for the tutorials, Tutorial Assignments, Case Problems, and Additional Cases. If your instructor gives you Student Disks, you can skip this section.

To make the student disks, you need 2 blank, formatted, high-density disks. Label each disk as follows:

Tutorial	**Student Disk #**
1–4 Tutorials and Tutorial Assignments	1
1–4 Case Problems and Additional Cases	2

1. Launch WIndows, make sure the Program Manager is open, and place your formatted Disk 1 in drive A.
2. Locate the group icon labeled **CTI WinApps**, and double-click it to open the CTI Winapps Group Windows.
3. Double-click the **Make Access2 Comprehensive Student Disks** icon. In the window that opens, make sure that the drive that contains your disk corresponds to the drive option button selected.

The Make Your Student Disk program, by default, will make all the disks for Tutorials 1–10 and Additional Cases for CTI's Comprehensive Access book. For these Intermediate tutorials, you want to make student disks only for Tutorials 7–10 and Additional Cases, which have been renumbered as Tutorials 1 through 4 here. *Do not be concerned that the tutorial numbering in the disk program is different from the numbering of these Intermediate tutorials. The file names on your student disks will match those referenced in the Intermediate tutorials.*

4. In the first screen that appears, you are asked if you want to create a student disk for Tutorials 1-6. Click **Skip Disk**.
5. The next screen asks if you want to create a student disk for Tutorial 7–10 Tutorials and Tutorial Assignments. Click **Make Disk**.
6. The next screen asks if you want to make disks for Tutorials 7–10 Case Problems and Additional Cases. Click **Make Disk**. Insert the second disk when requested.
7. When the copying is complete, click the OK button, then close the CTI Winapps window.

To the Instructor

Making the Student Disks To complete the tutorials in this book, your students must have a copy of the Student Disks. To relieve you of having to make multiple Student Disks from a single master copy, we provide you with the CTI WinApps Setup Disk, which contains an automatic Student Disk generating program. Once you install the Setup Disk on a network or standalone workstation, students can easily make their own Student Disks by double-clicking the "Make Access2 Comprehensive Student Disks" icon in the CTI WinApps icon group. Double-clicking this icon transfers all the data files students will need to complete the tutorials, Tutorial Assignments, Case Problems, and Additional Cases to high-density disks in drive A or B. If some of your students will use their own computers to complete the tutorials and exercises in this book, they must first get the Student Disks. The section called "Making Your Student Disks" above provides instructions on how to make the Student Disks.

Obtaining the Setup Disk from the World Wide Web The Setup Disk Files for these tutorials is also available at the Course Technology Student Center at **http://coursetools.com**. If you want to obtain these files from the site, be sure to click the book title *Comprehensive Microsoft Access 2.0 for Windows*, which will prompt you to download the self-extracting file called 987-5.exe. After extracting this file, copy each directory to a floppy disk, and README file for setup instructions. (See the inside front or back cover of this book and the Student Center page for more information.) *Once you install the Make Your Student Disk icon for Comprehensive Access, students will make their disks for Comprehensive tutorials 7–10 and Additional Cases, which have been renumbered as Tutorials 1–4 here.*

Installing the CTI WinApps Setup Disk To install the CTI WinApps icon group from the Setup Disk, follow the instructions on the Setup Disk label and in the README File on the Setup Disk. By adopting this book, you are granted a license to install this software on any computer or computer network used by you or your students.

README File A README.TXT file located on the Setup Disk provides complete installation instructions, additional technical notes, troubleshooting advice, and tips for using the CTI WinApps software in your school's computer lab. You can view the README.TXT file using any word processor you choose.

T U T O R I A L 1

OBJECTIVES

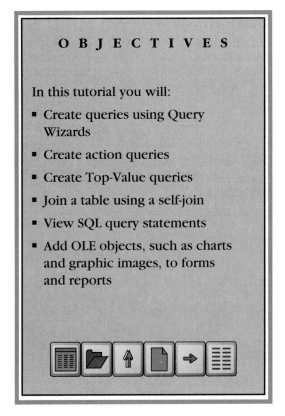

In this tutorial you will:

- Create queries using Query Wizards
- Create action queries
- Create Top-Value queries
- Join a table using a self-join
- View SQL query statements
- Add OLE objects, such as charts and graphic images, to forms and reports

Advanced Queries and OLE Objects

Enhancing the User Interaction with the Issue25 Database

CASE

Vision Publishers Brian Murphy is the president of Vision Publishers, which produces five specialized monthly magazines from its Chicago headquarters. Brian founded the company in March 1970 when he began publishing *Business Perspective*, a magazine featuring articles, editorials, interviews, and investigative reports that are widely respected in the financial and business communities.

Because the staff at Vision Publishers are using databases more and more in their work, Brian Murphy sends Elena Sanchez, special projects editor, to a one-week Access training seminar. Elena learns many intermediate and advanced concepts and features of Access at the seminar. After learning about Query Wizards, action queries, and SQL at the seminar, Elena can create more complex queries that answer important questions her team has been raising about the 25th-anniversary issue that they have been planning. She finishes her day's work by providing Brian with a set of financial charts for a stockholders' meeting.

Using Query Wizards

This tutorial assumes you have created select queries that used selection criteria, sorts, calculations, table joins, and parameters. These select queries are prepared in the Query Design window, bypassing Access's Query Wizards feature. Using Query Wizards, Elena can easily create more complicated queries that address specific needs. Access has four Query Wizards: the Crosstab Query Wizard, the Find Duplicates Query Wizard, the Find Unmatched Query Wizard, and the Archive Query Wizard.

- Use the **Crosstab Query Wizard** to guide you through the steps for creating crosstab queries. A **crosstab query** performs aggregate-function calculations on the values of one database field and displays the results in a spreadsheet format. (Aggregate functions perform arithmetic operations on the records in a database.) Figure 1-1 shows the aggregate functions you can use in a crosstab query. A crosstab query can also display one additional aggregate-function value that summarizes each row's set of values. The crosstab query uses one or more fields for the row headings on the left and one field for the column headings at the top.

Aggregate Function	Meaning
Avg	Average of the field values
Count	Number of non-full field values
First	First field value
Last	Last field value
Min	Lowest field value
Max	Highest field value
StDev	Standard deviation of the field values
Sum	Total of the field values
Var	Variance of the field values

Figure 1-1
Aggregate functions used in crosstab queries

Figure 1-2 shows two dynasets, the first from a select query and the second from a related crosstab query. Both queries use the Article Type Query that joins the WRITERS and PAST ARTICLES tables, but the crosstab query gives more readable information. For each record in the PAST ARTICLES table, the select query displays the Last Name and First Name fields from the WRITERS table and the Type and Article Length fields from the PAST ARTICLES table. There are, for example, four rows for Chong Kim—one row for each article he wrote. On the other hand, the crosstab query displays just one row for Chong Kim. The Last Name and First Name fields in the leftmost columns identify each row, and the field values for the Type field identify the rightmost columns. The crosstab query uses the Sum aggregate function on the Article Length field to produce the displayed values in the remainder of the dynaset. The third column, labeled Writer Total, represents the total of the Article Length values for each row.

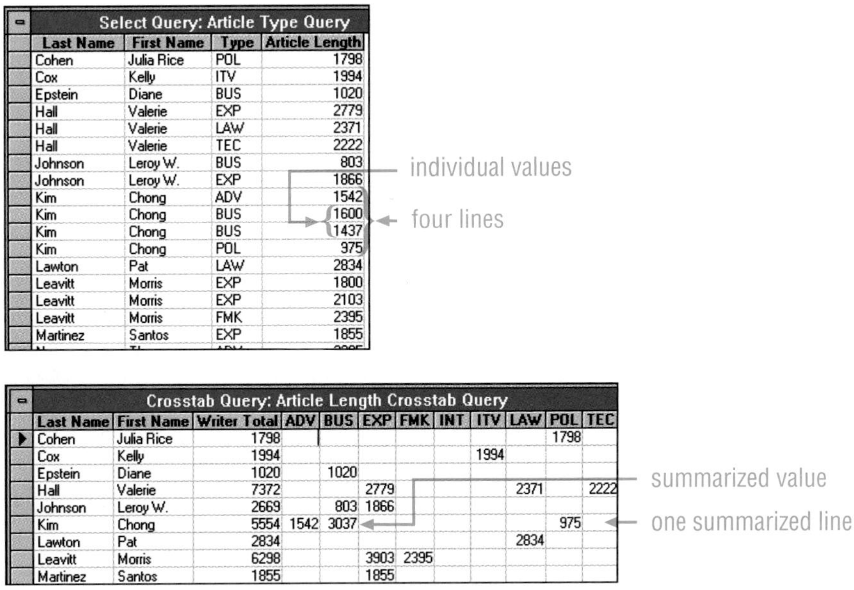

Last Name	First Name	Type	Article Length
Cohen	Julia Rice	POL	1798
Cox	Kelly	ITV	1994
Epstein	Diane	BUS	1020
Hall	Valerie	EXP	2779
Hall	Valerie	LAW	2371
Hall	Valerie	TEC	2222
Johnson	Leroy W.	BUS	803
Johnson	Leroy W.	EXP	1866
Kim	Chong	ADV	1542
Kim	Chong	BUS	1600
Kim	Chong	BUS	1437
Kim	Chong	POL	975
Lawton	Pat	LAW	2834
Leavitt	Morris	EXP	1800
Leavitt	Morris	EXP	2103
Leavitt	Morris	FMK	2395
Martinez	Santos	EXP	1855

Last Name	First Name	Writer Total	ADV	BUS	EXP	FMK	INT	ITV	LAW	POL	TEC
Cohen	Julia Rice	1798								1798	
Cox	Kelly	1994						1994			
Epstein	Diane	1020		1020							
Hall	Valerie	7372			2779				2371		2222
Johnson	Leroy W.	2669		803	1866						
Kim	Chong	5554	1542	3037						975	
Lawton	Pat	2834							2834		
Leavitt	Morris	6298			3903	2395					
Martinez	Santos	1855			1855						

Figure 1-2
Contrasting a select query (top dynaset) with a crosstab query (bottom dynaset)

- Use the **Find Duplicates Query Wizard** to create a select query that locates duplicate records in a table or query. The query searches for duplicates based on the fields you choose as you answer the Wizard questions. For example, you might want to display all customers who live at the same address, all students who have the same phone number, all products that have the same description, or all writers who have the same names. Using this query, you can locate duplicates that might indicate a potential problem (for example, you might have inadvertently assigned two different numbers to the same product), and you can eliminate duplicates that cost you money (for example, you could send just one advertising brochure to all the customers having the same address).
- Use the **Find Unmatched Query Wizard** to create a select query that finds all the records in a table or query that have no related records in a second table or query. For example, you could display all customers who have not placed orders, all non-degree students who are not currently enrolled in classes, or all writers who have not written articles. This query might help you solicit business from the inactive customers, contact the students to find out their future educational plans, or delete the non-producing writers from your database.
- Use the **Archive Query Wizard** to create a query that **archives**, or copies, designated records from a table into a new table. As you create the query you can choose to retain or delete the records from the original table. You typically archive records when you no longer need them in your main database tables. You might archive records of discontinued products, records for graduated students, or records for inactive customers. Usually you delete the archived records from the original table, but in rare cases you might want to keep the records in the original table.

Elena wants to practice the skills she learned at the seminar, so she spends the afternoon using the Query Wizards to create new queries that will answer questions her team has raised.

Creating a Crosstab Query

In planning for the special 25th-anniversary issue of *Business Perspective*, Elena must balance the total length of articles among the different types of articles, such as political and advertising, and among the featured writers. Elena creates a crosstab query using the Crosstab Query Wizard to provide the needed information.

REFERENCE WINDOW

Using the Crosstab Query Wizard

- Click the toolbar New Query button from the Database window, click the Query Wizards button, click Crosstab Query in the list box, and then click the OK button.
- Click the Tables, Queries, or Both radio button to display the corresponding objects in the list box. In the list box click the name of the table or query that will be the basis for the crosstab query and then click the Next > button.
- Select the row heading field or fields and then click the Next > button.
- Click the column heading field and then click the Next > button.
- Click the calculation field and then click its aggregate function. Turn the Calculate Summary for Each Row check box on if you want a row-summary column, and click it off if you do not. Finally, click the Next > button.
- Type the new query name in the text box and then click the Finish button to save and run the query.

The crosstab query Elena creates is similar to the one shown in Figure 1-2. This crosstab query has the following characteristics:

- The Article Type Query is the basis for the new crosstab query; it includes the fields named Article Title, Type, Article Length, Last Name, and First Name.
- The Last Name and First Name fields from the WRITERS table are the leftmost columns and identify each crosstab-query row. If two writers have the same first and last names, as do the two Chong Kims, then they are summarized in one row.
- The field values that appear in the PAST ARTICLES table for the Type field identify the rightmost columns of the crosstab query.
- The crosstab query applies the Sum aggregate function to the Article Length field from the PAST ARTICLES table and displays the resulting total values in the main part of the dynaset. If one writer has two or more articles of the same type, then the sum of the article lengths appears in the intersecting cell of the dynaset.
- The Calculate Summary for Each Row check box is turned on in the Crosstab Query Wizard so that the total of the Article Length values for each row appears. The default name for this column is changed to Writer Total.

To create a crosstab query using the Crosstab Query Wizard:

1. Place your Student Disk that contains the files for this tutorial in the appropriate drive, launch Access, and open the Issue25 database on the Student Disk.

   TROUBLE? Be sure you are using the Student Disk for this tutorial. Refer to the table on the "Read This Before You Begin" page before the tutorials.

2. Click the toolbar **New Query button** to open the New Query dialog box and then click the **Query Wizards button** in the dialog box. Access opens the Query Wizards dialog box.

3. If Crosstab Query is not already highlighted, click it, and then click the **OK button**. The first Crosstab Query Wizard dialog box opens.

4. Click the **Queries radio button** to display a list of the queries in the Issue25 database and then click **Article Type Query** in the list box at the top of the dialog box. See Figure 1-3.

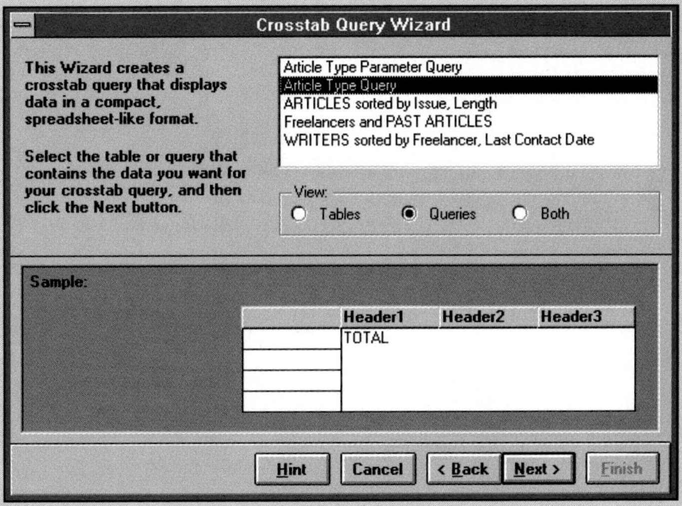

Figure 1-3 Choosing the table or query for a crosstab query

5. Click the **Next > button** to open the second Crosstab Query Wizard dialog box, in which you choose the fields for the row headings.

6. In the Available Fields list box, double-click **Last Name** and then double-click **First Name** to select these fields for the row headings in the selected order. As you select a field, Access changes the sample crosstab query in the bottom of the dialog box to illustrate your choice. Click the **Next > button** to open the third Crosstab Query Wizard dialog box, in which you select the field whose values will serve as column headings.

7. Click **Type** in the list box to select it as the column-headings field and then click the **Next > button**. Access opens the fourth Crosstab Query Wizard dialog box. Here you choose the field that will appear in the middle of the dynaset and its calculation method.

8. Click **Article Length** in the Available fields list box and then click **Sum** in the Functions list box. Be sure that the Calculate Summary for Each Row check box is selected. See Figure 1-4.

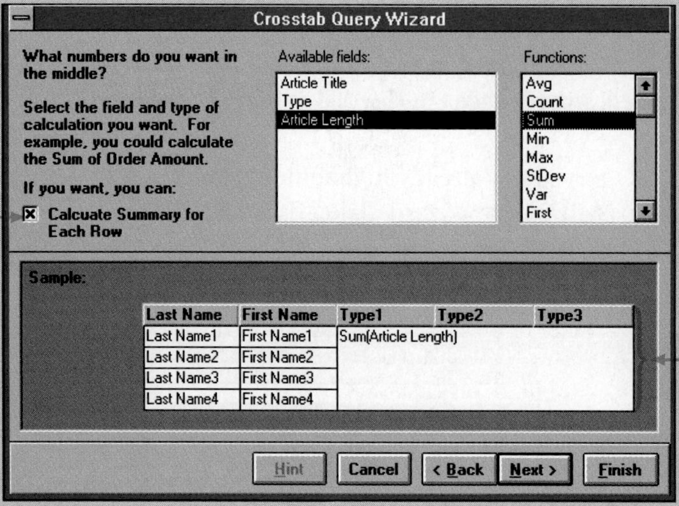

Figure 1-4 The completed crosstab query design

9. Click the **Next > button** to open the final Crosstab Query Wizard dialog box in which you choose the query name. Type **ArticleLengthCrosstabQuery** in the text box, be sure the "Open the query to view the data" radio button is turned on, and then click the **Finish button**. Access saves the crosstab query and, after a short pause, opens the query dynaset. See Figure 1-5.

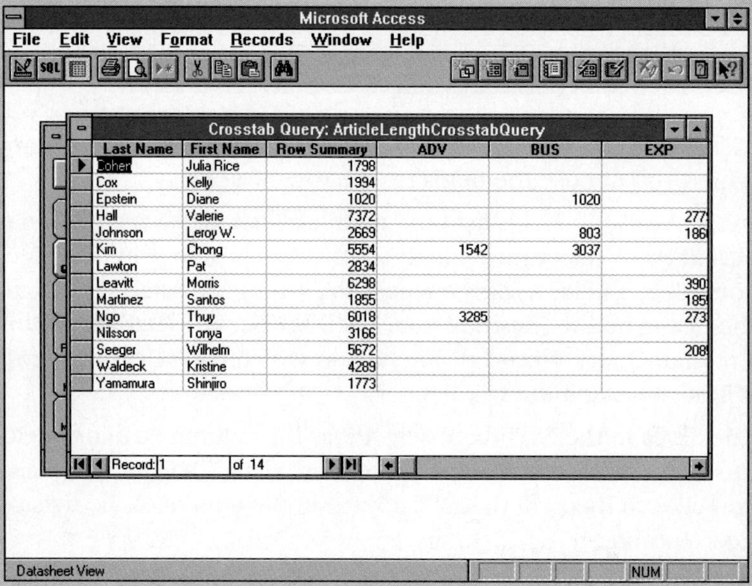

Figure 1-5 The crosstab query dynaset

Notice that you need to change the third column heading from Row Summary to Writer Total. Also, all the column widths in the dynaset are wider than necessary, so you should resize them. You make the first change in the Query Design window and the second change in the dynaset.

To rename and resize the dynaset columns:

1. Click the toolbar **Design View button** to switch to the Query Design window.
2. If necessary, scroll to the right until the fifth column, which begins with the name Row Summary, is visible. Highlight Row Summary and then type **Writer Total**. Be sure you do not delete the colon that separates the dynaset column name, Writer Total, from the table field name, Article Length.
3. Click the toolbar **Run button**. Access opens the dynaset and shows Writer Total instead of Row Summary as the dynaset column name.
4. Move the mouse pointer to the Last Name column selector. When it changes to ⬇, click and drag the pointer to the right, scrolling until all columns are highlighted, and then release the mouse button.
5. Move the mouse pointer to the right edge of any highlighted-column selector. When it changes to ✥, double-click the left mouse button to resize all highlighted columns to their best fits. Click anywhere in the dynaset to remove the highlighting. See Figure 1-6.

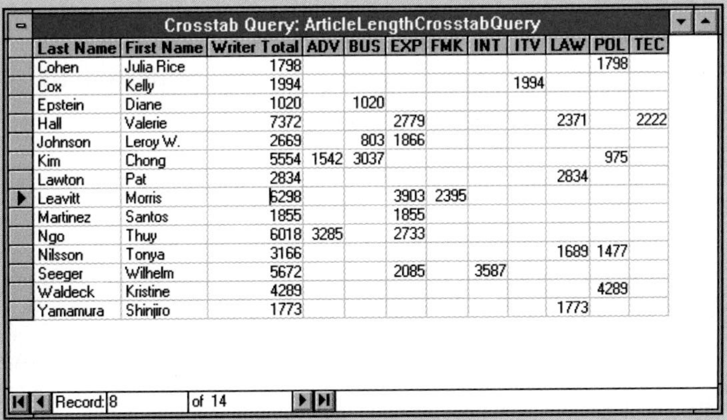
Crosstab Query: ArticleLengthCrosstabQuery

Last Name	First Name	Writer Total	ADV	BUS	EXP	FMK	INT	ITV	LAW	POL	TEC
Cohen	Julia Rice	1798								1798	
Cox	Kelly	1994						1994			
Epstein	Diane	1020		1020							
Hall	Valerie	7372			2779				2371		2222
Johnson	Leroy W.	2669		803	1866						
Kim	Chong	5554	1542	3037						975	
Lawton	Pat	2834							2834		
Leavitt	Morris	6298			3903	2395					
Martinez	Santos	1855			1855						
Ngo	Thuy	6018	3285		2733						
Nilsson	Tonya	3166							1689	1477	
Seeger	Wilhelm	5672			2085		3587				
Waldeck	Kristine	4289								4289	
Yamamura	Shinjiro	1773							1773		

Record: 8 of 14

Figure 1-6
The resized crosstab query dynaset

Elena closes the completed query dynaset. Because this dynaset shows the number of words for each type and each writer, Elena can use it to balance the total length of articles among the types and writers.

To close the query dynaset:

1. Double-click the dynaset window **Control menu box.**
2. Click the **Yes button** to close the dialog box, save the query, and activate the Database window.

The icon appearing in the Queries list box to the left of ArticleLengthCrosstabQuery is different from the icon for the select and parameter queries. The select and parameter queries, the crosstab query, and each of the four action queries have a unique icon, as shown in Figure 1-7. (Action queries, which modify table values, are covered later in this tutorial.)

Figure 1-7
Database window icons identifying the Access query type

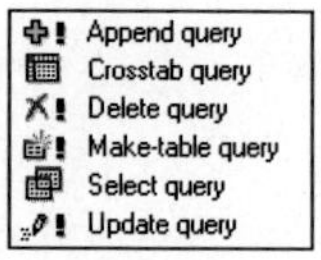

Using the Crosstab Query Wizard is the quickest way to create a crosstab query. Alternatively, you can change a select query to a crosstab query by clicking the toolbar Crosstab Query button in the Query Design window. In response, Access changes the title bar from Select Query to Crosstab Query and adds Total and Crosstab rows to the QBE grid between the Field and the Sort rows. For more details on this more complicated method, click Help, click Search..., type crosstab queries, click Show Topics, and then go to the Summarizing Data Using a Crosstab Query topic.

Creating a Find Duplicates Query

Elena wants to be sure that Chong Kim is the only duplicate writer name, so she uses the Find Duplicates Query Wizard to display writers having the same names. She uses the WRITERS table as the basis for this query, selects records that have duplicate values for *both* the Last Name and First Name fields, and displays all fields from the WRITERS table.

REFERENCE WINDOW

Using the Find Duplicates Query Wizard

- Click the toolbar New Query button from the Database window, then click the Query Wizards button.
- Click Find Duplicates Query in the list box and then click the OK button.
- Click the Tables, Queries, or Both radio button to display the corresponding objects in the list box, click the name of the table or query that will be the basis for the query, and then click the Next > button.
- Select the field or fields you want checked for duplicate values and then click the Next > button.
- Select the additional fields you want to see in the dynaset and then click the Next > button.
- Type the new query name in the text box and then click the Finish button to save and run the query.

Elena uses the Find Duplicates Query Wizard to create and run this new query.

To create a query using the Find Duplicates Query Wizard:

❶ Click the toolbar **New Query button** to open the New Query dialog box, then click the **Query Wizards button** in the New Query dialog box. Access opens the Query Wizards dialog box.

❷ Click **Find Duplicates Query** and then click the **OK button**. The first Find Duplicates Query Wizard dialog box opens.

❸ Click **WRITERS** in the list box to select this table as the basis for the query and then click the **Next > button**. Access opens the second Find Duplicates Query Wizard dialog box, in which you choose the fields you want checked for duplicate values.

❹ In the Available fields list box, double-click **Last Name** and then double-click **First Name** to select these fields for duplicate-value checking.

❺ Click the **Next > button** to open the third Find Duplicates Query Wizard dialog box, in which you select the additional fields you want to display in the query dynaset. You choose to display all the remaining fields in the WRITERS table.

❻ Click the **>> button** to select all remaining fields from the WRITERS table. Access moves all fields listed in the Available fields list box to the Selected fields list box.

❼ Click the **Next > button** to open the final Find Duplicates Query Wizard dialog box, in which you choose the query name.

❽ Type **DuplicateWritersNameQuery** in the text box, be sure the "Open the query to view the data" radio button is turned on, and then click the **Finish button**. Access saves the query and, after a short pause, opens the query dynaset for the select query, as shown in Figure 1-8. Access displays the records with duplicate names for the two writers named Chong Kim.

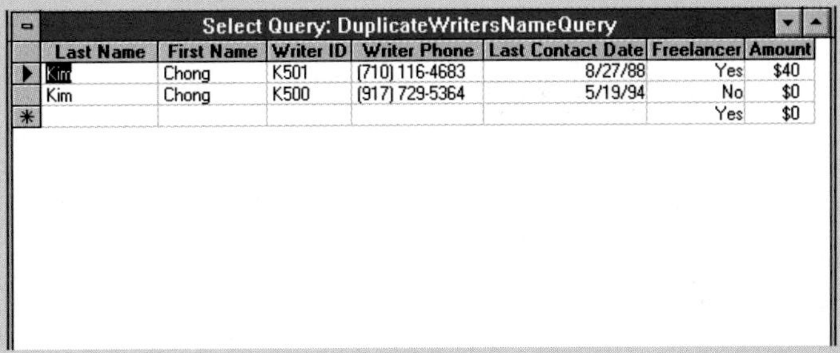

Select Query: DuplicateWritersNameQuery

Last Name	First Name	Writer ID	Writer Phone	Last Contact Date	Freelancer	Amount
Kim	Chong	K501	(710) 116-4683	8/27/88	Yes	$40
Kim	Chong	K500	(917) 729-5364	5/19/94	No	$0
					Yes	$0

Figure 1-8
The query dynaset opened by the Find Duplicates Query Wizard

❾ Double-click the dynaset window **Control menu box** to close the dynaset and activate the Database window.

Elena has confirmed that the two Chong Kims are the only writers with the same names. She takes this duplication into consideration as she uses the crosstab query to balance article types and writers.

Creating a Find Unmatched Query

Elena next uses the Find Unmatched Query Wizard to display the Type and Description fields from the TYPES table, but only when there are no records in the PAST ARTICLES table having that Type field value. She asks this question to be sure that all types of articles are represented in the PAST ARTICLES table.

REFERENCE WINDOW

Using the Find Unmatched Query Wizard

- Click the toolbar New Query button from the Database window, then click the Query Wizards button.
- Click Find Unmatched Query in the list box and then click the OK button.
- Click the Tables, Queries, or Both radio button to display the corresponding objects in the list box. In the list box, click the name of the table or query that contains the records you want to see in the dynaset and then click the Next > button.
- Click the Tables, Queries, or Both radio button to display the corresponding objects in the list box. Click the name of the table or query that contains the related records and then click the Next > button.
- Click the common field in each table or query, click the <=> button, and then click the Next > button.
- Select the fields you want to see in the dynaset and then click the Next > button.
- Type the new query name in the text box and then click the Finish button to save and run the query.

Elena uses the Find Unmatched Query Wizard to create and run this new query.

To create a query using the Find Unmatched Query Wizard:

1. Click the toolbar **New Query button** to open the New Query dialog box, click the **Query Wizards button** in the New Query dialog box, click **Find Unmatched Query**, and then click the **OK button**. Access opens the first Find Unmatched Query Wizard dialog box.
2. Click **TYPES** in the list box to select this table—its records will appear in the dynaset. Then click the **Next > button** to open the second Find Unmatched Query Wizard dialog box. Here you choose the table that contains the related records.
3. Click **PAST ARTICLES** in the list box and then click the **Next > button** to open the third Find Unmatched Query Wizard dialog box. Here you choose the common field for both tables.
4. Click **Type** in each list box and then click the **<=> button**. Access shows the Matching fields as "Type <=> Type".
5. Click the **Next > button** to open the fourth Find Unmatched Query Wizard dialog box, in which you choose the fields you want to see in the dynaset.

6. Click the >> **button** to select all fields from the TYPES table. Access moves all fields listed in the Available Fields list box to the Selected Fields list box.
7. Click the **Next > button** to open the final Find Unmatched Query Wizard dialog box, in which you choose the query name.
8. Type **TypesWithoutMatchingPastArticlesQuery**, be sure the "Open the query to view the data" radio button is turned on, and then click the **Finish button**. Access saves the query and, after a short pause, opens the query dynaset. The query created by the Find Unmatched Query Wizard is a select query. See Figure 1-9. Access displays the monetary and statistical article type codes and descriptions in the dynaset.

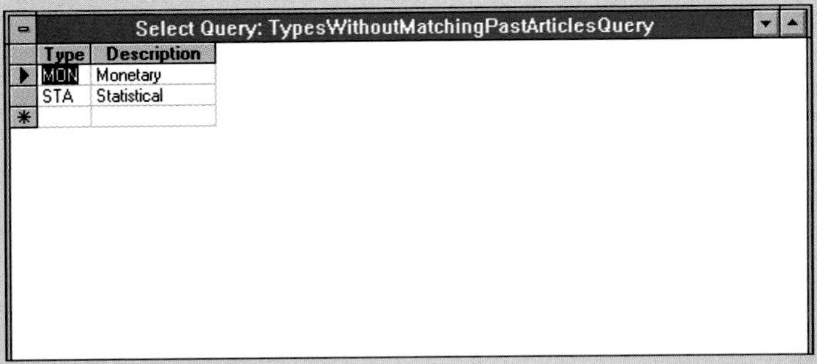

Figure 1-9
The query dynaset opened by the Find Unmatched Query Wizard

9. Double-click the dynaset window **Control menu box** to close the dynaset and activate the Database window.

Elena now knows that there are no monetary or statistical articles among those selected for the 25th-anniversary issue, because these were the only two records from the TYPES table that did not have a record with a matching Type field value in the PAST ARTICLES table. Elena asks an aide to give Brian Murphy several monetary and statistical articles. From these articles, Brian can choose his favorites for the 25th-anniversary issue.

Eight queries now appear in the Queries list box—seven select queries and one crosstab query.

Creating an Archive Query

Vision Publishers needs to pay all the freelancers for their articles appearing in the 25th-anniversary issue of *Business Perspective*. Elena must communicate the freelancer payment information to the payroll department. Elena uses the Archive Query Wizard to create a new table containing just the freelancer records from the WRITERS table. She asks Access to place all the fields from the WRITERS table into the new table but to retain the records in the WRITERS table. Elena will then tell the payroll department to use the new table to pay the freelancers. Elena could provide this information by printing a simple query or report. However, the payroll department wants its own table to restructure and modify without interfering with the Issue25 database work.

REFERENCE WINDOW

Using the Archive Query Wizard

- Click the toolbar New Query button from the Database window, then click the Query Wizards button.
- Click Archive Query in the list box and then click the OK button.
- In the list box, click the name of the table that contains the records you want to archive and then click the Next > button.
- If you want to archive all the table records, click the check box. If you want to archive selected records, select a field name, a comparison operator, type the value you want to match, then click the Next > button.
- Access displays the selected records. If the wrong records appear, click the < Back button to return to the previous dialog box and change the selection criterion. When the correct records appear, click the Next > button.
- Click either the delete radio button to delete the original records or the keep radio button to keep the original records and then click the Next > button.
- Type the new archive table name in the text box and then click the Finish button. Click Yes to copy the records, and then click OK to run the query, create the new archive table, and create a new query. The name of the new query is the same as the table name preceded by "Append to."

Elena uses the Archive Query Wizard to create a table named FREELANCER ARCHIVE. This new table will contain all the fields from the WRITERS table for just the freelancers and will not delete these records from the WRITERS table.

To create a new table using the Archive Query Wizard:

1. Click the toolbar **New Query button** and then click the **Query Wizards button** in the New Query dialog box.
2. Click **Archive Query** and then click the **OK button**. The first Archive Wizard dialog box opens.
3. Click **WRITERS** in the list box to select this table as the one that contains the records you want to archive and then click the **Next > button** to open the second Archive Wizard dialog box, in which you indicate which records you want to archive.
4. Click the **down arrow button** in the "This value" drop-down list box and then click **Freelancer**. Access will archive values for the Freelancer field that match the remaining parts of your selection criterion. Click the **down arrow button** in the "Is" drop-down list box and then click **=**. Finally, click the "This value" **text box** and then type **Yes**. Records to be archived from the WRITERS table are those whose Freelancer field values are equal to Yes—that is, the freelancer records will be selected. See Figure 1-10.

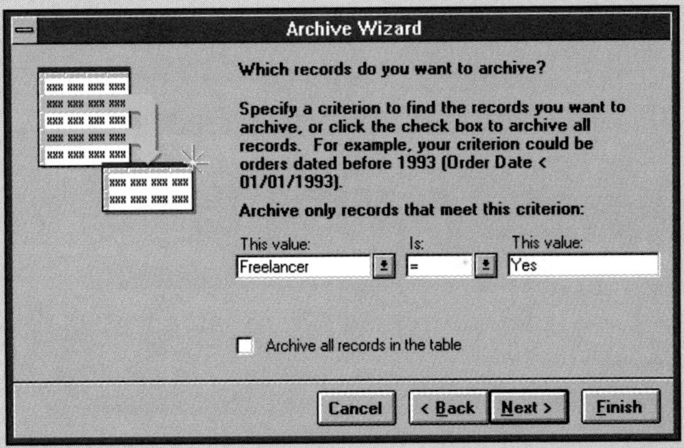

Figure 1-10 The selection criterion for an archive query

5. Click the **Next > button** to open the third Archive Wizard dialog box, in which Access displays the records that will be archived. See Figure 1-11.

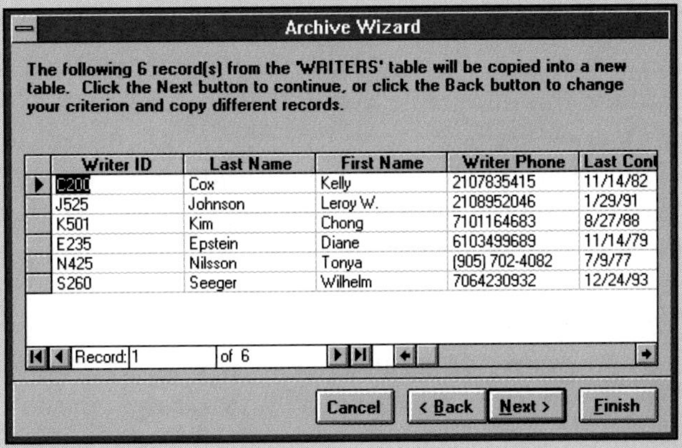

Figure 1-11 The records to be archived

TROUBLE? If the wrong records are displayed, click the < Back button and correct the selection criterion in Step 4.

6. Click the **Next > button** to open the fourth Archive Wizard dialog box. Here you choose whether or not to delete the selected records from the existing table. You do not want to delete the records from the WRITERS table, so be sure the "No, I want to keep the original records" radio button is selected.

7. Click the **Next > button** to open the fifth Archive Wizard dialog box and type **FREELANCER ARCHIVE** as the new table name in the text box. Be sure the "Archive the records" radio button is selected and then click the **Finish button**.

8. In response to the next two dialog boxes, click the **Yes button** to confirm the copying process and then click the **OK button** to acknowledge the successfully archived message. Access has created the FREELANCER ARCHIVE table and has archived, or copied, the six selected records from the WRITERS table to the new table. Access closes all dialog boxes and activates the Database window.

❾ Click the Database window **maximize button** to see the full names of all the queries in the Issue25 database. See Figure 1-12.

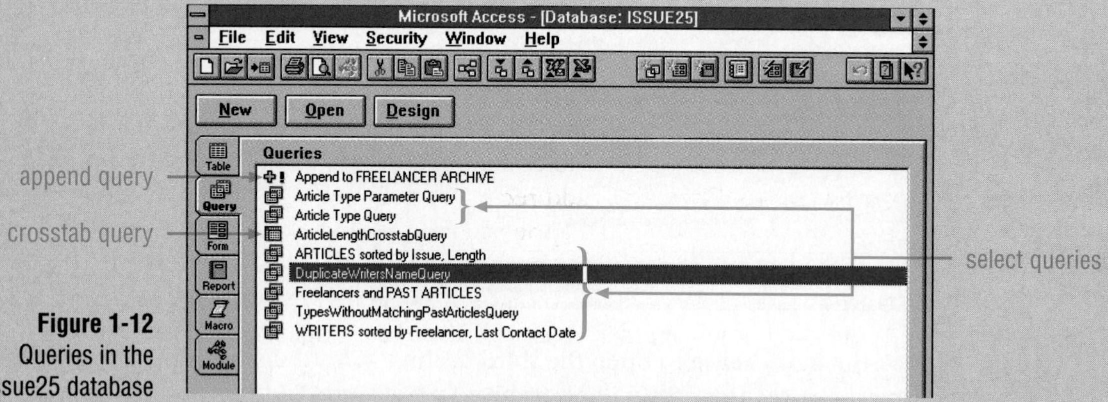

Figure 1-12
Queries in the Issue25 database

In addition to creating the FREELANCER ARCHIVE table, Access created and saved the query used to produce the new table giving it the query name Append to FREELANCER ARCHIVE. In the Queries list box, Access precedes this query's name with the append query icon. The FREELANCER ARCHIVE table is independent from the WRITERS table. If you update one table, the other table is not updated. Moreover, if you run the "Append to FREELANCER ARCHIVE" query again, you append, or add, a new set of selected records to the FREELANCER ARCHIVE table.

Using the Query Wizards is a convenient, organized way to produce queries. As you did with the crosstab query, you can change any query developed using the Query Wizards, or you can develop any Access query on your own in the Query Design window, completely bypassing the Query Wizards.

If you want to take a break and resume the tutorial at a later time, you can exit Access by double-clicking the Microsoft Access window Control menu box. When you resume the tutorial, place your Student Disk in the appropriate drive, launch Access, open the Issue25 database on your Student Disk, maximize the Database window, and click the Query object button.

■ ■ ■

Action Queries

Queries can do more than display answers to the questions you ask; they can also perform actions on the data in your database. For example, the Append to FREELANCER ARCHIVE query actually created a table and moved, or appended, data to the table. To perform this and other actions on the data in a database, you can use action queries. An **action query** is a query that adds, changes, or deletes multiple table records at one time. Because action queries modify many records in a table at a time, you should first create a select query to test the effects of your query design. When the select query works correctly, you then convert it to an action query.

Access has four types of action queries: the make-table query, the append query, the update query, and the delete query.

- Use a **make-table query** to create a new table from one or more existing tables. The new table can be an exact copy of an existing table, a subset of the fields and records of an existing table, or a combination of the fields and records from two or more tables. Access does not delete the selected fields and records from the existing tables. You can use make-table queries, for example, to create backup copies of tables or to create customized tables for others to use. Because the new table reflects data at a point in time, you need to run the make-table query periodically if you want the created table to contain reasonably current data.
- Use an **append query** to add records from an existing table or query to the end of another table. Although an append query is similar to a query you create using the Archive Query Wizard, it does not have the same capabilities. An Archive Query Wizard query selects entire records from a single table; you can choose either to delete or to keep the selected records in the original table. For an append query, you choose the fields to append from one or more tables or queries; the selected data remains in the original tables. Usually you append records to history tables. A **history table** contains data that is no longer needed for current processing but that might need to be referenced to answer questions in the future. Tables containing cleared bank checks, former employees, inactive customers, and obsolete products are examples of history tables. Because the records you append to a history table are no longer needed for current processing, you delete the records from the original table. If you want to append records to a history table and delete the records from the original table with a single query, you use an Archive Query Wizard query, not an append query.
- Use an **update query** to change selected fields and records in one or more tables. You choose the fields and records you want to change by entering the selection criteria and the update rules. You can use update queries, for example, to increase the salaries of selected employee groups by a specified percent and to change an article type from one value to another value.
- Use a **delete query** to delete a group of records from one or more tables. You choose which records you want to delete by entering the selection criteria. Once the records are deleted, they are gone from the database. Quite often, delete queries are run after append queries have added those same records to history tables. In this way you have a way to recapture records from the history tables if they were deleted in error from the original tables.

Creating a Make-Table Query

Elena wants her secretary to coordinate a conference call with all the freelance writers. Because the secretary needs to know only the freelance writers' names and phone numbers, Elena creates a new table with the name FREELANCERS. This table contains the freelance writers' Last Name, First Name, and Writer Phone fields. Although she could create a query instead of a table, Elena wants her secretary to keep notes of her phone conversations. Thus, Elena will eventually add a field to the new table; this new field will be a memo field, in which the secretary will enter notes.

Elena uses a make-table query to create the FREELANCERS table. She first creates a select query to choose the correct fields and records, tests the select query, and then changes the query to a make-table query.

To create a make-table query:

1. Click the **New command button** to open the New Query dialog box and then click the **New Query button** in the New Query dialog box. The Add Table dialog box opens on top of the Query Design window.
2. Double-click **WRITERS** in the Table/Query list box to add the WRITERS field list to the Query Design window and then click the **Close button** to close the Add Table dialog box.
3. Scrolling the WRITERS field list as necessary, double-click **Last Name**, **First Name**, **Writer Phone**, and then **Freelancer** to add these fields to the QBE grid.
4. Because the new table is to contain freelancers only, click the **Criteria text box** for the Freelancer field and then type **Yes**. The select query is now ready to test.
5. Click the toolbar **Run button** . The dynaset opens, showing the Last Name, First Name, Writer Phone, and Freelancer fields for Freelancer field values of Yes. The select query is correct, except for the Freelancer field, which you want to exclude from the new table.
6. Click the toolbar **Design View button** to switch back to the Query Design window and then click the **Freelancer Show box** to remove the X from it. The new table will contain only the fields whose Show boxes contain an X. You are now ready to change the select query to a make-table query.
7. Click the toolbar **Make-Table Query button** . Access opens the Query Properties dialog box, in which you enter the name of the new table. See Figure 1-13.

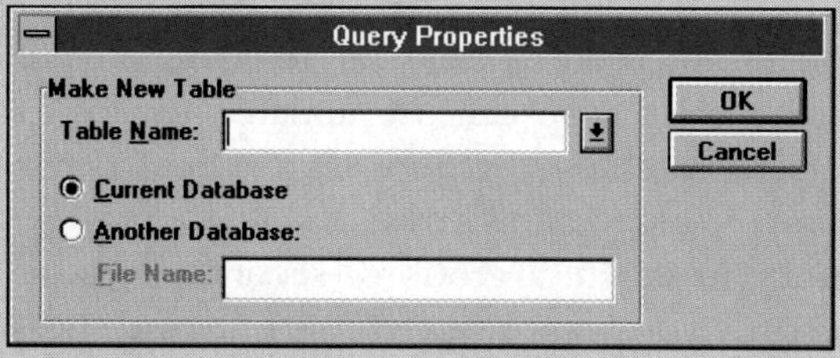

Figure 1-13 The Query Properties dialog box

8. In the Make New Table text box, type **FREELANCERS**, be sure that the Current Database radio button is selected, and then click the **OK button**.

Elena can now run and then save the make-table query.

To run and save a make-table query:

1. Click the toolbar **Run button** . Access opens a dialog box, which warns you about the upcoming copy operation.
2. Click the **OK button** to acknowledge the warning. Access closes the dialog box, runs the make-table query to create the FREELANCERS table, and leaves you in the Query Design window. If you check the Tables list box in the Database window, you will see the new FREELANCERS table listed there.
3. Click the toolbar **Save button** . Access opens the Save As dialog box.
4. Type **MakeFreelancersTableQuery** in the Query Name text box and then press **[Enter]** to name and save the query.
5. Double-click the Query Design window **Control menu box** to close this window and activate the Database window.

If you run this query again, Access will ask you if it can delete the existing FREELANCERS table before creating a new version of the table. Click the Yes button to delete the existing table or click the No button to cancel the make-table query without deleting the existing table.

Creating an Append Query

Suppose Elena needed a table containing the Last Name, First Name, and Writer Phone fields for all writers. She could change the make-table query she just created by deleting the Yes from the Criteria text box for the Freelancer field. Making this change would cause the three fields for all writers, not just the freelancers, to be placed in a new table. Alternatively, Elena could create an append query to add records for the writers who are not freelancers to the FREELANCERS table she already created. Because Elena wants to experiment with an append query, she first makes a copy of the FREELANCERS table, which she created for her secretary's use. She uses the name PHONE NUMBERS for the new table. Then Elena creates and runs an append query to add records for the staff writers' Last Name, First Name, and Writer Phone fields to the PHONE NUMBERS table, which already contains these same three fields for the freelancers. In summary, Elena's steps are:

- Copy the FREELANCERS table and paste it to the new PHONE NUMBERS table.
- Create a select query to choose the correct fields and records.
- Test the select query.
- Change the query to an append query.
- Run the append query.

To create an append query:

❶ Click the **Table object button**, click **FREELANCERS** in the Tables list box, click **Edit** in the menu bar, and then click **Copy**. Access copies the FREELANCERS table to the Clipboard. Finally, click **Edit** and then click **Paste**. Access opens the Paste Table As dialog box.

❷ Type **PHONE NUMBERS** in the Table Name text box, be sure that the Structure and Data radio button is selected, and then press **[Enter]**. Access creates the PHONE NUMBERS table and places a copy of the records from the FREELANCERS table into this new table.

❸ Click the **Query object button**, click the **New command button** to open the New Query dialog box, and then click the **New Query button** in the New Query dialog box. The Add Table dialog box opens on top of the Query Design window.

❹ Double-click **WRITERS** in the Table/Query list box to add the WRITERS field list to the Query Design window and then click the **Close button** to close the Add Table dialog box.

❺ Scrolling the WRITERS field list as necessary, double-click **Last Name**, **First Name**, **Writer Phone**, and then **Freelancer** to add these fields to the QBE grid.

❻ Because just staff writers are needed in the new table, click the **Criteria text box** for the Freelancer field, type **No**, then click the toolbar **Run button** [!]. The dynaset opens, showing the Last Name, First Name, Writer Phone, and Freelancer fields for Freelancer field values of No. The select query is correct, except for the Freelancer field, which you want to exclude from the new table.

❼ Click the toolbar **Design View button** to switch back to the Query Design window and then click the **Freelancer Show box** to remove the X from it. You can now change the select query to an append query.

8. Click the toolbar **Append Query button**. Access opens the Query Properties dialog box, in which you enter the name of the table to which you want to append the data.
9. Click the **down arrow button** on the right side of the Table Name text box, click **PHONE NUMBERS**, be sure that the Current Database radio button is selected, and then click the **OK button**. Between the Sort and Criteria rows in the QBE grid, Access replaces the Show row with the Append To row. See Figure 1-14.

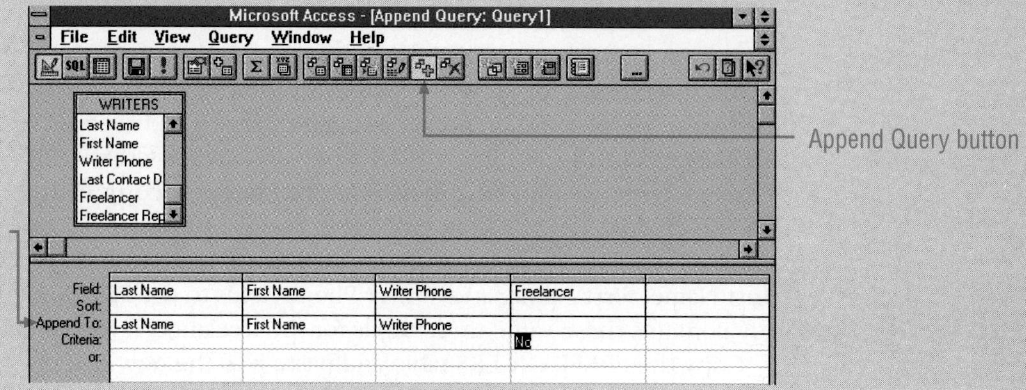

Figure 1-14
The Query Design window for an append query

The Append To row in the QBE grid identifies the fields that will be appended to the designated table. The Last Name, First Name, and Writer Phone fields for staff writers are to be appended to the PHONE NUMBERS table, which already contains these three fields for freelancers.

Elena can now run and then save the append query.

To run and save an append query:

1. Click the toolbar **Run button**. Access opens a dialog box, which warns you about the upcoming copy operation.
2. Click the **OK button** to acknowledge the warning. Access closes the dialog box, runs the append query to add records to the PHONE NUMBERS table, and leaves you in the Query Design window.
3. Click the toolbar **Save button**. Access opens the Save As dialog box.
4. Type **AppendToPhoneNumbersTableQuery** in the Query Name text box and then press **[Enter]** to name and save the query.
5. Double-click the Query Design window **Control menu box** to close this window and activate the Database window.

If you run the AppendToPhoneNumbersTableQuery query again, Access asks permission to append the data before it does so. Click the OK button to continue with the append query or click the Cancel button to cancel the append query.

Creating an Update Query

Brian Murphy tells Elena that freelancers will be paid $25 more than planned but staff writers will still not be paid for their article reprints in the 25th-anniversary issue. Elena must update each freelancer's Freelancer Reprint Payment Amount field value in the WRITERS table but not change the field value for staff writers. She could change each value in the table's datasheet individually, but using an update query to change all freelancers' field values at one time is faster and more accurate. As she has done before, Elena will create a select query to choose the correct records, test the select query, and then change the query to an update query. Several workable ways to construct the select query occur to Elena before she finally decides on her method. The select query Elena creates will display just the Freelancer Reprint Payment Amount field for all writers having a Freelancer Reprint Payment Amount field value greater than zero. Only freelancer records meet this requirement, because they are the only ones being paid for their reprinted articles.

To create an update query:

1. Click the **New command button** to open the New Query dialog box, and then click the **New Query button** in the New Query dialog box. The Add Table dialog box opens on top of the Query Design window.
2. Double-click **WRITERS** in the Table/Query list box to add the WRITERS field list to the Query Design window and then click the **Close button** to close the Add Table dialog box.
3. Scroll the WRITERS field list and then double-click **Freelancer Reprint Payment Amount** to add this field to the QBE grid.
4. Click the **Criteria text box** for the Freelancer Reprint Payment Amount field and then type **>0**. Access will select a record only if the Freelancer Reprint Payment Amount field value is greater than zero.
5. Click the toolbar **Run button** [!]. The dynaset opens, showing one column heading with a name of Amount, which is the caption value for the Freelancer Reprint Payment Amount field, and values for the six freelancer records. The select query is correct.
6. Click the toolbar **Design View button** to switch back to the Query Design window and then click the toolbar **Update Query button**. In the QBE grid, Access replaces the Sort and Show rows with the Update To row. See Figure 1-15.

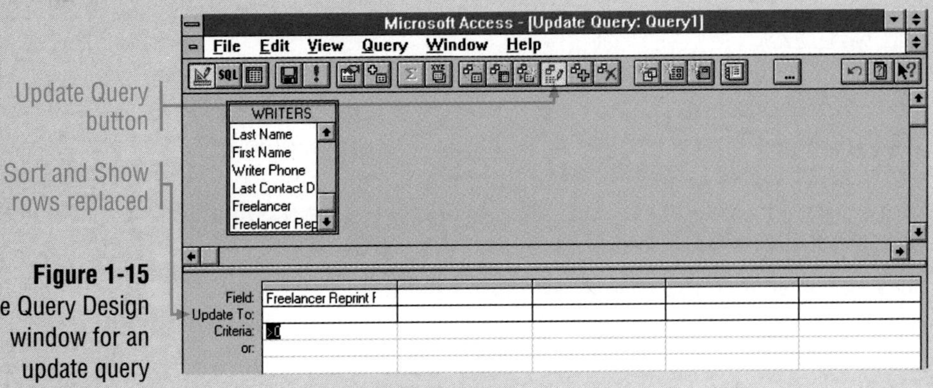

Figure 1-15 The Query Design window for an update query

You tell Access how you want to change a field value for the selected records by entering an expression in the field's Update To text box. An **expression** is a calculation resulting in a single value. You can either type it in or generate it using the **Expression Builder**, an Access tool that contains an Expression box for entering the expression, buttons for common operators, and one or more lists of expression elements, such as table and field names.

To use the Expression Builder to complete an update query:

1. Click the **Update To text box** for the Freelancer Reprint Payment Amount field, click it with the right mouse button, and then click **Build....** Access opens the Expression Builder dialog box. See Figure 1-16.

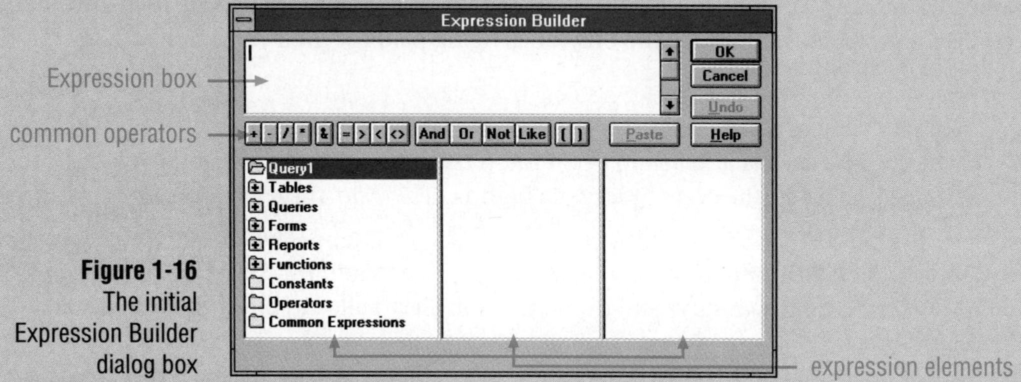

Figure 1-16 The initial Expression Builder dialog box

2. In the first column of expression elements, double-click **Tables** to display the Issue25 tables, scroll the list and double-click **WRITERS**. Access displays the field names for the WRITERS table. See Figure 1-17.

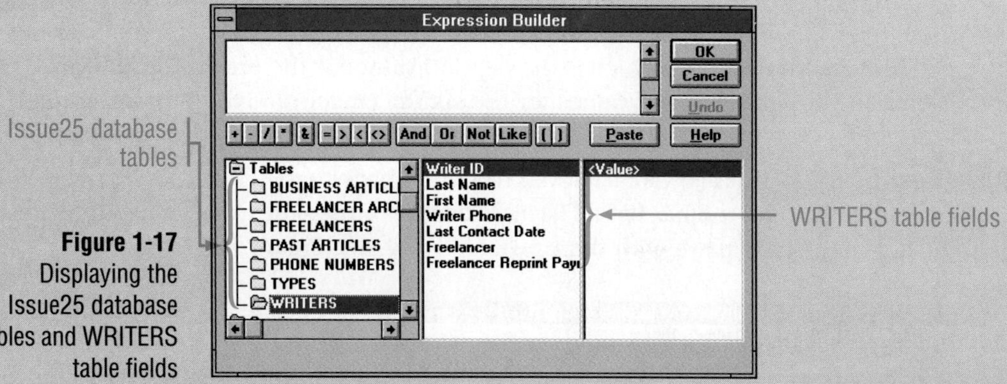

Figure 1-17 Displaying the Issue25 database tables and WRITERS table fields

3. Double-click **Freelancer Reprint Payment Amount** in the middle column of expression elements. Access places [WRITERS]![Freelancer Reprint Payment Amount] in the Expression box to indicate that, so far, your expression contains the Freelancer Reprint Payment Amount field, which is part of the WRITERS table.

4. Click the **+ button** in the row of common operators and then type **25**. You have completed the construction of the expression. See Figure 1-18.

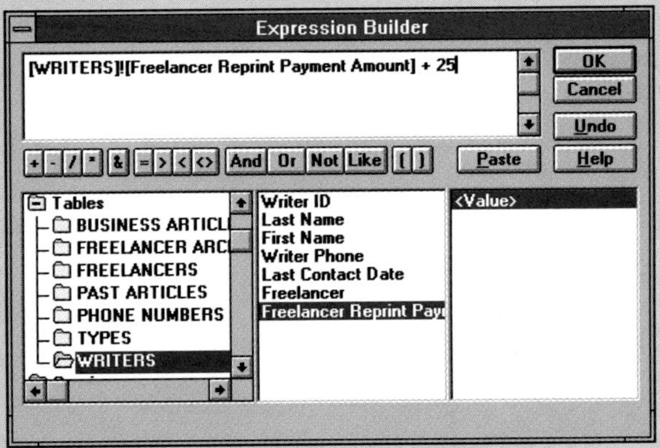

Figure 1-18 Completed expression for an update query

5. Click the **OK button**. Access closes the Expression Builder dialog box and adds the expression to the Update To text box for the Freelancer Reprint Payment Amount field.
6. Click the toolbar **Run button**. Access opens a dialog box, which warns you about the upcoming update operation.
7. Click the **OK button** to close the dialog box and run the update query. Access leaves the Query Design window open.
8. Click the toolbar **Save button** to open the Save As dialog box, type **UpdateWritersAmountQuery** in the Query Name text box, and then press **[Enter]** to name and save the query.
9. Double-click the Query Design window **Control menu box**, click the **Table object button**, and then double-click **WRITERS** in the Tables list box.

The freelancers Amount column shows $125, $55, $150, $65, $475, and $375. These figures are all $25 more than they were before the update query was run. Because you usually run an update query once, you would not normally need to save it. If you do happen to run a saved update query again, Access asks permission to modify the data. Click the OK button to continue with the change or click the Cancel button to cancel the update query.

Creating a Delete Query

Four writers visit the Vision Publishers offices and meet with Elena, who briefs them on the 25th-anniversary plans for *Business Perspective*. Because her secretary no longer needs to contact these four writers, Elena wants to delete their records from the PHONE NUMBERS table. She can delete the table records individually. Because these writers are the only ones who have 210 or 917 area codes, however, Elena creates a delete query to remove the four table records. Elena creates a select query to choose the correct records, tests the select query, and then changes the query to a delete query.

To create a delete query:

1. Double-click the Datasheet View window **Control menu box** to close the WRITERS table, click the **Query object button**, click the **New command button**, and then click the **New Query button**. The Add Table dialog box opens on top of the Query Design window.
2. Double-click **PHONE NUMBERS** in the Table/Query list box to add the PHONE NUMBERS field list to the Query Design window and then click the **Close button** to close the Add Table dialog box.
3. Double-click the **title bar** of the PHONE NUMBERS field list to select all the fields in the table and then drag the pointer from the highlighted area of the PHONE NUMBERS field list to the QBE grid's first column Field box. Access adds all the fields to the QBE grid.
4. Click the **Criteria text box** for the Writer Phone field, type **Like "210*"**, press [↓], and then type **Like "917*"**. Access will select a record only if the Writer Phone field value starts with either 210 or 917.
5. Click the toolbar **Run button** [!]. The dynaset appears, showing four records, each one with either a 210 or 917 area code. The select query is correct.
6. Click the toolbar **Design View button** to switch back to the Query Design window and then click the toolbar **Delete Query button**. In the QBE grid, Access replaces the Sort and Show rows with the Delete row. See Figure 1-19.

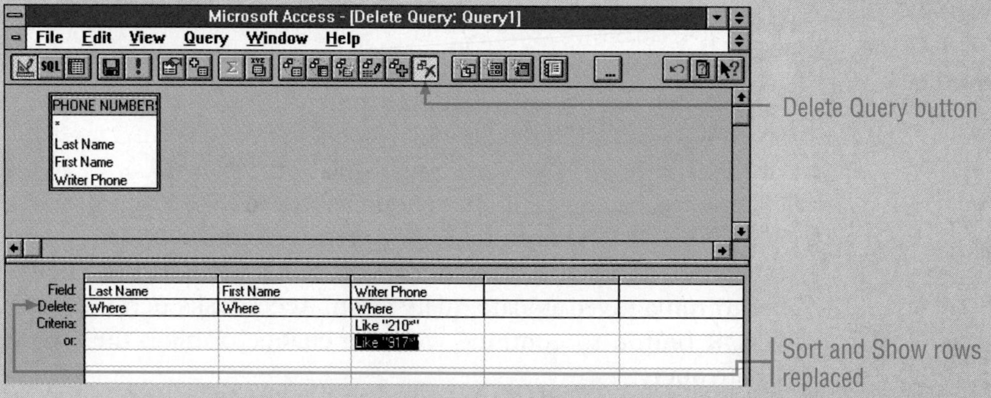

Figure 1-19
The Query Design window for a delete query

7. Click the toolbar [!]. Access opens a dialog box, which warns you about the upcoming delete operation.
8. Click the **OK button** to close the dialog box and run the delete query. Access keeps the Query Design window open. Because this query needs to be run only once, Elena doesn't bother to save it.
9. Double-click the Query Design window **Control menu box**, click the **No button** in the "Save changes to Query" dialog box, click the **Table object button**, and then double-click **PHONE NUMBERS** in the Tables list box. Access opens the Datasheet View window for the PHONE NUMBERS table.

Access displays the 11 remaining records in the PHONE NUMBERS table; four records were correctly deleted. As is the case with update queries, you do not usually need to save delete queries. If you do happen to run a delete query again, Access asks permission to modify the data. Click the OK button to continue with the delete or click the Cancel button to cancel the delete query.

Elena returns to the Database window before taking a short break.

To display the Queries list in the Database window:

1. Double-click the Datasheet View window **Control menu box** and then click the **Query object button**. Access activates the Database window and displays the Queries list box.

If you want to take a break and resume the tutorial at a later time, you can exit Access by double-clicking the Microsoft Access window Control menu box. When you resume the tutorial, place your Student Disk in the appropriate drive, launch Access, open the Issue25 database on your Student Disk, maximize the Database window, and click the Query object button.

■ ■ ■

Top-Value Queries

If you have a query that displays thousands of records, you might want to limit the number to a more manageable size by, for example, showing just the first 20 records. The **Top Values property** for a query lets you limit the number of records in a select, append, or make-table query dynaset. For the Top Values property you enter either an integer (like 20, to show the first 20) or percent (like 50%, to show the first half). Suppose you have a select query that displays 45 records. If you want the dynaset to show only the first five records, you can change the query by entering a Top Values property of either 5 or 10%. If the query contains a sort, Access displays the records in order by the primary sort key. Whenever the last record that Access can choose to display is one of two or more records because they have the same value for the primary sort key, Access displays all of them.

Let's experiment with the Top Values property by using the query named ARTICLES sorted by Issue, Length. For this example, you'll need to remove the existing sort keys and add a sort key for the Type field to see the effects of the Top Values property better.

To limit records in a dynaset using the Top Values property:

1. Double-click **ARTICLES sorted by Issue, Length** in the Queries list box. Access displays 27 records in the dynaset. First, you will change the query sort keys.
2. Click the **Design View button** to switch back to the Query Design window, click the **Sort text box** for the Issue of Business Perspectives field, click the **down arrow button** that appears, and then click **(not sorted)**. Similarly, click the **Sort text box** for the Article Length field, click the **down arrow button** that appears, and then click **(not sorted)**. Finally, click the **Sort text box** for the Type field, click the **down arrow button** that appears, and then click **Ascending**. The sort keys are now correctly modified.
3. Click the toolbar **Run button**. The dynaset opens, again showing 27 records. The records are in order by the Type field, and records 7 through 13 have a Type field value of EXP.

4. Click the **Design View button** to switch back to the Query Design window, click the blank area to the right of the WRITERS field list (as shown in Figure 1-20) to remove the cursor from the Type field, and then click the toolbar **Properties button**. Access opens the property sheet for the query. See Figure 1-20.

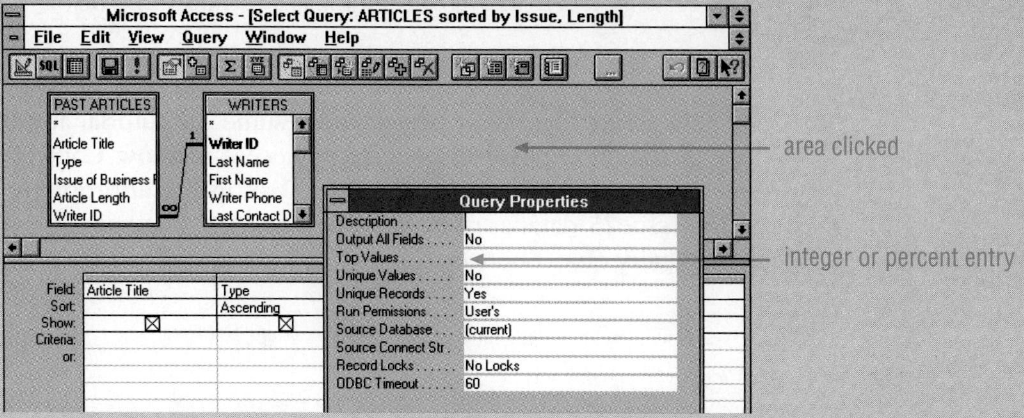

Figure 1-20
The property sheet for a query

5. Click the **Top Values box** in the property sheet, type **6**, and then click . Access displays the top six records in the dynaset.
6. Click , click to the right of the WRITERS field list, double-click **6** in the Top Values box, type **7**, and then click . Access displays the top 13 records, rather than the top seven, because the last seven records have the same Type field value.
7. Click , click to the right of the WRITERS field list, double-click **7** in the Top Values box, type **50%**, and then click . Access displays the top 14 records, which is just over 50% of the records. End your work without saving your query changes.
8. Double-click the Datasheet View window **Control menu box** and click the **No button** in response to the "Save changes to Query" dialog box. Access activates the Query list box in the Database window.

Reacting to a New Requirement

Freelance and staff writers have been voicing concern about not being kept informed of future writing opportunities at Vision Publishers. To correct this problem, Brian Murphy promotes Pat Lawton and Kristine Waldeck to senior writer positions. In addition, he assigns Lawton the responsibility of keeping the other staff writers informed of future projects and assigns Waldeck a similar responsibility with the freelancers.

Brian asks Elena to add the contact information to the database and then to create a new query that shows which junior writers are assigned to Lawton and which to Waldeck. She first adds a field named Contact to the WRITERS table that will contain either Lawton's or Waldeck's Writer ID field value. Then, she creates a query that displays the writers and their senior contacts.

To add a new field to the WRITERS table:

1. Click the **Table object button**, click **WRITERS** in the Tables list box, and then click the **Design command button**. Access opens the Table Design View window for the WRITERS table.

❷ Click the **Field Name box** just below the Freelancer Reprint Payment Amount field, type **Contact**, press **[Tab]**, press **[Tab]** again, and then type **Senior Writer contact for this writer** in the new field's Description box. Finally, double-click **50** in the Field Size box and then type **4**. This completes the addition of the Contact field to the WRITERS table. See Figure 1-21.

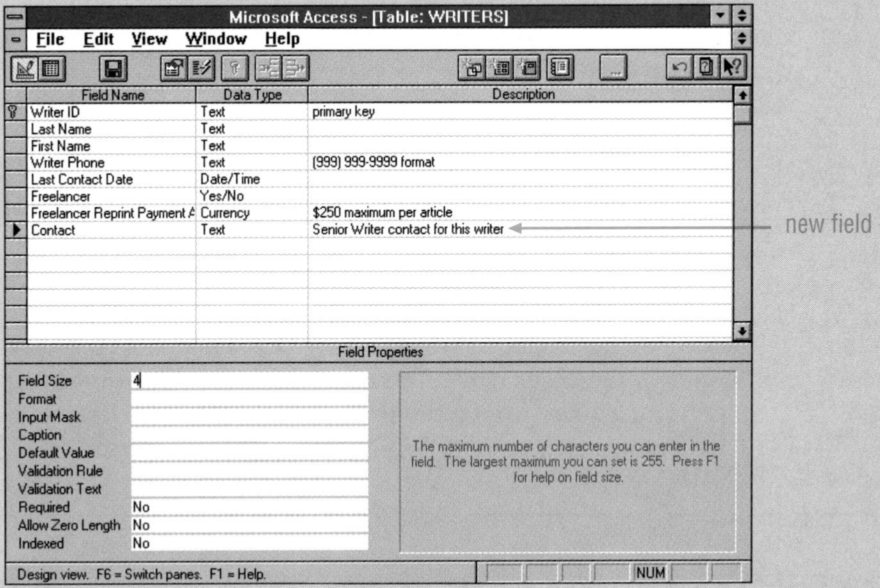

Figure 1-21
Contact field added to the WRITERS table

❸ Click the toolbar **Datasheet View button** and then click the **OK button** in response to the "Save now?" dialog box. Access saves the table structure changes and then opens the Datasheet View window.

❹ For each freelance writer (a value of Yes in the Freelancer field), type **W432** in the record's Contact field box. This is the Writer ID field value for Kristine Waldeck.

❺ For all other records, except those for Lawton and Waldeck, which must be kept null, type **L350** in the Contact field box. This is the Writer ID field value for Pat Lawton.

❻ Resize the Contact column to its best-fit column width. See Figure 1-22.

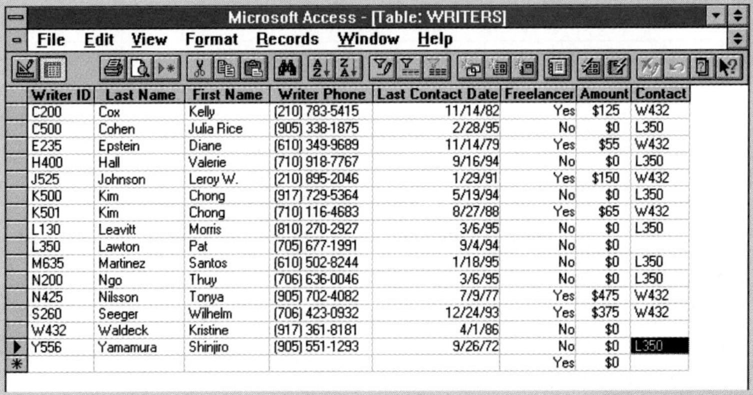
Microsoft Access - [Table: WRITERS]
File Edit View Format Records Window Help
Writer ID | Last Name | First Name | Writer Phone | Last Contact Date | Freelancer | Amount | Contact
C200 | Cox | Kelly | (210) 783-5415 | 11/14/82 | Yes | $125 | W432
C500 | Cohen | Julia Rice | (905) 338-1875 | 2/28/95 | No | $0 | L350
E235 | Epstein | Diane | (610) 349-9689 | 11/14/79 | Yes | $55 | W432
H400 | Hall | Valerie | (710) 918-7767 | 9/16/94 | No | $0 | L350
J525 | Johnson | Leroy W. | (210) 895-2046 | 1/29/91 | Yes | $150 | W432
K500 | Kim | Chong | (917) 729-5364 | 5/19/94 | No | $0 | L350
K501 | Kim | Chong | (710) 116-4683 | 8/27/88 | Yes | $65 | W432
L130 | Leavitt | Morris | (810) 270-2927 | 3/6/95 | No | $0 | L350
L350 | Lawton | Pat | (705) 677-1991 | 9/4/94 | No | $0
M635 | Martinez | Santos | (610) 502-8244 | 1/18/95 | No | $0 | L350
N200 | Ngo | Thuy | (706) 636-0046 | 3/6/95 | No | $0 | L350
N425 | Nilsson | Tonya | (905) 702-4082 | 7/9/77 | Yes | $475 | W432
S260 | Seeger | Wilhelm | (706) 423-0932 | 12/24/93 | Yes | $375 | W432
W432 | Waldeck | Kristine | (917) 361-8181 | 4/1/86 | No | $0
Y556 | Yamamura | Shinjiro | (905) 551-1293 | 9/26/72 | No | $0 | L350
Yes | $0

Figure 1-22
The Datasheet View window after the Contact field is added to the WRITERS table

❼ Double-click the Datasheet View window **Control menu box** and click the **Yes button** in response to the "Save layout changes" dialog box. Access saves the table layout changes and activates the Database window.

Now that the contact ID numbers are in place, Elena can generate the query Brian requested.

Joining Tables

Elena needs to create a query to display the new contact relationships in the WRITERS table. To do so, she creates a special join using the WRITERS table. In Access you can establish a relationship between two tables having a common field, and then join the tables to run a query with data from both tables. This type of join is called an equi-join, which is one of four available Access joins. The others are the left outer join, the right outer join, and the self-join.

- An **equi-join**, or **inner join**, is a join in which Access selects records from two tables only when the records have the same value in the common field that links the tables. For example, Writer ID is the common field for the WRITERS and PAST ARTICLES tables. As shown in Figure 1-23, an equi-join of these two tables includes only those records that have a matching Writer ID value. The Writer ID W432 record in the WRITERS table and the Writer ID N425 record in the PAST ARTICLES table are not included because they fail to match a record with the same Writer ID value in the other table. The equi-join is the join you ordinarily use whenever you perform a query from more than one table; it is the default join we have been using right along.

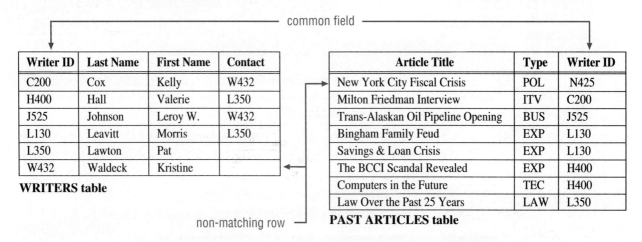

common field

Writer ID	Last Name	First Name	Contact
C200	Cox	Kelly	W432
H400	Hall	Valerie	L350
J525	Johnson	Leroy W.	W432
L130	Leavitt	Morris	L350
L350	Lawton	Pat	
W432	Waldeck	Kristine	

WRITERS table

Article Title	Type	Writer ID
New York City Fiscal Crisis	POL	N425
Milton Friedman Interview	ITV	C200
Trans-Alaskan Oil Pipeline Opening	BUS	J525
Bingham Family Feud	EXP	L130
Savings & Loan Crisis	EXP	L130
The BCCI Scandal Revealed	EXP	H400
Computers in the Future	TEC	H400
Law Over the Past 25 Years	LAW	L350

non-matching row

PAST ARTICLES table

Writer ID	Last Name	First name	Contact	Article Title	Type
C200	Cox	Kelly	W432	Milton Friedman Interview	ITV
H400	Hall	Valerie	L350	Computers in the Future	TEC
H400	Hall	Valerie	L350	The BCCI Scandal Revealed	EXP
J525	Johnson	Leroy W.	W432	Trans-Alaskan Oil Pipeline Opening	BUS
L130	Leavitt	Morris	L350	Bingham Family Feud	EXP
L130	Leavitt	Morris	L350	Savings & Loan Crisis	EXP
L350	Lawton	Pat		Law Over the Past 25 Years	LAW

Equi-join dynaset

Figure 1-23
Equi-join

- A **left outer join** is a join in which Access selects all records from the first, or left, table and only those records from the second table that have matching common field values. Figure 1-24 shows a left outer join for the WRITERS and PAST ARTICLES tables. All records from the WRITERS table, which is the left table, appear in the dynaset. The Writer ID W432 record appears even though it does not match a record in the PAST ARTICLES table. The Writer ID N425 record in the PAST ARTICLES table does not appear, however, because it does not match a record in the WRITERS table.

common field

Writer ID	Last Name	First Name	Contact
C200	Cox	Kelly	W432
H400	Hall	Valerie	L350
J525	Johnson	Leroy W.	W432
L130	Leavitt	Morris	L350
L350	Lawton	Pat	
W432	Waldeck	Kristine	

WRITERS table

Article Title	Type	Writer ID
New York City Fiscal Crisis	POL	N425
Milton Friedman Interview	ITV	C200
Trans-Alaskan Oil Pipeline Opening	BUS	J525
Bingham Family Feud	EXP	L130
Savings & Loan Crisis	EXP	L130
The BCCI Scandal Revealed	EXP	H400
Computers in the Future	TEC	H400
Law Over the Past 25 Years	LAW	L350

non-matching row

PAST ARTICLES table

Writer ID	Last Name	First name	Contact	Article Title	Type
C200	Cox	Kelly	W432	Milton Friedman Interview	ITV
H400	Hall	Valerie	L350	Computers in the Future	TEC
H400	Hall	Valerie	L350	The BCCI Scandal Revealed	EXP
J525	Johnson	Leroy W.	W432	Trans-Alaskan Oil Pipeline Opening	BUS
L130	Leavitt	Morris	L350	Bingham Family Feud	EXP
L130	Leavitt	Morris	L350	Savings & Loan Crisis	EXP
L350	Lawton	Pat		Law Over the Past 25 Years	LAW
W432	Waldeck	Kristine			

Left outer join dynaset

Figure 1-24
Left outer join

- A **right outer join** is a join in which Access selects all records from the second, or right, table and only those records from the first table that have matching common field values. Figure 1-25 shows a right outer join for the WRITERS and PAST ARTICLES tables. All records from the PAST ARTICLES table, which is the right table, appear in the dynaset. The Writer ID N425 record appears even though it does not match a record in the WRITERS table. The Writer ID W432 record in the WRITERS table does not appear, however, because it does not match a record in the PAST ARTICLES table.

common field

Writer ID	Last Name	First Name	Contact
C200	Cox	Kelly	W432
H400	Hall	Valerie	L350
J525	Johnson	Leroy W.	W432
L130	Leavitt	Morris	L350
L350	Lawton	Pat	
W432	Waldeck	Kristine	

WRITERS table

Article Title	Type	Writer ID
New York City Fiscal Crisis	POL	N425
Milton Friedman Interview	ITV	C200
Trans-Alaskan Oil Pipeline Opening	BUS	J525
Bingham Family Feud	EXP	L130
Savings & Loan Crisis	EXP	L130
The BCCI Scandal Revealed	EXP	H400
Computers in the Future	TEC	H400
Law Over the Past 25 Years	LAW	L350

PAST ARTICLES table

non-matching row

Writer ID	Last Name	First name	Contact	Article Title	Type
C200	Cox	Kelly	W432	Milton Friedman Interview	ITV
H400	Hall	Valerie	L350	Computers in the Future	TEC
H400	Hall	Valerie	L350	The BCCI Scandal Revealed	EXP
J525	Johnson	Leroy W.	W432	Trans-Alaskan Oil Pipeline Opening	BUS
L130	Leavitt	Morris	L350	Bingham Family Feud	EXP
L130	Leavitt	Morris	L350	Savings & Loan Crisis	EXP
L350	Lawton	Pat		Law Over the Past 25 Years	LAW
N425				New York City Fiscal Crisis	POL

Right outer join dynaset

Figure 1-25
Right outer join

- A **self-join**, which can be either an equi- or outer join, joins a table with itself, so that Access selects records from a table and other records from the same table. Figure 1-26 shows a self-join for the WRITERS table. In this case, the self-join is an equi-join because records appear in the dynaset only if the Contact field value matches a Writer ID field value. If you use Access to create this self-join, you add two copies of the WRITERS table to the Query Design window and link the Contact field of one WRITER table to the Writer ID field of the other WRITER table.

common field

Writer ID	Last Name	First Name	Contact
C200	Cox	Kelly	W432
H400	Hall	Valerie	L350
J525	Johnson	Leroy W.	W432
L130	Leavitt	Morris	L350
L350	Lawton	Pat	
W432	Waldeck	Kristine	

WRITERS table

non-matching row

Writer ID	Last Name	First name	Contact	Contact Last Name	Contact First Name
C200	Cox	Kelly	W432	Waldeck	Kristine
H400	Hall	Valerie	L350	Lawton	Pat
J525	Johnson	Leroy W.	W432	Waldeck	Kristine
L130	Leavitt	Morris	L350	Lawton	Pat

Self-join dynaset

Figure 1-26
Self-join

Creating a Self-Join

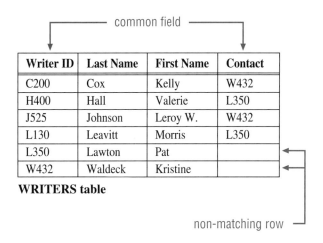

Elena creates a query to display the new contact relationships in the WRITERS table. This equi-join query requires a self-join on the table. Elena adds two copies of the WRITERS field list to the Query Design window. Next, Elena adds a join line from the Writer ID field in the right field list to the Contact field in the left field list to establish a relationship between the WRITERS table and itself; the Contact field is a foreign key that matches the primary key field of Writer ID. Finally, Elena adds the Writer ID, Last Name, First Name, and Contact fields from the left field list, adds the Last Name and First Name fields from the right field list, and then chooses an ascending sort on the Writer ID field. The dynaset displays, in increasing Writer ID order, all writers and their contacts, except for the two senior writers, who have null Contact field values.

To create a self-join query:

1. Click the **Query object button**, click the **New command button**, and then click the **New Query button** in the New Query dialog box. The Add Table dialog box opens on top of the Query Design window.
2. Double-click **WRITERS** in the Add Table dialog box, double-click **WRITERS** again to add a second copy of the WRITERS field list, click the **Close button**, and then click the toolbar **Properties button** to close the property sheet. Access identifies the left field list as WRITERS and the right field list as WRITERS_1 to distinguish the two copies of the table.

❸ Scroll the left field list until the Contact field is visible. Then click and drag the **Writer ID field** from the right field list to the **Contact field** in the left field list. Access adds a join line between the two fields. You can verify that this is an equi-join query by displaying the Join Properties dialog box.

❹ Double-click the **join line** between the two tables to open the Join Properties dialog box. See Figure 1-27.

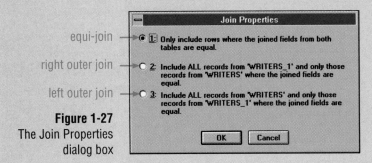

equi-join

right outer join

left outer join

Figure 1-27
The Join Properties dialog box

TROUBLE? If double-clicking the join line does not work, click View and then click Join Properties... to open the Join Properties dialog box.

The top radio button is selected; this button indicates an equi-join. You would click the middle radio button for a right outer join or the bottom radio button for a left outer join. Because the equi-join is correct, cancel the dialog box and then add fields to the QBE grid.

❺ Click the **Cancel button** and then, scrolling as necessary, double-click, in order from the left field list, the **Writer ID**, **Last Name**, **First Name**, and **Contact** fields to add them to the QBE grid. Then double-click, in order from the right field list, the **Last Name** and **First Name** fields to add them to the QBE grid.

❻ Click the **Sort text box** for the Writer ID field, click the **down arrow button** that appears, and then click **Ascending** to establish the sort order for the dynaset.

❼ Click the toolbar **Run button** [!]. The dynaset opens in increasing Writer ID order and shows six fields and 13 records. See Figure 1-28.

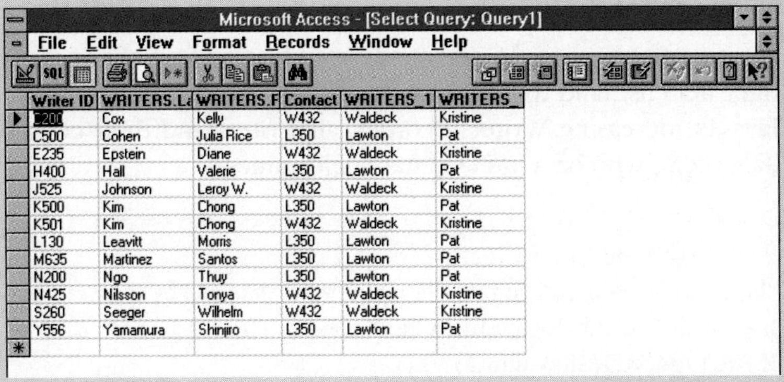

Figure 1-28
The initial self-join on the WRITERS table

Access displays 13 of the 15 records from the WRITERS table; Lawton and Waldeck, who are senior writers with a null Contact field value, are not displayed. Four field names at the top of the dynaset columns now have prefixes indicating either WRITERS or WRITERS_1 to distinguish fields in one table from fields in the other table.

Elena looks at the entire name for one of the fields and then switches back to the Query Design window to rename the four fields that have the table name prefixed to the field name. When they are renamed, the field names, from left to right, will be Writer ID, Last Name, First Name, Contact, Contact Last Name, and Contact First Name.

To rename fields in a self-join query:

❶ Resize the rightmost dynaset column to its best-fit column width. The full name displayed is WRITERS_1.First Name, which means the First Name field from the WRITERS_1 table.

❷ Click the toolbar **Design View button** to switch back to the Query Design window.

❸ Place the insertion point in front of the first character in the second column's Field box, which displays Last Name, and then type **Last Name:**. Be sure the colon is the last character you type.

❹ Repeat the previous step for the third, fifth, and sixth columns, typing **First Name:**, **Contact Last Name:**, and **Contact First Name:**, respectively.

❺ Click the toolbar **Run button**. The dynaset displays the new names for each column.

❻ Resize all columns to their best-fit column widths. See Figure 1-29.

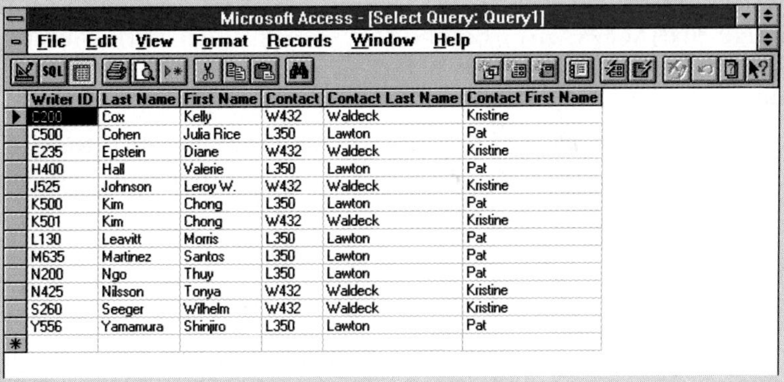

Writer ID	Last Name	First Name	Contact	Contact Last Name	Contact First Name
C200	Cox	Kelly	W432	Waldeck	Kristine
C500	Cohen	Julia Rice	L350	Lawton	Pat
E235	Epstein	Diane	W432	Waldeck	Kristine
H400	Hall	Valerie	L350	Lawton	Pat
J525	Johnson	Leroy W.	W432	Waldeck	Kristine
K500	Kim	Chong	L350	Lawton	Pat
K501	Kim	Chong	W432	Waldeck	Kristine
L130	Leavitt	Morris	L350	Lawton	Pat
M635	Martinez	Santos	L350	Lawton	Pat
N200	Ngo	Thuy	L350	Lawton	Pat
N425	Nilsson	Tonya	W432	Waldeck	Kristine
S260	Seeger	Wilhelm	W432	Waldeck	Kristine
Y556	Yamamura	Shinjiro	L350	Lawton	Pat

Figure 1-29
The final self-join on the WRITERS table

Elena can now give Brian a list of writers and their contacts for future article opportunities. She saves the query with the name WritersContactQuery and returns to the Database window.

To save and close a query:

1. Click **File**, click **Save Query As...**, type **WritersContactQuery** in the Save As dialog box, and then press **[Enter]**. Access saves the new self-join query.
2. Double-click the dynaset **Control menu box** to close the window and activate the Database window. See Figure 1-30.

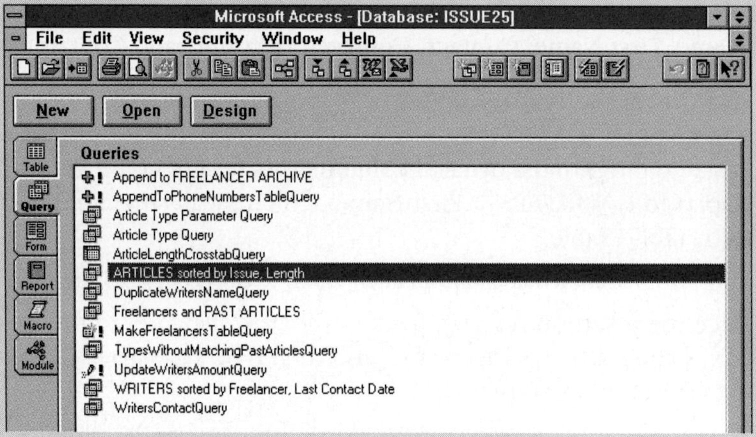

Figure 1-30
Saved queries in the Issue25 database

Elena has now saved 13 queries that she and others can use, thanks to the confidence she gained at the training seminar and her efforts to practice what she learned there. She recalls that one of the things that kept coming up at the seminar was the SQL language that Access uses behind the scenes when performing many of its operations. Elena knows that if she ever wants to take full advantage of Access's query abilities, she'll have to take the time to master SQL. She decides to familiarize herself with SQL statements by regularly looking them over after she performs queries. Perhaps that way she can become more comfortable with SQL so that when she does put in the effort to learn it, she'll already have some idea of how it works.

SQL

SQL (Structured Query Language) is a standard language used in querying, updating, and managing relational databases. Every full-featured relational DBMS has its version of the current standard SQL, which is called **SQL-92**. If you learn SQL for one relational DBMS, it's a relatively easy task to begin using SQL for other relational DBMSs. This is particularly important when you work with two or more relational DBMSs, which is the case in most companies.

Much of what Access accomplishes behind the scenes is done with SQL. For example, whenever you create a query by example (QBE) in the Query Design window, Access automatically constructs an equivalent SQL statement. And when you save a query, Access saves the SQL-statement version of the query rather than the QBE version.

When you are in the Query Design window or are viewing a dynaset, you can see the SQL statement that is equivalent to your QBE query if you click the toolbar SQL View button or choose SQL from the View menu. In response, Access displays the SQL statement in the SQL View window.

REFERENCE WINDOW

Viewing an SQL Statement for an Existing Query

- Open the Query Design window or the dynaset for an existing query.
- Click the toolbar SQL button, or click View and then click SQL.

Elena examines the SQL statements that are equivalent to two existing queries: WRITERS sorted by Freelancer, Last Contact Date; and ARTICLES sorted by Issue, Length.

To view the SQL statement for the query named WRITERS sorted by Freelancer, Last Contact Date:

1. Double-click **WRITERS sorted by Freelancer, Last Contact Date** in the Queries list box. Access opens the dynaset for this saved query and shows all 15 records from the WRITERS table in descending order by the Freelancer field as the primary sort key and the Last Contact Date field as the secondary sort key. The fields displayed are Writer ID, Last Name, First Name, Writer Phone, Freelancer, Last Contact Date, and Amount.
2. Click the toolbar **Design View button**. Access opens the Query Design window for this saved query.
3. Click the toolbar **SQL View button** to open the SQL View window. See Figure 1-31.

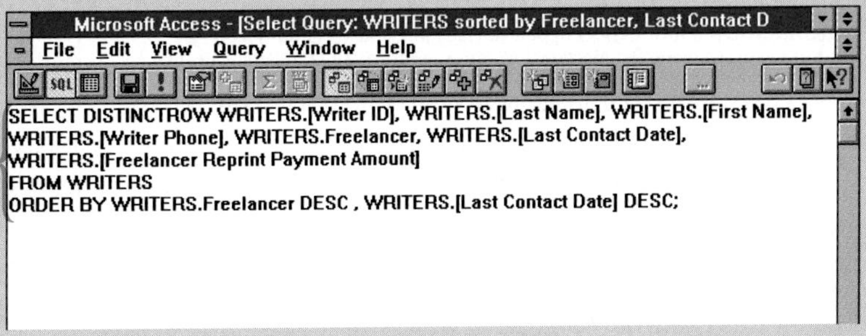

SQL statement

Figure 1-31
The SQL View window

SQL uses the **SELECT statement** to define what data it retrieves from a database and how it presents the data. If you learn SQL to the point where you can use it efficiently, you will be able to enter your own SELECT and other SQL statements in the SQL View window. For the work you've done so far, the Access menu commands and dialog box options have sufficed, but you might find if you work with more complicated databases that you need the extra power of the SQL language to implement your database strategies fully.

The rules that SQL uses to construct an SQL statement, similar to the SELECT statement shown in Figure 1-31, are summarized as follows:

- The basic form of an SQL statement is: SELECT-FROM-ORDER BY. After the SELECT, list the fields you want to display. After the FROM, list the tables used in the query. After the ORDER BY, list the sort keys.
- Enclose a field name in brackets and precede it by the name of its table. Connect the table name to the field name with a period. For example, enter Writer ID as "WRITERS.[Writer ID]."

- Separate field names and table names by commas, and end a statement with a semicolon.
- Use DESC to indicate a descending sort order; ascending is the default.
- Use DISTINCTROW to omit records that are entirely duplicates of other records in a table.

You can enter or change SQL statements directly in the SQL View window. If you enter an SQL statement and then switch to the Query Design window, you will see its equivalent QBE query.

Elena examines the SQL statement for the query named ARTICLES sorted by Issue, Length.

To view the SQL statement for the query named ARTICLES sorted by Issue, Length:

1. Double-click the SQL View window **Control menu box**. Access closes the SQL View window and displays the Queries list box in the Database window.
2. Double-click **ARTICLES sorted by Issue, Length** in the Queries list box. Access opens the dynaset for this saved query and shows 27 records from the PAST ARTICLES table in descending order by the Issue field as the primary sort key and in ascending order by the Article Length field as the secondary sort key. The fields displayed are Article Title, Type, Issue, and Article Length from the PAST ARTICLES table and Last Name and First Name from the WRITERS table.
3. Click the toolbar **SQL View button** to open the SQL View window. See Figure 1-32.

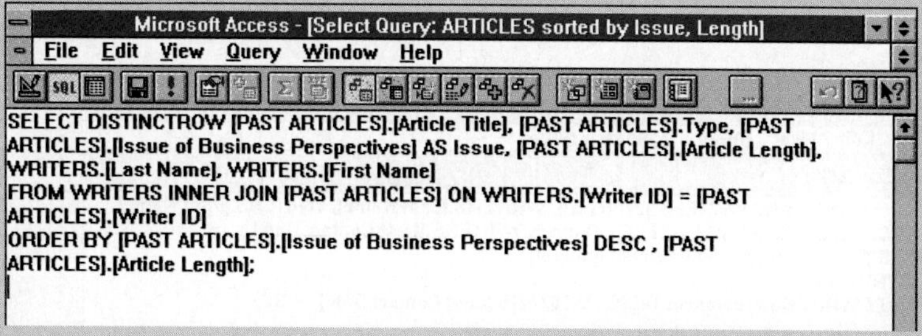

Figure 1-32 The SQL View window

4. Double-click the SQL View window **Control menu box** to return to the Queries list box in the Database window.

The SELECT statement for this second query is similar to the previous one, except for the following added features:

- Use AS to rename a field. For example, the Issue of Business Perspective field in the PAST ARTICLES table is renamed Issue.
- To link two tables with an equi-join, use INNER JOIN between the two file names, followed by ON, and then followed by the names of the fields serving as the common field, connected by an equals sign.
- If DESC does not follow a sort key field, then SQL uses ascending sort order.

Elena can see how the SQL SELECT statements mirror the options she selected in the Query Design window. In effect, every choice she made there is reflected as an SQL SELECT statement. She realizes that looking over SQL statements generated from queries that she designs really is an effective way to learn the SQL language, and she resolves to continue doing so. If you want to pursue SQL further, you can also use the Access Help system and search on SQL.

If you want to take a break and resume the tutorial at a later time, you can exit Access by double-clicking the Microsoft Access window Control menu box. When you resume the tutorial, place your Student Disk in the appropriate drive, launch Access, open the Issue25 database on your Student Disk, maximize the Database window, and click the Query object button.

■ ■ ■

Using Microsoft Graph

The first quarter of the fiscal year has just ended and Brian Murphy reviews the advertising revenue for his five magazines (Figure 1-33): *Business Perspective, Media Scene, Science Outlook, Total Sports,* and *Travel Vista*. All magazines continue to grow and prosper. Brian is especially pleased with the advertising revenue for *Business Perspective* and plans to focus on its record at the stockholders' meeting to be held later that week. He asks Elena to prepare two graphs for his presentation at the meeting—one graph to highlight *Business Perspective's* quarterly record, the other to illustrate the quarter's advertising revenue for all five magazines.

Vision Publishers

Advertising Revenue
for the First Quarter 1996–97

	July	August	September	First Quarter Total
Business Perspective	$327,000	$284,750	$377,115	$988,865
Media Scene	166,185	165,500	183,350	515,035
Science Outlook	132,840	119,900	143,300	396,040
Total Sports	203,000	221,680	237,750	662,430
Travel Vista	114,440	131,315	136,650	382,405
	$943,465	$923,145	$1,078,165	$2,944,775

Figure 1-33
First-quarter advertising revenue for Vision Publishers

Using a Chart

A **chart** is a display of numeric data in the form of a diagram. When you use Access to create a chart, you are actually using Microsoft Graph, a separate software application that comes with Access, Word, PowerPoint, and some of the other Microsoft applications. Figure 1-34 shows the 14 chart types that Graph offers to represent numeric data.

Figure 1-34
Microsoft Graph chart types

Icon	Chart Type	Purpose
	Area	Shows the magnitude of change of different items over a period of time
	Bar	Compares data represented as bars
	Column	Compares data represented as columns
	Doughnut	Shows the proportions of parts to a whole for one or more data series
	Line	Shows trends over time
	Pie	Shows the proportions of parts to a whole for one data series
	Radar	Compares data relative to a center point and to one another
	XY (Scatter)	Shows relationships among data for two or more data series
	3-D Area	Shows three-dimensional view of an area chart
	3-D Bar	Shows three-dimensional view of a bar chart
	3-D Column	Shows three-dimensional view of a column chart
	3-D Line	Shows three-dimensional view of a line chart; also called a ribbon chart
	3-D Pie	Shows three-dimensional view of a pie chart
	3-D Surface	Shows relationships among large amounts of data

On Access forms and reports, you can create charts using Graph, or you can use the Graph Wizard to create a chart for you. The **Graph Wizard** asks you a series of questions about your requirements and then creates a chart based on your answers. Whether you use the Graph Wizard or create your own chart, you can use Graph to change a chart design after it is created. Graph Wizard offers 12 of the 14 chart types; the radar and 3-D surface chart types are not available. However, you can change any chart type to another chart type, even the radar and 3-D surface chart types, while you make design changes in Graph.

When you launch Graph to change a chart on a form or report, you are no longer working in Access. Access is still running in the background, however. This process of running two or more application programs at the same time is known as **multitasking**. After launching Graph, you change the chart. When finished with your changes, you exit and return to Access, and Graph automatically inserts your changed chart into your form or report.

The inserted chart is called an **embedded object**, an object (such as a chart, spreadsheet, or picture) that is created and changed in one application (such as Graph) but stored and used in another (such as Access). In the Windows environment, the embedded object is more generally called an OLE object, short for "object linking and embedding."

Figure 1-35 shows a typical Graph window for a column chart. When you launch Graph, the Graph window appears with two document windows inside it: a datasheet window and a chart window. The **datasheet** contains the data used to create the chart in the chart window. You can size and move these document windows just like windows in other Windows packages.

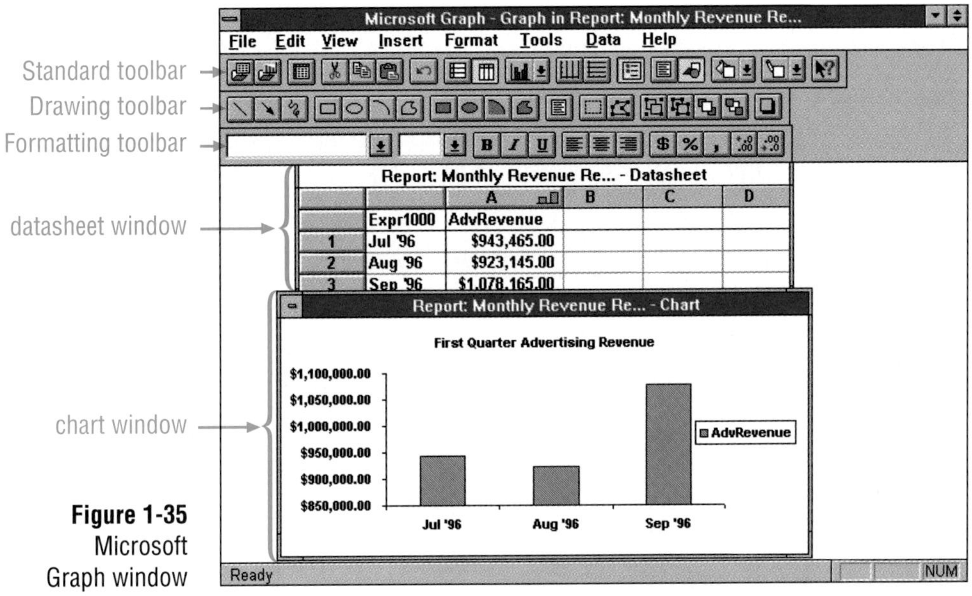

Figure 1-35 Microsoft Graph window

Graph offers three toolbars that help you create and edit your charts.

- The **Standard toolbar** contains buttons for the most common commands (for instance, buttons to cut, copy, paste, undo, get help, and select a chart type).
- The optional **Drawing toolbar** contains buttons that help you create and format graphic objects.
- The optional **Formatting toolbar** contains buttons that help you format graphic objects, datasheet cell contents, and chart objects, such as text and gridlines.

When you start Graph, the first thing you do is enter the data you want to chart into the datasheet (usually by importing). Figure 1-36 shows a typical Graph datasheet.

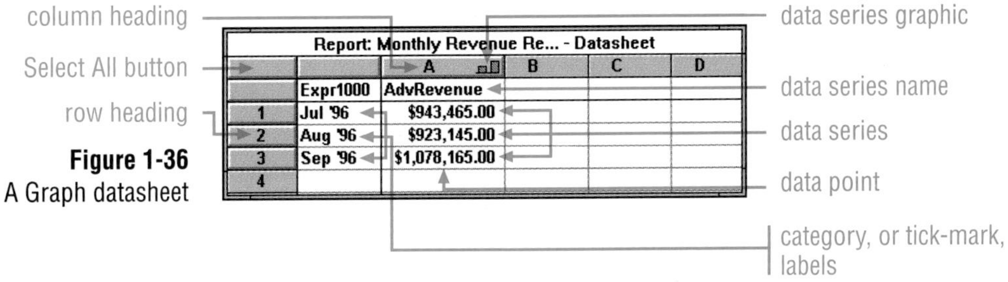

Figure 1-36 A Graph datasheet

On a datasheet, the letters A, B, and so on, serve as column headings, and the numbers 1, 2, and so on, serve as row headings. The intersections of each column and row are called **cells**, the boxes that contain the data values themselves. Figure 1-37 contains the name of each datasheet element in Figure 1-36, along with a brief description.

Datasheet Element	Description
Column heading (A, B, C, etc.)	Column identifier; click to select an entire column
Row heading (1, 2, 3, etc.)	Row identifier; click to select an entire row
Data point	Value in a cell
Data series	Row or column of data, used to graph one line or pie or one set of columns of bars on a chart
Data series name	Label for values in a data series; appears in the legend of a chart
Tick-mark labels	Category labels that appear along the horizontal axis of a column, line, or area chart, and along the vertical axis of a bar chart
Select All button	Click to select the entire datasheet for formatting
Data series graphic	Identifies the chart type associated with the datasheet

Figure 1-37
Elements of a Graph datasheet

Figure 1-38 shows a typical chart.

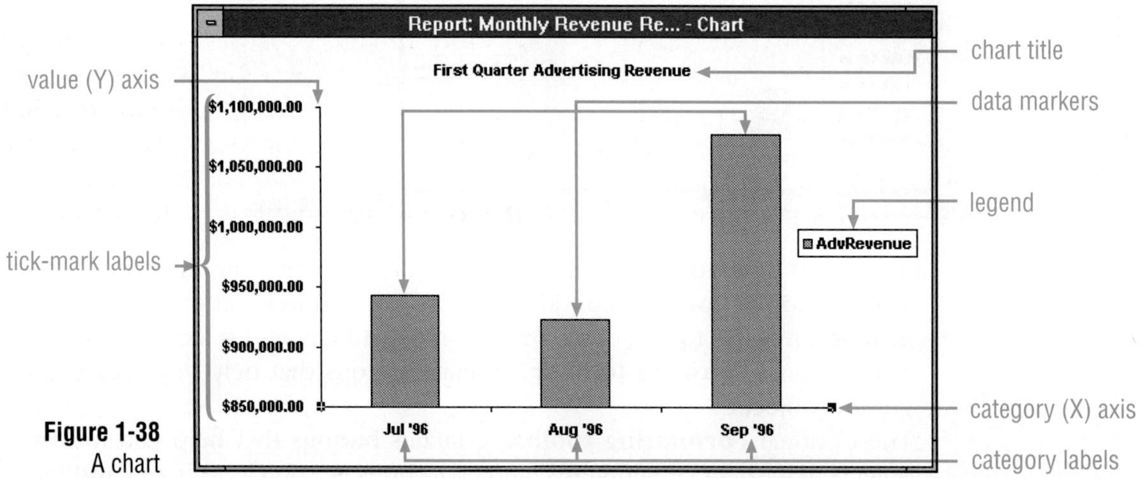

Figure 1-38
A chart

The chart has three columns, which taken together represent one data series. If a chart has more than one data series, each is a different color or is shaded differently. Figure 1-39 identifies each chart element and offers a brief description.

Chart Element	Description
Chart title	Identifies contents of a chart
Data marker	Marks a single point of data, like a column (as in Figure 1-38), a dot in a line chart, or a shape in a chart
X-axis	Horizontal or category axis
Y-axis	Vertical or value axis
Tick mark	Small line that intersects an axis and marks the scale or categories of chart data
Tick-mark label	Shows scale for value (Y) axis
Category label	Identifies data points on category (X) axis
Legend	Key that identifies which data markers represent each data series

Figure 1-39
Elements of a chart

Creating a Chart Using the Graph Wizard

Elena first tackles Brian's graph highlighting *Business Perspective's* quarterly record and sketches out the report design shown in Figure 1-40. She decides to insert a pie chart with a title and legend in the Page Footer section of the report. In addition to inserting the chart, Elena will place the magazine name and a column heading label in the Page Header section, the month and year and the advertising revenue amount for each month in the Detail section, and the total advertising revenue for the period in the Group Footer section.

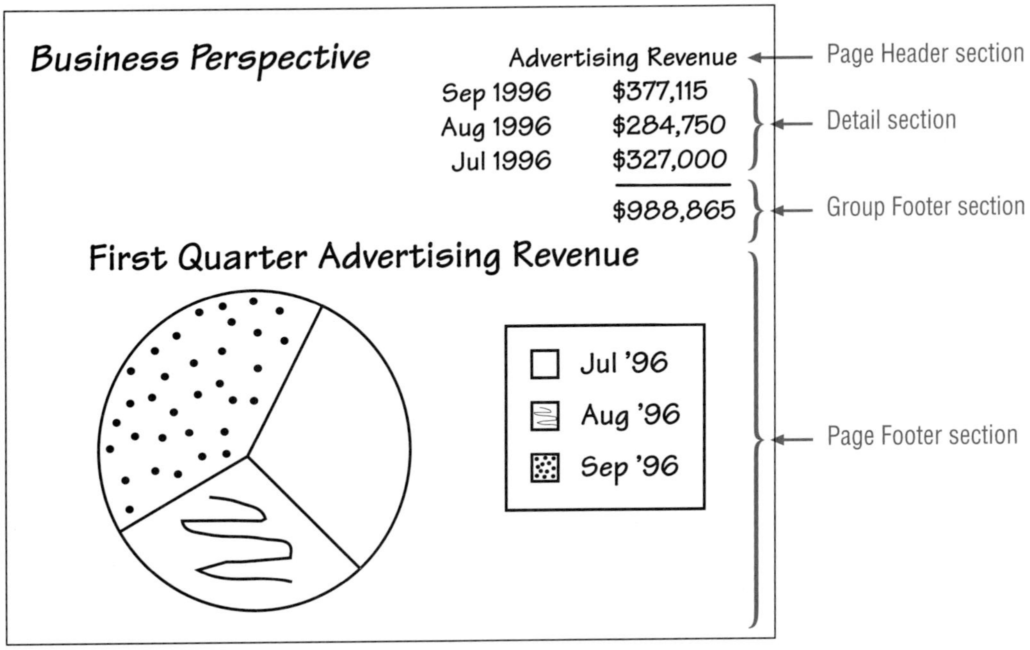

Figure 1-40
The design for the Business Perspective report

Before beginning her work on the chart, Elena checks with Brian for the location of the quarterly advertising data. Brian gives her a printout that describes the Lastfour database tables and queries, shown in Figure 1-41. She sees that the Lastfour database contains two tables and two queries that she can use for her work with charts.

```
tblMagazines table
MagazineCode        text       PK; two-character magazine code

MagazineTitle       text       20 characters

tblAdvRevenue table
MagazineCode        text       PK; 2 characters

MagazineIssue       date       PK; mmm yyyy format; magazine date
                               (month and year)

AdvRevenue          currency   0 decimals; advertising revenues for
                               this issue

qryAdvRevenueBPDetail query
Equi-join between the tblMagazines and tblAdvRevenue tables

Displayed: MagazineCode, MagazineTitle, MagazineIssue, and AdvRevenue

Ascending order on MagazineIssue as the sort key field

Select just those records whose MagazineCode = "BP"

qryAdvRevenueQuarterly query
Equi-join between the tblMagazines and tblAdvRevenue tables

Displayed: MagazineCode and AdvRevenue

Group By MagazineCode and Sum AdvRevenue
```

Figure 1-41
Quarterly advertising tables and queries

The tblMagazines table contains a two-character MagazineCode field, which is the primary key field (denoted by PK), and a 20-character MagazineTitle field. One record in this table, for example, contains the code BP and the title Business Perspective. The tblAdvRevenue table contains the two-character MagazineCode field, a MagazineIssue field in mmm yyyy format, and an AdvRevenue field in currency format. The MagazineCode and MagazineIssue fields together represent the primary key field, and the AdvRevenue field contains the advertising revenue for a given issue of a magazine. The two queries are qryAdvRevenueBPDetail, which Elena can use for her first chart, and qryAdvRevenueQuarterly, which she can use for her second chart.

Elena imports the two tables and the two queries from the Lastfour database to the Issue25 database. This saves her the time of entering the table data and possibly making mistakes.

To import tables and queries:

1. Click the toolbar **Import button** to open the Import dialog box.
2. Be sure that Microsoft Access is highlighted in the Data Source list box and then click the **OK button**. Access opens the Select Microsoft Access Database dialog box. Click **lastfour.mdb** in the File Name list box and then click the **OK button** to open the Import Objects dialog box.
3. Click the Object Type **drop-down list box down arrow button** to open the drop-down list box, click **Tables** in the list box, click **tblAdvRevenue** in the Objects in LASTFOUR.MDB list box, be sure that the Structure and Data radio button is selected, and then click the **Import button**. Access imports the table and displays the Successfully imported dialog box. Click the **OK button** to close the dialog box.
4. Click **tblMagazines** in the Objects in LASTFOUR.MDB list box, be sure that the Structure and Data radio button is selected, click the **Import button**, then click the **OK button**.
5. Click the Object Type **drop-down list box down arrow button** to display the drop-down list box, click **Queries** in the list box, click **qryAdvRevenueBPDetail** in the Objects in LASTFOUR.MDB list box, click the **Import button**, and then click the **OK button**.
6. Click **qryAdvRevenueQuarterly** in the Objects in LASTFOUR.MDB list box, click the **Import button**, and then click the **OK button**.
7. Click the **Close button** to close the Import Objects dialog box.

You can open the two imported tables and two imported queries to review their contents. If you do, be sure that you return to the Queries list in the maximized Database window when you are done.

Elena is ready to create her first chart. She will use the Graph Wizard to embed the chart in a report. You can use Graph Wizard from the Form Design window or from the Report Design window; simply click the toolbox Graph tool to start the Graph Wizard. Alternatively, for a form, you can start the Graph Wizard by clicking Graph in the Form Wizards dialog box.

Elena creates a one-page report with an embedded chart, similar to the sketch in Figure 1-40.

To launch Graph Wizard for a report:

1. Click the toolbar **New Report button** to open the New Report dialog box, click the Select A Table/Query **drop-down list box down arrow button** to display the list of the Issue25 database tables and queries, and then click **qryAdvRevenueBPDetail** in the list box, scrolling as necessary. Finally, click the **Blank Report button** to open the Report Design window.
2. If the toolbox is not on the screen, click the toolbar **Toolbox button** to open it. Click the toolbox **Graph tool**.

❸ Move the pointer into the Page Footer section. As you move the pointer into the report, the pointer changes to ⁺ılı. Click the mouse button when the pointer's plus symbol (+) is positioned on the grid dot in the upper-left corner of the Page Footer section. After several seconds, Access increases the height of the Page Footer section and then opens the first Graph Wizard dialog box. See Figure 1-42.

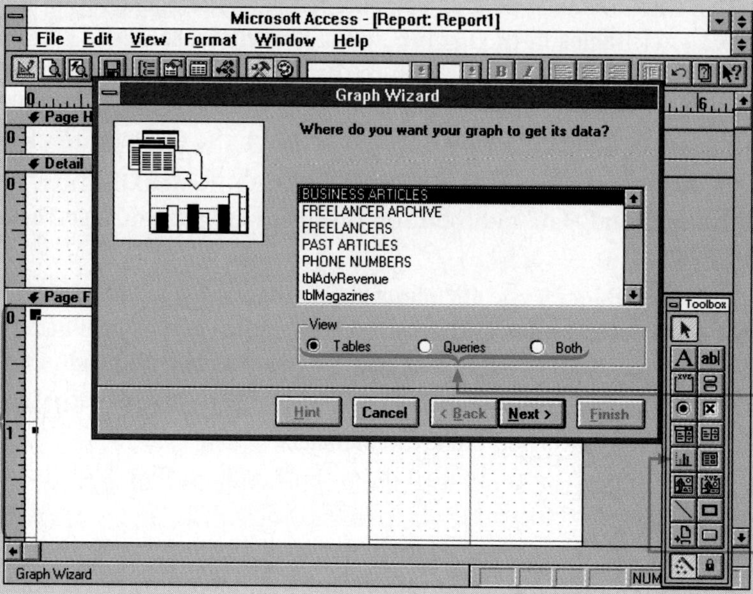

Figure 1-42
The first Graph Wizard dialog box

Even though the qryAdvRevenueBPDetail query is the basis for this report, Elena can choose it or any other table or query to be the source for her chart data. In this case, Elena will select the same query for her chart.

To create a chart using Chart Wizard:

❶ Click the **Queries radio button** to display the list of Issue25 queries, click **qryAdvRevenueBPDetail**, and then click the **Next > button**. Access opens the second Graph Wizard dialog box, in which you choose the fields for the chart.

❷ In order, double-click **MagazineTitle**, **MagazineIssue**, and **AdvRevenue** to move them from the Available Fields list box to the Fields for graph list box. Click the **Next > button** to open the third Graph Wizard dialog box. See Figure 1-43.

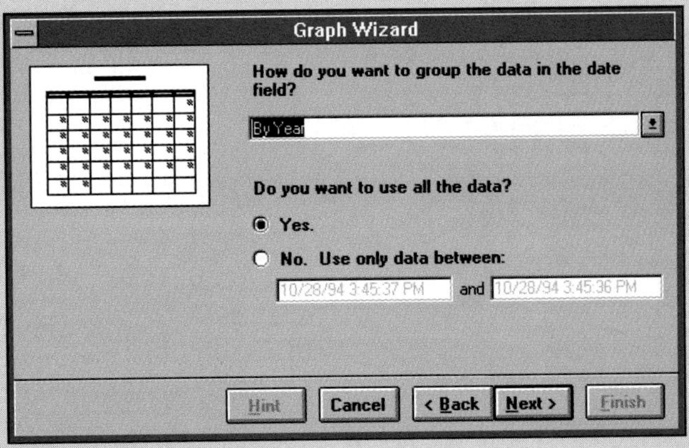

Figure 1-43
Choosing the data markers for a chart

3. To use all the data grouped by month, click the **drop-down list box arrow button**, click **By Month**, be sure the Yes radio button is selected, and then click the **Next > button**. Access opens the next Graph Wizard dialog box, in which you choose the calculation method for the chart's data points.
4. Click the **Add (sum) the numbers radio button** if necessary, and then click the **Next > button**. Access opens a dialog box with the question, "Do you want to link the data in your graph to a field on the report?" You do not want to link the data.
5. Click the **No button**. After a long pause, Access opens the next dialog box, in which you select the chart type. See Figure 1-44.

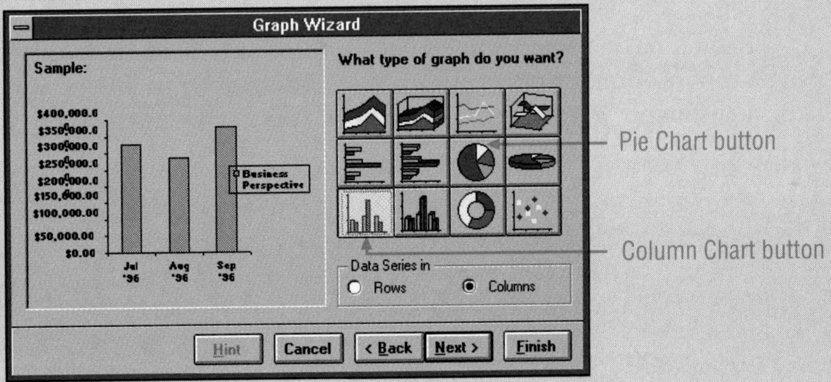

Figure 1-44
Choosing the chart type

6. The column chart is the selected, default chart type, and you want your chart to be a pie chart. Click the **Pie Chart button**, which is in the second row and the third column. After several seconds, the sample chart on the left of the dialog box changes to a pie chart.
7. Make sure the Columns radio button is selected and click the **Next > button**. Access opens the last Graph Wizard dialog box, in which you enter an optional chart title and choose whether to display a legend on the chart.

❽ Type **First Quarter Advertising Revenue**, be sure that the Yes radio button is selected so that a legend will appear on the chart, and then click the **Finish button**. After a long pause, Access closes Graph Wizard and shows the chart inserted in the Report Design window. See Figure 1-45.

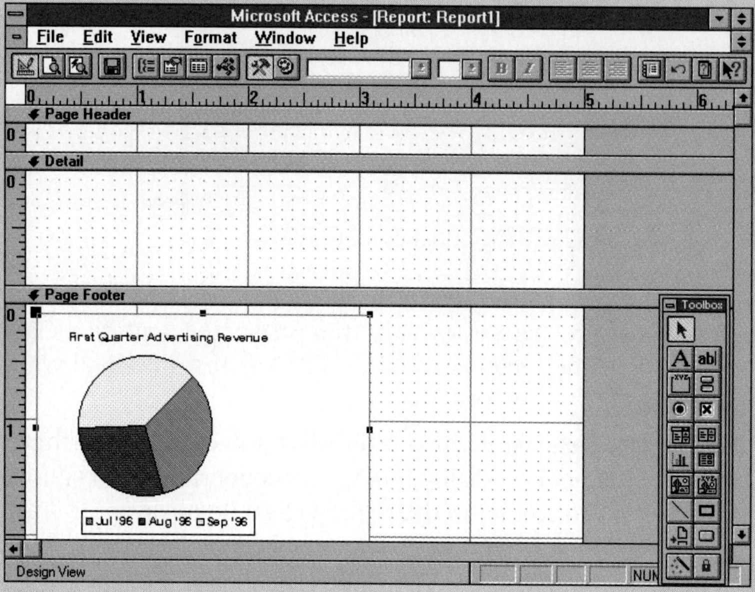

Figure 1-45
Chart inserted in the Report Design window

Before making some refinements to the chart, Elena saves the report. Periodically saving a report, form, or other object is a good practice to follow. If you are not happy with the adjustments you make to your object, you can always revert to the saved version.

To save a report:

❶ Click **File**, click **Save As...** to open the Save As dialog box, type **BusinessPerspective** in the Report Name box, and then press **[Enter]**. Access saves the report and displays the report name in the title bar.

Changing a Chart

Elena compares the newly created chart to her design and decides to make the following changes to the chart:

- Increase the width of the chart to 4.5" wide and 2.75" high.
- Make the chart title larger.
- Move the legend to the right of the pie chart if necessary; and increase the legend's size.
- Change the pie slices from color to black, white, and gray, because Vision Publishers does not have a color printer for its computers.

To change a chart's elements, such as the chart title, scale, and color, you must launch Graph from Access and change these elements using Graph. You can resize a chart's boundaries, however, in either Access or Graph. When you resize the chart, Access and Graph automatically reformat the axes, legend, and all other chart elements to accommodate the new size of the chart.

To resize a chart in Access:

❶ Move the pointer to the middle sizing handle on the right side of the chart. When the pointer changes to ↔, drag the right border to the right to the 4.5" mark on the horizontal ruler. Next, move the pointer to the middle sizing handle on the bottom of the chart. When the pointer changes to ↕, drag the bottom border down to the 2.75" mark on the vertical ruler.

To make the other chart changes, you must launch Graph from Access. To do so, double-click anywhere in the chart; after several seconds the Microsoft Graph window appears.

To launch Graph to change a chart:

❶ Double-click anywhere in the chart that appears in the Page Footer section. After several seconds, Access opens the Microsoft Graph window. If necessary, click the datasheet to activate it and place it on top. See Figure 1-46.

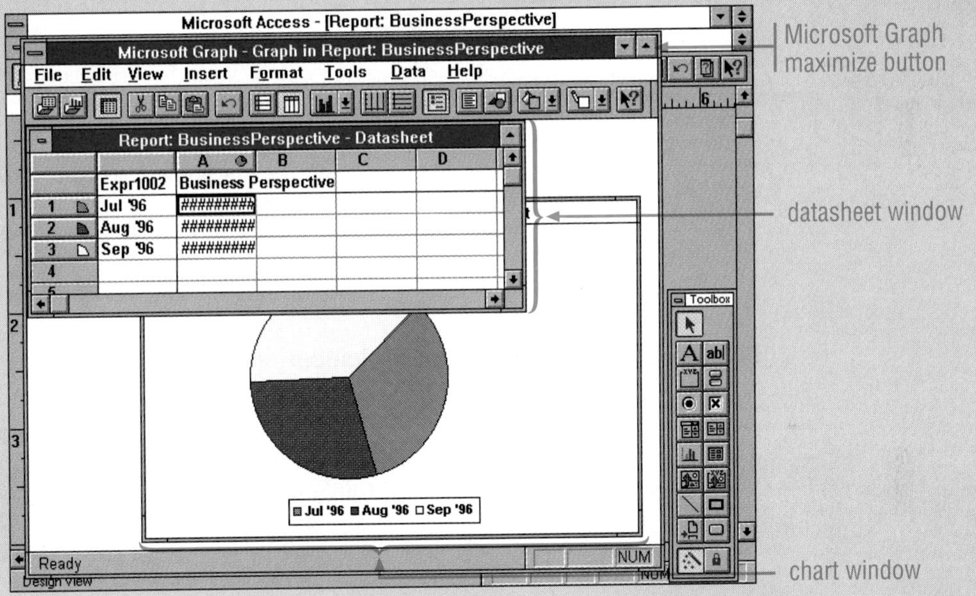

Figure 1-46
Revising a chart in the Microsoft Graph window

Before changing the chart, Elena completes a few preliminary steps in the Microsoft Graph window. First, she maximizes the Microsoft Graph window so that more space is available for working with the chart. Next, the pound signs (#) in column A of the datasheet indicate that the column is too narrow to display the values, so she widens the column to see the values. Finally, the chart window is partially hidden by the datasheet window. To activate the chart window and place it on top of the datasheet window, Elena clicks anywhere in the chart window. Even though Elena enlarged the chart in Access, she might also need to resize the chart in Graph.

To complete preparation steps for changing a chart:

❶ Click the Microsoft Graph **maximize button**.

❷ Double-click the right edge of the column heading for column A to widen it to the best fit.

❸ Click anywhere in the chart window to activate it and place it on top of the datasheet window. See Figure 1-47.

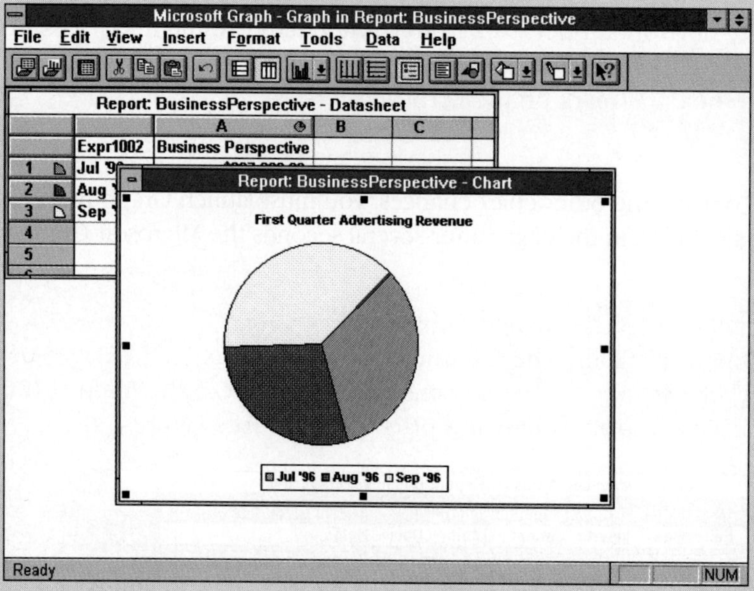

Figure 1-47
The chart window

TROUBLE? If your chart window is smaller than the one shown in Figure 1-47, you need to resize it. Move the pointer to the middle, right edge of the chart window. When the pointer changes to ⇔, drag the edge to the right about 2". Then move the pointer to the middle, bottom edge of the chart window. When the pointer changes to ⇕, drag the edge down about 1".

Before you can change a chart element, such as the chart title or legend, you must select that element by clicking it. Graph places a box around selected text and handles around selected graphics. Once it is selected, you can make changes to an element by using toolbar buttons, menu commands, and shortcut menu commands.

Elena changes the chart title font size and then moves the legend to the right of the pie chart.

To select a chart element and open a Graph dialog box:

❶ Click **First Quarter Advertising Revenue**. Graph places a box around this chart title to indicate it is the selected chart element.

❷ Click **Format** and then click **Font...** to open the Format Chart Title dialog box. See Figure 1-48.

tabs for dialog box option groups

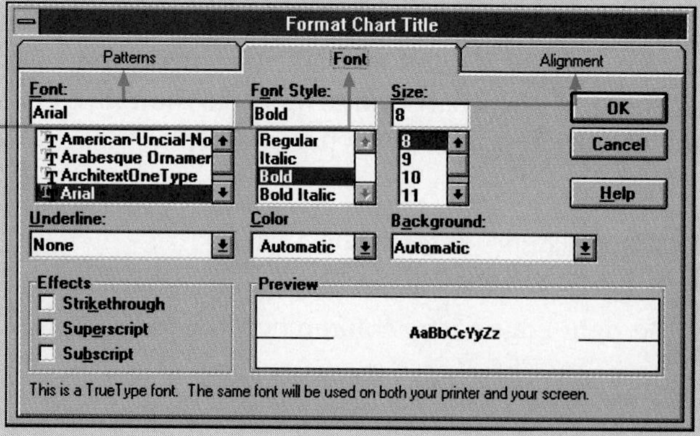

Figure 1-48
The Format Chart Title dialog box

TROUBLE? If your Format Chart Title dialog box looks different from the one shown in Figure 1-48, either the Patterns or Alignment tab at the top of the dialog box is active. Click the Font tab to choose the Font option group.

Many Graph dialog boxes provide groups of options, each group on a separate tab. For example, the Format Chart Title dialog box has three tabs: Patterns, Font, and Alignment. To select a tab to display its group of options, simply click the tab.

Elena changes the chart title font size to 11, moves the legend to the right of the pie chart, and then resizes the legend.

To change a chart title and legend:

1. Click **11** in the Size list box and then click the **OK button**. Graph changes the chart title font size from 8 to 11.
2. Click the legend below the pie chart to select it.

   TROUBLE? If your legend is already to the right of the pie chart, skip Steps 3 and 4.
3. Use the right mouse button to click the legend again. Graph opens the shortcut menu. Click **Format Legend...** in the shortcut menu to open the Format Legend dialog box and then click the **Placement tab**. Graph displays the Placement group options.
4. Click the **Right radio button** and then click the **OK button**. Graph positions the legend to the right of the pie chart.
5. Move the pointer to the upper-left corner of the box around the legend. When the pointer changes to ⤡, click and drag the corner approximately .5" up and to the left to enlarge the box.
6. Use the right mouse button to click inside the legend and then click **Format Legend...** in the shortcut menu. To change the legend font size, click the **Font tab**, click **10** in the Size list box, and then click the **OK button**.
7. Move the pointer inside the legend and drag the legend to the left. See Figure 1-49 for the placement of the legend box.

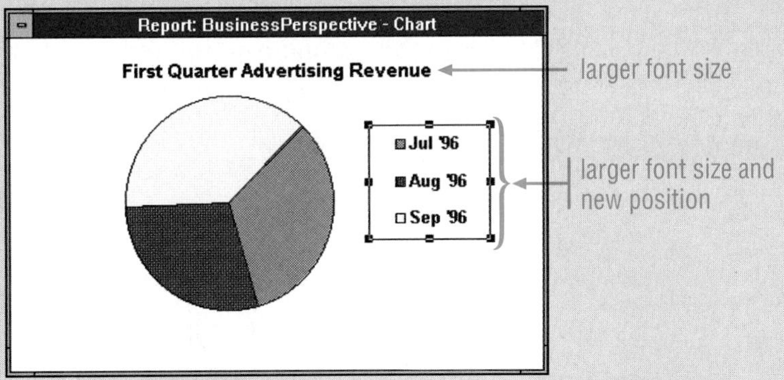

Figure 1-49
The chart title and legend after they are changed

Elena changes the pie slices from colors to black, white, and gray for printing on her black and white printer.

To change a chart's colors:

1. Click inside the uppermost pie slice and, after a second or two, click again inside the same pie slice. Graph places handles around the pie slice.

   TROUBLE? If handles appear around the entire pie, you need to click inside the pie slice one more time. You probably did not wait long enough before clicking the second time. If Graph displays the Format Data Series dialog box, click the Cancel box and then repeat Step 1.

2. Click the toolbar **Color button** **down arrow** to open the color palette. See Figure 1-50.

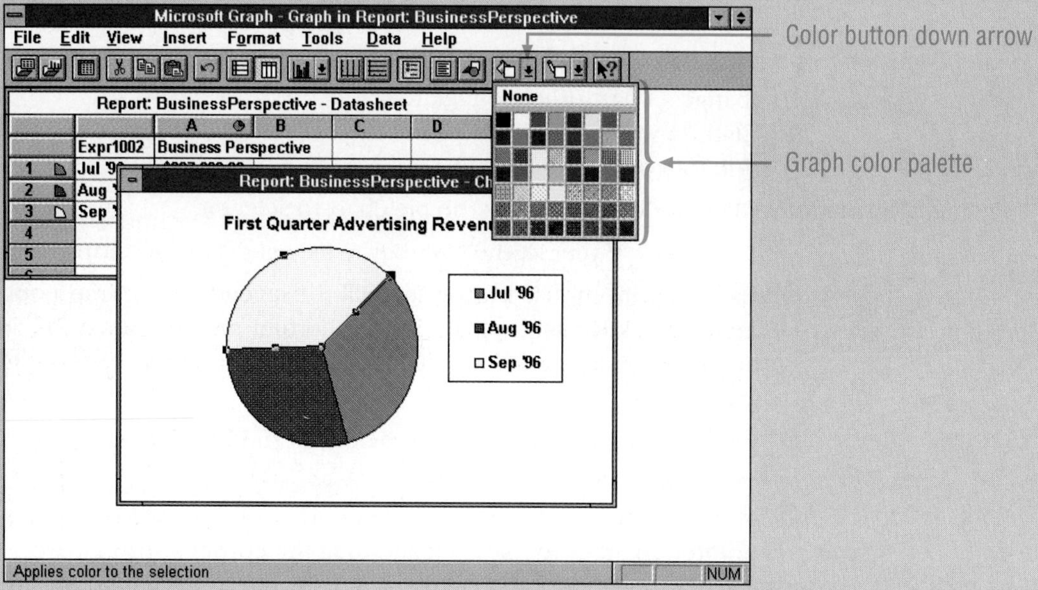

Figure 1-50 The Graph color palette

3. Click the **black color**, which is in the upper-left corner of the color palette. Graph changes the color of the selected pie slice to black.

4. Click inside the rightmost pie slice to select it, click the **down arrow**, and then click the **white color**, which is to the right of the black color. Graph changes the color of the selected pie slice to white.

5. Click inside the remaining pie slice to select it, click the **down arrow**, and then click the **gray color**, which is in the second row and the second column from the right. Graph changes the color of the selected pie slice to gray. See Figure 1-51.

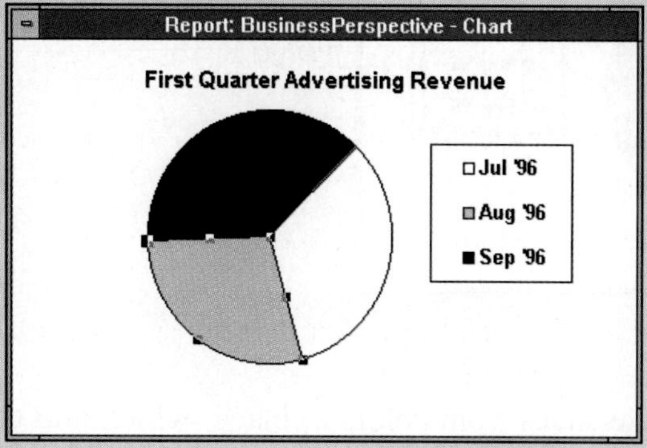

Figure 1-51 Chart colors changed

Having completed her chart changes, Elena exits Graph, returns to Access, and saves the report.

To exit Graph:

❶ Click **File** and then click **Exit & Return to Report: Business Perspective**. Graph ends, the Microsoft Graph window closes, and Access's Report Design window opens.

TROUBLE? Don't be concerned if "Exit & Return to Report: Business Perspecti..." is the option on the File menu instead, because the option wording does vary from one computer to another.

❷ Click the toolbar **Save button**. Access saves the report, including the changes to the chart.

Printing a Chart

Elena previews the report and then prints it to look at the pie chart's placement on the page. To print a report with a chart you take the same steps you take when printing a report without a chart.

To print a report with a chart:

❶ Click the toolbar **Print Preview button** to open the Print Preview window.

❷ Scroll down the screen until you see the entire chart. See Figure 1-52.

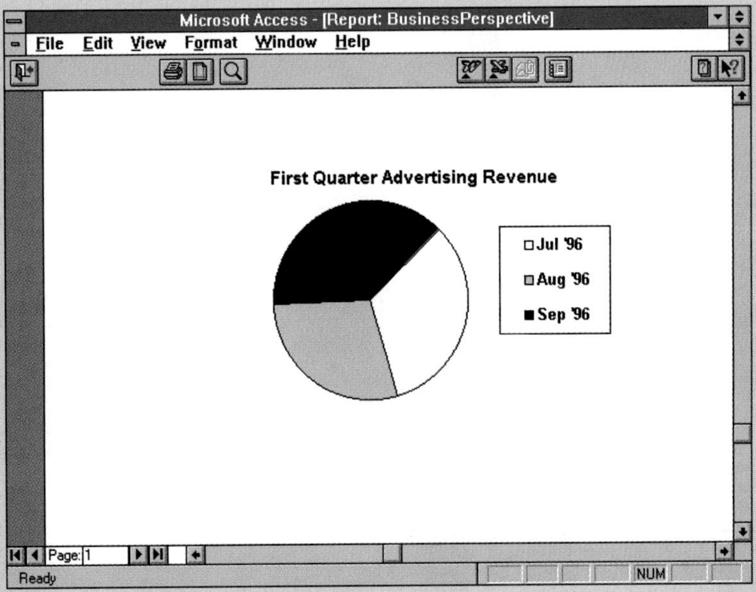

Figure 1-52
The chart in the Print Preview window

❸ Make sure your printer is on line and ready to print. Click the toolbar **Print button** to open the Print dialog box.

❹ Check the Printer section of the dialog box to make sure your computer's printer is selected.

❺ Click the **OK button** to initiate printing. After a printing dialog box opens briefly and then closes, Access prints the report page and returns you to the Print Preview window.

❻ Click the toolbar **Close Window button** to close the Print Preview window and open the Report Design window.

Changing the Chart Type

Elena recognizes that a pie chart is not appropriate for showing the differences in each month's advertising revenue. Each pie slice appears to be approximately the same size. A column chart would be a better choice for showing the differences. Elena changes the chart type from a pie chart to a column chart. To do this, she once again launches Graph.

To change the chart type:

1. Double-click anywhere inside the chart in the Report Design window. After several seconds, the Microsoft Graph window opens.
2. Use the right mouse button to click anywhere inside the pie chart. Graph selects the pie chart, places handles around it, and displays the shortcut menu.
3. Click **Chart Type...** in the shortcut menu. Graph opens the Chart Type dialog box. See Figure 1-53.

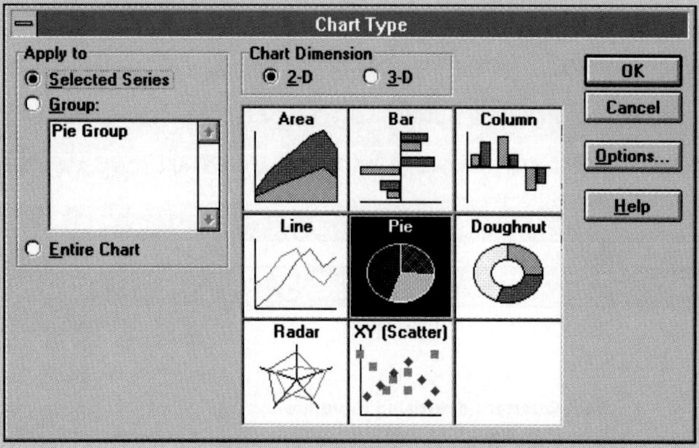

Figure 1-53
The Chart Type dialog box

4. The Pie button is selected. To change the chart to a column chart, click the **Column button** and then click the **OK button**. Graph changes the chart to a column chart. See Figure 1-54.

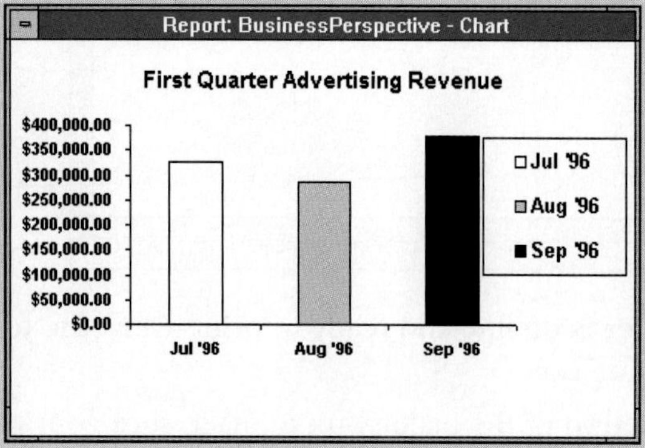

Figure 1-54
Chart changed to a column chart

The column chart does a better job than the pie chart does of showing each month's relative difference in advertising revenue. Note that the Chart Type dialog box displayed only eight chart types. To see the other six, you click the 3-D radio button. Each chart type has several different built-in formats, and you can create your own customized formats. Elena reviews the built-in format choices available for column charts to be sure she has the best format.

To display the built-in formats for a chart type:

❶ Click the right mouse button anywhere inside the column chart to display the shortcut menu and then click **AutoFormat...** in the shortcut menu. Graph opens the AutoFormat dialog box. See Figure 1-55.

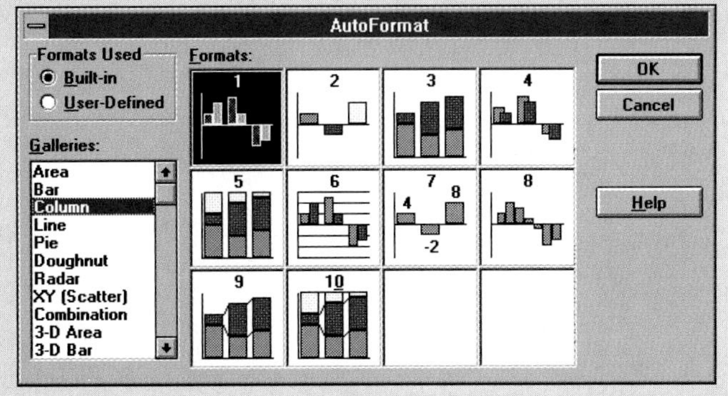

Figure 1-55
The AutoFormat dialog box

Elena decides not to change the format of the column chart, because the default choice appears to be the most appropriate choice. However, Elena decides to make a final change to the chart; she changes the range of the tick-mark labels along the value axis from a starting value of $0.00 to one of $225,000, thereby making the column differences more prominent, and she eliminates the decimals.

To change tick-mark labels:

❶ Click the **Cancel button** to close the AutoFormat dialog box.

❷ Click the right mouse button on any of the **tick-mark labels** along the Y-axis to open the shortcut menu and then click **Format Axis...** in the shortcut menu. Graph opens the Format Axis dialog box.

❸ Click the **Scale tab**. See Figure 1-56.

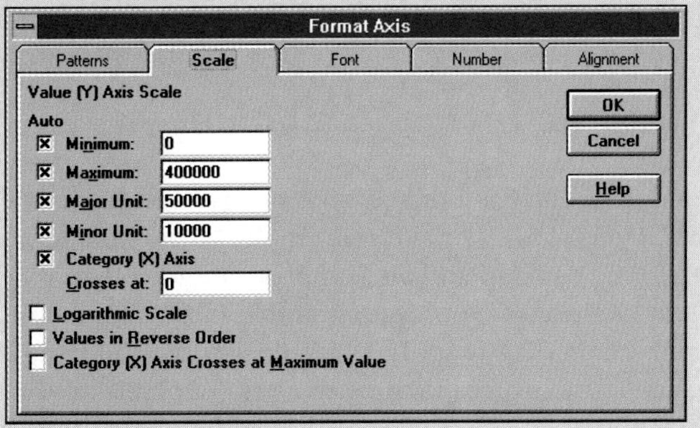

Figure 1-56
The Format Axis dialog box Scale options

❹ Click the **Minimum check box** to remove the check mark. Graph places the insertion point at the start of the Minimum text box. Type **22500** to make the value 225000 (the original zero remains following the insertion point).

❺ Click the **Major Unit check box** to remove the check mark, highlight only the **50** in the Major Unit text box, and then type **25**. The tick-mark labels will now have an increment of 25000.

6. Click the **Number tab**, click **$#,##0_];[Red][$#,##0]** in the Format Codes list box, and then click the **OK button**. This will eliminate the decimals from the tick mark labels. Graph closes the dialog box and activates the Microsoft Graph window. See Figure 1-57.

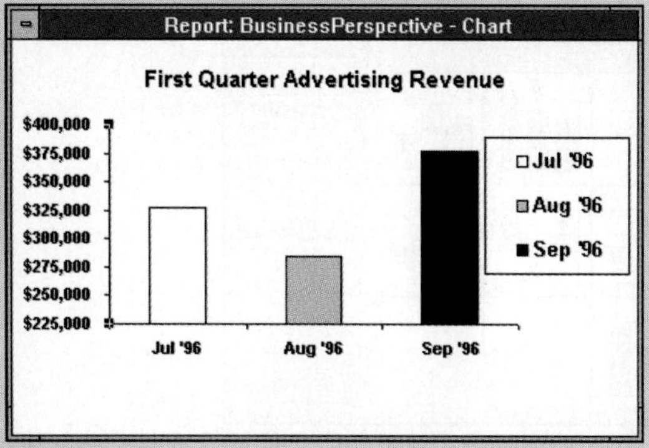

Figure 1-57
The completed chart

Elena is pleased with the new appearance of the chart, so she returns to Access and saves the changed report. She decides to finish the other portions of the report and to create the other chart that Brian wants later that day. Thus, she also closes the Report Design window. (You will finish the report and create the other chart in the Tutorial Assignments.)

To exit Graph and close the Report Design window:

1. Click **File** and then click **Exit & Return to Report: Business Perspective**. Graph ends, the Microsoft Graph window closes, and Access's Report Design window opens.
2. Click the toolbar **Save button**. Access saves the report, including the changes to the chart.
3. Double-click the Report Design window **Control menu box** to activate the Queries list in the Database window.

Adding a Graphic Image to a Form

The marketing department has created a company logo using the Windows Paintbrush drawing program. Elena gets a copy of this graphic image the next workday and adds it to the Article Type form. You can add visual impact to your forms and reports by using pictures or other graphic images. Sources of graphic images include Paintbrush, other drawing programs, and scanners. A graphic image created by Paintbrush is a **bitmap**, which is an image consisting of bits corresponding to a grid of pixels on the screen. Access treats a bitmap as an OLE object; this is similar to the way it treats other objects, such as graphs and sounds, as OLE objects.

The company logo, which is stored on your Student Disk, is a bitmap that you can add to an Access form or report. To add a graphic image to a form or report, you first position an unbound object frame on the design screen where you want the graphic to appear. An **unbound object frame** is a control on a form or report that displays any OLE object not stored in a table in an Access database. You use this control to create and change the graphic from within a form or report using the application in which the object was originally created. Elena can insert her company's logo into a form and can change it, if necessary, using Paintbrush. To create an unbound object frame you click the toolbox **Object Frame tool**.

REFERENCE WINDOW

Adding a Graphic Image

- Click the toolbox Object Frame tool and position the pointer in the form or report.
- Click Paintbrush Picture or another object type, click the Create from File radio button, click the Browse... button, select the drive and directory, double-click the file name, and then click the OK button.

Elena adds the graphic image into the unbound object frame.

To add a graphic image to a form:

❶ From the Database window, click the **Form object button**, click **Article Type form**, and then click the **Design command button**. Access opens the Form Design window. See Figure 1-58.

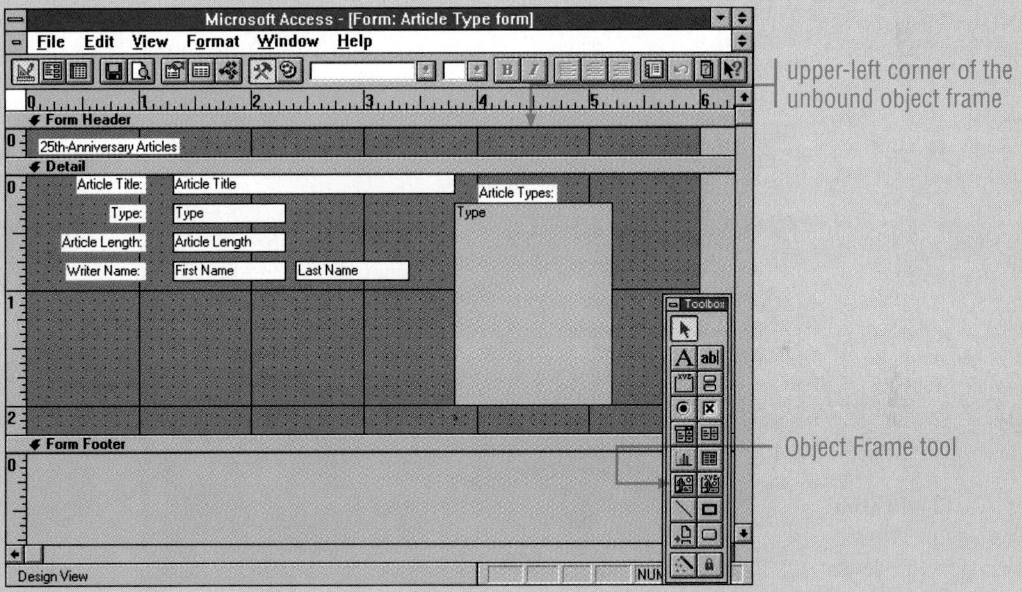

Figure 1-58 The form named Article Type form in the Form Design window

TROUBLE? If the property sheet is open, click the toolbar Properties button to close it.

❷ Click the toolbox **Object Frame tool**. As you move the pointer to the form, it changes to +. Click the mouse button when the pointer's plus symbol (+) is positioned at the top of the Form Header section at the 4.5" mark on the horizontal ruler. Access opens the Insert Object dialog box.

❸ Scroll the Object Type list box and click **Paintbrush Picture**. Click the **Create from File radio button**. Access displays a File text box and a Browse... button.

❹ Click the **Browse... button** to open the Browse dialog box.

❺ Change the Drives drop-down list box to the drive containing your Student Disk and, scrolling the box as necessary, double-click **vision.bmp** in the File Name list box. Finally, click the **OK button** in the Insert Object dialog box. After several seconds, Access inserts the graphic image in the unbound object frame. See Figure 1-59.

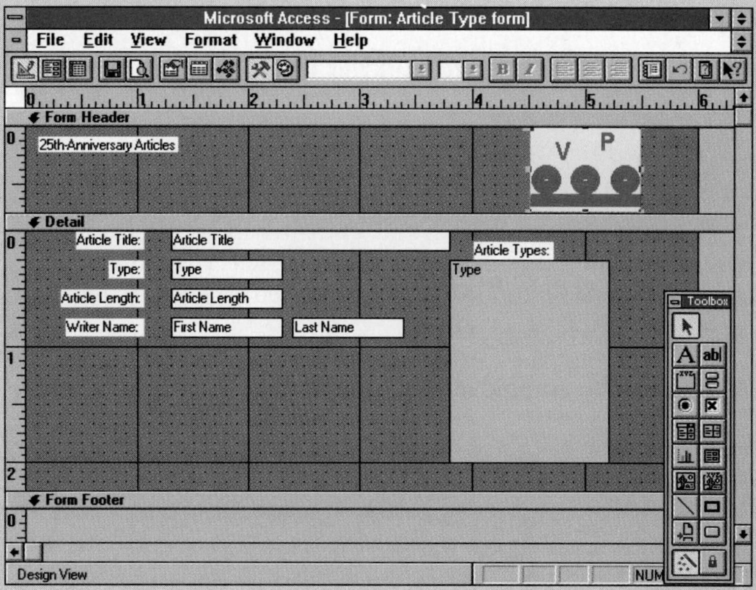

Figure 1-59 Adding a graphic image to a form

6. Click the toolbar **Save button**, click the Form Design window **restore button** if necessary, and then click the toolbar **Form View button**. Access saves the changed form and opens the Form View window. See Figure 1-60.

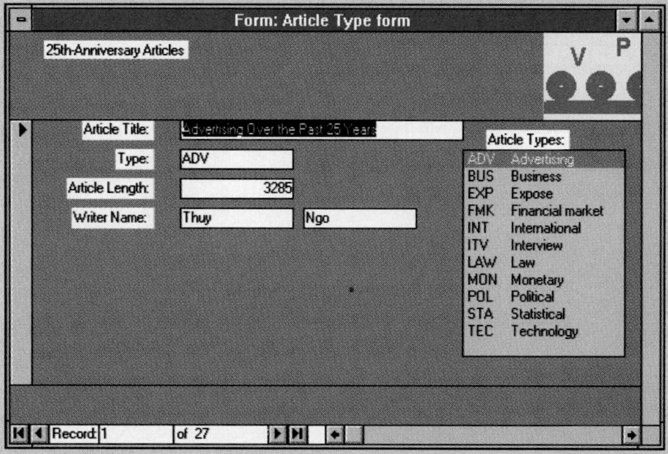

Figure 1-60 Displaying a graphic image on a form

7. Double-click the Form View window **Control menu box**. Access closes the Form View window and activates the Database window.

Elena has finished her work for the day, so she exits Access.

To exit Access:

1. Double-click the Microsoft Access window **Control menu box**.

■ ■ ■

Elena is ready to present her information to Brian.

Questions

1. With which Query Wizard must you use aggregate functions?
2. What precaution should you take before running an action query?
3. What happens if you enter 23 for the Top Values property? Give an example of an alternative entry for this property.
4. What is the difference between an equi-join and an outer join?
5. In what form does Access save a query?
6. What is an embedded object?
7. When do you use an unbound object frame?

E 8. Figure 1-61 lists the field names from two tables: tblTelephones and tblPhoneCalls.

tblTelephones	tblPhoneCalls
TelephoneNumber	CallingTelephoneNumber
BillingName	CalledTelephoneNumber
BillingAddress	CallDate
	CallStartTime
	CallEndTime
	BilledTelephoneNumber

Figure 1-61

a. What is the primary key for each table?
b. Which fields are foreign keys?
c. What type of relationship exists between the two tables?
d. Is an equi-join possible between the two tables? If so, give one example of an equi-join.
e. Is either type of outer join possible between the two tables? Is so, give one example of an outer join.
f. Is a self-join possible for one of the tables? If so, give one example of a self-join.

Tutorial Assignments

Launch Access and open the Issue25 database on your Student Disk.

1. Figure 1-62 shows Elena's revised design for the BusinessPerspective report. She has finished placing the chart in the Report Design window and you must complete the report according to the following specifications. Use Figure 1-62 for guidance. When you finish your revisions, save and print the report.

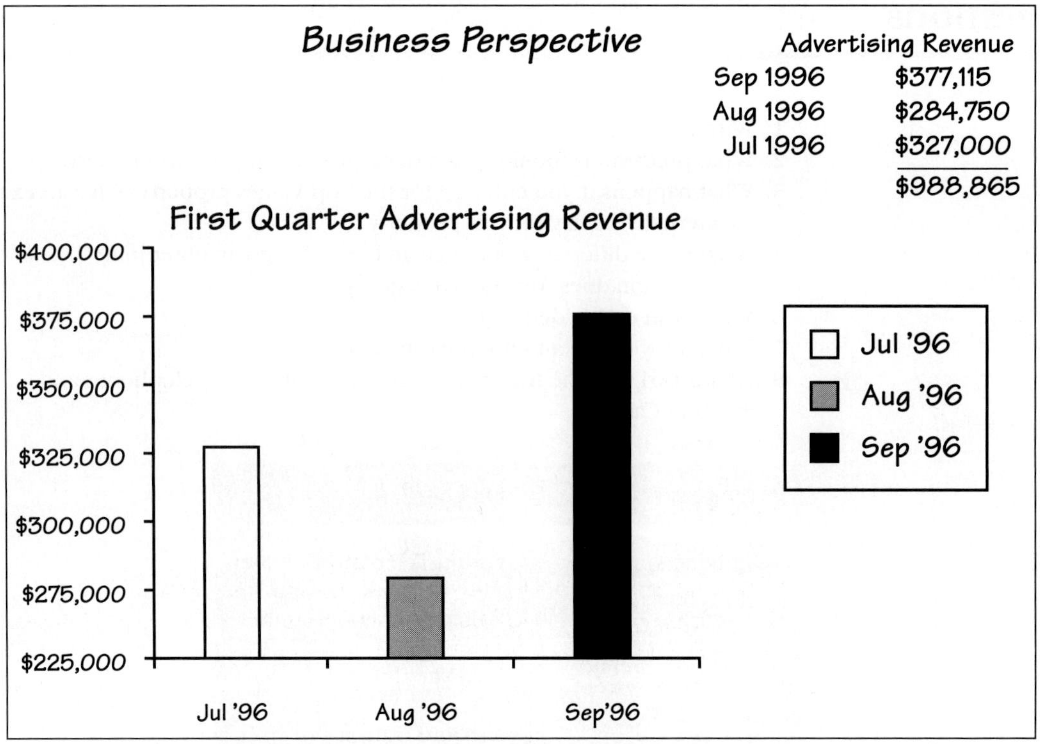

Figure 1-62

a. The entire report must fit on one page.
b. The qryAdvRevenueBPDetail query is the basis for the report.
c. Place in the Page Header section: the MagazineTitle field value from the query and "Advertising Revenue" as a column heading. Change the MagazineTitle field value font to italics and size to 12.
d. Place in the Detail section: the MagazineIssue field value from the query and the AdvRevenue field value from the query.
e. Add the MagazineTitle Footer section and place in this section one line and the total of the AdvRevenue field values.
f. As a very rough spacing guideline, there should be two or three rows of grid dots in the Page Header section and in the MagazineTitle Footer section and one row of grid dots in the Detail section. To position the chart close to the rest of the report, you should change its Height property in the property sheet to a value in the range 7.6" to 8.2".

2. Figure 1-63 shows Elena's design for the QuarterlyAdvertisingRevenues report. This is the other report that Brian wants for the stockholders' meeting. It illustrates the quarter's advertising revenue for all five magazines. Complete the report according to the following specifications. Use Figure 1-63 for guidance. When you finish creating the report, save it with the name QuarterlyAdvertisingRevenues and print the report.

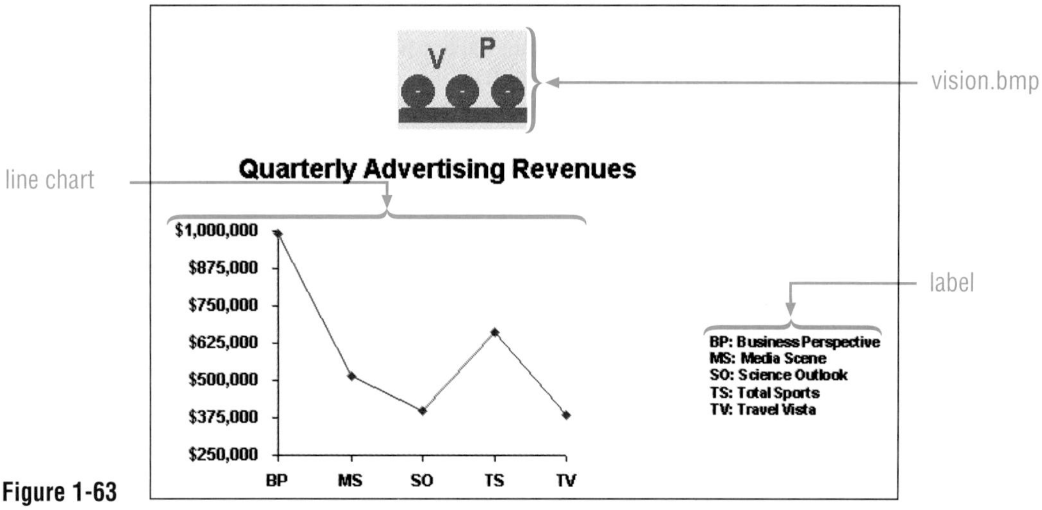

Figure 1-63

a. The entire report must fit on one page.
b. The qryAdvRevenueQuarterly query is the basis for the report.
c. Place the logo at the top of the Page Header section and its left side at approximately the 1.75" mark on the horizontal ruler. The logo is the same vision.bmp Paintbrush file that you used earlier in this tutorial; it is found on your Student Disk.
d. Place the line chart in the Page Header section beneath the logo. The qryAdvRevenueQuarterly query is the basis for the chart. Change the size of the chart title to 14. Change the size of the category labels to 9. Change the size of the tick-mark (Y-axis) labels to 9, change their scale, and eliminate their decimals.
e. In the Report Design window, place a label to the right of the line chart to serve as a legend explaining the category labels. (*Hint:* Press [Shift][Enter] to go to the start of a new line in a label box.)

3. Create a crosstab query (save it with the name qryAdvRevenueCrosstab) based on the tblAdvRevenue table. Use MagazineCode for the row headings, MagazineIssue for the column headings (by month), and AdvRevenue for the numbers to be summed in the middle. Calculate a summary for each row. Print the query results.
4. Create an outer join between the TYPES table and the TypesWithoutMatchingPastArticlesQuery query, printing all the Type and Description fields from the table and only those Type field values from the query that have matching records. Print the query results and save the query with the name qryTypesOuterJoin.

Case Problems

1. Walkton Daily Press Carriers

Launch Access and open the Press database on your Student Disk.

1. Create a query that displays Balance Amount (renamed Balance) from the BILLINGS table and Birthdate, Carrier Last Name, and Carrier First Name from the CARRIERS table. Sort the output in ascending order, using Carrier Last Name as the primary sort key and Carrier First Name as the secondary sort key. Save the query with the name Balance and Birthdate Query. Then create a crosstab query that is based on Balance and Birthdate Query. The crosstab query will have Carrier Last Name and Carrier First Name as row headings and Birthdate (grouped by Year) as a column heading. It will display Balance for the numbers to be summed in the middle. Do not calculate a summary for each row. Print the query results and save the query with the name Balance and Birthdate Crosstab Query.

2. Create an outer join between the CARRIERS and BILLINGS tables, printing the Carrier Last Name, Carrier First Name, Carrier ID, and Birthdate fields from the CARRIERS table and only those Route ID field values from the BILLINGS table that have matching records. Print the query results and save the query with the name CARRIERS Outer Join to BILLINGS Query.
3. Carrier routes form groups based on the first character of the Route ID. For example, all Route IDs starting with G form the G route group, all the Route IDs starting with J form the J route group, and so on. Grant Sherman needs to create a line chart showing the total carrier balances for each route group. Figure 1-64 shows his design for the new form. It consists of a line chart created with Graph Wizard. You must complete the form according to the following specifications. Save it with the name Route Group Balance Chart. Print the form when you finish creating it.

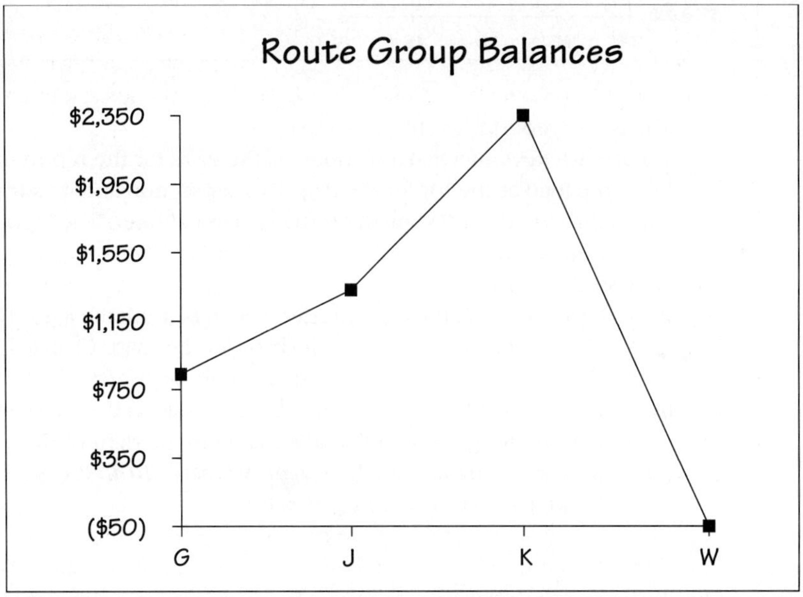

Figure 1-64

   a. Create a query (saved with the name Route Group Balance Query) that will be the basis for the chart. The query uses the Route ID field (renamed RouteGroup) and the Balance Amount field (renamed Balance) from the BILLINGS table. Sort the dynaset in ascending order by RouteGroup, group by RouteGroup, and sum the Balance field. The Field box for the RouteGroup field should be RouteGroup: Left([Route ID],1). The Left function, in this case, extracts the first character of Route ID, so that RouteGroup becomes a one-character text field output to the dynaset and input later to Graph Wizard.
   b. Place the line chart in the Detail section of the form. The form should not have any other sections. Use font size 14 for the chart title and font size 10 for both axes. Change the lines from the default colors to black. Change the scale of the tick-mark (Y-axis) labels and eliminate their decimals.
4. Add case.bmp, which is a bitmap stored on your Student Disk, to the CARRIERS By Name, Route ID form. Position the bitmap in the upper-left corner of the Form Header section. Print the form and save it.

2. Lopez Used Cars

Launch Access and open the Usedcars database on your Student Disk.

1. Create a crosstab query (save it with the name Sedan Inventory Crosstab Query) that uses the USED CARS and LOCATIONS tables. Row headings are based on the Location Name field, column headings are based on the Class field, and the numbers in the middle are based on the sum of the Cost field. The query includes only sedans—the Class of sedans have values that start with the letter S. Do not calculate a summary for each row. Print the query results.
2. Create a query (save it with the name TRANSMISSIONS Without Matching USED CARS) that displays the Transmission Type and Transmission Desc fields from the TRANSMISSIONS table for those records that do not match a record in the USED CARS table. Print the query results.
3. Maria Lopez creates a column chart comparing the total costs and selling prices for used cars in the cities of El Paso, Houston, Laredo, and Pecos. Figure 1-65 shows her design for the form. It consists of a column chart created with Graph Wizard. You must complete the form according to the following specifications. (Save it with the name Selected City Chart.) Print the form when you finish creating it.

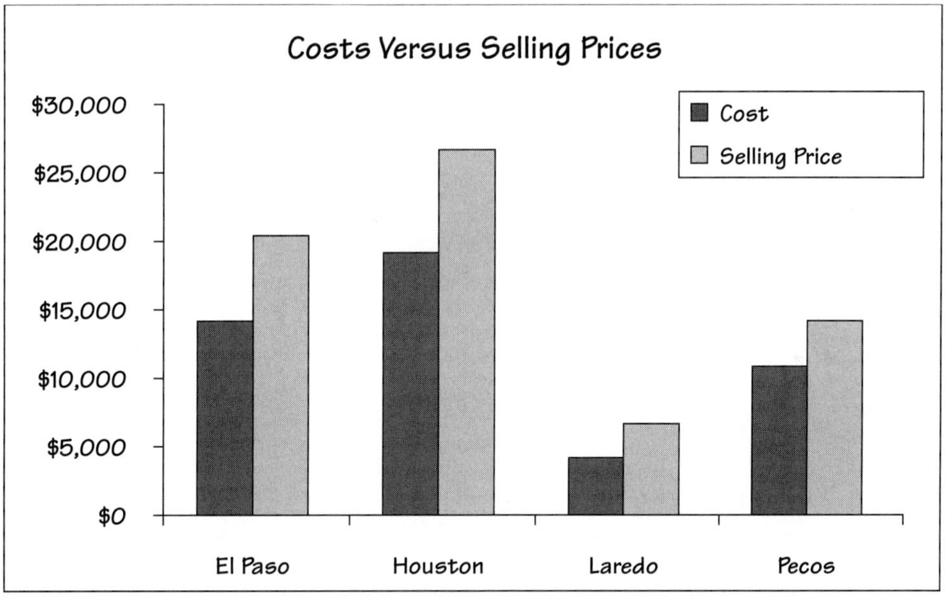

Figure 1-65

   a. Create a query (save it with the name Selected City Query) that will be the basis for the chart. The query uses the Location Name field from the LOCATIONS table and the Cost and Selling Price fields from the USED CARS table. Include in this query just those used cars from El Paso, Houston, Laredo, and Pecos. Print the query results.
   b. Place the line chart in the Detail section of the form. The form should not have any other sections. Use font size 14 for the chart title and font size 10 for both axes. Change the columns from the default colors to more printable colors or patterns. Change the scale of the tick-mark (Y-axis) labels and eliminate their decimals.
4. Add case.bmp, which is a bitmap stored on your Student Disk, to the USED CARS by Manufacturer and Model form. Position the bitmap on the left side of the form and near the top of the Detail section. Print the form and save it.

3. Tophill University Student Employment

Launch Access and open the Parttime database on your Student Disk.

1. Create a crosstab query (save it with the name JOBS Crosstab Query) that uses the JOBS table. Row headings are based on the Employer ID field, column headings are based on the Hours/Week field, and the numbers in the middle are based on the sum of the Weekly Wages field. The Weekly Wages field is a calculated field equal to Hours/Week times Wages. Do not calculate a summary for each row. Print the query results.
2. Create an outer join between the EMPLOYERS and JOBS tables, printing all the Employer Name and Contact Name fields from the EMPLOYERS table and only those Job Title field values from the JOBS table that have matching records. Print the query results and save the query with the name EMPLOYERS Outer Join to JOBS Query.
3. Create an XY (scatter) chart comparing the average wages per hour versus the number of hours worked per week. Figure 1-66 shows a design for the form. It consists of an XY (scatter) chart created with Graph Wizard. You must complete the form according to the following specifications. Save the form with the name Average Wages Per Hour Chart. Print the form when you finish creating it.

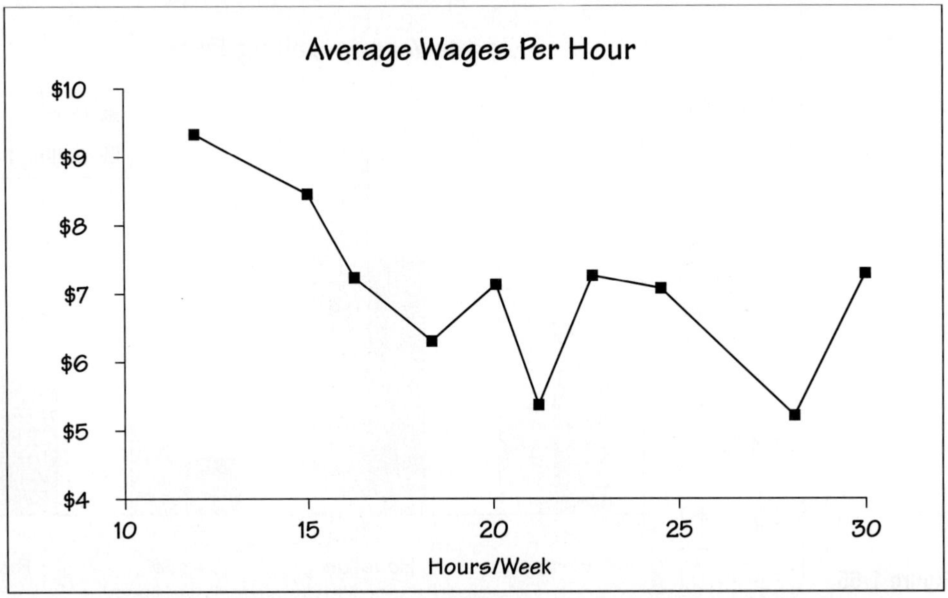

Figure 1-66

   a. Use the Hours/Week and Wages fields from the JOBS table as the basis for the chart. Average the numbers from the Wages field for the chart.
   b. Place the XY (scatter) chart in the Detail section of the form. The form should not have any other sections. Use font size 14 for the chart title and font size 10 for both axes. Change the scale of the tick-mark (Y-axis) labels and eliminate their decimals. Add the category label Hours/Week with font size 10.

4. Add case.bmp, which is a bitmap stored on your Student Disk, to the JOBS by Employer and Job Title form. Position the bitmap at the top of the Form Header section with its left side at the 2" mark on the horizontal ruler. Print the form and save it.

4. Rexville Business Licenses

Launch Access and open the Buslic database on your Student Disk.

1. Create a crosstab query (save it with the name ISSUED LICENSES Crosstab Query) that uses the ISSUED LICENSES and LICENSES tables. Row headings are based on the License Description field, column headings are based on the Date Issued field, and the numbers in the middle are based on the sum of the Amount field. The Field box for the Date Issued field should be Expr1: Month([Date Issued]). The Month function returns a value of 1 for January, 2 for February, and so on. Do not calculate a summary for each row. Print the query results.
2. Create an outer join between the LICENSES and ISSUED LICENSES tables, printing all the License Type and License Description fields from the LICENSES table and only those Amount field values from the ISSUED LICENSES table that have matching records. Print the query results and save the query with the name LICENSES Outer Join to ISSUED LICENSES Query.
3. Create a column chart that shows the total license amount by month. Figure 1-67 shows a design for the form. It consists of a column chart created with Graph Wizard. You must complete the form according to the following specifications. Save it with the name License Amount by Month Chart. Print the form when you finish creating it.

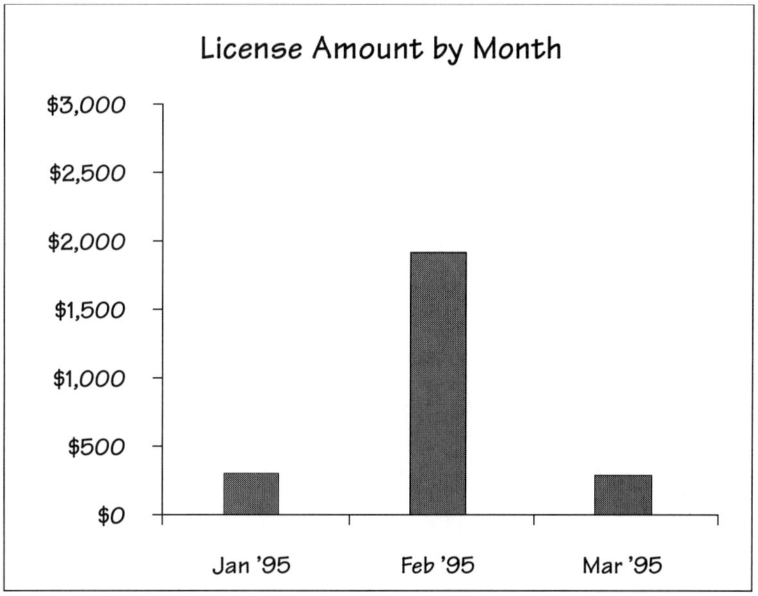

Figure 1-67

   a. Use the Amount and Date Issued fields from the ISSUED LICENSES table as the basis for the chart. Sum the numbers from the Amount field for the chart.
   b. Place the column chart in the Detail section of the form. The form should not have any other sections. Use font size 14 for the chart title and font size 10 for both axes. Change the scale of the tick-mark (Y-axis) labels and eliminate their decimals.

4. Add case.bmp, which is a bitmap stored on your Student Disk, to the BUSINESSES by License Type and Business Name form. Position the bitmap in the upper-left corner of the Form Header section. Print the form and save it.

Macros

OBJECTIVES

In this tutorial you will:

- Create and run macros
- Learn about actions, events, and event properties
- Design a switchboard and dialog boxes for a graphical user interface
- Create a control table and its queries
- Create dialog boxes
- Create a switchboard and the macro group for its command buttons

Using Macros with the Issue25 Database

CASE

Vision Publishers During Elena Sanchez's one-week Access training seminar, the instructors demonstrated several database applications they had developed. Elena and the other seminar attendees judged the instructors' database applications to be more professional looking and easier to use than those any attendee had created before the seminar. The main difference was that the instructors' applications used several advanced Access features to automate and control how a user interacts with Access. Elena explains these automation and control features to Brian Murphy, who asks her to develop a plan for applying what she learned at the seminar to the Issue25 database.

Designing the User Interface

A **user interface** is what you see and how you communicate with a computer application. A decade ago, you communicated with an application by typing in commands that you had to remember from a command language, but most of the applications developed for today's popular operating environments, such as Microsoft Windows, use graphical user interfaces. A **graphical user interface (GUI)** displays windows, menu bars, pull-down menus, dialog boxes, and graphical pictures called icons, which you use to communicate with your application. Microsoft Windows applications all use the same visual interface, so once you learn one Windows application, you can easily learn another. Overall, a GUI benefits a user by simplifying work, improving productivity, and decreasing errors.

Switchboards

Elena reviews the notes from her seminar and designs a special GUI for the Issue25 database, shown in Figure 2-1 as it will appear when she finishes creating it. This interface is called a **switchboard**, a user-created form that appears when you open a database and that provides controlled access to the database's tables, forms, queries, and reports. When a user opens the Issue25 database, Access will open this switchboard and the user will choose one of the options on the switchboard.

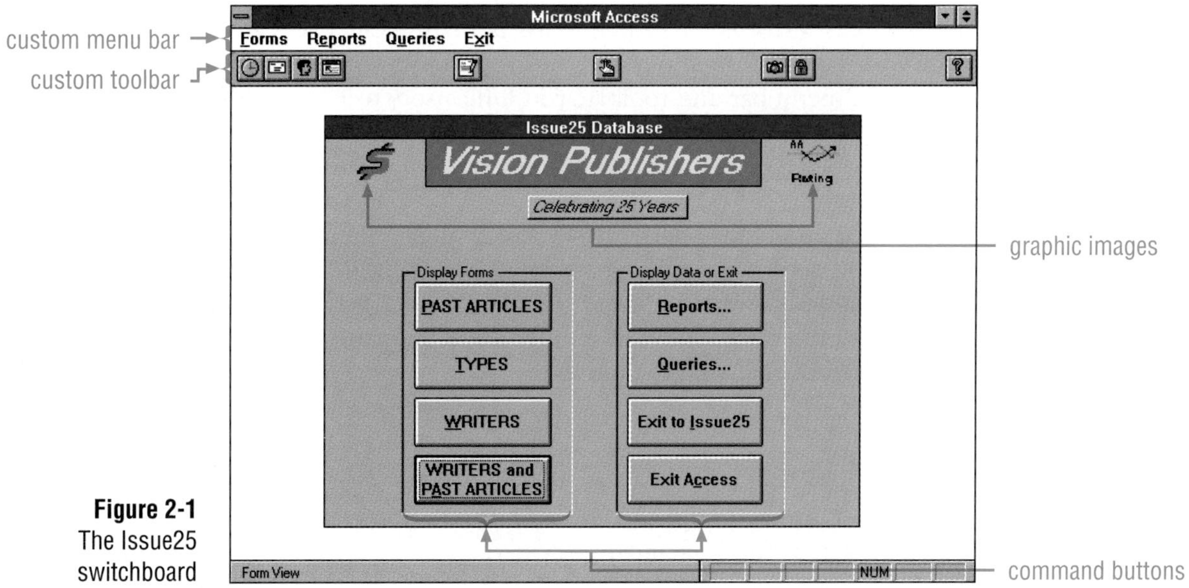

Figure 2-1
The Issue25 switchboard

When you create a switchboard, you are essentially creating a new interface, and it's up to you to decide what options you want to give the user. A typical switchboard has the following features:

- Command buttons that provide all the options available to the user. In Figure 2-1, for example, a user can click command buttons to open one of four forms or lists of available queries or reports, to exit from the switchboard to the Database window for the Issue25 database, or to exit Access. When a selected form, or a query or report list, is closed, Access redisplays the switchboard, allowing the user to choose the next option. In other words, you start and end with the switchboard and navigate between options from the switchboard.

- A custom menu bar, which provides another way for a user to make selections. Clicking each of the four menu names opens a pull-down menu of commands. You can choose options from the menu bar and menus or from the command buttons.
- A custom toolbar, which provides a third way for a user to make selections. When creating a custom toolbar, you can use standard Access toolbar buttons or create your own buttons. You can also change the icon on the face of a button to another icon or to text.
- Underlined letters in each menu name and on each command button option, are a fourth way for a user to make selections. Each underlined letter identifies a **shortcut key** or **hot key**, which you press while holding down [Alt] to make a selection, instead of clicking the mouse on a command button, menu name, or toolbar button.
- Text boxes and graphic images which provide identification and visual appeal. Using a small number of attractively designed graphic images and text boxes can help users understand the switchboard's functions, but beware that too many can confuse and distract.

A switchboard gives an attractive look to your user interface, but there are two more important reasons to use a switchboard. First, a switchboard lets you develop a custom organization to the user interface. If you wanted to allow users to open more than the four forms shown in Figure 2-1, for example, you could display one command button labeled Forms... instead of the four Display Forms command buttons. You would then, of course, reposition the command buttons to improve the switchboard design and add a dialog box in which a user selects the form to open.

Another reason to use a switchboard is to prevent users from changing the final design of your tables, forms, queries, and reports. By hiding the Database window and using a custom menu bar and toolbar, you limit users to just those database features you want them to use. You would not include any menu, toolbar, or command-button option that lets users open a design window. In this way, they cannot inadvertently change your application design.

Then why does Elena include the Exit to Issue25 command button, which closes the switchboard and activates the Database window for the Issue25 database? Because Elena needs a quick-and-easy way to change and test the interface while she is creating it. Once she perfects the interface, she will remove the command button and, with its removal, prevent others from changing the interface.

Dialog Boxes

Two command buttons on the switchboard, the Reports and Queries buttons, have three trailing dots. As a Windows standard, these dots signify that a dialog box containing further detailed options opens when you click that command button. To display the report and query names and their options, Elena designs the two custom dialog boxes shown in Figure 2-2 as they will appear when she finishes creating them. A **custom dialog box** is a form that you create to resemble a dialog box, both in appearance and function. You use a custom dialog box to ask for user input, selection, or confirmation before an action, such as the opening of a query dynaset or the printing of a report, is performed.

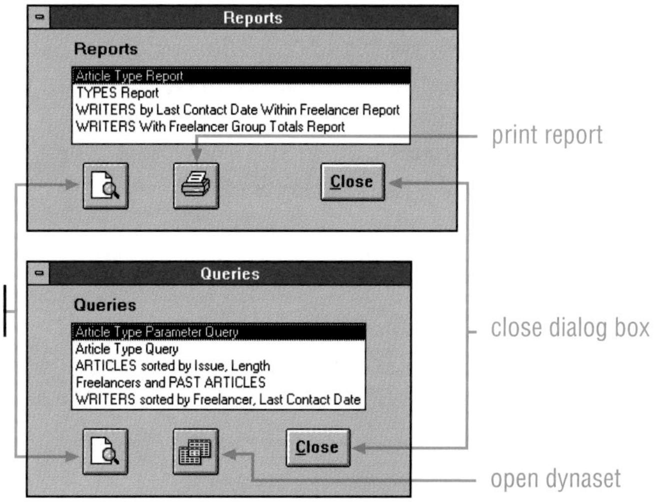

Figure 2-2
The Reports and Queries dialog boxes

Both dialog boxes contain list boxes that display the queries and reports available for selection. Clicking the Close command buttons returns you to the switchboard. The other command buttons use graphic images to identify their functions. Each dialog box has a command button on the left with a magnifying glass over a piece of paper. This is the same graphic image Access uses on its toolbar Print Preview button to open the Print Preview window for the selected query or report; these command buttons perform the same function. The middle command buttons in the dialog boxes print the selected report or open the dynaset for the selected query. Command buttons can contain text, standard graphic images available from Access, or graphic images you supply.

Macros

The command buttons on Elena's switchboard and custom dialog boxes gain their power from macros and Access Basic code. A **macro** is a command or a series of commands you want Access to perform automatically for you. Macros automate repetitive tasks, such as opening forms, printing reports, and running queries. Each command in a macro is called an **action** or instruction. Clicking the WRITERS command button on Elena's switchboard, for example, causes Access to perform a macro containing the action that opens the WRITERS form.

Access lets you automate most tasks using either macros or Access Basic. As a beginner, you will find it easier to write macros than to program using Access Basic. With macros, you simply select a series of actions from a list so that the macro does what you want it to do. To use Access Basic you need to understand the Access Basic command language well enough to be able to write your own code. Access Basic does provide advantages over macros, including better error-handling capabilities, and it makes your application easier to change. Macros, however, are useful for small applications and for simple tasks, such as opening and closing objects. Additionally, you cannot use Access Basic and must use macros in the following four situations.

- Assigning actions to a specific keyboard key or key combination
- Creating custom menu bars
- Opening an application in a special way, such as displaying a switchboard
- Performing actions from a toolbar button

Access has 47 actions you can use in your macros. Figure 2-3 lists the actions grouped under five categories. Actions in the Data Navigation category move the focus from one record to another record. **Focus** refers to the record and control that is currently active and awaiting user action. For example, a field has the focus when it is highlighted or has an I-beam pointer, and a command button has the focus when a dotted box appears around its label.

Action	Purpose
Data Navigation	
FindNext	Find the next record matching the previous FindRecord action.
FindRecord	Find the first record matching the criteria.
GoToControl	Move the focus to the named control.
GoToPage	Move the focus to the first field on the specified page.
GoToRecord	Move the focus to the specified record.
Import/Export	
OutputTo	Export data in Excel, rich-text, or text format.
SendObject	Output an e-mail message in Excel, rich-text, or text format.
TransferDatabase	Import or export data between the active database and another database.
TransferSpreadsheet	Import or export data between the active database and a spreadsheet file.
TransferText	Import or export data between the active database and a text file.
Object Manipulation	
Close	Close the specified window.
CopyObject	Copy a database object to the same or a different database.
DeleteObject	Delete the specified object.
Maximize	Maximize the active window.
Minimize	Minimize the active window to an icon.
MoveSize	Move or resize the active window.
OpenForm	Open a form.
OpenModule	Open an Access Basic module.
OpenQuery	Open a query.
OpenReport	Open or print a report.
OpenTable	Open a table.
Print	Print the active object.
Rename	Rename the specified object.
RepaintObject	Update the screen for the specified object.
Requery	Update the data in the specified control.
Restore	Restore a window to its previous size.
SelectObject	Select the specified object.
SetValue	Set the value of a control, field, or property.
ShowAllRecords	Remove a filter from the active object.

Figure 2-3
Actions grouped by category

Action	Purpose
Perform or Stop	
CancelEvent	Cancel the event that caused Access to run the macro.
DoMenuItem	Perform a menu command.
Quit	Exit Access.
RunApp	Run another DOS or Windows application.
RunCode	Run an Access Basic function.
RunMacro	Run another macro.
RunSQL	Run an SQL query.
StopAllMacros	Stop all macros currently running.
StopMacro	Stop the current macro.
Miscellaneous	
AddMenu	Add a drop-down menu to a custom menu bar.
ApplyFilter	Restrict or sort data in the underlying table or query.
Beep	Output a beep sound through the computer's speaker.
Echo	Display or hide a macro's results on the screen.
Hourglass	Display an hourglass pointer while the macro runs.
MsgBox	Display a message box.
SendKeys	Send keystrokes to an application.
SetWarnings	Turn system messages on or off.
ShowToolbar	Display or hide a toolbar.

Figure 2-3 ***(continued)***
Actions grouped by category

Actions in the Import/Export category transfer data between the active database and other applications. Actions in the Object Manipulation category open, close, size, and otherwise work with Access objects. Actions in the Perform or Stop category either start or stop tasks. The Miscellaneous category contains actions that inform the user (Echo, Hourglass, MsgBox, SetWarnings, and ShowToolbar), emit a sound (Beep), send keystrokes (SendKeys), create a custom menu bar (AddMenu), and filter data (ApplyFilter).

Do not be concerned about learning all 47 actions. You will rarely need to use more than a dozen actions in most database applications. In this tutorial you will gain experience with several macro actions.

Creating Macros

At her seminar Elena learned how to use macros by creating some simple macros and experimenting with them. To refresh her knowledge of macros, she creates a macro to open the TYPES form.

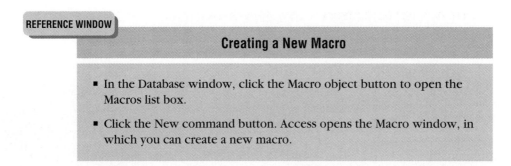

REFERENCE WINDOW

Creating a New Macro

- In the Database window, click the Macro object button to open the Macros list box.
- Click the New command button. Access opens the Macro window, in which you can create a new macro.

Elena opens the Issue25 database and then the Macro window in preparation for creating a new macro.

To open the Macro window:

1. Place your Student Disk in the appropriate drive, launch Access, and open the Issue25 database on your Student Disk.
2. Click the **Macro object button** in the Database Window to display the Macros list box.
3. Click the **New command button**. Access opens the Macro window. See Figure 2-4.

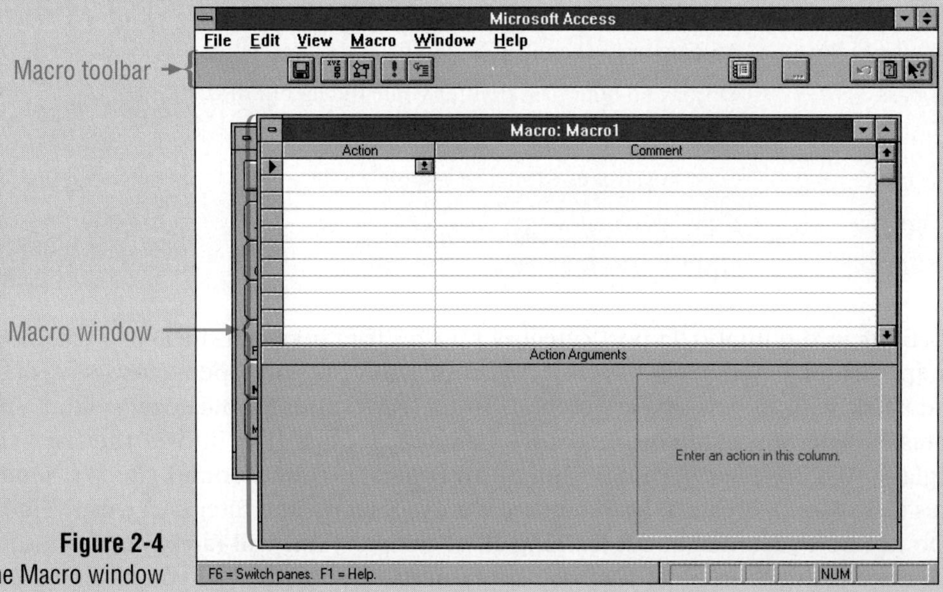

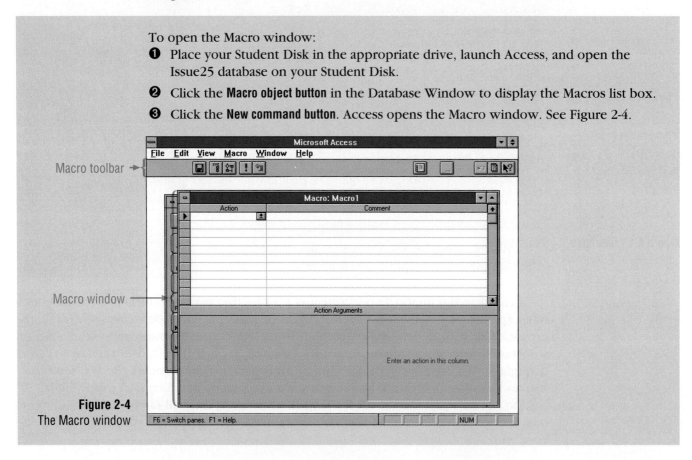

Figure 2-4
The Macro window

You use the **Macro window** to create and modify macros. Both the menu bar and toolbar for the Macro window have options that are specifically related to macros. The Macro window has an **Action column**, in which you enter the action you want Access to perform, and a **Comment column**, in which you enter optional comments to document the specific action.

When you choose your first action (as you'll see in a moment), Access displays a hint for the current macro property in the bottom half of the Macro window on the right. On the left, Access lists the arguments associated with the actions you choose. **Arguments** are additional facts needed by Access to execute an action. The action for opening a form, for example, needs the form name and the window name as arguments.

Choosing an Action

Elena creates a simple macro to open the TYPES form.

To create a macro to open a form:

1. Click the **down arrow button** in the first row's Action drop-down list box.
2. Scroll and then click **OpenForm** in the drop-down list box. Access closes the drop-down list box, displays OpenForm as the first action, and displays six arguments for this action.
3. Press **[Tab]** and then type **Open the TYPES form** in the Comment text box.
4. In the lower half of the Macro Window, click the **Form Name text box**, click the **down arrow button** that appears, and then click **TYPES form**. See Figure 2-5.

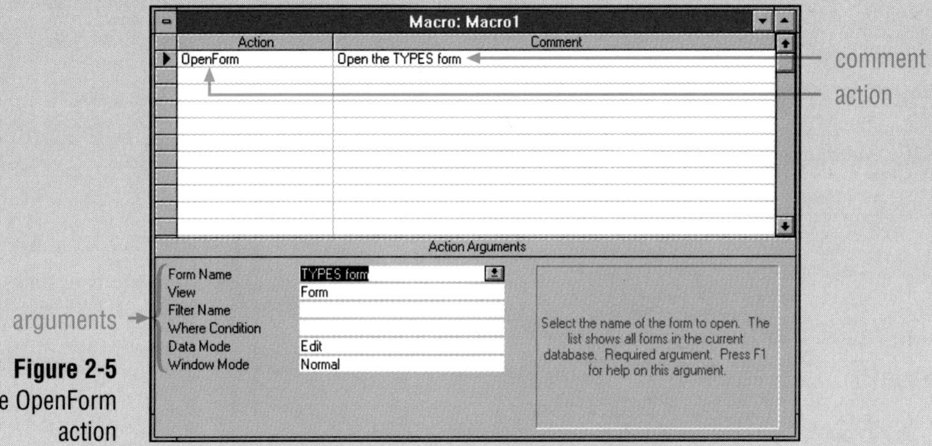

Figure 2-5
The OpenForm action

For now, do not change any other argument. When you run the macro, Access opens the TYPES form in the Form View window, does not use a filter or special condition, allows edits or changes to the data, and treats the Form View window normally.

Saving a Macro

Before running the macro Elena saves it using the macro name zOpenPractice, so that it sorts to the bottom of the Macros list box.

To save a new macro:

1. Click the toolbar **Save button** .
2. Type **zOpenPractice** in the Macro Name text box and then press **[Enter]**. Access closes the dialog box and saves the macro.

Running a Macro

You can directly run a macro in three different ways:

- In the Macro window, click the toolbar Run button.
- Click File, click Run Macro..., scroll the Macro Name drop-down list box, click the macro name, and then click the OK button.
- In the Database window, click the Macro object button and then double-click the macro in the Macros list box.

Elena uses the first method to run the macro she just created and saved. If she had not already saved the macro, Access would tell her to save the macro before she could run it.

To run the macro that is open in the Macro window:

❶ Click the toolbar **Run button** [!]. Access opens the TYPES form in the Form View window, placing it on top of the Macro window. See Figure 2-6.

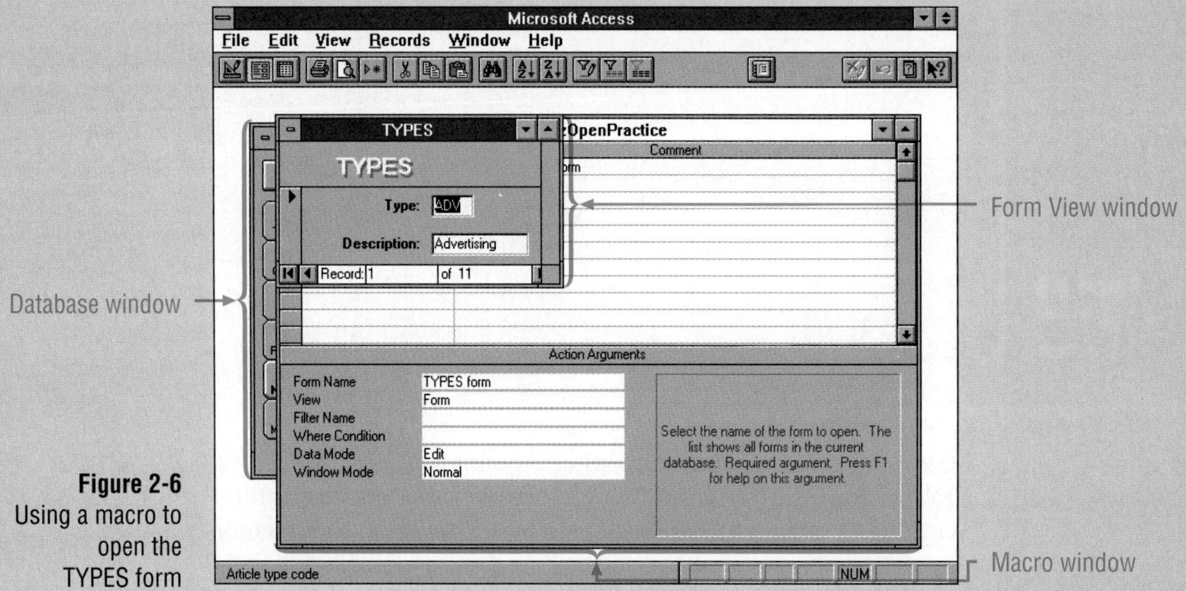

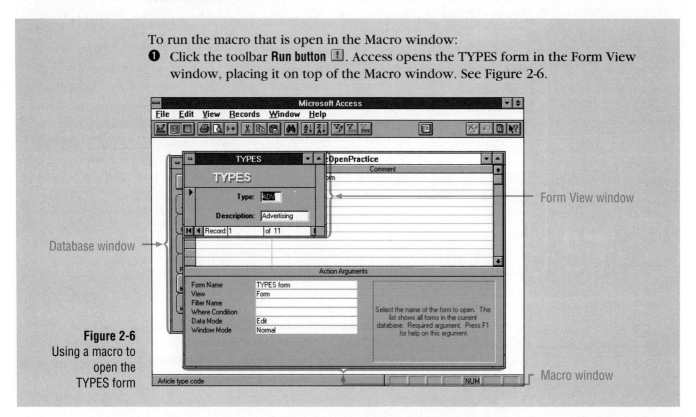

Figure 2-6 Using a macro to open the TYPES form

Access executes the macro by opening the TYPES form in the Form View window; you can now work with the fields and records of the TYPES form. This first macro is not a very exciting one; it involves only one action. It has, however, given you a chance to become comfortable with creating and using macros.

Adding Actions to a Macro

To create a macro with more than one action, Elena adds a few actions to the zOpenPractice macro. Before the OpenForm action, she adds the Hourglass and Beep actions. Following the OpenForm action, she adds actions to open the Article Type Query, perform the Beep action, close the Article Type Query, close the TYPES form, and then perform the Beep action. The **Hourglass action** displays an hourglass pointer while the macro is being executed, and the **Beep action** sounds a beep tone through the computer's speaker. Because the Hourglass and Beep action names are self-descriptive, Elena does not need to add comments to document them.

When the execution of the changed macro is finished, Elena will have heard three beep tones, two object windows will have opened and closed, and the hourglass pointer will have appeared from the start to the end of the macro's execution. The net effect is not useful, except to demonstrate the power of a macro with multiple actions.

To add actions to an existing macro:

1. Double-click the Form View window **Control menu box** to close that window and activate the Macro window.
2. Highlight the first two rows in the Macro window by dragging the pointer from the first to the second **row selectors,** located at the far left of the window. Click the right mouse button in one of the two highlighted row selectors to open the shortcut menu and then click **Insert Row**. Access adds two rows above the OpenForm action.
3. Click the first row's **Action text box**, click the **down arrow button**, scroll down the Action drop-down list box, and then click **Hourglass**. The default value for the Hourglass On argument is Yes. This is the value you want, so you are done adding the first action.
4. Click the second row's **Action text box**, click the **down arrow button**, and then click **Beep**. The Beep action has no arguments, so you are done adding this action.
5. To add the Beep action to the fifth and eighth rows, click the right mouse button in the second **row selector** and then click **Copy** in the shortcut menu. Click the right mouse button in the fifth **row selector**, and click **Paste** in the shortcut menu. Repeat this step for the eighth row. Access adds the Beep action to the fifth and eighth rows.
6. Click the fourth row's **Action text box**, click the **down arrow button**, scroll down the Action drop-down list box, and then click **OpenQuery**. Press **[Tab]** and then type **Open the Article Type Query** in the Comment text box. Click the **Query Name text box**, click the **down arrow button**, and then click **Article Type Query**.
7. Click the sixth row's **Action text box**, click the **down arrow button**, and then click **Close**. Press **[Tab]** and then type **Close the Article Type Query** in the Comment text box. Click the **Object Type text box**, click the **down arrow button**, and then click **Query**. Click the **Object Name text box**, click the **down arrow button**, and then click **Article Type Query**.
8. Click the seventh row's **Action text box**, click the **down arrow button**, and then click **Close**. Press **[Tab]** and then type **Close the TYPES form** in the Comment text box. Click the **Object Type text box**, click the **down arrow button**, and then click **Form**. Click the **Object Name text box**, click the **down arrow button**, and then click **TYPES form**. See Figure 2-7.

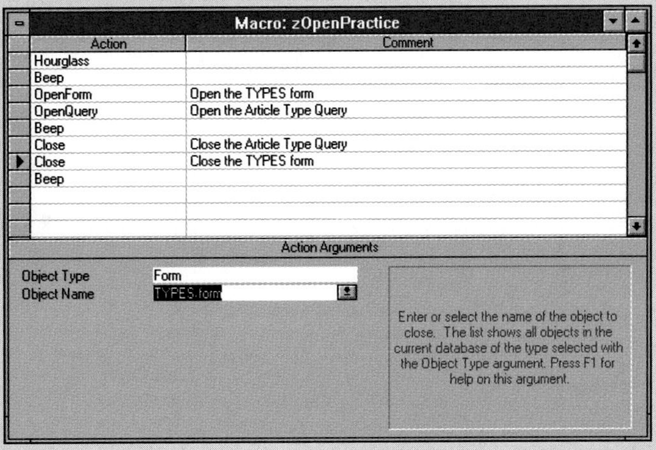

Figure 2-7
A macro with several actions

Elena executes the macro, again using the toolbar Run button.

To execute directly a macro with several actions:

1. Click the toolbar **Run button**. Access opens the "Save now?" dialog box.
2. Click the **OK button**. Access closes the dialog box, saves the macro, and executes the macro.

Depending on the speed of your computer, the form and query windows might appear and vanish too quickly to be seen clearly, but you should be able to hear the three beeps distinctly. Elena runs the macro again, but this time she single steps through it.

Single Stepping a Macro

Single stepping executes a macro one action at a time, pausing between actions. Use single stepping to make sure you have placed actions in the right order and with the right arguments. If you ever have problems with a macro, use single stepping to find the cause of the problems and to determine their proper corrections. Click the toolbar Single Step button to turn single stepping on and off. Once you turn on single stepping, it stays on for all macros until you turn it back off.

REFERENCE WINDOW

Single Stepping a Macro

- In the Macro window, click the toolbar Single Step button.
- Click the toolbar Run button.
- In the Macro Single Step dialog box, click the Step button to execute the next action, click the Halt button to stop the macro, or click the Continue button to execute all remaining actions in the macro and turn off single stepping.

Elena single steps through the zOpenPractice macro.

To start single stepping through a macro:

1. Click the toolbar **Single Step button** to turn on single stepping.
2. Click the toolbar **Run button**. Access opens the Macro Single Step dialog box. See Figure 2-8.

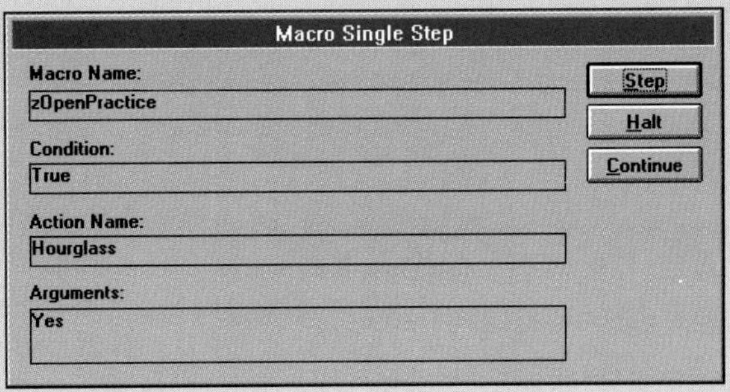

Figure 2-8
The Macro Single Step dialog box

When you single step through a macro, Access displays the Macro Single Step dialog box before performing each action. The **Macro Single Step dialog box** shows the macro name and the action's name, arguments, and condition. The action will be executed or not executed, depending on whether the condition is true or false. The three command buttons let you step one action at a time through the macro, halt the macro and return to the Macro window, or continue by executing all remaining actions without pause. Note that single stepping is turned off if you click the Continue button.

Elena single steps through the entire macro.

To single step through a macro:

1. Click the **Step button**. Access runs the first action and shows the macro's second action in the Macro Single Step dialog box. Because the Hourglass action changes the pointer to an hourglass for the duration of the macro, you can see the hourglass pointer if you move the pointer outside the Macro Single Step dialog box.
2. Click the **Step button** a second time. Access runs the second action by sounding a beep and shows the macro's third action. Each remaining action is executed by a single click on the Step button.
3. Click the **Step button** six times, making sure you read the Macro Single Step dialog box carefully and observe the windows opening and closing on the screen in between each click.
4. Double-click the Macro window **Control menu box**. Access closes the Macro window and activates the Database window.

Adding Actions by Dragging

Another way to add an action to a macro is by dragging an object from the Database window to a new row in the Macro window. Figure 2-9 shows the effect of dragging each of the six Access objects to a new row in the Macro window. For example, dragging a table creates an OpenTable action that opens the table's Datasheet View window and permits editing or updating. To use this dragging technique, be sure that the Macro and Database windows are both visible. You can move the two windows until you see all the critical components of each window, or use the Tile command on the Window menu.

Object Dragged	Action Created	Arguments and Their Default Values
Table	OpenTable	View—Datasheet, Data Mode—Edit
Query	OpenQuery	View—Datasheet, Data Mode—Edit
Form	OpenForm	View—Form, Data Mode—Edit, Filter Name—none, Where Condition—none, Window Mode—Normal
Report	OpenReport	View—Print Preview, Filter Name—none, Where Condition—none
Macro	RunMacro	Repeat Count—none, Repeat Expression—none
Module	OpenModule	Procedure Name—none

Figure 2-9
Actions created by dragging objects from the Database window

Elena uses the dragging technique to add an action that opens the Article Type form. She starts a new macro that she names zMorePractice.

To add an action to a macro using the dragging method:

1. Click the **New command button** to open the Macro window.
2. Click the toolbar **Database Window button** to place the Database window on top of the Macro window. Then drag the Database window **title bar** down and to the right, so that you move the Database window to the lower-right corner of the screen. See Figure 2-10.

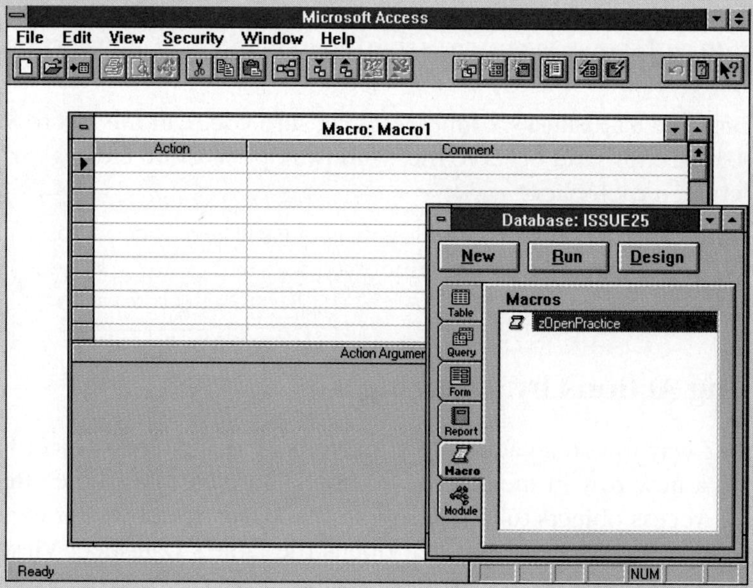

Figure 2-10
Macro and Database windows visible on

3. Click the **Form object button** in the Database window to display the Forms list box.
4. Drag **Article Type form** from the Forms list box to the first row's Action text box in the Macro window. Access adds the OpenForm action for the Article Type form, sets the arguments to their default values, and places the Macro window on top of the Database window.
5. Press **[Tab]** and then type **Open the Article Type form** in the Comment text box.

Elena next adds the MsgBox action to the macro to open a dialog box containing an informational or warning message. Before adding the dialog box, Elena first uses the Access Help system to learn more about macros and actions.

Using Help to Learn Macros and Actions

When you buy Access, you receive several manuals that describe, in detail, all the software's available features. You need to refer to dozens of different parts of these manuals, however, to find specific information about macros and actions. Fortunately, the Access Help system is a more complete and convenient reference. It's more complete because it has Cue Cards and a glossary added to the full set of manuals. The Access Help system is more convenient because the information in the full set of manuals is all contained in a single reference source with one index, available to answer your questions while you are working with Access. You can even print more complicated topics for study at your leisure away from the computer.

Elena uses the Access Help system to learn more about macros and actions and to print one of the macro topics. She uses the Glossary and the Search features to find rapidly the specific information she wants.

To use Access Help to learn about macros and actions:

1. Click **Help**, click **Contents**, click the **Glossary button**, click the **M button**, and then click **macro**. Access Help displays the definition of a macro.
2. Click **macro** again to close the definition window and then click the **A button** to display Glossary entries beginning with the letter A.
3. Click **action** to see its definition, and then click **action** to close the definition window. In the same way, open and read the definitions for **action argument**, **action list**, and **action row**, one at a time.
4. Click the **Search button**, type **action**, and then scroll until you see "actions: grouped by task" in the list box. Notice the many topics beginning with "action" and "actions."

5. Click **actions: grouped by task**, click the **Show Topics button**, and then click the **Go To button**. If the Microsoft Access 2.0 Help window is not maximized, click its **maximize button**. Access opens the Actions Grouped by Task topic, which is a complete list of the 47 actions. See Figure 2-11.

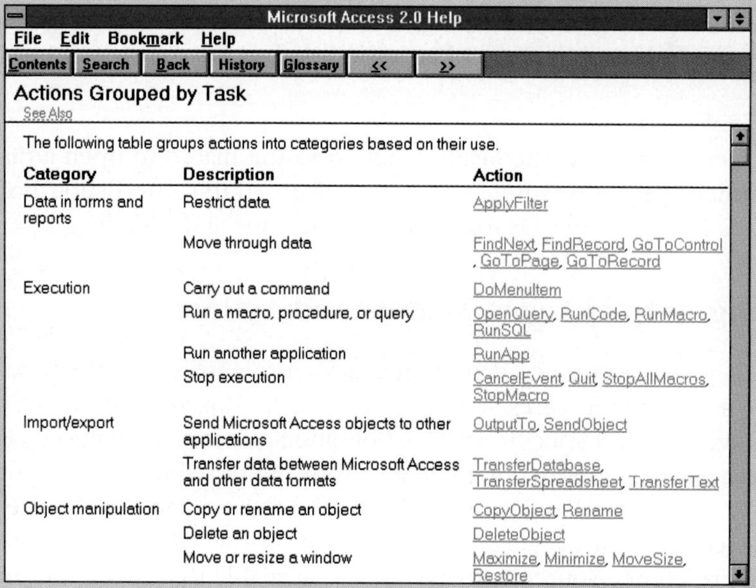
Microsoft Access 2.0 Help
File Edit Bookmark Help
Contents Search Back History Glossary << >>

Actions Grouped by Task
See Also

The following table groups actions into categories based on their use.

Category	Description	Action
Data in forms and reports	Restrict data	ApplyFilter
	Move through data	FindNext, FindRecord, GoToControl, GoToPage, GoToRecord
Execution	Carry out a command	DoMenuItem
	Run a macro, procedure, or query	OpenQuery, RunCode, RunMacro, RunSQL
	Run another application	RunApp
	Stop execution	CancelEvent, Quit, StopAllMacros, StopMacro
Import/export	Send Microsoft Access objects to other applications	OutputTo, SendObject
	Transfer data between Microsoft Access and other data formats	TransferDatabase, TransferSpreadsheet, TransferText
Object manipulation	Copy or rename an object	CopyObject, Rename
	Delete an object	DeleteObject
	Move or resize a window	Maximize, Minimize, MoveSize, Restore

Figure 2-11
The Actions Grouped by Task topic in the Help system

Next, Elena opens the MsgBox Action topic and prints the Using Shortcuts to Build Macros topic. She will use information from both the Using Shortcuts to Build Macros and the MsgBox Action topics to complete the macro she is creating.

To open and print Help topics:

1. Scroll down the Actions Grouped by Task topic to the Miscellaneous category and then click **MsgBox**. Access opens the MsgBox Action topic. See Figure 2-12.

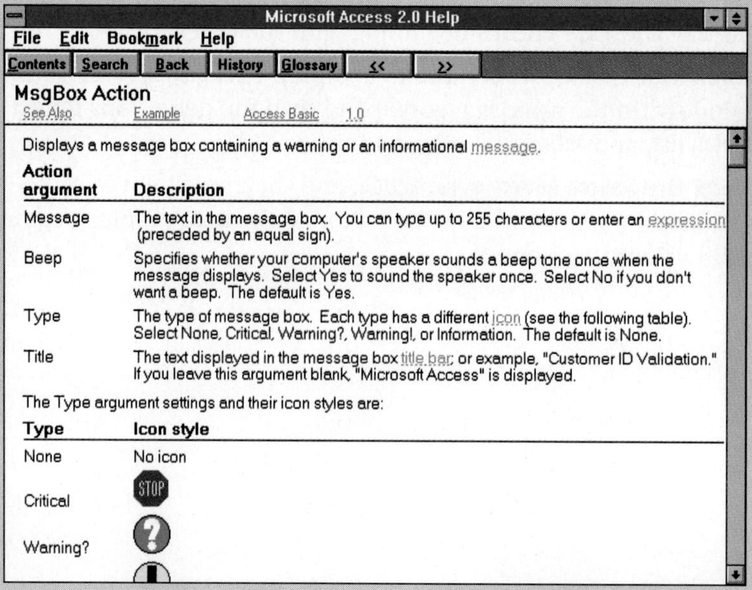
Microsoft Access 2.0 Help
File Edit Bookmark Help
Contents Search Back History Glossary << >>

MsgBox Action
See Also Example Access Basic 1.0

Displays a message box containing a warning or an informational message.

Action argument	Description
Message	The text in the message box. You can type up to 255 characters or enter an expression (preceded by an equal sign).
Beep	Specifies whether your computer's speaker sounds a beep tone once when the message displays. Select Yes to sound the speaker once. Select No if you don't want a beep. The default is Yes.
Type	The type of message box. Each type has a different icon (see the following table). Select None, Critical, Warning?, Warning!, or Information. The default is None.
Title	The text displayed in the message box title bar; or example, "Customer ID Validation." If you leave this argument blank, "Microsoft Access" is displayed.

The Type argument settings and their icon styles are:

Type	Icon style
None	No icon
Critical	STOP
Warning?	

Figure 2-12
The MsgBox Action topic in the Help system

2. Read through the MsgBox Action topic to get a general idea of its purpose and arguments.

❸ Click the **Search button**, type **macros: s**, click the **Show Topics button**, and then click the **Go To button**. Access opens the Using Shortcuts to Build Macros topic. You have already used the first part of this topic to create an action by dragging. Because you will be using the last part of the topic in just a moment, print the entire topic to serve as a reference.

❹ Click **File** and then click **Print Topic**. Access opens an informational dialog box for a few seconds and then prints the topic.

The Access Help system also has an alphabetical list of actions. Elena opens and reads this topic, so that she can easily reference it in her future work.

To open the alphabetical list of actions:

❶ Click the **Search button**, type **actions: r**, click the **Show Topics button**, click **Actions Reference**, and then click the **Go To button**. Access opens the Actions Reference topic. Scroll the topic to familiarize yourself with its contents.

❷ Double-click the Microsoft Access 2.0 Help window **Control menu box** to close the window and return to the Macro window.

Adding a MsgBox Action

If you add the MsgBox action to your macro it will open a dialog box that remains on the screen until you click the OK button. Because the macro does not proceed to the next action until you click the OK button, you have as much time as you need to look at the opened Article Type form. You will provide the following action arguments for the MsgBox action:

- Message: Click OK to resume the macro
- Beep: No
- Type: Information
- Title: MsgBox Action Practice

As you move from one macro argument to the next, Access changes the description that appears to the right of the argument text boxes. The description is a brief explanation of the current macro argument. If you need a more detailed explanation, press [F1]. When you are working with the MsgBox action in the Macro window and press [F1], for example, the Access Help system opens the MsgBox Action topic. This is the same topic you saw using the Access Help System.

To add a MsgBox action to a macro:

❶ Click the second row's **Action text box**, click the **down arrow button**, scroll down the Action drop-down list box, and then click **MsgBox**. Press **[Tab]** and then type **Display a practice message box** in the Comment text box.

❷ Click the **Message text box** and type **Click OK to resume the macro**.

❸ Click the **Beep text box**, click the **down arrow button**, and then click **No**.

❹ Click the **Type text box**, click the **down arrow button**, and then click **Information**.

❺ Click the **Title text box** and type **Message Box Practice**.

The macro now has two actions: the first action opens the Article Type form, and the second action displays a message box. To complete the macro, Elena adds the Close action for the Article Type form. She once again drags the Article Type form from the Database window, but this time to set the Close action's arguments.

Setting Action Arguments by Dragging

The last part of the Using Shortcuts to Build Macros topic Elena printed from the Access Help system explains how to set an action argument by dragging and shows a table of the arguments set for each action. Read it carefully before proceeding.

To set action arguments using the dragging method:

1. Click the third row's **Action text box**, click the **down arrow button**, and then click **Close**. Press **[Tab]** and then type **Close the Article Type form** in the Comment text box.
2. Click the toolbar **Database Window button** to place the Database window on top of the Macro window.
3. Drag **Article Type form** from the Forms list box to the Object Name **text box** in the Macro window. See Figure 2-13.

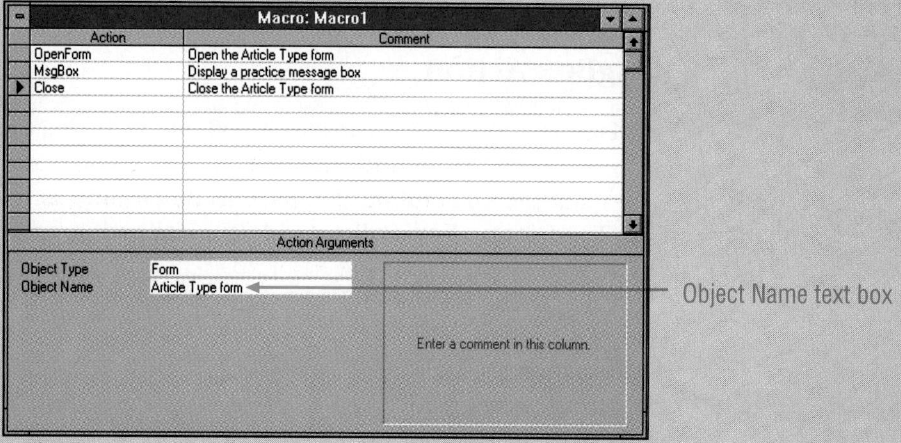

Figure 2-13 The Macro window after action arguments were set by the dragging method

When Elena releases the mouse button in the Object Name text box, Access sets the Object Type argument to Form and the Object Name argument to Article Type form. Because the macro is now complete, Elena runs it to be sure it is correct, saves it with the name zMorePractice, and then exits Access.

To run and save a macro:

1. If the toolbar Single Step button is selected, click it to deselect it.
2. Click the toolbar **Run button**. Access opens the "Save now?" dialog box.
3. Click the **OK button** to open the Save As dialog box, type **zMorePractice** in the Macro Name text box, and then press **[Enter]**. Access saves the macro and runs the first two macro actions. Access opens the dialog box after opening the Article Type form. See Figure 2-14.

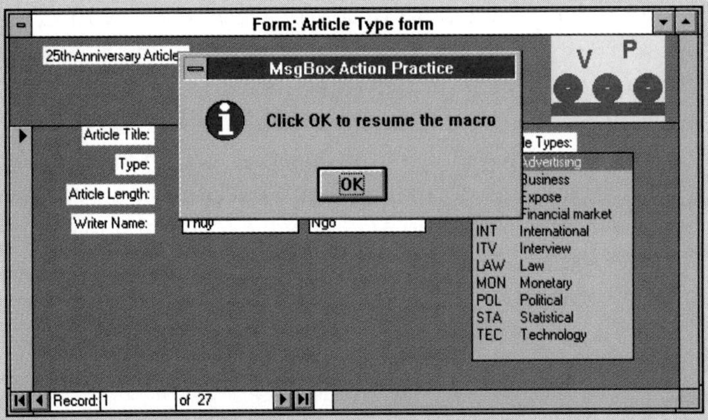

Figure 2-14 Running the MsgBox macro action

4. Click the **OK button**. Access closes the dialog box, runs the last macro action by closing the Article Type form, and displays the Macro window on top of the Database window.
5. Double-click the Microsoft Access window **Control menu box** to exit Access.

Elena has finished practicing with macros and is confident she can create the macros she needs for the Issue25 switchboard and dialog boxes.

When to Use Macros

In reviewing her seminar notes about macros, Elena reads that usually a macro is not initiated directly from the Macro window, as she did during her practice session. Instead, she should design her macros to be executed in the following situations:

- When a user opens a database. If a macro with the special name **AutoExec** is created, Access automatically executes the macro when a user opens the database.
- When a user presses a specific key combination.
- When a macro is executed from within another macro that uses the RunMacro action.
- When a user chooses a command on a custom menu bar.
- When a user clicks a toolbar button, especially a button on a custom toolbar.
- When a user clicks a command button or another special control on a form or report.
- When a user opens a form or report that has a macro attached to it.

For the last two situations, you can attach a macro to an event on a form or report.

Events

An **event** is an action to which you can define a response. Events occur, for example, when you click a button using the mouse or press a key to choose an option. In your work with Access you've initiated hundreds of events: on forms, controls, records, and reports. For example, three form events are: Open, which occurs when you open a form; Activate, which occurs when the form becomes the active window; and Close, which occurs when you close a form and it disappears from the screen. Each event has an associated event property. An **event property** is a named attribute of a control, section, form, or report to which the control, section, form, or report can respond. For example, each form has OnOpen, OnActivate, and OnClose event properties associated with the Open, Activate, and Close events, respectively.

Event properties appear in the property sheet when you create forms and reports. Unlike most properties you've likely used before in property sheets, event properties do not have an initial value. If an event property contains no value, it means the event property has not been **set.** In this case Access takes no special action when the associated event occurs. For example, if a form's OnOpen event property is not set and you open the form, then the form opens, the Open event occurs, and no special action occurs. You can set an event property value to a macro name, and Access will execute the macro when the event occurs.

Access has 35 events and 35 associated event properties. Figure 2-15 shows the events, their event properties, and when they occur.

Event	Event Property	Occurs With	Occurs
Activate	OnActivate	Forms, reports	After form or report receives the focus and becomes the active window
AfterDelConfirm	AfterDelConfirm	Forms	After user confirms the deletions and the records are deleted or the deletions are cancelled
AfterInsert	AfterInsert	Forms	After record is added
AfterUpdate	AfterUpdate	Forms, controls	After changed data in a control or record is updated
BeforeDelConfirm	BeforeDelConfirm	Forms	After user deletes records but before Access displays a dialog box for confirmation
BeforeInsert	BeforeInsert	Forms	After user types the first character in a new record but before the record is created
BeforeUpdate	BeforeUpdate	Forms, controls	After data are changed in a control or record but before they are updated
Change	OnChange	Controls	After contents of a text or combo box changes
Click	OnClick	Forms, controls, form sections	After user presses and releases the mouse button over an object
Close	OnClose	Forms, reports	After form or report is closed and removed from the screen
Current	OnCurrent	Forms	After focus moves to a record, making it the current record
DblClick	OnDblClick	Forms, controls, form sections	After user presses and releases the mouse button twice over an object
Deactivate	OnDeactivate	Forms, reports	After form or report loses the focus or is closed
Delete	OnDelete	Forms	After user acts to delete a record, such as pressing [Del], but before the record is deleted
Enter	OnEnter	Controls	Before a control receives the focus from a control on the same form

Figure 2-15
Events and event properties

Event	Event Property	Occurs With	Occurs
Error	OnError	Forms, reports	After a run-time error in Access
Exit	OnExit	Controls	Before a control loses the focus to another control on the same form
Format	OnFormat	Report sections	When data are placed in a report section but before formatting the section for previewing or printing
GotFocus	OnGotFocus	Forms, controls	When form or control receives the focus
KeyDown	OnKeyDown	Forms, controls	When user presses a key while the form or control has the focus
Key Press	OnKeyPress	Forms, controls	When user presses and releases a key
KeyUp	OnKeyUp	Forms, controls	When user releases a key while the form or control has the focus
Load	OnLoad	Forms	When form is opened and records are displayed
LostFocus	OnLostFocus	Forms, controls	When form or control loses the focus
MouseDown	OnMouseDown	Forms, controls, form sections	When user presses a mouse button
MouseMove	OnMouseMove	Forms, controls, form sections	When user moves the mouse
MouseUp	OnMouseUp	Forms, controls, form sections	When user releases a mouse button
NotInList	OnNotInList	Controls	When user enters a text box value not in the combo box
Open	OnOpen	Forms, reports	After form or report is opened but before the first record is displayed or the report is previewed or printed
Print	OnPrint	Reoprt sections	When report-section data is format-ted but not yet printed
Resize	OnResize	Forms	When form is opened and then resized
Retreat	OnRetreat	Report sections	When Access returns to a previous report section during formatting
Timer	OnTimer	Forms	At regular intervals, controlled by the form's TimerInterval property
Unload	OnUnload	Forms	After form is closed but before it is removed from the screen
Updated	OnUpdated	Controls	When an OLE object's data have been modified

Figure 2-15 *(continued)* Events and event properties

As with actions, you do not need to learn all 35 events. You will gain experience with several event properties in these tutorials, and if you need other event properties, use the Access Help system as a reference tool. Figure 2-16 lists two Help topics that are particularly useful when you work with events.

Search Entry	Help Topic
events: reference	Events and Event Properties Reference
events: order of	Order of Events

Figure 2-16 Important Help topics for events

Planning the User Interface

Elena lists the work she must do to create the user interface for the Issue25 database. She will create forms for the switchboard and the two dialog boxes, build a custom menu bar, and create a custom toolbar. In addition, the dialog boxes will contain lists of available reports and queries. For these lists, Elena will create a special control table that contains the names of all the available reports and queries. Using the control table, she will then create two queries. One query will select all report names in alphabetical order, and the other query will select all query names in alphabetical order. Figure 2-17 shows the objects Elena will create and their names.

Create	Object Name
Switchboard form	frmSwitchboard
Queries dialog box	frmQueries
Reports dialog box	frmReports
Custom menu bar	menSwitchboard
Custom toolbar	tolSwitchboard
Query and report names table	tblObjectNames
Query names query	qryQueryNames
Report names query	qryReportNames

Figure 2-17 Objects to be created for the Issue25 database

So far, Elena has assigned names to objects without using a specific naming convention. A **naming convention** is a consistent, standard way of naming objects in a database, making it easier to identify the type of object and its relationship to other objects. Elena will follow her seminar instructor's naming convention, which is based on guidelines by Stan Leszynski and Greg Reddick.

- Each object name starts with a lowercase **tag**, or prefix, that identifies the object type. Figure 2-18 shows the tags Elena will use for Access objects and for Access controls on forms and reports.

Object or Control	Tag
Access Basic module	bas
Control—label	lbl
Control—other	ctl
Form	frm
Macro—custom menu	men
Macro—other	mcr
Query	qry
Report	rpt
Table	tbl
Toolbar—custom	tol

Figure 2-18
Tags for Access objects and controls

- The tag is followed by a base name that describes the object contents, instead of the type of object. Examples of good base names with their tags are ctlWriterPhone, frmArticles, lblLastName, qryMagazines, rptPastArticles, rptTypes, and tblMagazines. Capitalize separate words in a base name and do not use spaces.

Following these naming conventions, Elena will be able to identify objects more easily in Access list boxes that display more than one type of object. Because these Access list boxes display object names in alphabetical order, the tag will group together all names for each object type.

Creating a Control Table and Its Queries

The switchboard command buttons run macros to display four forms, display two dialog boxes, exit the switchboard, and exit Access, as shown in Figure 2-1. To test the switchboard design, the forms and dialog boxes must be available. Elena has previously created the four forms, so she creates the dialog boxes before she creates the switchboard. Furthermore, each dialog box uses a query and a table of available reports and queries, so Elena creates the queries and table before she creates the dialog boxes.

Creating the Control Table Structure

Elena's first step is to create the control table containing the report and query names. The table design consists of the following three fields.

- ObjectId is a counter field and is the table's primary key.
- ObjectType is a one-character text field with two valid field values; Q for query and R for report.
- ObjectName is a 53-character text field whose field values contain the report and query names.

Elena launches Access and creates the table named tblObjectNames.

To create the tblObjectNames table:

❶ Place your Student Disk in the appropriate drive, launch Access, and open the Issue25 database on your Student Disk.

❷ Click the **New command button** in the Database window and then click the **New Table button** in the New Table dialog box. Access opens the Table Design View window.

❸ Type **ObjectID** in the Field Name text box, press **[Tab]**, type **co** in the Data Type text box, press **[Tab]**, type **primary key** in the Description text box, and then press **[Tab]**. The first table field is now defined.

❹ Type **ObjectType** in the Field Name text box, press **[Tab]** twice, and then type **Q for a query, R for a report** in the Description text box.

To complete the second table field's definition, you set the Field Size, Default Value, Validation Rule, and Validation Text properties.

❺ Double-click **50** in the Field Size text box, type **1**, click the **Default Value text box**, type **Q**, click the **Validation Rule text box**, type **Q Or R**, click the **Validation Text text box**, and then type **Must be Q or R**. The second table field is now defined.

❻ Click the third row's **Field Name text box**, type **ObjectName**, press **[Tab]** twice, double-click **50** in the Field Size text box, and then type **53**.

The third table field is now defined, and you can now choose ObjectID to be the primary key.

❼ Click the **row selector** for the ObjectID field to highlight the row and then click the toolbar **Set Primary Key button** . Access places the primary key field symbol in the row selector for the ObjectID field. See Figure 2-19.

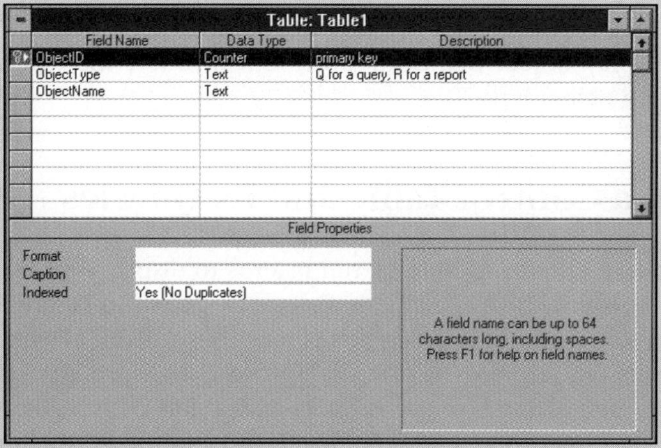

Figure 2-19
Structure of the tblObjectNames table

❽ Click the toolbar **Datasheet View button** . Access opens the "Save now?" dialog box.

❾ Click the **OK button** to open the Save As dialog box, type **tblObjectNames** in the Table Name text box, and then press **[Enter]**. Access saves the new table structure, closes the Table Design View window, and opens the datasheet.

Adding Records to the Control Table

Elena adds records to the tblObjectNames table. She first chooses the reports and queries that will be available to users of the Issue25 database and writes out the list shown in Figure 2-20. The list includes the field values to be entered for the ObjectType and ObjectName fields. You do not enter a field value for the ObjectID field, because it is a counter field that Access automatically controls.

ObjectType	ObjectName
R	TYPES Report
R	WRITERS by Last Contact Date Within Freelancer Report
R	WRITERS With Freelancer Group Totals Report
Q	Article Type Query
Q	Article Type Parameter Query
Q	WRITERS sorted by Freelancer, Last Contact Date
R	Article Type Report
Q	ARTICLES sorted by Issue, Length
Q	Freelancers and PAST ARTICLES

Figure 2-20
The reports and queries for the Issue25 database

Using her list, Elena adds the records to the table.

To add records to the tblObjectNames table:

1. Press **[Tab]**, type **R**, press **[Tab]**, type **TYPES Report**, and then press **[Tab]**. The first record is added to the table.
2. Enter the remaining eight records, using the field values from Figure 2-20.
3. Resize the widths of all three datasheet columns to their best fit. See Figure 2-21. Take a moment to check the values you entered and correct any that do not appear exactly as shown in Figure 2-20 and Figure 2-21. Capitalization and spelling are important.

Table: tblObjectNames

ObjectID	ObjectType	ObjectName
1	R	TYPES Report
2	R	WRITERS by Last Contact Date Within Freelancer Report
3	R	WRITERS With Freelancer Group Totals Report
4	Q	Article Type Query
5	Q	Article Type Parameter Query
6	Q	WRITERS sorted by Freelancer, Last Contact Date
7	R	Article Type Report
8	Q	ARTICLES sorted by Issue, Length
9	Q	Freelancers and PAST ARTICLES
(Counter)	Q	

Figure 2-21
The completed datasheet for the tblObjectNames table

TROUBLE? Depending on how you resized the columns, your datasheet might have a field value, a column, or all columns highlighted. This is okay, as long as all the values in the ObjectType and ObjectName columns are correct.

4. Double-click the datasheet **Control menu box** and then click the **Yes button** in the "Save layout changes?" dialog box. Access saves the datasheet changes, closes the datasheet, and activates the database window.

Now that she has created and updated the control table, Elena creates the two new queries.

Creating the Queries

Both queries use the tblObjectNames table, select the ObjectID and ObjectName fields, and perform an ascending sort using the ObjectName field. One query selects only query-object records and the other query selects only report-object records.

Elena first creates the qryQueryNames query.

To create the qryQueryNames query:

1. Click **tblObjectNames** in the Tables list box, click the toolbar **New Query button**, and then click the **New Query button** in the New Query dialog box.
2. Double-click the **title bar** of the tblObjectNames field list to highlight all the fields in the table and then drag all the fields from the highlighted area to the QBE grid's first column Field box. Access adds all three fields to the QBE grid.
3. Click the **ObjectID Show box** to uncheck the box, so that the field does not appear in the dynaset, click the **Criteria text box** for the ObjectType field, and then type **Q** to select just the query-object records.
4. Click the **Sort text box** for the ObjectName field, click the **down arrow button** that appears, and then click **Ascending** in the Sort list to perform an ascending sort using the ObjectName field.
5. Click the toolbar **Run button**. Access opens the query dynaset. See Figure 2-22. Be sure you have spelled each query name correctly.

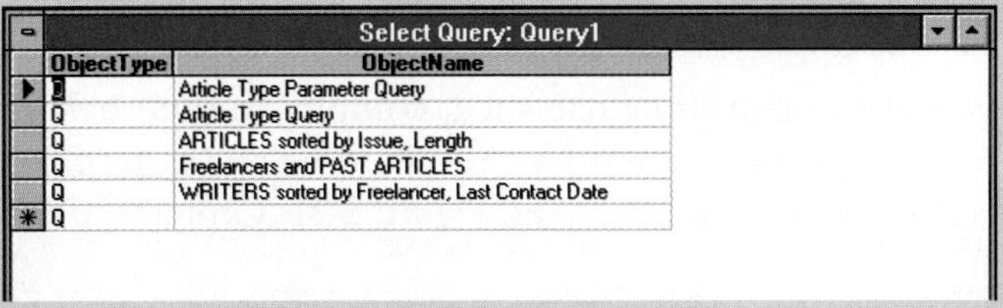

Figure 2-22 Queries from the tblObjectNames table

6. Click the toolbar **Design View button** to switch back to the Query Design window.
7. Click the toolbar **Save button**, type **qryQueryNames** in the Query Name text box, and then press **[Enter]**. Access saves the query with a name of qryQueryNames.

Elena modifies the qryQueryNames query and saves it using the name qryReportNames. She changes the Q in the Criteria text box for the ObjectType field to an R, runs the query to test it, and then saves it as qryReportNames.

To create the qryReportNames query:

1. Highlight the **Q** in the Criteria text box for the ObjectType field and then type **R**.
2. Click the toolbar **Run button**. Access opens the query dynaset. See Figure 2-23. Be sure you have spelled each report name correctly.

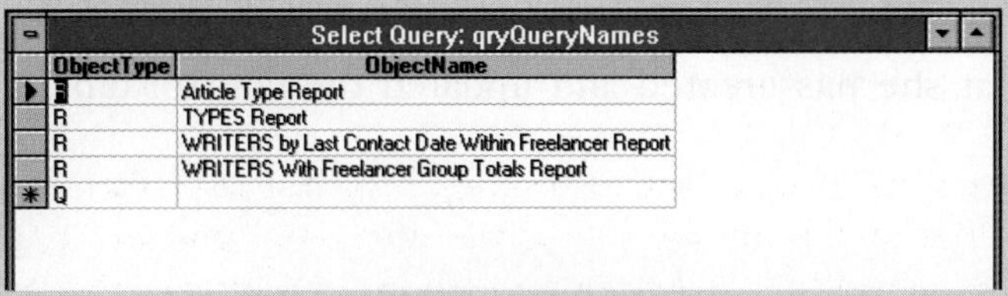

Figure 2-23 Reports from the tblObjectNames table

❸ Click **File**, click **Save Query As...**, highlight **Query** in qryQueryNames, type **Report** making the name qryReportNames, and then press **[Enter]**. Access saves the query with the name qryReportNames.

❹ Double-click the dynaset **Control menu box**. Access closes the dynaset and activates the Database window.

Elena has completed the first major step for her user interface. Her second step is to create the two dialog boxes. The queries she just created will appear as the lists in the dialog boxes. Figure 2-24 shows how the lists will look in each dialog box.

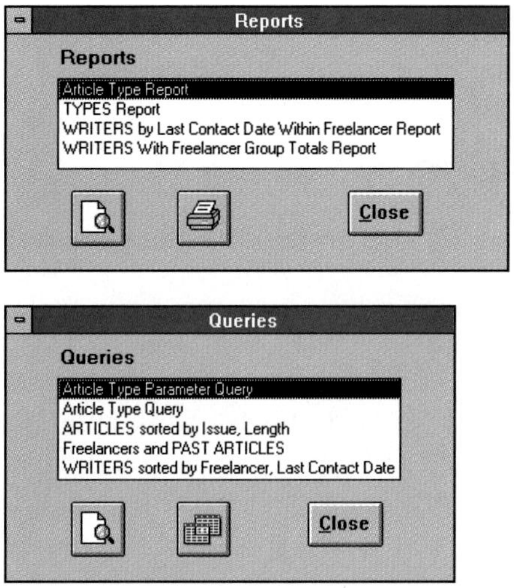

Figure 2-24
The Reports (frmReports) and Queries (frmQueries) dialog boxes

If you want to take a break and resume the tutorial at a later time, you can exit Access by double-clicking the Microsoft Access window Control menu box. When you resume the tutorial, place your Student Disk in the appropriate drive, launch Access, and open the Issue25 database on your Student Disk.

■ ■ ■

Creating Dialog Boxes

Elena creates the frmReports form to serve as a dialog box in the user interface. She then creates the frmQueries form by modifying the frmReports form. See Figure 2-24 for Elena's design of the dialog boxes. Both dialog boxes will have similar appearances and behaviors.

- Neither dialog box has scroll bars, navigation buttons, record selectors, or sizing buttons.
- Double-clicking a report or query name opens that report or query in the Print Preview window, as does clicking a name and then clicking the leftmost command button that contains the Print Preview icon.
- Clicking a report name and then clicking the middle command button prints that report. Clicking a query name and then clicking the middle command button opens that query's dynaset.
- Clicking the Close button closes the dialog box and activates the switchboard.
- The underlined C in the two Close command buttons identifies the button's hot key; pressing [Alt][C] closes the dialog box, just as clicking the Close command button does. To underline the C and make it the hot key, enter &Close as the

Caption property value for the command button control on the form. Placing an ampersand (&) in front of a character in a Caption (it doesn't need to be the first letter of a word) underlines the character on the open form and makes it that control's hot key.

- After a user makes a choice in the dialog box and finishes with the choice, the dialog box once again becomes the active window.
- The queries based on the tblObjectNames table supply the values that appear in the list boxes.
- A macro cannot handle the complex interaction between selecting a report or query in a list box and clicking a command button, but Access Basic code can. Thus, the OnClick event properties for the command buttons and the OnDblClick event properties for the list-box entries are attached to Access Basic code instead of macros. You will create this code in the tutorial entitled "Access Basic."

Creating the First Dialog Box

Elena creates a blank form based on the qryReportNames query to start the frmReports custom form.

To create the blank form for the frmReports custom form:

1. Click the toolbar **New Form button**, click the Select A Table/Query drop-down list box **down arrow button** in the New Form dialog box, scroll the list box until qryReportNames appears, click **qryReportNames**, and then click the **Blank Form button**. Access opens the Form Design window.

Before adding any controls to the form, Elena sets the overall form properties. The property values she sets are:

- Caption property, whose value appears in the form's title bar, set to Reports
- DefaultView property set to Single Form
- **ShortcutMenu property** set to No, which disables the display of a shortcut menu when the right mouse button is clicked on the form
- **ScrollBars property** set to Neither, which removes the horizontal and vertical scroll bars from the form
- RecordSelectors, NavigationButtons, MinButton, and MaxButton properties set to No, which removes all these components from the form
- **AutoResize property** set to No, which opens a form with its last saved size
- **Modal property** set to Yes, which prevents users from opening the Form Design window to make changes to the form
- **BorderStyle property** set to Dialog, which prevents a user from resizing the form (Elena sets this property after she completes the rest of the form, so that she can size the form properly before disabling the ability to do so)
- Width property set to 3.8"

To set properties for a form:

1. If the property sheet is not visible, click the toolbar **Properties button**. If the toolbox is not visible, click the toolbar **Toolbox button**. If the toolbox Control Wizards tool is not selected, click the toolbox **Controls Wizards tool**. If the Record Source property is not the first property listed in the property sheet, scroll up until it is at

the top. If All Properties does not appear in the text box above the Record Source property, click the drop-down list box **down arrow button** and then click **All Properties**.

2. Click the property sheet's **Caption text box** and type **Reports**.
3. Click the property sheet's **Default View text box**, click the **down arrow button**, and then click **Single Form**.
4. Click the property sheet's **Shortcut Menu text box**, click the **down arrow button**, and then click **No**.
5. Click the property sheet's **Scroll Bars text box**, click the **down arrow button**, and then click **Neither**.
6. Scroll down the property sheet, click the **Record Selectors text box**, click the **down arrow button**, and then click **No**. In the same way, set to No the **Navigation Buttons**, **Auto Resize**, **Min Button**, and **Max Button** properties.
7. Click the **Modal text box**, click the **down arrow button**, and then click **Yes**.
8. Click the beginning of the **Width text box**, press **[Del]** to delete the default value 5, and then type **3.8**.
9. Click [icon] to close the property sheet.

Elena saves the form, so that her work is not lost if hardware or software problems occur. She then adds the label and the list box to the form, using the Control Wizards tool for the list box.

To save a form and add controls:

1. Click the toolbar **Save button** [icon], type **frmReports** in the Form Name text box, and then press **[Enter]**. Access saves the form and changes the Form Design window title bar to Form: frmReports.
2. Click the toolbox **Label tool** [icon], position the pointer + in the top line of grid dots on the fourth grid dot from the left, and then click the mouse button. Type **Reports** and then press **[Enter]**. Next, change the label's default font size from 8 to 10, make the label boldface, and then resize the label box.
3. Click the toolbar **Font Size button** [icon], click **10**, click the toolbar **Bold button** [icon], click **Format**, click **Size**, and then click **to Fit**.
4. To start the List Box Wizard, click the toolbox **List Box tool** [icon], position the pointer + on the fourth grid dot from the left and the fourth grid dot down, and then click the mouse button. After a few seconds, Access opens the first List Box Wizard dialog box. The qryReportNames query will supply the values for the list box, so click the **radio button** that says "I want the list box to look up the values in a table or query." Then click the **Next > button**. The second List Box Wizard dialog box opens.
5. Click the **Queries radio button**, scroll the list box, click **qryReportNames**, and then click the **Next > button**. The third List Box Wizard dialog box opens.
6. Double-click **ObjectName** to move it to the list box on the right and then click the **Next > button**. The fourth List Box Wizard opens.
7. Double-click the right edge of the **column selector** to get the best column fit and then click the **Next > button**. The fifth List Box Wizard opens.
8. Click the **radio button** that says "Remember the value for later use." Then click the **Next > button**. The sixth List Box Wizard opens. Because you will delete the label box attached to the list box, you do not need to supply a label name.

9. Press **[Del]** to remove the default label name from the text box and then click the **Finish button**. Access closes the List Box Wizard dialog box and displays the completed list box in the form's Detail section. See Figure 2-25.

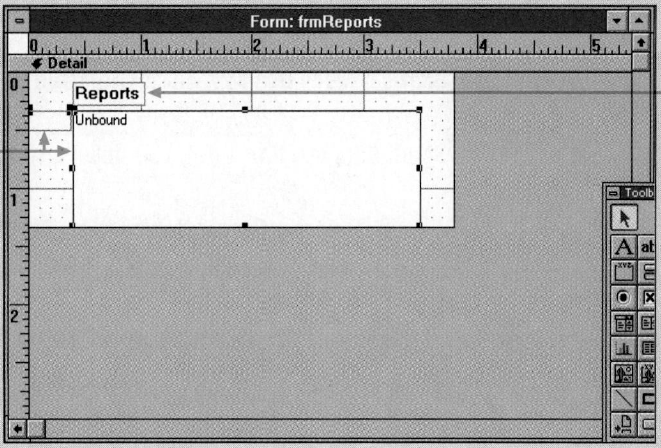

Figure 2-25
Form design after a label and a list box are added

Elena saves the form and then checks her progress by switching to the Form View window.

To save a form and switch to the Form View window:

1. Click the toolbar **Save button** to save the form.
2. Click the toolbar **Form View button**. Access closes the Form Design window and opens the Form View window.

Even though the MinButton and MaxButton properties are set to No, the buttons appear on the form in the Form View window. However, if you open the form directly in the Form View window from the Database window, instead of from the Form Design window, the buttons will not appear.

Elena makes three form changes before adding the command buttons. She deletes the label attached to the list box, reduces the list box height, and changes the form background color and the label box color to light gray.

To make minor form modifications:

1. Click the **Design View button** to switch to the Form Design window.
2. Click the **label box** attached to the list box to select it.
3. Click the right mouse button in the **label box** to open the shortcut menu and then click **Cut** to delete the label box.
4. Click the **list box** to select it. Drag the middle sizing handle on the bottom border upward to the row of grid dots at the 1" mark on the vertical ruler.
5. Click anywhere in the Detail section but not in the label box or list box, click the toolbar **Palette button** to open the Palette, and then click the **light gray color box** on the Back Color line. The Back Color line is the middle color line and the light gray color box is the third box from the left.
6. Click the label box containing the word "Reports" and then click the **light gray color box** on the Back Color line.
7. Click to close the Palette.

Elena now adds the Print Preview command button to the form. She does not use the Control Wizards tool, because she will attach Access Basic code to the OnClick event property for the command button at a later point. First, she saves the form.

To add a command button to a form:

1. Click the toolbar **Save button** to save the form.
2. Click the toolbox **Control Wizards tool** to deselect it.
3. Click the toolbox **Command Button tool**, position the pointer + in the line of grid dots just below the list box and on the fifth grid dot from the left, and then click the mouse button. Access adds a command button to the form.
4. Right-click the **command button** and then click **Properties...** in the shortcut menu to open the property sheet.
5. Scrolling the property sheet as necessary, click the property sheet's **Picture text box** and then click the **Build button** that appears next to the text box. Access opens the Picture Builder dialog box.
6. Scroll the Available Pictures list box and click **Preview Document**. Access shows the picture on the command button in the Sample box.
7. Click the **OK button**. Access closes the Picture Builder dialog box, resizes the command button, and places the picture on the command button.

Instead of repeating the steps to add the middle command button, Elena copies the first command button and pastes it in the Detail section. After moving the button into position, she changes the picture on the command button.

To create a command button by copying another command button:

1. Right-click the **command button** and then click **Copy** in the shortcut menu.
2. Click **Edit** and then click **Paste**. Access adds a copy of the command button to the Detail section.
3. Move the new command button into position to the right of the original command button. See Figure 2-26.

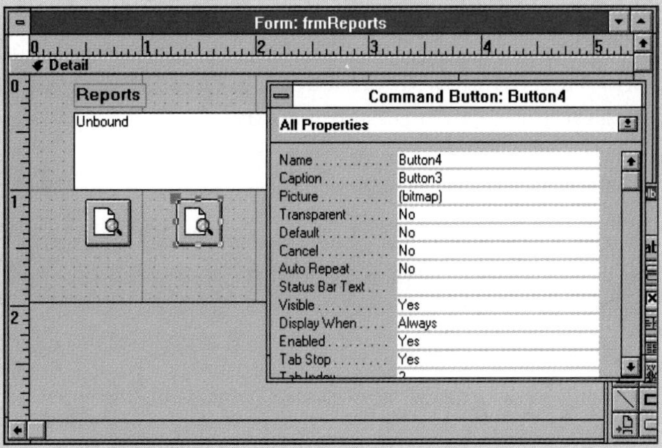

Figure 2-26 Adding a copy of a command button

4. Click the property sheet's **Picture text box** and then click the **Build button**.
5. Scroll the Available Pictures list box and click **Printer**. Access shows the picture on the command button in the Sample box.
6. Click the **OK button**. Access closes the Picture Builder dialog box and places the new picture on the command button.
7. Click the toolbar **Properties button** to close the property sheet.

Elena now adds the final command button that closes the dialog box. She uses the Control Wizards tool, because the tool automatically attaches the correct Access Basic code to the command button. Standard operations, such as opening and closing forms, are perfect candidates for using the Control Wizards tool. Elena also sets the command button's Caption property to &Close to define the C as the command button's hot key. Once again, Elena saves the form before she adds the command button.

To add a command button using the Control Wizards tool:

1. Click the toolbar **Save button** to save the form.
2. Click the toolbox **Control Wizards tool** to select it.
3. Click the toolbox **Command Button tool**, position the pointer + in the line of grid dots just below the list box and just beyond the 2.5" mark on the horizontal ruler, and then click the mouse button. Access adds a command button to the form and, after a few seconds, opens the first Command Button Wizard dialog box.
4. Click **Form Operations** in the Categories list box, click **Close Form** in the "When button is pressed" list box, and then click the **Next > button**. Access opens the second Command Button Wizard dialog box.
5. Click the **Text radio button**, highlight **Close Form** in the text box, type **&Close**, and then click the **Next > button**. Access opens the third Command Button Wizard dialog box.
6. Type **ctlClose** in the text box to conform with the naming conventions for controls and then click the **Finish button**. Access closes the Command Button Wizard dialog box and shows the new command button on the form.

Because the Access Basic code she will create in a later tutorial needs to refer to it, Elena enters the name ctlReportName for the list box control. She resizes and saves the form in the Form View window, then sets the form's BorderStyle property to Dialog, and saves the form again in the Form Design window.

To set properties and resize a form:

1. Click the **list box**, click the toolbar **Properties button** to open the property sheet, scroll as necessary to the top of the property sheet, double-click the **Name text box**, type **ctlReportName**, and press **[Enter]**.
2. Click the toolbar **Form View button**.
3. Drag the bottom edge of the form up and then drag the right edge of the form to the left until the form is properly sized. See Figure 2-27.

Figure 2-27
After the form is resized

4. Click **File**, click **Save Form**, and then click the toolbar **Design View button** to switch to the Form Design window.
5. Click the **white box** below the Control menu box in the Form Design window so that Form appears in the property sheet's title bar. Scroll down the property sheet, click the **Border Style text box**, click the **down arrow button**, and then click **Dialog**.
6. Click the toolbar to close the property sheet and then click the toolbar **Save button**.
7. Double-click the Form Design window **Control menu box**. Access closes the Form Design window and activates the Database window.

Elena tests the form by opening it in the Form View window from the Database window. Clicking the Print Preview command button on the left, clicking the Printer command button in the middle, or double-clicking a report name in the list box should have no effect, because Elena has not yet set these event properties. However, clicking the Close button or pressing [Alt][C] should close the form.

To test a form's design:

1. If necessary, click the **Form object button**. Double-click **frmReports** in the Forms list box. Access opens the form in the Form View window.
2. Double-click any report name in the list box, click the **Print Preview command button**, and then click the **Printer command button**. Each double-click or click moves the focus but leaves the form on the screen—steps in the tutorial entitled "Access Basic" will make these work as they should.
3. Either click the **Close button** or press **[Alt][C]**. Access closes the form and activates the Database window.

Elena has finished her initial work on the frmReports form. Her next task is to create the frmQueries form.

If you want to take a break and resume the tutorial at a later time, you can exit Access by double-clicking the Microsoft Access window Control menu box. When you resume the tutorial, place your Student Disk in the appropriate drive, launch Access, open the Issue25 database on your Student Disk, and click the Form object button.

■ ■ ■

Creating the Second Dialog Box

Because the forms are so similar, Elena starts the frmQueries form by making a copy of the frmReports form. Then she modifies the frmQueries form to work correctly with the list of available queries.

REFERENCE WINDOW

Copying an Object in the Same Database

- In the Database window, click the appropriate object button, click the name of the object you want to copy, click Edit, and click Copy.
- Click Edit, click Paste, type the new object name, and press [Enter].

Elena copies the frmReports form.

To copy a form in the same database:

1. Click **frmReports** in the Forms list box of the Database window, click **Edit**, and then click **Copy**. Access copies the form to the Windows Clipboard.
2. Click **Edit**, click **Paste**, type **frmQueries** in the Form Name text box on the Paste As dialog box, and then press **[Enter]**. Access creates a new form with the name frmQueries, which is a copy of the frmReports form.

Elena opens the frmQueries form in the Form Design window and changes the form's design so that it matches her design. Her changes include the following:

- The form's Record Source property is changed to qryQueryNames and the Caption property is changed to Queries.
- The label above the list box is changed to contain the value Queries.
- The Row Source property for the list box is changed to the qryQueryNames query, and the height of the list box is increased.
- The icon on the middle command button is changed, and all command buttons are moved down to make room for the resized list box.

To change a copied form:

1. Click **frmQueries** in the Forms list box, click the **Design command button**, and then click the toolbar **Properties button** to open the property sheet, which has Form in its title bar.
2. Click the **Record Source text box** in the property sheet, click the **down arrow button**, scroll up, and then click **qryQueryNames**. Double-click the **Caption text box** and type **Queries**.
3. Click the **label box** in the form's Detail section, double-click the same **label box** to highlight its value, Reports, type **Queries**, and then press **[Enter]**.
4. Click the **list box**, double-click the **Name text box** in the property sheet to highlight the value, and type **ctlQueryName**. Click the **Row Source text box**, press **[→]** until [qryReportNames]; appears, highlight **Report**, type **Query** so that it now reads [qryQueryNames]; and then press **[Enter]**.
5. Click the Form Design window **maximize button**, click the **Printer command button** in the middle, click the **Picture text box**, and then click the **Build button** that appears to the right of the Picture text box to open the Picture Builder dialog box.
6. Scroll the Available Pictures list box, click **MS Access Query**, and then click the **OK button**. Access closes the Picture Builder dialog box and places the new picture on the command button.
7. Click the toolbar **Save button**, click the toolbar to close the property sheet, and then click the toolbar **Form View button**. Access opens the Form View window.

Only the top of the fifth query name appears in the list box. Elena moves the command buttons down and increases the height of the list box.

To move controls and resize a list box:

1. Click the toolbar **Design View button** to switch back to the Form Design window.
2. Click the **Print Preview command button**, which is on the left. While holding down [Shift], click the **middle command button** and then click the **right command button**.
3. Place the pointer over one of the selected command buttons and, when the pointer changes to , drag the three command buttons straight down one grid row to make room for the list box.
4. Click the **list box** and then drag the middle sizing handle on the bottom border of the list box down one grid row.
5. Click the Form Design window **restore button**, click the toolbar **Save button**, and then double-click the Form Design window **Control menu box**.

Elena tests the frmQueries form in the same way she tested the frmReports form.

To test a form's design:

1. Double-click **frmQueries** in the Forms list box. Access opens the form in the Form View window. See Figure 2-28.

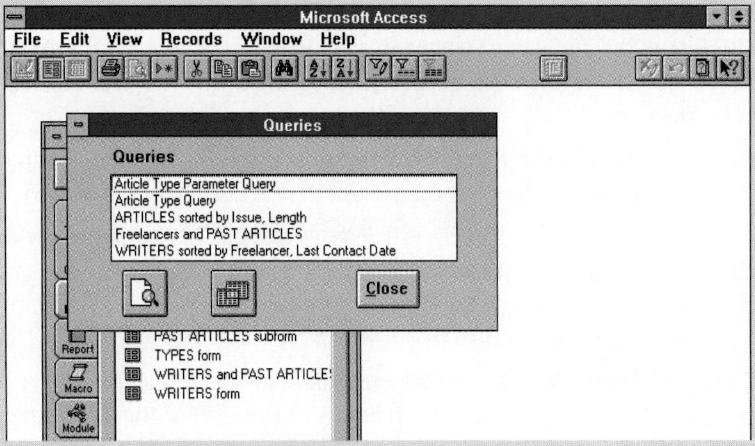

Figure 2-28
A copied form showing completed changes

2. Double-click any query name in the list box, click the **left command button**, and then click the **middle command button**. Each click or double-click moves the focus but leaves the form on the screen. Steps in the tutorial entitled "Access Basic" will make these work as they should.

3. Either click the **Close button** or press **[Alt][C]**. Access closes the form and activates the Database window.

Elena has now created one table, two queries, and two forms for the Issue25 user interface. Her next task is to create the frmSwitchboard form.

If you want to take a break and resume the tutorial at a later time, you can exit Access by double-clicking the Microsoft Access window Control menu box. When you resume the tutorial, place your Student Disk in the appropriate drive, launch Access, open the Issue25 database on your Student Disk, and click the Form object button.

■ ■ ■

Creating a Switchboard

Elena creates the frmSwitchboard form to serve as the primary user interface for the Issue25 database. Figure 2-29 shows the switchboard as it will look when Elena is done.

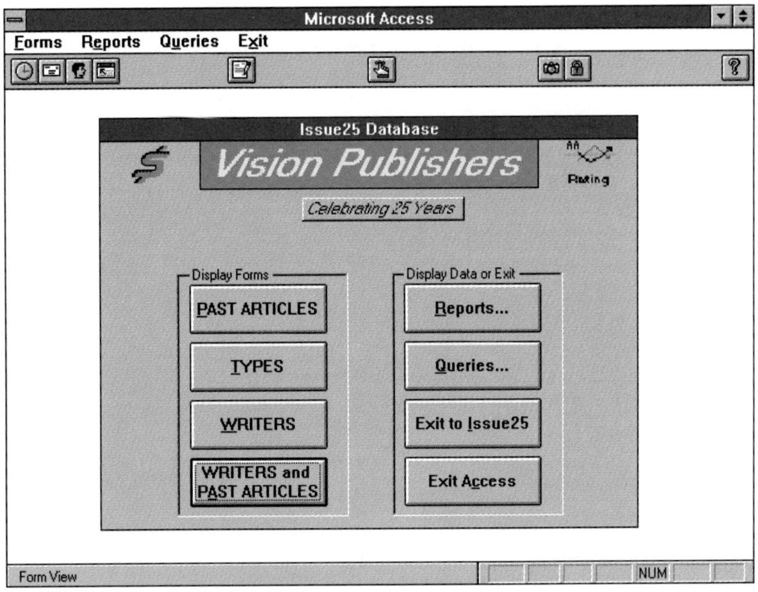

Figure 2-29
The Issue25 switchboard

Elena jots down several features of the frmSwitchboard form:

- The form has no Control menu box, scroll bars, navigation buttons, record selectors, or sizing buttons and cannot be resized.
- Graphic images appear in the upper left and upper right of the form.
- The Celebrating 25 Years label is raised.
- Sunken rectangles surround both sets of command buttons.
- The command buttons are all the same size.
- Macros are attached to each command button's OnClick event property.

Creating the Macros

Elena first creates the eight macros that she will attach to the command buttons. Instead of creating eight separate macros, she places the eight macros in a macro group. A **macro group** is a macro that contains more than one macro. Macro groups allow you to consolidate related macros and provide a means to manage large numbers of macros.

To create a macro group, you use the same Macro window you used to create a single macro. Recall that when you worked with the Macro window earlier in this tutorial, you entered actions in the Action column and comments in the Comment column. Now, you'll add a third column, the Macro Name column, that lets you distinguish macros in your macro group. First you'll name one macro, you'll list the actions for that macro, and then you'll name the second macro, list the actions for the second macro, and so on. You can group as many macros as you want in the Macro window.

Elena uses the name mcrSwitchboard for the macro group. Figure 2-30 shows the names and actions for the eight macros in the macro group.

Macro Name	Actions	Form Name
mcrPastArticles	OpenForm	PAST ARTICLES form
mcrTypes	OpenForm	TYPES form
mcrWriters	OpenForm	WRITERS form
mcrWritersPastArticles	OpenForm	WRITERS and PAST ARTICLES form
mcrReports	OpenForm	frmReports
mcrQueries	OpenForm	frmQueries
mcrExitToIssue25	SendKeys	
	Close	frmSwitchboard
mcrExitAccess	Close	frmSwitchboard
	Quit	

Figure 2-30
Macros and actions in the mcrSwitchboard macro group

Elena creates the mcrSwitchboard macro group for the eight command buttons on the frmSwitchboard form. She starts a new macro, enters the first two macros, and then saves the macro group.

To create a macro group:

❶ In the Database window, click the **Macro object button** and then click the **New command button**. Access opens the Macro window.

❷ Click the toolbar **Macro Names button** . Access adds the Macro Name column to the left of the Action column. See Figure 2-31.

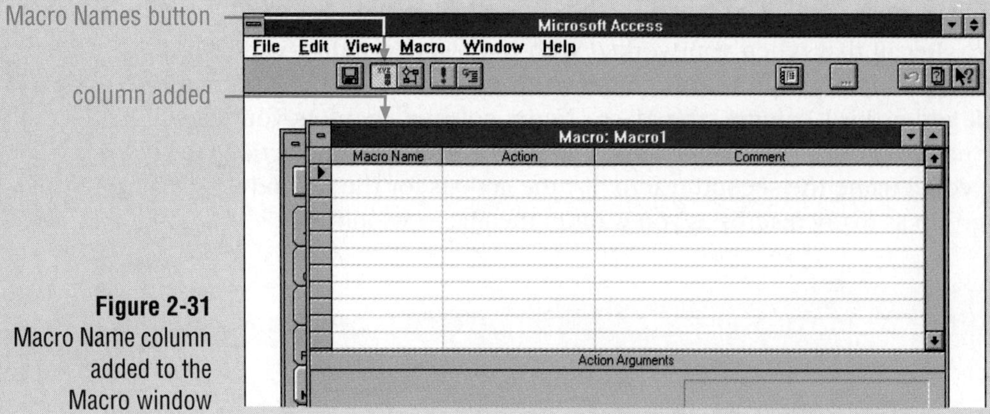

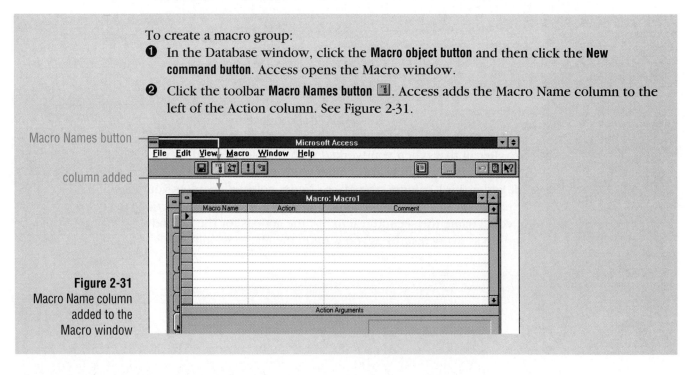

Figure 2-31
Macro Name column added to the Macro window

3. Type **mcrExitAccess**, press **[Tab]**, click the **down arrow button** in the Action text box, click **Close**, press **[Tab]**, type **Close frmSwitchboard**, click the **Object Type text box**, click the **down arrow button** in the Object Type text box, click **Form**, click the **Object Name text box**, and then type **frmSwitchboard**. This completes the first action for the first macro.
4. Click the second row's **Action text box**, click the **down arrow button** in the Action text box, scroll the drop-down list box, and then click **Quit**. This completes the first macro, which contains two actions.
5. Click the third row's **Macro Name text box**, type **mcrPastArticles**, press **[Tab]**, click the **down arrow button**, scroll the drop-down list box, click **OpenForm**, press **[Tab]**, type **Open "PAST ARTICLES form"**, click the **Form Name text box**, click the **down arrow button**, and then click **PAST ARTICLES form**. This completes the second macro, which contains one action.
6. Click the toolbar **Save button**, type **mcrSwitchboard** in the Macro Name text box, and then press **[Enter]**. See Figure 2-32.

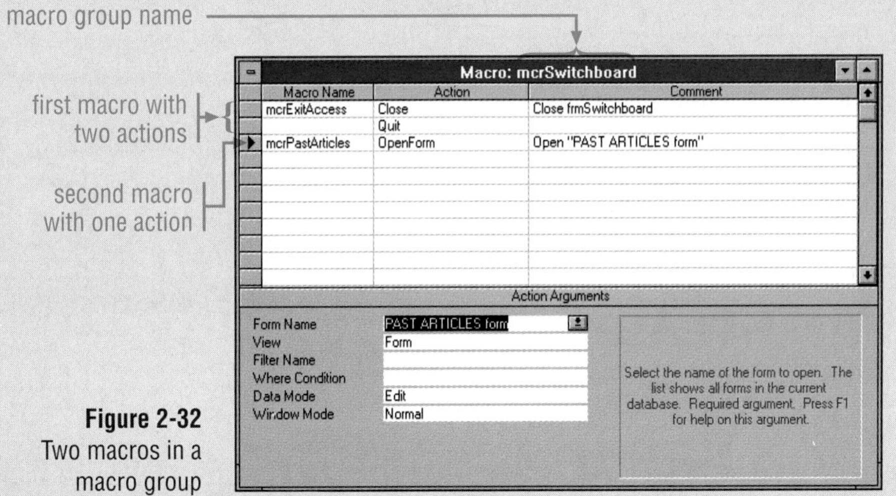

Figure 2-32
Two macros in a macro group

The macro name, which appears in the Macro window title bar, is mcrSwitchboard. This is also the name of the macro group, because the mcrSwitchboard macro comprises more than one macro. The first macro in the macro group is mcrExitAccess, and the second macro in the macro group is mcrPastArticles. A macro in a macro group starts in the row containing the macro name and continues until the row before the next macro name. When Access executes the mcrExitAccess macro, it runs the Close action and then the Quit action and ends because the next macro starts. The mcrPastArticles macro begins with the OpenForm action and then ends when it reaches the end of the macro group. The **Quit action**, which you may not have used before, appears in the first macro and simply exits Access.

Elena completes the macro group by entering the remaining six macros.

To finish creating a macro group:

1. Click the next row's **Macro Name text box**, type **mcrTypes**, press **[Tab]**, click the **down arrow button**, scroll the drop-down list box, click **OpenForm**, press **[Tab]**, type **Open "TYPES form"**, click the **Form Name text box**, click the **down arrow button**, and then click **TYPES form**. This completes the third macro, which contains one action.

❷ Click the next row's **Macro Name text box** and repeat the previous step with these changes: type **mcrWriters** instead of mcrTypes, type **Open "WRITERS form"** instead of Open "TYPES form", and click **WRITERS form** instead of TYPES form. This completes the fourth macro, which contains one action.

❸ Click the next row's **Macro Name text box** and repeat Step 1 with these changes: type **mcrWritersPastArticles**, type **Open "WRITERS and PAST ARTICLES form"** , and click **WRITERS and PAST ARTICLES form**. This completes the fifth macro, which contains one action.

❹ Click the next row's **Macro Name text box** and repeat Step 1 with these changes: type **mcrReports**, type **Open frmReports** , and click **frmReports**. This completes the sixth macro, which contains one action.

❺ Click the next row's **Macro Name text box** and repeat Step 1 with these changes: type **mcrQueries**, type **Open frmQueries**, and click **frmQueries**. This completes the seventh macro, which contains one action.

❻ Click the next row's **Macro Name text box**, type **mcrExitToIssue25**, press **[Tab]**, click the **down arrow button**, scroll the drop-down list box, click **SendKeys**, press **[Tab]**, type **Activate Database window**, click the **Keystrokes text box**, and then type **{F11}**. Be sure to type the braces. (The SendKeys action is explained after this series of steps.) This macro has a second action.

❼ Click the next row's **Action text box**, click the **down arrow button**, click **Close**, press **[Tab]**, type **Close frmSwitchboard**, click the **Object Type text box**, click the **down arrow button**, click **Form**, click the **Object Name text box**, type **frmSwitchboard**, and then press **[Enter]**. This completes the second of two actions for the last macro. See Figure 2-33.

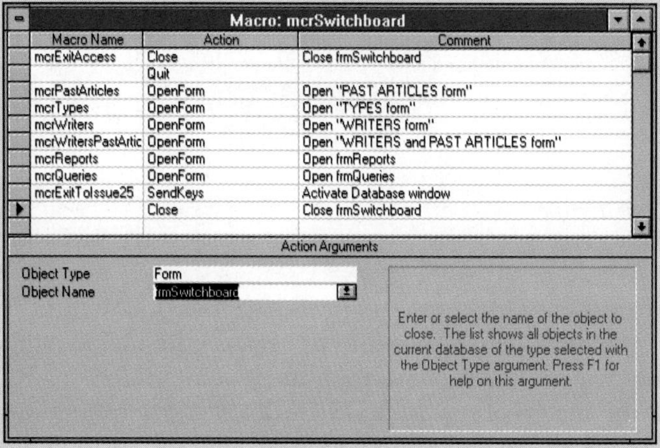

Figure 2-33
A completed macro group having eight macros

❽ Click the toolbar **Save button** and then double-click the Macro window **Control menu box**. Access saves the macro group, closes the Macro window, and activates the Database window.

A new action, the SendKeys action, appears in the last macro. The **SendKeys action** sends keystrokes to an application. In this case, the Keystrokes argument value {F11} is the same as pressing [F11], which activates the Database window.

Creating the Form

Now that the switchboard macros are done, Elena begins to create the switchboard by opening a blank form in the Form Design window. She first sets the overall form properties. While creating the switchboard, Elena takes a cautious approach and saves the form frequently.

To create the switchboard form and set its form properties:

1. Click the toolbar **New Form button** and then click the **Blank Form button** in the New Form dialog box to open the Form Design window.
2. If the property sheet is not visible, click the toolbar **Properties button**.
3. Click the **Caption text box** and type **Issue25 Database**. This value will appear in the switchboard's title bar.
4. Click the property sheet's **Default View text box**, click the **down arrow button**, and then click **Single Form**.
5. Click the property sheet's **Shortcut Menu text box**, click the **down arrow button**, and then click **No**.
6. Click the property sheet's **Scroll Bars text box**, click the **down arrow button**, and then click **Neither**.
7. Scroll down the property sheet, click the **Record Selectors text box**, click the **down arrow button**, and then click **No**. In a similar way, set to No the **Navigation Buttons**, **Auto Resize**, **Control Box**, **Min Button**, and **Max Button** properties.
8. Click the property sheet's **Modal text box**, click the **down arrow button**, and then click **Yes**.
9. Click the toolbar to close the property sheet, click the toolbar **Save button**, type **frmSwitchboard** in the Form Name text box, and then press **[Enter]**.

Next, Elena adds a label with a Caption property value of Vision Publishers in large, bold, italic letters at the top of the form. She adds background and foreground colors to the label using the Back Color and Fore Color properties, instead of the Palette, because these properties offer a larger choice of colors.

To add a form label:

1. Click the toolbox **Label tool**, position the pointer + at the top of the Detail section in the column of grid dots to the left of the 1" mark on the horizontal ruler, and then click the mouse button. Next, type **Vision Publishers** and press **[Enter]**.
2. Click the toolbar **Bold button**, click the toolbar **Italic button**, click the toolbar **Font Size button**, and then click **24** in the Font Size drop-down list box.
3. Click **Format**, click **Size**, and then click **to Fit**. Access resizes the label box to display the entire Caption value.

4. Click the toolbar **Properties button** to open the property sheet, scroll the property sheet if necessary, click the **Back Color text box**, and then click the **Build button** that appears to the right of the Back Color text box. Access opens the Color dialog box. See Figure 2-34.

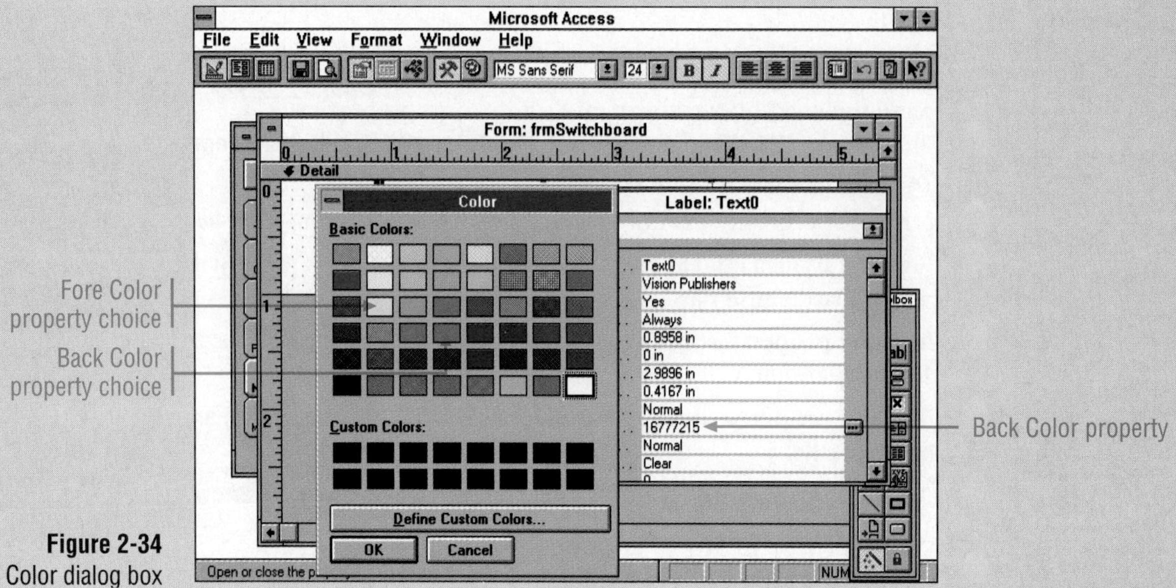

Figure 2-34
The Color dialog box

5. Click the **green color**, which is located in the fourth row down from the top and in the fourth column from the left, and then click the **OK button**.
6. Click the property sheet's **Border Style text box**, click the **down arrow button**, and then click **Normal**.
7. Scroll down the property sheet, click the **Border Width text box**, click the **down arrow button**, and then click **1 pt**.
8. Click the **Fore Color text box**, and then click to open the Color dialog box. Click the **yellow color**, which is located in the third row from the top and in the second column from the left, and then click the **OK button**.
9. Click the toolbar to close the property sheet and then click the toolbar **Save button**. The label box border properties, foreground color, and background color appear with their new settings.

Next, Elena adds a graphic image to the left of the label in the form's Detail section and another graphic image to the right of the label (both are bitmaps stored on your Student Disk). For each graphic image, Elena sets the Size Mode property value to Stretch. The **Stretch Size Mode property** setting lets you size an OLE object to fit the control. That is, increasing the size of the control also increases the size of the graphic image without distortion.

To add graphic images to a form:

1. Click the toolbox **Object Frame tool**, position the pointer + at the top of the Detail section in the second column of grid dots from the left, and then click the mouse button. Access opens the Insert Object dialog box.
2. Scroll the Object Type list box, click **Paintbrush Picture**, click the **Create from File radio button**, and then click the **Browse... button**. Access opens the Browse dialog box.

3. Change the Drives drop-down list box to the drive containing your Student Disk and then, scrolling the File Name list box as necessary, double-click **vis01.bmp**. Next, click the **OK button** in the Insert Object dialog box. After several seconds, Access inserts the graphic image in the unbound object frame.
4. Click the toolbar **Properties button**, click the property sheet's **Size Mode text box**, click the **down arrow button**, click **Stretch**, and then click the toolbar. Next, use the unbound object frame's sizing handles to increase its size to five grid dots in both width and height, dragging to the right and to the bottom. See Figure 2-35.

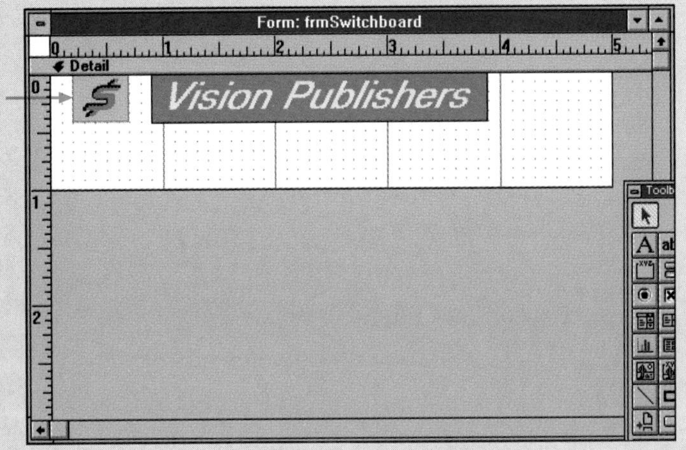

Figure 2-35
The first graphic image added to the form

TROUBLE? If your objects are placed differently, adjust them accordingly.

5. Click the toolbar **Save button** to save the form.
6. Click the toolbox, position the pointer + at the top of the Detail section in the second column of grid dots to the right of the label, and then click the mouse button. Access opens the Insert Object dialog box.
7. Repeat Steps 2 through 4, but use vis02.bmp instead of vis01.bmp for the graphic image.
8. Click the toolbar to save the form. See Figure 2-36.

Figure 2-36
The second graphic image added to the form

Elena now adds a second label below the first label. She sets this label's **Special Effect property** to Raised for a three-dimensional appearance.

To add a raised label to a form:

1. Click the toolbox **Label tool**, position the pointer + at the 1.8" mark on the horizontal ruler in the row of grid dots just below the Vision Publishers label, and then click the mouse button.
2. Type **Celebrating 25 Years** and press **[Enter]**.

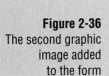

3. Click the toolbar **Italic button**, click the toolbar **Font Size button**, and then click **10** in the Font Size drop-down list box.
4. Click **Format**, click **Size**, and then click **to Fit**. Access resizes the label box to display the entire Caption value.
5. Click the toolbar **Properties button**, click the property sheet's **Special Effect text box**, click the **down arrow button**, and then click **Raised**.
6. Click the toolbar **Save button** and then click the toolbar to close the property sheet.

Before adding the eight command buttons, Elena changes the background color of the form and the raised label to light gray.

To change background colors:

1. Click the toolbar **Palette button** to open the Palette.
2. In the Back Color row, click the Palette's **light gray color**, which is the third color from the left. Access changes the label's background color to light gray.
3. Click inside the Detail section, but do not click any of the controls.
4. In the Back Color row, click the Palette's **light gray color**. Access changes the Detail section's background color to light gray.
5. Click the toolbar **Save button** and then click the toolbar to close the Palette. See Figure 2-37.

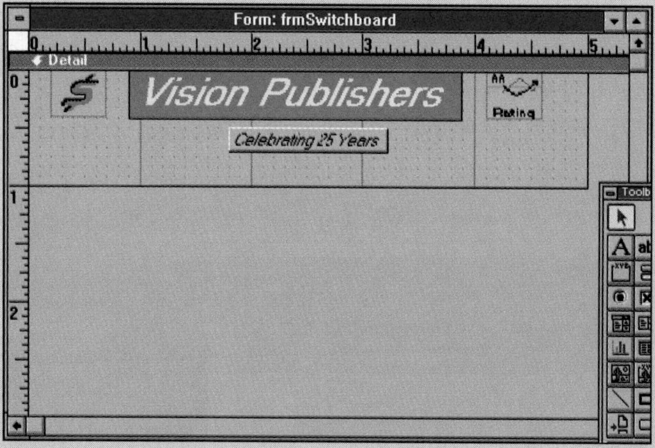

Figure 2-37
The form ready for the addition of command buttons

TROUBLE? If your form doesn't look the same as the form shown in Figure 2-37, make changes as necessary. For example, you might need to resize the form or controls, move controls, change colors, or change properties.

Elena now adds the command buttons to the form. Because she has already created the macros for the command buttons, she does not use Control Wizards to create the command buttons. She first creates the command button to open the WRITERS and PAST ARTICLES form, because it has the largest number of characters. Before adding the first command button, Elena increases the height of the Detail section to make room for the command buttons.

To place a command button on a form:

1. If the Control Wizards tool is selected, click the tool to deselect it.
2. Click the Form Design window **maximize button**. Then drag the bottom of the Detail section down to the 3.4" mark on the vertical ruler.
3. Click the **Command Button tool**, position the pointer + anywhere in the middle area of the Detail section, and then click the mouse button. You will move this command button into its correct position in a moment.
4. Click the toolbar **Properties button** to open the property sheet.
5. If the Name text box in the property sheet is not highlighted, double-click the **Name text box** to select it, type **ctlWritersPastArticles**, and then press **[Enter]**. In the Caption text box, which is now highlighted, type **WRITERS and P&AST ARTICLES**, and then press **[Enter]**. Because of the ampersand in front of the A in the Caption property, this letter is the hot key for the command button.
6. To make the property sheet temporarily wider, drag the left edge to the left approximately .75", remembering the original position of the left edge. Scroll the property sheet, click the **On Click text box**, click the **down arrow button**, scroll the drop-down list box, and then click **mcrSwitchboard.mcrWritersPastArticles**. Drag the left edge of the property sheet back to its original position.
7. Click the toolbar to close the property sheet.

The macro for this command button has the name mcrWritersPastArticles and is located in the mcrSwitchboard macro group. The full name of a macro in a macro group, therefore, is the group name, then a period, and finally the macro name. When a user clicks this command button, the Click event occurs and the OnClick event property value causes Access to execute the attached macro.

Elena resizes the command button to display the entire caption and then places it in its correct position in the Detail section.

To resize and position a command button:

1. Using the middle sizing handle on the bottom, drag the command button border down until you see "WRITERS" on the top of the button and "and PAST" on the bottom of the button. Next, using the middle sizing handle on the left, drag the command button border to the left until you see "WRITERS and" on the top of the button and "PAST ARTICLES" on the bottom of the button.

❷ Using the command button's move handle, move the command button until its left edge is at the .8" mark on the horizontal ruler and its top edge is at the 2.75" mark on the vertical ruler. See Figure 2-38.

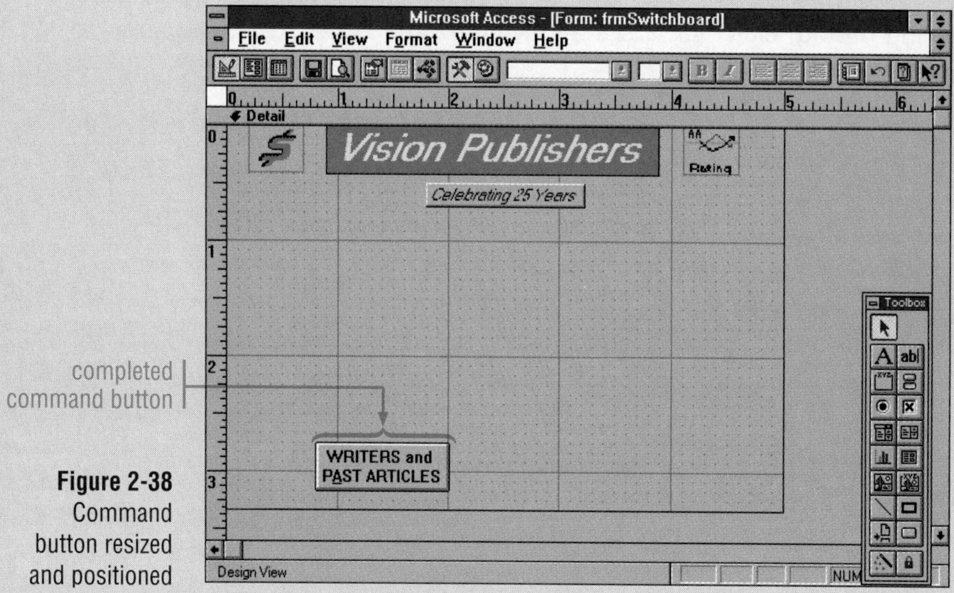

Figure 2-38 Command button resized and positioned

❸ Click the toolbar **Save button**.

Elena tests the command button by switching to the Form View window and clicking it. When you click the command button, the Click event takes place and Access runs the macro attached to the OnClick event property. The macro opens the WRITERS and PAST ARTICLES form.

To test a command button:

❶ Click the toolbar **Form View button** to switch to the Form View window and then click the **WRITERS and PAST ARTICLES command button**. Access opens the WRITERS and PAST ARTICLES form.

❷ Double-click the WRITERS and PAST ARTICLES form **Control menu box** to close the form.

❸ Click the toolbar **Design View button** to switch back to the Form Design window.

Elena wants all command buttons to be the same size, so she copies and pastes from the first command button. Then she changes each new command button's properties and positions it correctly in the Detail section.

To copy and change a command button:

❶ Click **Edit**, click **Copy**, click the pointer anywhere in the Detail section except on a control, click **Edit**, and then click **Paste**. Access places a second copy of the command button in the Detail section. This copy might end up on top of another control. Because the new command button has the focus, you can easily move it into position.

❷ Drag the command button so that its left edge is at the .8" mark on the horizontal ruler and its top edge is at the 1.25" mark on the vertical ruler.

❸ Click the toolbar **Properties button**. Scroll to the top of the property sheet, double-click the **Name text box**, type **ctlPastArticles**, and then press **[Enter]**. In the Caption text box, which is now highlighted, type **&PAST ARTICLES** and press **[Enter]**.

❹ Scroll the property sheet, click the **On Click text box**, click the **down arrow button**, scroll the drop-down list box, and then click **mcrSwitchboard.mcrPastArticles**. You might need to widen the property sheet temporarily to complete this step.

❺ Click the toolbar **Save button**.

The next copy-and-paste operation should place the new command button below the command button that has the focus. If you perform two consecutive paste operations, the two new command buttons should be perfectly positioned.

To copy and paste command buttons on a form:

❶ The new command button should have move and sizing handles on its edges. If it does not, click the command button. Then click **Edit**, click **Copy**, click **Edit**, click **Paste**, click **Edit**, and then click **Paste**. Two new command buttons should appear in perfect position. See Figure 2-39.

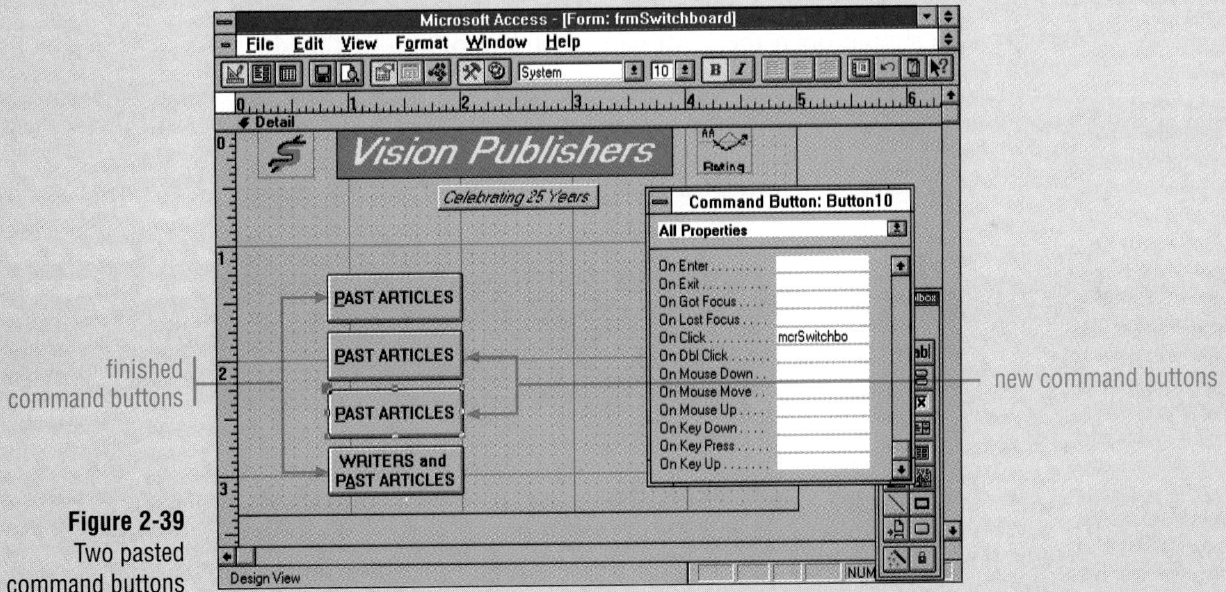

Figure 2-39
Two pasted command buttons

TROUBLE? If one or both of the command buttons are incorrectly positioned, click the command button and move it into position.

Elena changes the properties of these two command buttons.

To change command button properties:

1. The third command button from the top is the last one pasted and should have the focus. If it does not, click the command button to select it.
2. Scroll to the top of the property sheet, double-click the **Name text box**, type **ctlWriters**, and then press **[Enter]**. In the Caption text box, which is now highlighted, type **&WRITERS**, and then press **[Enter]**.
3. Scroll the property sheet, click the **On Click text box**, click the **down arrow button**, scroll the drop-down list box, and then click **mcrSwitchboard.mcrWriters**. You might need to widen the property sheet temporarily to complete this step.
4. Click the second command button from the top to select it.
5. Click the **On Click text box**, click the **down arrow button**, scroll the drop-down list box, and then click **mcrSwitchboard.mcrTypes**. You might need to widen the property sheet temporarily to complete this step.
6. Scroll to the top of the property sheet, double-click the **Name text box**, type **ctlTypes**, and then press **[Enter]**. In the Caption text box, which is now highlighted, type **&TYPES**, and then press **[Enter]**.
7. Click the toolbar **Save button** and then click the toolbar **Properties button** to close the property sheet.

Elena tests all four command buttons in the Form View window. Clicking a command button should open the form named on the button. If this does not happen, Elena will have to correct the command button in the Form Design window.

To test command buttons:

1. Click the toolbar **Form View button** to switch to the Form View window.
2. Click a command button. Access should open the associated form and make it the active window. After the associated form opens, double-click the form's Control menu box to close the form and activate the switchboard.
3. Repeat Step 2 for each of the four command buttons.
4. Click the toolbar **Design View button** to switch back to the Form Design window.

Next, Elena selects all four command buttons, copies them, and then pastes them in the Detail section so that she can format the final four command buttons, according to her switchboard design. Then she moves all four into position and changes their properties.

To copy, paste, and change a group of command buttons:

1. Click in a blank portion of the Detail section to deselect the command buttons. Then click a **command button** and, while holding down [Shift], click each of the remaining three **command buttons**. All four command buttons are selected.
2. Click **Edit**, click **Copy**, click in a blank area of the Detail section, click **Edit**, and then click **Paste**. Access pastes four command buttons into the Detail section. These new command buttons are all selected. See Figure 2-40.

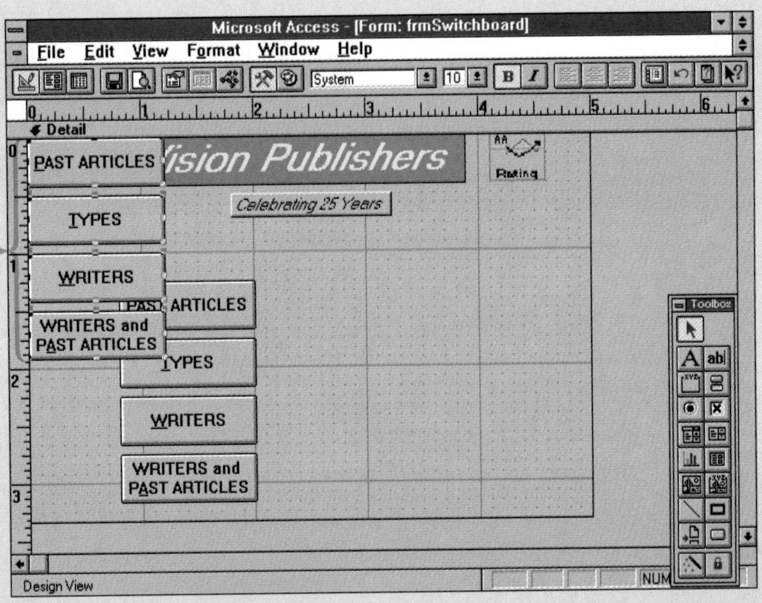

Figure 2-40
Four command buttons pasted as a group

3. Drag all four **command buttons** until the top command button's left edge is at the 2.7" mark on the horizontal ruler and its top edge is at the 1.25" mark on the vertical ruler. Use the grid dots, which should be .1" apart, as a guideline.
4. Click in a blank area of the Detail section and then click the top-right **command button** to select it. Next, click the toolbar **Properties button** to open the property sheet.
5. Scroll to the top of the property sheet, double-click the **Name text box**, type **ctlReports**, and then press **[Enter]**. In the Caption text box type **&Reports...** (be sure to type three periods) and then press **[Enter]**. Scroll the property sheet, click the **On Click text box**, click the **down arrow button**, scroll the drop-down list box, and then click **mcrSwitchboard.mcrReports**.
6. Click the second command button on the right to select it. Click the **On Click text box**, click the **down arrow button**, scroll the drop-down list box, and then click **mcrSwitchboard.mcrQueries**. Scroll to the top of the property sheet, double-click the **Name text box**, type **ctlQueries**, and then press **[Enter]**. In the Caption text box type **&Queries...** and then press **[Enter]**.
7. Click the third command button on the right to select it. Double-click the **Name text box**, type **ctlExitToIssue25**, and then press **[Enter]**. In the Caption text box type **Exit to &Issue25** and then press **[Enter]**. Scroll the property sheet, click the **On Click text box**, click the **down arrow button**, scroll the drop-down list box, and then click **mcrSwitchboard.mcrExitToIssue25**.
8. Click the bottom command button on the right to select it. Click the **On Click text box**, click the **down arrow button**, scroll the drop-down list box, and then click **mcrSwitchboard.mcrExitAccess**. Scroll to the top of the property sheet, double-click the **Name text box**, type **ctlExitAccess**, and then press **[Enter]**. In the Caption text box type **Exit A&ccess** and then press **[Enter]**.
9. Click the toolbar to close the property sheet and then click the toolbar **Save button**.

The switchboard is nearly complete. Before adding the final controls, however, Elena tests the command buttons one more time. This time she tries both clicking the command button to start the associated macro and pressing the character that is underlined on the command button while holding down [Alt].

To test command buttons:

1. Click the toolbar **Form View button** to switch to the Form View window. You should select each button, in turn, from top to bottom and left to right, so that the Exit Access command button is the last button you test.
2. For the command buttons on the left, press the character underlined on the command button while holding down [Alt]. After the associated form opens, double-click the form's **Control menu box** to close the form and activate the switchboard.
3. Repeat Step 2 for each of the four command buttons on the left.
4. Test the Reports... and the Queries... command buttons, this time using the Close command button to close each of those forms.
5. Click the **Exit to Issue25 command button** to close the form and activate the Database window. Click the **Form object button**, then double-click **frmSwitchboard**.
6. Click the **Exit Access command button** to exit Access.
7. Launch Access, open the Issue25 database on your Student Disk, click the **Form object button**, open the switchboard in the Form Design window, and click the Form Design window **maximize button**.

Now Elena is ready to add the finishing touches to her switchboard. She draws rectangles with light gray backgrounds around each set of command buttons, giving the rectangles the sunken special effect that makes the command buttons appear to pop out more.

You draw a rectangle using the toolbox **Rectangle tool**. When you draw a rectangle around a set of command buttons, the rectangle hides the command buttons. To expose the command buttons, use the **Send to Back command** on the Format menu.

To add rectangles to a form:

1. Click the toolbox **Rectangle tool**, position the pointer + in the row of grid dots above the top command button on the left and in the column of grid dots to its left, click the mouse button, and then drag a rectangle down and to the right, releasing the mouse button when the pointer + is in the row of grid dots below the bottom command button and in the column of grid dots two to its right. See Figure 2-41.

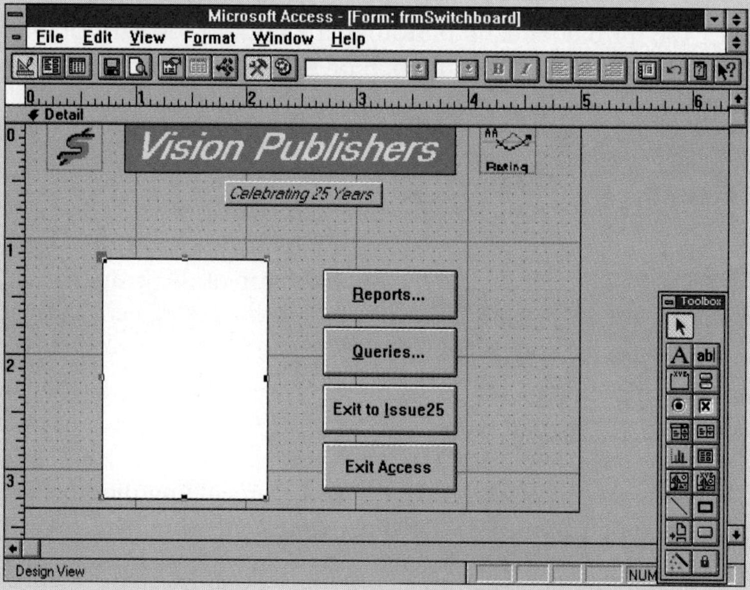

Figure 2-41 Rectangle hiding four command buttons

❷ Click **Format** and then click **Send to Back**. Access places the rectangle behind the command buttons.

❸ Click the toolbar **Palette button** to open the Palette, click the **light gray color** on the Back Color line, and then click the toolbar. Access changes the rectangle color to light gray.

❹ Click the toolbar **Properties button** to open the property sheet, click the **Special Effect text box**, click the **down arrow button**, click **Sunken**, and then click the toolbar. The rectangle now appears sunken around the command buttons.

❺ Repeat Steps 1-4 for the set of command buttons on the right, adjusting the placement of the rectangle as necessary. See Figure 2-42.

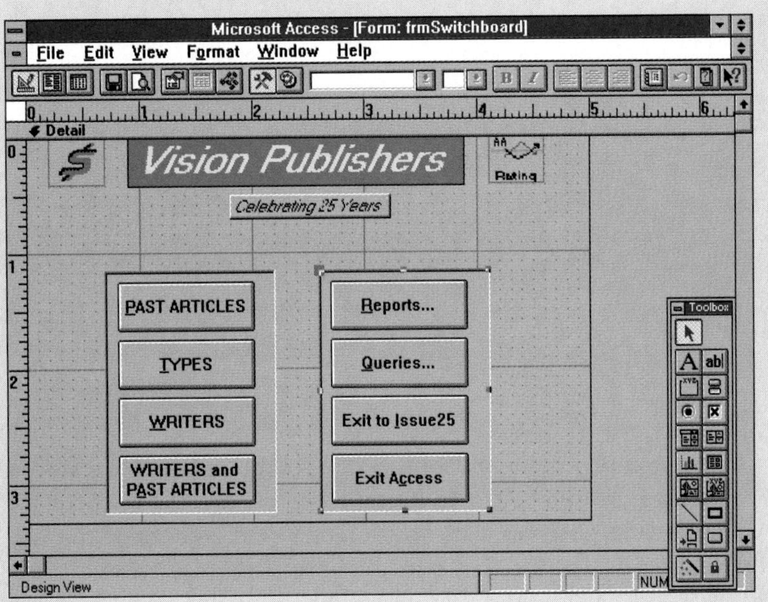

Figure 2-42 Rectangles around both sets of command buttons

❻ Click the toolbar **Save button**.

Elena's final task to complete the switchboard is to add labels with light gray backgrounds on the top line of each rectangle. These labels serve to identify each group of command buttons enclosed by the rectangles.

To add labels to a form:

❶ Click the toolbox **Label tool**, position the pointer + in the row of grid dots above the left rectangle and at the .8" mark on the horizontal ruler, click the mouse button, type **Display Forms**, and then press **[Enter]**. A label appears on the top line of the left rectangle.

❷ Click the toolbar **Palette button** to open the Palette, click the **light gray color** on the Back Color line, and then click the toolbar. Access changes the label background color to light gray.

❸ Click the toolbox, position the pointer + in the row of grid dots above the right rectangle and at the 2.7" mark on the horizontal ruler, click the mouse button, type **Display Data or Exit**, and then press **[Enter]**. A label appears on the top line of the right rectangle.

4. Click the toolbar to open the Palette, click the **light gray color** on the Back Color line, and then click the toolbar. Access changes the label background color to light gray.
5. Click the toolbar **Save button**. See Figure 2-43.

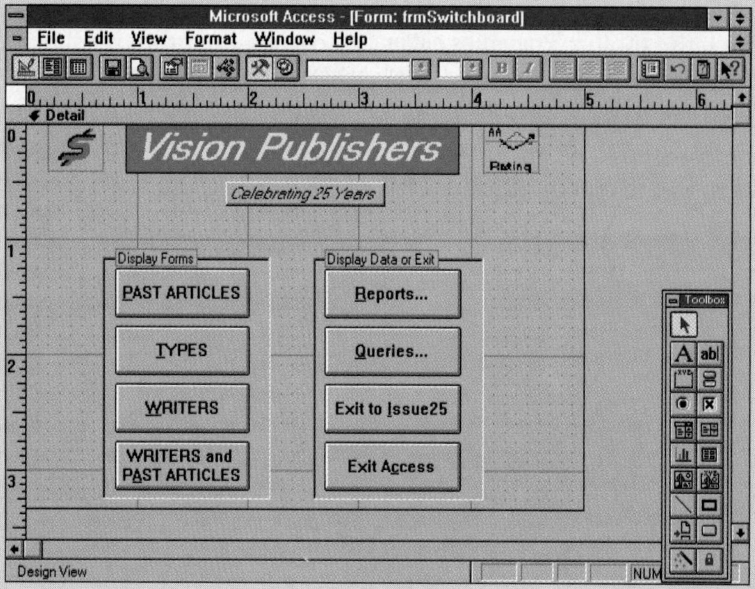

Figure 2-43 The switchboard with all controls added

Elena increases the height of the Detail section to 3.6", restores the Form Design window, and then switches to the Form View window to inspect the switchboard visually and to resize and position it on the screen. Next, she saves the final screen placement of the switchboard, switches back to the Form Design window to set the BorderStyle property to Dialog, saves the form, and then closes the Form Design window.

To resize and position a switchboard in the Form View window:

1. Scroll down the Form Design window and then drag the bottom border of the Detail section down to the 3.6" mark on the vertical ruler.

   TROUBLE? If you do not have .3" between the bottom command buttons and the bottom border of the Detail section, adjust the bottom border until you do.

2. Click the Form Design window **restore button** and then click the toolbar **Form View button** to switch to the Form View window.
3. Drag the switchboard's bottom border up or down, if necessary, and then drag the switchboard's right border to the left until the switchboard appears properly proportioned.

❹ Drag the switchboard **title bar** to center the form horizontally and position it down near the bottom of the screen. See Figure 2-44.

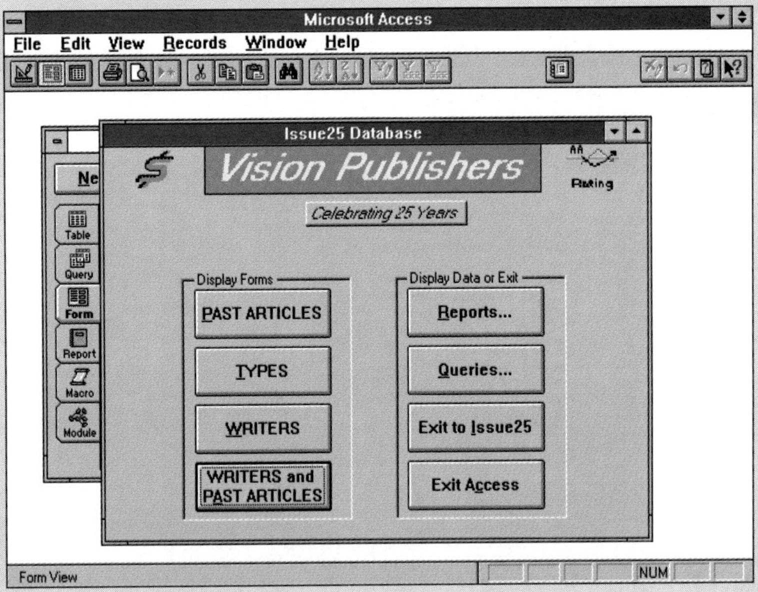

Figure 2-44
The resized and repositioned switchboard in the Form View window

❺ Click **File** and click **Save Form** to save the position and size of the switchboard.

❻ Click the toolbar **Design View button** to switch back to the Form Design window, click the **white box** below the Control menu box in the Form View window, click the toolbar **Properties button** to open the property sheet, scroll the property sheet as necessary, click the **Border Style text box**, click the **down arrow button**, click **Dialog**, and then click the toolbar .

❼ Click the toolbar **Save button** , click **File**, and then click **Close** to close the window and activate the Database window.

Elena opens the switchboard in the Form View window to see its final appearance. The only changes to the switchboard from your previous view of it should be the absence of the sizing buttons in the upper-right corner and a narrower border.

To view the completed switchboard:

1. Double-click **frmSwitchboard** to open the Form View window for the frmSwitchboard form. See Figure 2-45.

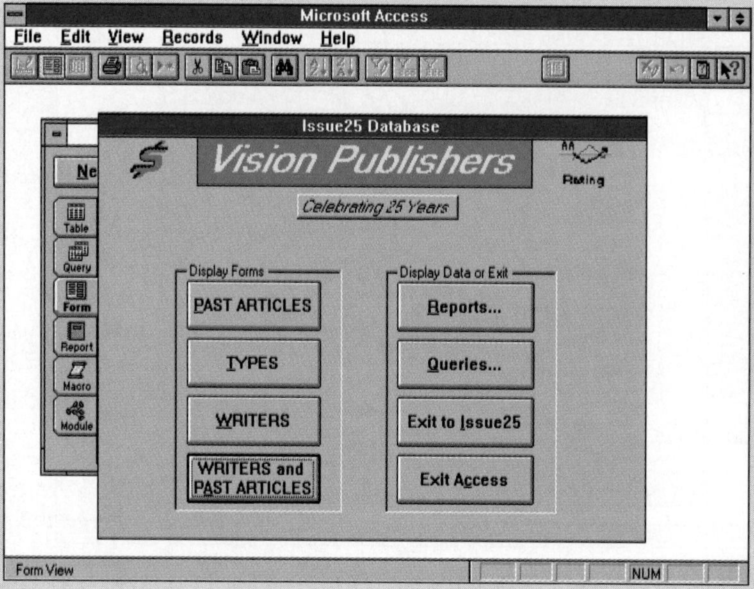

Figure 2-45
The completed switchboard in the Form View window

2. Click the **Exit to Issue25 button**. Access closes the switchboard and activates the Database window.

Elena has reached the end of the workday, so she exits Access.

To exit Access:

1. Double-click the Microsoft Access window **Control menu box** to exit Access.

■ ■ ■

Elena's plans for the next day include adding a custom menu bar and a custom toolbar to the switchboard, as she continues her work with the graphical user interface and macros.

Questions

1. Give a definition of a switchboard, describe its significant features, and provide two reasons for using one.
2. What is a macro and what is the relationship between a macro and an action?
3. What is an action argument? Give an example of an action argument.
4. What are you trying to accomplish when you single step through a macro?
5. When does an AutoExec macro run?
6. What is an event property?
7. What form components do not appear on a dialog box? What additional component does not appear on a switchboard?
8. What are two reasons for using macro groups?
9. When do you use the Stretch Size Mode property?
10. What are two special effects you can use for a control?

Tutorial Assignments

Launch Access and open the Issue25 database on your Student Disk.

1. Design and create a dialog box that has the following components and characteristics.
   a. When you save the form, use the name frmQueriesReports.
   b. The title bar contains Print Queries and Reports.
   c. A list box displays all the query and report names contained in the tblObjectNames table. The names appear in alphabetical order. (Create a new query with the name qryQueryReportNames that does an ascending sort on the ObjectName field and has no criteria for the ObjectType field.)
   d. Queries/Reports appears as a heading above the list box.
   e. Two command buttons appear below the list box. The left command button displays the printer icon, and the right command button displays the word Close with the C underlined.
   f. Double-clicking a query or report name has the same effect as clicking the left command button. Both events cause Access to display the Print Preview window for the selected query or report. (You will add the Access Basic code for the event properties in the tutorial entitled "Access Basic." For now, double-clicking or clicking should cause no action to occur.)
   g. Clicking the Close command button causes Access to close the dialog box.
2. Design and create a switchboard that has the following components and characteristics.
   a. When you save the form, use the name frmMySwitchboard.
   b. The title bar contains your name.
   c. The title of your course appears centered at the top of the switchboard. Use appropriate choices of background and foreground colors, special effects, and font size and characteristics.
   d. Two command buttons appear on the switchboard. One command button displays the dialog box you just created, and the other command button closes the switchboard and activates the Database window. Create a macro group for these command buttons.
   e. Use an appropriate background color for the overall switchboard, and size and position the switchboard in the Form View window.

Case Problems

1. Walkton Daily Press Carriers

Launch Access and open the Press database on your Student Disk.

1. Design and create a switchboard that has frmSwitchboard as a saved form name and that has the following components and characteristics.
   a. Provide appropriate wording for the title bar and a heading at the top center of the switchboard.
   b. Add the walk01.bmp and walk02.bmp graphic images from your Student Disk to appropriate positions on the switchboard.
   c. Place five command buttons on the switchboard. The command buttons perform these actions: open the "BILLINGS" table, open the "CARRIERS form" form, open the "CARRIERS sorted by Name, Route ID" query, open the "CARRIERS Report" report, and close the switchboard and activate the Database window. Create a macro group for these command buttons.
   d. Use appropriate background and foreground colors and visual effects for the switchboard and its components, and size and position the switchboard in the Form View window.

2. Lopez Used Cars

Launch Access and open the Usedcars database on your Student Disk.

1. Design and create a switchboard that has frmSwitchboard as a saved form name and that has the following components and characteristics.
   a. Provide appropriate wording for the title bar and a heading at the top center of the switchboard.
   b. Add the lopez01.bmp and lopez02.bmp graphic images from your Student Disk to appropriate positions on the switchboard.
   c. Place five command buttons on the switchboard. The command buttons perform these actions: open the "LOCATIONS" table, open the "USED CARS form" form, open the "USED CARS by Manufacturer, Model" query, open the "USED CARS by Year Report" report, and close the switchboard and activate the Database window. Create a macro group for these command buttons.
   d. Use appropriate background and foreground colors and visual effects for the switchboard and its components, and size and position the switchboard in the Form View window.

3. Tophill University Student Employment

Launch Access and open the Parttime database on your Student Disk.

1. Design and create a switchboard that has frmSwitchboard as a saved form name and that has the following components and characteristics.
   a. Provide appropriate wording for the title bar and a heading at the top center of the switchboard.
   b. Add the top01.bmp and top02.bmp graphic images from your Student Disk to appropriate positions on the switchboard.
   c. Place five command buttons on the switchboard. The command buttons perform these actions: open the "EMPLOYERS" table, open the "EMPLOYERS and JOBS form" form, open the "JOBS sorted by Employer, Job Title" query, open the "JOBS Report" report, and close the switchboard and activate the Database window. Create a macro group for these command buttons.
   d. Use appropriate background and foreground colors and visual effects for the switchboard and its components, and size and position the switchboard in the Form View window.

4. Rexville Business Licenses

Launch Access and open the Buslic database on your Student Disk.

1. Design and create a switchboard that has frmSwitchboard as a saved form name and that has the following components and characteristics.
   a. Provide appropriate wording for the title bar and a heading at the top center of the switchboard.
   b. Add the rex01.bmp and rex02.bmp graphic images from your Student Disk to appropriate positions on the switchboard.
   c. Place five command buttons on the switchboard. The command buttons perform these actions: open the "LICENSES" table, open the "BUSINESSES form" form, open the "BUSINESSES sorted by License Type, Business Name" query, open the "BUSINESSES Report" report, and close the switchboard and activate the Database window. Create a macro group for these command buttons.
   d. Use appropriate background and foreground colors and visual effects for the switchboard and its components, and size and position the switchboard in the Form View window.

T U T O R I A L 3

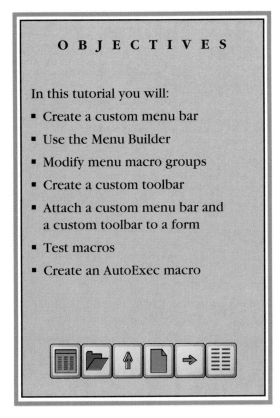

Additional Macros

Completing the Macros for the Issue25 Database User Interface

OBJECTIVES

In this tutorial you will:

- Create a custom menu bar
- Use the Menu Builder
- Modify menu macro groups
- Create a custom toolbar
- Attach a custom menu bar and a custom toolbar to a form
- Test macros
- Create an AutoExec macro

CASE

Vision Publishers Elena Sanchez has been developing a graphical user interface for the Issue25 database. She reviews her progress and plans the remaining tasks. So far, she has created the switchboard, two dialog boxes, and a macro group. The next tasks she undertakes are to create a custom menu bar and a custom toolbar for the switchboard. Once she creates the menu bar and toolbar, the only unfinished tasks involve adding Access Basic code to selected event properties to complete the two dialog boxes.

Creating a Custom Menu Bar

For the Issue25 database graphical user interface, Elena designs a custom menu bar, shown in Figure 3-1.

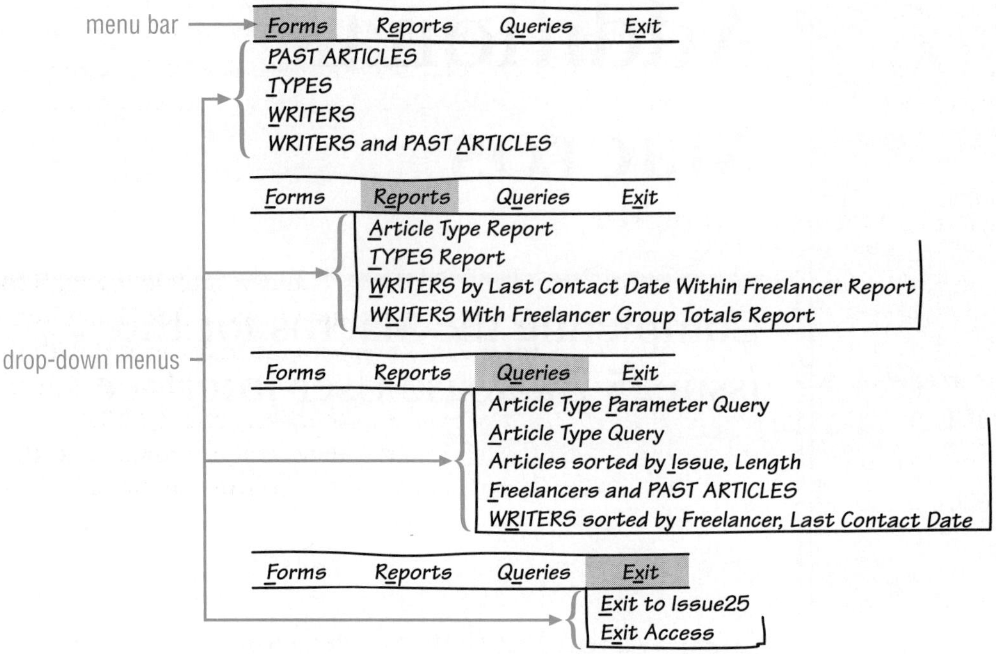

Figure 3-1 Elena's design for the Issue25 custom menu bar

A **custom menu bar** is a menu bar you create for an application. Custom menu bars are similar to standard Access menu bars, which are called **built-in menu bars**, in the following ways.

- A custom menu bar appears immediately below the title bar, replacing the built-in menu.
- A custom menu bar contains one or more menu names. Elena's menu names are Forms, Reports, Queries, and Exit.
- A list of menu-item names, which are usually the names of commands, appears in a drop-down menu when you click a menu name. The menu-item names for the Forms menu are PAST ARTICLES, TYPES, WRITERS, and WRITERS and PAST ARTICLES.
- Each menu name has an underlined letter that identifies the hot key to the menu. Pressing [Alt] and F, for example, opens the Forms menu to display the four menu items shown under it in Figure 3-1.
- Each menu-item name has an underlined letter that identifies the hot key for selecting that option. Pressing W when Elena's Forms menu is open, for example, opens the WRITERS form.

When you create a custom menu bar, you attach macros to the menu names and items. When the user clicks a menu name or item, an event occurs, and your macro responds and takes the appropriate action (for example, opens a form). To get your custom menu bar to function, you need to create a menu bar macro and menu macro groups. A **menu bar macro** displays a custom menu bar; the macro contains a series of AddMenu actions, one action for each menu name. Each **AddMenu action** adds a drop-down menu to the custom menu bar. A **menu macro group**, also called a **menu macro**, defines the commands for a drop-down menu. The commands on the four drop-down menus in Figure 3-1 are defined by four menu macro groups.

You can attach a custom menu bar to a form or report so that Access displays the custom menu bar only when it displays the form or report. Alternatively, your custom menu bar can be **global**, so that Access displays the custom menu bar in all windows of your application. Finally, you can create all the macros for a custom menu bar or use the **Menu Builder** to help you create the macros. You start the Menu Builder from the Menu Bar event property on a form or report or from the Add-ins command in the File menu. An **add-in** is an Access Basic program that adds features to the basic Access database command set. Several add-ins, such as the Menu Builder and Wizards, are included with the Access software. You can buy add-ins from third-party companies or you can create your own add-ins.

Planning a Custom Menu Bar

Elena uses the Menu Builder to create the Issue25 custom menu bar. Interacting with the Menu Builder, she enters each menu name and each menu-item name. After Elena assigns menSwitchboard as the menu bar name, Menu Builder creates a menu bar macro with the same name and four menu macro groups named menSwitchboard_Forms, menSwitchboard_Reports, menSwitchboard_Queries, and menSwitchboard_Exit.

Next, Elena adds the appropriate actions to the four menu macro groups. She then attaches menSwitchboard to the MenuBar event property of the frmSwitchboard form. Finally, Elena tests all custom menu bar options.

Using the Menu Builder

Elena starts the Menu Builder using the File menu's Add-ins command. She enters all menu and menu-item names and saves her work with the name menSwitchboard.

REFERENCE WINDOW

Creating a Custom Menu Bar with Menu Builder

- Click File, click Add-ins, click Menu Builder, click the New button, click <Empty Menu Bar>, and then click the OK button.
- Enter a menu or menu-item name in the Caption box, type a description in the Status Bar Text box, click an arrow button to distinguish between menu names and menu-item names, and click the Next button to complete each definition.
- After entering all menu and menu-item names, click the OK button, type the custom menu bar name, and press [Enter].

Elena starts the add-in Menu Builder to create a custom menu bar to attach to the frmSwitchboard form.

To start the Menu Builder:

1. Place your Student Disk in the appropriate drive, launch Access, and open the Issue25 database on your Student Disk.
2. Click **File**, click **Add-ins**, and then click **Menu Builder**. Access opens the first Menu Builder dialog box.
3. Click the **New button** in the dialog box to open the second Menu Builder dialog box.
4. Click **<Empty Menu Bar>** in the Template for New Menu Bar list box and then click the **OK button**. Access opens the third Menu Builder dialog box. See Figure 3-2.

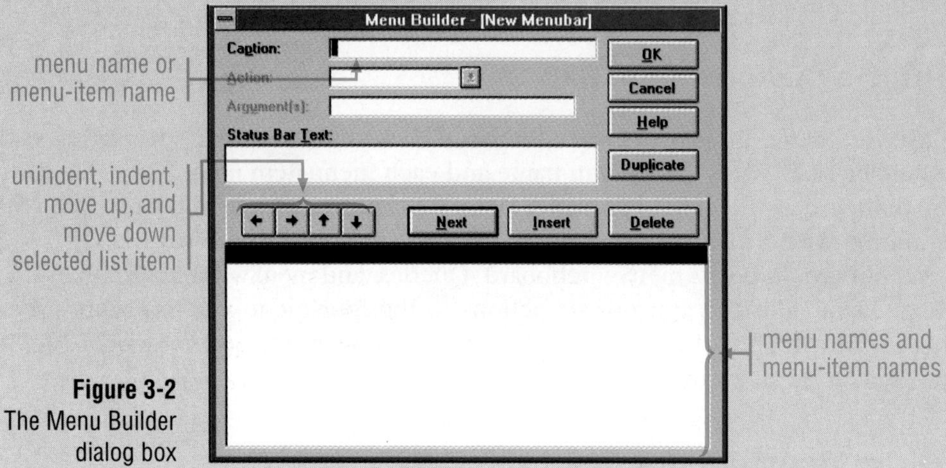

Figure 3-2
The Menu Builder dialog box

In the Caption text box, Elena enters the menu and menu-item names. In the Status Bar Text text box, she enters the comment or description she wants to be displayed in the status bar for the menu or menu item. Because she wants Menu Builder to create the menu bar macro and menu macro groups for her, Elena does not use the Action or Argument(s) text boxes.

Elena enters the first menu name and learns the purpose of the command buttons on the dialog box as she proceeds.

To use Menu Builder to enter a menu name:

1. Type **&Forms** in the Caption text box, press **[Tab]**, type **Open forms** in the Status Bar Text text box, and then click the **Next button**. Access adds &Forms to the lower portion of the dialog box, moves the highlight below the &Forms entry, and places the insertion point at the start of the Caption text box.
2. Type **&PAST ARTICLES**, press **[Tab]**, type **Open PAST ARTICLES form** in the Status Bar Text text box, and then click the **indent button**. See Figure 3-3.

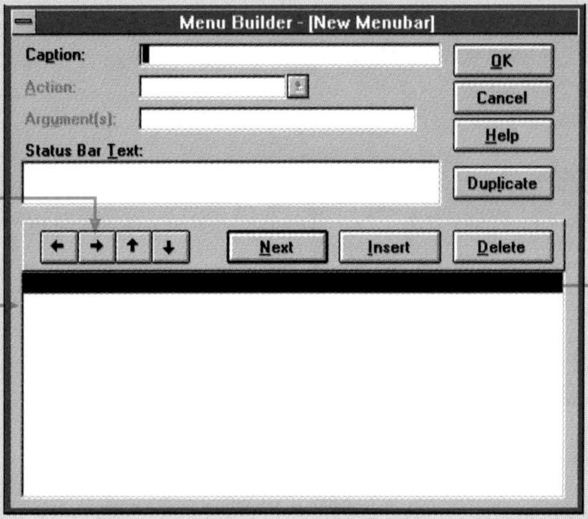

Figure 3-3
Entering menu names and menu-item names

You place menu names flush left in the list box and indent menu-item names one level. For more complicated menu bars that have submenus, you indent the submenu commands one additional level below a menu-item name. In this case, the menu-item name becomes the submenu name. Recall from the previous chapter that a letter preceded by an ampersand (&) in a menu name or menu-item name appears underlined on the custom menu bar or drop-down menu and functions as a hot key.

Elena continues entering menu-item names in the order she wants them to appear in the custom menu bar.

To continue entering the menu and menu-item names in a custom menu bar:

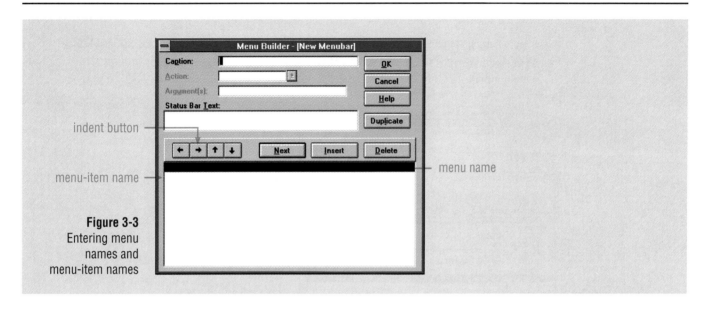

1. Click the **Next button**, type **&TYPES** in the Caption text box, press **[Tab]**, type **Open TYPES form** in the Status Bar Text text box, and then click the **indent button**. Elena is now ready to start the third menu item for the Forms menu.
2. Click the **Next button**, type **&WRITERS** in the Caption text box, press **[Tab]**, type **Open WRITERS form** in the Status Bar Text text box, and then click the **indent button**.
3. Click the **Next button**, type **WRITERS and PAST &ARTICLES** in the Caption text box, press **[Tab]**, type **Open WRITERS and PAST ARTICLES form** in the Status Bar Text text box, and then click the **indent button**. Elena has completed entering the four menu-item names for the Forms menu, so now she builds the Reports menu.
4. Click the **Next button**, type **R&eports** in the Caption text box, press **[Tab]**, and then type **Open reports** in the Status Bar Text text box. Elena now enters the first menu-item name for the Reports menu.

5. Click the **Next button**, type **&Article Type Report** in the Caption text box, press **[Tab]**, type **Open Article Type Report** in the Status Bar Text text box, and then click the **indent button**. See Figure 3-4.

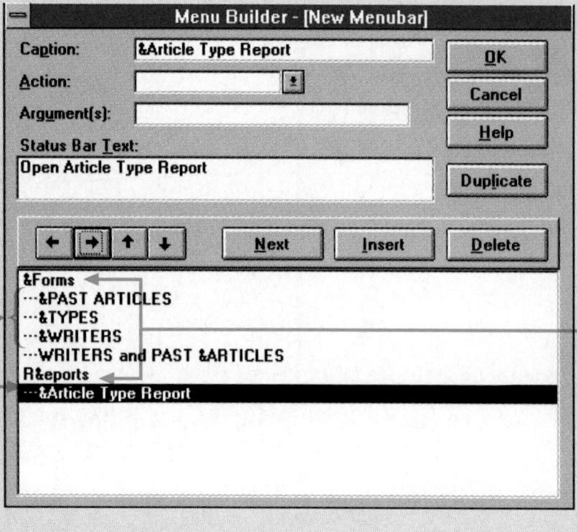

Figure 3-4
Defining the second drop-down menu

Elena completes the construction of the custom menu bar in the Menu Builder dialog box. She enters the remaining menu-item names for the Reports menu, the Queries menu name and its five menu-item names, and then the Exit menu name and its two menu-item names.

To complete a custom menu bar using the Menu Builder:

1. Click the **Next button**, type **&WRITERS by Last Contact Date Within Freelancer Report** in the Caption text box, press **[Tab]**, type **Open WRITERS by Last Contact Date Within Freelancer Report** in the Status Bar Text text box, and then click the **indent button**.
2. Click the **Next button**, type **W&RITERS With Freelancer Group Totals Report** in the Caption text box, press **[Tab]**, type **Open WRITERS With Freelancer Group Totals Report** in the Status Bar Text text box, and then click the **indent button**.
3. Click the **Next button**, type **Q&ueries** in the Caption text box, press **[Tab]**, and then type **Open queries** in the Status Bar Text text box. See Figure 3-5.

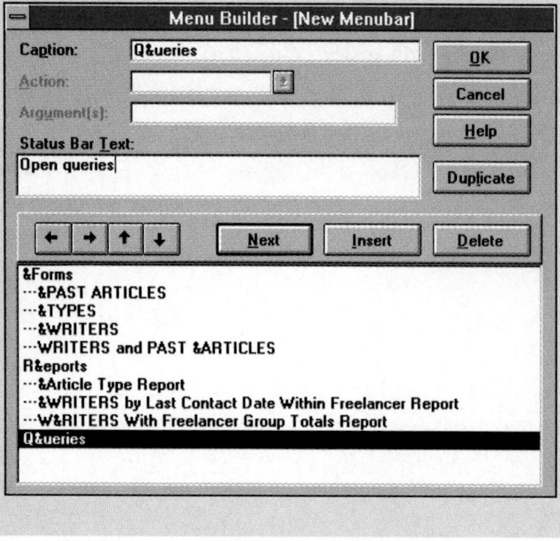

Figure 3-5
Defining the third menu name

4. Click the **Next button**, type **Article Type &Parameter Query** in the Caption text box, press **[Tab]**, type **Open Article Type Parameter Query** in the Status Bar Text text box, and then click the **indent button**.
5. Repeat Step 4 for the four remaining menu items for the Queries menu. Type **&Article Type Query; Articles sorted by &Issue, Length; &Freelancers and PAST ARTICLES;** and **W&RITERS sorted by Freelancer, Last Contact Date** for the four menu-item entries in the Caption text box and type corresponding entries in the Status Bar Text text box.
6. Click the **Next button**, type **E&xit** in the Caption text box, press **[Tab]**, and then type **Exit Switchboard** in the Status Bar Text text box.
7. Click the **Next button**, type **&Exit to Issue25** in the Caption text box, press **[Tab]**, type **Exit to Issue25 database** in the Status Bar Text text box, and then click the **indent button**.
8. Click the **Next button**, type **E&xit Access** in the Caption text box, press **[Tab]**, type **Exit Access** in the Status Bar Text text box, and then click the **indent button**.
9. Click the **OK button**, type **menSwitchboard** in the Menu Bar Name text box in the Save As dialog box, and then press **[Enter]**. Access saves the custom menu bar and activates the Database window.
10. Click the **Macro object button**. Access opens the Macros list box. See Figure 3-6.

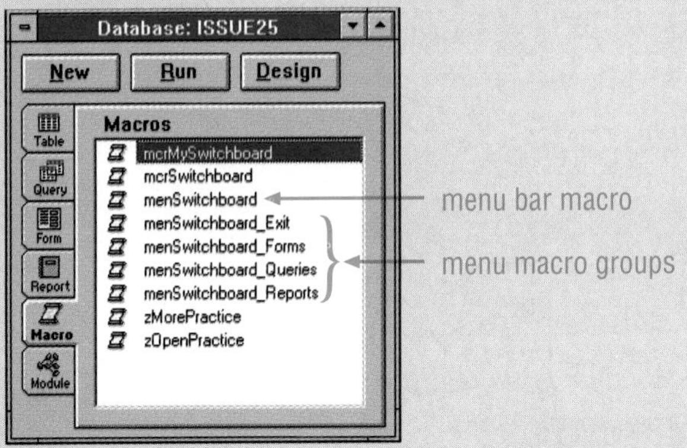

Figure 3-6
Macros created by the Menu Builder

The Menu Builder created the five macros whose names start with menSwitchboard. Elena now adds the required actions to the macros that will make them open the indicated objects.

Adding Actions to Menu Macro Groups

Now that Elena has the outline of her custom menu bar, she needs to add actions to the macros created by the Menu Builder. She doesn't need to change the menSwitchboard macro, which already contains AddMenu actions to display the custom menu bar and to define the four drop-down menus, although she does open it to be sure it's okay. Then she makes macro changes that fall into two categories:

- The menSwitchboard_Queries and menSwitchboard_Reports macros are menu macro groups that define the commands for the Queries and the Reports drop-down menus. For the macros in the menSwitchboard_Queries macro, Elena adds OpenQuery actions and sets the View action arguments to Print Preview. For the macros in the menSwitchboard_Reports macro, Elena adds OpenReport actions.

- The menSwitchboard_Exit and menSwitchboard_Forms macros are menu macro groups that define the commands for the Exit and Forms drop-down menus. Elena already created macros in the mcrSwitchboard macro group that perform the actions needed to exit and to open forms, so she adds **RunMacro actions** to the menu macro groups to run those other macros.

Elena opens the menSwitchboard macro to review its actions and to verify she does not need to make any changes.

To review a menu bar macro:

1. Click **menSwitchboard** in the Macros list box and then click the **Design command button** to open the Macro window. See Figure 3-7. The first AddMenu action displays Forms on the custom menu bar, displays "Open forms" on the status bar, and runs the menSwitchboard_Forms macro. This first macro is correct.

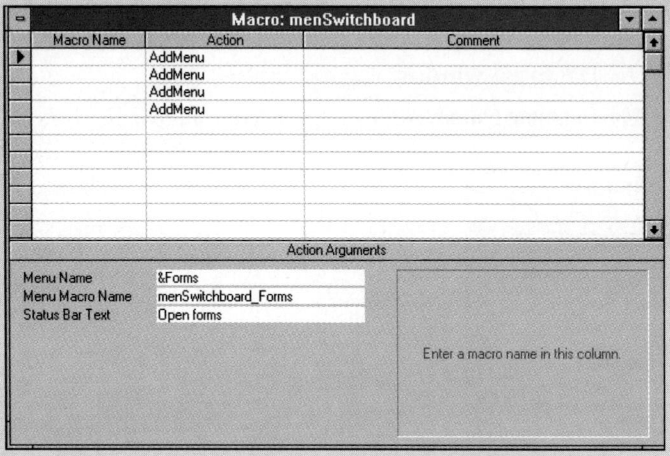

Figure 3-7 The menSwitchboard menu bar macro

2. Pausing between each keystroke to review each Addmenu action, press [↓] three times.

Elena closes the Macro window, opens the menSwitchboard_Exit menu macro group, and adds the RunMacro action to the group's two macros. The RunMacro action runs macros Elena previously created in the mcrSwitchboard macro group.

To add actions to a menu macro group:

1. Double-click the Macro window **Control menu box** to close the Macro window.
2. Click **menSwitchboard_Exit** in the Macros list box and then click the **Design command button**. Access opens the Macro window.
3. Click the first row's **Action text box**, click the **down arrow button**, scroll down the Action drop-down list box, and then click **RunMacro**.

4. Click the **Macro Name text box**, click the **down arrow button**, and then click **mcrSwitchboard.mcrExitToIssue25**. Access runs this macro whenever you select the Exit to Issue25 command on the Exit menu.
5. Click the second row's **Action text box**, click the **down arrow button**, scroll down the Action drop-down list box, and then click **RunMacro**.
6. Click the **Macro Name text box**, click the **down arrow button**, scroll, and then click **mcrSwitchboard.mcrExitAccess**. Access runs this macro whenever you select the Exit Access command on the Exit menu. See Figure 3-8.

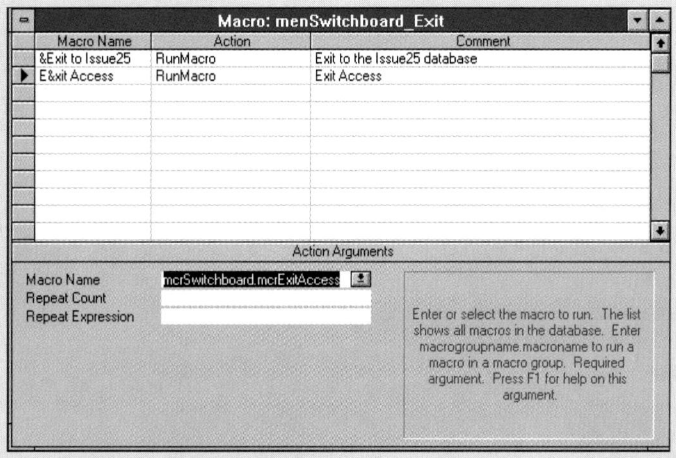

Figure 3-8
RunMacro macros added to a menu macro group

7. Click the toolbar **Save button** to save the macro changes and then double-click the Macro window **Control menu box** to close the Macro window and activate the Database window.

Next, Elena opens the Macro window for the menSwitchboard_Forms menu macro group and adds the RunMacro action to the group's four macros. The RunMacro action runs macros Elena previously created in the mcrSwitchboard macro group; these macros open the forms specified by the menu-item name.

To add RunMacro actions to a menu macro group:

1. Click **menSwitchboard_Forms** in the Macros list box and then click the **Design command button**. Access opens the Macro window.
2. Click the first row's **Action text box**, click the **down arrow button**, scroll down the Action drop-down list box, and then click **RunMacro**.
3. Click the **Macro Name text box**, click the **down arrow button**, and then click **mcrSwitchboard.mcrPastArticles**. Access runs this macro whenever you select the PAST ARTICLES command on the Forms menu.
4. Click the second row's **Action text box**, click the **down arrow button**, scroll down the Action drop-down list box, click **RunMacro**, click the **Macro Name text box**, scroll down the drop-down list box, click the **down arrow button**, and then click **mcrSwitchboard.mcrTypes**. Access runs this macro whenever you select the TYPES command on the Forms menu.

5. Click the third row's **Action text box**, click the **down arrow button**, scroll down the Action drop-down list box, click **RunMacro**, click the **Macro Name text box**, click the **down arrow button**, scroll down the drop-down list box, and then click **mcrSwitchboard.mcrWriters**. Access runs this macro whenever you select the WRITERS command on the Forms menu.
6. Click the fourth row's **Action text box**, click the **down arrow button**, scroll down the Action drop-down list box, click **RunMacro**, click the **Macro Name text box**, click the **down arrow button**, scroll down the drop-down list box, and then click **mcrSwitchboard.mcrWritersPastArticles**. Access runs this macro whenever you select the WRITERS and PAST ARTICLES command on the Forms menu. See Figure 3-9.

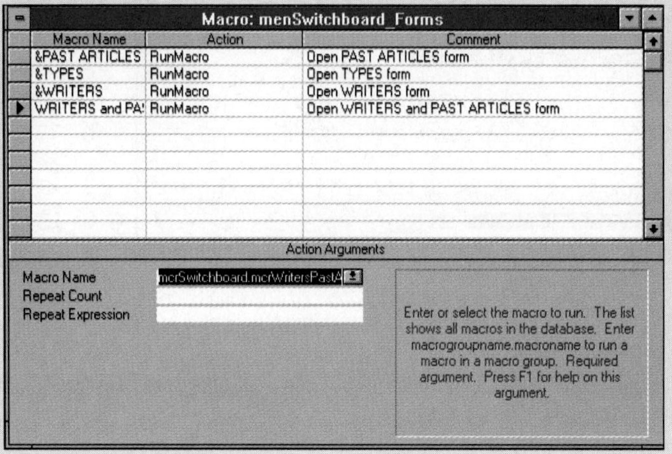

Figure 3-9
The completed menu macro group

7. Click the toolbar **Save button** and then double-click the Macro window **Control menu box**.

Elena does not have existing macros for the menSwitchboard_Queries menu macro group. Therefore, instead of adding RunMacro actions, Elena adds OpenQuery actions to each macro in the group.

To add OpenQuery actions to a menu macro group:

1. Click **menSwitchboard_Queries** in the Macros list box and then click the **Design command button**. Access opens the Macro window.
2. Click the first row's **Action text box**, click the **down arrow button**, scroll down the Action drop-down list box, and then click **OpenQuery**.
3. Click the **Query Name text box**, click the **down arrow button**, click **Article Type Parameter Query**, click the **View text box**, click the **down arrow button**, and then click **Print Preview**. Access opens this form in the Print Preview window whenever you select the corresponding command on the Queries menu.

4. Repeat Steps 2 and 3 for the four remaining macros. Click **Article Type Query**; **Articles sorted by Issue, Length**; **Freelancers and PAST ARTICLES**; and **WRITERS sorted by Freelancer, Last Contact Date** for the four macros in the Query Name text box. See Figure 3-10.

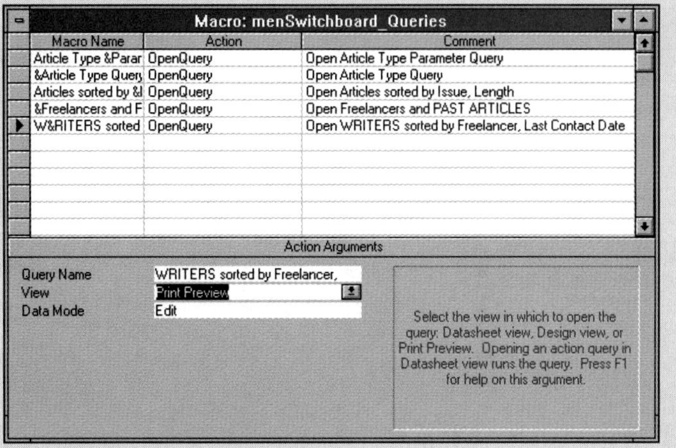

Figure 3-10
The completed menu macro group

5. Click the toolbar **Save button** and then double-click the Macro window **Control menu box**.

The changes Elena will make to the menSwitchboard_Reports menu macro group are similar to those she made to the menSwitchboard_Queries menu macro group. Instead of adding OpenQuery actions, however, Elena adds OpenReport actions to each macro in the group. She also notices that the TYPES Report is missing—she must have failed to add it in the Menu Builder dialog box. For minor mistakes like this one, Elena can make corrections in the Macro window rather than re-open the Menu Builder add-in.

To add OpenReport actions to a menu macro group:

1. Click **menSwitchboard_Reports** in the Macros list box and then click the **Design command button**. Access opens the Macro window.
2. Click the **second row selector** to highlight the entire row, use the right mouse button to click the **row selector** again, and then click **Insert Row** in the shortcut menu.
3. Click the second row's **Macro Name text box**, type **&TYPES Report**, press **[Tab]**, press **[Tab]**, and then type **Open TYPES Report**.
4. Click the first row's **Action text box**, click the **down arrow button**, scroll down the Action drop-down list box, and then click **OpenReport**.
5. Click the **Report Name text box**, click the **down arrow button**, and then click **Article Type Report**. Access opens this report in the Print Preview window whenever you select the corresponding command on the Reports menu.

❻ Repeat Steps 4 and 5 for the three remaining macros. Click **TYPES Report**, **WRITERS by Last Contact Date Within Freelancer Report**, and **WRITERS With Freelancer Group Totals Report** for the three macros in the Report Name text box. See Figure 3-11.

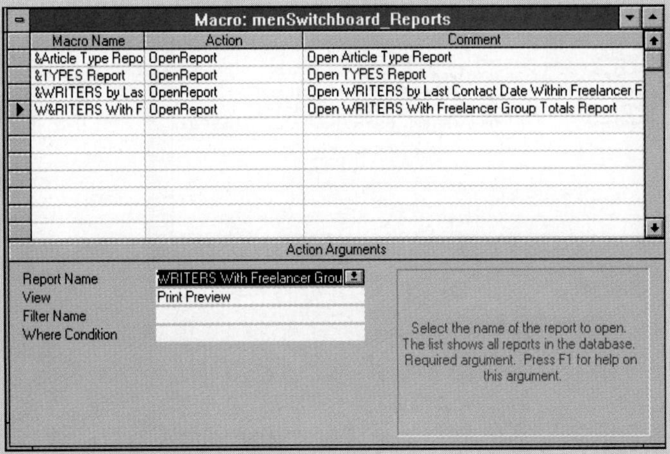

Figure 3-11
The completed menu macro group

❼ Click the toolbar **Save button** and then double-click the Macro window **Control menu box**.

Attaching a Custom Menu Bar to a Form

When Access displays the frmSwitchboard form, Elena wants the custom menu bar to appear instead of the built-in Form View window menu bar. For any other object in the Issue25 database, including the two dialog boxes opened from the frmSwitchboard form, Access should display the associated built-in menu bar. Thus, Elena attaches the custom menu bar to the frmSwitchboard form. Specifically, she sets the form's **MenuBar property** to the name of the custom menu bar.

To attach a custom menu bar to a form:

❶ Click the **Form object button**, click **frmSwitchboard**, and then click the **Design command button**. Access opens the Form Design window for the frmSwitchboard form.

❷ Click the toolbar **Properties button** to open the property sheet.

❸ Click the **Menu Bar text box** in the property sheet, click the **down arrow button**, scroll the drop-down list box, and then click **menSwitchboard**. You might need to widen the property sheet temporarily to complete this step.

❹ Click the toolbar **Save button** to save the form-design changes and then click to close the property sheet.

❺ Double-click the Form Design window **Control menu box** to close the window and activate the Database window and then double-click **frmSwitchboard** to open the form in the Form View window. See Figure 3-12.

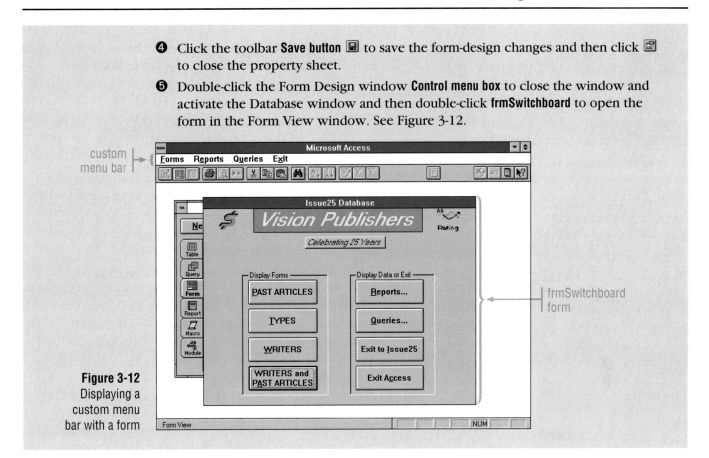

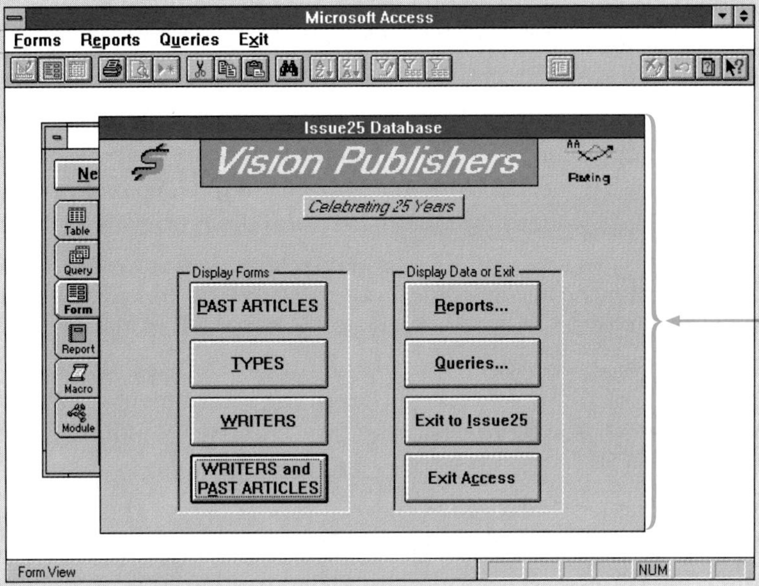

Figure 3-12
Displaying a custom menu bar with a form

Access opens the frmSwitchboard form and displays the custom menu bar below the Microsoft Access title bar. Elena successfully attached the custom menu bar to the frmSwitchboard form.

Testing a Custom Menu Bar

Elena tests all the menus and menu items on the custom menu bar. To test each menu, Elena clicks each menu name and verifies that the drop-down menu opens in response. To test keyboard access to the menus, she presses [Alt] and the underlined menu character to open a drop-down menu, and then presses [Esc] to close that drop-down menu.

In a similar way, Elena tests the mouse and keyboard access to the menu items on each drop-down menu. For keyboard access to the menu items, she simply presses the underlined character and does not use [Alt].

Elena makes the Exit Access menu item on the Exit menu her last choice and takes her lunch break at that point.

To test a custom menu bar:

1. Click each menu name, in turn, from left to right, to verify that each drop-down menu appears.
2. Press **[Alt]F** to display the Forms drop-down menu and then press **[Esc]** to close the drop-down menu.

   TROUBLE? Whenever a menu, command button, or other object provides a hot key, the hot key can be pressed either as a lowercase or uppercase letter.
3. Repeat Step 2 for the underlined character in each of the other three menu names.
4. Click **Forms** to display its drop-down menu. Then either click **PAST ARTICLES** or press **P** to open the PAST ARTICLES form. Double-click the Form View window **Control menu box** for the PAST ARTICLES form to close the form. Repeat this step for each of the other three menu items on the Forms menu.

   TROUBLE? If you are tempted to skip these testing steps, remember that there are many points in the menu building process where things can go wrong. If other users will be using your switchboard, you should be sure to test every part of it.
5. Click **Reports** to display its drop-down menu. Then either click **Article Type Report** or press **A** to open Article Type Report in the Print Preview window. Click the toolbar **Close Window button** to close the Print Preview window. Repeat this step for each of the other three menu items on the Reports menu.
6. Click **Queries** to display its drop-down menu. Then either click **Article Type Parameter Query** or press **P**, type **law** and press **[Enter]** to open Article Type Parameter Query in the Print Preview window. Double-click the Print Preview window **Control menu box** to close the Print Preview window. Repeat this step for each of the other four menu items on the Queries menu.
7. Click **Exit** to display its drop-down menu. Then either click **Exit to Issue25** or press **E**. Access closes the form and activates the Database window.
8. Click the **Open command button** to open the frmSwitchboard form in the Form View window.
9. Click **Exit** and then either click **Exit Access** or press **X**. Access closes all windows and exits.

Elena has now completed the custom menu bar. After she breaks for lunch she will create a custom toolbar for the Issue25 graphical user interface.

Creating a Custom Toolbar

You can customize the standard Access toolbars, called **built-in toolbars**, by replacing standard toolbar buttons with ones you choose (or create from scratch). You can position, or **float**, a toolbar anywhere on the screen. In this way, toolbars are similar to the toolbox and the Palette. In any Access window you can also display two or more toolbars on the screen.

Instead of customizing a built-in toolbar, Elena designs a new custom toolbar for the Issue25 database graphical user interface. A **custom toolbar** is a toolbar you create for an application. Your toolbar can replace one or more of the built-in Access toolbars or can appear in addition to other built-in toolbars.

Elena names her custom toolbar tolSwitchboard. When the frmSwitchboard form is open, Elena wants the custom toolbar to replace the built-in Form View window toolbar and to be the only toolbar on the screen. In all other situations the built-in Access toolbars appear. Macros control when the custom toolbar appears and disappears. The tolSwitchboard toolbar will contain nine buttons that duplicate the functions of the switchboard command buttons and the custom menu bar in the following ways:

- Four buttons on the left will be grouped together, and each will open a different one of the four forms that make up the user interface.
- Four more buttons will in turn open the Reports dialog box, open the Queries dialog box, exit to the Issue25 database, and exit Access.
- A button at the far right will open the Access Help system.

As she adds buttons to the custom toolbar, Elena changes the images appearing on the button faces. Elena will then make final adjustments to the toolbar button positions.

Placing Buttons on a Custom Toolbar

Elena creates the custom toolbar by adding a new toolbar and naming it tolSwitchboard. She adds buttons to the toolbar, changing the button faces, and positions the buttons on the toolbar.

REFERENCE WINDOW

Creating a Custom Toolbar

- Click anywhere on any toolbar with the right mouse button, click Toolbars..., click the New... button, type the new toolbar name, and then press [Enter].
- Click the Customize... button and drag the appropriate buttons to the custom toolbar.
- Click a button on the custom toolbar with the right mouse button, click Choose Button Face..., click a button in the Choose Button Face dialog box, type a Description value, and then click the OK button.
- Position the buttons on the custom toolbar, position the toolbar on the screen, and click the Close button in the Customize Toolbars dialog box.

Elena's first step is to create a new toolbar with the name tolSwitchboard.

To create a new toolbar:

1. Launch Access and open the Issue25 database.
2. Using the right mouse button, click anywhere on any toolbar to open the shortcut menu, and then click **Toolbars...** in the shortcut menu. Access opens the Toolbars dialog box.
3. Click the **New... button**. Access opens the New Toolbar dialog box.

❹ Type **tolSwitchboard** in the Toolbar name text box and then press **[Enter]**. Access closes the New Toolbar dialog box, activates the Toolbars dialog box, and opens the custom toolbar. See Figure 3-13.

tolSwitchboard custom toolbar

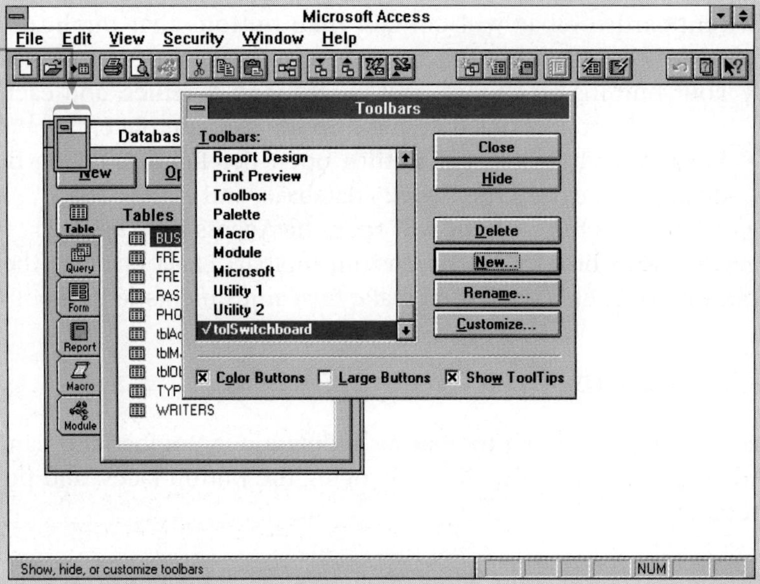

Figure 3-13
Displaying a new custom toolbar

❺ Click the **Customize... button**. Access opens the Customize Toolbars dialog box. See Figure 3-14.

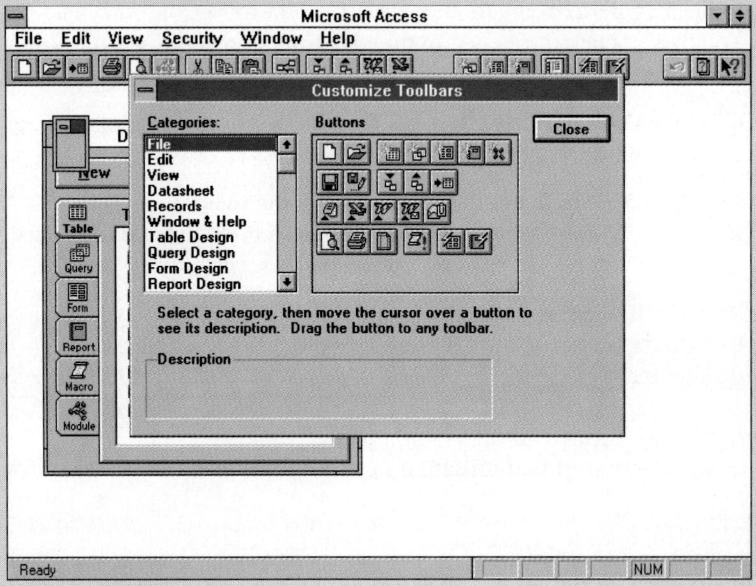

Figure 3-14
The Customize Toolbars dialog box

You add a button to a toolbar by dragging it from the Buttons list box in the Customize Toolbars dialog box to the toolbar. As you add buttons, Access increases the toolbar size to fit around the buttons. You can add buttons to a toolbar in any order. When you drag a new button and place it on top of an already positioned button, Access positions the new button to the left of the other button.

Elena positions the buttons on the new custom toolbar from right to left. The button farthest to the right is the Help button, and to find that button Elena selects the Window and Help category in the Customize Toolbars dialog box.

To place a button on the toolbar:

1. Click **Window & Help** in the Categories list box. Access displays buttons for the selected category in the Buttons list box.
2. Drag the **F1 Help button** from the Buttons list box to the center of the custom toolbar. Access adds it to the custom toolbar.

   TROUBLE? If you place the wrong button on the custom toolbar, drag the button off the custom toolbar to any screen location except another toolbar and then repeat the drag operation for the correct button.

Now Elena drags the second button (the one that will appear immediately to the left of the Help button) to the custom toolbar. Clicking the new button runs the mcrSwitchboard.mcrExitAccess macro, which closes the frmSwitchboard form and exits Access. Elena selects the All Macros category in the Customize Toolbars dialog box to display the choices she needs. After dragging her button choice, Elena takes a moment to stop the pointer over the new button and observes the button's ToolTip and status bar description. Then she changes the button face to a more interesting picture and changes the button's ToolTip caption and status bar description.

To add a toolbar button and change its button face:

1. Scroll the Categories list box and then click **All Macros**. Access displays the Issue25 database macros in the Objects list box.
2. Drag **mcrSwitchboard.mcrExitAccess** from the Objects list box to the custom toolbar, being sure you place the new button on top and slightly to the left of the Help button. When you release the mouse button, Access places the new button to the left of the existing button. Leave the pointer resting on the new button so that the ToolTip appears. See Figure 3-15.

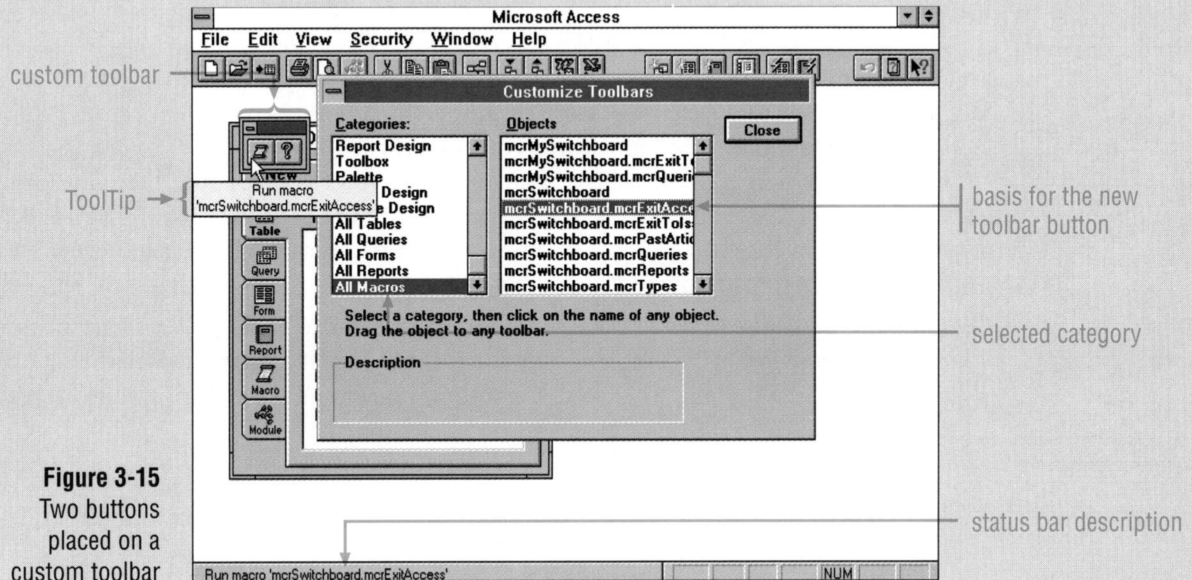

Figure 3-15
Two buttons placed on a custom toolbar

TROUBLE? If you drag the button too far off target, Access might create another custom toolbar. Simply drag the button from this newly created toolbar to its correct position on the tolSwitchboard toolbar and then click the empty toolbar's Control menu box to delete the extra custom toolbar.

3. Using the right mouse button, click the **new button** in the custom toolbar to open the shortcut menu and then click **Choose Button Face...** to open the Choose Button Face dialog box. See Figure 3-16.

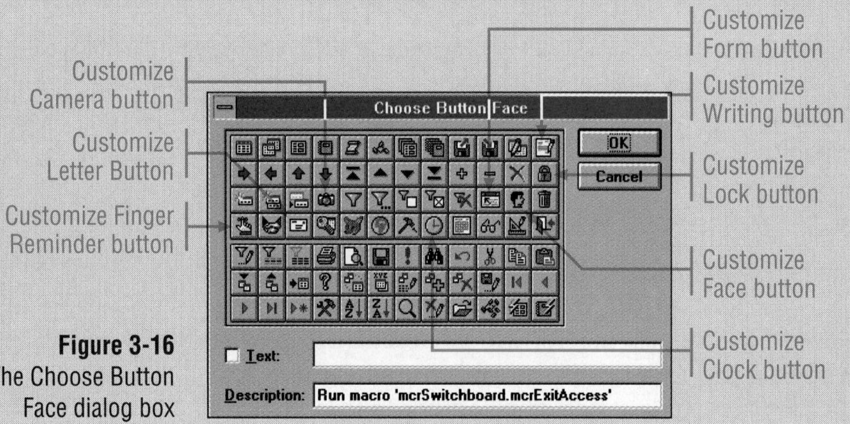

Figure 3-16
The Choose Button Face dialog box

4. Click the **Customize Lock button** in the Choose Button Face dialog box, highlight the entire value in the Description text box, type **Exit Access**, and then click the **OK button**. Access closes the Choose Button Face dialog box. Leave the pointer resting on the new button so that the ToolTip appears. Both the ToolTip caption and status bar description now read Exit Access.

   TROUBLE? The positions of the buttons in the Choose Button Face dialog box might differ from those shown in Figure 3-16. For example, Figure 3-16 shows the Customize Lock button at the far right in the second row but this button might appear elsewhere on your screen. Use Figure 3-16 to guide your selection of the correct button faces.

Elena adds the third button to the custom toolbar and then changes its button face and description. This button runs the mcrSwitchboard.mcrExitToIssue25 macro.

To add the third button to the custom toolbar:

1. Drag **mcrSwitchboard.mcrExitToIssue25** from the Objects list box to the custom toolbar, being sure you place the new button on top and slightly to the left of the last button added. When you release the mouse button, Access places the new button to the left of the existing buttons. Using the right mouse button, click the **new button** in the custom toolbar to open the shortcut menu and then click **Choose Button Face...** to open the Choose Button Face dialog box.

2. Click the **Customize Camera button**, highlight the entire value in the Description text box, type **Exit to Issue25**, and then click the **OK button**. Access closes the Choose Button Face dialog box. The ToolTip caption and status bar description now read Exit to Issue25.

The custom toolbar becomes partially blocked when another window gets the focus. To keep the custom toolbar visible, Elena can drag the custom toolbar to an open area at the bottom of the screen.

To reposition the custom toolbar:

1. Drag the custom toolbar **title bar** down near the bottom of the screen. See Figure 3-17.

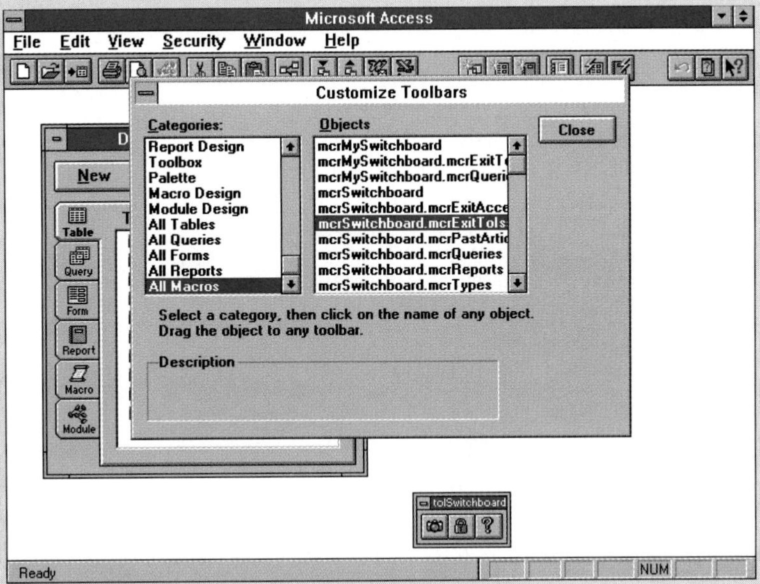

Figure 3-17 The repositioned custom toolbar

TROUBLE? As is always the case, do not be concerned if your screen is different from the screen shown in the figure. Your monitor's size and resolution are among the factors that account for legitimate differences in appearance among systems. For example, the custom toolbar's title might not appear on the title bar until you add another button.

Elena drags the remaining six buttons to the custom toolbar and then changes their button faces and descriptions. In right-to-left order, these buttons open the frmQueries form, the frmReports form, the WRITERS and PAST ARTICLES form, the WRITERS form, the TYPES form, and the PAST ARTICLES form.

To add the remaining buttons to the custom toolbar:

1. Click **All Forms** in the Categories list box. Access displays the Issue25 database forms in the Objects list box.
2. Drag **frmQueries** from the Objects list box to the custom toolbar, being sure you place the new button on top and slightly to the left of the last button added. When you release the mouse button, Access places the new button to the left of the existing buttons. Using the right mouse button, click the **new button** in the custom toolbar to open the shortcut menu and then click **Choose Button Face...** to open the Choose Button Face dialog box.
3. Click the **Customize Finger Reminder button** , highlight the entire value in the Description text box, type **Queries list**, and then click the **OK button**. Access closes the Choose Button Face dialog box. The ToolTip caption and status bar description now read Queries list.

4. Repeat Steps 2 and 3 for the five remaining buttons. Drag **frmReports**, **WRITERS and PAST ARTICLES form**, **WRITERS form**, **TYPES form**, and **PAST ARTICLES form** for the five forms in the Objects text box. Respectively, click the **Customize Writing button**, the **Customize Form button**, the **Customize Face button**, the **Customize Letter button**, and the **Customize Clock button**. In the Description text box, respectively enter **Reports list**, **WRITERS and PAST ARTICLES form**, **WRITERS form**, **TYPES form**, and **PAST ARTICLES form**. See Figure 3-18.

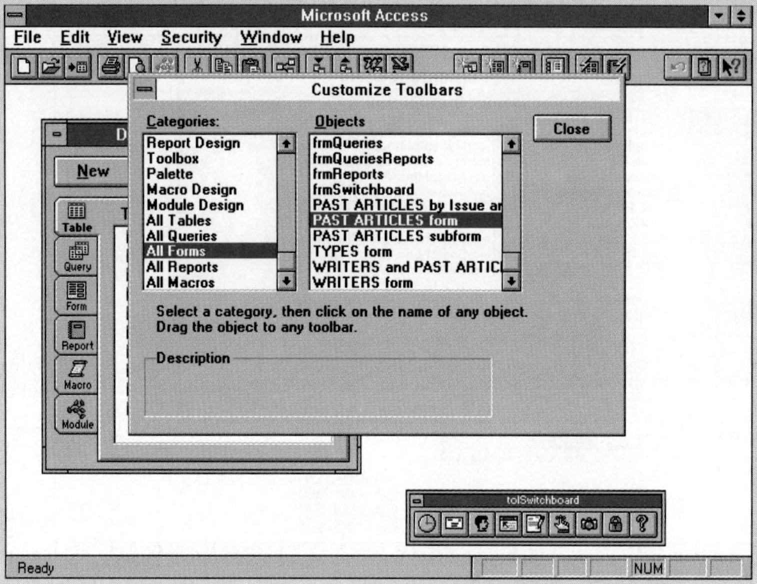

Figure 3-18
All custom-toolbar buttons added and modified

When you add a button to a toolbar, Access places the button so that it touches the button to its left. Elena further customizes the toolbar by grouping buttons and adding space between buttons and button groups. Holding down the Shift key while you drag a button to the right adds space between buttons and fixes the button's position on the toolbar.

Elena now improves the appearance of the custom toolbar by adding space between the five buttons on the right, leaving the four buttons on the left grouped together. She starts with the right button and works from right to left.

Elena first docks (that is, moves to a fixed location) the custom toolbar to the bottom of the screen, so that the toolbar is just above the status bar. This positioning expands the toolbar's width to full-screen size.

To move buttons on a custom toolbar:

1. Drag the custom toolbar **title bar** down so that its outline touches the status bar and then drag down slightly more. Access places the custom toolbar above the status bar and spreads the custom toolbar across the screen. See Figure 3-19.

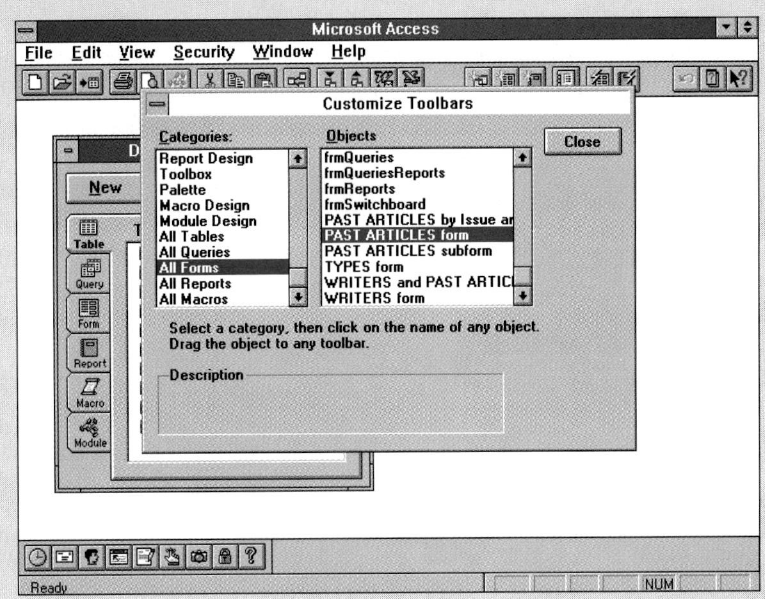

Figure 3-19 Custom toolbar docked at the bottom of the screen

TROUBLE? If the custom toolbar retains its original shape, you dragged it too little or too much. Drag the custom toolbar title bar back to its original position and then repeat Step 1.

❷ Now group the buttons by holding the **[Shift]** key and then dragging one button at a time to the right, starting with the Help button, so that your custom tool bar looks like Figure 3-20.

TROUBLE? Don't be concerned if your toolbar buttons aren't spaced indentically to Figure 3-20.

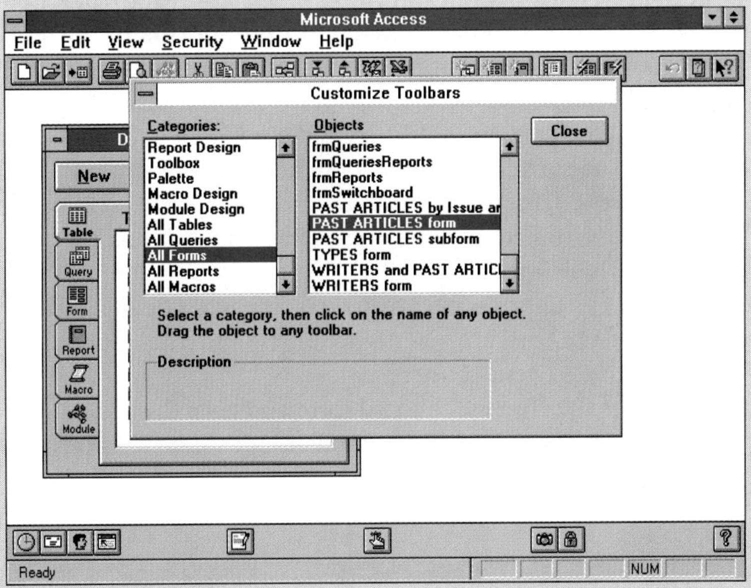

Figure 3-20 Buttons positioned on the custom toolbar

❸ Click the **Close button** in the Customize Toolbars dialog box. Access closes the dialog box and activates the Database window.

❹ Click anywhere in the custom toolbar's background but not on a toolbar button.

5. Drag the toolbar's background to the top of the screen, and position it just below the built-in toolbar. See Figure 3-21.

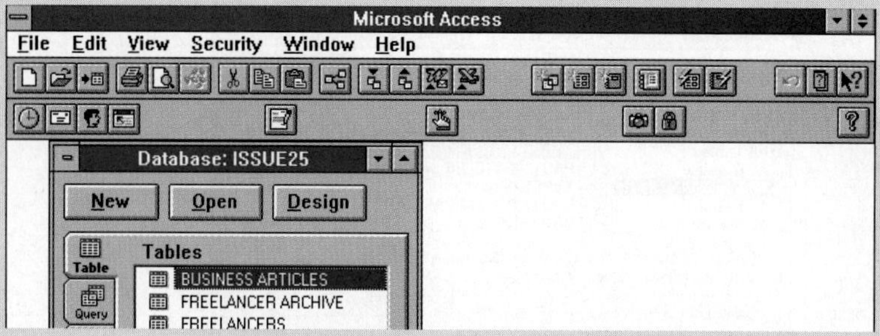

Figure 3-21
Custom toolbar positioned below the built-in toolbar

The custom toolbar is complete. Elena now tells Access when to show and hide the custom toolbar.

Using a Custom Toolbar with a Form

When a user opens the frmSwitchboard form, the custom toolbar should appear and the Form View toolbar should be hidden. To control the showing and hiding of these toolbars, Elena creates two macros and attaches them to the frmSwitchboard form's OnActivate and OnDeactivate event properties. When a form receives the focus and becomes the active window, the **Activate event** occurs and Access runs the macro attached to the **OnActivate event property**. Similarly, when a form loses the focus or is closed, the **Deactivate event** occurs and Access runs the macro attached to the **OnDeactivate event property**. Elena can add **ShowToolbar actions** to the attached macros that hide, show, or show where appropriate built-in and custom toolbars. To finish the custom toolbar for the Issue25 database, Elena performs four tasks:

- She hides the custom toolbar so that it no longer appears on the screen all the time.
- She adds two macros to the mcrSwitchboard macro group. The mcrActivate macro hides the Form View toolbar and shows the tolSwitchboard toolbar. The mcrDeactivate macro hides the tolSwitchboard toolbar and shows the Form View toolbar where appropriate.
- She attaches the two macros to the frmSwitchboard form—the mcrActivate macro with the OnActivate event property and the mcrDeactivate macro with the OnDeactivate event property.
- She opens the frmSwitchboard form and tests the tolSwitchboard toolbar.

Elena hides the tolSwitchboard toolbar, adds the two macros to the mcrSwitchboard macro group, and finally tests her work.

To hide a toolbar and add macros to a macro group:

1. Using the right mouse button, click the **custom toolbar** to open the shortcut menu, and then click **tolSwitchboard**. Access hides the tolSwitchboard toolbar.
2. Click the **Macro object button** to display the Macros list box, click **mcrSwitchboard** and then click the **Design command button**. Access opens the Macro window.

❸ Scroll the Macro window until several blank rows appear. Click the first blank row's **Macro Name text box**, type **mcrActivate**, press **[Tab]**, click the **down arrow button**, scroll the drop-down list box, click **ShowToolbar**, press **[Tab]**, and then type **Hide the Form View toolbar**. Next, click the **Toolbar Name text box**, click the **down arrow button**, and then click **Form View**. Notice the Show text box is set to No, so this action tells Access not to show the Form View toolbar. This completes the first of two actions for the mcrActivate macro.

❹ Click the next row's **Action text box**, click the **down arrow button**, scroll the drop-down list box, click **ShowToolbar**, press **[Tab]**, and then type **Show the tolSwitchboard toolbar**. Next, click the **Toolbar Name text box**, click the **down arrow button**, scroll the drop-down list box, click **tolSwitchboard**, click the **Show text box**, click the **down arrow button**, and then click **Yes**. This completes the second of two actions for the mcrActivate macro.

❺ Click the next row's **Macro Name text box**, type **mcrDeactivate**, press **[Tab]**, click the **down arrow button**, scroll the drop-down list box, click **ShowToolbar**, press **[Tab]**, and then type **Show the Form View toolbar where appropriate**. Next, click the **Toolbar Name text box**, click the **down arrow button**, click **Form View**, click the **Show text box**, click the **down arrow button**, and then click **Where Appropriate**. This completes the first of two actions for the mcrDeactivate macro.

❻ Click the next row's **Action text box**, click the **down arrow button**, scroll the drop-down list box, click **ShowToolbar**, press **[Tab]**, and then type **Hide the tolSwitchboard toolbar**. Next, click the **Toolbar Name text box**, click the **down arrow button**, scroll the drop-down list box, and then click **tolSwitchboard**. This completes the second of two actions for the mcrDeactivate macro. See Figure 3-22.

macro for the OnActivate event property

macro for the OnDeactivate event property

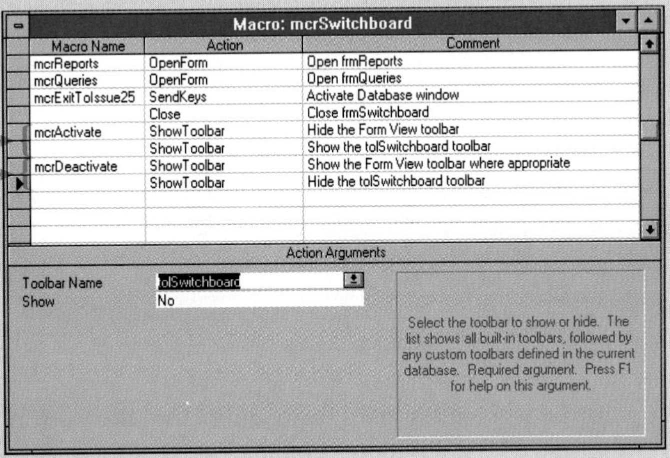

Figure 3-22
Macros to control the frmSwitchboard form's toolbars

❼ Click the toolbar **Save button** and then double-click the Macro window **Control menu box**. Access saves the macro group changes, closes the Macro window, and activates the Database window.

Elena attaches the new macros to the frmSwitchboard form's OnActivate and OnDeactivate event properties.

To attach macros to a form's event properties:

1. Click the **Form object button** in the Database window, click **frmSwitchboard**, and then click the **Design command button**. Access opens the Form Design window.
2. Click the toolbar **Properties button** to open the property sheet, scroll the property sheet, click the **OnActivate text box**, click the **down arrow button**, and then click **mcrSwitchboard.mcrActivate**. You might need to widen the property sheet temporarily to complete this step and the next step.
3. Click the **OnDeactivate text box**, click the **down arrow button**, and then click **mcrSwitchboard.mcrDeactivate**.
4. Click the toolbar **Save button** to save the form-design changes and then click to close the property sheet.
5. Double-click the Form Design window **Control menu box** to close the Form Design window and activate the Database window.
6. Double-click **frmSwitchboard** to open the form in the Form View window. See Figure 3-23.

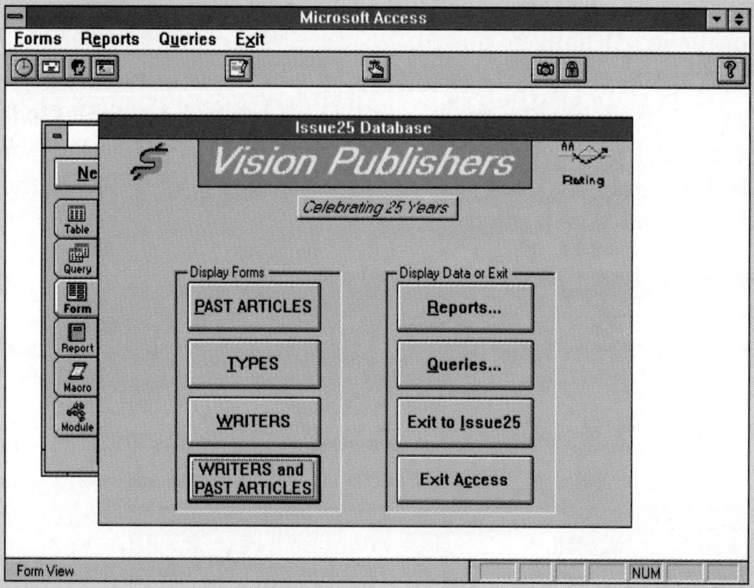

Figure 3-23 Displaying a custom toolbar with a form

Access opens the frmSwitchboard form and below the custom menu bar displays the custom toolbar in place of the built-in toolbar. The custom toolbar, therefore, is properly attached to the frmSwitchboard form.

Testing a Custom Toolbar

Elena tests each button on the custom toolbar. She stops the pointer on each button and verifies that its ToolTip and status bar description are correct. Then, starting with the left button and moving to the right, she clicks each button to test that the proper response occurs.

To test a custom toolbar:

1. Stop the pointer on each toolbar button and verify that the correct ToolTip and status bar description appear.
2. Click the toolbar **PAST ARTICLES form button** to open the PAST ARTICLES form. Double-click the Form View window **Control menu box** for the PAST ARTICLES form to close the form. Repeat this step for the three toolbar buttons to the right of this button.
3. Click the toolbar **Reports list button** to open the Reports dialog box. Then click the **Close button** to return to the frmSwitchboard form. Repeat this step for the **Queries list button**.
4. Click the toolbar **F1 Help button** to open the Microsoft Access 2.0 Help window and then double-click the Microsoft Access 2.0 Help **Control menu box** to close the window.
5. Click the toolbar **Exit to Issue25 button**. Access closes the form and activates the Database window.
6. Click the **Open command button** to open the frmSwitchboard form in the Form View window.
7. Click the toolbar **Exit Access button**. Access closes all windows and exits.

Elena has completed the custom toolbar, and the Issue25 graphical user interface is nearing completion. One of the tasks remaining for the user interface is the creation of an AutoExec macro.

Creating an AutoExec Macro

An **AutoExec macro** is a special macro that automatically runs when you open an Access database. If you want to bypass the AutoExec macro, you can hold down the Shift key when you open the database. Elena wants users to be able to open the Issue25 database and have her switchboard appear automatically so they don't have to use the Form object list to access it.

She creates an AutoExec macro that hides the Database window and opens the frmSwitchboard form. To hide the Database window, Elena's macro executes the **DoMenuItem** action, which executes a command on an Access menu, to select the Hide command on the Window menu. Elena's AutoExec macro also contains the OpenForm action to open the frmSwitchboard form. (What happens when a user clicks the Exit to Issue25 button? When a user clicks this button, Access runs the mcrExitToIssue25 macro. This macro closes the frmSwitchboard form and activates the Database window.)

To create an AutoExec macro:

1. Launch Access and then open the Issue25 database on your Student Disk.
2. Click the **Macro object button** and then click the **New command button** to open the Macro window.
3. Click the **down arrow button**, click **DoMenuItem** in the drop-down list box, press **[Tab]**, type **Hide the Database window**, click the **Menu Bar text box**, click the **down arrow button**, click **Database**, click the **Menu Name text box**, click the **down arrow button**, click **Window**, click the **Command text box**, click the **down arrow button**, and then click **Hide**. This completes the first macro for the AutoExec macro.

4. Click the second row's **Action text box**, click the **down arrow button**, scroll the drop-down list box, click **OpenForm**, press **[Tab]**, type **Open frmSwitchboard**, click the **Form Name text box**, click the **down arrow button**, and then click **frmSwitchboard**. This completes the AutoExec macro.
5. Click the toolbar **Save button**, type **AutoExec** in the Macro Name text box of the Save As dialog box, and then press **[Enter]**. See Figure 3-24.

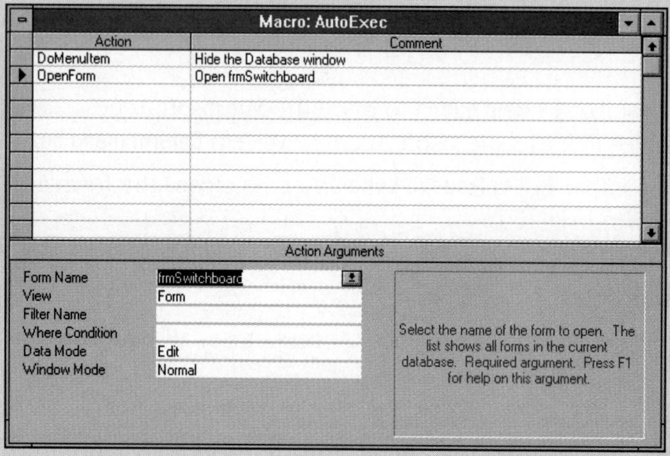

Figure 3-24
The AutoExec macro

6. Double-click the Macro window **Control menu box**. Access activates the Database window.

Elena tests the AutoExec macro by closing and then opening the Issue25 database.

To test an AutoExec macro:

1. Double-click the Database window **Control menu box** to close the Issue25 database.
2. Click **File** and then click **1 A:\ISSUE25.MDB** to open the Issue25 database. See Figure 3-25.

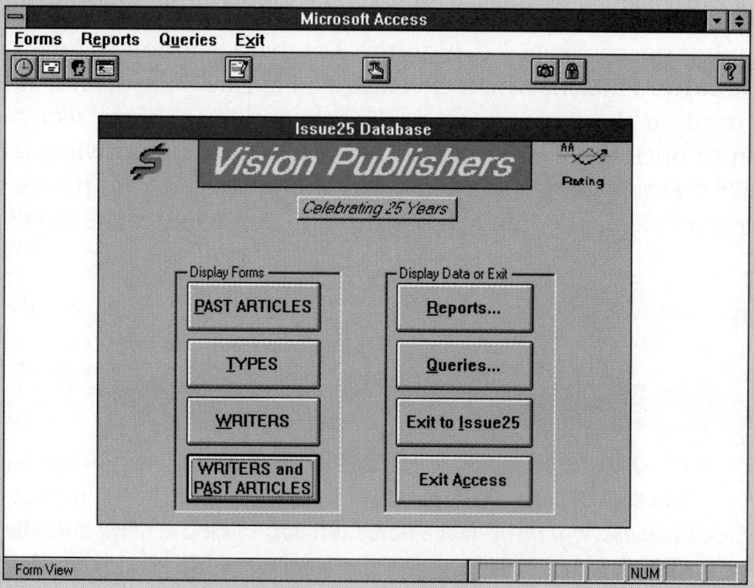

Figure 3-25
The Issue25 graphical user interface

Access opens the Issue25 database and automatically runs the AutoExec macro to hide the Database window and to display the frmSwitchboard form. Elena's test shows that the AutoExec macro runs correctly.

Elena's development of the graphical user interface for the Issue25 database is nearly complete. Her remaining tasks are to finish the Reports and Queries dialog boxes. These dialog boxes have list boxes containing the available reports and queries, respectively. To allow a user to select a report or query and then ask Access to take the next action, Elena cannot use macros. Instead she must create Access Basic procedures.

Before she can start planning the Access Basic procedures, however, managing editor Judith Rossi calls to set up a meeting with Elena. Deciding that the meeting is more important, Elena agrees to meet immediately and defers her Access Basic work until the next day.

To exit Access:

1. Click the **Exit Access button** to close the switchboard and exit Access.

■ ■ ■

Elena exits Access and then leaves for the meeting in Judith's office.

Questions

1. What is the difference between a menu bar macro and a menu macro group?
2. What is a global custom menu bar?
3. When you use the Menu Builder, how do you distinguish between a menu name and a menu-item name?
4. What three Access "tools" can you float anywhere on the screen?
5. When does the Deactivate event occur?
6. What are the three options for the ShowToolbar action?
7. What is an AutoExec macro?

Tutorial Assignments

Launch Access and open the Issue25 database on your Student Disk.

1. For the frmQueriesReports form, which you created in the previous tutorial, design and create a custom menu bar and a custom toolbar that have the following characteristics.
   a. Enter the name menQueriesReports for the custom menu bar and the name tolQueriesReports for the custom toolbar.
   b. Display the custom menu bar and the custom toolbar only when the frmQueriesReports form has the focus.
   c. Add two menus to the custom menu bar: one menu named QueriesAndReports and the other named Exit. Place enough menu-item names on the QueriesAndReports menu to open each of the nine queries and reports from the tblObjectNames table in the Print Preview window. Allow both mouse and keyboard selection. Place two menu items on the Exit menu: one menu item named Close to close the form and activate the Database window, and the other menu item named Exit Access to close the form and exit Access. Make Q the hot key for the QueriesAndReports menu and E the hot key for the Exit menu.

   d. Place enough buttons on the custom toolbar to perform the same operations performed on the custom menu bar.
2. Test the custom menu bar and the custom toolbar.

Case Problems

1. Walkton Daily Press Carriers

Launch Access and open the Press database on your Student Disk.

1. For the frmSwitchboard form, which you created in the previous tutorial, design and create a custom menu bar and a custom toolbar that have the following characteristics.
   a. Enter the name menSwitchboard for the custom menu bar and the name tolSwitchboard for the custom toolbar.
   b. Display the custom menu bar and the custom toolbar only when the frmSwitchboard form has the focus.
   c. Add two menus to the custom menu bar: one menu named OpenObjects and the other named Exit. Place three menu items on the OpenObjects menu to open the "BILLINGS" table in Datasheet View, the "CARRIERS form" form in Form View, and the "CARRIERS sorted by Name, Route ID" query in Datasheet View. Allow both mouse and keyboard selection. Place two menu items on the Exit menu: one menu item named Close to close the form and activate the Database window, and the other menu item named Exit Access to close the form and exit Access. Make O the hot key for the Open Objects menu and E the hot key for the Exit menu.
   d. Place enough buttons on the custom toolbar to perform the same operations performed on the custom menu bar.
2. Add an AutoExec macro to hide the Database window and open the frmSwitchboard form whenever you open the Press database.
3. Test the custom menu bar, the custom toolbar, and the AutoExec macro.

2. Lopez Used Cars

Launch Access and open the Usedcars database on your Student Disk.

1. For the frmSwitchboard form, which you created in the previous tutorial, design and create a custom menu bar and a custom toolbar that have the following characteristics.
   a. Enter the name menSwitchboard for the custom menu bar and the name tolSwitchboard for the custom toolbar.
   b. Display the custom menu bar and the custom toolbar only when the frmSwitchboard form has the focus.
   c. Add two menus to the custom menu bar: one menu named OpenObjects and the other named Exit. Place four menu items on the OpenObjects menu to open the "LOCATIONS" table in Datasheet View, the "USED CARS form" form in Form View, the "USED CARS by Manufacturer, Model" query in Datasheet View, and the "USED CARS by Year Report" report in Print Preview. Allow both mouse and keyboard selection. Place two menu items on the Exit menu: one menu item named Close to close the form and activate the Database window, and one menu item named Exit Access to close the form and exit Access. Make O the hot key for the Open Objects menu and E the hot key for the Exit menu.
   d. Place enough buttons on the custom toolbar to perform the same operations performed on the custom menu bar.
2. Add an AutoExec macro to hide the Database window and open the frmSwitchboard form whenever you open the Usedcars database.
3. Test the custom menu bar, the custom toolbar, and the AutoExec macro.

3. Tophill University Student Employment

Launch Access and open the Parttime database on your Student Disk.

1. For the frmSwitchboard form, which you created in the previous tutorial, design and create a custom menu bar and a custom toolbar that have the following characteristics.
   a. Enter the name menSwitchboard for the custom menu bar and the name tolSwitchboard for the custom toolbar.
   b. Display the custom menu bar and the custom toolbar only when the frmSwitchboard form has the focus.
   c. Add two menus to the custom menu bar: one menu named OpenObjects and the other named Exit. Place four menu items on the OpenObjects menu to open the "EMPLOYERS" table in Datasheet View, the "EMPLOYERS and JOBS form" form in Form View, the "JOBS sorted by Employer, Job Title" query in Datasheet View, and the "JOBS Report" report in Print Preview. Allow both mouse and keyboard selection. Place two menu items on the Exit menu: one menu item named Close to close the form and activate the Database window, and one menu item named Exit Access to close the form and exit Access. Make O the hot key for the Open Objects menu and E the hot key for the Exit menu.
   d. Place enough buttons on the custom toolbar to perform the same operations performed on the custom menu bar.
2. Add an AutoExec macro to hide the Database window and open the frmSwitchboard form whenever you open the Parttime database.
3. Test the custom menu bar, the custom toolbar, and the AutoExec macro.

4. Rexville Business Licenses

Launch Access and open the Buslic database on your Student Disk.

1. For the frmSwitchboard form, which you created in the previous tutorial, design and create a custom menu bar and a custom toolbar that have the following characteristics.
   a. Enter the name menSwitchboard for the custom menu bar and the name tolSwitchboard for the custom toolbar.
   b. Display the custom menu bar and the custom toolbar only when the frmSwitchboard form has the focus.
   c. Add two menus to the custom menu bar: one menu named OpenObjects and the other named Exit. Place four menu items on the OpenObjects menu to open the "LICENSES" table, the "BUSINESSES form" form, the "BUSINESSES sorted by License Type, Business Name" query, and the "BUSINESSES Report" report. Allow both mouse and keyboard selection. Place two menu items on the Exit menu: one menu item named Close to close the form and activate the Database window, and one menu item named Exit Access to close the form and exit Access. Make O the hot key for the Open Objects menu and E the hot key for the Exit menu.
   d. Place enough buttons on the custom toolbar to perform the same operations performed on the custom menu bar.
2. Add an AutoExec macro to hide the Database window and open the frmSwitchboard form whenever you open the Buslic database.
3. Test the custom menu bar, the custom toolbar, and the AutoExec macro.

TUTORIAL 4

Access Basic

Using Access Basic with the Issue25 Database

OBJECTIVES

In this tutorial you will:

- Learn about Access Basic functions, sub procedures, and modules
- Create functions in a global module
- Create event procedures
- Compile and test functions, sub procedures, and event procedures
- Hide text and change colors during execution

CASE **Vision Publishers** Elena Sanchez is ready to finish her graphical user interface for the Issue25 database. She uses Access Basic to control the events in her two new dialog boxes, the frmReports and frmQueries forms (you'll work on the frmReports dialog box in this tutorial and the frmQueries dialog box in the Tutorial Assignments at the end of the tutorial). Although she learned the fundamentals of Access Basic at her Access seminar, this is the first time Elena uses Access Basic on the job at Vision Publishers. To refresh her memory about Access Basic before she works on the two dialog boxes, Elena practices some of the Access Basic she learned at the seminar. First, she adds two functions to help with the capitalization of data entered in forms. Then, she adds a message in color that appears only when freelancers are displayed in the WRITERS form.

Access Basic

Access Basic is Access's programming language. It is similar to, but not the same as, the Microsoft Visual Basic programming language. For example, both languages have the same instructions, which are called **statements** or **code**, to test conditions, to assign values to fields and controls, and to repeat one or more statements multiple times. Access Basic has statements, however, to manipulate Access databases that Visual Basic does not have.

The process of writing Access Basic statements is called **coding**. You write Access Basic statements to respond to events that occur with the objects in a database. A language such as Access Basic is therefore called both an **event-driven language** and an **object-oriented language**. Experience with macros, which are also event driven and object oriented, will help ease your learning of Access Basic. You can do almost anything with Access Basic that you can do with macros, but Access Basic allows you to do much more than you can with macros. For example, with Access Basic you can create your own functions to perform special calculations and you can change an object's properties dynamically, based on predefined conditions.

Procedures

When you work with Access Basic, you code a group of statements in Design view and attach the group to the event property of an object. Access then executes, or **calls**, these statements every time the event occurs for that object. Each group of statements is called a **procedure**. The two types of procedures are functions and sub procedures, or subroutines.

- A **function** is a procedure that performs operations, returns a value, can accept arguments, and can be used in expressions (An expression is a calculation resulting in a single value). For example, you may have used two built-in functions that come with Access (Sum and Avg) to calculate a sum and an average. Elena plans to create a function named CapOnlyFirst, which will accept a field value as an argument, capitalize the first character of the field value, change all other characters to lowercase, and return the changed field value. Elena can use the CapOnlyFirst function in an expression on a form or report.
- A **sub procedure**, or **subroutine**, performs operations and can accept arguments but does not return a value and cannot be used in expressions. Elena uses a sub procedure that adds a message on the WRITERS form that appears only when freelancers are displayed.

Modules

You store a group of related procedures together in a **module**. Figure 4-1 shows the structure of a typical module.

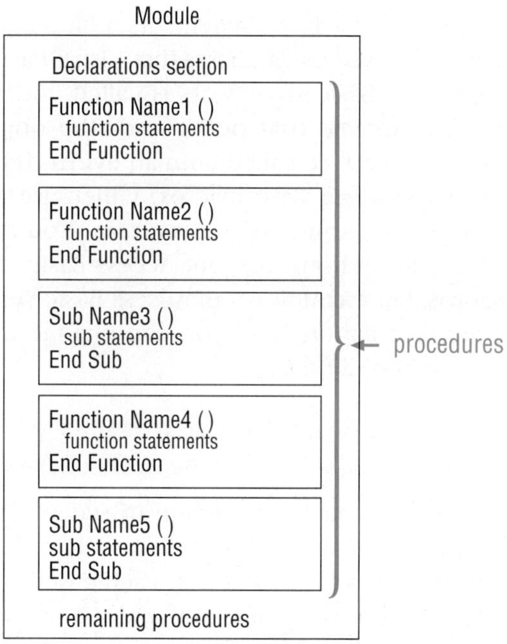

Figure 4-1
An Access Basic module outline and its procedures

Each module starts with a **Declarations section**, which contains statements that apply to all procedures in the module. One or more procedures, which follow the Declarations section, comprise the rest of the module. A module is either global or it is contained in a form or report.

- A **global module** is a separate database object that is stored in memory with other database objects when you open the database. You can use the procedures in global modules from anywhere in a database, even from procedures in other modules, or from more than one place.
- Access automatically creates a form module for each form and a report module for each report. Also called **Code Behind Forms (CBF)** and **Code Behind Reports (CBR)**, each form or report module contains event procedures. An **event procedure** is a procedure you code to respond to an event that occurs for that specific form or report. Event procedures are local, or private, and cannot be used outside the form or report. Unlike global modules, a CBF or CBR module is stored with its form or report and is loaded into memory only when you open the form or report.

Using Help and Sample Applications

The most difficult part of becoming proficient with Access is learning how to code effective Access Basic procedures. Access Basic is a powerful programming language containing hundreds of statements and built-in functions, along with hundreds of event properties, object properties, and methods. Deciding when and how to use each Access Basic feature can be intimidating to programming novices and even experts. Fortunately, you can perform many fundamental operations without using Access Basic by setting control properties and by using macros.

When you do need to use Access Basic, take advantage of the excellent Access Help system as a reference tool. Figure 4-2 lists several Help topics that are particularly useful when you work with Access Basic. You can also find help for every Access Basic statement, function, and property; most of these topics have an Example jump that displays sample Access Basic code. If you find sample code similar to what you need, simply copy the statements to the Windows Clipboard, paste them into a procedure in your own database, and modify the statements to work for your special case.

Search Entry	Help Topic
Access Basic	Language and Technical Reference
	Programming Topics
	Running Access Basic Code
event properties	Events and Event Properties Reference

Figure 4-2
Important Help Topics for Access Basic

Another source for sample Access Basic code is the set of sample databases that comes with Access. Three databases appear in the sampapps subdirectory under the access directory: the Northwind Traders database (nwind.mdb), the Orders Application database (orders.mdb), and the Solutions Application database (solution.mdb). Each database has a variety of simple and complex examples of Access Basic procedures. You can view the effects of these procedures by using them in the sample databases. Microsoft encourages you to copy and use the proven procedures in the sample databases as a way to learn Access Basic more quickly.

Creating Functions in a Global Module

Elena decides to practice with one of the procedures she coded at her seminar, a function named CapOnlyFirst, which capitalizes the first character of a field value and changes all other characters to lowercase. In other words, if a user types the words "social Justice," the CapOnlyFirst function corrects the entry to "Social justice." Elena thinks this would be a helpful function to use in the Description field on the TYPES form. The data entry staff might not always be consistent about capitalizing entries in that field, and having this function running in the background will ensure consistency.

Elena can program code that runs whenever a user enters or changes a value in the Description field. Whenever a user enters or changes a field value in a control on a form, Access automatically triggers the **AfterUpdate event**, which by default simply accepts the new or changed entry. However, Elena can set the Description field's AfterUpdate event property to [Event Procedure], and she can then code an event procedure to call the CapOnlyFirst function.

Because Elena might use the function in several other forms and reports in the Issue25 database, she places the procedure in a new global module, which she names basIssue25Functions. This global module name conforms to Elena's naming convention; bas is the tag for an Access Basic module, and Issue25Functions is the base name describing the module's contents.

REFERENCE WINDOW

Creating a New Global Module

- In the Database window, click the Module object button to open the Modules list box.
- Click the New command button. Access opens the Module window, in which you create a new module.

Elena creates the new global module.

To create a new global module:

1. Launch Access, open the Issue25 database on your Student Disk, and then click the switchboard's **Exit to Issue25 button**.
2. Click the **Module object button** and then click the **New command button**. Access opens the Module window. See Figure 4-3.

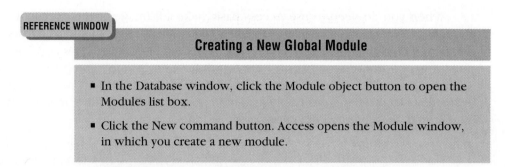

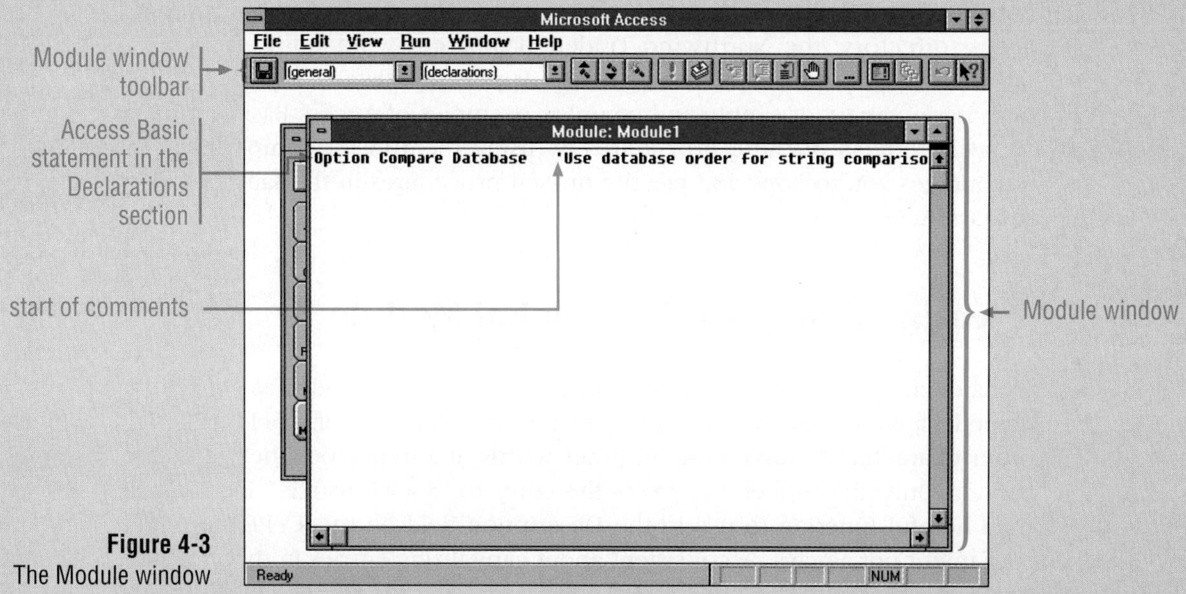

Figure 4-3
The Module window

TROUBLE? If the Module window toolbar is missing from your screen, click View, click Toolbars..., scroll the Toolbars list box, click Module, click Reset, click the OK button, and then click the Close button.

You use the **Module window** to create and modify Access Basic procedures. Access automatically includes the Option Compare statement in the Declarations section of a new module, followed by an argument specifying the technique Access uses when executing Option Compare (in Figure 4-3, the word "Database"). The **Option Compare statement** designates the technique Access uses to compare and sort text data. You use the default argument **Database** for this statement, so that Access compares and sorts letters in normal alphabetical order.

The final part of the Option Compare statement is a short comment describing the purpose of the statement. In Figure 4-3, this comment begins with the word "Use." You can include comments to explain an Access Basic statement on the same line as the statement, using a single quote (') to identify the start of the comments.

Creating a Function

Each function begins with a **Function statement** and ends with an **End Function statement**. Elena enters "Function CapOnlyFirst (FValue)" on the line below the Option Compare statement. CapOnlyFirst is the **function name** and FValue is an argument name. In other words, the value passed to the function is assigned to the argument named FValue. All Access Basic names you create must conform to the following rules:

- They must begin with a letter.
- They cannot exceed 40 characters.
- They must use letters, numbers, and the underscore character; other characters and spaces cannot be used.
- They cannot contain **reserved words**, such as Function, Sub, and Option, that the language uses for its regular statements.

Elena begins entering the function.

To start a new function:

❶ With the insertion point on the line below the Option Compare statement, type **Function CapOnlyFirst (FValue)** and then press **[Enter]**. Access places the statement at the top of the Module window, adds the End Function statement, and places the insertion point at the beginning of a blank line between the two statements. See Figure 4-4.

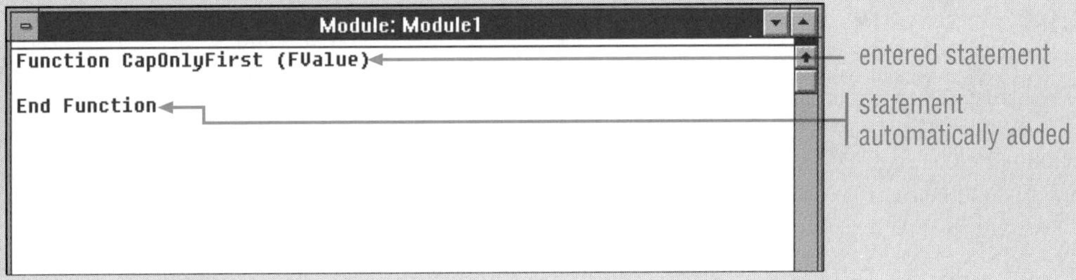

Figure 4-4
Starting a new function

Elena's CapOnlyFirst function consists of a single executable statement, called an assignment statement, that she places between the Function and End Function statements. An **assignment statement** assigns the value of an expression to a memory location. Because the content of the memory location varies depending on the values used in the expression, the memory location is called a **variable**. Associated with a variable is its **variable name**, which must follow the Access Basic naming rules. The general format of an assignment statement is "variable name = expression." Elena needs to enter the following assignment statement: "CapOnlyFirst = UCase(Left(FValue, 1)) & LCase(Mid(FValue, 2))." CapOnlyFirst is the variable name and "UCase(Left(FValue, 1)) & LCase(Mid(FValue, 2))" is the expression. The expression in Elena's assignment statement uses four built-in Access functions (UCase, Left, LCase, and Mid) and the **concatenation operator** (&), which concatenates or combines two strings. Figure 4-5 describes the value returned by each function.

Function	Returned Value
UCase(expression)	An expression converted to uppercase letters
Left(expression, n)	The leftmost *n* characters of expression
LCase(expression)	An expression converted to lowercase letters
Mid(expression, start, [length])	Portion of an expression from character number *start*, for *length*, or to the end of the expression, if *length* is omitted

Figure 4-5
The built-in functions in Elena's assignment statement

Figure 4-6 shows the order in which Access evaluates the functions and shows the values each function returns, using as an example the parameter value "aDvErTiSiNg" (the parameter value appears in the expression as the argument "FValue;" this is what the expression is evaluating). After all the functions to the right of the equals symbol are executed, the & operator combines the two strings and produces Advertising, which Access assigns as a value to CapOnlyFirst.

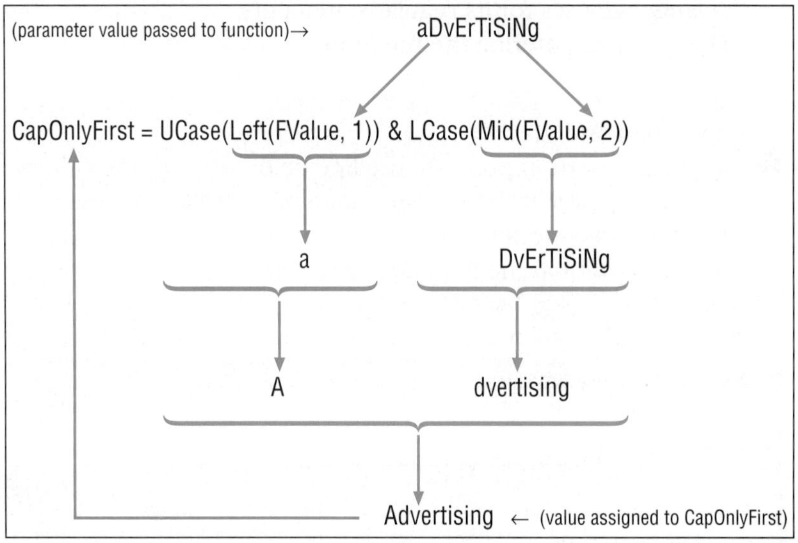

Figure 4-6
Evaluation of Elena's assignment statement

Before entering the assignment statement, Elena adds two lines of comments to explain the procedure's purpose. You use the **Rem statement**, or **single quote (')**, to signify that comments follow on that line. Also, Elena indents these three lines; indenting statements is a common practice to make code easier to read.

To add comments and statements to a function:

1. Press **[Tab]**, type **'Capitalize only the first letter of a field value;**, press **[Enter]**, type **'Change to lowercase all other letters.**, and then press **[Enter]**. After entering these two comment lines, you can now enter the assignment statement.
2. Type **CapOnlyFirst = UCase(Left(FValue, 1)) & LCase(Mid(FValue, 2))**. See Figure 4-7. Access scans each statement for errors when you press [Enter] or change the focus to another statement. Because the function is complete and Elena wants Access to scan for errors, she moves the insertion point to another line.

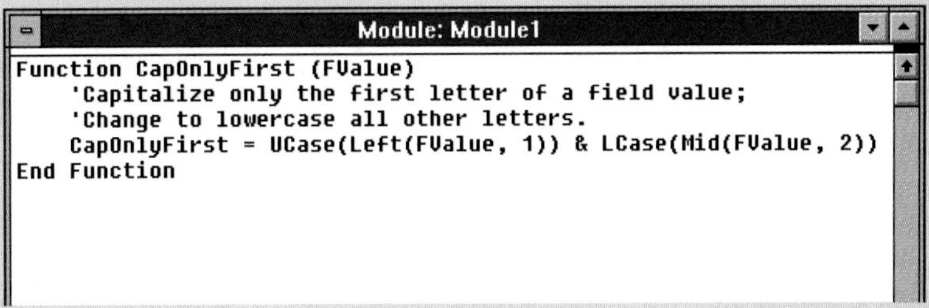

Module: Module1
Function CapOnlyFirst (FValue)
'Capitalize only the first letter of a field value;
'Change to lowercase all other letters.
CapOnlyFirst = UCase(Left(FValue, 1)) & LCase(Mid(FValue, 2))
End Function

Figure 4-7
A completed function

❸ Press [↓] to move the insertion point to the next line. Because Access finds no errors, the insertion point continues to blink in the last line.

TROUBLE? If Access finds an error in the assignment statement, it highlights the error and opens a dialog box with a message describing the nature of the error. Click the OK button and change the highlighted error by comparing each character you entered against what you should have entered. Then press [Down Arrow] so that Access again scans the statement for errors.

Elena has finished entering the function, so she saves it before continuing with her work.

Saving a Module

When you click the toolbar Save button from the Module window, Access saves the module and its procedures. If you are entering a long procedure, periodically save your work.

Elena saves the module with the name basIssue25Functions.

To save a module:

❶ Click the toolbar **Save button**, type **basIssue25Functions** in the Module Name text box, and then press **[Enter]**. Access saves the module and places the new module name in the title bar.

Before making the changes to the TYPE form so that the CapOnlyFirst function automatically acts on every entry in the Description field, Elena tests the function using the Immediate window.

Testing a Procedure in the Immediate Window

Even the simplest procedure can have errors. Be sure to test each procedure thoroughly to ensure it does exactly what you expect it to do in all situations. When working in the Module window, use the **Immediate window** to test Access Basic procedures. Clicking the toolbar Immediate Window button opens the Immediate window on top of the Module window. In the Immediate window, you can enter different parameter values to test the procedure you just entered. To test a procedure, use the **Print statement**, or **question mark (?)**, followed by the procedure name and the parameter value you want to test in parentheses. For example, to test the CapOnlyFirst function in the Immediate window on the word "advertising," type "?CapOnlyFirst ("advertising")" and press [Enter]. Access executes the function and prints the value returned by the function (you expect it to return "Advertising"). Note that you enclose a **string** of characters, with double quotes (").

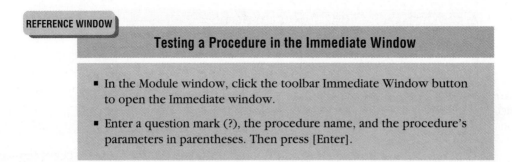

REFERENCE WINDOW

Testing a Procedure in the Immediate Window

- In the Module window, click the toolbar Immediate Window button to open the Immediate window.
- Enter a question mark (?), the procedure name, and the procedure's parameters in parentheses. Then press [Enter].

Elena uses the Immediate window to test the CapOnlyFirst function.

To test a function in the Immediate window:

1. Click the toolbar **Immediate Window button**. Access opens the Immediate window on top of the Module window and places the insertion point inside the window.
2. Type **?CapOnlyFirst("advertising")** and press **[Enter]**. Access executes the function and prints the function result, Advertising, on the next line. See Figure 4-8.

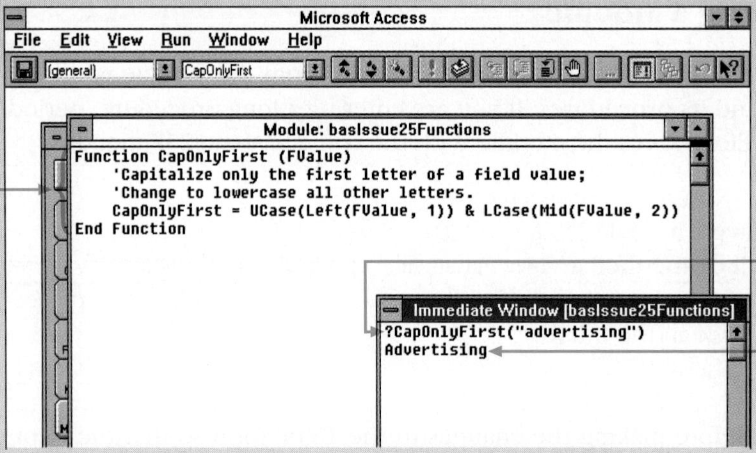
Microsoft Access
File Edit View Run Window Help
(general)
CapOnlyFirst
Module: basIssue25Functions
Function CapOnlyFirst (FValue)
'Capitalize only the first letter of a field value;
'Change to lowercase all other letters.
CapOnlyFirst = UCase(Left(FValue, 1)) & LCase(Mid(FValue, 2))
End Function
Immediate Window [basIssue25Functions]
?CapOnlyFirst("advertising")
Advertising
function being executed
function call statement
function execution results

Figure 4-8
A function executed in the Immediate window

To test the CapOnlyFirst function further, Elena enters several other parameter values. She could retype the entire statement each time. Instead, she highlights the parameter value, types the next parameter value, and presses [Enter].

To continue testing a function in the Immediate window:

1. Highlight **advertising** in the first line of the Immediate window; this line now is ?CapOnlyFirst("advertising"). Type **aDVERTISING** and then press **[Enter]**. Access executes the function and prints the function result, Advertising, on the next line.
2. Repeat Step 1 two more times, using **ADVERTISING** and then **stock MARket** as parameter values. Access prints the correct values, Advertising and Stock market.
3. Click the toolbar **Immediate Window button** and then double-click the Module window **Control menu box** to return to the Database window.

Elena's initial testing of the CapOnlyFirst function is successful. Next she modifies the TYPES form to call the CapOnlyFirst function for the Description field.

Creating an Event Procedure

Access automatically creates a form module (called Code Behind Forms or CBF) for each form and a report module (called Code Behind Reports or CBR) for each report. When you add a procedure to one of these modules, Access stores the procedure with the form or report and treats the procedure as a local procedure that can be used with only that form or report. Each of these procedures is called an event procedure; Access runs a procedure when a specific event occurs.

For the TYPES form, Elena codes an event procedure to call the CapOnlyFirst function for the Description field's AfterUpdate event. Whenever a user enters or changes a Description field value, the AfterUpdate event occurs and Access runs Elena's event procedure.

What exactly happens when Access calls a procedure? Figure 4-9 shows the following information for the CapOnlyFirst procedure:

- The event procedure statement that calls the CapOnlyFirst procedure
- The CapOnlyFirst function in the basIssue25Functions global module
- The interaction between the **calling statement** and the function statements as a series of steps

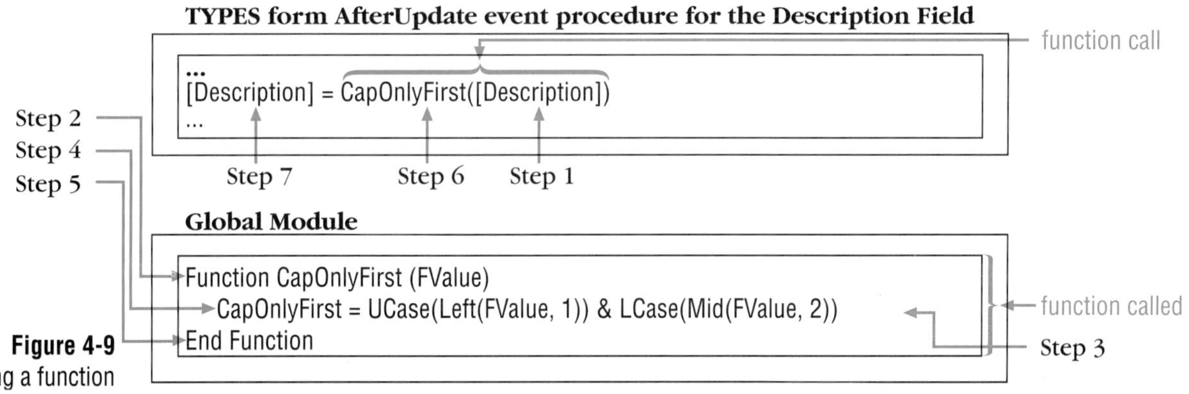

Figure 4-9
Executing a function

The steps in Figure 4-9 are numbered in the order in which they occur as Access processes the statement and the function. Access goes through the following steps:

- Step 1 Call to function CapOnlyFirst passes the value of the argument [Description]
- Step 2 Function CapOnlyFirst starts and argument FValue receives the value of [Description]
- Step 3 First character of FValue changed to uppercase; all remaining characters changed to lowercase
- Step 4 Value of CapOnlyFirst set equal to the results of Step 3
- Step 5 Function CapOnlyFirst ends
- Step 6 Value of CapOnlyFirst returned to the point of the call to the function
- Step 7 Value of [Description] set equal to the returned value of CapOnlyFirst

Although it looks complicated, the general function process is simple—a statement contains a function call; when the statement is executed, Access performs the function call, executes the function called, returns a single value back to the original statement, and completes that statement's execution. Study the steps in Figure 4-9 and trace their placement until you understand the complete process.

Designing an Event Procedure

Elena plans her changes to the TYPES form to use the CapOnlyFirst function for the Description field. Whenever a user enters a new value or modifies an existing value in the Description field on the TYPES form, Elena wants Access to execute the CapOnlyFirst function. Therefore, she makes the following changes to the TYPES form.

- After a user changes a Description field value, the AfterUpdate event automatically occurs. Elena can set the AfterUpdate event property to run a macro, call a built-in Access function, or execute an event procedure. Because Elena wants to call her user-defined function from within the event procedure, she sets the AfterUpdate event property to [Event Procedure].
- All event procedures are sub procedures. Access automatically adds the Sub and End Sub statements to an event procedure. All Elena needs to do is place the statements between the Sub and End Sub statements. Figure 4-10 shows her design for the event procedure. The following text describes the parts of the procedure.

If statement — sub procedure statement — comments

```
Sub Description_AfterUpdate ( )
   'Capitalize the first letter of the
   'Description field value
   If Not IsNull([Description]) Then
      [Description] = CapOnlyFirst([Description])
   End If
End Sub
```

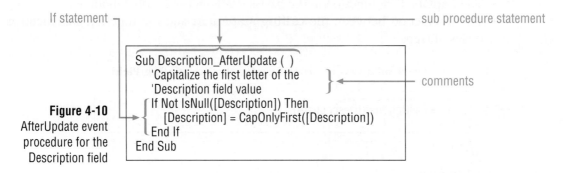

Figure 4-10
AfterUpdate event procedure for the Description field

Access names each event procedure in a standard way: name of the control, an underscore (_), and the event name. No parameters are passed to an event procedure, so Access places nothing in the parentheses following the name of the sub procedure. If the name of the control contains spaces, Access substitutes underscores for the spaces in the event procedure name.

Elena adds two lines of comments to explain what the event procedure does.

A user might delete an existing Description field value, so that it contains no value, or becomes null. In this case, calling the function accomplishes nothing. Elena designs the procedure code to call the CapOnlyFirst function only when a user changes the Description field to a nonnull value. Elena uses the If statement to screen out the null values. In its simplest form, an **If statement** executes one of two groups of statements based on a condition, similar to common English usage. For example, consider the English statement, "If I work the nightshift, I'll earn extra spending money, or else I'll go to the movies and I'll dip into my savings." In this sentence, the two groups of statements come before and after the "else," based on the condition, "if I work the nightshift." The general **syntax**, or valid form, of an Access Basic If statement is:

```
If condition Then
      true-statement group
[Else
      false-statement group]
End If
```

Access executes the true-statement group when the condition is true and the false-statement group when the condition is false. Bracketed portions of a statement's syntax are optional parts of the statement. Therefore, omit the Else and its related false-statement group when you want Access to execute a group of statements only when the condition is true.

In Figure 4-10, Elena's If statement uses Access's **IsNull function**, which returns True when the Description field value is null and False when it is not null. The Not is the same logical operator you've used before to negate an expression. Thus, Access executes the statement "[Description] = CapOnlyFirst([Description])" only when the Description field value is not null.

Elena is ready to make her changes to the TYPES form.

Adding an Event Procedure

Elena opens the TYPES form in the Form Design window and adds an event procedure for the Description field's AfterUpdate event property.

REFERENCE WINDOW

Adding an Event Procedure

- Open the form or report in the Design window, open the property sheet, and click the control whose event property you want to set.
- Set the appropriate event property to [Event Procedure] and click the Build button.
- Enter the sub procedure statements in the Module window, compile the procedure, fix any statement errors, and save the event procedure.

Elena adds her event procedure to the TYPES form.

To add an event procedure:

❶ Click the **Form object button**, click **TYPES form**, and then click the **Design command button** to open the Form Design window. Then click the Form Design window **maximize button** to see the entire form.

❷ Click the field-value **text box** for the Description field to make it the current control; this text box is to the right of the Description label box.

❸ Click the toolbar **Properties button** to open the property sheet, click the **down arrow button** at the very top of the property sheet, and then click **Event Properties**. Access shows only the event properties in the property sheet.

❹ Click the **AfterUpdate box**, click the **down arrow button** that appears, click **[Event Procedure]**, and then click the **Build button** to the right of the AfterUpdate property. Access opens the Module window, which is maximized and contains the Sub and End Sub statements. See Figure 4-11.

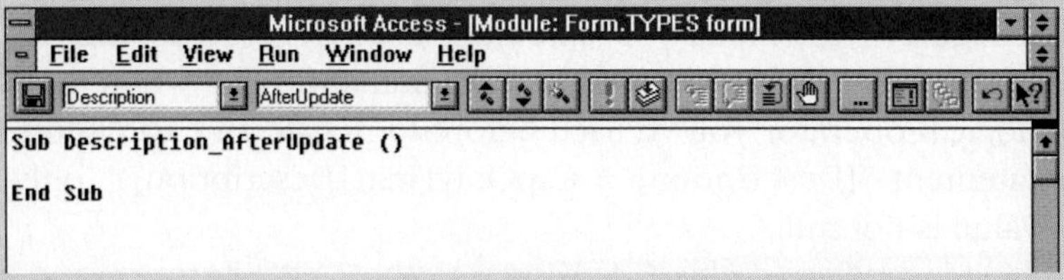

Figure 4-11 The initial event procedure in the Module window

❺ Press **[Tab]**, type **'Capitalize the first letter of the**, press **[Enter]**, type **'Description field value**, press **[Enter]**, type **If Not IsNull([Description]) Then**, press **[Enter]**, press **[Tab]**, type **[Description] = CapOnlyFirst([Description])**, and then press **[Enter]**.

❻ Press **[Shift][Tab]** to move the insertion point one tab setting to the left and then type **End If**. This completes the event procedure. Compare your screen to Figure 4-12 and make any necessary corrections.

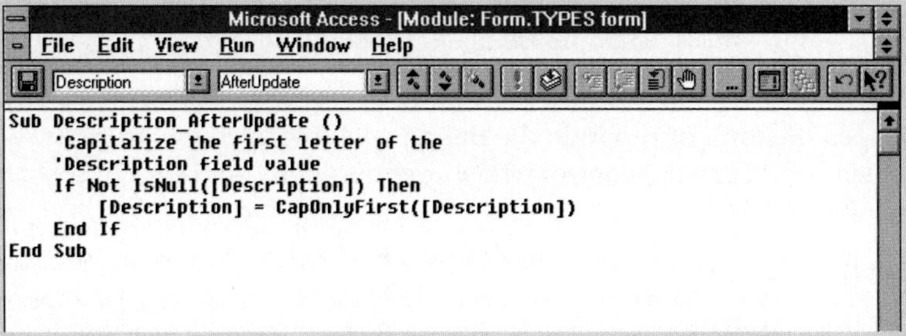

Figure 4-12 The completed event procedure

Before saving the event procedure, Elena compiles the procedure so that Access can run it.

Compiling a Procedure

Access cannot execute the Access Basic statements you enter in a procedure without compiling them first. **Compiling** a procedure translates Access Basic statements into a form Access can execute and checks the procedure for errors. When you run a procedure for the first time, Access compiles it for you automatically and opens a dialog box only if it finds errors in the procedure. If it finds an error, Access does not translate the procedure statements. If no errors are detected, Access translates the procedure and does not display a confirmation. You can also compile a procedure at any point as you enter it. Just click the toolbar **Compile Loaded Modules button**. In response, Access compiles the procedure and all other procedures in all modules in the database. Access does not, however, compile CBF and CBR for closed forms and reports.

REFERENCE WINDOW

Compiling Procedures in Modules

- In the Module window, click the toolbar Compile Loaded Modules button.

Elena compiles and saves the CBF for the TYPES form.

To compile and save CBF:

1. Click the toolbar **Compile Loaded Modules button**. Access compiles the CBF for the TYPES form and dims.
2. Click the toolbar **Save button**, double-click the Module window **Control menu box** to close the Module window, click the toolbar **Properties button** to close the property sheet, click the Form Design window **restore button**, and then double-click the Form Design window **Control menu box** to activate the Database window.

Elena has created the function and the event procedure and has set the event property. She now tests the event procedure.

Testing an Event Procedure

Elena opens the Form View window for the TYPES form and tests the Description field's event procedure by entering a few different test Description field values in the first record of the form. Moving the focus to another control on the form or to another record triggers the AfterUpdate event for the Description field and executes the attached event procedure. Consequently, after entering a value for the Description field, Elena changes the focus by clicking the first record's Type text box.

To test an event procedure:

1. Double-click **TYPES form** in the Forms list box on the Database window to open the Form View window.
2. Press **[Tab]**, type **stock MARKET** in the Description text box, and click the **Type text box**. Access executes the AfterUpdate event procedure for the Description field and changes the Description field value to "Stock market." See Figure 4-13.

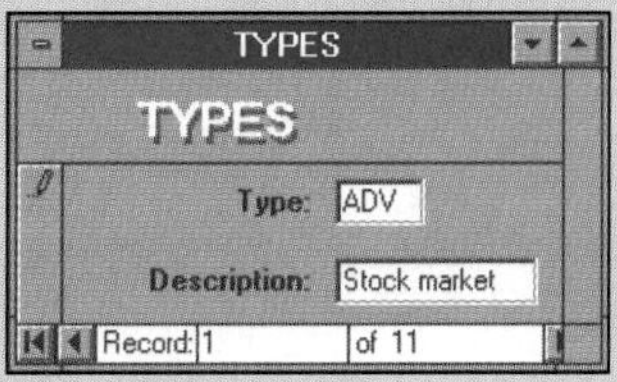

Figure 4-13
After an event procedure is executed

3. Repeat Step 2 three more times, entering **advertising**, then **ADVERTISING**, and finally **aDVERTISING** in the Description field box. Access prints the correct value, Advertising, each time.
4. Double-click the Form View window **Control menu box** to activate the Database window.

Elena has finished her work on the CapOnlyFirst function. Next, she creates a similar, but more complicated, function for the Article Title field on the PAST ARTICLES form.

If you want to take a break and resume the tutorial at a later time, you can exit Access by double-clicking the Microsoft Access window Control menu box. When you resume the tutorial, place your Student Disk in the appropriate drive, launch Access, open the Issue25 database on your Student Disk, click the switchboard's Exit to Issue25 button, and click the Form object button.

■ ■ ■

Adding a Second Function to a Global Module

Elena now decides to practice with a second function she learned at the seminar. This function, named CapAllFirst, capitalizes the first letter of all words in a field value and leaves unchanged all other letters. Using this function for the Article Title field on the PAST ARTICLES form changes the field value "the bCCI scandal revealed," for example, to "The BCCI Scandal Revealed." Because Elena wants a field value like "computers in the future" changed to "Computers in the Future," the CapAllFirst function does not capitalize the first letter of the following five words when they are not the first word of the title: and, in, of, on, the.

The Design of the CapAllFirst Function

Figure 4-14 shows the CapAllFirst function that Elena learned about at the seminar. You've already seen several of the statements in this function in your work with the CapOnlyFirst function. Except for the function name, the Function and End Function statements are the same. Elena enters comments on the second and third lines of the function; these comments are specific to the CapAllFirst function. An explanation of the new statements and the purpose of each group of statements appear in the following paragraphs.

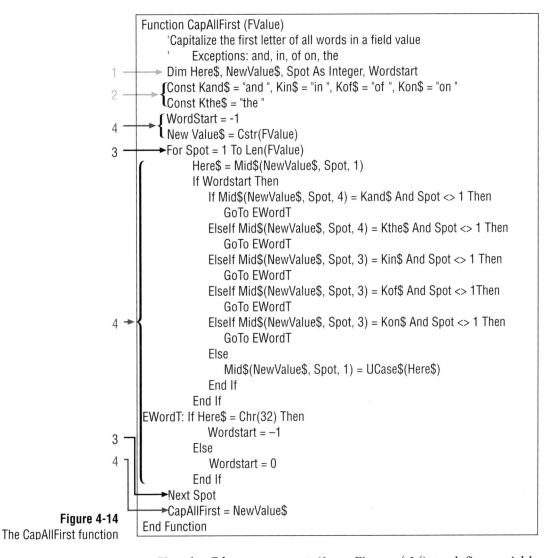

```
Function CapAllFirst (FValue)
    'Capitalize the first letter of all words in a field value
    '    Exceptions: and, in, of on, the
1 → Dim Here$, NewValue$, Spot As Integer, Wordstart
2 → {Const Kand$ = "and ", Kin$ = "in ", Kof$ = "of ", Kon$ = "on "
     Const Kthe$ = "the "
4 → {WordStart = -1
     New Value$ = Cstr(FValue)
3 → For Spot = 1 To Len(FValue)
        Here$ = Mid$(NewValue$, Spot, 1)
        If Wordstart Then
            If Mid$(NewValue$, Spot, 4) = Kand$ And Spot <> 1 Then
                GoTo EWordT
            ElseIf Mid$(NewValue$, Spot, 4) = Kthe$ And Spot <> 1 Then
                GoTo EWordT
            ElseIf Mid$(NewValue$, Spot, 3) = Kin$ And Spot <> 1 Then
                GoTo EWordT
            ElseIf Mid$(NewValue$, Spot, 3) = Kof$ And Spot <> 1Then
                GoTo EWordT
4 →         ElseIf Mid$(NewValue$, Spot, 3) = Kon$ And Spot <> 1 Then
                GoTo EWordT
            Else
                Mid$(NewValue$, Spot, 1) = UCase$(Here$)
            End If
        End If
EWordT: If Here$ = Chr(32) Then
            Wordstart = –1
3       Else
4           Wordstart = 0
        End If
    Next Spot
    CapAllFirst = NewValue$
End Function
```

Figure 4-14
The CapAllFirst function

Use the **Dim statement** (1 on Figure 4-14) to define variables in a procedure (in Figure 4-14, the variables are Here$, NewValue$, spot, and Wordstart). You'll see what these variables do in a moment. You also assign each variable an associated data type. Figure 4-15 shows the primary data types for Access Basic variables. Choose a data type for a variable by adding the associated suffix to the variable name or by following the variable name with As and the data type. In the CapAllFirst function, for example, the two variables Here$ and NewValue$ are string variables, Spot is an integer variable, and Wordstart is a variant variable. The **variant data type** is the default data type, and a variant variable can store numeric, string, date/time, and null values.

Data Type	Suffix
Currency	@
Double	#
Integer	%
Long	&
Single	!
String	$
Variant	None

Figure 4-15
Access Basic data types

Use the **Const statement** (2 on Figure 4-14) to define constants in a procedure. A **constant**, unlike a variable, is a memory location that contains a value that does not change in value. In a Const statement, you assign a constant name and a value to each separate constant. In the CapAllFirst function, for example, Kand$ is a constant name, has the string data type, and is assigned the string value "and ". Each of the other four constants is similarly defined. The space at the end of each constant ensures that only these five words are not capitalized; for "industry," "office," and other words beginning with the letters of these words, the CapAllFirst function capitalizes their first letters.

The **For...Next statement** (all the occurrences of 3 on Figure 4-14) repeats a group of statements a fixed number of times. A group of statements repeatedly executed is called a **loop**. In the CapAllFirst function, the For statement establishes how many times to repeat the statement group, the Next statement marks the end of the For...Next statement pair, and the statements between these two statements are repeated a fixed number of times.

- A For statement uses one of the variables that you've defined as a counter. You define a range that the variable will take on and tell Access, "For this range, do these steps." This tells the For statement for which values it should execute the loop. The general syntax for the For statement is "For counter = start To end [Step increment]," where increment has a default value of 1. The "For Spot = 1 To Len(FValue)" statement in the CapAllFirst function sets the starting value of Spot, which is an integer variable, to 1 and the ending value of Spot to Len(FValue). The **Len function** returns the number of characters in a string. For example, if FValue is the string "An Article Title" Len(FValue) returns 16 as the number of characters, including spaces. In this case, the statements in the loop will be executed 16 times.
- Then Access executes the group of statements that follow the For statement, ending with the statement before the Next Spot statement.
- When execution reaches the Next Spot statement, Access adds one to Spot, goes back to the For statement, and compares the value of Spot to Len(FValue). If Spot is less than or equal to Len(FValue), Access executes the loop statements again, reaches the Next Spot statement, and repeats the cycle. When Spot becomes greater than Len(FValue), Access terminates the loop and executes the statement following the Next Spot statement.

The rest of the CapAllFirst function (all the occurrences of 4 on Figure 4-14) finds the first character of a word and capitalizes it, when it isn't one of the exception words (that is, the words defined by the Const statements). Access uses the **CStr function** to convert the value of the parameter FValue, which has the variant data type, to a string and assigns this converted value to the variable NewValue$. Access changes the first character of a word to uppercase using the UCase$ function. After inspecting all characters and changing appropriate characters to uppercase, Access assigns the changed value of NewValue$ to CapAllFirst, whose value is returned to the calling statement.

Access sets the variable Wordstart to a value of -1 whenever the current character is the first character of a word and to a value of zero otherwise. (The statement "If Here$ = Chr(32)" uses the **Chr function** to convert an ANSI character code—a number assigned to a letter or other symbol—to a string character; for example, ANSI character code 32 is assigned to the space character.) The statement "If Wordstart Then" is true when Wordstart is nonzero, or equal to -1, and is false when Wordstart is zero. This simply means that the If statement is true when the current character is the first character of a word and is false in all other cases. Notice that Wordstart is set to -1 at the outset, telling Access that the first time it goes through the loop, it is at the beginning of a word.

After Access has evaluated a word to be sure it isn't one of the words defined in the Const statement (this evaluation takes place in the If and Else statements, as you'll see in a moment), the code tells it to go to a line beginning with the word "EWordT." This is short for EndWordTest, and all EWordT does is serve as a name for the line so Access knows what statement to execute next (for this reason it's called a **line label**). The EWordT line starts a new If statement that tests whether the next character is a space or not.

Finally, for an **If...Then...ElseIf** set of statements, only one of the If or ElseIf conditions will be true. For example, if it's summer, we'll go to the beach, else if it's fall, we'll view the fall foliage, else if it's winter, we'll ski, else we'll plant our garden. In these four mutually exclusive possibilities, only one can be true. Access evaluates the very first If statement (in this case, testing to see if the word is "and"). If the statement is true, then it skips all the rest of the statements between the If and End If and jumps to the EWordT line label. If the first statement Access evaluates is not true (that is, the word is not "and,") Access moves on to the next statement to see if the word is "the." The point is that Access is checking to be sure the word isn't one of the ones you don't want capitalized. The CapAllFirst function's If...Then...ElseIf statement either capitalizes the first character of a word (the assignment following the Else) or does not when the first character is for one of the exception words.

Elena adds the CapAllFirst function to the basIssue25Functions module.

Creating a Second Function

Elena opens the basIssue25Functions module in the Module window and adds the CapAllFirst function.

REFERENCE WINDOW

Adding a New Procedure to a Global Module

- In the Database window, click the Module object button, click the module name, and click the Design command button.
- In the Module window, click the toolbar New Procedure button, type the new procedure name, click the Sub or Function radio button, and click the OK button.
- Enter the new procedure, click the toolbar Compile Loaded Modules button, and click the toolbar Save button.

To add a function to an existing module:

1. Click the **Module object button**, click the **Design command button**, and then click the Module window **maximize button**.
2. Click the toolbar **New Procedure button**, type **CapAllFirst** in the Name text box, be sure the Function radio button is selected, and then press **[Enter]**. Access starts a new procedure named CapAllFirst and displays the Function and End Function statements in the Module window.
3. Click between the parentheses in the Function statement, type **FValue**, press **[↓]**, press **[Home]**, and then press **[Tab]**.
4. Enter the statements for the CapAllFirst function. See Figure 4-16 and Figure 4-17. Be sure to use the Edit menu's Copy and Paste commands to duplicate similar statements, and recall that pressing [Shift][Tab] moves the insertion point one tab stop to the left.

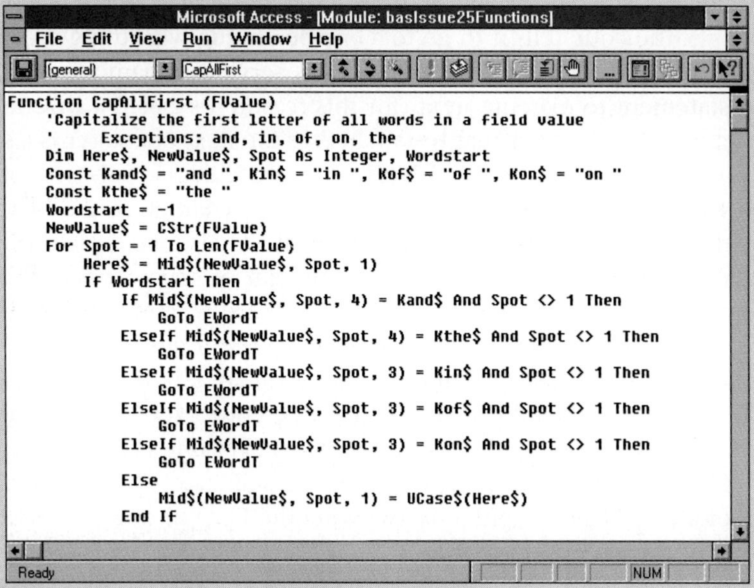

Figure 4-16 The top of the CapAllFirst function in the Module window

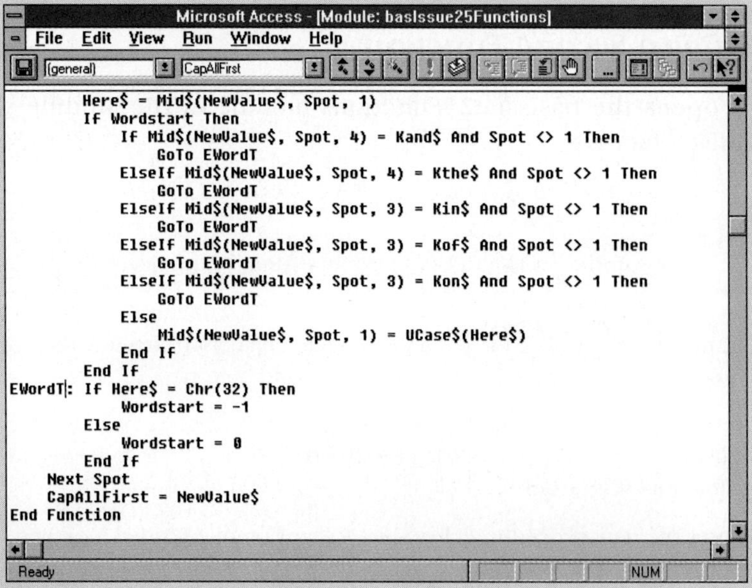

Figure 4-17 The bottom of the CapAllFirst function in the Module window

❺ Click the toolbar **Compile Loaded Modules button** to compile the CapAllFirst function and then click the toolbar **Save button** to save the basIssue25Functions module.

TROUBLE? If Access finds an error, it highlights the error and opens a dialog box with a message describing the nature of the error. Click the OK button and change the statemnt contained in the highlighted area by comparing each character you entered to what you should have entered. Then repeat Step 5.

❻ Click the toolbar **Next Procedure button**. Access displays the CapOnlyFirst function and displays CapOnlyFirst in the toolbar Procedure box, which is to the left of the Previous Procedure button. You can easily move from procedure to procedure in a module by clicking the Next Procedure or Previous Procedure buttons.

❼ Click a second time. Access displays the module's Declarations section. Click the toolbar **Previous Procedure button**, and then click a second time to redisplay the top of the CapAllFirst function.

❽ Double-click the Module window **Control menu box** to activate the maximized Database window.

Creating a Second Event Procedure

Elena uses the CapAllFirst function with the Article Title field on the PAST ARTICLES form. She opens the PAST ARTICLES form in the Form Design window and adds an event procedure for the Article Title field's AfterUpdate event property. The new event procedure looks exactly like the event procedure for the Description field on the TYPES form, except for the Sub statement, the function call statement, and the sub procedure comments.

To add an event procedure for the Article Title field on the PAST ARTICLES form:

❶ Click the **Form object button**, click **PAST ARTICLES form**, and then click the **Design command** button to open the Form Design window.

❷ Click the field-value **text box** for the Article Title field to make it the current control; this text box is to the right of the Article Title label box.

❸ Click the toolbar **Properties button** to open the property sheet, click the **AfterUpdate box**, click the **down arrow button** that appears, click **[Event Procedure]**, and then click the **Build button** to the right of the AfterUpdate property. Access opens the Module window, which is maximized and contains the Sub and End Sub statements.

❹ Press **[Tab]** and type the sub procedure statements. See Figure 4-18.

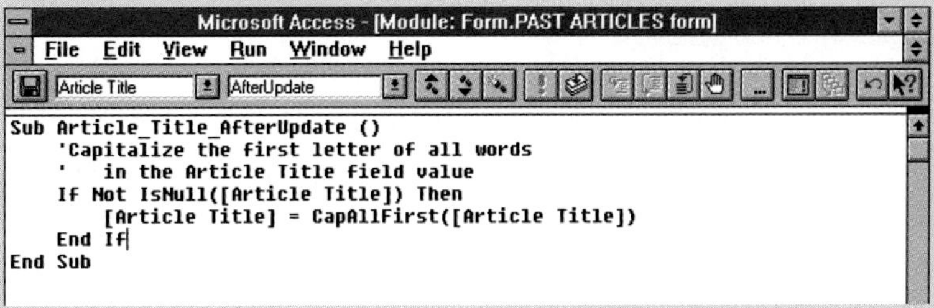
Microsoft Access - [Module: Form.PAST ARTICLES form]
File Edit View Run Window Help
Article Title
AfterUpdate
Sub Article_Title_AfterUpdate ()
'Capitalize the first letter of all words
' in the Article Title field value
If Not IsNull([Article Title]) Then
[Article Title] = CapAllFirst([Article Title])
End If
End Sub

Figure 4-18 The event procedure for the Article Title field

❺ Click the toolbar **Compile Loaded Modules button**, click the toolbar **Save button**, double-click the Module window **Control menu box** to close the Module window, click to close the property sheet, click the Form Design window **restore button**, and then double-click the Form Design window **Control menu box** to activate the Database window.

Elena has entered the function and the event procedure and has set the event property. She now tests the event procedure. Elena opens the Form View window for the PAST ARTICLES form and tests the Article Title field's event procedure by entering different Article Title field values.

To test an event procedure:

1. Double-click **PAST ARTICLES form** in the Forms list box on the Database window to open the Form View window.
2. Type **the first of the tests on this field** in the Article Title text box and then press **[Tab]**. Access executes the AfterUpdate event procedure for the Article Title field and changes the Article Title field value to "The First of the Tests on This Field." Press **[Shift][Tab]** to highlight the Article Title field value.
3. Repeat Step 2 two more times, entering **and the second in the field and function** (correctly changed to "And the Second in the Field and Function"), and then entering **milton friedman interview** (correctly changed to "Milton Friedman Interview").
4. Double-click the Form View window **Control menu box** to activate the Database window.

Elena has finished all work on her second function, the CapAllFirst function.

If you want to take a break and resume the tutorial at a later time, you can exit Access by double-clicking the Microsoft Access window Control menu box. When you resume the tutorial, place your Student Disk in the appropriate drive, launch Access, open the Issue25 database on your Student Disk, click the switchboard's Exit to Issue25 button, and click the Form object button.

■ ■ ■

Hiding Text and Changing Color During Execution

Next, Elena adds a message to the WRITERS form that will remind users when freelancers need to be paid. Access displays the message in red when the writer is a freelancer but does not display the message otherwise. Also, Access displays the value in the Amount text box in red for freelancers and in black for staff writers. See Figure 4-19.

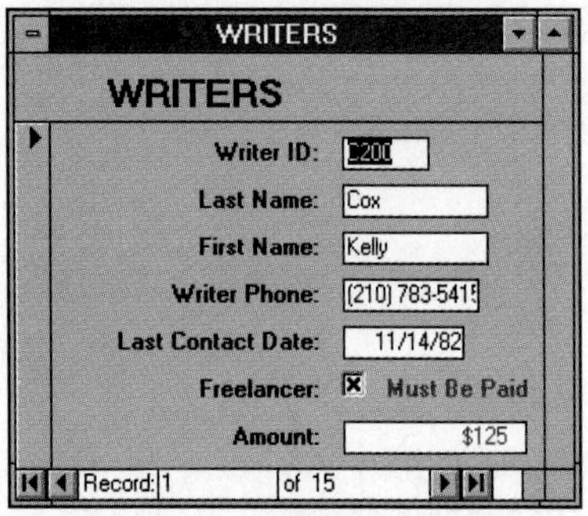

Figure 4-19 WRITERS form with highly visible Freelancer message

On the WRITERS form, Elena adds a label to the right of the Freelancer check box. In red letters, the text is "Must Be Paid." Because Elena wants the text to appear in some cases and not in others, she changes the label's Visible property during execution. The

Visible property determines when Access displays a control. Access displays a control when its Visible property is True, which is the default, and hides the control when its Visible property is False.

Elena also changes the foreground color of the Amount field to red for freelancers and to black for staff writers. The field's **ForeColor property** determines a field's foreground color. A ForeColor value of zero displays black characters, and a value of 255 displays red characters.

Because the change to the visible property takes place during execution, Elena adds code to the Current event procedure on the WRITERS form. The **Current event** occurs every time Access displays a new record in a form. Figure 4-20 shows Elena's code. To set a property in an Access Basic statement, use the object name followed by the property name, separating the two with a period. For example, if the label name for the message is FreelancerMsg, then "[FreelancerMsg].Visible = False" hides the label on the form.

```
Sub Form_Current ( )
    'For freelancers, display a message and the "Amount" field value in red
    'For others, display the "Amount" field value in black without a message
    If [Freelancer] = True Then
        [FreelancerMsg].Visible = True
        [Freelancer Reprint Payment Amount].ForeColor = 255
    Else
        [FreelancerMsg].Visible = False
        [Freelancer Reprint Payment Amount].ForeColor = 0
    End If
End Sub
```

Figure 4-20
The Current event procedure for the WRITERS form

To add the Current event procedure to the WRITERS form:

❶ Click the Database window **maximize button**, click **WRITERS form**, and then click the **Design command** button to open the Form Design window.

❷ Click the toolbox **Label tool** A, position the pointer's plus symbol (+) in the grid dots to the right of the Freelancer check box, click the mouse button, type **Must Be Paid**, and then press **[Enter]**. Using the move handle in the upper-left corner of the label box, drag the label box just to the right of the Freelancer check box. See Figure 4-21.

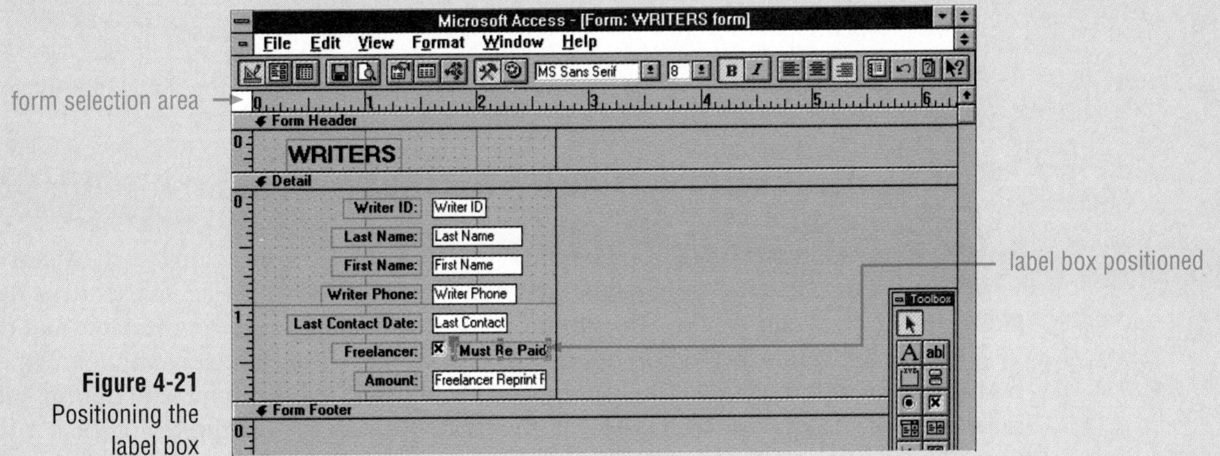

Figure 4-21
Positioning the label box

3. Click the toolbar **Properties button** to open the property sheet, click the **down arrow button** at the top of the property sheet, click **All Properties** in the drop-down list box, double-click the value in the Name box, type **FreelancerMsg**, scroll the property sheet, double-click **0** in the ForeColor box, type **255**, and then press **[Enter]**. Access changes the foreground color of the label box to red.
4. Click the **white box** shown in Figure 4-21 in the upper-left corner between the horizontal and vertical rulers to select the form as the current control, scroll the property sheet, click the **OnCurrent box**, click the **down arrow button**, click **[Event Procedure]**, and then click the **Build button**. Access opens the Module window, displaying the Sub and End Sub statements.
5. Press **[Tab]** and type the sub procedure statements. See Figure 4-22.

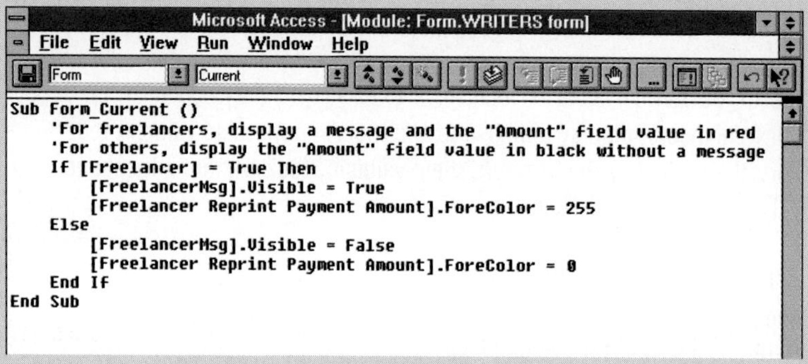

Figure 4-22
The Current event procedure for the WRITERS form

6. Click the toolbar **Compile Loaded Modules button**, click the toolbar **Save button**, double-click the Module window **Control menu box** to close the Module window, click to close the property sheet, click the Form Design window **restore button**, and then double-click the Form Design window **Control menu box** to activate the Database window.
7. Double-click **WRITERS form** in the Forms list box on the Database window to open the Form View window. Access displays the first record for Kelly Cox, who is a freelancer. The message is in red, as is the Amount value $125.
8. Click the **Next Record navigation button** several times to be sure each freelancer's message and Amount value appear in red and each staff writer's Amount value is in black without the message appearing.
9. Double-click the Form View window **Control menu box** to activate the Database window.

Elena has finished all work on the Current event procedure for the WRITERS form.

Creating the Event Procedures for the frmReports Dialog Box

Finally, Elena addresses the procedures for the frmReport form dialog box. When the form first opens, Access highlights the first item in the list box by placing the focus on it. Next, double-clicking a report name in the list box or highlighting a report name and then clicking the left command button opens that report in the Print Preview window. Finally, highlighting a report name in the list box and clicking the middle command button immediately prints that report. Elena designs the three procedures for the dialog box to perform these functions. Figure 4-23 shows the procedure names she chooses in relation to the way they are used.

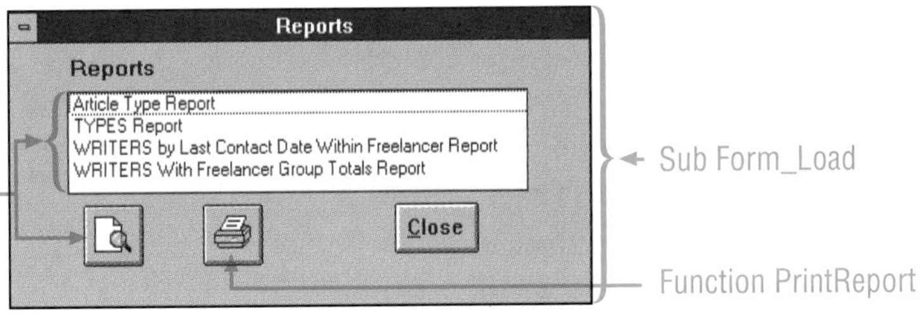

Figure 4-23 The frmReports form's procedures

The Load Event Procedure for the Dialog Box

When a user opens the frmReports dialog box, Elena wants Access to place the focus on the top report in the list box on the form automatically. Figure 4-24 shows the code she designs for the form's Load event.

Figure 4-24 The Load event procedure for the frmReports form

```
Sub Form_Load ( )
    'Move the focus to the list box and highlight the first report
    [ctlReportName].SetFocus
    SendKeys "{Down}"
End Sub
```

The **Load event** occurs when Access opens a form. **SetFocus** is a method that moves the focus to the specified object or control, and a **method** is an action that operates on specific objects or controls. The statement [ctlReportName].SetFocus moves the focus to the ctlReportName control, which is the name for the form's list box. The SendKeys "{Down}" statement sends the Down Arrow keystroke to the list box; Access highlights the top report in the list box in response to this statement. The end result of these statements is that when the user opens the dialog box, the top report is highlighted and has the focus.

Elena opens the frmReports form in the Form Design window and creates the Load event procedure.

To add the Load event procedure for the frmReports form:

1. Click **frmReports** in the Forms list box, click the **Design command button** to open the Form Design window, and then click the Form Design window **maximize button**.
2. Click the toolbar **Properties button** to open the property sheet. If Form does not appear in the property sheet title bar, click the **white box** in the upper-left corner between the horizontal and vertical rulers to select the form as the current control, scroll the property sheet, click the **On Load box**, click the **down arrow button**, click **[Event Procedure]**, and then click the **Build button**. Access opens the Module window, displaying the Sub and End Sub statements.
3. Press **[Tab]** and type the sub procedure statements. See Figure 4-25.

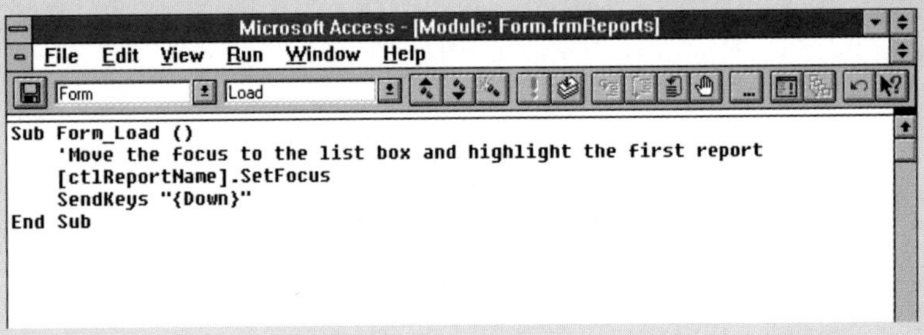

Figure 4-25 The Load event procedure for the frmReports form

❹ Click the toolbar **Compile Loaded Modules button**, click the toolbar **Save button**, double-click the Module window **Control menu box** to close the Module window, click the toolbar to close the property sheet, click the Form Design window **restore button**, and then double-click the Form Design window **Control menu box** to activate the Database window.

❺ Double-click **frmReports** in the Forms list box on the Database window to open the Form View window for the frmReports form. The top report in the list box is selected.

❻ Click the **Close button** on the dialog box to close it and activate the Database window.

Elena has finished her work with the Load event procedure for the frmReports form. Next, she creates the form's PreviewReport and PrintReport functions.

The PreviewReport and PrintReport Functions for the Dialog Box

Double-clicking a report name in the list box or highlighting a report name and then clicking the left command button must open that report in the Print Preview window. Highlighting a report name in the list box and clicking the middle command button must immediately print that report. Figure 4-26 shows the code Elena designs to handle these processes.

```
Function PreviewReport ( )
    'Open the selected report in the Print Preview window
    DoCmd OpenReport [ctlReportName], A_PREVIEW
End Function
```

```
Function PrintReport ( )
    'Print the selected report
    DoCmd OpenReport [ctlReportName], A_NORMAL
End Function
```

Figure 4-26 The PreviewReport and PrintReport functions for the frmReports form

An Access Basic **DoCmd statement** executes an action. Elena uses the DoCmd statements in her functions to run the OpenReport action. The parameter choices for the selected report of [ctlReportName] in the OpenReport action are: A_PREVIEW to open the Print Preview window, A_NORMAL to print the report, and A_DESIGN to open the Report Design window. Because the OpenReport action and its parameter values A_PREVIEW, A_NORMAL, and A_DESIGN are standard features of Access, you do not define them in a Dim statement as you do for variables you create.

Elena opens the frmReports form in the Form Design window, creates the two functions, and attaches the functions to the appropriate control properties.

To add the two functions to the frmReports form:

❶ Click the **Design command** button to open the Form Design window, click the toolbar **Code button** to open the Module window for the form's CBF, click the toolbar **New Procedure button**, type **PreviewReport** in the Name text box, be sure the Function radio button is selected, and then click the **OK button**. Access displays the Function and End Function statements for a new procedure.

❷ Press **[Tab]** and type the function statements. See Figure 4-27.

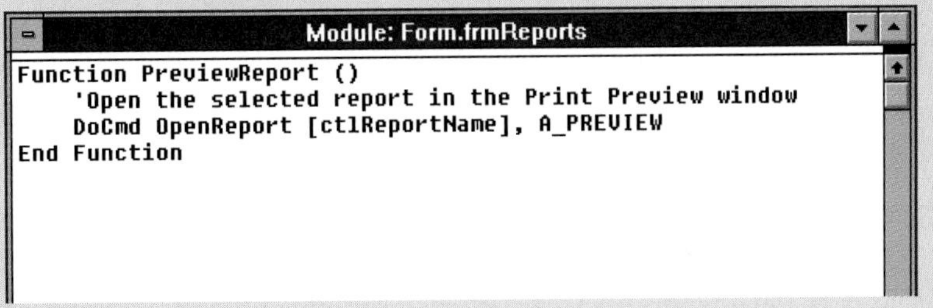


```
Function PreviewReport ()
    'Open the selected report in the Print Preview window
    DoCmd OpenReport [ctlReportName], A_PREVIEW
End Function
```

Figure 4-27
The PreviewReport function for the frmReports form

❸ Click the toolbar **Save button**, click the toolbar, type **PrintReport** in the Name text box, be sure the Function radio button is selected, and then click the **OK button**.

❹ Press **[Tab]** and type the function statements. See Figure 4-28.

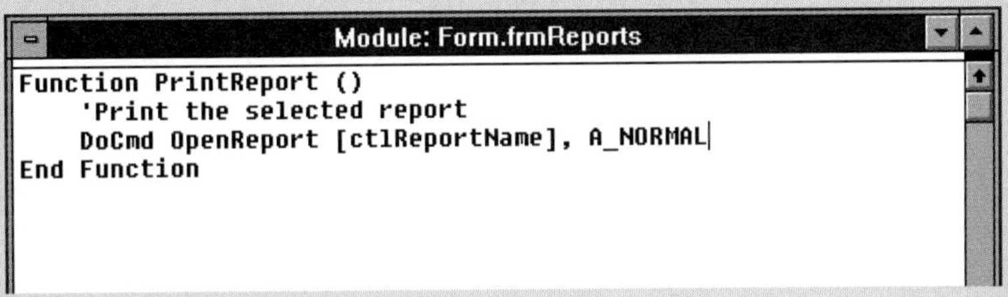


```
Function PrintReport ()
    'Print the selected report
    DoCmd OpenReport [ctlReportName], A_NORMAL
End Function
```

Figure 4-28
The PrintReport function for the frmReports form

❺ Click the toolbar **Compile Loaded Modules button**, click, double-click the Module window **Control menu box** to close the Module window, click the Form Design window **maximize button**, click the form's **list box** to make it the current control, and then click the toolbar **Properties button** to open the property sheet.

❻ Scrolling the property sheet as necessary, click the **On Dbl Click box**, and type **=PreviewReport()**.

❼ Click the form's **left command button**, click the property sheet's **On Click box**, and type **=PreviewReport()**.

❽ Click the form's **middle command button**, click the property sheet's **On Click box**, and type **=PrintReport()**.

❾ Click to save all form changes, click the toolbar to close the property sheet, click the Form Design window **restore button**, and then double-click the Form Design window **Control menu box** to activate the Database window.

Elena tests the changes made to the frmReports form.

To test the changes to the frmReports form:

❶ Double-click **frmReports** in the Forms list box on the Database window to open the form in the Form View window.

❷ Double-click each of the report names, in turn, in the list box to verify that the correct report opens in the Print Preview window. From the Print Preview window, click the toolbar **Close Window button** each time to return to the dialog box in the Form View window.

❸ Click a report name in the list box and then click the **left command button** to verify that the correct report opens in the Print Preview window. From the Print Preview window, click the toolbar **Close Window button** to return to the dialog box in the Form View window.

❹ Repeat Step 3 for each report name in the form's list box.

❺ Click a report name in the list box and then click the **middle command button** to verify that the correct report prints.

❻ Repeat Step 5 for each report name in the form's list box.

❼ Click the **Close button** on the dialog box to close it and activate the Database window.

Elena makes one final test of the frmSwitchboard form. She has completed all the form's features, except for the options on the frmQueries form (you will add procedures in the Tutorial Assignment to finish this form), and wants to be sure everything works properly. When she finishes her final testing, Elena exits Access.

To test the features on the frmSwitchboard form:

❶ Double-click **frmSwitchboard** in the Forms list box on the Database window to open the form in the Form View window.

❷ Make one final pass through all menu, toolbar, and command button options to verify all features work properly on the frmSwitchboard form.

❸ Click the form's **Exit Access button** as your last test to close the form, close the Issue25 database, and exit Access.

■ ■ ■

Elena's graphical user interface for the Issue25 database gives users controlled, easy access to the database's forms, queries, and reports. To complete the interface, she needs to complete the frmQueries form and remove the Exit to Issue25 command button from the switchboard. Elena has a fundamental understanding of Access macros and the Access Basic language and now can tackle more ambitious database projects for Vision Publishers.

Questions

1. Why is Access Basic called an event-driven, object-oriented language?
2. What are the differences between a function and a sub procedure?
3. What are the two different types of modules?
4. What is an event procedure?
5. What can you accomplish in the Immediate window?
6. What does Access do when you compile a procedure?
7. What is the difference between a variable and a constant?
8. How many times would the following loop be executed?
   For MyCounter = 2 To 11 Step 3
9. What is a method?

Tutorial Assignments

Launch Access and open the Issue25 database on your Student Disk.

1. Elena's CapOnlyFirst function will change names like joAnn and deYoung to Joann and Deyoung. Figure 4-29 shows the CapFirstLetter function, which correctly changes names like joAnn and deYoung to JoAnn and DeYoung. Add the CapFirstLetter function to the basIssue25Functions module and create event procedures for the Last Name and First Name fields' AfterUpdate events on the WRITERS form.

```
Function CapFirstLetter (FValue)
    'Capitalize only the first letter of a field value;
    'Leave unchanged all other letters.
    CapFirstLetter = UCase(Left(FValue, 1)) & Mid(FValue, 2)
End Function
```

Figure 4-29

2. Create the procedures for the frmQueries form dialog box. Highlighting a query name in the list box and clicking the left command button opens the query in the Print Preview window (use the OpenQuery action, the parameter value A_PREVIEW, and name the CBF function PreviewQuery). Double-clicking a query name in the list box or highlighting a query name and then clicking the middle command button opens the query dynaset (use the OpenQuery action, the parameter value A_NORMAL, and name the CBF function DisplayDynaset). Be sure to create an event procedure for the form's Load event to highlight the top query name in the list box.

E

3. Now that you have completed the frmSwitchboard form, remove the Exit to Issue25 command button from the form, remove the Exit to Issue25 button from the custom toolbar, and remove the Exit to Issue25 menu item from the Exit menu on the custom menu bar.

   To retain a secured way of closing the frmSwitchboard form and activating the Database window for the Issue25 database, create an AutoKeys macro to assign to the [F2] key the same actions that the Exit to Issue25 options used to have. (See the "Assigning a Macro to a Key" topic in Access online Help for the key assignment macro search value.) Reposition the form's controls so that the form has a professional look, and test the form.

Case Problems

1. Walkton Daily Press Carriers

Launch Access and open the Press database on your Student Disk.

1. To the "CARRIERS by Name, Route ID form" form, add the message "Carrier has a Positive Balance" above the Balance field. Use a ForeColor value of 128 for the message and make the message font bold. Display the message only when the Balance field value is greater than zero. Display the Balance field value in black when no message appears and in the same color as the message otherwise.

2. Lopez Used Cars

Launch Access and open the Usedcars database on your Student Disk.

1. To the "USED CARS form" form, add the message "BIG PROFIT" to the right of the Year field. Use a ForeColor value of 30000 for the message and be sure the message font is bold and italic. Beneath this message, on the same line as Location field, display the profit amount (difference between the Selling Price and Cost field values). Use the same ForeColor and font effects for the profit amount as for the message. Display the message and the profit amount only when the profit amount is greater than $1,500.

3. Tophill University Student Employment

Launch Access and open the Parttime database on your Student Disk.

1. To the "JOBS by Employer and Job Title form" form, add the message "High Hours" to the right of the Hours/Week field value and the message "High Wages" to the right of the Wages field value. Use a ForeColor value of 255 for the messages and be sure the message font is bold. Display the first message when the Hours/Week field value is greater than 18 and the second message when the Wages field value is greater than $7.00.

4. Rexville Business Licenses

Launch Access and open the Buslic database on your Student Disk.

1. To the "BUSINESSES by License Type and Business Name form" form, add the message "Collect NOW!" to the right of the Basic Cost field. Use a ForeColor value of 128 for the message and make the message font bold. Display the message only when the Basic Cost field value is greater than or equal to $100. Display the Basic Cost field value with a ForeColor value of 30000 when no message appears and in the same color as the message otherwise.

Additional Case 1

Company Financial Information by FINSTAT Inc.

OBJECTIVES

In this case you will:

- Change field properties
- Add a table and add relationships between tables
- Create select, parameter, and crosstab queries
- Create a form using Form Wizards
- Create a custom form
- Create custom reports
- Prepare a chart
- Design and create a switchboard
- Add macros and event procedures

CASE

FINSTAT Inc. When Pat Mitchell graduated from an eastern business college, she had her pick of job offers. Companies could see, from her internship record and her grades, that she was a bright, ambitious worker who would be an asset. Pat had always dreamed of being her own boss, however, so after careful market analysis and planning, she founded FINSTAT Inc., an electronic information service that markets financial information to its clients. Since the time Pat started her company, competing vendors have begun to appear on the market, offering similar databases of financial information.

Pat and her team of financial analysts are now realizing that to remain competitive, not only must their products supply current and complete data, but equally importantly, their clients need to be able to access the data effortlessly and with as many options as possible. Pat decides to take the current databases she has and upgrade them with ease of use in mind. Her most successful database contains recent financial statement data on the leading U.S. corporations, so she starts her new campaign by reorganizing the information to make it more accessible, and then designing an interface that is easier for clients to use.

Pat's corporation database currently consists of two tables, tblCOMPANY and tblFINANCE. Figure 1 shows the structure of the tblCOMPANY table, which stores general data about each company. The tblCOMPANY table contains an ID number and name for each company, a code classifying the company's industry, and a symbol that uniquely identifies the company on the stock exchange and in financial publications.

Field Name	Data Type	Properties
CompanyID	Text	Field Size—3 Input Mask—>L00 Caption—Company ID
CompanyName	Text	Field Size—30 Caption—Company Name
Industry	Text	Field Size—2 Input Mask—>LL
Symbol	Text	Field Size—6

Figure 1
Structure of the tblCOMPANY table

Figure 2 shows the structure of the tblFINANCE table, which tracks the yearly financial data for each company. The tblFINANCE table contains the same ID number used in the tblCOMPANY table and contains additional data on the sales, assets, and profits for each company for a given year, 1993 or later.

Field Name	Data Type	Properties
CompanyID	Text	Field Size—3 Input Mask—>L00 Caption—Company ID
Year	Number	Field Size—Integer
Sales	Currency	Description—Rounded to the nearest million. Decimal Places—0
Assets	Currency	Description—Rounded to the nearest million. Decimal Places—0
Profits	Currency	Description—Rounded to the nearest million. Decimal Places—0

Figure 2
Structure of the tblFINANCE table

Pat wants to create a new customized version of the database so that clients can choose information more easily. She formulates the following plan: she will modify the field properties in the tblCOMPANY and tblFINANCE tables, add a table for industry codes and descriptions, add relationships for the three tables, and create and save four queries. She will then create the form shown in Figure 3 using Form Wizards. This new form makes it easier for both her own staff and her clients to add current financial data to the database.

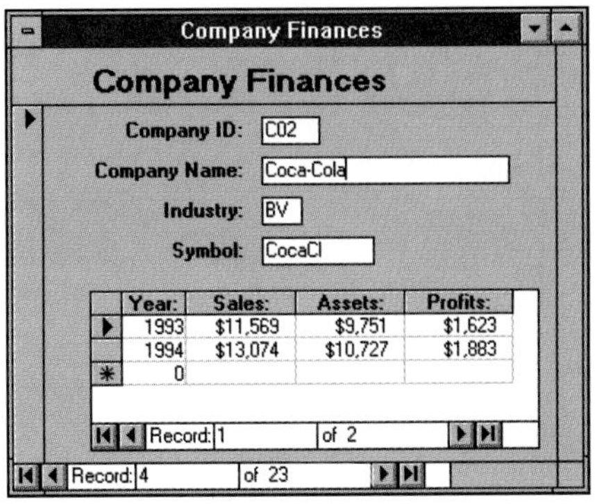

Figure 3 The frmCompanyFinance form created by Form Wizards

Pat plans to create a custom form, shown in Figure 4, that uses all three tables to display a company's financial information, a year at a time. Calculations are included on this form for the company's rate of return and profit margin.

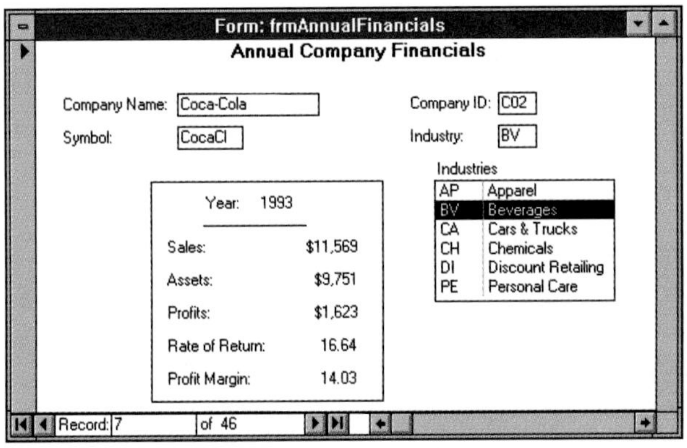

Figure 4 The custom frmAnnualFinancials form

Next, Pat plans to create two reports that are easy to generate and are of presentation quality. The first report, shown in Figure 5, groups companies by industry and provides industry and overall totals. The second report, shown in Figure 6, summarizes sales, assets, and profits by industry.

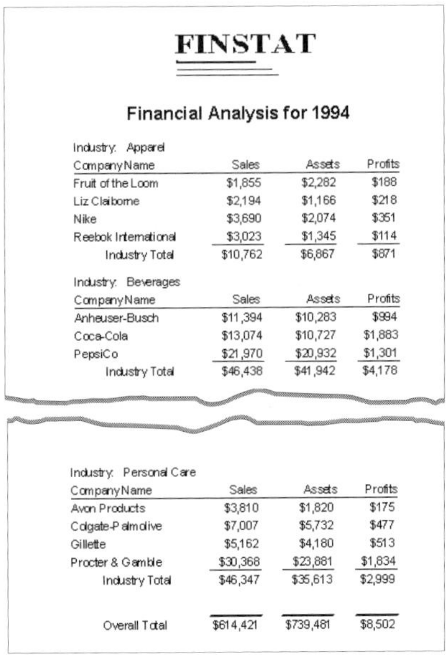

FINSTAT

Financial Analysis for 1994

Industry: Apparel

Company Name	Sales	Assets	Profits
Fruit of the Loom	$1,855	$2,282	$188
Liz Claiborne	$2,194	$1,166	$218
Nike	$3,690	$2,074	$351
Reebok International	$3,023	$1,345	$114
Industry Total	$10,762	$6,867	$871

Industry: Beverages

Company Name	Sales	Assets	Profits
Anheuser-Busch	$11,394	$10,283	$994
Coca-Cola	$13,074	$10,727	$1,883
PepsiCo	$21,970	$20,932	$1,301
Industry Total	$46,438	$41,942	$4,178

Industry: Personal Care

Company Name	Sales	Assets	Profits
Avon Products	$3,810	$1,820	$175
Colgate-Palmolive	$7,007	$5,732	$477
Gillette	$5,162	$4,180	$513
Procter & Gamble	$30,368	$23,881	$1,834
Industry Total	$46,347	$35,613	$2,999
Overall Total	$614,421	$739,481	$8,502

Figure 5 The custom rptIndustry1994 report

FINSTAT

Industry Summary for 1994

Industry Desc	Sales	Assets	Profits
Apparel	$10,762	$6,867	$871
Beverages	$46,438	$41,942	$4,178
Cars & Trucks	$268,062	$406,313	($2,616)
Chemicals	$64,533	$73,315	$1,125
Discount Retailing	$178,279	$175,431	$1,945
Personal Care	$46,347	$35,613	$2,999
Grand Total:	$614,421	$739,481	$8,502

Figure 6 The custom rptIndustry-1994Summary report

After creating a crosstab query showing the sales by company name and by year, and a bar chart showing average sales and average profits by year, Pat plans to design and create a switchboard, add an AutoExec macro, and create an event procedure for one of the new forms. Figure 7 shows the switchboard Pat eventually creates.

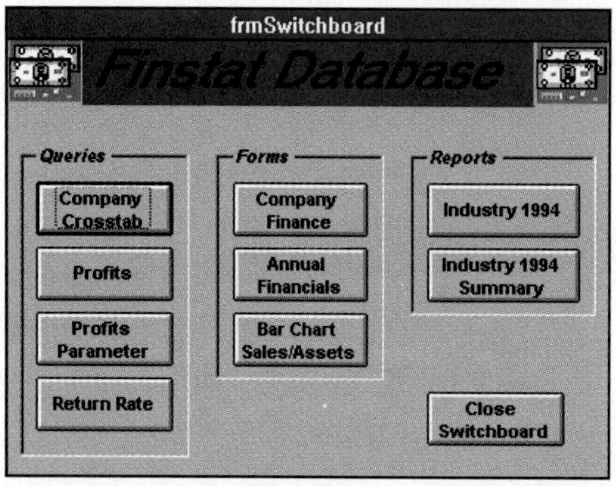

Figure 7 The Finstat database switchboard

Complete the following to create the customized database:

1. Place your Student Disk in the appropriate drive, launch Access, and open the Finstat database on your Student Disk.
2. Review the tblCOMPANY and tblFINANCE tables to become familiar with their structures and datasheet contents. If you are unfamiliar with any property setting, use the Access Help system for an explanation of that property.
3. For the tblCOMPANY table, make CompanyName a required field and make CompanyID the primary key. For the tblFINANCE table, add a validation rule for the Year field to allow values greater than or equal to 1993, add an appropriate validation-text message, and make the combination of CompanyID and Year the primary key. Finally, add a one-to-many relationship between the primary tblCOMPANY table and the related tblFINANCE table using CompanyID as the common field and enforcing referential integrity.

4. The tblCOMPANY table contains the Industry field, which stores a two-character industry code. The acceptable industry codes and associated industry descriptions are: AP (Apparel), BV (Beverages), CA (Cars & Trucks), CH (Chemicals), DI (Discount Retailing), PE (Personal Care). Design and create a new table to store the industry codes and industry descriptions, using the field names Industry and IndustryDesc and making Industry the primary key. Name this table tblINDUSTRY and add the six industry records to the table. Add a one-to-many relationship between the primary tblINDUSTRY table and the related tblCOMPANY table using the two-character industry code as the common field and enforcing referential integrity. Print the six records from the tblINDUSTRY table.
5. Create and save a query with the name qryProfits that displays the CompanyID, CompanyName, Year, IndustryDesc, Sales, and Profits for all companies with sales above 4000 and profits above 300. Print the query results in ascending order by profits.
6. For all companies, display the CompanyName, Sales, Assets, Profits, and RateOfReturn for the year 1994. Calculate RateOfReturn by dividing Profits by Assets (format RateOfReturn as a percent with one decimal place). Print the query results in descending order by RateOfReturn and save the query with the name qryReturnRate.
7. For all companies, display the CompanyID, CompanyName, Industry, Symbol, Year, Sales, Assets, Profits, RateOfReturn, and ProfitMargin. Calculate RateOfReturn by dividing Profits by Assets and then multiplying by 100. Calculate ProfitMargin by dividing Profits by Sales and then multiplying by 100. For both RateOfReturn and ProfitMargin, use a fixed format with two decimal places. Print the query results in ascending order by CompanyName as the primary sort key and Year as the secondary sort key and save the query with the name qryCompany.
8. Create and save a parameter query with the name qryProfitsParameter that displays the CompanyName, Symbol, Sales, Assets, Profits, and Industry for companies during 1994 in a selected industry (use Industry as the parameter). Print the query results in ascending order by Profits using the parameter value PE.
9. Use Form Wizards to create the form shown in Figure 3. Use the tblCOMPANY and tblFINANCE tables, save the subform with the name frmSubFinance and the main/subform form with the name frmCompanyFinance, and print the first record.

E 10. Create the custom form shown in Figure 4 and save it with the name frmAnnualFinancials. Use the qryCompany query as the basis for the form, position label boxes and text boxes as shown in Figure 4, add a list box to display data from the tblINDUSTRY table, and draw a rectangle around the financial information. Use the Border Style property to remove the boxes from the financial text boxes. Print the first and last records of the custom form.

E 11. Create a query using the tblCOMPANY, tblFINANCE, and tblINDUSTRY tables to select all the financial records for the year 1994. Refer to Figure 5 to determine which fields to include in the query and which fields to use as sort keys. Name and save the query as qryIndustry1994. Then create the custom report shown in Figure 5, using the qryIndustry1994 query as the basis for the report, save it with the name rptIndustry1994, and print the report. (***Note:*** The FINSTAT logo at the top of the report is stored as finlogo.bmp on the Student Disk.)

12. Create the Industry Summary for 1994 report shown in Figure 6. Base the report on the qryIndustry1994 query. Save the report with the name rptIndustry1994Summary. Print the report. (***Hint:*** Use the previous report as a guide, but include only summary information for this report.)

13. Create a crosstab query showing the sales by company name and by year. Include a row summary, save the query with the name qryCompanyCrosstab, and print the query results.
14. Create a form with a bar chart showing average sales and average assets by year for all companies. Because the Sales and Assets fields are rounded to the nearest million, eliminate the decimals from the Y-axis labels. Save the form with the name frmBarChartSales&Assets and print the form.

E 15. Design and create a switchboard, using Figure 7 as a model, and save it with the name frmSwitchboard. Provide appropriate wording for the title bar and a heading at the top center of the switchboard. Add the finmoney.bmp graphic image from your Student Disk to an appropriate location on the switchboard. On the switchboard, place 10 command buttons to perform these actions:
   - open the qryProfits query,
   - open the qryReturnRate query,
   - open the qryProfitsParameter query,
   - open the qryCompanyCrosstab query,
   - open the frmCompanyFinance form,
   - open the frmAnnualFinancials form,
   - open the frmBarChartSales&Assets form,
   - open the rptIndustry1994 report,
   - open the rptIndustry1994Summary report, and
   - close the switchboard and activate the Database window.

   Create a macro group for these command buttons. Use appropriate background and foreground colors and visual effects for the switchboard and its components, and size and position the switchboard in the Form View window. Test the switchboard.

E 16. Add an AutoExec macro to hide the Database window and open the frmSwitchboard form whenever you open the Finstat database.

E 17. For the frmAnnualFinancials form, display the Rate of Return field value with a ForeColor value of 128 when it's over 10 and with the default black color otherwise. Similarly, display the Profit Margin field value with a ForeColor value of 128 when it's over 10 and with the default black color otherwise.

Additional Case 2

Customer Orders for Pet Provisions

OBJECTIVES

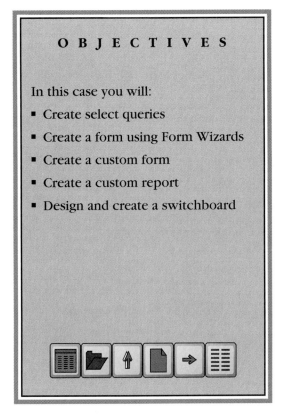

In this case you will:

- Create select queries
- Create a form using Form Wizards
- Create a custom form
- Create a custom report
- Design and create a switchboard

CASE

Pet Provisions Pet Provisions, started by Manny Cordova in 1991, sells pet food and pet supplies to pet shops around the world. His company has enjoyed steady annual increases in sales, but profits have lagged behind. Manny asks his office manager, Kerri Jackson, to tighten the company's collection methods as a first step in improving profits.

Currently the office maintains an Access database that contains information on its customers. After looking over the database, Kerri realizes that there is no easy way to tell which client accounts are paid in full and which have outstanding balances. She decides to create the necessary forms, queries, and reports to automate the collection process. Her work will include creating an all-important invoice report that she can automatically generate to send to any client with an outstanding balance.

Kerri uses the Pet database, an Access database, as the starting point for her work. Among the tables in the Pet database are the tblCUSTOMER and tblORDER tables. Figure 8 shows the structure for the tblCUSTOMER table, which contains one record for each customer. CustomerNum is the primary key for the table, which has 26 customer records. The other fields in the table are CustomerName, Street, City, State/Prov, Zip/PostalCode, Country, Phone, and FirstContact.

Field Name	Data Type	Properties
CustomerNum	Number	Primary Key Field Size—Integer Format—Fixed Decimal Places—0 Caption—Customer Num Required—Yes
CustomerName	Text	Field Size—35 Caption—Customer Name
Street	Text	Field Size—30
City	Text	Field Size—20
State/Prov	Text	Field Size—20
Zip/PostalCode	Text	Field Size—10 Caption—Zip/Postal Code
Country	Text	Field Size—20
Phone	Text	Field Size—15
FirstContact	Date/Time	Format—m/d/yy Caption—First Contact

Figure 8
Structure of the tblCUSTOMER table

Figure 9 shows the structure for the tblORDER table, which contains one record for each customer order. OrderNum is the table's primary key. CustomerNum is a foreign key in the tblORDER table, and the tblCUSTOMER table has a one-to-many relationship with the tblORDER table.

Field Name	Data Type	Properties
OrderNum	Number	Primary Key Field Size—Integer Format—Fixed Decimal Places—0 Caption—Order Num Required—Yes
CustomerNum	Number	Field Size—Integer Format—Fixed Decimal Places—0 Caption—Customer Num Required—Yes
SaleDate	Date/Time	Format—m/d/yy Caption—Ship Via
Ship Via	Text	Field Size—7 Caption—Ship Via
TotalInvoice	Number	Field Size—Double Format—Standard Decimal Places—2 Caption—Total Invoice
AmountPaid	Number	Field Size—Double Format—Standard Decimal Places—2 Caption—Amount Paid
PayMethod	Text	Field Size—5 Caption—Pay Method

Figure 9
Structure of the tblORDER table

Kerri plans to create special queries, forms, and reports to help her analyze the 144 orders in the tblORDER table. One of the special forms, shown in Figure 10, displays all orders for a customer along with totals for the customer's invoices, amount paid, and amount owed. Kerri also creates a special report, shown in Figure 11, that she can send to customers owing money to Pet Provisions.

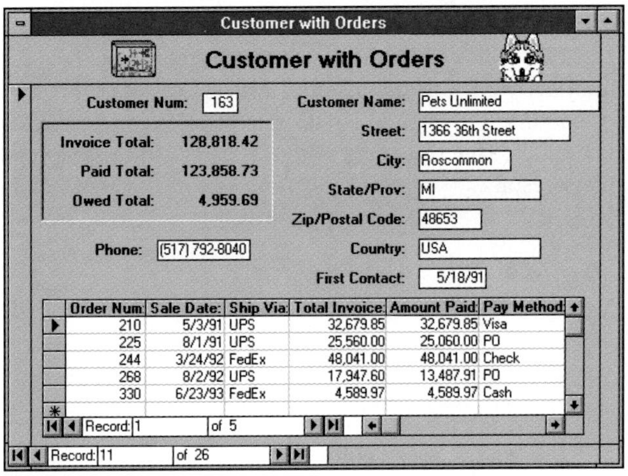

Figure 10
The frmCustomerWith-Orders form

Customer 163
Pets Unlimited
1366 36th Street
Roscommon MI
USA 48653 (517) 792-8040

Pet Provisions

Please pay your outstanding balance of: $4,959.69
for these orders:

Order Num	Sale Date	Invoice Total	Amount Paid	Balance
225	8/1/91	25,560.00	25,060.00	500.00
268	8/2/92	17,947.60	13,487.91	4,459.69

Figure 11
The custom rptCustomer-Statement report

Complete the following to analyze profits at Pet Provisions:

1. Place your Student Disk in the appropriate drive, launch Access, and open the Pet database on your Student Disk.
2. Review the tblCUSTOMER and tblORDER tables to become familiar with their structures and datasheet contents. If you are unfamiliar with any property settings, use the Access Help system for an explanation of that property.
3. Create and save a query with the name qryOrderTotals that displays the grand total number of orders and grand totals for the TotalInvoice, AmountPaid, and TotalOwed fields. TotalOwed, a calculated field, is the difference between the TotalInvoice and AmountPaid fields. Print the query results.
4. For all orders that have not been paid in full, display the CustomerName, Phone, SaleDate, TotalInvoice, AmountPaid, and AmountOwed. Print the query results in descending order by AmountOwed and save the query with the name qryOpenOrders.
5. For all orders that have not been paid in full, create and save a query with the name qryOwedByCustomer that displays the total number of orders and totals for the TotalInvoice, AmountPaid, and AmountOwed fields, grouped by CustomerName. Print the query results. (***Hint***: Use the qryOpenOrders query as the basis for this query. The query dynaset contains five columns, including one for the CustomerName field.)
6. Use Form Wizards to create a form to maintain all fields in the tblCUSTOMER table and a second form to maintain all fields in the tblORDER table. Save the forms with the names frmCUSTOMER and frmORDER, respectively. Use the forms to print the first record from each table.
7. Create and save two special queries that will be used with the special form shown in Figure 10. For the first query, use the tblORDER table to display totals for the TotalInvoice, AmountPaid, and AmountOwed fields, grouping by CustomerNum and using the column names Invoice Total, Paid Total, and Owed Total, respectively. Save the query with the name qryCustomerOrderTotals and print the query results. For the second query, use the qryCustomerOrderTotals query and the tblCUSTOMER table; display the CustomerNum, TotalInvoice, AmountPaid, AmountOwed, CustomerName, Street, City, State/Prov, Zip/PostalCode, Country, Phone, and FirstContact fields; and sort in ascending order by CustomerNum. Save the query with the name qryCustomerWithTotals and print the query results.

E 8. Create the custom form shown in Figure 10 and save it with the name frmCustomerWithOrders. To create an initial approximation of the form, use Form Wizards to create a main/subform form, using the qryCustomerWithTotals query for the main form and the tblORDER table for the subform. Save the subform with the name frmSubOrder. (Click OK in the dialog box warning you that the "Main/Subform Form Wizard couldn't establish a link between the main form and the subform.") Then change the form so that it looks similar to the form shown in Figure 10. Use the Border Style property to remove the boxes from the three text boxes between the Customer Num and Phone boxes. To establish the link between the main form and the subform, click the subform box in the Form Design window and type CustomerNum in the Link Child Fields box and the Link Master Fields box in the property sheet. Print the first record of the custom form. (***Note***: The bitmaps that appear on the top of the form are stored as petfish.bmp and petdog.bmp on your Student Disk.)

E 9. Create and save a query with the name qryForSpecialReport that selects customers who owe money to Pet Provisions and unpaid orders for these customers. Refer to Figure 11 to determine which fields to include in the query. (***Hint***: Use the qryCustomerWithTotals query and the tblORDER table to create this query, create a join line between the CustomerNum fields, and sort in ascending order by CustomerNum as the primary sort key and OrderNum as the secondary sort key.) Then create the custom report shown in Figure 11, using the qryForSpecialReport query as the basis for the report, using a Group Header section based on CustomerNum, and placing orders in the Detail section. Set the ForceNewPage property in the Group Header section to the value Before Section so that one customer statement prints per page. Save the report with the name rptCustomerStatement and print pages six to eight of the report. (***Note***: The logo on the upper right of the report is stored as petlogo.bmp on your Student Disk.)

E 10. Design and create a switchboard with frmSwitchboard as the saved form name. Place command buttons on the switchboard to coordinate the running of these three forms, three queries, and one report: frmCUSTOMER, frmORDER, frmCustomerWithOrders, qryOpenOrders, qryOrderTotals, qryOwedByCustomer, and rptCustomerStatement. Also provide a command button to close the switchboard and activate the Database window.

Additional Case 3

Internship Program for Pontiac College

OBJECTIVES

In this case you will:

- Design a database and draw its entity-relationship diagram
- Create the tables and relationships for the database
- Create forms to maintain the database
- Design and enter test data for the database
- Create queries and reports from the database
- Design and create a switchboard

CASE

Pontiac College Pontiac College provides students with opportunities for professional development and field study through its internship program, administered by the Office of Internships and Field Experience. Students complement their courses with a structured training experience provided by qualified professionals in selected fields. Internships are offered in several hundred areas, including law, counseling, government, administration, public relations, communications, health care, computer programming, and marketing.

Anjali Bhavnani has just been hired as Pontiac's new Internship Coordinator. She is eager to make information about the sponsoring agencies, potential internships, and current student interns more readily available to her office and to the students who qualify for the program. Anjali's most ambitious project is to develop a computerized database for the internship program to help meet these goals.

Instead of visually scanning all internship possibilities, Anjali, her staff, and interested students will be able to select internships of specific interest to them. The new database will allow potential interns to view only the internships that meet the criteria they specify. Anjali asks Roula Mendes, an information systems major working in the Office of Internships and Field Experience, to help the office develop a computerized database system for the internship system.

Anjali first outlines for Roula the steps in the internship program process:

- Identify and document the available internships
- Arrange for student intern placements
- Assign and track student interns

As the first step in the internship program process, Anjali receives a letter or phone call from a potential sponsoring agency. After some discussions, a sponsoring agency proposes an internship possibility and fills out the Agency/Internship Information form, shown in Figure 12 (Anjali's office currently maintains this form on a word processor).

AGENCY/INTERNSHIP INFORMATION

AGENCY INFORMATION

NAME OF AGENCY ____________________

DEPARTMENT ____________________

ADDRESS ____________________
Street

____
City State Zip

CONTACT ____________________ PHONE ____________

INTERNSHIP INFORMATION

TITLE ____________________

DESCRIPTION OF DUTIES ____________________

ORIENTATION & TRAINING ____________________

ACADEMIC BACKGROUND REQUIRED ____________________

SUPERVISOR ____________________ PHONE ____________

Office Use

Agency ID ________

Intership ID ________

Category ________

Figure 12 The Agency/Internship Information form

Many agencies offer more than one type of internship possibility. For each possible internship, the agency fills out a separate form and assigns one person as the contact for all internship questions and problems. In addition, each internship lists a supervisor who will work with the student intern. The internship remains active until the agency notifies the Internship Office that the internship is filled or no longer available.

Anjali assigns a three-digit Agency ID to each new agency and a four-digit Internship ID to each new internship. These are sequential numbers. She also classifies each internship into a category that helps students identify internships that are related to their major or interests. For example, a student might be interested in health care, accounting, social service, or advertising.

A copy of each Agency/Internship Information form is placed in reference books in the Office of Internships and Field Experience. Students browse through these books to find internships that are of interest to them. If an internship interests a student, the student copies the information about the internship and contacts the sponsoring agency directly to request an interview.

When a student gets an internship, the student and agency establish a Learning Contract, outlining the goals to be accomplished during the internship. The student then fills out the Student Internship form, shown in Figure 13, to provide basic information on the student for the office files.

STUDENT INTERNSHIP

NAME ______________________________ SS# ____________

ADDRESS ______________________________
Street

____
City State ZIP

PHONE ____________

MAJOR ____________ GPA ________ CLASS ____ Junior _____ Senior

Office Use

Internship ID ____________
Internship Term ___ Fall ___ Spring ___ Summer
Internship Year ____________

Figure 13
The Student Internship form

Anjali enters the Internship ID and year on the Student Internship form and checks the term for the internship. Next, a clerk enters information from the form into a word processor to prepare lists of current interns and internships and then places the form in a binder.

Anjali and Roula determine that getting these two forms into an on-line Access database is their first priority, and then they will work on creating several new reports. The first report, whose design is shown in Figure 14, lists all student interns, alphabetically by last name, for a selected term. In order to identify the student interns who should be included in the report, the system prompts the user for the term and year.

<today's date>		**Student Interns** As of <term><year>	Page x
Last Name	First Name	Agency Name	Internship Title
X-----------------X	X-----------X	X-----------------------X	X-----------------X
X-----------------X	X-----------X	X-----------------------X	X-----------------X
X-----------------X	X-----------X	X-----------------------X	X-----------------X
X-----------------X	X-----------X	X-----------------------X	X-----------------X
		End of Report	

Figure 14
Student Interns report design

A second new report, whose design is shown in Figure 15, lists all agencies in the database alphabetically by agency name.

<today's date>		**Internship Agencies**	Page x
Agency Name	Department	Contact	Phone
X------------------X	X-----------------X	X-----------------X	X-------------------X
X------------------X	X-----------------X	X-----------------X	X-------------------X
X------------------X	X-----------------X	X-----------------X	X-------------------X
X------------------X	X-----------------X	X-----------------X	X-------------------X
		End of Report	

Figure 15
Internship Agencies report design

The Internship by Category report, whose design is shown in Figure 16, lists internships grouped by category. The staff will use this report when talking with students about the internship program.

<today's date>	**Internship by Category**		Page x
Category x____________x			
Internship ID	Internship Title	Internship Description	
XXXX	X__________________X	X____________________________________X	
		X____________________________________X	
		X____________________________________X	
XXXX	X__________________X	X____________________________________X	
XXXX	X__________________X	X____________________________________X	
		X____________________________________X	
Category x____________x			
Internship ID	Intership Title	Internship Description	
XXXX	X__________________X	X____________________________________X	
XXXX	X__________________X	X____________________________________X	
		X____________________________________X	
		X____________________________________X	
	End of Report		

Figure 16 Internship by Category report design

At the end of an internship, the intern's supervisor evaluates the intern's work experience, using an evaluation form mailed from the Office of Internships and Field Experience. Anjali needs mailing labels addressed to the supervisor of each intern for the current term and year. The mailing labels should contain the supervisor name on the first line; the agency name on the second line; the agency's street on the third line; and the agency's city, state, and zip on the fourth line.

Complete the following to create the complete database system:

1. Identify each entity (relation) in the database for the internship system.
2. Draw an entity-relationship diagram showing the entities and the relationships between the entities.
3. Design the database for the internship system. For each relation, list the fields and their attributes, such as data types, field sizes, and validation rules. Place the set of relations in third normal form and identify all primary, alternate, and foreign keys.
4. Create the database structure using Access and the database name Intern. Be sure to add relationships between appropriate tables.
5. Create forms to maintain data on agencies, internships, student interns, and any other entity in your database structure. The forms should be used to view, add, edit, and delete records in the database.
6. Create test data for each table in the database, and add it, using the forms created in Step 5.
7. Create the Student Interns report, Internship Agencies report, Internship by Category report, and mailing labels report. The layouts shown in Figures 14 through 16 are guides—improve the formats as you see fit.

8. Design and create a form that a student can use to view internships for a selected category. Display one internship at a time on the screen. For each internship, display the category, internship ID, title, description of duties, orientation and training, academic background, agency name, department, agency address, contact name, and contact phone. Provide an option to print the internship displayed on the screen.
9. Design and create a switchboard to coordinate the running of the internship system. (***Note***: Two graphic images, intmatch.bmp and inttrack.bmp, are available on your Student Disk for use on the switchboard or the form created in Step 8.)
10. Test all features of the internship system.

Microsoft Access 2.0 References

1 **Menu Commands**

2 **Functions**

3 **Toolbar Buttons**

ACCESS SECTION 1

Menu Commands

Menus Without an Open Database

File Menu (No Open Database)

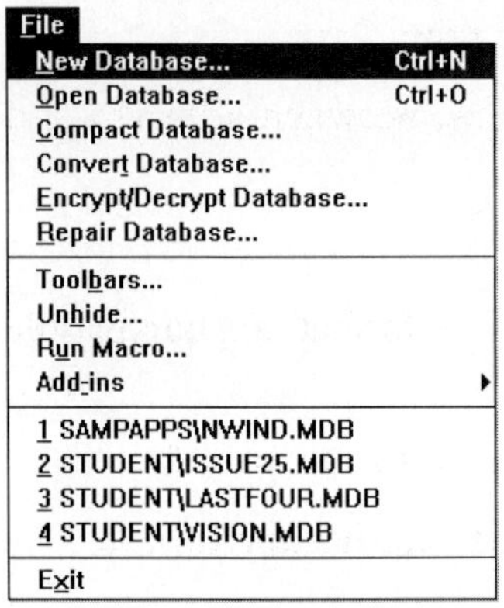

New Database Creates an empty database file.

Open Database Opens a previously existing database file.

Compact Database Reduces the amount of hard disk space that the database occupies.

Convert Database Upgrades a database created in an earlier version of Access to Access 2.0 format.

Encrypt/Decrypt Database Encodes (decodes) the database so that it cannot (can) be deciphered by a word processor or other application.

Repair Database Fixes a damaged database and recovers corrupted files.

Toolbars Specifies which toolbars will be visible while Access is used.

Unhide Reveals a window that is currently hidden.

Run Macro Begins a predetermined chain of events tied to a macro.

Add-ins Displays a list of additional options you can make available for use during a session.

File Names Displays the four most recently opened files; select any one to open it.

Exit Quits Access and returns to Windows. If files have been modified and not saved, Access presents a save option now.

Help Menu (No Open Database)

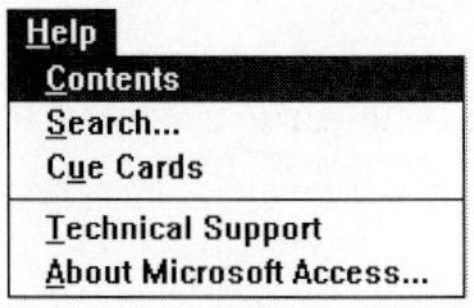

Contents Opens the Help window with the Table of Contents displayed.

Search Opens the Search window to locate specific help on a topic.

Cue Cards Displays the on-line tutorial for assistance.

Technical Support Provides an on-line listing of Microsoft Product Support.

About Microsoft Access Displays the current version of Microsoft Access and information on the computer system in use.

Database Window Menu Commands

File Menu (Database Window)

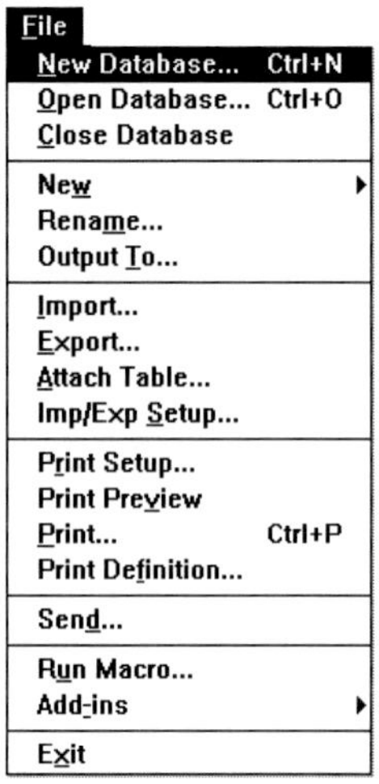

New Database Creates an empty database file.

Open Database Opens a previously existing database file.

Close Database Closes the current database. If modifications have been made since the last save, Access presents a save option now.

New Displays list of options for a new object; choose between a wizard and a blank option.

Rename Changes the name of the highlighted object.

Output To Saves the data to another application in the format of a compatible application such as Microsoft Excel or MS DOS Text.

Import Takes data from a non-Access source and creates a database file.

Export Transfers data from an Access database to an external application.

Attach Table Creates a new relationship between the Access database and a table from another application.

Imp/Exp Setup Opens a screen with options to modify the settings for importing and exporting data.

Print Setup Selects and modifies the printer used by Access. The printer settings can be changed as well.

Print Preview Shows how the database will appear on paper when printed.

Print Creates a paper copy of the document.

Print Definition Creates a paper copy of the selected database object.

Send Transmits the current object to another computer via electronic mail.

Run Macro Begins a predetermined chain of events tied to a macro.

Add-ins Displays a list of additional options you can make available for use during a session.

Exit Quits Access and returns to Windows. If files have been modified and not saved, Access presents a save option now.

Edit Menu (Database Window)

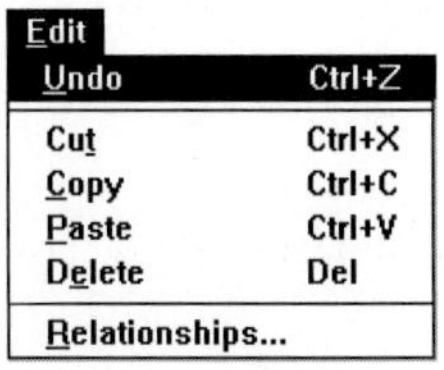

Undo (Can't Undo) Reverses most recent change. Selecting this option multiple times reverses actions in order of latest to earliest.

Cut Removes selected object from the database and places it on the clipboard.

Copy Creates a copy of the selected data and places it on the clipboard.

Paste Inserts data from the clipboard to the current cursor location.

Delete Removes the selected data or object permanently from the database.

Relationships Shows and edits relationships between the database objects in the current application.

View Menu (Database Window)

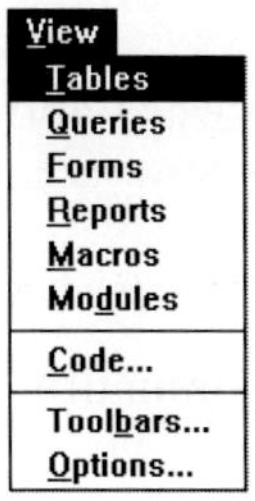

Tables Shows a list of all tables in the current database.

Queries Shows a list of all queries in the current database.

Forms Shows a list of all forms in the current database.

Reports Shows a list of all reports in the current database.

Macros Shows a list of all macros in the current database.

Modules Shows a list of all modules in the current database.

Code Opens a new form module or report module to create, edit, or view procedures.

Toolbars Shows, hides, and modifies the toolbars on the screen.

Options Modifies the user options for Access, including screen display and database applications.

Security Menu (Database Window)

Permissions Grants or denies access to the current database and objects for greater or reduced security.

Users Modifies the list of users on the database by creating (removing) user codes; also allows the assignment of users to groups.

Groups Defines or modifies collections of individual users that store user accounts.

Change Password Modifies the password of the current user to a new password.

Change Owner Assigns and modifies the owner/operator of the selected database or object.

Print Security Creates a paper copy of the user and group information related to security of the database.

Window Menu (Database Window)

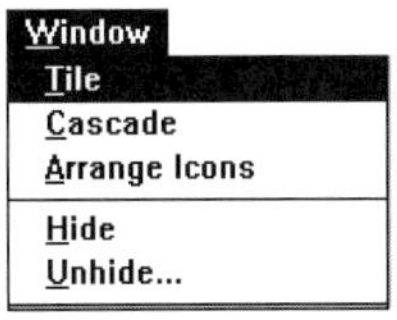

Tile Arranges open windows in a pattern side by side.

Cascade Arranges open windows in a diagonal stack.

Arrange Icons Arranges minimized windows (icons) in a row along the bottom of the screen.

Hide/Unhide Hides or reveals open windows.

(Window Name) Switches to one of the other open windows.

Help Menu (Database Window)

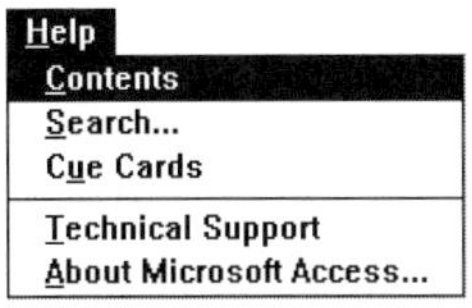

Contents Opens the Help window with the Table of Contents displayed.

Search Opens the Search window to locate specific help on a topic.

Cue Cards Displays the on-line tutorial for assistance.

Technical Support Provides an on-line listing of Microsoft Product Support.

About Microsoft Access Displays the current version of Microsoft Access and information on the computer system in use.

Table Window Menu Commands

(* indicates commands available in Design View or in other circumstances)

File Menu (Table Window)

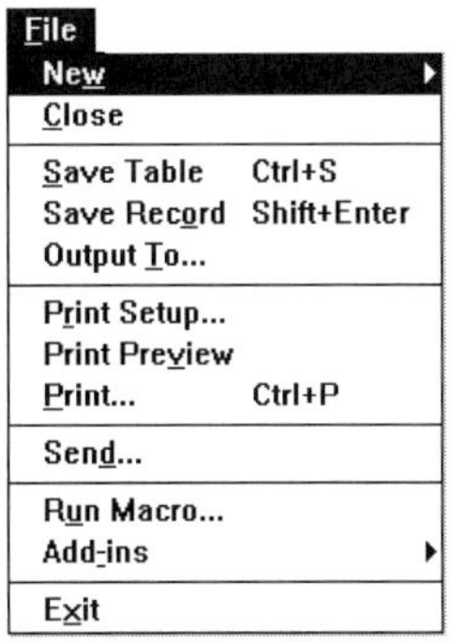

New Displays list of options for a new object; choose between a Wizard and a blank option.

Close Closes the current table. If modifications have been made since the last save, Access presents a save option now.

Save Table Saves the data and setup of the current table to the database.

Save Record Saves the current record to the database.

***Save** Saves the data and setup of the current report to the database.

***Save As** Saves the current database object to a new file with a new name.

Output To Saves the data to another application in the format of a compatible application such as Microsoft Excel or MS DOS Text.

Print Setup Selects and modifies the printer used by Access.

Print Preview Shows how the database will appear on paper when printed.

Print Creates a paper copy of the document.

***Print Definition** Creates a paper copy of the selected database object.

Send Transmits the current object to another computer via electronic mail.

Run Macro Begins a predetermined chain of events tied to a macro.

Add-ins Displays a list of additional options you can make available for use during a session.

Exit Quits Access and returns to Windows. If files have been modified and not saved, Access presents a save option now.

Edit Menu (Table Window)

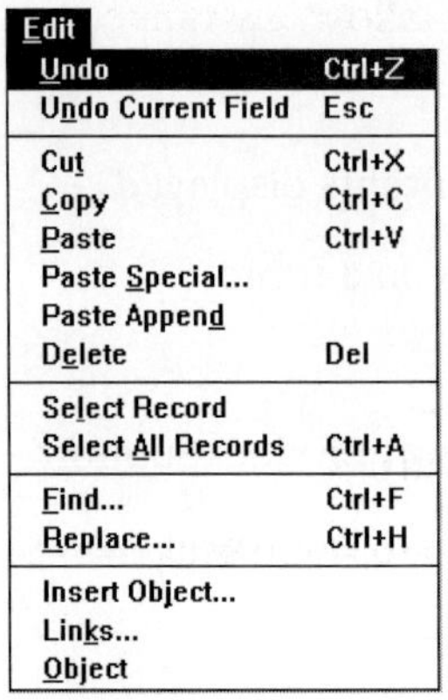

Undo (Can't Undo) Reverses most recent change. Selecting this option multiple times reverses actions in order of latest to earliest.

Undo Current Field Changes the current value of the specified field to its values prior to the most recent change.

Cut Removes selected object from the database and places it on the clipboard.

Copy Creates a copy of the selected data and places it on the clipboard.

Paste Inserts data from the clipboard to the current cursor location.

Paste Special Inserts objects from a compatible application to a database and formats the data to conform.

Paste Append Adds records from the clipboard to the end of the current database object.

Delete Removes the selected data or object permanently from the database.

Select Record Highlights data to be cut, copied, or deleted. Allows multiple records to be modified at once.

Select All Records Selects all of the records on the current database object.

***Select All** Highlights all of the data to be cut, copied, or deleted. Allows multiple records to be modified at once.

***Insert Row** Adds a new, empty row above the current row.

***Delete Row** Removes the highlighted row from the database.

Find Locates specified text for rapid access.

Replace Locates specified text and replaces it with new text.

Insert Object Adds an object or data from a compatible application into the current database object.

Links Changes, breaks, or adds a connection between multiple objects or files.

Object Activates an object that has been inserted or linked to another.

***Set Primary Key** Modifies which field provides identification for each record in the table.

View Menu (Table Window)

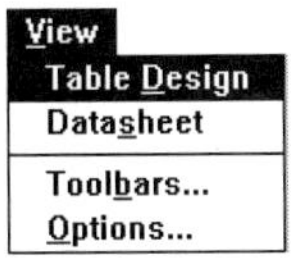

Table Design Shows the design characteristics of the current table.

Datasheet Shows the table and data in spreadsheet format.

***Indexes** Opens the Indexes window which allows the modification and creation of indexes in the database object.

***Table Properties** Opens the window that allows modifications to the attributes of the display of the table.

Toolbars Shows, hides, and modifies the toolbars on the screen.

Options Modifies the user options for Access. Options allow customization of the screen display and database applications.

Format Menu (Table Window)

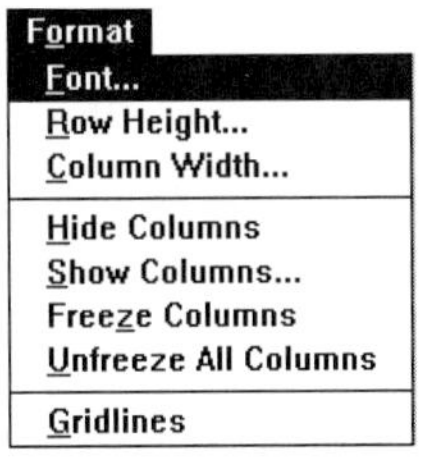

Font Selects the font used in the current datasheet.

Row Height Selects how tall the rows on the datasheet are.

Column Width Selects how wide the columns on the datasheet are.

Hide Columns Hides the selected column(s) from view.

Show Columns Selects columns on the datasheet. Also reveals hidden column(s).

Freeze Columns Prevents the selected column(s) from scrolling off the screen.

Unfreeze All Columns Removes freeze command from all columns and allows normal scrolling.

Gridlines Hides or shows the gridlines on the current datasheet.

Records Menu (Table Window)

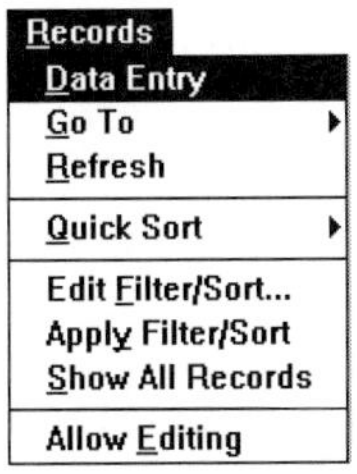

Data Entry Opens a new datasheet to store information and hides the current datasheet.

Go To Moves the cursor to the selected record on the current datasheet. The options are First, Last, Next, Previous, and New.

Refresh Adds data input by other users on the network to the current database object.

Quick Sort Arranges the data in either ascending or descending order in the current datasheet.

Edit Filter/Sort Modifies the filters that determine how the records are sorted or to which group they belong.

Apply Filter/Sort Uses the criteria of the filters to sort the records into groups on the current database object.

Show All Records Shows the most recent records on the current database object.

Allow Editing Permits (restricts) changes to the current datasheet.

Query Window Menu Commands

(* indicates commands available in Design View or in other circumstances)

File Menu (Query Window)

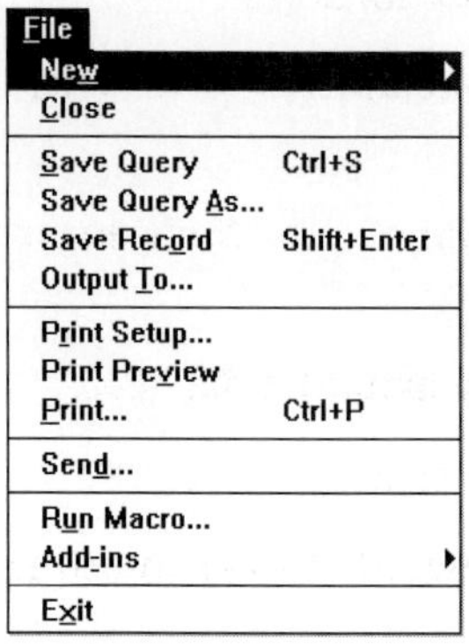

New Displays list of options for a new object; choose between a Wizard and a blank option.

Close Closes the current query. If modifications have been made since the last save, Access presents a save option now.

Save Query Saves the data and setup of the current query to the database.

Save Query As Saves the current database object to a new file with a new name.

***Save** Saves the data and setup of the current report to the database.

***Save As** Saves the current database object to a new file with a new name.

Save Record Saves the current record to the database.

Output To Saves the data to another application in the format of a compatible application such as Microsoft Excel or MS DOS Text.

Print Setup Selects and modifies the printer used by Access. The printer settings can be changed as well.

Print Preview Shows how the database will appear on paper when printed.

Print Creates a paper copy of the document.

***Print Definition** Creates a paper copy of the selected database object.

Send Transmits the current object to another computer via electronic mail.

Run Macro Begins a predetermined chain of events tied to a macro.

Add-ins Displays a list of additional options you can make available for use during a session.

Exit Quits Access and returns to Windows. If files have been modified and not saved, Access presents a save option now.

Edit Menu (Query Window)

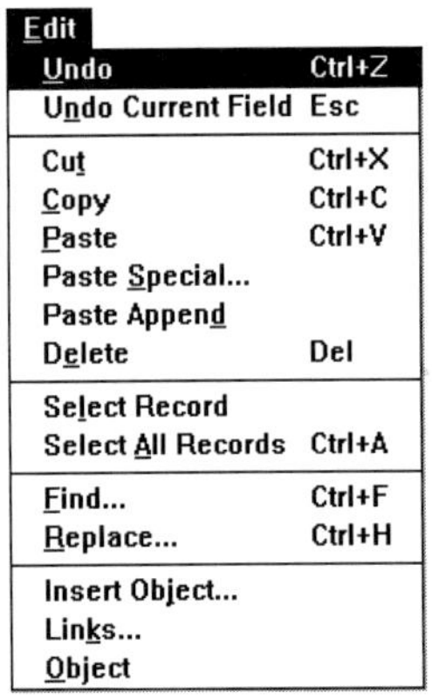

Undo (Can't Undo) Reverses most recent change. Selecting this option multiple times reverses actions in order of latest to earliest.

***Undo All** Reverses all of the changes made to the SQL text on the current query.

Undo Current Field Changes the current value of the specified field to its value prior to the most recent change.

Cut Removes selected object from the database and places it on the clipboard.

Copy Creates a copy of the selected data and places it on the clipboard.

Paste Inserts data from the clipboard to the current cursor location.

Paste Special Inserts objects from a compatible application to a database and formats the data to conform.

Paste Append Adds records from the clipboard to the end of the current database object.

Delete Removes the selected data or object permanently from the database.

***Clear Grid** Deletes the data from the current query or grid.

Select Record Highlights data to be cut, copied, or deleted. Allows multiple records to be modified at once.

Select All Records Selects all of the records on the current database object.

Find Locates specified text for rapid access.

Replace Locates specified text and replaces it with new text.

Insert Object Adds an object or data from a compatible application into the current database object.

Links Changes, breaks, or adds a connection between multiple objects or files.

Object Activates an object that has been inserted or linked to another.

***Insert Row** Adds a new, empty row above the current row.

***Delete Row** Removes the highlighted row from the database.

***Insert Column** Adds a new, empty column to the left of the current column.

***Delete Column** Removes the highlighted column from the database.

View Menu (Query Window)

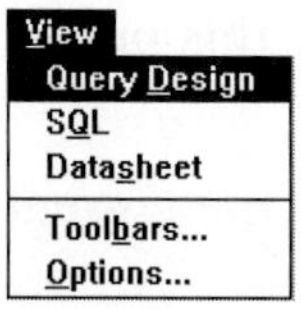

Query Design Shows the design characteristics of the current query and allows modification.

SQL Shows the query table in Structured Query Language, which is used to manage relational databases.

Datasheet Shows the table and data in spreadsheet format.

***Totals** Shows or hides the totals on the current query datasheet.

***Table Names** Shows or hides the table names involved in the current query.

***Properties** Modifies the attributes of the display of the current database object.

***Join Properties** Modifies how the queries are joined to one another.

Toolbars Shows, hides, and modifies the toolbars on the screen.

Options Modifies the user options for Access. Options allow customization of the screen display and database applications.

Query Menu (Query Window)

Run Begins the active query.

Add Table Includes an additional table into the current query.

Remove Table Excludes one of the tables already involved in the current query.

Select Makes the current query ask questions about the current data without changing the data.

Crosstab Changes the current query to a spreadsheet format with specified row and column headings.

Make Table Allows the current query to modify tables or create new tables.

Update Allows the current query to modify tables based on specified criteria.

Append Copies records from the current query to specified tables.

Delete A toggle that allows the current query to delete records from table based on given criteria.

SQL Specific Offers three options for queries based on Standard Query Language. **Union** makes snapshots of multiple tables, even when not related. **Pass-through** allows a client machine direct access to a server's tables. **Data-definition** modifies tables and indexes.

Join Tables Provides helpful messages on how to join tables in the current query.

Parameters Changes the current query to locate records based on specified criteria that will be used on a regular basis.

Form Window Menu Commands

(* indicates commands available in Design View or in other circumstances)

File Menu (Form Window)

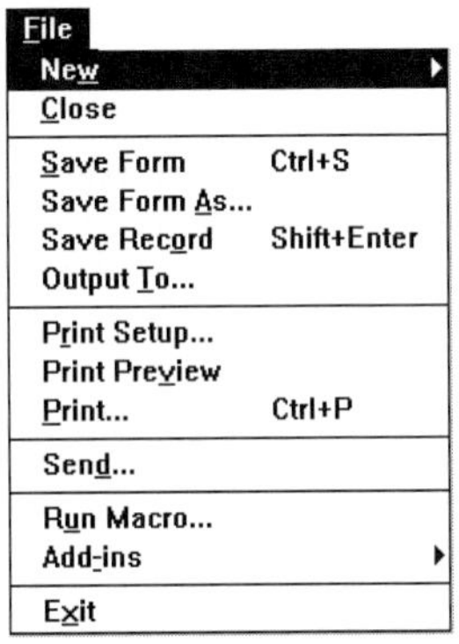

New Displays list of options for a new object; choose between a Wizard and a blank option.

Close Closes the current form. If modifications have been made since the last save, Access presents a save option now.

Save Form Saves the data and setup of the current form to the database.

Save Form As Saves the current database object to a new file with a new name.

Save Record Saves the current records to the database.

***Save** Saves the data and setup of the current report to the database.

***Save As** Saves the current database object to a new file with a new name.

***Save As Report** Copies the current form to the database in the form of a report.

Output To Saves the data to another application in the format of a compatible application such as Microsoft Excel or MS DOS Text.

Print Setup Selects and modifies the printer used by Access. The printer settings can be changed as well.

Print Preview Shows how the database will appear on paper when printed.

Print Creates a paper copy of the document.

***Print Definition** Creates a paper copy of the selected database object.

Send Transmits the current object to another computer via electronic mail.

Run Macro Begins a predetermined chain of events tied to a macro.

Add-ins Displays a list of additional options you can make available for use during a session.

Exit Quits Access and returns to Windows. If files have been modified and not saved, Access presents a save option now.

Edit Menu (Form Window)

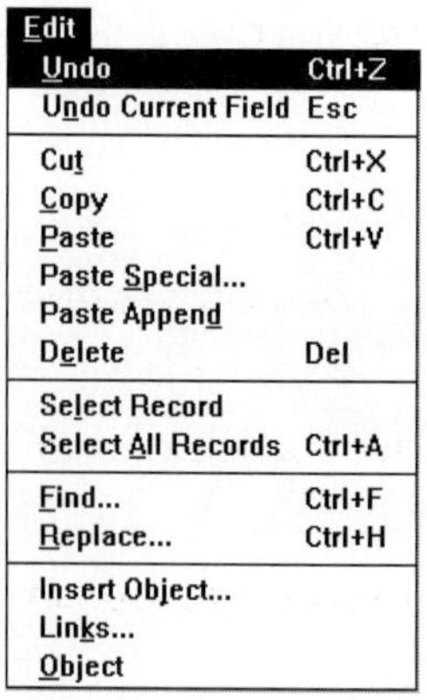

Undo (Can't Undo) Reverses most recent change. Selecting this option multiple times reverses actions in order of latest to earliest.

Undo Current Field Changes the current value of the specified field to its value prior to the most recent change.

Cut Removes selected object from the database and places it on the clipboard.

Copy Creates a copy of the selected data and places it on the clipboard.

Paste Inserts data from the clipboard to the current cursor location.

Paste Special Inserts objects from a compatible application to a database and formats the data to conform.

Paste Append Adds records from the clipboard to the end of the current database object.

Delete Removes the selected data or object permanently from the database.

***Duplicate** Copies the selected graphical object on the current database object.

Select Record Highlights data to be cut, copied, or deleted. Allows multiple records to be modified at once.

Select All Records Selects all of the records on the current database object.

***Select All** Highlights all of the data to be cut, copied, or deleted. Allows multiple records to be modified at once.

***Select Form** When displayed, chooses the form in design view.

Find Locates specified text for rapid access.

Replace Locates specified text and replaces it with new text.

Insert Object Adds an object or data from a compatible application into the current database object.

Links Changes, breaks, or adds a connection between multiple objects or files.

Object Activates an object that has been inserted or linked to another.

***Tab Order** Modifies the order in which the Tab key selects fields in the form.

View Menu (Form Window)

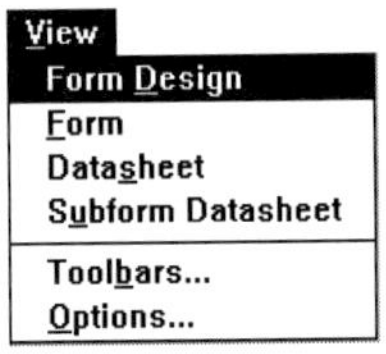

Form Design Shows the design characteristics of the current form.

Form Shows the form in its standard format.

Datasheet Shows the form and data in spreadsheet format.

Subform Datasheet Shows forms nested within the current database object in spreadsheet format.

***Field List** Opens and closes the field list that contains fields that exist in the database. These fields can be added to the report.

***Properties** Shows the property form of the selected record or object. Allows modifications to the properties of the selected item.

***Code** Opens the Module window.

***Ruler** Shows (hides) the measuring strip on the design view.

***Grid** Shows (hides) the dot grid on the design view.

***Toolbox** Shows (hides) the toolbox icon menu on the design screen.

***Palette** Shows (hides) the selection of colors on the design screen.

***Control Wizards** Activates (deactivates) the control wizards.

Toolbars Shows, hides, and modifies the toolbars on the screen.

Options Modifies the user options for Access. Options allow customization of the screen display and database applications.

Format Menu (Form Window)

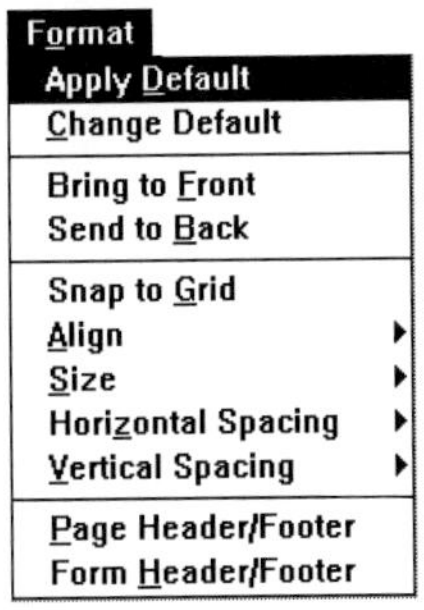

Apply Default Changes the settings of the current report to the default settings.

Change Default Modifies the default settings of the database to the current settings and saves them.

Bring to Front Brings a selected graphical object to the front of the current report.

Send to Back Puts the selected graphical object behind the current report.

Snap to Grid Aligns controls to the grid.

Align Presents a list of options on the alignment of objects in the form (left, right, top, bottom, or on a grid).

Size Modifies the size of objects in the form based on the criteria.

Horizontal Spacing Modifies the horizontal spacing of the report to the chosen criteria.

Vertical Spacing Modifies the vertical spacing of the report to the chosen criteria.

Page Header/Footer Creates or deletes the headers and footers of the current page.

Form Header/Footer Creates of deletes the headers and footers of the current form.

***Font** Selects the font used in the current datasheet.

***Row Height** Selects how tall the rows on the datasheet are.

***Column Width** Selects how wide the columns on the datasheet are.

***Hide Columns** Hides the selected column(s) from view.

***Show Columns** Selects columns on the datasheet. Also reveals hidden column(s).

***Freeze Columns** Prevents the selected columns from scrolling off the screen.

***Unfreeze All Columns** Removes freeze command from all columns and allows normal scrolling.

***Gridlines** A toggle that hides or shows the gridlines on the current datasheet.

Records Menu (Form Window)

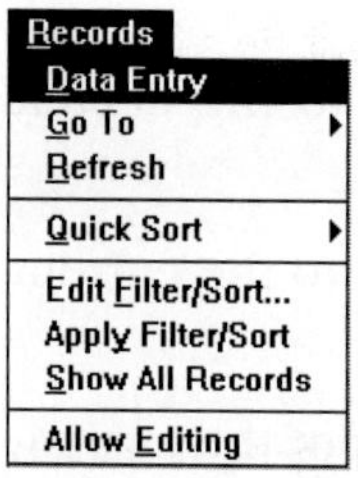

Data Entry Opens a new datasheet to store information and hides the current datasheet.

Go To Moves the cursor to the selected record on the current datasheet. The options are First, Last, Next, Previous, and New.

Refresh Adds data input by other users on the network to the current database object.

Quick Sort Arranges the data in either ascending or descending order in the current datasheet.

Edit Filter/Sort Modifies the filters that determine how the records are sorted or to which group they belong.

Apply Filter/Sort Uses the criteria of the filters to sort the records into groups on the current database object.

Show All Records Shows the most recent records on the current database object.

Allow Editing Permits (restricts) changes to the current datasheet.

Report Window Menu Commands

File Menu (Report Window)

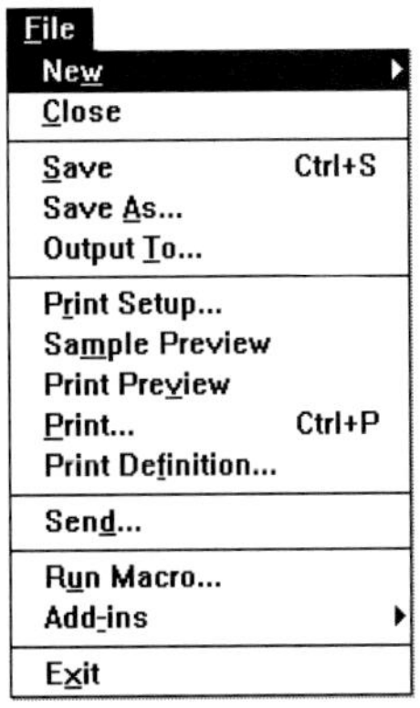

New Displays list of options for a new object; choose between a wizard and a blank option.

Close Closes the current report. If modifications have been made since the last save, Access presents a save option now.

Save Saves the data and setup of the current report to the database.

Save As Saves the current database object to a new file with a new name.

Output To Saves the data to another application in the format of a compatible application such as Microsoft Excel or MS DOS Text.

Print Setup Selects and modifies the printer used by Access. The printer settings can be changed as well.

Sample Preview Shows how the data looks in a quick preview.

Print Preview Shows how the database will appear on paper when printed.

Print Creates a paper copy of the document.

Print Definition Creates a paper copy of the selected database object.

Send Transmits the current object to another computer via electronic mail.

Run Macro Begins a predetermined chain of events tied to a macro.

Add-ins Displays a list of additional options you can make available for use during a session.

Exit Quits Access and returns to Windows. If files have been modified and not saved, Access presents a save option now.

Edit Menu (Report Window)

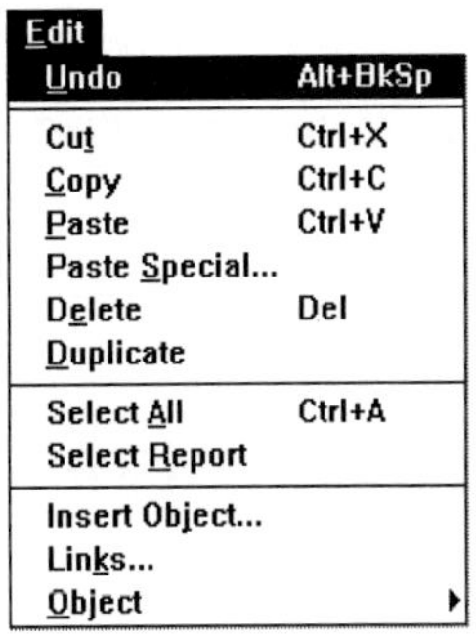

Undo (Can't Undo) Reverses most recent change. Selecting this option multiple times reverses actions in order of latest to earliest.

Cut Removes selected object from the database and places it on the clipboard.

Copy Creates a copy of the selected data and places it on the clipboard.

Paste Inserts data from the clipboard to the current cursor location.

Paste Special Inserts objects from a compatible application to a database and formats the data to conform.

Delete Removes the selected data or object permanently from the database.

Duplicate Copies the selected graphical object on the current database object.

Select All Selects all objects in the report.

Select Report When displayed in design view, chooses the report.

Insert Object Adds an object or data from a compatible application into the current database object.

Links Changes, breaks, or adds a connection between multiple objects or files.

Object Activates an object that has been inserted or linked to another.

View Menu (Report Window)

Sorting and Grouping Modifies the group levels of the report.

Field List Opens and closes the field list, which contains fields that are used in the report.

Properties Shows the property form of the selected record or object. Allows modifications to the properties of the selected item.

Code Opens the Module window.

Ruler Shows (hides) the measuring strip on the design view.

Grid Shows (hides) the dot grid on the design view.

Toolbox Shows (hides) the toolbox icon menu on the design screen.

Palette Shows (hides) the selection of colors on the design screen.

Control Wizards Activates (deactivates) the control wizards.

Toolbars Shows, hides, and modifies the toolbars on the screen.

Options Modifies the user options for Access. Options allow customization of the screen display and database applications.

Format Menu (Report Window)

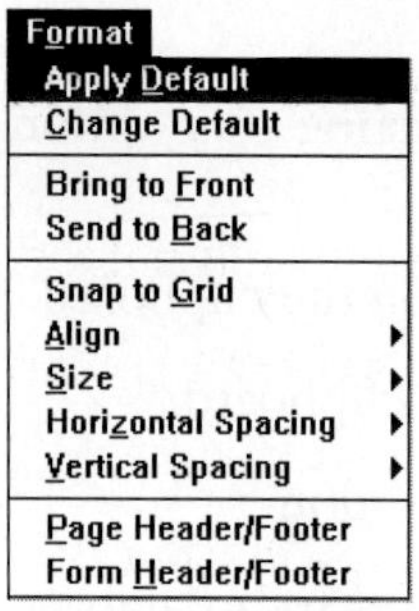

Apply Default Changes the settings of the current report to the default settings.

Change Default Modifies the default settings of the database to the current settings and saves them.

Bring to Front Brings a selected graphical object to the front of the current report.

Send to Back Puts the selected graphical object behind the current report.

Snap to Grid Aligns controls to the grid.

Align Presents a list of options on the alignment of the objects in a report (left, right, top, bottom, or on a grid).

Size Modifies the size of the objects in a report based on the criteria.

Horizontal Spacing Modifies the horizontal spacing of the objects in a report to the chosen criteria.

Vertical Spacing Modifies the vertical spacing of the report to the chosen criteria.

Page Header/Footer Creates or deletes the headers and footers of the current page.

Report Header/Footer Creates or deletes the headers and footers of the current report.

Macro Window Menu Commands

File Menu (Macro Window)

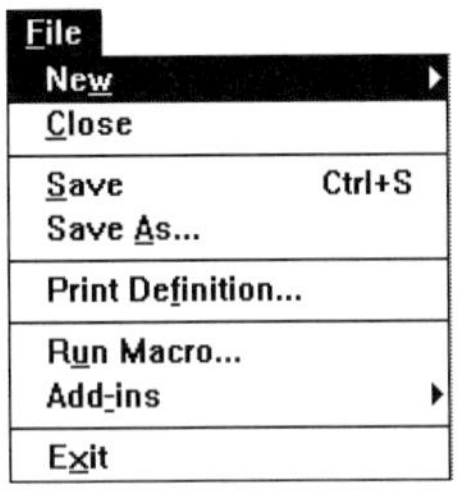

New Displays list of options for a new object; choose between a wizard and a blank option.

Close Closes the current macro. If modifications have been made since the last save, Access presents a save option now.

Save Saves the data and setup of the current macros to the database.

Save As Saves the current database object to a new file with a new name.

Print Definition Creates a paper copy of the selected database object.

Run Macro Begins a predetermined chain of events tied to a macro.

Add-ins Displays a list of additional options you can make available for use during a session.

Exit Quits Access and returns to Windows. If files have been modified and not saved, Access presents a save option now.

Edit Menu (Macro Window)

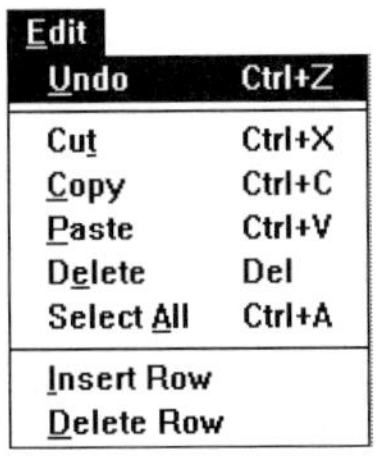

Undo (Can't Undo) Reverses most recent change. Selecting this option multiple times reverses actions in order of latest to earliest.

Cut Removes selected object from the database and places it on the clipboard.

Copy Creates a copy of the selected data and places it on the clipboard.

Paste Inserts data from the clipboard to the current cursor location.

Delete Removes the selected data or object permanently from the database.

Select All Highlights all of the data to be cut, copied, or deleted. Allows multiple records to be modified at once.

Insert Row Adds a new, empty row above the current row.

Delete Row Removes the highlighted row from the database.

View Menu (Macro Window)

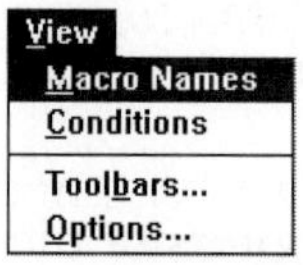

Macro Names Shows or hides the names of all of the macros on the datasheet.

Conditions Shows or hides the conditions column of the datasheet.

Toolbars Shows, hides, and modifies the toolbars on the screen.

Options Modifies the user options for Access. Options allow customization of the screen display and database applications.

Macro Menu (Macro Window)

Run Begins the operation of the specified macros.

Single Step Toggles the single step function of the current macros. Single stepping runs the actions in a macro individually in order.

Module Window Menu Commands

File Menu (Module Window)

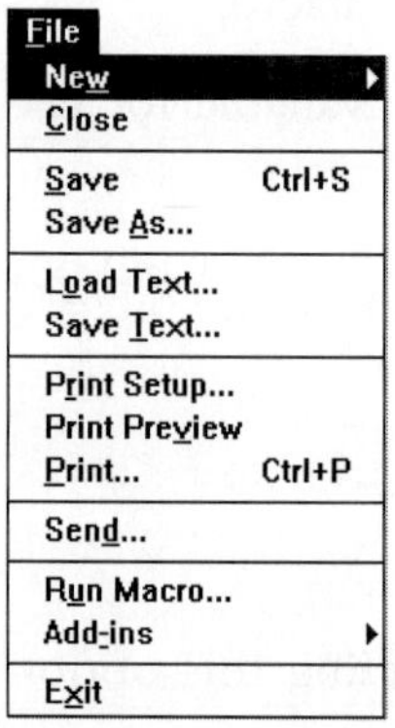

New Displays list of options for a new object; choose between a wizard and a blank option.

Close Closes the current module. If modifications have been made since the last save, Access presents a save option now.

Save Saves the data and setup of the current modules to the database.

Save As Saves the current database object to a new file with a new name.

Load Text Imports text/code from other text files; can replace or merge the text/code already in the module.

Save Text Saves code in a module to a text file.

Print Setup Selects and modifies the printer used by Access. The printer settings can be changed as well.

Print Preview Shows how the database will appear on paper when printed.

Print Creates a paper copy of the document.

Send Saves output to a file and attaches file to electronic mail message.

Run Macro Begins a predetermined chain of events tied to a macro.

Add-ins Displays a list of additional options you can make available for use during a session.

Exit Quits Access and returns to Windows. If files have been modified and not saved, Access presents a save option now.

Edit Menu (Module Window)

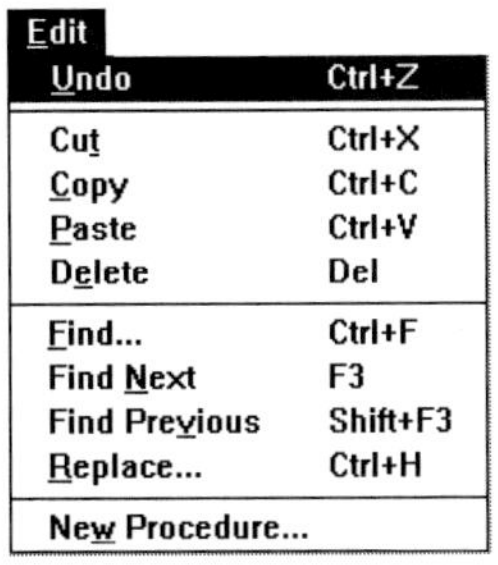

Undo (Can't Undo) Reverses the last action performed.

Cut Removes selected text from the module.

Copy Creates a copy of the selected data and places it on the clipboard.

Paste Inserts data from the clipboard to the current cursor location.

Delete Removes the selected data or object permanently from the database.

Find Locates specified text for rapid access.

Find Next Locates the next occurrence of a specific piece of text.

Find Previous Locates the last occurrence of a specific piece of text.

Replace Locates specified text and replaces it with new text.

New Procedure Creates a new procedure, either a sub or function, within the current module.

View Menu (Module Window)

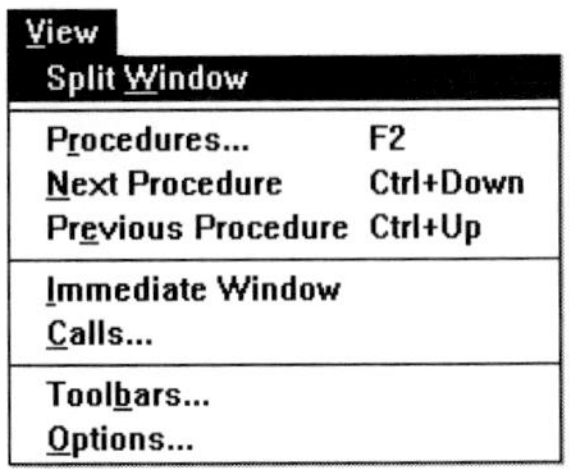

Split Window Allows the user to view two different portions of the module at the same time.

Procedures Shows all of the procedures in use in the current database object.

Next Procedure Views the next procedure in the list.

Previous Procedure Views the previous procedure in the list.

Immediate Window Displays the immediate window, which allows for the debugging and testing of procedures in the module.

Calls Locates and identifies all of the active procedures that are called by the code.

Toolbars Shows, hides, and modifies the toolbars on the screen.

Options Modifies the user options for Access. Options allow customization of the screen display and database applications.

Run Menu (Module Window)

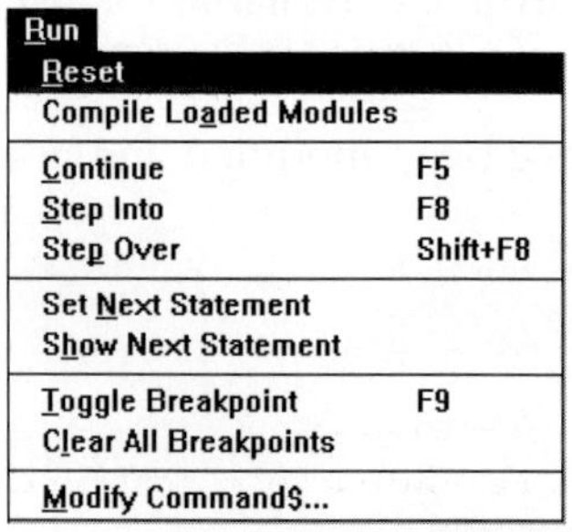

Reset Stops the use of all of the procedures in Access and clears the variables they hold.

Compile Loaded Modules Compiles all procedures in all modules in the database.

Continue Resumes code usage unless the codes have been specifically stopped by a previous action.

Step Into Slows the debugging process to one step at a time. This allows the effects of each statement to be registered before the next is begun. Step Into will enter a procedure within a statement.

Step Over Slows the debugging process to one step at a time. This allows the effects of each statement to be registered before the next is begun. Step Over will skip a procedure within a statement.

Set Next Statement Allows the insertion of a statement at the point of the cursor. The next statement must be a part of the same procedure.

Show Next Statement Displays the next sequential statement in the procedure.

Toggle Breakpoint Creates or deletes a line that will stop the execution of a procedure at that point to allow debugging of the procedure.

Clear All Breakpoints Removes all of the breakpoints in all of the modules in the current database.

Modify Command$ Enables the user to modify or add an argument to a command and test code's response to it.

Functions

The function name appears in boldface. Arguments are italicized and appear in parenthesis. Optional arguments are enclosed in brackets.

Abs Abs(*number*) returns the absolute value of *number*.

Asc Asc(*stringexpression*) returns the ANSI code for the first character of *stringexpression*.

Atn Atn(*number*) returns the inverse tangent of *number*.

Avg Avg(*expr*) returns the average (arithmetic mean) of the values in the field specified by *expr*.

Choose Choose(*indexnum*, *varexpr* [, *varexpr*] . . .) returns the value of the *varexpr* specified by *indexnum*, a numeric expression from 1 to the number of *varexpr* expressions (up to 13).

Chr Chr[$](*charcode*) returns the character specified by the ANSI code *charcode*. Chr returns a Variant data type, and Chr$ returns a String.

CodeDB CodeDB() returns a database object that specifies the database in which the code is running.

Command Command[$][()] returns the argument portion (anything following /cmd) of the command line that launched Access. Command returns a Variant data type, and Command$ returns a String.

Count Count(*expr*) returns the number of selected records in the field specified by *expr*.

CreateControl CreateControl(*formname* As String, *controltype* As Integer [, *section* As Integer [, *parent* As String [, *fieldname* As String [, *left* As Integer [, *top* As Integer [, *width* As Integer [, *height* As Integer]]]]]]]) creates a control on the open form.

CreateForm CreateForm([*database* [, *formtemplate*]]) creates a form, returning a Form object.

CreateGroupLevel CreateGroupLevel(*report*, *expression*, *header*, *footer*) creates a new group level on the specified *report*, sorting or grouping by *expression*, giving the group a *header* or *footer* if True (!1).

CreateObject CreateObject(*class*) creates an OLE Automation object, specified by *class*, an argument with two parts (separated by a period), the name of the application used to create the object and the type of object created.

CreateReport CreateReport([*database* [, *reporttemplate*]]) creates a report, returning a Report object.

CreateReportControl CreateReportControl (*reportname* As String, *controltype* As Integer [, *section* As Integer [, *parent* As String [, *fieldname* As String [, *left* As Integer [, *top* As Integer [, *width* As Integer [, *height* As Integer]]]]]]]) creates a control on the open report.

CurDir CurDir[$][(*drive*)] returns the directory in the Open Database dialog box, as Variant data type, or as a String if $ is included.

CurrentUser CurrentUser() returns the current user's name.

CVDate CVDate(*expression*) converts an *expression* that can be interpreted as a date to the Variant data type VarType 7.

Data Type Conversion Functions CCur, CDbl, CInt, CLng, CSng, CStr, and CVar (all with the argument *expression*) convert *expression* to the data types Currency, Double, Integer, Long, Single, String, and Variant, respectively.

Date Date[$][()] returns the current system date, as Variant data type (VarType 7) if $ is omitted, or as a String, if $ is included.

DateAdd DateAdd(*interval*, *number*, *date*) returns a date (as Variant data type VarType 7) after or before *date*, the length of time being *number* times *interval*, which is *yyyy* (years), *q* (quarters), *m* (months), *y* (day of year), *d* (days), *w* (weekdays), *ww* (week), *h* (hours), *n* (minutes), or *s* (seconds).

DateDiff DateDiff(*interval*, *date1*, *date2*[, *firstweekday*][, *firstweek*]) returns a Variant data type that contains the number of time intervals between *date1* and *date2*; *interval* is as in DateAdd.

DatePart DatePart(*interval*, *date*[, *firstweekday*][, *firstweek*]) returns the part of *date* specified by *interval*, as in DateAdd.

DateSerial DateSerial(*year*, *month*, *day*) returns the date for the specified *year*, *month*, and *day* as Variant date type VarType 7.

DateValue DateValue(*stringexpression*) returns the date specified by *stringexpression* as Variant data type VarType 7.

DAvg DAvg(*expr*, *domain*[, *criteria*]) calculates and returns the arithmetic mean of the values in the records specified by *domain*, in the field *expr*.

Day Day(*number*) returns the day of the month (an integer from 1 to 31) of the date represented by *number*.

DCount DCount(*expr*, *domain*[, *criteria*]) returns the number of selected records in the *domain* of the field *expr*.

DDB DDB(*cost*, *salvage*, *life*, *period*) returns the depreciation of an item with initial price *cost*, salvage value *salvage*, and useful lifetime *life*, using the double-declining balance method.

DDE DDE(*application*, *topic*, *item*) initiates dynamic data exchange with *application*, and returns the *item* of information in *topic* (two arguments recognizable by the *application*).

DDEInitiate DDEInitiate(*application*, *topic*) initiates dynamic data exchange with *application*, and returns a Variant data type containing a channel number, which is used by other DDE functions and statements to refer to this link.

DDERequest DDERequest(*channum*, *item*) requests information via the DDE link *channum*.

DDESend DDESend(*application*, *topic*, *item*, *data*) initiates dynamic data exchange with *application*, and sends *data* to the *item* in the *topic* of the other application.

Derived Math Functions Here is a list of derived mathematical functions available in Access Basic:

Arccos(*x*)	Inverse cosine
Arccosec(*x*)	Inverse cosecant
Arccotan(*x*)	Inverse cotangent
Arcsec(*x*)	Inverse secant
Arcsin(*x*)	Inverse sine
Cos(*x*)	Cosine
Cosec(*x*)	Cosecant
Cotan(*x*)	Cotangent
HArccos(*x*)	Inverse hyperbolic cosine
HArccosec(*x*)	Inverse hyperbolic cosecant
HArccotan(*x*)	Inverse hyperbolic cotangent
HArcsec(*x*)	Inverse hyperbolic secant
HArcsin(*x*)	Inverse hyperbolic sine
HArctan(*x*)	Inverse hyperbolic tangent
HCos(*x*)	Hyperbolic cosine
HCosec(*x*)	Hyperbolic cosecant
HCotan(*x*)	Hyperbolic cotangent
HSec(*x*)	Hyperbolic secant
HSin(*x*)	Hyperbolic sine
HTan(*x*)	Hyperbolic tangent
LogN(*x*)	Logarithm
Sec(*x*)	Secant
Sin(*x*)	Sine
Tan(*x*)	Tangent

DFirst DFirst(*expr*, *doman in*[, *criteria*]) returns a field value from the first record of *domain*.

Dir Dir[$][(*filespec*)] returns a file name matching the path or file name *filespec*, as a Variant, or a String if $ is included.

DLast DLast(*expr*, *domain*[, *criteria*]) returns a field value from the last record of *domain*.

DLookup DLookup(*expr*, *domain*[, *criteria*]) returns a field value from the set of records *domain*; *expr* identifies the field or performs calculations using data in a field.

DMax DMax(*expr*, *domain*[, *criteria*]) returns the maximum value of the values in the field specified by *expr*, in the records of *domain*.

DMin DMin(*expr*, *domain*[, *criteria*]) returns the minimum value of the values in the field specified by *expr*, in the records of *domain*.

DStDev DStDev(*expr*, *domain*[, *criteria*]) returns an estimate of the sample standard deviation of the values in the field specified by *expr*, in the records of *domain*.

DStDevP DStDevP(*expr*, *domain*[, *criteria*]) returns an estimate of the population standard deviation of the values in the field specified by *expr*, in the records of *domain*.

DSum DSum(*expr*, *domain*[, *criteria*]) returns the sum of the values in the field specified by *expr*, in the records of *domain*.

DVar DVar(*expr*, *domain*[, *criteria*]) returns an estimate of the sample variation of the values in the field specified by *expr*, in the records of *domain*.

DVarP DVarP(*expr*, *domain*[, *criteria*]) returns an estimate of the population variation of the values in the field specified by *expr*, in the records of *domain*.

Environ Environ[$](*environmentstring*) returns the string associated with the operating system environment variable *environmentstring*, as Variant data type if $ is omitted, or as a String if $ is included. Environ[$](*n*) returns the *n*th string of the environment string table.

EOF EOF(*filenumber*) returns True if the end of a file has been reached, and False if not.

Erl Erl returns an Integer that is the line number of the line where the error occurred.

Err Err returns the error status, an Integer runtime error code.

Error Error[$][(*errorcode*)] returns the error message corresponding to *errorcode*, or the message corresponding to the most recent run-time error, as Variant data type if $ is omitted, or as a String if $ is included.

Eval Eval(*stringexpr*) returns the value of *stringexpr* evaluated.

Exp Exp(*number*) returns *e* raised to the power *number*.

FileAttr FileAttr(*filenumber*, *attribute*) returns file handle information about the open file specified by *filenumber*, the number used in the Open statement that opened the file. If *attribute* is 2, the operating system handle for the file is returned; if *attribute* is 1, the return indicates the file's mode: 1 for Input, 2 for Output, 4 for Random, 8 for Append, and 32 for Binary.

First First(*expr*) returns the field value of the field specified by *expr*, from the first record.

Fix Fix(*number*) returns the integer portion of a positive number, or the first negative integer greater than or equal to *number*, if it is negative.

Format Format[$](*expression*[, *fmt*][, *firstweekday*][, *firstweek*]) formats *expression* to the format specified by *fmt*. If *fmt* is omitted and *expression* is numeric, Format[$] converts *expression* to the appropriate data type, as the Str[$] function.

FreeFile FreeFile[()] returns the next unused file number.

FV FV(*rate*, *nper*, *pmt*, *pv*, *due*) returns the future value of an annuity with *rate* interest rate per period, *nper* payments of size *pmt*, and present value *pv*; *due* is 0 if payments are due at the end of each period, and 1 if at the beginning.

GetObject GetObject(*filename*[, *class*]) returns an OLE object from the specified file; *class* represents the object class, and is a two-part argument, *appname.objecttype*.

Hex Hex[$](*number*) converts *number* from decimal to hexadecimal, and returns the result as Variant data type if $ is omitted, or as a String if $ is included.

Hour Hour(*number*) returns an integer between 0 and 23, the hour of the day of the time *number*.

IIf IIf(*expr*, *truepart*, *falsepart*) returns *truepart* if *expr* is true, and *falsepart* if *expr* is false.

Input Input[$](*n*, [#]*filenumber*) returns the first *n* characters read from the file specified by *filenumber*, the number used in the open statement that opened the file, as Variant data type if [$] is omitted, or as a String if $ is included.

InputBox InputBox[$](*prompt*[, [*title*] [, [*default*][, *xpos*, *ypos*]]]) displays a prompt in the dialog box, allowing input or a button choice, and returns the contents of the text box; *prompt* is the message displayed in the dialog box, *title* appears in the title bar, *default* is the default return, *xpos* is the distance in twips from the left edge of the screen to the left edge of the box, and *ypos* is the distance in twips from the top of the screen to the top of the box.

InStr InStr([*start*,] *strexpr1*, *strexpr2*) returns the position of the first occurrence of *strexpr2* within *strexpr1*, starting the search from character number *start*. InStr(*start*, *strexpr1*, *strexpr2*, *compare*) performs a case-sensitive search if *compare* is 0; if *compare* is 1, the search is not case sensitive; if *compare* is 2, the string comparison method is Database, using the New Database Sort Order.

Int Int(*number*) returns the integer portion of *number* if it is positive; if it is negative, the first negative integer less than or equal to *number* is returned.

IPmt IPmt(*rate*, *per*, *nper*, *pv*, *fv*, *due*) returns the interest payment for the payment period *per*, on an annuity with *rate* interest rate per period, *nper* total periods, *pv* present value, *fv* future value; *due* is 0 if payments are due at the end of the periods, and 1 if payments are due at the beginning.

IRR IRR(*valuearray*(), *guess*) returns the internal rate of return for periodic cash flows contained in *valuearray*; *guess* is a guess at the return (usually 0.1).

IsDate IsDate(*variant*) returns True if *variant* can be converted to a date, and False if not.

IsEmpty IsEmpty(*variant*) returns True if *variant* contains the Empty value (has not been initialized), and False if not.

IsNull IsNull(*variant*) returns True if *variant* contains Null, and False if not.

IsNumeric IsNumeric(*variant*) returns True if *variant* can be converted to a number, and False if not.

Last Last(*expr*) returns the field value of the field specified by *expr*, from the last record.

LBound LBound(*array*[, *dimension*]) returns the smallest available subscript for *array; dimension* determines which dimension of the array is examined; if omitted, the default is 1, for the first dimension.

LCase LCase[$](*strexpr*) converts *strexpr* to lowercase, and returns as Variant data type, if $ is omitted, or as a String, if $ is included.

Left Left[$](*strexpr*, *n*) returns the *n* left characters of *strexpr*, as Variant data type if $ is omitted, and as a String if $ is included.

Len Len(*strexpr*) returns the number of characters (length) of *strexpr*. Len(*variablename*) returns the number of bytes used to store *variablename*.

Loc Loc(*filenumber*) returns the current position within the file specified by *filenumber*, the number used in the Open statement that opened the file.

LOF LOF(*filenumber*) returns the size (in bytes) of the file specified by *filenumber*, the number used in the Open statement that opened the file.

Log Log(*number*) returns the natural logarithm of *number*.

LTrim LTrim[$](*stringexpr*) returns *stringexpr* with the leftmost spaces removed, as Variant data type if $ is omitted, and as a String if $ is included.

Max Max(*expr*) returns the largest of a set of values in the field specified by *expr*.

Mid Mid[$](*stringexpr*, *start*[, *length*]) returns the portion of *stringexpr* starting from character number *start*, of length *length*, or to the end of *stringexpr*, if *length* is omitted. Returns Variant data type if $ is omitted, and a String if $ is included.

Min Min(*expr*) returns the smallest of a set of values in the field specified by *expr*.

Minute Minute(*number*) returns a number between 0 and 59, the minutes after the hour of the time *number*.

MIRR MIRR(*valuearray*(), *financerate*, *reinvestrate*) calculates and returns the modified internal rate of return for the cash flows in *valuearray*, where *financerate* is the rate paid on payments, and *reinvestrate* is the rate earned on receipts.

Month Month(*number*) returns a number between 1 and 12, the month of the year of the date *number*.

Now Now[()] returns the current system date and time as Variant data type VarType 7.

NPer NPer(*rate*, *pmt*, *pv*, *fv*, *due*) returns the number of payment periods for an annuity with *rate* interest rate per period, payment size *pmt*, present value *pv*, and future value *fv*; *due* is 0 if payments are due at the end of the payment period, and 1 if they are due at the beginning.

NPV NPV(*rate*, *valuearray*()) returns the net present value of cash flows in *valuearray*, with discount rate *rate*.

Oct Oct[$](*number*) returns the decimal number *number* in octal form, as Variant data type if $ is omitted, and as a String if $ is included.

Partition Partition(*number*, *start*, *stop*, *interval*) returns a range of numbers that includes *number*. The ranges are calculated from *start* to *stop* (nonnegative integers) with length *interval*, and the one that contains *number* is returned.

Pmt Pmt(*rate*, *nper*, *pv*, *fv*, *due*) returns the payment for an annuity with *rate* interest rate per period, *nper* payment periods, present value *pv*, and future value *fv; due* is 0 if payments are due at the end of each period, and 1 if they are due at the beginning.

PPmt PPmt(*rate*, *per*, *nper*, *pv*, *fv*, *due*) returns the principal payment for payment period *per*, for an annuity with *rate* interest rate per period, *nper* payment periods, present value *pv*, and future value *fv*; *due* is 0 if payments are due at the end of each period, and 1 if they are due at the beginning.

PV PV(*rate*, *nper*, *pmt*, *fv*, *due*) returns the present value of an annuity with *rate* interest rate per period, *nper* payment periods, payment size *pmt*, and future value *fv*; *due* is 0 if payments are due at the end of each period, and 1 if they are due at the beginning.

QBColor QBColor(*qbcolor*) returns the red-green-blue color value corresponding to color number *qbcolor*.

Rate Rate(*nper*, *pmt*, *pv*, *fv*, *due*, *guess*) returns the interest rate per period of an annuity with *nper* payment periods, payment size *pmt*, present value *pv*, and future value *fv*; *due* is 0 if payments are due at the end of each period, and 1 if they are due at the beginning; *guess* is your guess for the rate (usually .1).

RGB RGB(*red*, *green*, *blue*) returns a number of Long data type that represents the color with components *red*, *green*, and *blue*.

Right Right[$](*stringexpr*, *n*) returns the *n* rightmost characters of *stringexpr*, as Variant data type if $ is omitted, and as a String if $ is included.

Rnd Rnd[(*number*)] returns a random number less than 1 and greater than or equal to 0. If *number* is positive or omitted, the next random number in the sequence is generated; if *number* is negative, the same random number is returned every time; if *number* is 0, the most recently generated random number is returned.

RTrim RTrim[$](*stringexpr*) returns *stringexpr* with the rightmost spaces removed, as Variant data type if $ is omitted, and as a String if $ is included.

Second Second(*number*) returns a number between 0 and 59, the seconds of the time *number*.

Seek Seek(*filenumber*) returns the current file position of the file specified by *filenumber*, the number used in the Open statement used to open the file.

Sgn Sgn(*number*) returns 1 if *number* is positive, 0 if *number* is 0, and !1 if *number* is negative.

Shell Shell(*commandstring*[, *windowstyle*]) runs the program specified by *commandstring*.

SLN SLN(*cost*, *salvage*, *life*) returns the straight-line depreciation of an asset with initial price *cost*, salvage value *salvage*, and useful life *life*.

Space Space[$](*number*) returns *number* of spaces, as Variant data type if $ is omitted, and as a String if $ is included.

Spc Spc(*number*) prints *number* of blank spaces, in a Print # statement or Print method.

Sqr Sqr(*number*) returns the positive square root of *number*.

StDev StDev(*expr*) returns an estimate of the sample standard deviation of the values in the field specified by *expr*.

StDevP StDevP(*expr*) returns an estimate of the population standard deviation of the values in the field specified by *expr*.

Str Str[$](*number*) returns *number* as Variant data type if $ is omitted, and as a String if $ is included.

StrComp StrComp(*stringexpr1*, *stringexpr2*[, *compare*]) converts *stringexpr1* and *stringexpr2* to Variant data types and compares them; if *compare* is 0, the comparison is case sensitive; 1, the comparison is not case sensitive; 2, the comparison uses the New Database Sort Order; if *compare* is omitted, the comparison method is that set by the Option Compare statement. The return is !1 if *stringexpr2* is less than *stringexpr2*, 0 if they are equal, and 1 if *stringexpr1* is greater than *stringexpr2*.

String String[$](*number*, *charcode*) returns a string of the character with ANSI code *charcode*, repeated *number* times. String[$](*number*, *string*) returns a string of the first character of *string*, repeated *number* times.

Sum Sum(*expr*) returns the sum of the values in the field specified by *expr*.

Switch Switch(*varexpr1*, *var1*[, *varexpr2*, *var2* . . . [, *varexpr7*, *var7*]]) returns the *var* expression corresponding to the first *varexpr* expression that is True (!1).

SYD SYD(*cost*, *salvage*, *life*, *period*) returns the sum-of-years' digits depreciation for an asset with initial price *cost*, salvage value *salvage*, useful lifetime *life*, and period of depreciation *period*.

SysCmd ReturnValue = SysCmd(*action*[, *text*][, *value*]) is used to display a progress meter, return the version number of Access, information about .INI and .EXE files, or the state of the active database object.

Tab Tab(*column*) is used with the Print # statement and the Print method, and causes the next character to be printed starting at column number *column*.

Time Time[$][()] returns the current system time, as Variant data type if $ is omitted, and as a String if $ is included.

Timer Timer[()] returns the number of seconds elapsed since midnight.

TimeSerial TimeSerial(*hour*, *minute*, *second*) returns the specified time as Variant data type of VarType 7, a number between 0 and 0.99999.

TimeValue TimeValue(*stringexpression*) returns the time represented by the string argument *stringexpression*, as Variant data type of VarType 7, a number between 0 and 0.99999.

Trim Trim[$](*stringexpr*) returns *stringexpr* with leading and trailing spaces removed.

UBound UBound(*array*[, *dimension*]) returns the largest available subscript for *array*; *dimension* determines which dimension of the array is examined; if omitted, the default is 1, for the first dimension.

UCase UCase[$](*stringexpr*) returns *stringexpr* with all letters converted to uppercase, as Variant data type if $ is omitted, and as a String if $ is included.

Val Val(*stringexpression*) returns the numeric value of *stringexpression*, ignoring blanks and stopping at any character that is not part of a number.

Var Var(*expr*) returns an estimate of the sample variation of the values in the field specified by *expr*.

VarP VarP(*expr*) returns an estimate of the population variance of the values in the field specified by *expr*.

VarType VarType(*variant*) returns a number from 0 to 8, corresponding to the VarType of *variant* (Empty, Null, Integer, Long, Single, Double, Currency, Date, and String, respectively).

Weekday Weekday(*dateexpression* [, *firstweekday*]) returns a number between 1 (Sunday) and 7 (Saturday), the day of the week of the date *number*.

Year Year(dateexpression [, firstweekday][, firstweek]) returns a number between 100 and 9999, the year of the date number.

Toolbar Buttons

This section contains descriptions of toolbar buttons that appear in this text, categorized by type. Some buttons may appear on more than one access toolbar, but are only listed once here.

EDIT BUTTONS

 Removes selected object and places it on the clipboard

 Creates a copy of the selection and places it on the clipboard

 Inserts data from the clipboard to the current location

 Shows and edits relationships between the database tables and queries

 Locates specified text

 Adds a new, empty row above the current row

 Removes the highlighted row from the database

 Reverses newest change

 Changes the current value of the specified field or record to its previous value(s)

FILE BUTTONS

 Creates a new database

 Opens an existing database

 Attaches a table from another application to the current database

 Prints the current document

 Shows how the document will look when printed

 Takes data from another Access database or a non-Access source into the current database

 Transfers data from an Access database to an external application

 Inserts data into a Microsoft Word document

 Inserts data into a Microsoft Excel spreadsheet

 Makes a new query

 Makes a new form

 Makes a new report

Generates a simple form based on the parameters of the current database table or query

Generates a simple report based on the data of the current database table or query

Saves the data and setup of the current database object to the database

Selects and modifies the printer and print options

Exports data to Microsoft Word

FORM DESIGN BUTTONS

Opens and closes the field list, which contains fields that are used in a form/report

Opens the module window to create, edit, or view procedures

MS Sans Serif — Presents fonts available for text

8 — Modifies the size of the text

Makes (removes) boldface from the selected text

Makes (removes) italics from the selected text

Changes the text to be aligned along the left side

Centers the text

Changes the text to be aligned along the right side

MACRO DESIGN BUTTONS

Shows (hides) the Macro name column

Shows (hides) the Condition column of the macro

Toggles single stepping

MODULE DESIGN BUTTONS

Shows the previous procedure in the module

Shows the next procedure in the module

Adds a new procedure to the module

Stops procedures and clears all variables

Creates (deletes) a line that will stop a procedure at that point to allow debugging

Displays the Immediate window, which allows for the debugging and testing of Access procedures

Compiles all loaded procedures in the current database

Steps through Access Basic code one line at a time

Steps through Access Basic code one procedure at a time

Trace all active procedures called by Access Basic code

QUERY DESIGN BUTTONS

 Shows the Structured Query Language version of a query

 Includes an additional table

 Shows (hides) the Totals row for the query

 Shows (hides) the tables list

 Makes the current query ask questions about the data without changing it

 Changes the current query to a crosstab query with specified row and column headings

 Allows the current query to modify tables or create new tables

 Allows the current query to modify tables based on specified criteria

 Allows the current query to modify the current query to add records to tables

 Allows the current query to delete records from a table based on given criteria

RECORDS BUTTONS

 Moves the cursor to a blank record at the end of the current database object

 Arranges the data in ascending order in the current datasheet or form

 Arranges the data in descending order in the current datasheet or form

 Modifies the filter that determines how the records are sorted or which records are selected

 Uses the criteria of the filter to sort the records into groups and to select records

 Removes any existing filter

 Begins the active database object

REPORT DESIGN BUTTONS

 Shows how the report looks in a preview sample

 Modifies the sorting and grouping of the report

TABLE DESIGN BUTTONS

 Modifies indexes

 Modifies which fields provide identification for each record in the table

 Begins an Access builder

 Shows and edits direct relationships between the database tables and queries

 Shows and edits all relationships between the database tables and queries

TOOLBOX BUTTONS

Shows (hides) the toolbox

Highlights an item

Creates descriptive text

Creates a group that can contain other controls

Adds a single option control

Adds a list of options

Adds a graph

Frames an OLE object

Draws straight line

Inserts a page break

Toggles the Control Wizards

Inserts an area for text

Adds a toggle button

Adds a check-box control

Embeds a form or report

Frames an OLE object

Draws a rectangle

Adds a command button

Forces current tool to remain active

Adds a list of values

VIEW BUTTONS

Shows the design characteristics of the current database object

Shows the current database object in a spreadsheet format

Modifies the display attributes of the current database object, control or section

Shows the form in its standard format

Closes the active window

Toggle to magnify the report on the screen

WINDOW AND HELP BUTTONS

Returns to the Database window

Offers access to Cue Cards

Adds a question mark icon to the cursor; while it is active, clicking on any item will open the Help file on the topic related to the item

Relational Databases and Design

Relational Databases and Design

C H A P T E R

Relational Databases and Database Design

O B J E C T I V E S

In this section you will:

- Learn the characteristics of a relation
- Learn about primary, candidate, alternate, foreign, and composite keys
- Study one-to-one, one-to-many, and many-to-many relationships
- Learn to describe relations and relationships with entity-relationship diagrams and with a shorthand method
- Study database integrity constraints for primary keys, referential integrity, and domains
- Learn about determinants, functional dependencies, anomalies, and normalization

This chapter introduces you to the basics of database design. Before trying to master this material, be sure you have worked through at least the first tutorial, and that you have an understanding of the following concepts: data, information, field, field value, record, table, relational database, common fields, database management system (DBMS), and relational database management system.

Relations

A relational database stores its data in tables. A **table** is a two-dimensional structure made up of rows and columns. The terms table, row, and column are the popular names for the more formal terms **relation** (table), **tuple** (row), and **attribute** (column), as shown in Figure AP-1.

CLIENT

ClientID	ClientName	VetID
2173	Barbara Hennessey	27
4519	Vernon Noordsy	31
8005	Sandra Amidon	27
8112	Helen Wandzell	24

tuples (rows)

attributes (columns)

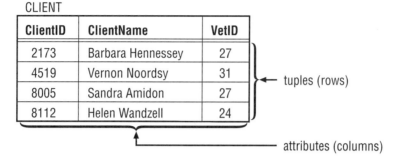

Figure AP-1
A relation consisting of tuples and attributes

The CLIENT table shown in Figure AP-1 is an example of a relation, a two-dimensional structure with the following characteristics:

- Each row is unique. Because no two rows are the same, you can easily locate and update specific data. For example, you can locate the row for ClientID 8005 and change the ClientName value, Sandra Amidon, or the VetID value, 27.
- The order of the rows is unimportant. You can add or view rows in any order. For example, you can view the rows in ClientName order instead of ClientID order.
- Table entries contain a single value. At the intersection of each row and column, you cannot have more than one value. For example, each row in Figure AP-1 contains one ClientID, one ClientName, and one VetID.
- The order of the columns is unimportant. You can add or view columns in any order.
- Each column has a unique name called the **attribute name**. The attribute name allows you to access a specific column without needing to know its position within the relation.
- The entries in a column are from the same domain. A **domain** is a set of values from which one or more columns draw their actual values. A domain can be broad, such as "all legitimate names of people" for the ClientName column, or narrow, such as "24, 27, or 31" for the VetID column. The domain of "all legitimate dates" could be shared by the BirthDate, StartDate, and LastPayDate columns in a company's employee relation.
- The columns in a relation describe, or are characteristics of, an entity. An **entity** is a person, place, object, event, or idea for which you want to store and process data. For example, ClientID, ClientName, and VetID are characteristics of the clients of a pet-sitting company. The CLIENT relation represents the client entity and its characteristics. That is, the sets of values in the rows of the CLIENT relation describe the different clients of the company. The CLIENT relation includes only characteristics of a client. Other relations would exist for the company's other entities. For example, a PET relation might describe the clients' pets and an EMPLOYEE relation might describe the company's employees.

Knowing the characteristics of a relation leads directly to a definition of a relational database. A **relational database** is a collection of relations.

Keys

Primary keys ensure that each row in a relation is unique. A **primary key** is an attribute, or a collection of attributes, whose values uniquely identify each row in a relation. In addition to being *unique*, a primary key must be *minimal* (that is, contain no unnecessary extra attributes) and *must not change in value*. For example, in Figure AP-2 the STATE relation contains one record per state and uses StateAbbrev as its primary key.

primary key

alternate key

STATE

State Abbrev	StateName	Entered Union Order	StateBird	State Population
CT	Connecticut	5	American robin	3,287,116
MI	Michigan	26	robin	9,295,297
SD	South Dakota	40	pheasant	696,004
TN	Tennessee	16	mockingbird	4,877,185
TX	Texas	28	mockingbird	16,986,510

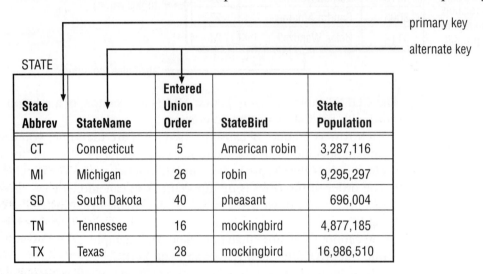

Figure AP-2
A relation and its keys

Could any other attribute, or collection of attributes, be the primary key of the STATE relation?

- Could StateBird serve as the primary key? No, because the column does not have unique values (for example, the mockingbird is the state bird of more than one state).
- Could StatePopulation serve as the primary key? No, because the column values change periodically and are not guaranteed to be unique.
- Could StateAbbrev and StateName together serve as the primary key? No, because the combination is not minimal. Something less, StateAbbrev by itself, can serve as the primary key.
- Could StateName serve as the primary key? Yes, because the column has unique values. In a similar way, you could select EnteredUnionOrder as the primary key for the STATE relation. One attribute, or collection of attributes, that can serve as a primary key is called a **candidate key**. The candidate keys for the STATE relation are StateAbbrev, StateName, and EnteredUnionOrder. You choose one of the candidate keys to be the primary key, and the remaining candidate keys are called **alternate keys**.

Figure AP-3 shows a CITY relation containing the attributes StateAbbrev, CityName, and CityPopulation.

primary key

CITY

State Abbrev	CityName	City Population
CT	Hartford	139,739
CT	Madison	14,031
CT	Portland	8,418
MI	Lansing	127,321
SD	Madison	6,257
SD	Pierre	12,906
TN	Nashville	488,374
TX	Austin	465,622
TX	Portland	12,224

Figure AP-3
A relation with a composite key

What is the primary key for the CITY relation? The values for CityPopulation periodically change and are not guaranteed to be unique, so CityPopulation cannot be the primary key. Because the values for each of the other two columns are not unique, StateAbbrev alone cannot be the primary key and neither can CityName (for example, there are two Madisons and two Portlands). The primary key is the combination of StateAbbrev and CityName. Both attributes together are needed to identify, uniquely and minimally, each row in the CITY relation. A multiple-attribute primary key is also called a **composite key** or a **concatenated key**.

The StateAbbrev attribute in the CITY relation is also a foreign key. A **foreign key** is an attribute, or a collection of attributes, in one relation whose values must match the values of the primary key of some relation. As shown in Figure AP-4, the values in the CITY relation's StateAbbrev column match the values in the STATE relation's StateAbbrev column. Thus, StateAbbrev, the primary key of the STATE relation, is a foreign key in the CITY relation. Although the attribute name StateAbbrev is the same in both relations, the names could be different. Most people give the same name to an attribute stored in two or more tables to broadcast clearly they are really the same attribute.

primary key → StateAbbrev

STATE

State Abbrev	StateName	Entered Union Order	StateBird	State Population
CT	Connecticut	5	American robin	3,287,116
MI	Michigan	26	robin	9,295,297
SD	South Dakota	40	pheasant	696,004
TN	Tennessee	16	mockingbird	4,877,185
TX	Texas	28	mockingbird	16,986,510

primary key → State Abbrev, CityName

foreign key → State Abbrev

CITY

State Abbrev	CityName	City Population
CT	Hartford	139,739
CT	Madison	14,031
CT	Portland	8,418
MI	Lansing	127,321
SD	Madison	6,257
SD	Pierre	12,906
TN	Nashville	488,374
TX	Austin	465,622
TX	Portland	12,224

Figure AP-4
StateAbbrev as a primary key (STATE relation) and a foreign key (CITY relation)

A **nonkey attribute** is an attribute that is not part of the primary key. In the two relations shown in Figure AP-4, all attributes are nonkey attributes except StateAbbrev in the STATE and CITY relations and CityName in the CITY relation. *Key* is an ambiguous word because it can refer to a primary, candidate, alternate, or foreign key. When the word key appears alone, however, it means primary key and the definition for a nonkey attribute consequently makes sense.

Relationships

The CAPITAL relation, shown in Figure AP-5, has one row for each state capital. The CapitalName and StateAbbrev attributes are candidate keys; selecting CapitalName as the primary key makes StateAbbrev an alternate key. The StateAbbrev attribute in the CAPITAL relation is also a foreign key, because its values match the values in the STATE relation's StateAbbrev column.

primary key

STATE

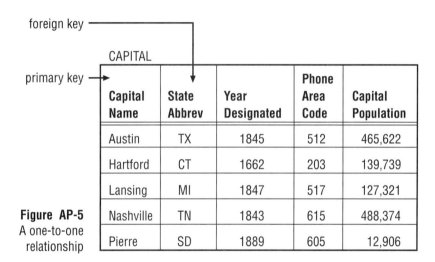

State Abbrev	StateName	Entered Union Order	StateBird	State Population
CT	Connecticut	5	American robin	3,287,116
MI	Michigan	26	robin	9,295,297
SD	South Dakota	40	pheasant	696,004
TN	Tennessee	16	mockingbird	4,877,185
TX	Texas	28	mockingbird	16,986,510

foreign key

CAPITAL

primary key

Capital Name	State Abbrev	Year Designated	Phone Area Code	Capital Population
Austin	TX	1845	512	465,622
Hartford	CT	1662	203	139,739
Lansing	MI	1847	517	127,321
Nashville	TN	1843	615	488,374
Pierre	SD	1889	605	12,906

Figure AP-5
A one-to-one relationship

One-to-One

The STATE and CAPITAL relations, shown in Figure AP-5, have a one-to-one relationship. A **one-to-one relationship** (abbreviated 1:1) exists between two relations when each row in one relation has at most one matching row in the other relation. StateAbbrev, which is a foreign key in the CAPITAL relation and the primary key in the STATE relation, is the common field that ties together the rows of each relation.

Should the STATE and CAPITAL relations be combined into one relation? Although the two relations in any 1:1 relationship can be combined into one relation, each relation describes different entities and should usually be kept separate.

One-to-Many

The STATE and CITY relations, shown once again in Figure AP-6, have a one-to-many relationship. A **one-to-many relationship** (abbreviated 1:M) exists between two relations when one row in the first relation matches many rows in the second relation and one row in the second relation matches only one row in the first relation. Many can mean zero rows, one row, or two or more rows. StateAbbrev, which is a foreign key in the CITY relation and the primary key in the STATE relation, is the common field that ties together the rows of each relation.

primary key

STATE

State Abbrev	StateName	Entered Union Order	StateBird	State Population
CT	Connecticut	5	American robin	3,287,116
MI	Michigan	26	robin	9,295,297
SD	South Dakota	40	pheasant	696,004
TN	Tennessee	16	mockingbird	4,877,185
TX	Texas	28	mockingbird	16,986,510

primary key

CITY

foreign key

State Abbrev	CityName	City Population
CT	Hartford	139,739
CT	Madison	14,031
CT	Portland	8,418
MI	Lansing	127,321
SD	Madison	6,257
SD	Pierre	12,906
TN	Nashville	488,374
TX	Austin	465,622
TX	Portland	12,224

Figure AP-6
A one-to-many relationship

Many-to-Many

In Figure AP-7 the STATE relation with a primary key of StateAbbrev and the CROP relation with a primary key of CropName have a many-to-many relationship. A **many-to-many relationship** (abbreviated as M:N) exists between two relations when one row in the first relation matches many rows in the second relation and one row in the second relation matches many rows in the first relation. You form a many-to-many relationship between two relations indirectly by adding a third relation that has the primary keys of the M:N relations as its primary key. The original relations now each have a 1:M relationship with the new relation. The StateAbbrev and CropName attributes represent the primary key of the PRODUCTION relation that is shown in Figure AP-7. StateAbbrev, which is a foreign key in the PRODUCTION relation and the primary key in the STATE relation, is the common field that ties together the rows of the STATE and PRODUCTION relations. Likewise, CropName is the common field for the CROP and PRODUCTION relations.

primary key

STATE

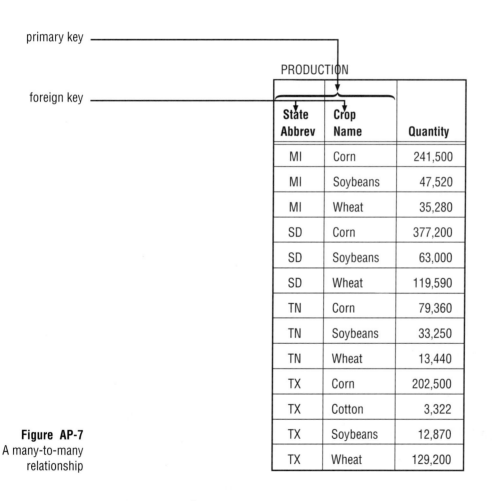

State Abbrev	StateName	Entered Union Order	StateBird	State Population
CT	Connecticut	5	American robin	3,287,116
MI	Michigan	26	robin	9,295,297
SD	South Dakota	40	pheasant	696,004
TN	Tennessee	16	mockingbird	4,877,185
TX	Texas	28	mockingbird	16,986,510

CROP

Crop Name	Exports	Imports
Corn	$4,965.8	$68.5
Cotton	$2,014.6	$11.4
Soybeans	$4,462.8	$15.8
Wheat	$4,503.2	$191.1

primary key

foreign key

PRODUCTION

State Abbrev	Crop Name	Quantity
MI	Corn	241,500
MI	Soybeans	47,520
MI	Wheat	35,280
SD	Corn	377,200
SD	Soybeans	63,000
SD	Wheat	119,590
TN	Corn	79,360
TN	Soybeans	33,250
TN	Wheat	13,440
TX	Corn	202,500
TX	Cotton	3,322
TX	Soybeans	12,870
TX	Wheat	129,200

Figure AP-7
A many-to-many relationship

Entity Subtype

Figure AP-8 shows a special type of one-to-one relationship. The SHIPPING relation's primary key is StateAbbrev and contains one row for each state having an ocean shoreline. Because not all states have an ocean shoreline, the SHIPPING relation has fewer rows than the STATE relation. However, each row in the SHIPPING relation has a matching row in the STATE relation with StateAbbrev serving as the common field; StateAbbrev is the primary key in the STATE relation and is a foreign key in the SHIPPING relation.

STATE

primary key → State Abbrev

State Abbrev	StateName	Entered Union Order	StateBird	State Population
CT	Connecticut	5	American robin	3,287,116
MI	Michigan	26	robin	9,295,297
SD	South Dakota	40	pheasant	696,004
TN	Tennessee	16	mockingbird	4,877,185
TX	Texas	28	mockingbird	16,986,510

SHIPPING

primary key → State Abbrev

foreign key → State Abbrev

State Abbrev	Ocean Shoreline	Export Tonnage	Import Tonnage
CT	618	3,377,466	2,118,494
TX	3,359	45,980,912	109,400,314

Figure AP-8
An entity subtype

The SHIPPING relation, in this situation, is called an **entity subtype**, a relation whose primary key is a foreign key to a second relation and whose attributes are additional attributes for the second relation. You can create an entity subtype when a relation has attributes that could have null values. A **null value** is the absence of a value. A null value is not blank, nor zero, nor any other value. You give a null value to an attribute when you do not know its value or when a value does not apply. For example, instead of using the SHIPPING relation, you could store the OceanShoreline, ExportTonnage, and ImportTonnage attributes in the STATE relation and allow them to be null for states not having an ocean shoreline. You should be aware that database experts are currently debating the validity of the use of nulls in relational databases and many experts insist that you should never use nulls. Part of this warning against nulls is based on the inconsistent way different relational DBMSs treat nulls and part is due to the lack of a firm theoretical foundation for how to use nulls. In any case, entity subtypes are an alternative to the use of nulls.

Entity-Relationship Diagrams

A common shorthand method for describing relations is to write the relation name followed by its attributes in parentheses, underlining the attributes that represent the primary key and identifying the foreign keys for a relation immediately after the relation. Using this method, the relations that appear in Figures AP-5 through AP-8 are described in the following way:

STATE (StateAbbrev, StateName, EnteredUnionOrder, StateBird, StatePopulation)

CAPITAL (CapitalName, StateAbbrev, YearDesignated, PhoneAreaCode, CapitalPopulation)

Foreign key: StateAbbrev to STATE relation
CITY (StateAbbrev, CityName, CityPopulation)
Foreign key: StateAbbrev to STATE relation
CROP (CropName, Exports, Imports)
PRODUCTION (StateAbbrev, CropName, Quantity)
Foreign key: StateAbbrev to STATE relation
Foreign key: CropName to CROP relation
SHIPPING (StateAbbrev, OceanShoreline, ExportTonnage, ImportTonnage)
Foreign key: StateAbbrev to STATE relation

Another popular way to describe relations *and their relationships* is with entity-relationship diagrams. An **entity-relationship diagram (ERD)** graphically shows a database's entities and the relationships among the entities. An entity and a relation are equivalent when you are dealing with an entity-relationship diagram. Figure AP-9 shows an entity-relationship diagram for the relations that appear in Figures AP-5 through AP-8.

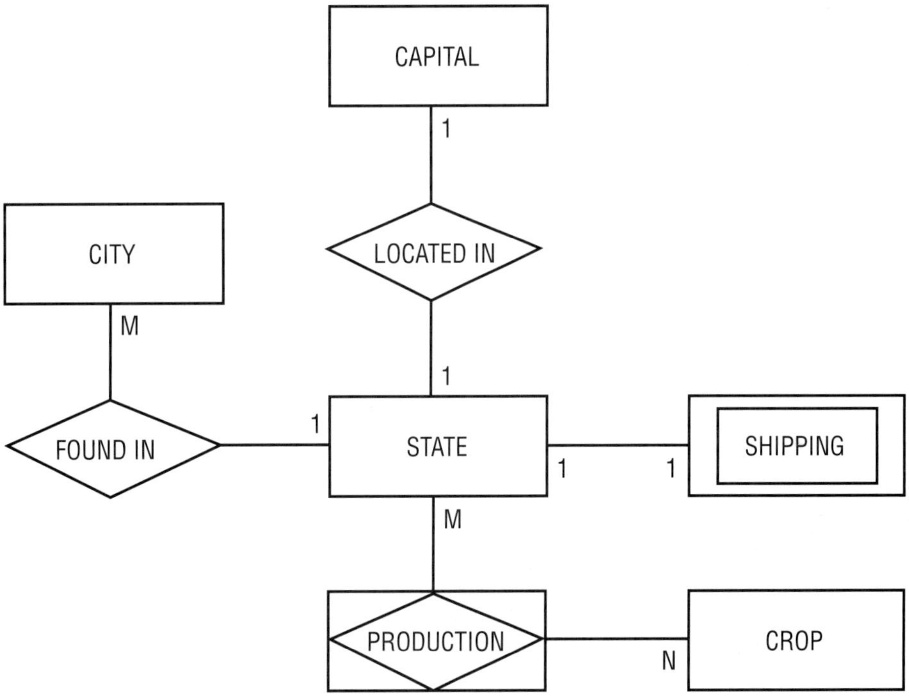

Figure AP-9
An entity–relationship diagram

Entity-relationship diagrams have the following characteristics:

- Entities, or relations, appear in rectangles and relationships appear in diamonds. The entity name appears inside the rectangle and a verb describing the relationship appears inside the diamond. For example, the CITY rectangle is connected to the STATE rectangle by the FOUND IN diamond and is read: "a city is found in a state."
- The 1 by the STATE entity and the M by the CITY entity identify a 1:M relationship between these two entities. In a similar manner, an M:N relationship exists between the STATE and CROP entities and 1:1 relationships exist between the STATE and CAPITAL entities and between the STATE and SHIPPING entities.
- A diamond inside a rectangle defines a composite entity. A **composite entity** is a relationship that has the characteristics of an entity. For example, PRODUCTION connects the STATE and CROP entities in an M:N relationship and acts as an entity by containing the Quantity attribute, along with the composite key of the StateAbbrev and CropName attributes.

- An entity subtype appears in a double rectangle and is connected without an intervening diamond directly to its related entity, STATE.

You can also show attributes in an ERD by placing each individual attribute in a bubble connected to its entity or relationship. However, typical ERDs have large numbers of entities and relationships, so including the attributes might confuse rather than clarify the ERD.

Integrity Constraints

A database has **integrity** if its data follows the rules, known as **integrity constraints**. The ideal is to have the DBMS enforce all integrity constraints. If a DBMS can enforce some integrity constraints but not others, the other integrity constraints must be enforced by programs or by people. Integrity constraints can be divided into three groups: primary key constraints, referential integrity, and domain integrity constraints.

- One primary key constraint is inherent in the definition of a primary key, which says that the primary key must be unique. The **entity integrity constraint** says that the primary key cannot be null. For a composite key, none of the individual attributes can be null. The uniqueness and nonnull properties of a primary key ensure that you can reference any data value in a database by supplying its table name, attribute name, and primary key value.
- Foreign keys provide the mechanism for forming a relationship between two tables, and referential integrity ensures that only valid relationships exist. **Referential integrity** is the constraint specifying that each nonnull foreign key must match a primary key value in the related relation. Specifically, referential integrity means that you cannot add a row with an unmatched foreign key value. Referential integrity also means that you cannot change or delete the related primary key value and leave the foreign key orphaned. In some relational DBMSs, if you try to change or delete a primary key value, you can specify one of these options: restricted, cascades, or nullifies. If you specify **restricted**, the DBMS updates or deletes the value only if there are no matching foreign key values. If you choose **cascades** and then change a primary key value, the DBMS changes the matching foreign keys to the new primary key value, or, if you delete a primary key value, the DBMS also deletes the matching foreign-key rows. If you choose **nullifies** and then change or delete a primary key value, the DBMS sets all matching foreign keys to null.
- A domain is a set of values from which one or more columns draw their actual values. **Domain integrity constraints** are the rules you specify for an attribute. By choosing a data type for a attribute, you impose a constraint on the set of values allowed for the attribute. You can create specific validation rules for an attribute to limit its domain further. As you make an attribute's domain definition more precise, you exclude more and more unacceptable values for an attribute. For example, in the STATE relation you could define the domain for the EnteredUnionOrder attribute to be a unique integer between 1 and 50 and the domain for the StateBird attribute to be any name containing 25 or fewer characters.

Dependencies and Determinants

Relations are related to other relations. Attributes are also related to other attributes. Consider the STATE CROP relation shown in Figure AP-10. Its description is:

STATE CROP (<u>StateAbbrev</u>, <u>CropName</u>, StateBird, BirdScientificName, StatePopulation, Exports, Quantity)

null value

primary key

STATE CROP

State Abbrev	Crop Name	StateBird	BirdScientificName	State Population	Exports	Quantity
CT	Corn	American robin	Planesticus migratorius	3,287,116	$4,965.8	
MI	Corn	robin	Planesticus migratorius	9,295,297	$4,965.8	241,500
MI	Soybeans	robin	Planesticus migratorius	9,295,297	$4,462.8	47,520
MI	Wheat	robin	Planesticus migratorius	9,295,297	$4,503.2	35,280
SD	Corn	pheasant	Phasianus colchicus	696,004	$4,965.8	277,200
SD	Soybeans	pheasant	Phasianus colchicus	696,004	$4,462.8	63,000
SD	Wheat	pheasant	Phasianus colchicus	696,004	$4,503.2	119,590
TN	Corn	mockingbird	Mimus polyglottos	4,977,185	$4,965.8	79,360
TN	Soybeans	mockingbird	Mimus polyglottos	4,977,185	$4,462.8	33,250
TN	Wheat	mockingbird	Mimus polyglottos	4,977,185	$4,503.2	13,440
TX	Corn	mockingbird	Mimus polyglottos	16,986,510	$4,965.8	202,500
TX	Cotton	mockingbird	Mimus polyglottos	16,986,510	$2,014.6	3,322
TX	Soybeans	mockingbird	Mimus polyglottos	16,986,510	$4,462.8	12,870
TX	Wheat	mockingbird	Mimus polyglottos	16,986,510	$4,503.2	129,200

Figure AP-10
A relation combining several attributes from the STATE, CROP, and PRODUCTION relations

The STATE CROP relation combines several attributes from the STATE, CROP, and PRODUCTION relations that appeared in Figure AP-7. The StateAbbrev, StateBird, and StatePopulation attributes are from the STATE relation. The CropName and Exports attributes are from the CROP relation. The StateAbbrev, CropName, and Quantity attributes are from the PRODUCTION relation. The BirdScientificName attribute is a new attribute for the STATE CROP relation, whose primary key is the combination of the StateAbbrev and CropName attributes.

Notice the null value in the Quantity attribute for the state of Connecticut (StateAbbrev CT). If you look back to Figure AP-7, you can see that there were no entries for Quantity for the state of Connecticut, which is why Quantity is null in the STATE CROP table. However, note that CropName requires an entry because it is part of the composite key for the relation. If you want the state of CT to be in the relation, you need to assign a dummy CropName for the CT entry, in this case, Corn.

In the STATE CROP relation, each attribute is related to other attributes. For example, a value for StateAbbrev determines the value of StatePopulation, and a value for StatePopulation depends on the value of StateAbbrev. In database discussions, the word *functionally* is used, as in: "StateAbbrev functionally determines StatePopulation" and "StatePopulation is functionally dependent on StateAbbrev." In this case, StateAbbrev is called a determinant. A **determinant** is an attribute, or a collection of attributes, whose values determine the values of another attribute. We also state that an attribute is **functionally dependent** on another attribute (or collection of attributes) if that other attribute is a determinant for it.

You can graphically show a relation's functional dependencies and determinants in a **bubble diagram**. Bubble diagrams are also called **data model diagrams** and **functional dependency diagrams**. Figure AP-11 shows the bubble diagram for the STATE CROP relation.

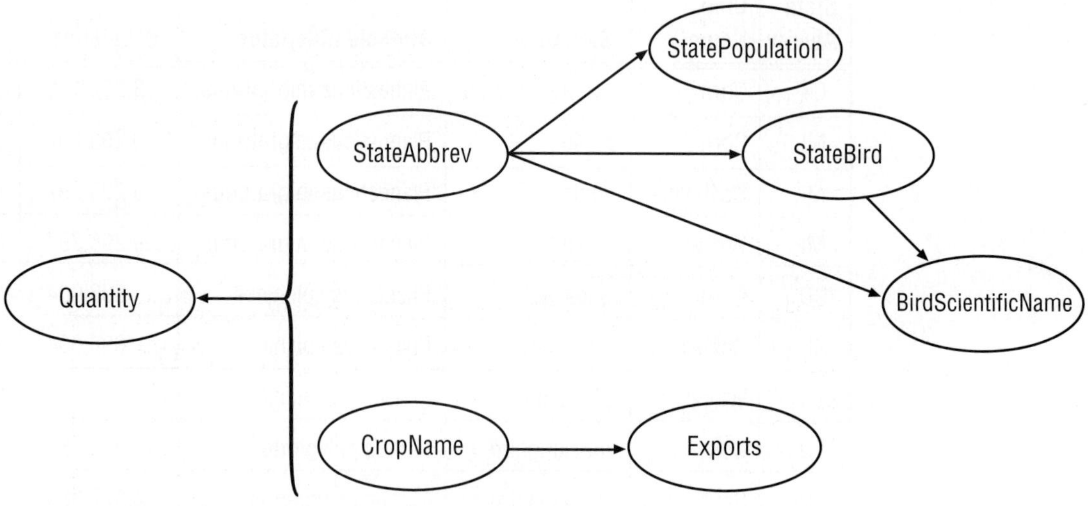

Figure AP-11 A bubble diagram for the STATE CROP relation

- StateAbbrev is a determinant for StatePopulation, StateBird, and BirdScientificName.
- CropName is a determinant for Exports.
- Quantity is functionally dependent on StateAbbrev and CropName together.
- StateBird is a determinant for BirdScientificName.

Only Quantity is functionally dependent on the relation's full primary key, StateAbbrev and CropName. StatePopulation, StateBird, and BirdScientificName have partial dependencies, because they are functionally dependent on StateAbbrev, which is part of the primary key. A **partial dependency** is a functional dependency on part of the primary key, instead of the entire primary key. Does another partial dependency exist in the STATE CROP relation? Yes, Exports has a partial dependency on CropName.

Because StateAbbrev is a determinant of both StateBird and BirdScientificName, and StateBird is a determinant of BirdScientificName, StateBird and BirdScientificName have a transitive dependency. A **transitive dependency** is a functional dependency between two nonkey attributes, which are both dependent on a third attribute.

How do you know which functional dependencies exist among a collection of attributes, and how do you recognize partial and transitive dependencies? The answers lie with the questions you ask as you gather the requirements for a database application. For each attribute and entity, you must gain an accurate understanding of its meaning and relationships in the context of the application. **Semantic object modeling** is an entire area of study within the database field devoted to the meanings and relationships of data.

Anomalies

When you use a DBMS, you are more likely to get results you can trust if you create your relations carefully. For example, problems might occur with relations that have partial and transitive dependencies, whereas you won't have as much trouble if you ensure that your relations include only attributes that are directly related to each other. Also, when you remove data redundancy from a relation, you improve that relation. **Data redundancy** occurs when you store the same data in more than one place.

The problems caused by data redundancy and by partial and transitive dependencies are called **anomalies**, because they are undesirable irregularities of relations. Anomalies are of three types: insertion, deletion, and update.

To examine the effects of these anomalies, consider the CLIENT relation that is shown in Figure AP-12. The CLIENT relation represents part of the database for Pet Sitters Unlimited, which is a company providing pet-sitting services for homeowners while they are on vacation. Pet Sitters Unlimited keeps track of the data about its clients and the clients' children, pets, and vets. The attributes for the CLIENT relation include the composite key ClientID and ChildName, along with ClientName, VetID, and VetName.

primary key

CLIENT

ClientID	ChildName	ClientName	VetID	VetName
2173	Ryan	Barbara Hennessey	27	Pet Vet
4519	Pat	Vernon Noordsy	31	Pet Care
4519	Dana	Vernon Noordsy	31	Pet Care
8005	Dana	Sandra Amidon	27	Pet Vet
8005	Dani	Sandra Amidon	27	Pet Vet
8112	Pat	Helen Wandzell	24	Pets R Us

Figure AP-12 The CLIENT relation with insertion, deletion, and update anomalies

- An **insertion anomaly** occurs when you cannot add a row to a relation because you do not know the entire primary key value. For example, you cannot add the new client Cathy Corbett with a ClientID of 3322 to the CLIENT relation when you do not know her children's names. Entity integrity prevents you from leaving any part of a primary key null. Because ChildName is part of the primary key, you cannot leave it null. To add the new client, your only option is to make up a ChildName, even if the client does not have children. This solution misrepresents the facts and is unacceptable, if a better approach is available.
- A **deletion anomaly** occurs when you delete data from a relation and unintentionally lose other critical data. For example, if you delete ClientID 8112 because Helen Wandzell is no longer a client, you also lose the only instance of VetID 24 in the database. Thus, you no longer know that VetID 24 is Pets R Us.
- An **update anomaly** occurs when you change one attribute value and either the DBMS must make more than one change to the database or else the database ends up containing inconsistent data. For example, if you change the ClientName, VetID, or VetName for ClientID 4519, the DBMS must change multiple rows of the CLIENT relation. If the DBMS fails to change all the rows, the ClientName, VetID, or VetName now has two different values in the database and is inconsistent.

Normalization

Database design is the process of determining the precise relations needed for a given collection of attributes and placing those attributes into the correct relations. Crucial to good database design is understanding the functional dependencies of all attributes;

recognizing the anomalies caused by data redundancy, partial dependencies, and transitive dependencies when they exist; and knowing how to eliminate the anomalies.

The process of identifying and eliminating anomalies is called **normalization**. Using normalization, you start with a collection of relations, apply sets of rules to eliminate anomalies, and produce a new collection of problem-free relations. The sets of rules are called **normal forms**. Of special interest for our purposes are the first three normal forms: first normal form, second normal form, and third normal form. First normal form improves the design of your relations, second normal form improves the first normal form design, and third normal form applies even more stringent rules to produce an even better design.

First Normal Form

Consider the CLIENT relation shown in Figure AP-13. For each client, the relation contains ClientID, which is the primary key; the client's name and children's names; the ID and name of the client's vet; and the ID, name, and type of each client's pets. For example, Barbara Hennessey has no children and three pets, Vernon Noordsy has two children and one pet, Sandra Amidon has two children and two pets, and Helen Wandzell has one child and one pet. Because the entries in a relation must contain a single value, the structure shown in Figure AP-13 is not even a relation, although it is called an **unnormalized relation**. ChildName, which can have more than one value, is called a **repeating group**. The set of attributes that includes PetID, PetName, and PetType is a second repeating group in the structure.

repeating group

CLIENT

ClientID	ClientName	ChildName	VetID	VetName	PetID	PetName	PetType
2173	Barabara Hennessey		27	Pet Vet	1 2 4	Sam Hoober Sam	Bird Dog Hamster
4519	Vernon Noordsy	Pat Dana	31	Pet Care	2	Charlie	Cat
8005	Sandra Amidon	Dana Dani	27	Pet Vet	1 2	Beefer Kirby	Dog Cat
8112	Helen Wandzell	Pat	24	Pets R Us	3	Kirby	Dog

Figure AP-13 Repeating groups of data in an unnormalized CLIENT relation

First normal form addresses this repeating-group situation. A relation is in **first normal form (1NF)** if it does not contain repeating groups. To remove a repeating group and convert to first normal form, you expand the primary key to include the primary key of the repeating group. You must perform this step carefully, however. If the unnormalized relation has independent repeating groups, you must perform the conversion step separately for each.

The repeating group of ChildName is independent from the repeating group of PetId, PetName, and PetType. That is, the number and names of a client's children is independent of the number, names, and types of a client's pets. Performing the conversion step to each independent repeating group produces the two 1NF relations shown in Figure AP-14.

primary key → ClientID, ChildName

CHILD

ClientID	ChildName	ClientName	VetID	VetName
4519	Pat	Vernon Noordsy	31	Pet Care
4519	Dana	Vernon Noordsy	31	Pet Care
8005	Dana	Sandra Amidon	27	Pet Vet
8005	Dani	Sandra Amidon	27	Pet Vet
8112	Pat	Henlen Wandzell	24	Pets R Us

primary key → ClientID, PetID

CLIENT

ClientID	PetID	ClientName	VetID	VetName	PetName	PetType
2173	1	Barbara Hennessey	27	Pet Vet	Sam	Bird
2173	2	Barbara Hennessey	27	Pet Vet	Hoober	Dog
2173	4	Barbara Hennessey	27	Pet Vet	Sam	Hamster
4519	2	Vernon Noordsy	31	Pet Care	Charlie	Cat
8005	1	Sandra Amidon	27	Pet Vet	Beefer	Dog
8005	2	Sandra Amidon	27	Pet Vet	Kirby	Cat
8112	3	Helen Wandzell	24	Pets R Us	Kirby	Dog

Figure AP-14 After conversion to 1NF

The alternative way to describe the 1NF relations is:

CHILD (ClientID, ChildName, ClientName, VetID, VetName)

CLIENT (ClientID, PetID, ClientName, VetID, VetName, PetName, PetType)

CHILD and CLIENT are now true relations and both have composite keys. Both relations, however, suffer from insertion, deletion, and update anomalies. (Find examples of the three anomalies in both relations.) In the CHILD and CLIENT relations, ClientID is a determinant for ClientName, VetID, and VetName, so partial dependencies exist in both relations. It is these partial dependencies that cause the anomalies in the two relations, and second normal form addresses the partial-dependency problem.

Second Normal Form

A relation in 1NF is in **second normal form (2NF)** if it does not contain any partial dependencies. To remove partial dependencies from a relation and convert it to second normal form, you perform two steps. First, identify the functional dependencies for every attribute in the relation. Second, if necessary, create new relations and place each attribute in a relation, so that the attribute is functionally dependent on the entire primary key. If you need to create new relations, restrict them to ones with a primary key that is a subset of the original composite key. Note that partial dependencies occur only when you have a composite key; a relation in first normal form with a single-attribute primary key is automatically in second normal form.

Figure AP-15 shows the functional dependencies for the 1NF CHILD and CLIENT relations.

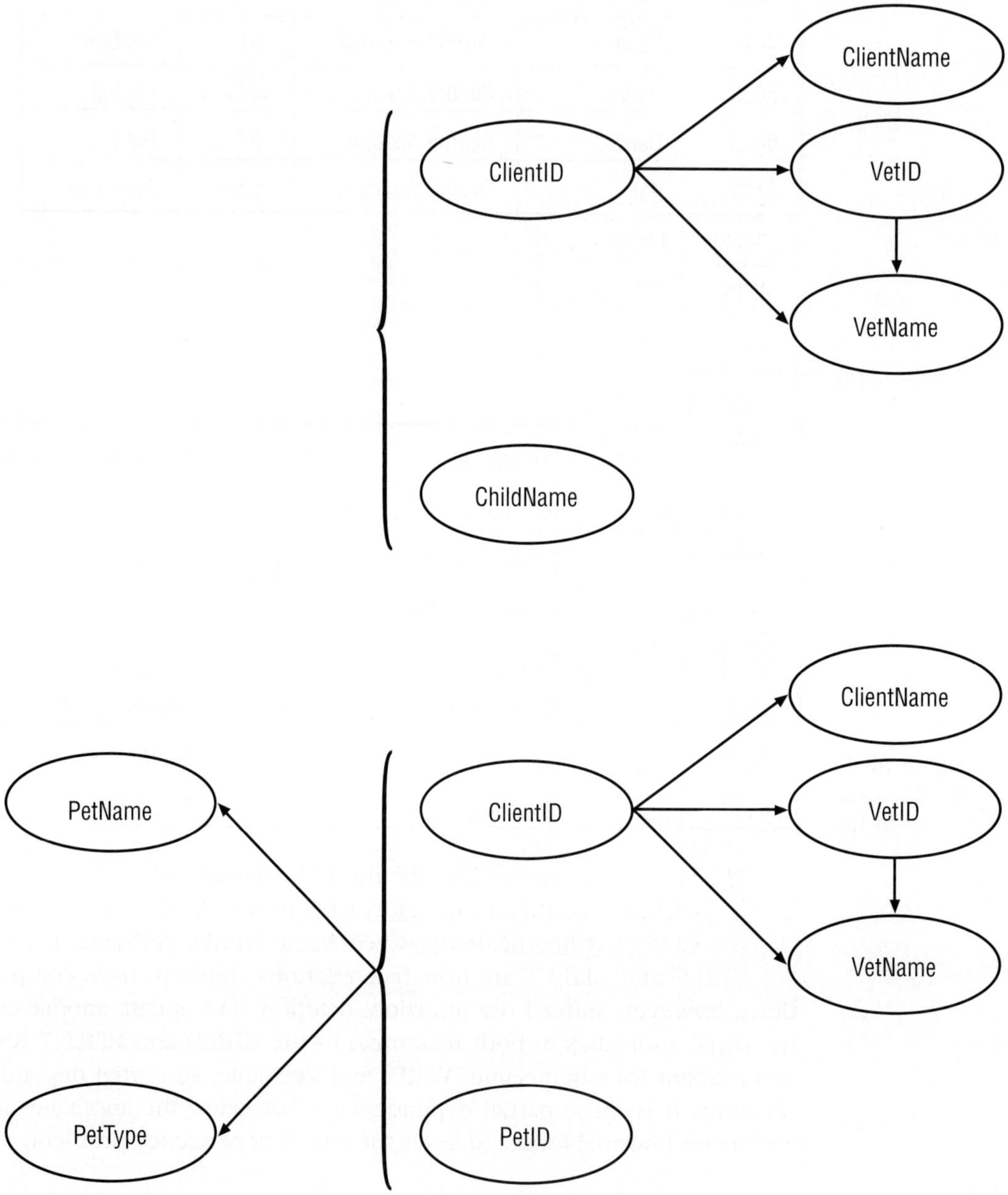

Figure AP-15
A bubble diagram for the 1NF CHILD and CLIENT relations

ClientID is a determinant for ClientName, VetID, and VetName in both relations. The composite key ClientID and PetID is a determinant for PetName and PetType. ChildName is not a determinant, nor is PetID. Is the composite key of ClientID and ChildName a determinant? No, it is not a determinant. What happens, however, if you do not have a relation with this composite key? You lose the names of the children of each client. You need to retain this composite key in a relation to preserve the important 1:M attribute relationship between ClientID and ChildName. Performing the second conversion step produces the three 2NF relations shown in Figure AP-16.

CLIENT

primary key → ClientID

ClientID	ClientName	VetID	VetName
2173	Barbara Hennessey	27	Pet Vet
4519	Vernon Noordsy	31	Pet Care
8005	Sandra Amidon	27	Pet Vet
8112	Helen Wandzell	24	Pets R Us

primary key → ClientID + ChildName

CHILD

ClientID	ChildName
4519	Pat
4519	Dana
8005	Dana
8005	Dani
8112	Pat

primary key → ClientID + PetID

PET

ClientID	PetID	PetName	PetType
2173	1	Sam	Bird
2173	2	Hoober	Dog
2173	4	Sam	Hamster
4519	2	Charlie	Cat
8005	1	Beefer	Dog
8005	2	Kirby	Cat
8112	3	Kirby	Dog

Figure AP-16
After conversion to 2NF

The alternative way to describe the 2NF relations is:

CLIENT (ClientID, ClientName, VetID, VetName)
CHILD (ClientID, ChildName)
Foreign key: ClientID to CLIENT relation
PET (ClientID, PetID, PetName, PetType)
Foreign key: ClientID to CLIENT relation

All three relations are in second normal form. Do anomalies still exist? The CHILD and PET relations show no anomalies, but CLIENT suffers from anomalies caused by the transitive dependency between VetID and VetName. (Find examples of the three anomalies caused by the transitive dependency.) You can see the transitive dependency in the bubble diagram shown in Figure AP-15; VetID is a determinant for VetName and ClientID is a determinant for VetID and VetName. Third normal form addresses the transitive-dependency problem.

Third Normal Form

A relation in 2NF is in **third normal form (3NF)** if every determinant is a candidate key. This definition for 3NF is referred to as **Boyce-Codd normal form (BCNF)** and is an improvement over the original version of 3NF.

To convert a relation to third normal form, remove the attributes that depend on the non-candidate-key determinant and place them into a new relation with the determinant as the primary key. For the CLIENT relation, you remove VetName from the relation, create a new VET relation, place VetName in the VET relation, and then make VetID the primary key of the VET relation. Note that only VetName is removed from the CLIENT relation; VetID remains as a foreign key in the CLIENT relation. Figure AP-17 shows the database design for the four 3NF relations.

VET

primary key → VetID

VetID	VetName
24	Pets R Us
27	Pet Vet
31	Pet Care

CLIENT

primary key → ClientID

ClientID	ClientName	VetID
2173	Barbara Hennessey	27
4519	Vernon Noordsy	31
8005	Sandra Amidon	27
8112	Helen Wandzell	24

CHILD

primary key → ClientID + ChildName

ClientID	ChildName
4519	Pat
4519	Dana
8005	Dana
8005	Dani
8112	Pat

PET

primary key → ClientID + PetID

ClientID	PetID	PetName	PetType
2173	1	Sam	Bird
2173	2	Hoober	Dog
2173	4	Sam	Hamster
4519	2	Charlie	Cat
8005	1	Beefer	Dog
8005	2	Kirby	Cat
8112	3	Kirby	Dog

Figure AP-17
After conversion to 3NF

The alternative way to describe the 3NF relations is:

VET (VetID, VetName)
CLIENT (ClientID, ClientName, VetID)
  Foreign key: VetID to VET relation
CHILD (ClientID, ChildName)
  Foreign key: ClientID to CLIENT relation
PET (ClientID, PetID, PetName, PetType)
  Foreign key: ClientID to CLIENT relation

The four relations have no anomalies, because you have eliminated all the data redundancy, partial dependencies, and transitive dependencies. Normalization provides the framework for eliminating anomalies and delivering an optimal database design, which you should always strive to achieve. You should be aware, however, that experts often denormalize relations to improve database performance—specifically, to decrease the time it takes the database to respond to a user's commands and requests. When you **denormalize** a relation, you reintroduce redundancy to the relation. At the same time, you reintroduce anomalies. Thus, improving performance exposes a database to potential integrity problems. Only database experts should denormalize relations, but even experts first complete the normalization of their relations.

Questions

1. What are the formal names for a table, for a row, and for a column?
2. What is a domain?
3. What is an entity?
4. What is the relationship between a primary key and a candidate key?
5. What is a composite key?
6. What is a foreign key?
7. **E** Look for an example of a one-to-one relationship, an example of a one-to-many relationship, and an example of a many-to-many relationship in a newspaper, magazine, book, or everyday situation you encounter. For each one, name the entities and select the primary and foreign keys.
8. When do you use an entity subtype?
9. What is a composite entity in an entity-relationship diagram?
10. What is the entity integrity constraint?
11. What is referential integrity?
12. What does the cascades option, which is used with referential integrity, accomplish?
13. What are partial and transitive dependencies?
14. What three types of anomalies can be exhibited by a relation, and what problems do they cause?
15. Figure AP-18 shows the VET, CLIENT, and CHILD relations with primary keys VetID, ClientID, and both ClientID and ChildName, respectively. Which two integrity constraints do these relations violate and why?

VET

VetID	VetName
24	Pets R Us
27	Pet Vet
31	Pet Care

CLIENT

ClientID	ClientName	VetID
2173	Barbara Hennessey	27
4519	Vernon Noordsy	31
8005	Sandra Amidon	37
8112	Helen Wandzell	24

CHILD

ClientID	ChildName
4519	Pat
4519	Dana
8005	
8005	Dani
8112	Pat

Figure AP-18

16. The STATE and CAPITAL relations, shown in Figure AP-5, are described as follows:

    STATE (<u>StateAbbrev</u>, StateName, EnteredUnionOrder, StateBird, StatePopulation)

    CAPITAL (<u>CapitalName</u>, StateAbbrev, YearDesignated, PhoneAreaCode, CapitalPopulation)

    Foreign key: StateAbbrev to STATE relation

    Add the attribute CountyName for the county or counties containing the state capital to this database, justify where you placed it (that is, in an existing relation or in a new one), and draw the entity-relationship diagram for all the entities. The counties for the state capitals shown in Figure AP-5 are Travis and Williamson counties for Austin TX; Hartford county for Hartford CT; Clinton, Eaton, and Ingham counties for Lansing MI; Davidson county for Nashville TN; Hughes county for Pierre SD.
17. Suppose you have a relation for a dance studio. The attributes are dancer's identification number, dancer's name, dancer's address, dancer's telephone number, class identification number, day that the class meets, time that the class meets, instructor name, and instructor identification number. Assume that each dancer takes one class, each class meets only once a week and has one instructor, and each instructor can teach more than one class. In what normal form is the relation currently, given the following shorthand description?

    DANCER (<u>DancerID</u>, DancerName, DancerAddr, DancerPhone, ClassID, ClassDay, ClassTime, InstrName, InstrID)

    Convert this relation to 3NF and then draw an entity-relationship diagram for this database.
18. Store the following attributes for a library database: AuthorCode, AuthorName, BookTitle, BorrowerAddress, BorrowerName, BorrowerCardNumber, CopiesOfBook, ISBN (International Standard Book Number), LoanDate, PublisherCode, PublisherName, and PublisherAddress. A one-to-many relationship exists between publishers and books. Many-to-many relationships exist between authors and books and between borrowers and books.
    a. Name the entities for the library database.
    b. Create the relations for the library database and describe them using the shorthand method. Be sure the relations are in third normal form.
    c. Draw an entity-relationship diagram for the library database.

Index

Index

Special Characters

A

B

C

D

E

F

N

Q

R

T

U

TASK REFERENCE

COMPREHENSIVE ACCESS 2.0 FOR WINDOWS

Italicized page numbers indicate the first discussion of each task.

TASK	MOUSE	MENU	KEYBOARD
Add a field to a table structure, *A 69*	See Reference Window: *Adding a Field to a Table Structure*		
Add a graphic image to a form or report, *IA 54*	See Reference Window: *Adding a Graphic Image*		
Add a label to a form or report, *A 189*	[A]		
Add a list box to a form, *A 189*	See *Adding a List Box Using Control Wizards*		
Add a record to a table, *A 171*	[▶|], [▶] or [▶*]	Click Records, click Go To, click New	[Ctrl] [+]
Add a rectangle to a form or report, *IA 112*	[□]		
Add a text box to a form or report, *A 233*	[ab|]		
Add an action by dragging, *IA 75*	See *Adding Actions by Dragging*		
Add aggregate functions to a query, *A 138*	See *Using Record Calculations*		
Add all fields to a query's QBE grid, *A 114*	See *The Query Design Window*		
Add an input mask to a field, *A 60*	See *Using Input Mask Wizard*		
Add calculated field to a query, *A 136*	See *Using Calculated Fields*		
Add fields to a form or report, *A 182*	See *Adding Fields to a Form*		
Add Form Header and Footer sections, *A 188*		Click Format, click Form Header/Footer	[Alt] [O], [H]
Add lines to a form or report, *A 229*	[\\]		
Add record group calculations to a query, *A 141*	See *Using Record Group Calculations*		
Add Report Header and Footer sections, *A 232*		Click Format, click Report Header/Footer	[Alt] [O], [H]
Add sort keys and grouping fields to a report, *A 230*	[≡]		
Align control boxes, *A 186*	See *Aligning Labels*		
Arrange controls on a form or report, *A 183*	See *Selecting, Moving, and Deleting Controls*		
Attach a macro to an event property, *IA 142*	See *Using a Custom Toolbar with a Form*		

TASK REFERENCE

COMPREHENSIVE ACCESS 2.0 FOR WINDOWS

Italicized page numbers indicate the first discussion of each task.

TASK	MOUSE	MENU	KEYBOARD
Back up a database, *A 102*	See *Backing Up a Database*		
Change a datasheet's font, *A 86*	See Reference Window: *Changing a Datasheet's Font Properties*		
Change a select query to a delete query, *IA 24*		Click Query, click Delete	Alt Q, D
Change a select query to a make-table query, *IA 18*		Click Query, click Make Table...	Alt Q, K
Change a select query to an append query, *IA 20*		Click Query, click Append...	Alt Q, P
Change a select query to an update query, *IA 21*		Click Query, click Update	Alt Q, U
Change colors on a form, *A 192*	See Reference Window: *Adding Colors to a Form*		
Change the number of decimal places for a field, *A 59*	See *Changing Decimal Places*		
Close a database, *A 25*	, double-click Database window Control menu box	Click File, click Close, click File, click Close Database	Alt F, C, Alt F, C
Close an object window, *A 22*	Double-click the object window Control menu box	Click File, click Close	Alt F, C
Close Print Preview window, *A 22*		Click File, click Close	Alt F, C
Compact a database, *A 103*	See *Compacting a Database*		
Compile procedures in a module, *IA 160*		Click Run, click Compile Loaded Modules	Alt R, A
Copy an object, *IA 96*	See Reference Window: *Copying an Object in the Same Database*		
Create a chart using Graph Wizard, *IA 41*	See *Creating a Chart Using the Graph Wizard*		
Create a crosstab query, *IA 6*	See Reference Window: *Using the Crosstab Query Wizard*		
Create a custom form, *A 179*	, select table or query, click Blank Form button		
Create a custom menu bar using Menu Builder, *IA 121*	See Reference Window: *Creating a Custom Menu Bar with Menu Builder*		
Create a custom report, *A 218*	, select table or query, click Blank Report button		
Create a custom toolbar, *IA 132*	See Reference Window: *Creating a Custom Toolbar*		
Create a database, *A 46*	See Reference Window: *Creating a Database*		

TASK REFERENCE

COMPREHENSIVE ACCESS 2.0 FOR WINDOWS

Italicized page numbers indicate the first discussion of each task.

TASK	MOUSE	MENU	KEYBOARD
Create a dialog box, *IA 89*	See *Creating the First Dialog Box*		
Create a filter, *A 174*	See *Using a Filter*		
Create a find-duplicates query, *IA 10*	See Reference Window: *Using the Find Duplicates Query Wizard*		
Create a find-unmatched query, *IA 11*	See Reference Window: *Using the Find Unmatched Query Wizard*		
Create a form with Form Wizards, *A 163*	See *Creating Forms Using Form Wizards*		
Create a function, *IA 153*	See *Creating a Function*		
Create a global module, *IA 152*	See Reference Window: *Creating a New Global Module*		
Create a macro group, *IA 100*	See *Creating the Macros*		
Create a multiple-table form, *A 166*	See *Creating Main/Subform Forms*		
Create a new macro, *IA 69*	Click the Macro object button, click the New command button	Click File, click New, click Macro	Alt F, W, M
Create a multiple-table query, *A 149*	See *Querying More Than One Table*		
Create a new query, *A 113*	Click table name, , click New Query	Click table name, click File, click New..., click Query, click New Query	Alt F, W, Q, N
Create a parameter query, *A 152*	See Reference Window: *Creating a Parameter Query*		
Create a report with Report Wizards, *A 210*	See *Creating Reports Using Report Wizards*		
Create a self-join, *IA 31*	See *Creating a Self-Join*		
Create a table, *A 47*	Click the New command button	Click File, click New, click Table	Alt N
Create a top-value query, *IA 25*	See *Top-Value Queries*		
Create an archive query, *IA 13*	See Reference Window: *Using the Archive Query Wizard*		
Create an AutoExec macro, *IA 143*	See *Creating an AutoExec Macro*		
Create an expression with Expression Builder, *IA 22*	See *Creating an Update Query*		
Create an AutoForm form, *A 162*	Click the table or query,		
Create an AutoReport report, *A 209*	Click the table or query,		

TASK REFERENCE

COMPREHENSIVE ACCESS 2.0 FOR WINDOWS

Italicized page numbers indicate the first discussion of each task.

TASK	MOUSE	MENU	KEYBOARD
Create an Event Procedure, *IA 157*	See Reference Window: *Adding an Event Procedure*		
Define a relationship between tables, *A 147*	See *Adding a Relationship Between Two Tables*		
Define fields in a table, *A 50*	See *Changing the Sample Field Properties*		
Delete a field from a table structure, *A 68*	Right-click the field, click Delete Row	Click Edit, click Delete Row	Alt E, D
Delete a field from the QBE grid, *A 116*	Click field selector, right-click field selector, click Cut	Click field selector, click Edit, click Cut	Click field selector, Del
Delete a form or report section, *A 188*	Drag section's bottom edge to 0" height		
Delete a record in a datasheet, *A 88*	Select record, right-click record selector, click Cut, click OK	Select record, click Edit, click Delete, click OK	Select record, Del, Enter
Delete a table, *A 92*	Right-click table name, click Delete, click OK	Click table name, click Edit, click Delete, click OK	Click table name, Del, Enter
Delete an index, *A 67*	Right-click the index, click Delete Row		
Delete selection criteria from QBE grid, *A 134*	See *The Or Logical Operator*		
Display a single record on a form, *A 192*	, click Default View box, click Single Form		
Display a table's indexes, *A 66*		Click View, click Indexes...	Alt V, I
Enter a default value for a field, *A 59*	See *Assigning Default Values*		
Enter record selection criteria in a query, *A 121*	See *Defining Record Selection Criteria*		
Exit Access, *A 12*	Double-click Microsoft Access window Control menu box	Click File, Exit	Alt F, X
Find data in a datasheet, *A 94*	See Reference Window: *Finding Data in a Table*		
Find data in a form, *A 173*	See *Using the Find Command*		
Help screens, *A 27*		Click Help, Contents or Click Help, Search...	Alt H, C or Alt H, S
Hide duplicate values in a group report, *A 235*	See *Hiding Duplicate Values in a Group Report*		

TASK REFERENCE

COMPREHENSIVE ACCESS 2.0 FOR WINDOWS

Italicized page numbers indicate the first discussion of each task.

TASK	MOUSE	MENU	KEYBOARD
Import an Access table, *A 90*	See Reference Window: *Importing an Access Table*		
Insert a field in the QBE grid, *A 119*	See *Inserting a Field*		
Launch Access, *A 11*	Double-click Microsoft Access icon		
Move a field or column, *A 117*	See *Moving a Field*		
Move the toolbar, *A 24*	See *Moving the Toolbar*		
Move to first record, *A 18*		Click Records, click Go To, click First	Alt R, G, F
Move to last record, *A 18*		Click Records, click Go To, click Last	Alt R, G, L
Move to next record, *A 18*		Click Records, click Go To, click Next	Alt R, G, N
Move to previous record, *A 18*		Click Records, click Go To, click Previous	Alt R, G, P
Open a database, *A 13*	See Reference Window: *Opening a Database*		
Open a filter saved as a query, *A 177*		Click File, click Load From Query...	Alt F, L
Open a form, *A 23*	Click Form object button, click the form name, click the Open command button		
Open a saved query, *A 132*	Click Query object button, click query name, click Open		
Open a table datasheet, *A 93*	Click Table object button, double-click the table name		
Open Cue Cards, *A 64*		Click Help, click Cue Cards	Alt H, U
Print a datasheet, *A 20*	See Reference Window: *Printing a Hardcopy of a Datasheet*		
Print a form, *A 25*		Click File, click Print...	Alt F, P
Print a report, *A 213*		Click File, click Print...	Alt F, P
Print selected records, *A 130*	See *Printing a Dynaset Selection*		
Print table documentation, *A 101*	See *Printing Table Documentation*		
Quick sort records, *A 99*	Click field, then or	Click field, click Records, click Quick Sort, click Ascending or Descending	Click field, Alt R, Q, A or D
Remove a filter, *A 176*		Click Records, click Show All Records	Alt R, S
Rename a field in a query, *A 120*	See *Renaming Fields in a Query*		

TASK REFERENCE

COMPREHENSIVE ACCESS 2.0 FOR WINDOWS

Italicized page numbers indicate the first discussion of each task.

TASK	MOUSE	MENU	KEYBOARD
Rename a table, *A 93*	Right-click table name, click Rename	Click table name, click File, click Rename...	Click table name, Alt F, M
Replace data in a datasheet, *A 97*	See Reference Window: *Replacing Data in a Table*		
Resize a column, *A 57*	See *Resizing Columns in a Datasheet*		
Resize a control, *A 185*	Click control box, drag sizing handle		
Run a macro, *IA 72*		Click File, click Run Macro...	Alt F, U
Save a filter as a query, *A 175*		Click File, click Save As Query...	Alt F, A
Save a form, *A 163*		Click File, click Save Form As...	Alt F, A
Save a macro, *A 309*		Click File, click Save As...	Alt F, A
Save a query, *A 131*		Click File, click Save Query As...	Alt F, A
Save a report, *A 210*		Click File, click Save As...	Alt F, A
Save a table's structure, *A 53*		Click File, click Save	Alt F, S
Select a primary key, *A 63*	See *Selecting the Primary Key*		
Set action arguments by dragging, *IA 80*	See *Setting Action Arguments by Dragging*		
Single step through a macro, *IA 74*	See Reference Window: *Single Stepping a Macro*		
Sort records in a query, *A 126*	See *Sorting Data*		
Switch to Datasheet View, *A 53*		Click View, click Datasheet	Alt V, S
Switch to editing mode from navigation mode, *A 84*			F2
Switch to Form View, *A 187*		Click View, click Form	Alt V, F
Switch to navigation mode from editing mode, *A 84*			F2
Switch to Table Design View, *A 54*		Click View, click Table Design	Alt V, D
Test a procedure, *IA 155*	See Reference Window: *Testing a Procedure in the Immediate Window*		
Undo a field change, *A 55*		Click Edit, click Undo Typing	Ctrl Z
Undo a quick sort, *A 100*		Click Records, click Show All Records	Alt R, S
View a query dynaset, *A 115*	or	Click View, click Datasheet	Alt V, S
View an SQL statement for an existing query, *IA 35*	SQL	Click View, click SQL	Alt V, Q